T0220792

Communications
in Computer and Information Science   915

Commenced Publication in 2007
Founding and Former Series Editors:
Phoebe Chen, Alfredo Cuzzocrea, Xiaoyong Du, Orhun Kara, Ting Liu,
Dominik Ślęzak, and Xiaokang Yang

More information about this series at http://www.springer.com/series/7899

Juan Carlos Figueroa-García
Eduyn Ramiro López-Santana
José Ignacio Rodriguez-Molano (Eds.)

Applied Computer Sciences in Engineering

5th Workshop on Engineering Applications, WEA 2018
Medellín, Colombia, October 17–19, 2018
Proceedings, Part I

 Springer

Editors
Juan Carlos Figueroa-García ⓘD
Department of Industrial Engineering
Universidad Distrital Francisco José de
Caldas
Bogotá
Colombia

José Ignacio Rodriguez-Molano ⓘD
Department of Industrial Engineering
Universidad Distrital Francisco José de
Caldas
Bogotá
Colombia

Eduyn Ramiro López-Santana ⓘD
Industrial Engineering Department
Univ. Distrital Francisco José de Caldas
Bogotá
Colombia

ISSN 1865-0929 ISSN 1865-0937 (electronic)
Communications in Computer and Information Science
ISBN 978-3-030-00349-4 ISBN 978-3-030-00350-0 (eBook)
https://doi.org/10.1007/978-3-030-00350-0

Library of Congress Control Number: 2018953754

This Springer imprint is published by the registered company Springer Nature Switzerland AG
The registered company address is: Gewerbestrasse 11, 6330 Cham, Switzerland

Preface

The fifth edition of the Workshop on Engineering Applications (WEA 2018) was focused on computer science, simulation, IoT, logistics, as well as computational intelligence and its applications. WEA has grown as a scientific forum for applied engineering and applied sciences in academia, industry, and goverment. WEA 2018 was one of the flagship events of the Faculty of Engineering of the Universidad Distrital Francisco José de Caldas, in Bogotá, Colombia.

WEA 2018 was held at the Universidad de Antioquia in Medellín – Colombia, one of the most beautiful cities in the country. The submissions covered topics such as computer science, IoT, logistics, operations research, simulation systems, systems dynamics, systems modeling, power and electrical applications, software engineering, computer informatics, computational intelligence, and intelligent computing among others. In this first volume, the proceedings are focused on computational intelligence, power applications, simulation systems and software engineering. Therefore, the main topic of our conference was "Applied Computer Sciences in Engineering."

WEA 2018 received over 200 submissions from 15 countries. All submissions were rigorously peer–reviewed via EasyChair and 91 papers were accepted for presentation at WEA 2018. The Program Committee divided all submissions into two volumes, and finally 50 high–quality papers were included in this volume of *Communications in Computer and Information Sciences* (CCIS) published by Springer. The Faculty of Engineering of the Universidad Distrital Francisco José de Caldas, the Universidad de Antioquia, the Corporación Unificada Nacional (CUN), the Faculty of Engineering of the National University of Colombia, and the Infantry School of the National Colombian Army made significant efforts to guarantee the success of the conference. We would like to thank all members of the Program Committee and the referees for their commitment to help in the review process and for spreading our call for papers. We would like to thank Alfred Hofmann and Jorge Nakahara from Springer for their helpful advice, guidance, and their continuous support in publishing the proceedings, and a special thanks to all authors for supporting WEA 2018; without all their high–quality submissions, the conference would not have been possible.

Finally, we are especially grateful to the University of Antioquia for supporting the organization of the event, particularly to the professors and students of the research groups INCAS and GITA, the Department of Industrial Engineering, Expoingeniería, the Universidad de Antioquia Foundation, the IEEE Universidad Distrital Francisco José de Caldas Student branch, the Institute of Industrial and Systems Engineers Chapter 985 (IISE) of the Universidad Distrital Francisco José de Caldas, the Laboratory for Automation and Computational Intelligence (LAMIC), the Acquisition and Representation of Knowledge Expert Systems and Simulation (ARCOSES) research groups of the Universidad Distrital Francisco José de Caldas, and the Algorithms and Combinatory (ALGOS) research group of the National University of Colombia.

October 2018   Juan Carlos Figueroa-García
                                                Eduyn Ramiro López-Santana
                                            José Ignacio Rodriguez-Molano

Organization

General Chair

Juan Carlos Figueroa–García   Universidad Distrital Francisco José de Caldas, Colombia

Finance Chair/Treasurer

Pablo Andres Maya Duque   Universidad de Antioquia, Colombia

Technical Chairs

Juan G. Villegas   Universidad de Antioquia, Colombia
Carlos Montenegro Marín   Universidad Distrital Francisco José de Caldas, Colombia

Publication Chair

Eduyn López–Santana   Universidad Distrital Francisco José de Caldas, Colombia

Track Chairs

Edwin Rivas   Universidad Distrital Francisco José de Caldas, Colombia
German Mendez–Giraldo   Universidad Distrital Francisco José de Caldas, Colombia
Juan G. Villegas   Universidad de Antioquia, Colombia
Juan Rafael Orozco–Arroyave   Universidad de Antioquia, Colombia

Logistics Chairs

Pablo Andres Maya Duque   Universidad de Antioquia, Colombia
Yesid Díaz   Corporación Unificada Nacional de Educación Superior (CUN), Colombia

Plenary Speakers

Vladik Kreinovich   The University of Texas at El Paso (UTEP), USA
Juan J. Merelo Guervoz   Universidad de Granada, Spain
Roberto Murphy   INAOE, Mexico
Carlos Cabrera   Miami Dade College, USA

Program Committee

Abdellah Kacha	University of Jijel, Algeria
Adil Usman	Indian Institute of Technology at Mandi, India
Adolfo Jaramillo–Matta	Universidad Distrital Francisco José de Caldas, Colombia
Alvaro D. Orjuela–Cañon	Universidad Antonio Nariño, Colombia
Alvaro Jaramillo	Universidad de Antioquia, Colombia
Andres M. Alvarez Mesa	Universidad Nacional de Colombia
Aydee Lopez	Universidade Estadual de Campinas (UNICAMP), Brazil
Carlos Franco–Franco	Universidad del Rosario, Colombia
Carlos Osorio–Ramírez	Universidad Nacional de Colombia
Christopher Mejía	MIT, USA
DeShuang Huang	Tongji University, China
Diana Ovalle	Universidad Distrital Francisco José de Caldas, Colombia
Diana P. Tobón Vallejo	Universidad del Valle, Colombia
Diego Botia	Universidad de Antioquia, Colombia
Eduyn López–Santana	Universidad Distrital Francisco Jose de Caldas, Colombia
Edwin Rivas	Universidad Distrital Francisco José de Caldas, Colombia
Eliana M. Toro	Universidad Tecnológica de Pereira, Colombia
Elmar Nöth	University of Erlangen–Nuremberg, Germany
Elvis Eduardo Gaona	Universidad Distrital Francisco José de Caldas, Colombia
Eugenio Yime	Universidad del Atlántico, Colombia
Feizar Javier Rueda–Velazco	Universidad Distrital Francisco José de Caldas, Colombia
Francisco Ramis	Universidad del Bío Bío, Chile
Germán Hernández–Pérez	Universidad Nacional de Colombia, Colombia
Giovanny Tarazona	Universidad Distrital Francisco José de Caldas, Colombia
Gonzalo Mejía	Universidad C. Valparaiso, Chile
Guadalupe González	Universidad Tecnológica de Panamá, Panama
Guillermo Cabrera	Universidad C. Valparaiso, Chile
Gustavo Gatica	Universidad de Santiago de Chile/Universidad Andrés Bello, Chile
Gustavo Puerto L.	Universidad Distrital Francisco José de Caldas, Colombia
Henry Diosa	Universidad Distrital Francisco José de Caldas, Colombia
Heriberto Román–Flores	Universidad de Tarapacá, Chile
I–Hsien Ting	National University of Kaohsiung, Taiwan
Isabel Agudelo	Logyca, Colombia

Ivan Santelices Manfalti	Universidad del Bío–Bío, Chile
Jair Cervantes–Canales	Universidad Autónoma de México, Mexico
Jairo R. Montoya–Torres	Universidad de La Sabana, Colombia
Jairo Serrano	Universidad Tecnológica de Bolívar, Colombia
Jairo Soriano–Mendez	Universidad Distrital Francisco José de Caldas, Colombia
Jan Rusz	CTU, Czech Republic
Javier Arturo Orjuela–Castro	Universidad Nacional de Colombia, Colombia
Javier F. Botia–Valderrama	Universidad de Antioquia, Colombia
Jesus Lopez	Universidad de Antioquia, Colombia
Jhon James Granada Torres	Universidad de Antioquia, Colombia
Jose Ignacio Rodríguez Molano	Universidad Distrital Francisco José de Caldas, Colombia
Jose Luis González–Velarde	Instituto Tecnológico de Monterrey, Mexico
Jose Luis Villa	Universidad Tecnológica de Bolívar, Colombia
Juan Carlos Figueroa–García	Universidad Distrital Francisco José de Caldas, Colombia
Juan Camilo Vásquez	Universidad de Antioquia, Colombia
Juan Carlos Rivera	Universidad EAFIT, Colombia
Juan Felipe Botero–Vega	Universidad de Antioquia, Colombia
Juan G. Villegas	Universidad de Antioquia, Colombia
Juan Rafael Orozco–Arroyave	Universidad de Antioquia, Colombia
Laura Lotero	UPB, Colombia
Laura Lotero	Universidad Pontificia Bolivariana, Colombia
Lindsay Alvarez	Universidad Distrital Francisco José de Caldas, Colombia
Luis J. Morantes Guzmán	Instituto Tecnológico Metropolitano, Colombia
Mabel Frías	Universidad de las Villas Marta Abreu, Cuba
Mario Chong	Universidad del Pacífico, Peru
Martha Centeno	University of Turabo, Puerto Rico
Martin Pilat	Charles University, Czech Republic
Mauricio Pardo Gonzalez	Universidad del Norte, Colombia
Michael Till Beck	LMU, Germany
Miguel Melgarejo	Universidad Distrital Francisco José de Caldas, Colombia
Milton Herrera	Universidad Piloto de Colombia, Colombia
Milton Orlando Sarria Paja	Universidad Santiago de Cali, Colombia
Nelson L. Diaz Aldana	Universidad Distrital Francisco José de Caldas, Colombia
Nicanor García	Universidad de Antioquia, Colombia
Nicolas Clavijo	Universidad Javeriana Cali, Colombia
Oscar Acevedo	Universidad Tecnológica de Bolívar, Colombia
Oswaldo Lopez Santos	Universidad de Ibagué, Colombia
Pablo Andres Maya Duque	Universidad de Antioquia, Colombia
Pablo Manyoma Colombia	Universidad del Valle, Colombia

Paulo Alonso Gaona	Universidad Distrital Francisco José de Caldas, Colombia
Rafael Bello–Pérez	Universidad de las Villas Marta Abreu, Cuba
Roberto Ferro	Universidad Distrital Francisco José de Caldas, Colombia
Rodrigo Linfati	Universidad del Bío–Bío, Chile
Roman Neruda	Charles University, Czech Academy of Sciences
Santiago Murillo Rendón	Universidad Nacional de Colombia, Colombia
Sergio Rojas–Galeano	Universidad Distrital Francisco José de Caldas, Colombia
Steven Latré	University of Antwerp, The Netherlands
Tomás Arias	Universidad de Antioquia, Colombia
Victor Cantillo	Universidad del Norte, Colombia
Victor Medina García	Universidad Distrital Francisco José de Caldas, Colombia
William Camilo Rodríguez	Universidad Distrital Francisco José de Caldas, Colombia
William Sarache	Universidad Nacional de Colombia, Colombia
Xavier Hesselbach	Universitat Politècnica de Catalunya, Spain
Yesid Díaz	Corporación Unificada Nacional de Educación Superior (CUN), Colombia
Yurilev Chalco–Cano	Universidad de Tarapacá, Chile

Contents – Part I

Simulation Systems

Contents – Part II

Internet of Things (IoT)

Miscellaneous Applications

Computational Intelligence

Optimization Under Fuzzy Constraints: From a Heuristic Algorithm to an Algorithm that Always Converges

Vladik Kreinovich[1]⬤ and Juan Carlos Figueroa-García[2(✉)]⬤

[1] University of Texas at El Paso, El Paso, TX 79968, USA
vladik@utep.edu
[2] Universidad Distrital Francisco José de Caldas, Bogotá D.C., Colombia
jcfigueroag@udistrital.edu.co
http://www.cs.utep.edu/vladik

Abstract. An efficient iterative heuristic algorithm has been used to implement Bellman-Zadeh solution to the problem of optimization under fuzzy constraints. In this paper, we analyze this algorithm, explain why it works, show that there are cases when this algorithm does not converge, and propose a modification that always converges.

Keywords: Optimization · Fuzzy constraints
Bellmna-Zadeh approach · Convergence

1 Formulation of the Problem

Need to Select the Best Alternative. In many practical situations, we want to select the best of the possible alternatives x.

To use mathematical and computational techniques in solving such problems, we need describe this problem in precise terms. For this, we need to describe what is meant by "the best", and what is meant by "possible alternatives".

What Does "The Best" Means. "The best" can usually be described in numerical form: we have an objective function $f(x)$ such that the larger the value of this function, the better the alternative. For example, in economics problems, we want to maximize profit.

In some cases, the better alternative corresponds to the smallest value of the corresponding function $g(x)$. For example, in economics, we may want to minimize the cost $g(x)$. In transportation problems, we may want to minimize travel time $g(x)$. Such problems can be easily reformulated in the maximization terms if we take $f(x) \stackrel{\text{def}}{=} -g(x)$.

The Objective Function Is Usually Continuous, Even Smooth. Tiny changes in the selected alternative usually do not change the output much, so

---

This work was supported in part by US National Science Foundation grant HRD-1242122 (Cyber-ShARE Center).

J. C. Figueroa-García et al. (Eds.): WEA 2018, CCIS 915, pp. 3–16, 2018.
https://doi.org/10.1007/978-3-030-00350-0_1

we expect that the values of the objective function $f(x)$ should not change much either. Thus, we expect the objective function to be continuous – or, if we interpret "not much" as bounded by a certain constant times Δx, as Lipschitz continuous, and thus, as differentiable almost everywhere. In practice, the objective function is usually smooth.

Which Alternatives Are Possible? An alternative is possible if it satisfies certain constraints. Usually, these constraints are equalities $g_i(x) = 0$ or inequalities $h_j(x) \geq 0$. For example, in chemical manufacturing, constraints are that the number of potential pollutants $p(x)$ released into the environment does not exceed some threshold t: $p(x) \leq t$. This constraint can be described as $h_1(x) \geq 0$, where $h_1(x) \stackrel{\text{def}}{=} t - p(x)$.

In principle, we can have more general constraints. Let us denote the set of all possible alternatives – i.e., of all the alternatives that satisfy all the constraints – by $S \subset R^N$ for an appropriate N.

It Is Reasonable to Assume that Constraints Describe a Closed Set. Selecting an alternative means selecting the parameters that describe this alternative. For example, in control applications, we select the values of the control parameters. For a car, we can select the acceleration and the torque, etc.

In practice, we can set up the desired values only with some accuracy – and we can only measure how well we have set them with some accuracy. As a result, if we have a sequence of possible alternative $x_1, x_2, \ldots$ that converges to a limit alternative x, then, for any desired implementation and/or measuring accuracy $\varepsilon > 0$, there is a possible state x_n which is ε-close to x and is, thus, practically indistinguishable from the alternative x. Since we cannot distinguish the limit alternative x from possible alternatives, no matter how much we increase our accuracy, it makes sense to assume that the limit alternative x is also possible.

Under this assumption, the set S of all possible alternatives has the property that is $x_i \in S$ for all i and $x_i \to x$, then $x \in S$. In mathematical terms, this means that the set S is *closed*.

Comment. This closeness assumption is the main reason why in traditional optimization problems, we consider constraints of the non-strict inequality type $h_j(x) \geq 0$ but not constraints of the strict inequality type $h_j(x) > 0$. Indeed, non-strict inequalities are preserved in the limit, while strict inequalities are not necessarily preserved: e.g., $2^{-i} > 0$, $2^{-i} \to 0$, but $0 \not> 0$.

In Practice, the Set of Possible Alternatives Is Always Bounded. In practice, the values of all the quantities are bounded. For example, the speeds are limited by the speed of light, the distances for Earth travel are bounded by the Earth's size, accelerations are bounded by our technical abilities, etc. Thus, in practice, the set S of possible alternatives is always bounded.

Mathematical Conclusion: The Set of Possible Alternatives Is a Compact Set. Since the set S is closed and bounded, it is a compact set. This means, in particular, that for every continuous function $F(x)$ on this set, there exists an alternative x_{opt} at which this function attains its maximum, i.e., at which $F(x_{\text{opt}}) = \max\limits_{x \in S} F(x)$.

Resulting Formulation: Optimization Under Constraints. Thus, the above practical problem takes the following form: maximize the objective function $f(x)$ under the constraint that $g_1(x) = 0$, ..., $g_m(x) = 0$, $h_1(x) \geq 0$, ..., $h_m(x) \geq 0$ (or, more generally, that $x \in S$ for some compact set S).

Since the set S of possible alternatives is compact, for continuous objective functions $f(x)$, there is always an alternative x_{opt} that solves this problem.

Algorithms for Optimization Under Constraints. There exist many efficient algorithms for optimization under constraints; see, e.g., [9].

The most well-known methods are based on Lagrange multiplier techniques, according to which maximizing a function $f(x)$ under the constraints $g_1(x) = 0$, ..., $g_m(x) = 0$ can be reduced to the unconstrained problem of maximizing the auxiliary function

$$f(x) + \lambda_1 \cdot g_1(x) + \ldots + \lambda_m \cdot g_m(x),$$

where the auxiliary constants λ_i (known as *Lagrange multipliers*) can be determined by the condition that the resulting solution x satisfies all m equality constraints $g_i(x) = 0$, $1 \leq i \leq m$.

Thus, equality-type constraint optimization problem can be reduced to an unconstraint optimization problem, and for such problems, many efficient optimization algorithms are known; see, e.g., [9].

If some of the constraints are inequalities, then the constrained maximum is attained when some of them are equalities, and some are not. In this case, we need to consider all 2^n possible subsets $I \subseteq \{1, \ldots, n\}$, and for each of these subsets, look for local maxima of the auxiliary function

$$f(x) + \sum_{i=1}^{m} \lambda_i(x) \cdot g_i(x) + \sum_{j \in I} \lambda'_j \cdot h_j(x).$$

For each I, we select the coefficients λ_i and λ'_j from the condition that $g_i(x) = 0$ for all i and $h_j(x) = 0$ for all $j \in I$; then, we check that $h_j(x) > 0$ for all $j \notin I$.

This procedure leads to several different possible maxima x; out of them, we select the one for which the value of the objective function $f(x)$ is the largest.

Need for Imprecise ("Fuzzy") Constraints. In many practical situations, constraints are imprecise. For example, when we select a hotel, we want it to be "comfortable" and/or "not very expensive". These are not precise terms: in many cases, we are not 100% sure what "not very expensive" means.

Fuzzy Logic: A Way to Describe Imprecise ("Fuzzy") Constraints. Situations where we have information described in such imprecise ("fuzzy") natural-language terms are ubiquitous. To take this imprecise information into account when using computers, it is necessary to describe this information in precise terms. Such a description was proposed by Lotfi Zadeh and is now known as *fuzzy logic*; see, e.g., [2,4,7,8,10,11].

The main idea behind fuzzy logic is that to describe an imprecise property like "not very expensive", we ask an expert, for each possible value of the corresponding quantity q (i.e., of the hotel daily rate) describe, on a scale from 0 to 1, the degree to which this amount is, in the opinion of this expert, not very expensive. For example, for a hotel in El Paso, Texas, a daily rate of $140 would definitely not satisfy this property, so we assign degree 0. The daily rate of $35 would definitely satisfy this property, so we assign degree 1. For some intermediate values like $80, we will assign intermediate degrees.

Instead of using the scale from 0 to 1, we can alternatively use a scale, e.g., from 0 to 10, and then divide the result by 10. For example, if an expert estimates his/her degree as 7 on a scale from 0 to 10, we get the degree $7/10 = 0.7$.

As a result, as a description of the desired imprecise property, we get a function that assigns, to each possible value q of this quantity, the degree $\mu(q)$ to which this value satisfies this property. This function is known as a *membership function*, or, alternatively, as a *fuzzy set*.

Tiny changes in x usually only slightly change the degree to which x is possible. So, similarly to our conclusion that the objective function be continuous and even smooth, we conclude that the membership function should also be continuous – and, if possible, smooth.

"And"-Operations. In most practical situations, we have several different constraints that describe different quantities. For example, when selecting a hotel, we want a hotel which is not very expensive (which is a limitation on the daily rate), not very noisy (which is a restriction on noise level), not too far from the city center (which is a restriction on the distance), etc.

By using the above procedure, we can find, for each of the related quantities, the degree to which the given value of this quantity satisfies the corresponding constraint. But what we are interested in is the degree to which the hotel as a whole satisfies all these properties, i.e., the degree to which the hotel is not very expensive *and* not very noisy *and* not too far from the city center, etc. How can we find this degree?

Theoretically, we could use the same procedure as above and ask the expert's opinion about all possible combinations of the corresponding quantities. However, the number of such combinations grows exponentially with the number of quantities, and even for reasonable number of quantities, becomes astronomically large. It is therefore not practically possible to ask for expert's opinion about all these combinations.

Thus, we need to be able to estimate the degree to which an "and"-combination $A \& B$ is satisfied if we know to what extent A and B are satisfied. In other words, we need to be able, given the degree a to which A is satisfied and the degree b to which b is satisfied, to come up with an estimate for the degree to which the combination $A \& B$ is satisfied. This estimate is usually denoted by $f_\&(a, b)$, and the corresponding function $f_\&$ is known as an *"and"-operation*, or, for historical reasons, a *t-norm*.

This operation must satisfy several reasonable conditions. For example, since $A \& B$ means the same as $B \& A$, it is reasonable to require that the estimates for these two combinations are the same, i.e., that $f_\&(a, b) = f_\&(b, a)$. In mathematical terms, this means that the "and"-operations be commutative.

Similarly, since $A \& (B \& C)$ means the same as $(A \& B) \& C$, we expect that the corresponding estimates are equal, i.e., that $f_\&(a, f_\&(b, c)) = f_\&(f_\&(a, b), c)$. In other words, the "and"-operations must be associative.

The degree to which we believe that $A \& B$ holds cannot exceed the degree to which A or B holds, so we must have $f_\&(a, b) \leq a$ and $f_\&(a, b) \leq b$.

If our degree of belief in A and/or in B increases, then the degree of belief in $A \& B$ will either increase or remain the same. So, the "and"-operation should be monotonic: if $a \leq a'$ and $b \leq b'$, then $f_\&(a, b) \leq f_\&(a', b')$.

It is also reasonable, since $A \& A$ means the same as A, to require that $f_\&(a, a) = a$ for all a. It turns out that the only "and"-operation that satisfies all these properties is the minimum $f_\&(a, b) = \min(a, b)$.

Proposition 1. *Let $f_\&(a, b)$ be a function from $[0, 1] \times [0, 1]$ to $[0, 1]$ that satisfies the following properties:*

- *it is monotonic, i.e., $a \leq a'$ and $b \leq b'$ imply $f_\&(a, b) \leq f_\&(a', b')$;*
- *it is idempotent, i.e., $f_\&(a, a) = a$ for all a, and*
- *it satisfies the inequalities $f_\&(a, b) \leq a$ and $f_\&(a, b) \leq b$ for all a and b.*

Then, $f_\&(a, b) = \min(a, b)$ for all a and b.

Comments.

- All the proofs are places in a special (last) proofs section.
- Please note that this result does not require that $f_\&$ be commutative and/or associative.
- Minimum is indeed one of the most widely use "and"-operations.

Fuzzy Constraints. After applying the appropriate "and"-operation to constraints describing individual quantities, we get a membership function (fuzzy set) $\mu(x)$ that describes, for each alternative x, to what extend this alternative satisfies all the given constraints, i.e., to what extent this alternative x is possible.

Alpha-Cuts: An Alternative Way of Describing Fuzzy Sets. Instead of a membership function $\mu(x)$, we can describe the same imprecise information if we describe, for each $\alpha \in (0, 1]$, the set $S_\alpha \stackrel{\text{def}}{=} \{x : \mu(x) \geq \alpha\}$ of all the alternatives for which the expert's degree of confidence that x is possible is at least α. Such sets are known as *alpha-cuts*.

Once we know all the α-cuts, we can uniquely reconstruct the membership function: namely, one can easily prove that for every x, $\mu(x)$ is the largest α for which $x \in S_\alpha$.

Alpha-Cuts Are Usually Closed and Compact. Since the membership functions are continuous, alpha-cuts are closed sets; since the set of possible alternatives is bounded, each α-cut is a compact set.

Additional Natural Property. Similar to our arguments that $f(x)$ and $\mu(x)$ be continuous, it is also reasonable to assume that the set S_α to also continuously depend on α – e.g., in terms of the usual Hausdorff metric

$$d_H(S, S') = \max\left(\max_{s \in S} d(s, S'), \max_{s' \in S'} d(s', S)\right),$$

where the distance $d(s', S)$ between an element s' and a set S is defined in the usual way $d(s', S) \overset{\text{def}}{=} \min_{s \in S} d(s', s)$. This is true for many known membership functions.

Optimization Under Fuzzy Constraints: Bellman-Zadeh Formulation of the Problem. Intuitively, it makes sense to say that the desired alternative should be optimal *and* satisfy all the constraints. For example, when we look for a hotel which is the cheapest among all the hotel which are not too far away from the city center, what we are really meaning is that we are looking for a hotel which is cheap and not too far away from the city center.

To describe this idea in precise terms, we need to be able to describe, for each alternative x, the degree $\mu_{\text{opt}}(x)$ to what extent this alternative is optimal. The corresponding degree depends on the value of the objective function $f(x)$, i.e., we must have $\mu_{\text{opt}}(x) = F(f(x))$ for some function $F(x)$.

When the value $f(x)$ is the smallest possible, i.e., when $f(x) = m \overset{\text{def}}{=} \min_{x \in X} f(x)$, where X is the set of all alternatives, then this degree is 0: $\mu_{\text{opt}}(x) = 0$. In other words, we must have $F(m) = 0$.

Similarly, when the value $f(x)$ is the largest possible, i.e., when $f(x) = M \overset{\text{def}}{=} \max_{x \in X} f(x)$, then this degree is 1: $\mu_{\text{opt}}(x) = 1$. In other words, we must have $F(M) = 1$.

It is reasonable to use the simplest linear interpolation to find the values $F(f(x))$ for $f(x) \in (m, M)$. Thus, we get $\mu_{\text{opt}}(x) = \dfrac{f(x) - m}{M - m}$. The degree to which the alternative x is optimal *and* satisfies the constraints can be obtained by applying the corresponding "and"-operation (which we agreed to be min) and is, thus, equal to

$$J(x) \overset{\text{def}}{=} \min\left(\frac{f(x) - m}{M - m}, \mu(x)\right). \tag{1}$$

We should select the alternative for which this degree of satisfaction is the largest, i.e., we should select the alternative for which $J(x)$ attains the largest possible value.

This formulation was proposed by Zadeh and Bellman in 1970 and is thus known as Bellman-Zadeh approach to optimization under fuzzy constraints [1]; see also [5, 6].

Comment. Since both the original objective function $f(x)$ and the membership function $\mu(x)$ are continuous, the function $J(x)$ is also continuous. Due to the fact that the set of all possible alternatives S is a compact set, there always exists an alternative at which the new objective function $J(x)$ attains its maximum. Thus, the Bellman-Zadeh formulation always leads to a solution.

Bellman-Zadeh Approach: Need for New Algorithms. At first glance, the situation is good: we have reduced the original practical problem to the problem of unconstrained optimization, and for this problem, as we have mentioned, there are many efficient algorithms.

However, from the computational viewpoint, the situation is not so good: most efficient optimization algorithms require that the objective function be smooth (everywhere differentiable), and the expression $J(x)$ is not differentiable – even when the original objective function $f(x)$ and the membership function $\mu(x)$ describing constraints is differentiable. This is because the function $\min(a, b)$ is not differentiable when $a = b$.

For non-smooth functions, optimization algorithms are not that efficient; thus, it is desirable to design new efficient algorithm for solving the corresponding problem.

A Known Heuristic Algorithm. A heuristic iterative algorithm for optimization under fuzzy constraints is known. This algorithm assumes that we can efficiently solve the corresponding crisp optimization problems. Specifically, we assume that for every α, we can efficiently maximize $f(x)$ under the constraint $x \in S_\alpha$, where S_α is the α-cut of the fuzzy constraint set $\mu(x)$.

In this algorithm, we start with an arbitrary value $\alpha_0 \in (0, 1)$, and then compute the values $\alpha_1, \alpha_2, \ldots$ as follows. Once we have the value α_k, we:

- solve the corresponding constraint optimization problem, i.e., find the maximum M_k of the original objective function $f(x)$ under the constraint $x \in S_{\alpha_k}$ (and find the value x_k at which this maximum is attained); and
- then compute $\alpha_{k+1} \stackrel{\text{def}}{=} \dfrac{M_k - m}{M - m}$.

We stop when the difference between the two consecutive values of α_k becomes sufficiently small, i.e., when $|\alpha_{k+1} - \alpha_k| \le \varepsilon$ for some pre-determined stopping threshold $\varepsilon > 0$. In this case, we return the corresponding alternative x_k as the optimal one.

The main advantage of this heuristic algorithm comes from the fact that for each α, the constraint $x \in S_\alpha$ has a traditional non-fuzzy form. For example, for the inequality constraint of the type $H_j(x) \ge A$ for some fuzzy number A, the α-cut usually has a form $H_j(x) \ge a$ for some crisp a, i.e., the form $h_j(x) \ge 0$, where $h_j(x) \stackrel{\text{def}}{=} H_j(x) - a$. Thus, to find x_k, we can use known and well-developed efficient algorithms for traditional (non-fuzzy) constraint optimization.

Results of Testing this Algorithm. In [3], one of the authors applied this heuristic algorithm to several different instances of optimization under fuzzy constraints. In all these instances, no matter what the initial value α_0 we selected, the above iterative process converged and let to the solution of the Bellman-Zadeh problem.

Theoretical Challenges. These empirical results led to the following theoretical challenges:

1. If the above process converges, do we always get the solution to the Bellman-Zadeh problem (and if yes, why)?
2. Why for each case when the process converged, the resulting limit $\lim\limits_{k} \alpha_k$ did not depend on the initial value α_0?
3. Does the above process always converge? and
4. If the above iterative process does not always converge, then how can we modify this algorithm to guarantee convergence?

In this paper, we provide answers to all these questions.

2   Analysis of the Problem

Definitions. Let us first describe the above ideas in precise terms.

Definition 1. *Let X be a compact set. By a* reasonable membership function *on X, we mean a continuous function $\mu : X \rightarrow [0,1]$ for which the family $S_\alpha \overset{\text{def}}{=} \{x : \mu(x) \geq \alpha\}$ continuously depends on α for $\alpha > 0$.*

Definition 2.

- *By a* problem of *optimization under fuzzy constraints, we mean the triple $\langle X, f, \mu \rangle$, where $X \subseteq R^N$ is a bounded closed (compact) set, $f : X \rightarrow \mathbb{R}$, and μ is a reasonable membership function on the set X.*
- *We say that an element x_{opt} is a* solution *to the problem of optimization under fuzzy constraints if $J(x_{\text{opt}}) = \max\limits_{x \in X} J(x)$, where $J(x)$ is defined by the formula (1).*

Simplifying Notations. To analyze our problem, it is useful to reformulate it by using simpler notations.

For every α, let us denote $M(\alpha) \overset{\text{def}}{=} \max\{f(x) : x \in S_\alpha\}$, and $G(\alpha) \overset{\text{def}}{=} \dfrac{M(\alpha) - m}{M - m}$.

In terms of the function $G(\alpha)$, the existing algorithm takes a very simple form: $\alpha_{k+1} = G(\alpha_k)$.

Properties of the Newly Defined Functions. Since $\alpha < \alpha'$ implies $S_\alpha \supseteq S_{\alpha'}$, we have $M(\alpha) \geq M(\alpha')$ and thus, $G(\alpha) \geq G(\alpha')$. So, the functions $M(\alpha)$ and $G(\alpha)$ are (non-strictly) decreasing functions.

Since S_α continuously depends on α and the function $f(x)$ is continuous, one can show that the function $M(\alpha)$ also continuously depends on α. Thus, the function $G(\alpha) = \dfrac{M(\alpha) - m}{M - m}$ is also continuous.

What Happens when the Process Converges. When the process converges, i.e., when $\alpha_k \to \alpha$, then, due to the continuity of the function $G(\alpha)$, in the limit $k \to \infty$, we get

$$G(\alpha) = \alpha. \qquad (2)$$

3 Answer to the First Challenge

The First Challenge: Reminder. The first challenge was to explain why finding the value α for which the above iterative process converges, i.e., for which $G(\alpha) = \alpha$, is helpful in solving the original problem of optimization under fuzzy constraint.

Proposition 2.

– *If $G(\alpha) = \alpha$, then there exists an optimal solution x_{opt} for which $\mu(x_{\text{opt}}) = J(x_{\text{opt}}) = \alpha$.*
– *Vice versa, for every problem of optimization under fuzzy constraints, there exists an optimal solution x_{opt} for which, for $\alpha \stackrel{\text{def}}{=} \mu(x_{\text{opt}})$, we have $G(\alpha) = \alpha = J(x_{\text{opt}})$.*

Comments.

– Thus, finding α for which $G(\alpha) = \alpha$ indeed leads to optimal solution – and vice versa.
– When the function $G(\alpha)$ is strictly decreasing, the second part of Proposition 2 becomes even more straightforward.

Proposition 3. *When the function $G(\alpha)$ is strictly decreasing, then for every optimal solution x_{opt}, we have $G(\alpha) = \alpha = J(x_{\text{opt}})$, where $\alpha \stackrel{\text{def}}{=} \mu(x_{\text{opt}})$.*

4 Answer to the Second Challenge

The Second Challenge: Reminder. The second challenge was to explain why for each case when the heuristic algorithm converged, the resulting limit $\lim_{k} \alpha_k$ did not depend on the initial value α_0.

Our Explanation. We know that when the process converges, the limit α satisfies the property $G(\alpha) = \alpha$. According to Proposition 2, this implies that $\alpha = \max_{x \in X} J(x)$. Thus, whenever the heuristic algorithm converges, it converges to the same value $\alpha = \max_{x \in X} J(x)$.

5   Answer to the Third Challenge

The Third Challenge: Reminder. The third challenge was to check whether the above process always converges.

Our Answer. We have a simple counter-example. Let $X = [0,1]$, $f(x) = x$ and let $\mu(x) = 1 - x$. In this case, $m = 0$ and $M = 1$, so $J(x) = \min(f(x), \mu(x)) = \min(x, 1 - x)$. This function increases for $x \leq 0.5$ and decreases for $x \geq 0.5$, so its largest possible value is attained for $x = 0.5$ and is equal to 0.5.

Here, for any α, we have $S_\alpha = \{x : 1 - x \geq \alpha\} = [0, 1 - \alpha]$. The largest possible value $M(\alpha)$ of $f(x) = x$ on this α-cut interval is equal to $1 - \alpha$. Since $m = 0$ and $M = 1$, we have $G(\alpha) = M(\alpha) = 1 - \alpha$.

Thus, whatever value $\alpha_0 \leq 0.5$ we start with, we get $\alpha_1 = G(\alpha_0) = 1 - \alpha_0$ and then $\alpha_2 = 1 - \alpha_1 = 1 - (1 - \alpha_0) = \alpha_0$ again. The iterative process oscillates between α_0 and $1 - \alpha_0$ and does not converge.

6   Answer to the Forth Challenge

The Fourth Challenge: Reminder. The fourth challenge was to modify the current heuristic algorithm to guarantee convergence.

Analysis of the Problem. According to Proposition 1, we need to find the value α for which $G(\alpha) = \alpha$. This is equivalent to finding the root of the equation $H(\alpha) < 0$, where $H(\alpha) \overset{\text{def}}{=} G(\alpha) - \alpha$.

If $G(\alpha_0) = \alpha_0$, we are done. What if $\alpha_1 \neq \alpha_0$?

- If $\alpha_1 = G(\alpha_0) < \alpha_0$, i.e., if $H(\alpha_0) < 0$, then, due to the fact that the function $G(\alpha)$ is non-strictly decreasing, we get $G(\alpha_1) \geq \alpha_1$, i.e., $H(\alpha_1) \geq 0$.
- Similarly, if $\alpha_1 = G(\alpha_0) > \alpha_0$, i.e., if $H(\alpha_0) > 0$, then, due to the fact that the function $G(\alpha)$ is non-strictly decreasing, we get $G(\alpha_1) \leq \alpha_1$, i.e., $H(\alpha_1) \leq 0$.

In both cases, we have two values $\underline{\alpha} < \overline{\alpha}$ for which $H(\underline{\alpha}) \geq 0 \geq H(\overline{\alpha})$. To always find the root α for which $H(\alpha) = 0$, we can use, e.g., bisection; see, e.g., [9]. Thus, we arrive at the following algorithm.

A Modified Algorithm that Always Converges. Start with an arbitrary value α_0 and compute $\alpha_1 = G(\alpha_0)$.

If $\alpha_1 = \alpha_0$, we are done, otherwise we form an interval $[\underline{\alpha}, \overline{\alpha}]$ for which $H(\underline{\alpha}) \geq 0 \geq H(\overline{\alpha})$: $\underline{\alpha} = \min(\alpha_0, \alpha_1)$ and $\overline{\alpha} = \max(\alpha_0, \alpha_1)$.

On each iteration, we take $m \overset{\text{def}}{=} \dfrac{1}{2} \cdot (\underline{\alpha} + \overline{\alpha})$ and compute $H(m) = G(m) - m$. Then:

- if $H(m) \geq 0$, we replace $\underline{\alpha}$ with m;
- otherwise, we replace $\overline{\alpha}$ with m.

In both cases, the size of the intervals halves. We stop when the difference $\overline{\alpha} - \underline{\alpha}$ becomes smaller than or equal to a pre-defined threshold ε.

7   Proofs

Proof of Proposition 1. Let us consider two possible cases: $a \leq b$ and $b \leq a$.

In the first case $a \leq b$, due to monotonicity, we have $f_{\&}(a, a) \leq f_{\&}(a, b)$. Since $f_{\&}(a, a) = a$, we conclude that $a \leq f_{\&}(a, b)$. On the other hand, we know that $f_{\&}(a, b) \leq a$. Thus, we conclude that $f_{\&}(a, b) = a$, i.e., that in this case, indeed $f_{\&}(a, b) = \min(a, b)$.

In the second case $b \leq a$, due to monotonicity, we have $f_{\&}(b, b) \leq f_{\&}(a, b)$. Since $f_{\&}(b, b) = b$, we conclude that $b \leq f_{\&}(a, b)$. On the other hand, we know that $f_{\&}(a, b) \leq b$. Thus, we conclude that $f_{\&}(a, b) = b$, i.e., that in this case, indeed $f_{\&}(a, b) = \min(a, b)$.

The proposition is proven.

Proof of Proposition 2.

1°. Let us first prove that if $G(\alpha) = \alpha$, then there exists an alternative x_{opt} for which $J(x_{\text{opt}}) = \max\limits_{x \in X} J(x) = \alpha$.

Indeed, let us take x' for which $f(x') = \max\limits_{x \in S_\alpha} f(x)$. Then us show that this is indeed the optimizing value. Indeed, for this x', we have $f(x') = M(\alpha)$ and thus, $\dfrac{f(x') - m}{M - m} = \dfrac{M(\alpha) - m}{M - m} = G(\alpha) = \alpha$. Since $x' \in S_\alpha$, we have $\mu(x') \geq \alpha$ thus $\mu(x') \geq G(\alpha)$. Thus,

$$J(x') = \min\left(\frac{f(x') - m}{M - m}, \mu(x')\right) = \min(G(\alpha), \mu(x')) = G(\alpha) = \alpha.$$

Let us prove that this is indeed the optimal solution, i.e., that $J(x) \leq J(x')$ for all $x \in X$. For this, let us consider two possible cases: $x \in S_\alpha$ and $x \notin S_\alpha$.

1.1°. If $x \in S_\alpha$, then, since the maximum of $f(x)$ on S_α is attained at the alternative x', we have $f(x) \leq f(x')$. Hence, $\dfrac{f(x) - m}{M - m} \leq \dfrac{f(x') - m}{M - m} = \alpha$. Thus,

$$J(x) = \min\left(\frac{f(x) - m}{M - m}, \mu(x)\right) \leq \frac{f(x) - m}{M - m} \leq \alpha = J(x').$$

So, in this case, indeed $J(x) \leq J(x')$.

1.2°. If $x \notin S_\alpha$, then $\mu(x) < \alpha$. Thus,

$$J(x) = \min\left(\frac{f(x) - m}{M - m}, \mu(x)\right) \leq \mu(x) < \alpha.$$

Since $J(x') = \alpha$, this also implies that $J(x) < J(x')$.

The first statement is thus proven.

2°. Let us now prove that there always exists an optimal solution x_{opt} for which, for $\alpha = \mu(x_{\text{opt}})$, we have $G(\alpha) = \alpha = J(x_{\text{opt}})$.

Since the new objective function $J(x)$ is continuous, and the set X is compact, there exists an alternative x' at which this objective function attains its maximum: $J(x') = \max\limits_{x \in X} J(x)$. Let us denote $\alpha' \overset{\text{def}}{=} \mu(x')$.

2.1°. Let us first prove that $G(\alpha') \leq \alpha'$. To prove this, let us assume that $G(\alpha') > \alpha'$ and let us derive a contradiction that will show that this inequality is impossible.

Let x'' be the value $x'' \in S_{\alpha'}$ at which the function $f(x)$ attains its maximum $M(\alpha')$ on the set $S_{\alpha'}$. Then, since $x' \in S(\alpha')$, we have $f(x'') \geq f(x')$ and thus,

$$\frac{f(x'') - m}{M - m} = \frac{M(\alpha') - m}{M - m} \geq \frac{f(x') - m}{M - m}.$$

Since $x'' \in S_{\alpha'}$, by definition of the α-cut, we have $\mu(x'') \geq \alpha'$. Thus,

$$\min\left(\frac{f(x'') - m}{M - m}, \mu(x'')\right) = \min(G(\alpha'), \mu(x')) \geq \min(G(\alpha'), \alpha') \geq$$

$$\min\left(\frac{f(x') - m}{M - m}, \alpha'\right) = J(x').$$

Since the value $J(x')$ is the largest possible value of the auxiliary, we cannot have strict inequality, so $\min(G(\alpha'), \alpha') = J(x')$. Since $G(\alpha') > \alpha'$, this means that $J(x') = \alpha'$, i.e., α' is the largest possible value of the function $J(x)$.

From $G(\alpha') > \alpha'$, it follows that $G(\alpha') > \alpha' + \delta$, where we denoted $\delta \overset{\text{def}}{=} \frac{1}{2} \cdot (G(\alpha') - \alpha')$. Since we assumed that the function $G(\alpha)$ is continuous, there exists a $\varepsilon > 0$ for which $|\alpha - \alpha'| \leq \varepsilon$ also implies $G(\alpha) > \alpha' + \delta$. Thus, for $\alpha'' \overset{\text{def}}{=} \alpha' + \min(\delta, \varepsilon)$, we have $\alpha'' > \alpha'$ and $G(\alpha'') > \alpha'$ hence $\min(G(\alpha''), \alpha'') > \alpha' = J(x')$. Let us now take the value x''' for which the maximum of $f(x)$ is attained on the set $S_{\alpha''}$, i.e., for which $f(x''') = M(\alpha'')$. Then, $\frac{f(x''') - m}{M - m} = \frac{M(\alpha'') - m}{M - m} = G(\alpha'')$ and – due to $x''' \in S(\alpha'')$ – we have $\mu(x''') \geq \alpha''$. Then, we have

$$\min\left(\frac{f(x''') - m}{M - m}, \mu(x''')\right) \geq \min(G(\alpha''), \alpha'') > \alpha' = J(x'),$$

which contradicts to our assumption that $J(x')$ is the largest possible value of the function $J(x)$.

Thus, the case $G(\alpha') > \alpha'$ is indeed impossible, and so $G(\alpha') \leq \alpha'$.

2.2°. Since $G(\alpha') \leq \alpha'$, we have two possible cases: $G(\alpha') < \alpha'$ and $G(\alpha') = \alpha'$. Let us show that in the first case, we can find some value α'' for which $G(\alpha'') = \alpha''$.

Indeed, let us assume that $G(\alpha') < \alpha'$. In this case, let us take x'' for which $f(x'') = \max_{x \in S_{\alpha'}} f(x)$. Then, $f(x'') = M(\alpha') \geq f(x')$ and $\mu(x'') \geq \alpha'$, hence

$$J(x'') = \min\left(\frac{f(x'') - m}{M - m}, \mu(x'')\right) \geq \min(G(\alpha'), \mu(x'')) \geq$$
$$\min(G(\alpha'), \alpha') \geq \min\left(\frac{f(x') - m}{M - m}, \alpha'\right) = J(x').$$

Since $J(x')$ is the largest possible value of x', we thus get $J(x'') = J(x') = \min(G(\alpha'), \alpha')$. Since $G(\alpha') < \alpha'$, this means that $J(x') = G(\alpha')$.

Let us now take $\alpha'' \stackrel{\text{def}}{=} G(\alpha')$. Then, $\alpha'' < \alpha'$. Since the function $G(\alpha)$ is non-strictly decreasing, we have $G(\alpha'') \geq \alpha''$. Thus, $\min(G(\alpha''), \alpha'') \geq \alpha'' = G(\alpha') = J(x')$. By taking the alternative $x'' \in S_{\alpha''}$ that maximizes $f(x)$, we get $J(x'') \geq J(x')$, and since $J(x')$ is the largest value, we get $J(x'') = J(x')$.

Similarly to Part 2.1 of this proof, we can prove that we cannot have $G(\alpha'') > \alpha''$, so we have $G(\alpha'') = \alpha''$.

2.3°. Once we have a value α for which $G(\alpha) = \alpha$, we can use Part 1 of this proof to show that $\max_{x \in X} J(x) = \alpha$. The proposition is proven.

Proof of Proposition 3. Let us assume that the function $G(\alpha)$ is strictly decreasing, that $J(x_{\text{opt}}) = \max_{x \in X} J(x)$. Let us prove that for $\alpha \stackrel{\text{def}}{=} \mu(x_{\text{opt}})$, we have $G(\alpha) = \alpha = J(x_{\text{opt}})$.

Indeed, let x' be the alternative for which the original objective function $f(x)$ attains its maximum on the set S_α. Since $x' \in S_\alpha$, we thus get $f(x') \geq f(x_{\text{opt}})$, hence $\dfrac{f(x') - m}{M - m} = \dfrac{M(\alpha) - m}{M - m} = G(\alpha) \geq \dfrac{f(x_{\text{opt}}) - m}{M - m}$; also, $\mu(x') \geq \alpha_{\text{opt}} = \mu(x')$. Thus,

$$J(x') = \min\left(\frac{f(x') - m}{M - m}, \mu(x')\right) \geq \min(G(\alpha), \alpha) \geq J(x_{\text{opt}}).$$

Since x_{opt} is the optimal alternative, we have $J(x_{\text{opt}}) = \min(G(\alpha), \alpha)$.

Similar to the proof of Part 2.1 of Proposition 2, we can conclude that $G(\alpha) \leq \alpha$. So, to complete our proof, we need to prove that $G(\alpha) = \alpha$, i.e., that the case $G(\alpha) < \alpha$ is not possible.

Indeed, in this case, we can take $\alpha' = \dfrac{1}{2} \cdot (G(\alpha) + \alpha)$. Here, $\alpha' > G(\alpha)$. Due to strict monotonicity, we have $G(\alpha') > G(\alpha)$, thus, $\min(G(\alpha'), \alpha') > G(\alpha) = J(x')$. By taking an alternative x'' that maximizes $f(x)$ on $S_{\alpha'}$, we will get $J(x'') \geq \min(G(\alpha'), \alpha') > G(\alpha) = J(x')$ and thus, $J(x'') > J(x')$, which contradicts to our assumption that $J(x')$ is the largest possible value of $J(x)$.

The proposition is proven.

References

1. Bellman, R.E., Zadeh, L.A.: Decision making in a fuzzy environment. Manag. Sci. **17**(4), B141–B164 (1970)
2. Belohlavek, R., Dauben, J.W., Klir, G.J.: Fuzzy Logic and Mathematics: A Historical Perspective. Oxford University Press, New York (2017)
3. Figueroa-García, J.C., Tenjo-García, J.S., Bustos-Tellez, C.A.: Solving transhipment problems with fuzzy delivery costs and fuzzy constraints. In: Barreto, G., Coelho, R. (eds.) NAFIPS 2018. CCIS, vol. 831, pp. 538–550. Springer, Cham (2018). https://doi.org/10.1007/978-3-319-95312-0_47
4. Klir, G., Yuan, B.: Fuzzy Sets and Fuzzy Logic. Prentice Hall, Upper Saddle River (1995)
5. Kosheleva, O., Kreinovich, V.: Why Bellman-Zadeh approach to fuzzy optimization. Appl. Math. Sci. **12**(11), 517–522 (2018)
6. Kreinovich, V., Kosheleva, O., Shahbazova, S.: Which t-norm is most appropriate for Bellman-Zadeh optimization. In: Proceedings of the World Conference on Soft Computing, Baku, Azerbaijan, 29–31 May 2018 (2018)
7. Mendel, J.M.: Uncertain Rule-Based Fuzzy Systems: Introduction and New Directions. Springer, Cham (2017). https://doi.org/10.1007/978-3-319-51370-6
8. Nguyen, H.T., Walker, E.A.: A First Course in Fuzzy Logic. Chapman and Hall/CRC, Boca Raton (2006)
9. Nocedal, J., Wright, S.: Numerical Optimization, 2nd edn. Springer, New York (2006). https://doi.org/10.1007/978-0-387-40065-5
10. Novák, V., Perfilieva, I., Močkoř, J.: Mathematical Principles of Fuzzy Logic. Kluwer, Boston, Dordrecht (1999)
11. Zadeh, L.A.: Information and control. Fuzzy sets **8**, 338–353 (1965)

Going Stateless in Concurrent Evolutionary Algorithms

Juan J. Merelo[1](✉) and José-Mario García-Valdez[2](✉)

[1] Universidad de Granada/CITIC, Granada, Spain
jmerelo@ugr.es
[2] Instituto Tecnológico de Tijuana, Calzada Tecnológico, s/n, Tijuana, Mexico
mario@tectijuana.edu.mx

Abstract. Concurrent languages such as Perl 6 fully leverage the power of current multi-core and hyper-threaded computer architectures, and they include easy ways of automatically parallelizing code. However, to achieve more computational capability by using all threads and cores, algorithms need to be redesigned to be run in a concurrent environment; in particular, the use of a reactive, fully functional patterns need to turn the algorithm into a series of stateless steps, with simple functions that receive all the context and map it to the next stage. In this paper, we are going to analyze different versions of these stateless, reactive architectures applied to evolutionary algorithms, assessing how they interact with the characteristics of the evolutionary algorithm itself and show how they improve the scaling behavior and performance. We will use the Perl 6 language, which is a modern, concurrent language that was released recently and is still under very active development.

Keywords: Concurrent algorithms · Distributed computing
Stateless algorithms · Algorithm implementation
Performance evaluation · Heterogeneous distributed systems

1 Introduction

Evolutionary algorithms (EA) [14] are currently one of the most widely used meta-heuristics to solve optimization problems in engineering. If the cost or adequacy of a solution can be measured in terms of a single function, called *fitness*, evolutionary algorithms are generally able to find a good solution given enough time. Furthermore, parallel and distributed evolutionary algorithms (pEAs) are useful to find solutions of problems with a time-consuming fitness function [15,25,27] or problems that need many evaluations to find a good solution; in either case, using several computing *nodes* speeds ups the algorithm; even some authors [1,12,20] state that using pEAs improves the quality of solutions in terms of the number of evaluations needed to find one. This reason, together with the improvement in evaluation time brought by running simultaneously in several nodes, have made parallel and distributed evolutionary algorithms a popular methodology.

© Springer Nature Switzerland AG 2018
J. C. Figueroa-García et al. (Eds.): WEA 2018, CCIS 915, pp. 17–29, 2018.
https://doi.org/10.1007/978-3-030-00350-0_2

One of the reasons for this popularity is that the implementation of EAs in parallel is relatively straightforward, by just dividing the population into computing nodes and using some messaging mechanism to interchange some members selected according to some optimality criterion [4] but programming paradigms used for the implementation of such algorithms are far from being an object of study in the wide evolutionary algorithm area; object oriented or procedural languages like Java and C/C++ are mostly used. Even when some researchers show that implementation matters [28], parallel approaches found in new languages/paradigms are not usually pursued; this is what we intend to do in this paper.

The main reason for doing this is that, despite having identified new parallel platforms as a challenge in EAs [25], in general, only advances in hardware are considered. Software platforms, specifically programming languages, remain poorly explored; only Ada [31], Scala [23] and Erlang [7,9,22,35] have been analyzed in the area of evolutionary computation. Even so, the number of works on this area has increased lately, since the challenge of multi-core, hyper-threaded architectures [17] need better applications, even simpler ones, to be parallelized. Eventually, this shows the need use and create design patterns for concurrent algorithms; the conversion of a pattern into a language feature is a common practice in the programming languages domain, and sometimes that means a language modification, others the creation of a new one.

That is the case of Perl6 [37], a relatively new and decidedly non main-stream language (since it is not included in the top ten of any of the most popular languages rankings), with concurrent and functional features in order to develop parallel versions of EAs through concurrency. Perl 6 started as a redesign of the implementation of Perl, given its inadequacy to work correctly, among other things, with threads. Perl 6 has a three-tier architecture, including a virtual machine (either MoarVM, specifically designed for Perl 6, JVM or, lately, GraalVM [41]; a second level with a minimal bootstrapping language called NQP (Not Quite Perl), which allows for easy portability among different VMs, and finally a compiler, of which there is just one version right now, called Rakudo. This paper, as well as similar ones preceding it [3,10,26], are motivated by the need to explore new language architectures that give you good insight on the nature of evolutionary algorithms, as well as the need to create fast implementations that can be run efficiently in current processor architectures.

This research is intended to show some possible areas of improvement on architecture and engineering best practices for concurrent-functional paradigms, as was made for Object Oriented Programming languages [30], by focusing on pEAs as a domain of application and describing how their principal traits can be modeled by means of concurrent-functional languages constructs. We are continuing the research reported in [2,10]. This paper is an extended version of [26], including new results with an updated version of the evolutionary algorithm library.

Previously [13,26], we explored stateless evolutionary algorithm architectures. In this paper we will also see how to work with implicit parallelism at the instruction level, what kind of changes are needed to make it work and the speedups that can be achieved in that case.

The rest of the paper is organized as follows. Next section presents the state of the art in concurrent and functional programming language in the area of parallel evolutionary algorithms. We present two different versions of a concurrent evolutionary algorithm in Sect. 3, to be followed by actual results in Sect. 4. Finally, we draw the conclusions and present future lines of work in Sect. 5.

2   State of the Art

Despite the emphasis on hardware-based techniques such as cloud computing or GPGPU, there are not many papers dealing with creating concurrent evolutionary algorithms that work in a single computing node.

The concurrent programming paradigm (or concurrency oriented programming [5]) is characterized by the presence of programming constructs for managing processes like first class objects. That is, with operators for acting upon them and the possibility of using them like parameters or function's result values. This changes the coding of concurrent algorithms due to the direct mapping between patterns of communications and processes with language expressions; on one hand it becomes simpler since the language provides an abstraction for communication, in the other hand it changes the paradigm for implementing algorithms, since these new communication constructs have to be taken into account.

This design has to take into account the communication/synchronization between processes, which nowadays will be mainly threads. One of the best efforts to formalize and simplify that is the Hoare's *Communicating Sequential Processes* [18], this interaction description language is the theoretical support for many libraries and new programming languages. This kind of concurrent programs is based on *channels*, which are used to interchange message between the different processes or threads; messages can be interchanged asynchronously or synchronously. The Go language uses this kind of model, and Perl 6 will use, among others (like *promises* or low-level access to the creation of threads), this one. Another, different, approach is actor-based concurrency, [32]. This actor model bans shared state, with different *actors* communicating through messages [11].

The fact that messages have to be processed without secondary effects and that actors do not share any kind of state makes concurrent programming specially fit for functional languages or languages with functional features; this has made this paradigm specially popular for late cloud computing implementations; however, its presence in the EA world is not so widespread, although some efforts have lately revived the interest for this kind of paradigm [36]. Several years ago was used in Genetic Programming [8,19,40] and recently in neuroevolution [33] but in EA its presence, despite being scarce in the previous years [16], has experimented a certain rise lately with papers such as [39] which perform program synthesis using functional programming or [6] which uses the functional and parallel language Erlang for an evolutionary multi-agent system.

Among languages with functional features, the languages Erlang and Scala have embraced the actor model of concurrency and get excellent results in many application domains; Clojure is another one with concurrent features such as promises/futures, Software Transaction Memory and agents; Kotlin [34] has been recently used for implementing a functional evolutionary algorithm framework.

On the other hand, Perl 6 [38] uses different concurrency models, that go from implicit concurrency using a particular function that automatically parallelizes operations on iterable data structures, to explicit concurrency using threads. These both types of concurrency will be analyzed in this paper, which uses the `Algorithm::Evolutionary::Simple` library for that language which was presented in the same conference [29].

3   Concurrent Evolutionary Algorithms and Its Implementation

The implementation of evolutionary algorithms in a concurrent environment must have several features:

- They must be *reactive*, that is, functions respond to events, and not procedural or sequential.
- Functions responding to events are also first class objects and are stateless, having no secondary effects. These functions have to be reentrant, that is, with the capability of being run in a thread without exclusion of other functions.
- Functions communicate with each other exclusively via channels, which can hold objects of any kind but are not cached or buffered. Channels can be shared, but every object can be read from a channel only once.

In general, an evolutionary algorithm consists of an iterative procedure where, after generating an initial set of individuals, these individuals are evaluated, and then they reproduce, with errors and combination of their features, with a probability that is proportional to their fitness. As long as there is variation and survival of the fittest, an evolutionary algorithm will work. However, the usual way of doing this is through a series of nested loops, with possibly asynchronous operation in a parallel context when communicating with other *islands* or isolated populations. However, the concept of loop itself implies state, in the shape of the generation counter, or even with the population itself that is handled from one iteration step to the next one.

Getting rid of these states, however, leads to many different algorithms which are not functionally equivalent to the canonical genetic algorithm above. Of course, a functional equivalent is also possible in this environment, with non-terminating *islands* running every one of them on a different thread, and communicating via channels. Although this version is guaranteed to succeed, we are looking for different implementations that, while keeping the spirit of the evolutionary algorithm, maps themselves better to a multithreaded architecture and a concurrent language such as Go, Scala or Perl 6.

This is why in this paper we are going to examine two different architectures, which basically differ in the granularity with which they perform the evolutionary algorithm.

The module used, as well as the code for the experiments, is available under a free license.

4   Experimental Setup and Results

The first experiments we have performed for this paper included using implicit autothreading, in the shape of the method called `race` or `hyper`. These methods auto-thread the processing of arrays or list, disregarding the order in the first case, using it in the second case. In order to check this we implemented the p-peaks function [21], which was considered more adequate for this task since it is, at the same time, deceptive from the point of view of the evolutionary algorithm and computing-intensive, involving computing the distance to a number of generated binary strings, which in this case were 100.

In order to do this implicitly parallel version, several changes had to be made to the function that evaluates the whole population:

- First, the cache had to be turned off. We were using a cache to keep all values that were already computed, and we had to stop using it. Since it is autothreaded, trying to store or retrieve from the cache simultaneously could result in deadlocks or crashes.
- Do all the computation in a functional way, without side effects. The auto-threaded code must take values, return values, without changing any external variable on the fly. All values are then computed and assigned to the data structure that holds them.

Perl 6, by default, uses 4 threads for auto-threading. We designed population evaluation so that it was autothreaded, and did some runtime tests. Without changing the algorithm, this resulted in an almost 4x speedup of the original code.

This implies that using implicitly parallel facilities might allow, without much changes to the underlying algorithm, to use multithreading and achieve speedups, as already observed in [29]. However, it is essential that what is being parallelized is a substantial amount of work. Using just MaxOnes, as in the above mentioned paper, will not offer any substantial speedups and might even result in performance taking a hit.

However, we were more interested in creating explicit concurrent version of the evolutionary algorithm, and do a set of experiments to make them work properly. In the next set of experiments we will concentrate not so much in runtime performance, but on algorithmic performance, that is, the number of evaluations needed to find the solution. In order to perform the experiments, we used Linux boxes (with Ubuntu 14.04 and 16.04), the latest version of the Perl 6 compiler and virtual machine. First we used a selecto-recombinative evolutionary algorithm, with no mutation, in order to find out what's the correct population for every problem size [24]. This method sizes populations looking for the minimal size that achieves a 95% success rate on a particular problem and problem size; in this case, size 512 was the ideal for the MaxOnes problem with size 64. This size was used as a base for the rest of the problem sizes; since the real evolutionary algorithm actually uses mutation, the population was halved for the actual experiments. This population size is more dependent on the problem itself than on the particular implementation, that is why we use it for all implementations.

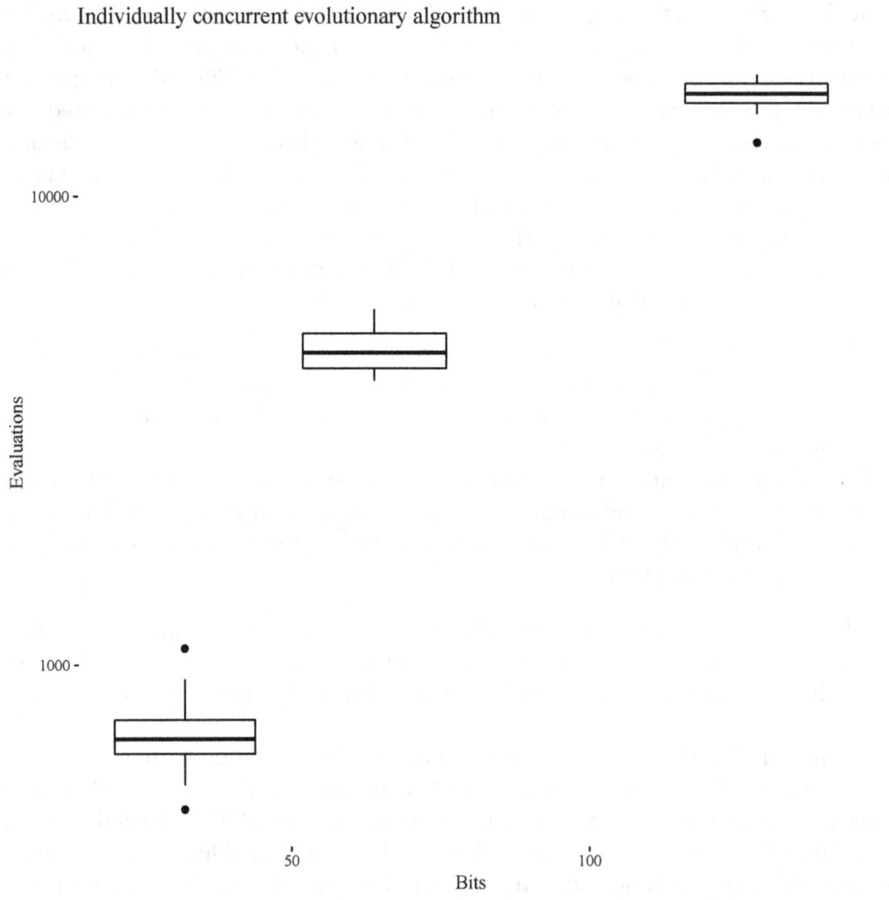

Individually concurrent evolutionary algorithm

Fig. 1. Boxplot of the number of evaluations needed for different number of bits in the MaxOnes problem. Please note that axes x and y both have a logarithmic scale.

First we run a basic evolutionary algorithm with different chromosome sizes, to get a baseline of the number of evaluations needed for finding the solution in that case. Time needed was the main requisite for choosing the different sizes, although we think that scaling should follow more or less the same trend as

Comparing population–level concurrent EA for different number of initial populations

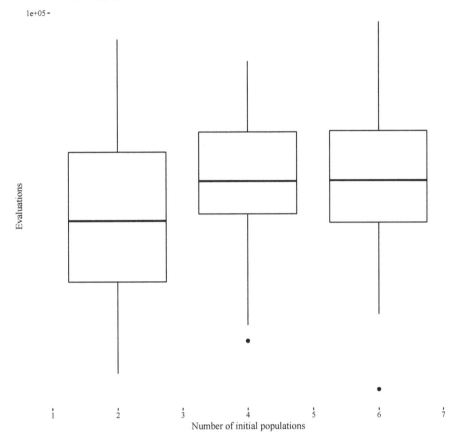

Fig. 2. Boxplot comparing the number of evaluations needed for solving the 64 bit onemax problem using the population-level concurrent algorithm with different number of initial populations.

shown for smaller sizes. We compared mainly the number of evaluations needed, since that is the main measure of the quality of the algorithm.

We show in Fig. 1 the logarithmic chart of the number of evaluations needed to find the solution for different, logarithmically growing, chromosome sizes using the individually concurrent evolutionary algorithm. There is a logical increase in the number of evaluations needed, but the fact that it is a low number and its scaling prove that this simple concurrent implementation is indeed an evolutionary algorithm, and does not get stuck in diversity traps that take it to local minimum. The number of evaluations is, in fact, quite stable.

We did the same for the population-level concurrent algorithm; however, since this one has got parameters to tune, we had to find a good result. In order to do that, we tested different number of initial populations placed in the

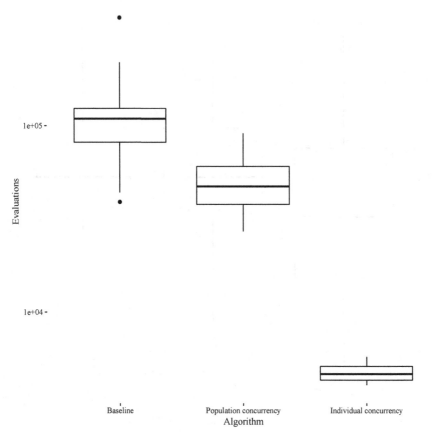

Comparing algorithms for the 64 bit onemax problem

Fig. 3. Boxplot comparing the number of evaluations needed for solving the 64 bit onemax problem in the individually concurrent and canonical EA version.

channel, since this seems to be the critical parameter, more than the number of generations until mixing. The results are shown in Fig. 2. The difference between using 4 and 6 initial populations is virtually none, but there is a slight advantage if you use only 2 initial populations to kickstart the channel. Please bear in mind that, in this case, the concept of *population* is slightly different from the one used in island EAs. While in the latter the population does not move from the island, in this case populations are read from channels and acted upon, and in principle there could be as many initial or unread populations as wanted or needed; every function in every thread will process a single population nonetheless.

We can now compare these two algorithms with the baseline EA. This is a canonical evolutionary algorithm using bitflip mutation and two-point crossover, using roulette wheel as a selection method. It has, as the rest of the implementations of the algorithms, been implemented using `Algorithm::Evolutionary::Simple`, the free software module in Perl 6.

The comparison is shown in Fig. 3, which shows, in a logarithmic y scale, a boxplot of the number of evaluations for the baseline, as well as the two different concurrent algorithms, at the population and individual level. As it can be seen, this last algorithm outperforms the other two, achieving the same result using many less evaluations, almost one order of magnitude less. In fact, both concurrent algorithms are better than the baseline, and please note this measures the number of evaluations, equivalent to the algorithmic complexity, and not time. This figure is the base to reach our conclusions.

5   Conclusions and Discussion

It is natural to take advantage of the multi-threading and multi-process capabilities of modern hardware architectures to make evolutionary or other population-based algorithms run faster by using all CPUs and threads at the same time; that can be done in a very straightforward way by parallelizing the evolutionary algorithm using the many available models, such as island model; however, it is possible that adapting the algorithm itself to the architecture makes its performance better, by actually adapting the resources consumed to the resources used, instead of allocating them in advance as it is done in island architectures.

The first exploration of the facilities for concurrent programming Perl 6 uses has been done through the auto-threading mechanism that allows the parallel execution of code on arrays or lists. After making small changes, this resulted in a speedup of the program in a number that is compatible with the number of threads used by default, four.

However, a change to a concurrent architecture implies looking at an algorithm in a different, non sequential way, that is why the first thing that has to be evaluated is the actual number of evaluations that need to be done to solve the problem, since the new implementation is not functionally equivalent to the old one. This is what we have done in this paper. We have proposed two different concurrent implementations of an evolutionary algorithms with different *grain*: a *fine-grained* one that acts at the individual level, and a *coarse-grained* one that acts at the level of populations.

The individual-level concurrent EA shows a good scaling across problem size; besides, when comparing it with the population-level concurrent EA and the canonical and sequential evolutionary algorithm, it obtains a much better performance, being able to obtain the solution with a much lower evaluation budget. Second best is the population-level concurrent algorithm, to be followed by the baseline canonical EA, which obtains the worse result. This proves that, even from the purely algorithmic point of view, concurrent evolutionary algorithms are better than sequential algorithms. If we consider time, the difference increases, since the only sequential part of the concurrent algorithms is reading from the channels, but once reading has been done the rest of the operations can be performed concurrently, not to mention every function can have as many copies as needed running in different threads.

These results are not so much inherent to the concurrency itself as dependent on the selection operators that have been included in the concurrent version of the algorithms. The selection pressure of the canonical algorithm is relatively low, depending on the roulette wheel selection algorithm, as opposed to the more greedy operation of the individual-level algorithm, which uses tournament selection. The population-level concurrent algorithm eliminates half the population with the worst fitness, although every generation it is running a canonical EA identical to the baseline; however, this exerts a high selective pressure on the population which, combined with the increased diversity of running two populations in parallel, results in better performance. Same happens with the individual-level concurrent EA: the worst of three is always eliminated, which exerts a big pressure on the population, which is thus able to find the solution much faster. Nothing prevents us from using these same mechanisms in an evolutionary algorithm, which would then be functionally equivalent to these concurrent algorithms, but we wanted to compare a canonical EA to *canonical* concurrent evolutionary algorithms, at the same time we compare different versions of them; in this sense, it is better to use this individual-level concurrent algorithm in future versions of the evolutionary algorithm library.

The main conclusion of this paper is that evolutionary algorithms can benefit from concurrent implementations, and that these should be as fine grained as possible. However, a lot of work remains to be done. One line of research will be to try and use the implicitly concurrent capabilities of Perl 6 to perform multi-threaded evaluation or any other part of the algorithm, which would delegate the use of the threading facilities to the compiler and virtual machine. That will have no implications on the number of evaluations, but will help make the overall application faster.

Of course, time comparisons will also have to be made, as well as a more thorough exploration of the parameter space of the population-level evolutionary algorithm. Since this type of algorithm has a lower overhead, communicating via channels with lower frequency, it could be faster than the individual-level concurrent EA. Measuring the scaling with the number of thread is also an interesting line to pursue; since our architecture is using single channels, this might eventually be a bottleneck, and will prevent scaling to an indefinite number of threads. However, that number might be higher than the available number of threads in a desktop processor, so it has to be measured in practice.

This paper has been intended mainly as a proof of concept, and thus does not really focuses on creating a scalable architecture for concurrent evolutionary algorithms. Preliminary results with the individual-level concurrency indicate that a basic redesign is probably needed to achieve good scaling performance. One of the problems with this architecture is that actually every thread is doing much less work than communication; since the application is communication-bound it will get worse as the number of threads increases. While keeping functional equivalence, it is probably better to work with bigger batch sizes instead of working with a single individual.

Finally, we would like to remark that this paper is part of the open science effort by the authors. It is hosted in GitHub, and the paper repository hosts the data and scripts used to process them, which are in fact embedded in this paper source code using Knitr [42].

Acknowledgements. This paper has been supported in part by projects TIN2014-56494-C4-3-P s (Spanish Ministry of Economy and Competitiveness) and DeepBio (TIN2017-85727-C4-2-P). I would like to express my gratefulness to the users in the #perl6 IRC channel, specially Elizabeth Mattijsen, Timo Paulsen and Zoffix Znet, who helped me with the adventure of programming efficient concurrent evolutionary algorithms.

References

1. Alba, E., Troya, J.M.: Analyzing synchronous and asynchronous parallel distributed genetic algorithms. Future Gener. Comput. Syst. - Spec. Issue Bioimpaired Solut. Parallel Process. Probl. **17**, 451–465 (2001)
2. Albert-Cruz, J., Acevedo-Martínez, L., Merelo, J., Castillo, P., Arenas, M.: Adaptando algoritmos evolutivos paralelos al lenguaje funcional erlang. In: MAEB 2013 - IX Congreso Español de Metaheurísticas, Algoritmos Evolutivos y Bioinspirados (2013)
3. Albert-Cruz, J., Merelo, J., Acevedo-Martínez, L., De Las Cuevas, P.: Implementing parallel genetic algorithm using concurrent-functional languages. In: Proceedings of the International Conference on Evolutionary Computation Theory and Applications, ECTA 2014, pp. 169–175 (2014). (since 1996)
4. Araujo, L., Guervós, J.J.M., Mora, A., Cotta, C.: Genotypic differences and migration policies in an island model. In: Rothlauf, F. (ed.) GECCO, pp. 1331–1338. ACM (2009)
5. Armstrong, J.: Concurrency oriented programming in Erlang (2003). http://ll2.ai.mit.edu/talks/armstrong.pdf
6. Barwell, A.D., Brown, C., Hammond, K., Turek, W., Byrski, A.: Using program shaping and algorithmic skeletons to parallelise an evolutionary multi-agent system in Erlang. Comput. Inform. **35**(4), 792–818 (2017)
7. Bienz, A., Fokle, K., Keller, Z., Zulkoski, E., Thede, S.: A generalized parallel genetic algorithm in Erlang. In: Proceedings of Midstates Conference on Undergraduate Research in Computer Science and Mathematics (2011)
8. Briggs, F., O'Neill, M.: Functional genetic programming and exhaustive program search with combinator expressions. Int. J. Know.-Based Intell. Eng. Syst. **12**(1), 47–68 (2008). http://dl.acm.org/citation.cfm?id=1375341.1375345
9. Butcher, S.G., Sheppard, J.W.: An actor model implementation of distributed factored evolutionary algorithms. In: Proceedings of the Genetic and Evolutionary Computation Conference Companion, pp. 1276–1283. ACM (2018)
10. Cruz, J.A., Merelo-Guervós, J.J., Mora-García, A., de las Cuevas, P.: Adapting evolutionary algorithms to the concurrent functional language Erlang. In: Blum, C., Alba, E. (eds.) GECCO (Companion), pp. 1723–1724. ACM (2013)
11. Erb, B.: Concurrent programming for scalable web architectures (2012)
12. García-Arenas, M., et al.: Speedup measurements for a distributed evolutionary algorithm that uses Jini. In: Depto. ATC, U.d.G. (ed.) XI Jornadas de Paralelismo, pp. 241–246 (2000)

13. García-Valdez, J.M., Merelo-Guervós, J.J.: A modern, event-based architecture for distributed evolutionary algorithms. In: Proceedings of the Genetic and Evolutionary Computation Conference Companion, GECCO 2018, pp. 233–234. ACM, New York (2018). http://doi.acm.org/10.1145/3205651.3205719
14. Goldberg, D.E.: Genetic Algorithms in Search, Optimization and Machine Learning. Addison Wesley (1989)
15. Gong, Y.J., et al.: Distributed evolutionary algorithms and their models: a survey of the state-of-the-art. Appl. Soft Comput. **34**, 286–300 (2015)
16. Hawkins, J., Abdallah, A.: A generic functional genetic algorithm. In: Proceedings of the ACS/IEEE International Conference on Computer Systems and Applications, AICCSA 2001, pp. 11-17. IEEE Computer Society, Washington (2001). http://dl.acm.org/citation.cfm?id=872017.872197
17. Sutter, H., Larus, J.R.: Software and the concurrency revolution. ACM Queue **3**(7), 54–62 (2005). http://doi.acm.org/10.1145/1095408.1095421
18. Hoare, C.A.R.: Communicating sequential processes. Commun. ACM **21**(8), 666–677 (1978). http://doi.acm.org/10.1145/359576.359585
19. Huelsbergen, L.: Toward simulated evolution of machine-language iteration. In: Proceedings of the First Annual Conference on Genetic Programming, GECCO 1996, pp. 315–320. MIT Press, Cambridge, MA, USA (1996). http://dl.acm.org/citation.cfm?id=1595536.1595579
20. Jiménez-Laredo, J.L., Eiben, A.E., van Steen, M., Merelo-Guervós, J.J.: EvAg: a scalable peer-to-peer evolutionary algorithm. Genet. Program. Evol. Mach. **11**(2), 227–246 (2010)
21. Kennedy, J., Spears, W.: Matching algorithms to problems: an experimental test of the particle swarm and some genetic algorithms on the multimodal problem generator. In: The 1998 IEEE International Conference on Evolutionary Computation Proceedings, IEEE World Congress on Computational Intelligence, pp. 78–83. IEEE (1998)
22. Kerdprasop, K., Kerdprasop, N.: Concurrent data mining and genetic computing implemented with Erlang Language. Int. J. Softw. Eng. Appl. **7**(3), 63–76 (2013)
23. Krzywicki, D., Turek, W., Byrski, A., Kisiel-Dorohinicki, M.: Massively concurrent agent-based evolutionary computing. J. Comput. Sci. **11**, 153–162 (2015)
24. Lobo, F.G., Lima, C.F.: A review of adaptive population sizing schemes in genetic algorithms. In: Proceedings of the 7th Annual Workshop on Genetic and Evolutionary Computation, GECCO 2005, pp. 228–234. ACM, New York (2005). http://doi.acm.org/10.1145/1102256.1102310
25. Luque, G., Alba, E.: Parallel models for genetic algorithms. In: Luque, G., Alba, E. (eds.) Parallel Genetic Algorithms: Theory and Real World Applications, pp. 15–30. Springer, Heidelberg (2011). https://doi.org/10.1007/978-3-642-22084-5_2
26. Merelo, J.J., García-Valdez, J.M.: Mapping evolutionary algorithms to a reactive, stateless architecture: using a modern concurrent language. In: Proceedings of the Genetic and Evolutionary Computation Conference Companion, GECCO 2018, pp. 1870–1877. ACM, New York (2018). http://doi.acm.org/10.1145/3205651.3208317
27. Merelo-Guervós, J.J.: Cloudy distributed evolutionary computation. In: Proceedings of the Genetic and Evolutionary Computation Conference Companion, pp. 1138–1140. ACM (2018)
28. Merelo, J.J., Romero, G., Arenas, M.G., Castillo, P.A., Mora, A.M., Laredo, J.L.J.: Implementation matters: programming best practices for evolutionary algorithms. In: Cabestany, J., Rojas, I., Joya, G. (eds.) IWANN 2011. LNCS, vol. 6692, pp. 333–340. Springer, Heidelberg (2011). https://doi.org/10.1007/978-3-642-21498-1_42

29. Merelo Guervós, J.J., Valdez, J.M.G.: Performance improvements of evolutionary algorithms in perl 6. In: Aguirre, H.E., Takadama, K. (eds.) Proceedings of the Genetic and Evolutionary Computation Conference Companion, GECCO 2018, Kyoto, Japan, 15–19 July 2018, pp. 1371–1378. ACM (2018). http://doi.acm.org/10.1145/3205651.3208273
30. Merelo-Guervós, J.J., et al.: Evolving objects. In: Wang, P.P. (ed.) Proceedings of JCIS 2000 (Joint Conference on Information Sciences), vol. 1, pp. 1083–1086 (2000). ISBN 0-9643456-9-2
31. Santos, L.: Evolutionary computation in Ada95: a genetic algorithm approach. Ada User J. **23**(4), 239 (2002)
32. Schippers, H., Van Cutsem, T., Marr, S., Haupt, M., Hirschfeld, R.: Towards an actor-based concurrent machine model. In: Proceedings of the 4th Workshop on the Implementation, Compilation, Optimization of Object-Oriented Languages and Programming Systems, pp. 4–9. ACM (2009)
33. Sher, G.I.: Handbook of Neuroevolution Through Erlang. Springer, Heidelberg (2013). https://doi.org/10.1007/978-1-4614-4463-3
34. Simson, J., Mayo, M.: Open-source linear genetic programming (2017)
35. Stypka, J.: The missing link! a new skeleton forevolutionary multi-agent systems in Erlang. Int. J. Parallel Program. **46**(1), 4–22 (2018). https://doi.org/10.1007/s10766-017-0503-4
36. Swan, J., et al.: A research agenda for metaheuristic standardization. In: Proceedings of the XI Metaheuristics International Conference (2015)
37. Tang, A.: Perl 6: reconciling the irreconcilable. In: Proceedings of the 34th Annual ACM SIGPLAN-SIGACT Symposium on Principles of Programming Languages, POPL 2007, p. 1. ACM, New York (2007). http://doi.acm.org/10.1145/1190216.1190218
38. Tang, A.: Perl 6: reconciling the irreconcilable. SIGPLAN Not. **42**(1), 1 (2007). http://doi.acm.org/10.1145/1190215.1190218
39. Valkov, L., Chaudhari, D., Srivastava, A., Sutton, C., Chaudhuri, S.: Synthesis of differentiable functional programs for lifelong learning. arXiv preprint arXiv:1804.00218 (2018)
40. Walsh, P.: A functional style and fitness evaluation scheme for inducting high level programs. In: Banzhaf, W., et al. (eds.) Proceedings of the Genetic and Evolutionary Computation Conference, vol. 2, pp. 1211–1216. Morgan Kaufmann, Orlando, Florida, USA, 13–17 July 1999. http://www.cs.bham.ac.uk/wbl/biblio/gecco1999/GP-455.ps
41. Würthinger, T., et al.: One VM to rule them all. In: Proceedings of the 2013 ACM International Symposium on New Ideas, New Paradigms, and Reflections on Programming & Software, pp. 187–204. ACM (2013)
42. Xie, Y.: knitr: a general-purpose package for dynamic report generation in R. R Package Vers. **1**(7), 1 (2013)

Thermal Vein Signatures, DNA and EEG Brainprint in Biometric User Authentication

Carlos Cabrera[1], German Hernández[2(✉)], Luis Fernando Niño[2],
and Dipankar Dasgupta[3]

[1] School of Engineering + Technology,
Miami Dade College-Kendall and School of Computing and Information,
Florida International University and GattaKX Inc., Miami, FL, USA
ccabrer3@mdc.edu
[2] Departamento de Ingeniería de Sistemas e Industrial,
Universidad Nacional de Colombia, Bogotá, Colombia
{gjhernandezp,lfninov}@unal.edu.co
[3] Department of Computer Science, The University of Memphis, Memphis, TN, USA
dsagupta@memphis.edu

Abstract. In this paper we present a survey of three recent developments in biometric user authentication based on physical human characteristics that are less prone to natural or intentional changes than other currently used techniques: thermal vein signatures, DNA and EEG brainprint obtained by stimulating the brain with cognitive events. This paper argues that biometric user authentication using these three human characteristics is already an everyday a reality or is going to be very soon.

Keywords: Biometrics · Physical biometrics
Facial and dorsal thermal vein signatures · DNA

1 Introduction

Biometrics comes from the Greek words $\beta\iota o\varsigma$ (bios-life) and *metrikós* (metric-measure). Initially, it was defined as the measurement and statistical analysis of body measurements that allowed to uniquely identify individuals. In recent year's this notion has been extended to include measurements of physiological and behavioral traits that are used in combination with physical measurements to improve the efficacy and precision of individual identification [1,2].

Due to the terrorism threat, the staggering number of identity thefts (one in every 14 Americans fell victim to identity theft during 2014 [3]) and the increasing number of attacks to computer networks, infrastructures and information systems, biometric authentication has become a popular and reliable approach for individual and user authentication. Biometric authentication relies in the fact that certain traits of the human body and the human behavior are unique in a large group of individuals. The biometric authentication methods are classified in (see Fig. 1):

© Springer Nature Switzerland AG 2018
J. C. Figueroa-García et al. (Eds.): WEA 2018, CCIS 915, pp. 30–41, 2018.
https://doi.org/10.1007/978-3-030-00350-0_3

– Physical biometrics, which analyzes physical human characteristics such as fingerprint, palmprint, iris, ear-shape, face recognition and heartbeat, see Fig. 2.
– Behavioral biometrics: that analyzes physiological, cognitive and behavioral traits and response patterns (continous behavioral biometrics [4], see Fig. 3) like voice, gait (walking pattern) keystroke analysis, mouse dynamics, handwriting, signature, on-line and social network activity and communications activity (devices, IP addresses, telecommunication providers - Google sends confirmation codes to the user's phone when they detect unfamiliar changes in the communications activity).

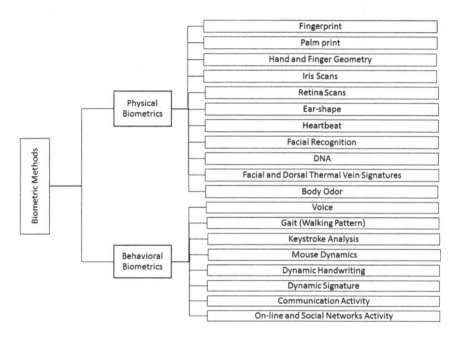

Fig. 1. An overview of biometric methods.

Currently, some authentication systems rely in a unique authentication method, but the tendency is to have Multi Factor Authentication (MFA) systems that combine biometric with non-biometric methods such as PINs, passwords, graphical patterns, security questions, hardware tokens, SMS or E-mail codes and phone callback to increase the resiliency en efficacy of the authentication; recently, some Adaptive MFAs have been proposed with the capacity of adapting the combination of methods to the user authentication history and the user operating environment [6].

Section 2 presents a survey of the current applications of biometric authentication. Section 3 presents an overview of the challenges of currently available

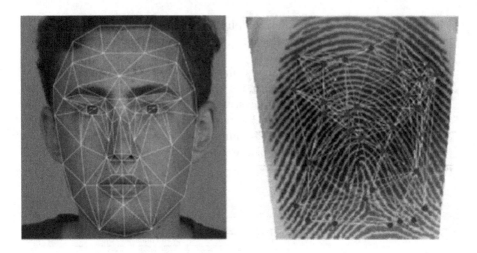

Fig. 2. Facial and fingerprint recognition (www.biocatch.com).

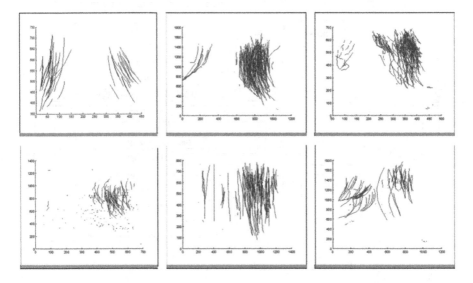

Fig. 3. Six different person scrolling patterns (www.biocatch.com).

biometric authentication techniques. Section 4 is dedicated to the study of biometric authentication using thermal signatures from dorsal and facial thermal images using Hough Transform. Section 5 presents the current state of biometric authentication is performed Using DNA. Section 6 reviews how biometric authentication is performed Using the EEG brainprint obtained stimulating the brain with cognitive events. Section 7 presents a summary.

2 Current Applications of Biometric Authentication

Biometric authentication methods are widely use today in both industry and government [7,8].

2.1 Industry Applications

The industry sector leading the application of biometric authentication is the smartphone industry, where fingerprints, face recognition and voice combined with other authentication methods like PINs, passwords and graphic patterns are being used millions of times on a daily basis to unlock smartphones around the world. Multiple studies have been conducted on how the authentication process impacts the usability, privacy and trust of smartphone users [9,10].

The second leading sector is the financial industry; some even call this area *financial biometrics*, due to the staggering impact of the frauds committed by identity theft and the fact commerce, retail and financial services are moving almost completely to the virtual world (on-line stores, mobile banking, e-loans, P2P loans, etc.). This area is developing methods on their own to identify, verify, authenticate and calculate credit scores for clients in remote locations around the world [11].

Other sectors are *healthcare biometrics*, specially in telecare, due to the importance of keeping patient security and privacy, and the on-line education industry, where students taking courses need to be identified from remote locations. Coursera, one of the major players in the Massive On-line Open Courses (MOOCs) industry, uses two biometric authentication approaches, face photos and typing patterns, to verify the connection between the student account and its real-world identity [12,13].

2.2 Government Applications

More than 150 countries are issuing now biometric passports with an embedded electronic microprocessor chip which contains biometric information that is used to authenticate the identity of the passport holder [14].

Iris recognition systems are becoming increasingly common around the worlds border crossings [15,16]. In the US, iris scans, photos and fingerprints are being used in pilot programs in major airports to be matched with iris scans, photos and fingerprints that were previously taken of the passengers at the arrival or from their passports, visas, or other government documentation [17]. In Colombia, the use of iris recognition started in 2018 and check individual's data with national police, intelligence service, Interpol data, and different national and international databases without the intervention of an immigration agent. Many intelligence services perform analysis of on-line and social network activity before awarding visas.

The number of countries using biometrics for voting registration or voting authentication has steadily increased in the past decade. According to the International Institute for Democratic and Electoral Assistance (IDEA), 35% of

National Electoral Commissions are capturing biometric data (such as finger-prints or photos) as part of their voter registration process [18].

In countries with compulsory identity cards, these are including biometric information that can be verified on-line by public offices and business to ensure a reliable identification of the holder. in Colombia the current national id card includes fingerprint information and photo, the fingerprint and photo can be verified on-line by the national registration office [19] and the country is moving to a new electronic biometric card that will include face recognition information verifiable on line [20] and now biometrics is being offered as a service in the cloud [21–23].

3   Challenges of Biometric Authentication Techniques

1. Some biometrics like fingerprints, palmprints, iris scans may change over time due to natural, accidental or inadvertent changes.
2. Some biometrics like iris scans, retina scans may cause discomfort to users.
3. Some biometrics like facial and iris scans may change because of fashion or makeover (e.g. color contact lenses, hair color and cosmetics, etc.)
4. Some biometrics may change due to surgery, skin drafting, nose implant, face lifting, anti-aging skin repair, amputation, botox, etc.
5. The development o sophisticated sin-like films and facemasks poses a challenge fingerprint and facial recognition. In 2014, hackers claimed to have cloned German defense minister Ursula von der Leyen's fingerprints just by taking a high-definition photo of her hands at a public event [24].

In the following sections we survey three biometric techniques that are resilient because they relate to internal and hard to change characteristics and that have recent developments making then.

4   Biometric Authentication Using Thermal Vein Signatures

Thermal imaging produces images –thermograms or heat signatures– in the infrared range of the electromagnetic spectrum (9,000–14,000 nanometers) that can be used to identify blood vessels patterns (thermal vein signatures) located just below the skin of a face/hand, which are unique to each individual [27].

There have been numerous studies investigating how to extract/match bio-metric thermal vein signatures [25,26]. Czajka et al. [27] used mutual informa-tion, PCA and LDA to extract biometric features; also k-NN and SVM were used for matching achieving a 93.33% accuracy. Guzman et al. [28] used morphologi-cal operators to extract features, and a simple similarity measure based on linear image records was used to match images achieving a 90.39% accuracy. Recently of Hough transform have been used to extract venous networks signatures.

4.1 The Hough Transform

The Hough transform [29] was introduced by Duda and Hart in 1972 [30] as an extension of the 1962 Hough's patent [31] to detect simple shapes (commonly lines, circles and ellipses) within an image. In some cases for detecting lines, an edge detector can be used but if the image has missing points or pixels, it becomes a difficult task.

The Hough transform addresses this problem by grouping edge points into object candidates and performing a voting procedure over a set of parameterized candidate shapes. One of the advantages of Hough transformation is its speed and easyness to implement in hardware which is a requirement in real biometric applications.

The simplest case of Hough transform is detecting straight lines. Thus, the straight line $y = mx + b$ can be represented as the point (b, m) in the parameter space. However, vertical lines pose a problem, so the Hesse line parameter representation (r, θ) (Hesse normal form) is more convenient

$$r = x \cos \theta + y \sin \theta,$$

where r is the distance from the origin to the closest point on the straight line, and θ is the angle between the x axis and the line connecting the origin with that closest point, and the problem of detecting collinear points becomes the problem of finding intersecting curves in the (r, θ) space.

4.2 Thermal Vein Signature Detection Algorithm

The common structure of thermal vein signature detection algorithms is shown in Algorithm 1. In Figs. 4 and 5 two examples of thermal image input images, contour segmentation, detecting thermal patterns (Using Hough transform) and filtering and thinning results, are shown.

Biometric authentication using thermal vein signatures is an every day reality already. Hitachi develop a finger vein biometric reader that Barclays is offering already to corporate banking customers [32] (see Fig. 6). And now with cell phones capable of thermal imaging [33] this will become even more accessible.

Algorithm 1. Thermal vein signature detection

1: Normalize the image
2: Contour segmentation [34]
3: Skeletonize and overlay
4: Detect thermal patterns
5: Filtering and thinning
6: Pattern recognition and match

---

5   Biometric Authentication Using DNA

The development of molecular biology technologies has allowed many scientific and technical applications. Among such applications, DNA technology has an amazing power as an identification tool. From a scientific perspective, DNA analysis has been used in the study of animals and plants, in the fields of zoology, botany, and agriculture. Also DNA analysis can be used to identify species, which is called DNA barcoding. But DNA technology can also be used to identify individuals rather than species, which has had a significant impact in criminal justice, among other tasks.

DNA biometric methods are generally used in applications where a high level of security is required. Forensics and law enforcement use DNA biometric methods for identification, since every person's DNA is unique, it is impossible to fake it. Even though is been proved that DNA suffer changes in extreme conditions (e.g. astronaut after spending a year-long in the space shuttle) [39]. In practice when compared to any other biometric method DNA posses 0% Failure to Enroll Rate (FTER) and its unique solution is absolute. FTER defines the probability of the system that could not extract distinctive characteristics from the given samples.

DNA databases become a very important information resource for the forensic DNA typing, where commonly short tandem repeat (STR) DNA markers are used. Blood and soft tissues in the human body are mainly used to extract DNA. The DNA can also be extracted from semen, saliva, hair roots and even from several skin cells. DNA obtained from these is commonly employed in forensic analysis. Extracting DNA from saliva has advantages over blood sample usage in the extraction process. Also self-administration is possible in extracting saliva samples. Saliva gets its DNA from the cells that degenerate from the inner walls of cheeks.

The main limitations for DNA biometric in real time applications were:

1. DNA matching was time consuming limiting real-time applications
2. Complex sample collection, aphysical sample must be taken, as opposed to other biometric systems that only need to use an image or a recording,
3. DNA procession was expensive for most authentication applications, and
4. Privacy issues, since DNA sample taken from an individual may show its health conditions and its susceptibility to some diseases.

But recent developments like the Rapid DNA devices, sponsored by the US government [35, 36], that now deliver a fully automated DNA profile usable as evidence in couple of hours from a reference sample buccal (cheek) swab. And also the small, credit card sized, device that can identity an individual from his DNA at low cost and in minutest, presented last year by researchers from Columbia University and the New York Genome Center [37, 38] are making real time DNA biometric authentication a real possibility.

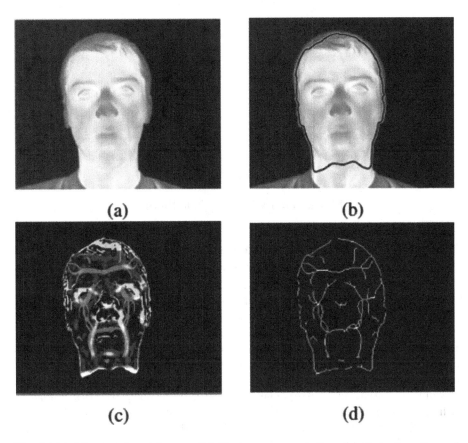

Fig. 4. (a) Thermal input image. (b) Contour segmentation. (c) Detecting thermal patterns. (d) Filtering and thinning.

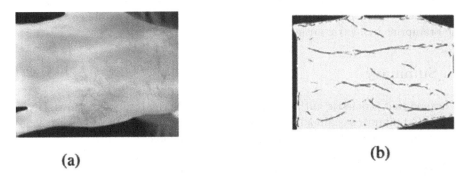

Fig. 5. (a) Thermal palm input image. (b) Filtering and thinning.

Fig. 6. Finger vein reader from Hitachi

6   Biometric Authentication Using the EEG Brainprint Obtained Stimulating the Brain with Cognitive Events

In 2016 Researchers from the State University of New York, Binghamton presented a biometric Brainprint system that identify individuals with 100% accuracy [40,41]. The system measures EEG signals of brain activities obtained by stimulating the brain with cognitive events, in the study they used series of images designed to elicit unique responses from person to person [42]. They found that the 50 participants' brains reacted differently to series of images and were able to match using pattern classifiers the EGG response to series of images with the registered EEG data with a 100% accuracy. In a previous 2015 study [43] using words instead of images and with 32 individuals they achieved a 97% accuracy. This technique is the intersection of physical and behavioral analytics.

This development matched with advances in EEG sensor and control headsets [44,45], that sense and interpret EEG signals to control other devices and many if which are now commercially available at very reasonable costs; make the brainprint biometric authentication also a reality.

7   Summary

In argued that biometric authentication based on thermal vein signatures, DNA and EEG brainprint is already an everyday a reality or is going to be very soon due to the fact that scientific groundings and the technological advances required for make its practical use widespread are mature enough.

We believe that the use of biometrics (internal or external) and their success depend on their appropriate application domain. In particular, physical identification of human beings (physical biometrics) is reaching the limits of its possibilities and the new advances biometric authentication will come from the profiling of human mind (behavior monitoring) which still is in a very early stage of development.

References

1. Dasgupta, D.: Biometrics and its use: viewpoint. Biostat. Biom. Open Acc. J. **7**(3) (2018). https://juniperpublishers.com/bboaj/pdf/BBOAJ.MS.ID.555714.pdf
2. Ricanek, K.: Beyond recognition: the promise of biometric analytics. IEEE Comput. Mag. **47**, 87–89 (2014). http://lifesciences.embs.org/wp-content/uploads/sites/53/2014/10/06898735.pdf
3. Williams, M.: One in every 14 Americans fell victim to identity theft last year, 27 September 2015. https://www.pcworld.com/article/2986810/security/identity-theft-hit-7-of-us-population-last-year.html
4. BioCatch: Behavioral Biometrics: A Primer on the Future of Cybersecurity, 2 March 2018. https://www.biocatch.com/blog/behavioral-biometrics-primer-future-cybersecurity
5. Tan, S.C., Yiap, B.C.: DNA, RNA, and protein extraction: the past and the present. J. Biomed. Biotechnol. **2009**, 1–10 (2009)
6. Dasgupta, D., Nag, A.K., Shrein, J., Swindle, M., Rahman, I.: Adaptive Multifactor Authentication (A-MFA) System, Center for Information Assurance (CfIA). The university of Memphis (2017)
7. Dasgupta, D., Roy, A., Nag, A.: Advances in User Authentication. ISFS. Springer, Cham (2017). https://doi.org/10.1007/978-3-319-58808-7
8. Jain, A.K., Ross, A., Prabhakar, S.: An introduction to biometric recognition. IEEE Trans. Circuits Syst. Video Technol. **14**(1), 4–20 (2004)
9. De Luca, A., Hang, A., Von Zezschwitz, E., Hussmann, H.: I feel like I'm taking selfies all day!: towards understanding biometric authentication on smartphones. In: Proceedings of the 33rd Annual ACM Conference on Human Factors in Computing Systems, CHI 2015, pp. 1411–1414. ACM, New York (2015)
10. Bhagavatula, C., Ur, B., Iacovino, K., Kywe, S.M., Cranor, L.F., Savvides, M.: Biometric authentication on iphone and android: usability, perceptions, and influences on adoption. In: Proceedings of USEC, pp. 1–2 (2015)
11. Wei, Y., Yildirim, P., Van den Bulte, C., Dellarocas, C.: Credit scoring with social network data. Mark. Sci. **35**(2), 234–258 (2016). https://pdfs.semanticscholar.org/35fe/6cb2a49aca15341f4af6224f7411269af601.pdf. Accessed 19 Jul 2018
12. Vrankulj, A.: Coursera looks to verify online student identity with photo, keystroke dynamic. Biometricupdate, 16 January 2013. https://www.biometricupdate.com/201301/coursera-looks-to-verify-online-student-identity-with-photo-keystroke-dynamics
13. Dehaye, P.O.: Coursera and keystroke biometrics. Medium, 12 February 2016. https://medium.com/personaldata-io/coursera-and-keystroke-biometrics-550762f2f61b
14. Gemalto: The electronic passport in 2018 and beyond. 25 June 2018. https://www.gemalto.com/govt/travel/electronic-passport-trends. Accessed 19 July 2018
15. Daugman, J.G.: How iris recognition works. IEEE Trans. Circuits Syst. Video Technol. **14**, 21–30 (2004)
16. Daugman, J.G.: Iris recognition at airports and border-crossings. In: Li, Z. (ed.) Encyclopedia of Biometrics. Springer, Heidelberg (2009). https://doi.org/10.1007/978-0-387-73003-5_24. Chapter 62
17. Mason, M.: Biometric Breakthrough How CBP is Meeting its Mandate and Keeping America Safe. U.S. Customs and Border Protection (2018). https://www.cbp.gov/frontline/cbp-biometric-testing

18. Wolf, P.: Introducing Biometric Technology in Elections. International IDEA Institute for Democracy and Electoral Assistance (2017). https://www.idea.int/sites/default/files/publications/introducing-biometric-technology-in-elections.pdf
19. Martins, A.: The Colombian Identification System. Keesing Journal of Documents and Identity, Annual Report: Identity Management 2012–2013
20. Businesswire: Colombia Selects IDEMIA to Upgrade Its Identification and Civil Registry Platform, 16 October 2017. https://www.businesswire.com/news/home/20171016005787/en/Colombia-Selects-IDEMIA-Upgrade-Identification-Civil-Registry
21. Das, R.: Biometrics in the cloud. Keesing Journal of Documents and Identity, pp. 21–23, February 2013
22. Talreja, V., Ferrett, T., Valenti, M.C., Ross, A.: Biometrics-as-a-Service: A Framework to Promote Innovative Biometric Recognition in the Cloud (2017) https://arxiv.org/pdf/1710.09183.pdf
23. Rose, J.: Biometrics as a service: the next giant leap? Biom. Technol. Today **2016**(3), 7–9 (2016)
24. Kleinman, Z.: Politician's fingerprint 'cloned from photos' by hacker. BBC News, 29 December 2014. https://www.bbc.com/news/technology-30623611
25. Cabrera, C., Guillen, M.R., Adjouadi, M.: Integrating palmprint and voice biometric for identity identification. In: 8th Latin American and Caribbean Conference (LACCEI 2010) (2010)
26. Cabrera, C., Guillen, M.R., Adjouadi, M.: Infrared thermal hand vein pattern recognition. In: 9th Latin American and Caribbean Conference (LACCEI 2011) (2011)
27. Czajka, A., Bulwan, P.: Biometric verification based on hand thermal images. In: 2013 International Conference on Biometrics (ICB). IEEE (2013)
28. Guzman, A.M.: Thermal imaging as a biometrics approach to facial signature authentication. IEEE J. Biomed. Health Inform. **17**(1), 214–222 (2013)
29. Hart, P.E.: How the hough transform was invented. IEEE Signal Process. Mag. **26**(6), 18–22 (2009)
30. Duda, R.O., Hart, P.E.: Use of the hough transformation to detect lines and curves in pictures. Comm. ACM **15**, 11–15 (1972)
31. Hough, P.V.C.: Method and means for recognizing complex patterns. U.S. Patent 3,069,654, 18 December 1962
32. Peaston, S.: The changing nature of identity: is biometrics the way forward? Cifas, 24 May 2017. https://www.cifas.org.uk/insight/fraud-risk-focus-blog/changing-nature-identity-biometrics-way-forward
33. Van Heerden, I.: 4 Ways to Turn Your Cell Phone into a Thermal Camera: FLIR vs Seek vs Therm-App vs CAT. TectoGizmo (2017). https://tectogizmo.com/4-ways-to-turn-your-cell-phone-into-a-thermal-camera/
34. Lankton, S., Tannenbaum, A.: Localizing region-based active contours. IEEE Trans. Image Process. **17**(11), 2029–2039 (2008)
35. FBI: Rapid DNA General Information. https://www.fbi.gov/services/laboratory/biometric-analysis/codis/rapid-dna
36. NIST: DNA Biometrics, 13 July 2017. https://www.nist.gov/programs-projects/dna-biometrics
37. Caughill, P.: Using DNA, New Software Can Verify Identity in Minutes. Futurim, 1 December 2017. https://futurism.com/software-verify-id-dna/

38. Zaaijer, S., Gordon, A., Speyer, D., Piccone, R., Groen, S.C., Erlich, Y.: Rapid re-identification of human samples using portable DNA sequencing. eLife **6**, e27798 (2017). https://doi.org/10.7554/eLife.27798. https://elifesciences.org/articles/27798

39. Benjamin, R.: NASA study reveals 7% percent of DNA has changed to an astronaut after spending a year-long in the space shuttle. US and World News from MLIVE.com, 12 March 2018

40. Moore, S.K.: "Brainprint" biometric ID hits 100% accuracy. IEEE Spectrum **53**, 14 (2016). https://spectrum.ieee.org/biomedical/devices/brainprint-biometric-id-hits-100-accuracy

41. Orpanidhes, K.G.: Your 'brainprint' can identify you with 100% accuracy. Wired, Tuesday 19 April 2016. https://www.wired.co.uk/article/eeg-brainprint-biometric-identification

42. Ruiz-Blondet, M.V., Jin, Z., Laszlo, S.: CEREBRE: a novel method for very high accuracy event-related potential biometric identification. IEEE Trans. Inf. Forensics Secur. **11**(7), 1618–1629 (2016)

43. Armstrong, B.C., Ruiz-Blondetb, M.V., Laszlobe, S., Khalifia, N., Kurtz, K.J., Jin, Z.: Brainprint: assessing the uniqueness, collectability, and permanence of a novel method for ERP biometrics. Neurocomputing **166**(20), 59–67 (2015). https://doi.org/10.1016/j.neucom.2015.04.025

44. Maskeliunas, R., Damasevicius, R., Martisius, R., Vasiljevas, M.: Consumer-grade EEG devices are they usable for control tasks? PeerJ **4**, e1746 (2016). https://doi.org/10.7717/peerj.1746

45. Grush, L.: Those 'mind-reading' EEG headsets definitely can't read your thoughts. The Verge, 12 January 2016. https://www.theverge.com/2016/1/12/10754436/commercial-eeg-headsets-video-games-mind-control-technology

46. Kataria, A.N., Adhyaru, D.M., Sharma, A.K., Zaveri, T.H.: A survey of automated biometric authentication techniques. In: Nirma University International Conference on Engineering (NUiCONE) (2013)

47. Ibrahim, D.R., Tamimi, A.A., Abdalla, A.M.: Performance analysis of biometric recognition modalities. In: IEEE 8th International Conference on Information Technology (ICIT) (2017)

48. Moren, D.: 7 Surprising Biometric Identification Methods. Popular Science, 30 December 2014. https://www.popsci.com/seven-surprising-biometric-identification-methods

49. Shachtman, O., Beckhusen, R.: 11 Body Parts Defense Researchers Will Use To Track You. Wired, 25 January 2013. https://www.wired.com/2013/01/biometrics/

Robust Kalman Filter for High-Frequency Financial Data

Tomáš Cipra[1]([⊠]), Radek Hendrych[1], and Michal Černý[2]

[1] Department of Probability and Mathematical Statistics,
Faculty of Mathematics and Physics, Charles University,
Sokolovsk á 83, 186 75 Prague 8, Czech Republic
{cipra,hendrych}@karlin.mff.cuni.cz
[2] Department of Econometrics, Faculty of Informatics and Statistics,
University of Economics in Prague,
W. Churchill Sq. 4, 130 67 Prague 3, Czech Republic
cernym@vse.cz

Abstract. The robust recursive algorithm for the parameter estimation
and the volatility prediction in GARCH models is proposed. The suggested technique employs principles of robustified Kalman filter. It seems
to be useful for (high-frequency) financial time series contaminated by
additive outliers. In particular, it can be effective in the risk control and
regulation when the prediction of volatility is the main concern since it is
capable of distinguishing and correcting outlaid bursts of volatility. This
conclusion is confirmed by simulations and real data examples.

Keywords: Kalman filter · Outlier · Robustification · Volatility

1 Introduction

Financial time series (in particular returns of financial assets) typically exhibit
significant kurtosis and volatility clustering. The assets are usually stocks, stock
indices, or currencies. The GARCH models are commonly applied in order to
model these typical properties with the aim to describe dynamics of conditional
variances and forecast financial volatility. However, when fitted to real time
series the estimated residuals have frequently excess kurtosis explainable by the
presence of outliers which are not captured by the GARCH models.

The parameters of the GARCH models are routinely estimated by the (conditional) maximum likelihood but they are rarely calibrated recursively. Nevertheless, recursive estimates performed using recursive algorithms are undoubt-
edly advantageous. To evaluate the parameter estimates at a time step, recursive
estimation methods operate only with the current measurements and parameters
estimated in previous steps. It is in sharp contrast to the non-recursive estimation where all data are collected at first and then the model is fitted. Therefore,

Supported by the grants P402/12/G097 (T. Cipra and R. Hendrych) and 16-00408S
(M. Černý) provided by the Grant Agency of the Czech Republic.

© Springer Nature Switzerland AG 2018
J. C. Figueroa-García et al. (Eds.): WEA 2018, CCIS 915, pp. 42–54, 2018.
https://doi.org/10.1007/978-3-030-00350-0_4

recursive estimation techniques are effective in terms of memory storage and computational complexity. This efficiency can be employed just in the framework of (high-frequency) financial time series data. Alternatively, it is possible to adopt these methods to monitor or forecast volatility on-line, to evaluate risk measures (e.g. Value at Risk or Expected Shortfall), to detect faults, to check model stability including detection of structural changes, etc. Moreover due to the previous arguments, the recursive GARCH estimation should be resistant (robust) to outliers. The primary goal of this paper is to suggest a robust recursive algorithm which is effective enough in the context of GARCH models to estimate and forecast volatility of contaminated (high-frequency) financial data.

As robust recursive estimation of GARCH model is concerned, one should remind a close connection to robustification of Kalman filter which is desirable including various engineering applications in the context of state space modeling with outliers (see e.g. [3,5,7,14,18,23–25,27,28]). Moreover, a special case of Kalman filter robustification is the robust exponential smoothing including Holt-Winters method (see e.g. [4,6,8–10,12,15,22]).

The following sections of the paper deal in sequence with (1) the presentation of self weighted recursive estimation algorithm for GARCH models, (2) its robustification, (3) the simulation study for various types of outliers, and finally (4) real data applications.

2 GARCH Models: Construction of Recursive Estimator

The GARCH(p, q) process $\{y_t\}_{t \in \mathbb{Z}}$ is commonly defined as

$$y_t = \sigma_t \varepsilon_t, \quad \sigma_t^2 = \omega + \sum_{i=1}^{p} \alpha_i y_{t-i}^2 + \sum_{j=1}^{q} \beta_j \sigma_{t-j}^2, \tag{1}$$

where $\{\varepsilon_t\}_{t \in \mathbb{Z}}$ is a sequence of i.i.d. random variables with zero mean and unit variance, and ω, $\alpha_1, \ldots, \alpha_p$, $\beta_1, \ldots, \beta_q$ are the parameters of the process. The first two conditional and unconditional moments can be simply expressed as

$$\mathbb{E}(y_t | \mathcal{F}_{t-1}) = 0, \ \mathbb{E}(y_t) = 0, \ \text{var}(y_t | \mathcal{F}_{t-1}) = \sigma_t^2, \ \text{var}(y_t) = \mathbb{E}(\sigma_t^2), \tag{2}$$

where $\mathcal{F}_t$ denotes the smallest σ-algebra with respect to which y_s is measurable for all $s \leq t$. Sufficient conditions for σ_t^2 being positive are $\omega > 0$, $\alpha_1, \ldots, \alpha_p$, $\beta_1, \ldots, \beta_q \geq 0$. If $\beta_1 = \cdots = \beta_q = 0$, the model is reduced to the ARCH(p) process. Additionally, sufficient conditions for y_t being (weakly) stationary are $\omega > 0$, $\alpha_1, \ldots, \alpha_p, \beta_1, \ldots, \beta_q \geq 0$, and $\sum_{i=1}^{p} \alpha_i + \sum_{j=1}^{q} \beta_j < 1$. The one-step ahead prediction of σ_t^2 is calculated as

$$\hat{\sigma}_{t+1|t}^2 = \omega + \sum_{i=1}^{p} \alpha_i y_{t+1-i}^2 + \sum_{j=1}^{q} \beta_j \sigma_{t+1-j}^2. \tag{3}$$

The GARCH models are routinely estimated by the non-recursive conditional maximum likelihood method with normal distribution being usually preferred since the corresponding estimates stay consistent. Aknouche and Guerbyenne [1] proposed a couple of two-stage recursive estimation schemes appropriate for the standard GARCH(p, q) models extending the ideas presented in [2]. However, they focused mainly on the derivation and convergence analysis of the algorithm and not on its numerical evaluation, which might be regarded as a (crucial) objection (consult [21]). In particular, the whole computational implementation is based on recursive pseudo-linear regression estimation scheme applied to the following representation of the GARCH(p, q) process y_t:

$$y_t^2 = \sigma_t^2(\boldsymbol{\theta}_0) + \nu_t, \tag{4}$$

where $\sigma_t^2(\boldsymbol{\theta}_0)$ is defined in (1) for the true values of model parameters collected in the vector $\boldsymbol{\theta}_0$ and $\nu_t = \sigma_t^2(\boldsymbol{\theta}_0)(\varepsilon_t^2 - 1)$ is white noise with $\mathbb{E}(\nu_t) = 0$ and $\mathsf{var}(\nu_t) = \mathbb{E}(\nu_t^2)$. Independently, such a recursive pseudo-linear regression algorithm has been also proposed in [17] following analogical derivation schemes (see [13]).

Hendrych and Cipra [16] derived an alternative recursive formulas for estimating parameters of the standard GARCH(p, q) model which is based on the principle of self-weighted estimation (see also [19,30], but Hendrych and Cipra [16] made use of the opportunity to formulate this principle conveniently in a recursive way). Even though the Gaussian QMLE approach was applied for this purpose, theoretically it could be generalized to other types of QMLE (see e.g. [29] for an overview), but with much higher computational complexity.

The recursive identification instruments introduced by [20,21,26] were applied to deliver one-stage recursive estimation procedures (in contrast to two-stage procedure suggested in [1]):

$$\widehat{\boldsymbol{\theta}}_t = \widehat{\boldsymbol{\theta}}_{t-1} + \frac{\widehat{\boldsymbol{P}}_{t-1}\widehat{\boldsymbol{\psi}}_t(y_t^2 - \widehat{\boldsymbol{\varphi}}_t^\top \widehat{\boldsymbol{\theta}}_{t-1})}{\lambda_t(\widehat{\boldsymbol{\varphi}}_t^\top \widehat{\boldsymbol{\theta}}_{t-1})^2 + \widehat{\boldsymbol{\psi}}_t^\top \widehat{\boldsymbol{P}}_{t-1}\widehat{\boldsymbol{\psi}}_t}, \tag{5a}$$

$$\widehat{\boldsymbol{P}}_t = \frac{1}{\lambda_t}\left\{\widehat{\boldsymbol{P}}_{t-1} - \frac{\widehat{\boldsymbol{P}}_{t-1}\widehat{\boldsymbol{\psi}}_t\widehat{\boldsymbol{\psi}}_t^\top \widehat{\boldsymbol{P}}_{t-1}}{\lambda_t(\widehat{\boldsymbol{\varphi}}_t^\top \widehat{\boldsymbol{\theta}}_{t-1})^2 + \widehat{\boldsymbol{\psi}}_t^\top \widehat{\boldsymbol{P}}_{t-1}\widehat{\boldsymbol{\psi}}_t}\right\}, \tag{5b}$$

$$\widehat{\boldsymbol{\varphi}}_{t+1} = (1, y_t^2, \ldots, y_{t+1-p}^2, \widehat{\boldsymbol{\varphi}}_t^\top \widehat{\boldsymbol{\theta}}_t, \ldots, \widehat{\boldsymbol{\varphi}}_{t+1-q}^\top \widehat{\boldsymbol{\theta}}_{t+1-q})^\top, \tag{5c}$$

$$\widehat{\boldsymbol{\psi}}_{t+1} = \widehat{\boldsymbol{\varphi}}_{t+1} + \sum_{j=1}^q \widehat{\beta}_{j,t}\widehat{\boldsymbol{\psi}}_{t+1-j}, \tag{5d}$$

$$\lambda_t = \tilde{\lambda} \cdot \lambda_{t-1} + (1 - \tilde{\lambda}), \quad \lambda_0, \tilde{\lambda} \in (0,1), \ t \in \mathbb{N}, \tag{5e}$$

where the recursive estimates are collected in $\widehat{\boldsymbol{\theta}}_t$ (the parameters in (1) are ordered to a single vector $\boldsymbol{\theta} = (\omega, \alpha_1, \ldots, \alpha_p, \beta_1, \ldots, \beta_q)^\top$). The *forgetting factor* $\{\lambda_t\}_{t\in\mathbb{N}}$ is a deterministic sequence of positive real numbers less or equal to one. It represents the observation weight over time. One commonly puts $\lambda_0 = 0.95$ and $\tilde{\lambda} = 0.99$. The initialization of the algorithm is thoroughly discussed in [16] (see p. 320). Finally, one should introduce the simple projection, which completes the algorithm (5) and ensures that it will not degenerate:

$$\left[\widehat{\boldsymbol{\theta}}_t\right]_{\boldsymbol{D}_{\mathcal{M}}} = \begin{cases} \widehat{\boldsymbol{\theta}}_t & \text{if } \widehat{\boldsymbol{\theta}}_t \in \boldsymbol{D}_{\mathcal{M}}, \\ \widehat{\boldsymbol{\theta}}_{t-1} & \text{if } \widehat{\boldsymbol{\theta}}_t \notin \boldsymbol{D}_{\mathcal{M}}, \end{cases} \tag{6}$$

where $\boldsymbol{D}_{\mathcal{M}} = \{\boldsymbol{\theta} \in \mathbb{R}^{p+q+1} | \tilde{\delta}_1 \leq \theta_1 \leq \tilde{\Delta}_1; \theta_i \geq 0, i = 2, \ldots, p+q+1; \sum_{j=2}^{p+q+1} \theta_j \leq 1 - \tilde{\delta}_2\}$ and one usually puts $0 < \tilde{\delta}_1 \leq \tilde{\Delta}_1 < \infty$, $0 < \tilde{\delta}_2 < 1$, e.g. $\tilde{\delta}_1 = 10^{-9}$ and $\tilde{\Delta}_1 = 10^2$.

The performance of this algorithm was (fairly) compared by means of the various Monte Carlo experiments with other methods mentioned above. The one-stage recursive estimate has proven to be at least competitive amongst the others (and usually better, see [16]). The simulations have also shown that the initialization of the algorithms must be handled carefully, since it can significantly influence the speed of its convergence. For more details, consult [16] and the references therein.

3   Robust Recursive Estimation of GARCH Models

Using GARCH models, it is necessary to be concerned about outliers that may occur in data (see also the first introduction section and the last section on real data applications). Outliers can be caused by many reasons, e.g. by additive innovations, measurement failures, operational risk problems, management decisions, etc. They can influence the estimation and prediction in the applied model considerably if no specific action is taken. Therefore, if such defects are expected in the data set, one should modify the estimation algorithms to make them more robust. The outliers tend to appear as spikes in the sequence of $\{y_t / \sqrt{\sigma_t^2}\}$, which obviously result in large contributions to the loss function. There exist various ways how to robustify recursive estimation algorithms (refer to the first introduction section above). In this contribution, a simple way of handling outliers is applied based on testing a measurement at each time t. If it is large compared with a given limit, it is indicated as erroneous and substituted immediately by another value (see e.g. [6,21,23], and others). According to simulations, this strategy seems to be efficient for additive outliers (AD) mainly.

Under the previous arguments, the algorithm (5) can be robustified to the following form:

$$\widehat{\boldsymbol{\theta}}_t^{rob} = \widehat{\boldsymbol{\theta}}_{t-1}^{rob} + \frac{\widehat{\boldsymbol{P}}_{t-1}^{rob} \widehat{\boldsymbol{\psi}}_t^{rob} \left[\left(\widehat{y}_t^{rob}\right)^2 - (\widehat{\boldsymbol{\varphi}}_t^{rob})^{\top} \widehat{\boldsymbol{\theta}}_{t-1}^{rob} \right]}{\lambda_t \left[(\widehat{\boldsymbol{\varphi}}_t^{rob})^{\top} \widehat{\boldsymbol{\theta}}_{t-1}^{rob} \right]^2 + (\widehat{\boldsymbol{\psi}}_t^{rob})^{\top} \widehat{\boldsymbol{P}}_{t-1}^{rob} \widehat{\boldsymbol{\psi}}_t^{rob}}, \tag{7a}$$

$$\widehat{\boldsymbol{P}}_t^{rob} = \frac{1}{\lambda_t} \left\{ \widehat{\boldsymbol{P}}_{t-1}^{rob} - \frac{\widehat{\boldsymbol{P}}_{t-1}^{rob} \widehat{\boldsymbol{\psi}}_t^{rob} (\widehat{\boldsymbol{\psi}}_t^{rob})^{\top} \widehat{\boldsymbol{P}}_{t-1}^{rob}}{\lambda_t \left[(\widehat{\boldsymbol{\varphi}}_t^{rob})^{\top} \widehat{\boldsymbol{\theta}}_{t-1}^{rob} \right]^2 + (\widehat{\boldsymbol{\psi}}_t^{rob})^{\top} \widehat{\boldsymbol{P}}_{t-1}^{rob} \widehat{\boldsymbol{\psi}}_t^{rob}} \right\}, \tag{7b}$$

$$\widehat{\boldsymbol{\varphi}}_{t+1}^{rob} = \left(1, \left(\hat{y}_t^{rob}\right)^2, \ldots, \left(\hat{y}_{t+1-p}^{rob}\right)^2, (\widehat{\boldsymbol{\varphi}}_t^{rob})^{\top} \widehat{\boldsymbol{\theta}}_t^{rob}, \ldots, (\widehat{\boldsymbol{\varphi}}_{t+1-q}^{rob})^{\top} \widehat{\boldsymbol{\theta}}_{t+1-q}^{rob} \right)^{\top}, \tag{7c}$$

$$\widehat{\psi}_{t+1}^{rob} = \widehat{\varphi}_{t+1}^{rob} + \sum_{j=1}^{q} \widehat{\beta}_{j,t}^{rob} \widehat{\psi}_{t+1-j}^{rob}, \tag{7d}$$

$$\lambda_t = \tilde{\lambda} \cdot \lambda_{t-1} + (1 - \tilde{\lambda}), \quad \lambda_0, \ \tilde{\lambda} \in (0,1), \ t \in \mathbb{N}, \tag{7e}$$

where the recursive estimates are collected in $\widehat{\boldsymbol{\theta}}_t^{rob}$ (the $\{\lambda_t\}_{t \in \mathbb{N}}$ is the same as in (5e)). To complete (7), one defines the outlier-corrected series $\{\hat{y}_t^{rob}\}$ as follows:

$$(\hat{y}_t^{rob})^2 = \begin{cases} (\widehat{\varphi}_t^{rob})^\top \widehat{\boldsymbol{\theta}}_{t-1}^{rob} \\ \quad + \operatorname{sign}\left(y_t^2 - (\widehat{\varphi}_t^{rob})^\top \widehat{\boldsymbol{\theta}}_{t-1}^{rob}\right)(u_{1-\alpha/2})^2 \sqrt{\left[(\widehat{\varphi}_t^{rob})^\top \widehat{\boldsymbol{\theta}}_{t-1}^{rob}\right]^2 + (\widehat{\psi}_t^{rob})^\top \widehat{\boldsymbol{P}}_{t-1}^{rob} \widehat{\psi}_t^{rob} / \lambda_t} \\ \quad \text{for } \left| y_t^2 - (\widehat{\varphi}_t^{rob})^\top \widehat{\boldsymbol{\theta}}_{t-1}^{rob} \right| > (u_{1-\alpha/2})^2 \sqrt{\left[(\widehat{\varphi}_t^{rob})^\top \widehat{\boldsymbol{\theta}}_{t-1}^{rob}\right]^2 + (\widehat{\psi}_t^{rob})^\top \widehat{\boldsymbol{P}}_{t-1}^{rob} \widehat{\psi}_t^{rob} / \lambda_t}, \\ y_t^2 \quad \text{otherwise.} \end{cases} \tag{7f}$$

Note that $\hat{y}_t^{rob} = \operatorname{sign}(y_t) \sqrt{(\hat{y}_t^{rob})^2}$ and that $u_{1-\alpha/2}$ denotes the corresponding quantile of the standard normal distribution, where one usually puts $\alpha = 0.05$. The initialization settings and projection rule (6) remain similar as in the previous section. The algorithm is based on the robustified version of Kalman filter derived in [6] (see Appendix) which is applied to the GARCH models written in the form (4). The assumption of normality can be replaced by other distributions.

Parallelly one can construct the robust recursive prediction of volatility, e.g. the one-step ahead prediction has the form (compare with (3)):

$$(\hat{\sigma}_{t+1|t}^{rob})^2 = \hat{\omega}_t^{rob} + \sum_{i=1}^{p} \hat{\alpha}_{it}^{rob} (\hat{y}_{t+1-i}^{rob})^2 + \sum_{j=1}^{q} \hat{\beta}_{jt} (\hat{\sigma}_{t+1-j}^{rob})^2. \tag{8}$$

A theoretical analysis of the introduced algorithm can follow the general schemes considered by [21]; it is rather technical and uses instruments known mainly in the ordinary differential equation theory. Under the corresponding (mostly technical) general assumptions, it can be shown that the estimated parameters converge to their true counterparts. Additionally, they are asymptotically normally distributed (consult [21]).

4   Simulations

The suggested procedure (7) has been studied by means of simulations $\{y_t^*\}$ using several simulation scenarios described in Table 1:

$$y_t^* = y_t + \delta_t, \ t = 1, \ldots, T, \ T = 20000, \tag{9a}$$

$$y_t = \sigma_t \varepsilon_t, \ \sigma_t^2 = 0.0001 + 0.05 y_{t-1}^2 + 0.94 \sigma_{t-1}^2, \ \varepsilon_t \sim i.i.d. \ \mathsf{N}(0,1), \tag{9b}$$

Table 1. Various simulation scenarios for additive outliers in (9) [$Alt \sim$ alternative distribution, $t(1) \sim$ Student t_1-distribution, $st(4) \sim$ skewed Student t_4-distribution with the skewness parameter $\xi = -1.5$]

Model 0	$\delta_t = 0$ for all t
Model 1	$\delta_t = 10 \times I_t,\ I_t = \begin{cases} 1, t = 10000 \\ 0, \text{otherwise} \end{cases}$
Model 2	$\delta_t = 10 \times I_t,\ I_t \sim i.i.d.\ Alt\left(\frac{1}{20000}\right)$ for all t
Model 3	$\delta_t = 10 \times I_t,\ I_t \sim i.i.d.\ Alt\left(\frac{4}{20000}\right)$ for all t
Model 4	$\delta_t = s_t \times I_t,\ I_t \sim i.i.d.\ Alt\left(\frac{4}{20000}\right),\ s_t \sim i.i.d.\ t(1)$ for all t
Model 5	$\delta_t = s_t \times I_t,\ I_t \sim i.i.d.\ Alt\left(\frac{20}{20000}\right),\ s_t \sim i.i.d.\ t(1)$ for all t
Model 6	$\delta_t = s_t \times I_t,\ I_t \sim i.i.d.\ Alt\left(\frac{200}{20000}\right),\ s_t \sim i.i.d.\ t(1)$ for all t
Model 7	$\delta_t = s_t \times I_t,\ I_t \sim i.i.d.\ Alt\left(\frac{4}{20000}\right),\ s_t \sim i.i.d.\ st(4)$ for all t
Model 8	$\delta_t = s_t \times I_t,\ I_t \sim i.i.d.\ Alt\left(\frac{20}{20000}\right),\ s_t \sim i.i.d.\ st(4)$ for all t
Model 9	$\delta_t = s_t \times I_t,\ I_t \sim i.i.d.\ Alt\left(\frac{200}{20000}\right),\ s_t \sim i.i.d.\ st(4)$ for all t

where the term δ_t represents the additive outlier. According to Table 1, this simulation study covers various ways of contamination of the generic processes in the first scenario (Model 0) without outliers (e.g., the t-distribution with the degree of freedom one denoted as $t(1)$ represents the contamination by outliers with heavy tails). For each scenarios one has simulated 1000 realizations of length 20000 and applied the robust recursive estimation procedure (7) with the same initialization settings and projection rule (6) (in particular, $\alpha = 0.05$, $\tilde{\delta}_1 = \tilde{\delta}_2 = 10^{-9}$, and $\tilde{\Delta}_1 = 10^2$). The simulation results for innovative outliers (IO) are not presented in this paper.

Figure 1 displays the boxplots of estimated parameters $\omega = 0.0001$, $\alpha_1 = 0.05$, and $\beta_1 = 0.94$ in times $t = 5000, 10000, 20000$ calculated over 1000 realizations in Model 1. Figure 2 shows the time records of medians of estimated parameters ω, α_1, and β_1 in Model 1 (i.e., the single additive outlier of size 10 in time $t = 10000$) before and after the robustification. Moreover, Table 2 reports the median absolute deviations (MAD) for all studied models.

Similar results have been obtained for other configurations of true parameters (the presented case corresponds to the extreme situation close to the border of model stability). In general, the simulations show that the robustification improves the behaviour of suggested recursive procedure in a substantial way.

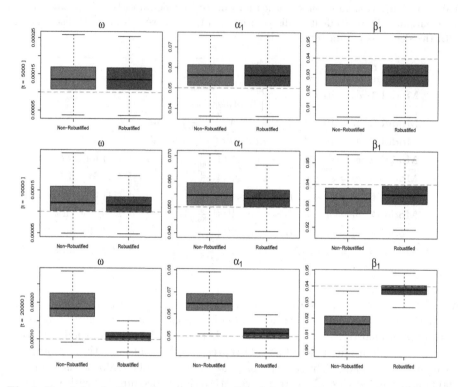

Fig. 1. Boxplots of estimated parameters in **Model 1** in times $t = 5000, 10000, 20000$ before and after robustification

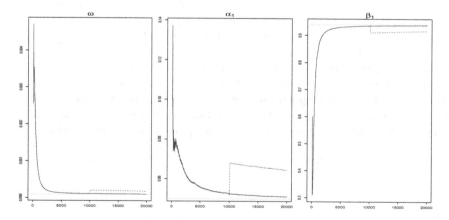

Fig. 2. Time records of medians of estimated parameters: **Model 1** [non-robustified estimates $\sim$ dashed lines, robustified estimates $\sim$ solid lines]

Table 2. Median absolute deviations MAD of estimated parameters [calculated in times $t = 5000, 10000, 20000$ over 1000 realizations]

Model 0	$\hat{\omega}_t$	$\hat{\omega}_t^{rob}$	$\hat{\alpha}_{1t}$	$\hat{\alpha}_{1t}^{rob}$	$\hat{\beta}_{1t}$	$\hat{\beta}_{1t}^{rob}$
5000	0.00003	0.00004	0.00635	0.00636	0.00940	0.00939
10000	0.00002	0.00002	0.00343	0.00341	0.00473	0.00480
20000	0.00001	0.00001	0.00240	0.00238	0.00292	0.00292
Model 1	$\hat{\omega}_t$	$\hat{\omega}_t^{rob}$	$\hat{\alpha}_{1t}$	$\hat{\alpha}_{1t}^{rob}$	$\hat{\beta}_{1t}$	$\hat{\beta}_{1t}^{rob}$
5000	0.00004	0.00004	0.00681	0.00673	0.01032	0.01022
10000	0.00002	0.00002	0.00499	0.00397	0.00654	0.00497
20000	0.00008	0.00001	0.01435	0.00227	0.02334	0.00298
Model 2	$\hat{\omega}_t$	$\hat{\omega}_t^{rob}$	$\hat{\alpha}_{1t}$	$\hat{\alpha}_{1t}^{rob}$	$\hat{\beta}_{1t}$	$\hat{\beta}_{1t}^{rob}$
5000	0.00005	0.00004	0.00885	0.00688	0.01281	0.00989
10000	0.00003	0.00002	0.00732	0.00371	0.00989	0.00478
20000	0.00007	0.00001	0.01267	0.00229	0.01972	0.00303
Model 3	$\hat{\omega}_t$	$\hat{\omega}_t^{rob}$	$\hat{\alpha}_{1t}$	$\hat{\alpha}_{1t}^{rob}$	$\hat{\beta}_{1t}$	$\hat{\beta}_{1t}^{rob}$
5000	0.00022	0.00004	0.02682	0.00694	0.05244	0.01073
10000	0.00027	0.00002	0.03274	0.00363	0.06364	0.00527
20000	0.00065	0.00001	0.04147	0.00235	0.08291	0.00321
Model 4	$\hat{\omega}_t$	$\hat{\omega}_t^{rob}$	$\hat{\alpha}_{1t}$	$\hat{\alpha}_{1t}^{rob}$	$\hat{\beta}_{1t}$	$\hat{\beta}_{1t}^{rob}$
5000	0.00007	0.00004	0.01030	0.00703	0.01660	0.01101
10000	0.00006	0.00002	0.00948	0.00370	0.01441	0.00523
20000	0.00009	0.00001	0.01221	0.00242	0.02092	0.00318
Model 5	$\hat{\omega}_t$	$\hat{\omega}_t^{rob}$	$\hat{\alpha}_{1t}$	$\hat{\alpha}_{1t}^{rob}$	$\hat{\beta}_{1t}$	$\hat{\beta}_{1t}^{rob}$
5000	0.00058	0.00007	0.03504	0.00765	0.09018	0.01327
10000	0.00077	0.00004	0.04377	0.00413	0.09973	0.00619
20000	0.00098	0.00003	0.04786	0.00280	0.10609	0.00378
Model 6	$\hat{\omega}_t$	$\hat{\omega}_t^{rob}$	$\hat{\alpha}_{1t}$	$\hat{\alpha}_{1t}^{rob}$	$\hat{\beta}_{1t}$	$\hat{\beta}_{1t}^{rob}$
5000	0.00630	0.00050	0.05000	0.01550	0.25070	0.04070
10000	0.00660	0.00040	0.05000	0.01440	0.17110	0.02000
20000	0.00630	0.00020	0.05000	0.01710	0.08070	0.01230
Model 7	$\hat{\omega}_t$	$\hat{\omega}_t^{rob}$	$\hat{\alpha}_{1t}$	$\hat{\alpha}_{1t}^{rob}$	$\hat{\beta}_{1t}$	$\hat{\beta}_{1t}^{rob}$
5000	0.00005	0.00004	0.00846	0.00683	0.01294	0.01030
10000	0.00004	0.00002	0.00600	0.00378	0.00897	0.00518
20000	0.00004	0.00001	0.00524	0.00237	0.00785	0.00300
Model 8	$\hat{\omega}_t$	$\hat{\omega}_t^{rob}$	$\hat{\alpha}_{1t}$	$\hat{\alpha}_{1t}^{rob}$	$\hat{\beta}_{1t}$	$\hat{\beta}_{1t}^{rob}$
5000	0.00032	0.00007	0.02200	0.00731	0.04770	0.01314
10000	0.00032	0.00004	0.02350	0.00429	0.04551	0.00650
20000	0.00033	0.00003	0.02198	0.00284	0.04369	0.00387
Model 9	$\hat{\omega}_t$	$\hat{\omega}_t^{rob}$	$\hat{\alpha}_{1t}$	$\hat{\alpha}_{1t}^{rob}$	$\hat{\beta}_{1t}$	$\hat{\beta}_{1t}^{rob}$
5000	0.00334	0.00055	0.04780	0.01405	0.14872	0.03644
10000	0.00331	0.00032	0.04805	0.01393	0.10392	0.01691
20000	0.00329	0.00022	0.04818	0.01706	0.09037	0.01086

5   Real Data Applications

Log returns of the daily currency rate CHF/EUR for the period from January 2000 to May 2017 show an apparent burst of volatility in January 2015 (see e.g. [11]). It has a clear explanation, i.e. the end of currency regulation of CHF by the Swiss National Bank in 2015: CHF was pegged to the Euro for around two years, with the minimum rate (or the floor) at 1.2. As of 15 January 2015, this link has been removed (a consequence of recent appreciation of USD against EUR and of CHF weakening against USD).

It was natural to apply the algorithm (7) to handle this time series. This estimation scheme has indeed identified the value of 15 January 2015 as an outlier and corrected it in a proper way. The one-day-ahead predictions of volatility (see (3) and (8)) would be out of reality without the robustification (see Fig. 3; the initial segment of the data is not displayed due to initialization of the recursive algorithm: the recursive estimates generally tend to be volatile here). It is also confirmed by the AIC values reported in Table 3 jointly with classical statistical tests on model adequacy (applied on standardized residuals). Point out that the results of these tests are rather indicative due to the presence of outlier. Furthermore, the estimation algorithm (7) has been applied to forty currency rates */EUR (daily log returns) and in some of them the declared robustification has been activated (see Table 4). The results for these daily log returns are not reported here since the figures are just of the type presented herein.

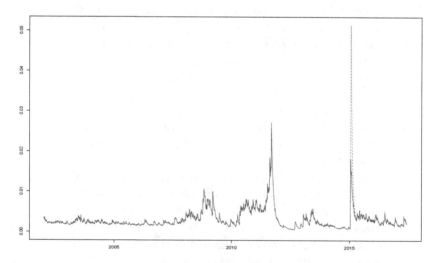

Fig. 3. One-day-ahead predictions of volatility for daily log returns of CHF/EUR [non-robustified predictions ∼ dashed line, robustified predictions ∼ solid line]

Table 3. Statistical characteristics of the GARCH(1,1) model for daily log returns of CHF/EUR [AIC, Ljung-Box test on standardized residuals with 8 degrees of freedom $Q(8)$, Ljung-Box test on squared standardized residuals with 8 degrees of freedom $Q^2(8)$, Jarque-Bera test on standardized residuals JB (p-values in brackets)]

Estimation algorithm	AIC	$Q(8)$	$Q^2(8)$	JB
Non-robustified	-1.29049	0.06614	0.00310	1598500000
		(0.99999)	(0.99999)	(0.00000)
Robustified	-8.08754	1.25470	0.01162	164470000
		(0.99610)	(0.99999)	(0.00000)

Table 4. Activation times of robustification in (7) [daily currency rates */EUR]

Currency	Identified outliers	Currency	Identified outliers
USD	1999-07-26	TRY	2006-05-12
UF	2003-01-17	CAD	2000-01-04
ROL	2000-01-04	CNY	2006-01-23
RON	2006-05-15	MYR	2006-04-18
CHF	2015-01-15	MYR	2008-03-17
ISK	2008-11-06	MYR	2008-03-20
TRL	2001-02-22	NZD	1999-08-25

6   Conclusion

The robust recursive algorithm for the estimation parameters and the corresponding volatility prediction of the GARCH model suggested in this paper seems to be effective for financial data, especially for contaminated log returns in the risk control and regulation when the prediction of volatility is the main concern. The one-stage recursive estimation procedure introduced for the GARCH process in [16] is robustified in such a way that it can distinguish and correct outlaid bursts of volatility. The simulations and real data examples also demonstrate that the suggested procedure enables corresponding adaptations in the case parameter changes.

Appendix

The robustified recursive algorithm for estimation of GARCH model (refer to (7) is based on the robustified version of Kalman filter derived in [6] with the aim to robustify the classical exponential smoothing in time series analysis:

Let us consider the dynamic linear model (DLM) in the form:

$$x_{t+1} = x_t, \tag{A1a}$$

$$y_t = h_t^\top x_t + \nu_t, \ \nu_t \sim i.i.d. \ \mathsf{N}(0, w_t^2), \tag{A1b}$$

where $\boldsymbol{x}_t$ is the state vector in the signal equation (A1a) and $\boldsymbol{h}_t$ is the vector of coefficients in the observation equation (A1b). Then the classical Kalman filter recursion is:

$$\hat{\boldsymbol{x}}_t = \hat{\boldsymbol{x}}_{t-1} + \frac{\boldsymbol{P}_{t-1}\boldsymbol{h}_t}{\boldsymbol{h}_t^{\top}\boldsymbol{P}_{t-1}\boldsymbol{h}_t + w_t^2}\left(y_t - \boldsymbol{h}_t^{\top}\hat{\boldsymbol{x}}_{t-1}\right), \tag{A2a}$$

$$\boldsymbol{P}_t = \boldsymbol{P}_{t-1} - \frac{\boldsymbol{P}_{t-1}\boldsymbol{h}_t\boldsymbol{h}_t^{\top}\boldsymbol{P}_{t-1}}{\boldsymbol{h}_t^{\top}\boldsymbol{P}_{t-1}\boldsymbol{h}_t + w_t^2}, \tag{A2b}$$

which can be rewritten by means of the filter gain $\boldsymbol{k}_t$ as

$$\hat{\boldsymbol{x}}_t = \hat{\boldsymbol{x}}_{t-1} + \boldsymbol{k}_t\left(y_t - \boldsymbol{h}_t^{\top}\hat{\boldsymbol{x}}_{t-1}\right), \tag{A3a}$$

$$\boldsymbol{P}_t = \boldsymbol{P}_{t-1} - \boldsymbol{k}_t\boldsymbol{h}_t^{\top}\boldsymbol{P}_{t-1}, \tag{A3b}$$

$$\boldsymbol{k}_t = \frac{\boldsymbol{P}_{t-1}\boldsymbol{h}_t}{\boldsymbol{h}_t^{\top}\boldsymbol{P}_{t-1}\boldsymbol{h}_t + w_t^2}. \tag{A3c}$$

The robust version according to [6] replaces (A3a) by

$$\hat{\boldsymbol{x}}_t^{rob} = \hat{\boldsymbol{x}}_{t-1}^{rob} + \boldsymbol{k}_t\Psi(e_t), \tag{A4}$$

i.e. the prediction error

$$e_t = y_t - \hat{y}_{t+1|t} = y_t - \boldsymbol{h}_t^{\top}\hat{\boldsymbol{x}}_{t-1} \sim \mathsf{N}(0, \boldsymbol{h}_t^{\top}\boldsymbol{P}_{t-1}\boldsymbol{h}_t + w_t^2) \tag{A5}$$

is trimmed by means of the robustifying function $\Psi(\cdot)$ defined as

$$\Psi(e_t) = \begin{cases} \text{sign}\,(e_t)u_{1-\alpha/2}\sqrt{\boldsymbol{h}_t^{\top}\boldsymbol{P}_{t-1}\boldsymbol{h}_t + w_t^2} & \text{for } |e_t| > u_{1-\alpha/2}\sqrt{\boldsymbol{h}_t^{\top}\boldsymbol{P}_{t-1}\boldsymbol{h}_t + w_t^2}, \\ e_t & \text{otherwise.} \end{cases}$$
$$\tag{A6}$$

For instance, if applying this scheme to the classical model AR(1) then the strong consistency of the recursive formulas for the robust estimation of the autoregressive parameter can be shown (see [7]).

References

1. Aknouche, A., Guerbyenne, H.: Recursive estimation of GARCH models. Commun. Stat. - Simul. Comput. **35**(4), 925–938 (2006)
2. Bose, A., Mukherjee, K.: Estimating the ARCH parameters by solving linear equations. J. Time Ser. Anal. **24**(2), 127–136 (2003)
3. Calvet, L.E., Czellar, V., Ronchetti, E.: Robust filtering. J. Am. Stat. Assoc. **110**(512), 1591–1606 (2015)
4. Cipra, T.: Robust exponential smoothing. J. Forecast. **11**(1), 57–69 (1992)
5. Cipra, T.: Robust recursive estimation in nonlinear time-series. Commun. Stat. - Theory Methods **27**(5), 1071–1082 (1998)
6. Cipra, T., Hanzák, T.: Exponential smoothing for time series with outliers. Kybernetika **47**(2), 165–178 (2011)

7. Cipra, T., Romera, R.: Robust Kalman filter and its applications in time series analysis. Kybernetika **27**(6), 481–494 (1991)
8. Crevits, R., Croux, C.: Forecasting using robust exponential smoothing with damped trend and seasonal components. Working paper KBI_1714, KU Leuven, Leuven (2016)
9. Croux, C., Gelper, S.: Computational aspects of robust Holt-Winters smoothing based on M-estimation. Appl. Math. **53**(3), 163–176 (2008)
10. Croux, C., Gelper, S., Mahieu, K.: Robust exponential smoothing of multivariate time series. Comput. Stat. Data Anal. **54**(12), 2999–3006 (2010)
11. ECB. www.ecb.europa.eu/stats/policy_and_exchange_rates/euro_reference_exchan ge_rates. Accessed 9 June 2017
12. Gelper, S., Fried, R., Croux, C.: Robust forecasting with exponential and Holt-Winters smoothing. J. Forecast. **29**(3), 285–300 (2009)
13. Gerencsér, L., Orlovits, Z., Torma, B.: Recursive estimation of GARCH processes. In: Edelmayer, A. (ed.) Proceedings of the 19th International Symposium on Mathematical Theory and Systems - MTNS, pp. 2415–2422. Eötvös Loránd University, Budapest (2010)
14. Grillenzoni, C.: Recursive generalized M-estimators of system parameters. Technometrics **39**(2), 211–224 (1997)
15. Hendrych, R., Cipra, T.: Robustified on-line estimation of the EWMA models: simulations and applications. In: Martinčák, D., Ircingová, J., Janeček, P. (eds.) Proceedings of the 33rd International Conference Mathematical Methods in Economics, pp. 237–242. University of West Bohemia, Pilsen (2014)
16. Hendrych, R., Cipra, T.: Self-weighted recursive estimation of GARCH models. Commun. Stat. - Simul. Comput. **47**(2), 315–328 (2018)
17. Kierkegaard, J., Nielsen, J., Jensen, L., Madsen, H.: Estimating GARCH models using recursive methods. Working paper, Technical University of Denmark, Lyngby (2000)
18. Koch, K.R., Yang, Y.: Robust Kalman filter for rank deficient observation models. J. Geod. **72**(7–8), 436–441 (1998)
19. Ling, S.: Self-weighted and local quasi-maximum likelihood estimators for ARMA-GARCH/ IGARCH models. J. Econ. **140**(2), 849–873 (2007)
20. Ljung, L.: System Identification: Theory for the User. Prentice Hall PTR, Upper Saddle River (1999)
21. Ljung, L., Söderström, T.S.: Theory and Practice of Recursive Identification. MIT Press, Cambridge (1983)
22. Michalek, J.: Robust methods in exponential smoothing. Kybernetika **32**(3), 289–306 (1996)
23. Romera, R., Cipra, T.: On practical implementation of robust Kalman filtering. Commun. Stat. - Simul. Comput. **24**(2), 461–488 (1995)
24. Ruckdeschel, P., Spangl, B., Pupashenko, D.: Robust Kalman tracking and smoothing with propagating and non propagating outliers. Stat. Pap. **55**(1), 93–123 (2014)
25. Shaolin, H.U., Meinke, K., Ouyang, H., Guoji, S.: Outlier-tolerant Kalman filter of state vectors in linear stochastic system. Int. J. Adv. Comput. Sci. Appl. **2**(12), 37–41 (2011)
26. Söderström, T.S., Stoica, P.: System Identification. Prentice Hall, New York (1989)

27. Yang, Y.: Adaptively robust Kalman filters with applications in navigation. In: Xu, G. (ed.) Sciences of Geodesy, pp. 49–82. Springer, Berlin (2010). https://doi.org/10.1007/978-3-642-11741-1_2
28. Yang, Y., Gao, W., Zhang, X.: Robust Kalman filtering with constraints: a case study for integrated navigation. J. Geod. **84**(6), 373–381 (2010)
29. Zhu, K., Li, W.K.: A new Pearson-type QMLE for conditionally heteroskedastic models. J. Bus. Econ. Stat. **33**(4), 552–565 (2015)
30. Zhu, K., Ling, S.: Global self-weighted and local quasi-maximum exponential likelihood estimators for ARMA-GARCH/IGARCH models. Ann. Stat. **39**(4), 2131–2163 (2011)

A Note on Partial Identification of Regression Parameters in Regression with Interval-Valued Dependent Variable

Michal Černý[1(✉)], Tomáš Cipra[2], Radek Hendrych[2], Ondřej Sokol[1], and Miroslav Rada[1]

[1] Department of Econometrics, Faculty of Informatics and Statistics, University of Economics, Winston Churchill Square 4, CZ13067 Prague, Czech Republic
{cernym,ondrej.sokol,miroslav.rada}@vse.cz
[2] Department of Probability and Mathematical Statistics, Faculty of Mathematics and Physics, Charles University, Sokolovská 83, CZ18675 Prague, Czech Republic
{cipra,radek.hendrych}@karlin.mff.cuni.cz

Abstract. We consider linear regression where the dependent variable is unobservable. Instead we can observe only an upper and lower bound. In this setup, the regression parameters need not be consistently estimable. We make certain stochastic assumptions, as weak as possible, on the random process generating the observable intervals and derive tight bounds for the regression parameters. The bounds are consistently estimable and the estimators are functions of the observable quantities only. We also restate the result in terms of set-estimators for regression models with interval-valued data.

Keywords: Interval data · Regression · Partial identification

1 Introduction

In data analysis we have to deal with various kinds of imprecision. One of the frequent forms is *interval imprecision*, meaning that we can observe only bounds $\underline{y}, \overline{y}$ on a data point y, such that $\underline{y} \leq y \leq \overline{y}$, but the number y is unobservable itself. One of many natural examples is rounding of data. Another example comes from measurement theory and theory of uncertain probabilities (for details see [5,6] and references therein): although we can observe y, the observation suffers from a systematic error which can be bounded by a known value $\Delta > 0$. Then, the "correct" value is only known to be in interval $[y - \Delta, y + \Delta]$.

The work was supported by the Czech Science Foundation under grants 16-00408S (M. Černý) and P402/12/G097 (T. Cipra and R. Hendrych). The work of O. Sokol was supported by University of Economics, Prague under project IGA 58/2017.

© Springer Nature Switzerland AG 2018
J. C. Figueroa-García et al. (Eds.): WEA 2018, CCIS 915, pp. 55–65, 2018.
https://doi.org/10.1007/978-3-030-00350-0_5

This paper contributes to the analysis of implications of interval imprecision for regression analysis. Namely, we consider the case when the endogenous (dependent) variable suffers from interval imprecision, while the regressor(s) are assumed to be observed exactly. To be more precise: the endogenous variable y is assumed to suffer from the "standard" stochastic random error, which is a traditional approach in statistics, and then, in addition, the resulting data point is hidden to the analyst and (s)he can observe only a lower bound $\underline{y}$ and upper bound $\overline{y}$ thereof. Formally, unobservability of y means that estimators and test statistics are not allowed to be functions of y, but only function of the observable quantities $\underline{y}, \overline{y}$ and the regressors. Of course, the interval imprecision gives an analyst weaker information and can result in the loss of consistent estimability of regression parameters (which is the main goal in regression analysis). But still, in some cases, we can derive at least bounds on the parameters.

In econometrics, this problem is known as *partial identification* [4,7,8]. When the data sampling process does not allow us to estimate a parameter of a distribution consistently (in the limit, when the number of observations grows unboundedly), but we can consistently estimate at least nontrivial upper and lower bounds thereof, we say that the parameter is partially identified.

First we motivate the problem by a very simple model of location, which, however, illustrates what needs to be done and why standard techniques, such as maximum likelihood, do not work. Then we derive tight asymptotic bounds for a linear regression model with a single regressor. Although the model is simple, it is sufficient for an illustration of the idea how to estimate the bound, and can be further generalized (with a lot of additional algebra). Moreover, as a main result, we improve our previous loose bounds [3] to a tight form.

2   Location Model

Assumptions. To illustrate the problem more formally, we start with the simple model of location

$$y_i = \mu + \varepsilon_i, \quad i = 1, \ldots, n,$$

where the error terms $\varepsilon_1, \ldots, \varepsilon_n$ are assumed to be $\mathcal{N}(0, \sigma^2)$ independent. The task is to estimate the model parameters μ and $\sigma \geq 0$. Clearly,

$$y_1, \ldots, y_n \sim \mathcal{N}(\mu, \sigma^2) \text{ independent.} \tag{1}$$

Assume further that the vector $y = (y_1, \ldots, y_n)^T$ is unobservable; instead, let the model contain also additional observable random variables $\underline{y} = (\underline{y}_1, \ldots, \underline{y}_n)^T$ $\overline{y} = (\overline{y}_1, \ldots, \overline{y}_n)^T$, where the joint distribution of $(\underline{y}, y, \overline{y})$ is assumed to satisfy

$$\underline{y}_i \leq y_i \leq \overline{y}_i \text{ a.s.} \quad i = 1, \ldots, n. \tag{2}$$

Formally, the *unobservability* of y means that estimators $(\widehat{\mu}, \widehat{\sigma})$ of (μ, σ) are allowed to be functions of $(\underline{y}, \overline{y})$ but not y. This is what makes the problem nontrivial.

We have assumed only the property (2), which gives essentially no information on the relation between the observable bounds $[\underline{y}_i, \overline{y}_i]$ and the unobservable quantity of interest y_i; we just know that y_i is almost surely covered by the interval $[\underline{y}_i, \overline{y}_i]$ but nothing more. In other words, *we do not assume any prior information on the interval-generating process.*

Likelihood Does Not Work. With the assumption (1) it is tempting to use the likelihood method for construction of the estimators (μ, σ) by maximizing the likelihood function

$$L_{\underline{y},\overline{y}}(\mu, \sigma) = \prod_{i=1}^{n} \left[\Phi\left(\frac{\overline{y}_i - \mu}{\sigma}\right) - \Phi\left(\frac{\underline{y}_i - \mu}{\sigma}\right) \right], \tag{3}$$

where $\Phi(\xi) = \int_{-\infty}^{\xi} \varphi(t)\, dt$ is the cumulative distribution function of $\mathcal{N}(0,1)$ and $\varphi(t) = (2\pi)^{-1/2} \exp(-t^2/2)$ is the density function.

To prove that the ML-estimates $(\widehat{\mu}, \widehat{\sigma})$ from (3) may be inconsistent, assume that $(\widehat{\mu}, \widehat{\sigma}) \to (\mu_0, \sigma_0)$ in probability with $n \to \infty$. Assume that y_i satisfy (1) and define

$$\underline{y}_i = y_i, \quad \overline{y}_i = \underline{y}_i + 1, \quad i = 1, \ldots, n. \tag{4}$$

Consider a new, "shifted" dataset $y' = (y'_1, \ldots, y'_n)$ defined as

$$y'_i = y_i + 1, \quad i = 1, \ldots, n.$$

Now, clearly, both triplets $(\underline{y}, y, \overline{y})$ and $(\underline{y}, y', \overline{y})$ satisfy the property (2), and we have $y_i \sim \mathcal{N}(\mu, \sigma^2)$ and $y'_i \sim \mathcal{N}(\mu', \sigma^2)$ with $\mu' = \mu + 1$. But the likelihood function $L_{\underline{y},\overline{y}}$ *is the same* for both cases $(\underline{y}, y, \overline{y})$ and $(\underline{y}, y', \overline{y})$. If $\widehat{\mu}$, the argmax of $L_{\underline{y},\overline{y}}$, converges, it cannot simultaneously converge to both μ and $\mu' = \mu + 1$.

The Argument Generalizes. Essentially, the same argument holds true not only for the ML-estimator, but for *any* function $f(\underline{y}, \overline{y})$ depending only on $(\underline{y}, \overline{y})$. Still assuming (4), we can define $y'_i = y_i + \Delta$ and the triple $(\underline{y}, y', \overline{y})$ satisfies (2) for any $\Delta \in [0, 1]$. So, $\mathsf{E}y'_i$ can attain any value from $[\mu, \mu+1]$. But the information available to $f(\underline{y}, \overline{y})$ does not depend on Δ, and thus f cannot be a consistent estimator of $\mu' := \mathsf{E}y'_i$. Indeed, if $f(\underline{y}, \overline{y}) \to \mu_0$ in probability with $n \to \infty$, it suffices to choose $\Delta \in [0, 1]$ so that $\mu + \Delta \neq \mu_0$.

This argument shows that the expectation of y'_i is partially identified—the observable random variables $\underline{y}, \overline{y}$ remain unchanged even if we change $\Delta \in [0, 1]$ (the datasets are said to be *observationally equivalent*). In other words, the observable variables $\underline{y}, \overline{y}$ are consistent with any value of $\mu' \in [\mu, \mu + 1]$. Partial identification basically means that we can consistently estimate only bounds on μ'. Here, the bounds are trivial: denoting $\underline{\mu} = \lim_{n\to\infty} \frac{1}{n} \sum_{i=1}^{n} \underline{y}_i$ and $\overline{\mu} = \lim_{n\to\infty} \frac{1}{n} \sum_{i=1}^{n} \overline{y}_i$ (where all limits are understood in probability and assuming that they exist), we have $\underline{\mu} \leq \mu' \leq \overline{\mu}$. Thus we have consistently estimated an interval provably covering μ', but no more information about μ' can be derived from $(\underline{y}, \overline{y}')$ unless we admit additional assumptions.

In other words, consistent estimability of μ is possible only at the cost of additional prior knowledge or assumptions. Such assumptions can shrink the class of distributions of $(\underline{y}, y', \overline{y})$ satisfying (2) so that μ' could be consistently estimable. The basic question is, in which situations such assumptions can be well justified.

Further Assumptions on the Interval Generating Process. A usual "treatment" of the partial identification problem is making additional assumptions, such as taking a particular distribution of y_i given $\underline{y}_i, \overline{y}_i$. For example, when we say that the conditional distribution of y_i is uniform on $[\underline{y}_i, \overline{y}_i]$, then $\mathsf{E}[y_i|\underline{y}_i, \overline{y}_i] = \frac{1}{2}(\underline{y}_i + \overline{y}_i)$ which implies that $\frac{1}{2n} \sum_{i=1}^{n} (\underline{y}_i + \overline{y}_i)$ consistently estimates $\mu = \mathsf{E}y_i$. However, the assumption of uniform distribution is strong—at least, the sampling process, allowing us to observe $\underline{y}$ and $\overline{y}$ only, reveals no information for testing the assumption.

It might be natural to make a weaker assumption: not to assume a particular distribution of y_i given $\underline{y}_i, \overline{y}_i$, but a certain *class* of distributions. It might be natural, for example, to restrict the class of allowed distributions to those satisfying

$$\mathsf{E}[y_i|\underline{y}_i, \overline{y}_i] = \tfrac{1}{2}(\underline{y}_i + \overline{y}_i). \tag{5}$$

The above arguments imply that this is sufficient for consistent estimability of μ. On the other hand, it still holds true that (5) is not testable from the observable data $(\underline{y}_i, \overline{y}_i)$. However, we will show that even (5) might be unnatural.

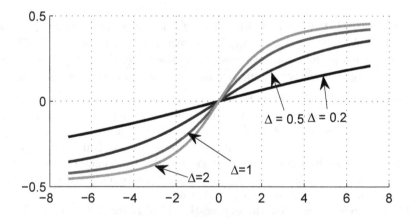

Fig. 1. The relative difference $D(y - \frac{1}{2}\Delta, y + \frac{1}{2}\Delta, \mu = 0, \sigma = 1)$ between (6) and (5) as a function of y, the center of the interval $[\underline{y}, \overline{y}] = [y - \frac{1}{2}\Delta, y + \frac{1}{2}\Delta]$.

The Example (Location Model) Continued. Assume that $(\underline{y}, y, \overline{y})$ satisfy (1) and (2). As an example consider that the interval imprecision resulted from downward rounding of data with precision $\Delta > 0$ but the analyst does not know that the interval was generated this way. So, put

$$\underline{y}_i = \max\{k\Delta \mid k\Delta \leq y_i, \ k \in \mathbb{Z}\}, \quad \overline{y}_i = \underline{y}_i + \Delta, \quad i = 1, \ldots, n.$$

This is an example of a very special interval generating process corresponding to the decomposition of the domain $\mathbb{R}$ into fixed bins $\ldots, [-2\Delta, -\Delta], [-\Delta, 0],$

$[0, \Delta], [\Delta, 2\Delta], \ldots$ and reporting only the bin into which y_i belongs. Since y_i is assumed to be normally distributed, it is easy to calculate

$$E[y_i | \underline{y}_i \leq y_i \leq \overline{y}_i] = \mu - \sigma \frac{\varphi\left(\frac{\overline{y}_i - \mu}{\sigma}\right) - \varphi\left(\frac{\underline{y}_i - \mu}{\sigma}\right)}{\Phi\left(\frac{\overline{y}_i - \mu}{\sigma}\right) - \Phi\left(\frac{\underline{y}_i - \mu}{\sigma}\right)}, \tag{6}$$

where the fraction is essentially a form of Mills Ratio. The function

$$D(\underline{y}, \overline{y}, \mu, \sigma) = \frac{\mu - \sigma \frac{\varphi\left(\frac{\overline{y} - \mu}{\sigma}\right) - \varphi\left(\frac{\underline{y} - \mu}{\sigma}\right)}{\Phi\left(\frac{\overline{y} - \mu}{\sigma}\right) - \Phi\left(\frac{\underline{y} - \mu}{\sigma}\right)} - \frac{1}{2}(\overline{y} + \underline{y})}{\overline{y} - \underline{y}},$$

(which is, for the sake of transparency, normalized by the width of the interval $[\overline{y}, \underline{y}]$ in the denominator), measures the difference between $E[y_i | \underline{y}_i \leq y_i \leq \overline{y}_i]$ and the "presumed" value of the expectation given by (5). A plot of

$$D(y - \tfrac{1}{2}\Delta, \ y + \tfrac{1}{2}\Delta, \ \mu = 0, \ \sigma = 1)$$

against $y \in [-7, 7]$ is depicted in Fig. 1 with $\Delta \in \{0.2, 0.5, 1, 2\}$. In other words, the horizontal axis describes the center point of the interval $[\underline{y}, \overline{y}] = [y - \tfrac{1}{2}\Delta, y + \tfrac{1}{2}\Delta]$ and Δ is the diameter. The example illustrates the crucial conclusion: *the relation (5) is valid only if the observed interval $[\underline{y}, \overline{y}]$ is exactly centered around μ.*

3   Regression with Interval-Valued Dependent Variable

Assumptions. Now we generalize the previous idea to the regression model

$$y_i = \theta_1 + \theta_2 x_i + \varepsilon_i, \quad i = 1, \ldots, n. \tag{7}$$

We consider this simple form to make algebra as simple as possible. The idea is similar to our previous work [3], but the bounds derived therein are redundant; here we derive tight bounds which cannot be generally improved.

Again, consider that the dependent variable y_i is unobservable; instead we can observe only bounds $\underline{y}_i, \overline{y}_i$ satisfying (2). The regressor x_i is assumed to be observable exactly. The rest—the disturbances ε_i and the constants θ_1, θ_2—are unobservable. The task is to estimate θ_1, θ_2.

Formally, our model contains a family of random variables $(\underline{y}_i, \overline{y}_i, x_i, \varepsilon_i)_{i=1,\ldots,n}$ which is restricted by (2), i.e., that $\underline{y}_i \leq \theta_1 + \theta_2 x_i + \varepsilon_i \leq \overline{y}_i$ a.s. In addition, we also need need some further assumptions:

(i) ε_i are iid with zero mean,
(ii) x_i are iid with mean ξ and variance π^2,
(iii) x_i and ε_i are pairwise independent,
(iv) $L_i := \overline{y}_i - \underline{y}_i$ are iid with mean Λ and with finite variance. (Observe that L_i are nonnegative random variables.)

Assumptions (i) and (iii) are standard in regression. Namely, (iii) justifies that the usage of Ordinary Least Squares (OLS) would be appropariate. Observe also that L_i, the widths of the observable intervals, and x_i, the regressor, may be dependent. Or, L_i and ε_i may be dependent.

Least Squares for (7) and Notation. The least-squares estimator $\widehat{\theta} = (\widehat{\theta}_1, \widehat{\theta}_2)^T$ of regression parameters in (7) has the form

$$\widehat{\theta}_2 = \frac{\frac{1}{n}\sum_{i=1}^n x_iy_i - \left(\frac{1}{n}\sum_{i=1}^n x_i\right)\left(\frac{1}{n}\sum_{i=1}^n y_i\right)}{\frac{1}{n}\sum_{i=1}^n x_i^2 - \left(\frac{1}{n}\sum_{i=1}^n x_i\right)^2}, \quad \widehat{\theta}_1 = \frac{1}{n}\sum_{i=1}^n y_i - \widehat{\theta}_2\frac{1}{n}\sum_{i=1}^n x_i. \quad (8)$$

To facilitate notation, we will use shorthands $\widetilde{x} = \frac{1}{n}\sum_{i=1}^n x_i$, $\widetilde{x^2} = \frac{1}{n}\sum_{i=1}^n x_i^2$, $\widetilde{xy} = \frac{1}{n}\sum_{i=1}^n x_iy_i$ etc. Now (8) reduces to

$$\widehat{\theta}_1 = \widetilde{y} - \frac{\widetilde{xy} - \widetilde{x}\widetilde{y}}{\widetilde{x^2} - \widetilde{x}^2}\widetilde{x}, \quad \widehat{\theta}_2 = \frac{\widetilde{xy} - \widetilde{x}\widetilde{y}}{\widetilde{x^2} - \widetilde{x}^2}. \quad (9)$$

It will be convenient to introduce centered data

$$z_i := x_i - \widetilde{x}, \quad i = 1, \ldots, n.$$

Observe that $\widetilde{z} = 0$. Using a pair of some further simple properties of averaging, such as $\widetilde{z} = 0$, $\widetilde{\widetilde{\alpha}} = \widetilde{\alpha}$, $\widetilde{\alpha + \beta} = \widetilde{\alpha} + \widetilde{\beta}$, $\widetilde{\widetilde{\alpha}\beta} = \widetilde{\alpha}\widetilde{\beta}$, we derive from (8) that

$$\widehat{\theta}_1 = \widetilde{y} - \frac{\widetilde{zy}}{\widetilde{z^2}}\widetilde{x}, \quad \widehat{\theta}_2 = \frac{\widetilde{zy}}{\widetilde{z^2}}.$$

Derivation of the Limit Bounds for θ_1, θ_2. Our aim is to derive consistently estimable bounds on θ_1 and θ_2 based on observable data

$$[x_i, \underline{y}_i, \overline{y}_i]_{i=1,\ldots,n} \quad (10)$$

in the limit $n \to \infty$. That is, we are to find functions

$$\underline{\theta}_1^{[n]}, \overline{\theta}_1^{[n]}, \underline{\theta}_2^{[n]}, \overline{\theta}_2^{[n]} \quad (11)$$

with input (10) such that, if $\underline{\theta}_1^{[n]} \to \underline{\theta}_1$, $\overline{\theta}_1^{[n]} \to \overline{\theta}_1$, $\underline{\theta}_2^{[n]} \to \underline{\theta}_2$ and $\overline{\theta}_2^{[n]} \to \overline{\theta}_2$, then

$$\underline{\theta}_1 \leq \theta_1 \leq \overline{\theta}_1, \quad \underline{\theta}_2 \leq \theta_2 \leq \overline{\theta}_2.$$

We can derive bounds for both θ_1 and θ_2 simultaneously by considering a general linear combination

$$\widehat{\theta}^c := c_1\widehat{\theta}_1 + c_2\widehat{\theta}_2 = c_1\widetilde{y} + \frac{\widetilde{zy}}{\widetilde{z^2}}(c_2 - c_1\widetilde{x}).$$

The bounds for θ_1, θ_2 will then result from the choices $c = \binom{1}{0}$ and $c = \binom{0}{1}$, respectively. We will need only the following easy properties:

$$y_i - L_i \leq \underline{y}_i \leq y_i \leq \overline{y}_i \leq y_i + L_i. \tag{12}$$

First we derive the upper bound. Writing $[\alpha]^+ = \max\{\alpha, 0\}$ and $[\alpha]^- = \max\{-\alpha, 0\}$, we have

$$
\widehat{\theta^c} = c_1(\widetilde{y} - \widehat{\theta}_2 \widetilde{x}) + c_2\widehat{\theta}_2 = c_1\widetilde{y} - c_1\frac{\widetilde{zy}}{\widetilde{z^2}}\widetilde{x} + c_2\frac{\widetilde{zy}}{\widetilde{z^2}}
$$

$$
= \frac{c_1\widetilde{y}\widetilde{z^2} - c_1\widetilde{zy}\widetilde{x} + c_2\widetilde{zy}}{\widetilde{z^2}} = \frac{\frac{1}{n}\sum_{i=1}^{n} y_i(c_1\widetilde{z^2} - z_i(c_1\widetilde{x} - c_2))}{\widetilde{z^2}}
$$

$$
= \frac{\frac{1}{n}\left(\sum_{i=1}^{n} y_i[c_1\widetilde{z^2} - z_i(c_1\widetilde{x} - c_2)]^+ - \sum_{i=1}^{n} y_i[c_1\widetilde{z^2} - z_i(c_1\widetilde{x} - c_2)]^-\right)}{\widetilde{z^2}} \tag{13}
$$

$$
\leq \frac{\frac{1}{n}\left(\sum_{i=1}^{n} \overline{y}_i[c_1\widetilde{z^2} - z_i(c_1\widetilde{x} - c_2)]^+ - \sum_{i=1}^{n} \underline{y}_i[c_1\widetilde{z^2} - z_i(c_1\widetilde{x} - c_2)]^-\right)}{\widetilde{z^2}}. \tag{14}
$$

After substitutions $c = \binom{1}{0}$ and $c = \binom{0}{1}$, expression (14) will give *the* functions $\overline{\theta}_1^{[n]}, \overline{\theta}_2^{[n]}$ from (11) for the upper bound. Indeed, the expression depends only on (10). Observe that the bound is tight since y_i do not occur in (13) repeatedly: at least one of the expressions $[c_1\widetilde{z^2} - z_i(c_1\widetilde{x} - c_2)]^+$, $[c_1\widetilde{z^2} - z_i(c_1\widetilde{x} - c_2)]^-$ is zero.

If we are able to determine the limit of (14), we get the desired upper bound $\overline{\theta^c}$ on θ^c. To derive a bound on (14) we can write

$$
(14) \leq \frac{\frac{1}{n}\sum_{i=1}^{n}(y_i + L_i)[c_1\widetilde{z^2} - z_i(c_1\widetilde{x} - c_2)]^+}{\widetilde{z^2}} \tag{15}
$$

$$
- \frac{\frac{1}{n}\sum_{i=1}^{n}(y_i - L_i)[c_1\widetilde{z^2} - z_i(c_1\widetilde{x} - c_2)]^-}{\widetilde{z^2}}
$$

$$
= \frac{\frac{1}{n}\sum_{i=1}^{n} y_i[c_1\widetilde{z^2} - z_i(c_1\widetilde{x} - c_2)] + \frac{1}{n}\sum_{i=1}^{n} L_i|c_1\widetilde{z^2} - z_i(c_1\widetilde{x} - c_2)|}{\widetilde{z^2}}
$$

$$
= c_1\widehat{\theta}_1 + c_2\widehat{\theta}_2 + \frac{\frac{1}{n}\sum_{i=1}^{n} L_i|c_1\widetilde{z^2} - z_i(c_1\widetilde{x} - c_2)|}{\widetilde{z^2}}
$$

$$
\leq c_1\widehat{\theta}_1 + c_2\widehat{\theta}_2 + \frac{\frac{1}{n}\sum_{i=1}^{n} L_i(|c_1\widetilde{z^2}| + |z_i||c_1\widetilde{x} - c_2|)}{\widetilde{z^2}} \tag{16}
$$

$$
= \underbrace{c_1\widehat{\theta}_1 + c_2\widehat{\theta}_2}_{=:A} + \underbrace{|c_1|\frac{1}{n}\sum_{i=1}^{n} L_i}_{=:B} + \underbrace{|c_1\widetilde{x} - c_2|\frac{\frac{1}{n}\sum_{i=1}^{n} L_i|z_i|}{\widetilde{z^2}}}_{=:C}.
$$

In the limit $n \to \infty$, we have $A \to \theta^c$ by standard consistency arguments for OLS and

$$B \to |c_1|\Lambda, \quad C \to |c_1\xi - c_2|\frac{\mathsf{E}[|z_i|L_i]}{\pi^2}.$$

The derivation of the lower bound is symmetric.

The Final form of the Limit Bounds for θ_1, θ_2. Putting the lower and upper bound together, we get the form

$$\theta^c \pm \left(|c_1|\Lambda + |c_1\xi - c_2|\frac{\mathsf{E}[|z_i|L_i]}{\pi^2} \right). \tag{17}$$

Substituting $c = \binom{1}{0}$ and $c = \binom{0}{1}$, we get bounds

$$\left[\theta_1 \pm \left(\Lambda + |\xi|\frac{\mathsf{E}[|z_i|L_i]}{\pi^2} \right) \right], \quad \left[\theta_2 \pm \frac{\mathsf{E}[|z_i|L_i]}{\pi^2} \right] \tag{18}$$

for θ_1 and θ_2, respectively.

Discussion. Recall what the bounds tell us: since we cannot observe y_i, we cannot estimate θ_1, θ_2 consistently. We must admit that it could happen that the interval-generating random process (which is also unknown to us) created the intervals $[\underline{y}, \overline{y}]$ in a really awkward way; for example in a way that (15) is satisfied with equality. (Recall that we admitted that $\underline{y}_i, \overline{y}_i$ may be dependent on the regressor.) But still, we can be sure that however we would select representatives $y_i \in [\underline{y}_i, \overline{y}_i]$ and use OLS with them, it need not consistently estimate θ_1, θ_2, but its limit (if exists) cannot be farther from the true values θ_1 and θ_2 more than $\Lambda + |\xi|\mathsf{E}[|z_i|L_i]\pi^{-2}$ and $\mathsf{E}[|z_i|L_i]\pi^{-2}$, respectively. And, moreover, the bounds *are* consistently estimable. Indeed, they depend only on the characteristics of distributions of the observable quantities, namely the mean width Λ of the intervals, mean ξ and variance π^2 of the regressor and $\mathsf{E}[|z_i|L_i]$, which is estimable by $n^{-1}\sum_{i=1}^n L_i|x_i - \tilde{x}|$.

Remark. Observe that, in general, the bound (17) is tight. We already observed that there exists an interval-generating process satisfying (15) with equality: it is the process

$$[\underline{y}_i, \overline{y}_i] = \begin{cases} [y_i, y_i + L_i] & \text{if } c_1\tilde{z}^2 - z_i(c_1\tilde{x} - c_2) \geq 0, \\ [y_i - L_i, y_i] & \text{if } c_1\tilde{z}^2 - z_i(c_1\tilde{x} - c_2) < 0. \end{cases}$$

Also the inequality (16) can be satisfied with equality: it suffices to choose $c_1 = 1$, $c_2 = \tilde{x}$. This shows that in general, the bound cannot be improved.

A Special Case. If x_i and L_i are independent, then the bounds (18) reduce to

$$\left[\theta_1 \pm \Lambda \left(1 + \frac{|\xi|\zeta}{\pi^2} \right) \right], \quad \left[\theta_2 \pm \frac{\Lambda\zeta}{\pi^2} \right],$$

where $\zeta = \mathsf{E}[|x_i - \xi|]$ is the mean absolute deviation of the regressor.

If, moreover, x_i is normally distributed, then

$$\frac{\zeta}{\pi} = \sqrt{\frac{2}{\pi}} \leq 0.8,$$

where $\pi = 3.14\ldots$ (to avoid misunderstanding, recall that π stands for the standard deviation of the regressor). In this special case we can restate the bounds into the form

$$\left[\theta_1 \pm \Lambda\left(1 + 0.8\frac{|\xi|}{\pi}\right)\right], \quad \left[\theta_2 \pm 0.8\frac{\Lambda}{\pi}\right]. \tag{19}$$

4 The Bounds and Set Estimators

We can also reformulate the bounds, derived in the previous section, into the context of set estimators. Recall that set-estimators can be viewed as statistical counterparts of interval-valued statistics [5] in the finite-sample case. The corresponding identification region then results as a limit set.

According to [1], given n-vectors $x, y, \overline{y}$, define the *OLS-set* (in $\mathbb{R}^2$) as

$$L^n \equiv L^n(x, \underline{y}, \overline{y}) = \left\{ \begin{pmatrix} \widetilde{v} - \frac{\widetilde{xv} - \widetilde{x}\widetilde{v}}{\widetilde{x^2} - \widetilde{x}^2}\widetilde{x} \\ \frac{\widetilde{xv} - \widetilde{x}\widetilde{v}}{\widetilde{x^2} - \widetilde{x}^2} \end{pmatrix} \;\middle|\; \underline{y}_i \leq v_i \leq \overline{y}_i, \; i = 1, \ldots, n \right\}.$$

Clearly, if the dependent variable y were observable, then $L^n(x, y, y)$ reduces to the traditional finite-sample point-estimate and standard consistency arguments show that $L^n(x, y, y) \to \theta$. So, the set L^n generalizes the traditional OLS-estimator. When $\underline{y}_i \leq \overline{y}_i$, then $L^n(x, \underline{y}, \overline{y})$ is a random set which can be shown to be a convex polytope a.s. [2]. Now the question is what happens with the set in the limit $n \to \infty$. If there exists a limit set L^∞, then it has the crucial property

$$\theta \in L^\infty,$$

and thus it is called an *identification region* for θ.

The bounds from Sect. 3 show us that L_∞ can be bounded to a "nice" region (namely, that it cannot grow and cover the whole plane $\mathbb{R}^2$). We state this result as a separate theorem without a formal proof, although it can be derived along the lines of the estimates from Sect. 3. (We apologize a reader for a "careful" formulation of the theorem to avoid topological issues on convergence of random sets.) For simplicity, we also use just the special-case bounds (19).

Theorem 1. *Define*

$$\underline{\lambda}_1^n = \inf\{\lambda_1 \mid (\exists \lambda_2)\, \begin{pmatrix}\lambda_1\\\lambda_2\end{pmatrix} \in L^n\}, \qquad \overline{\lambda}_1^n = \sup\{\lambda_1 \mid (\exists \lambda_2)\, \begin{pmatrix}\lambda_1\\\lambda_2\end{pmatrix} \in L^n\},$$

$$\underline{\lambda}_2^n = \inf\{\lambda_2 \mid (\exists \lambda_1)\, \begin{pmatrix}\lambda_1\\\lambda_2\end{pmatrix} \in L^n\}, \qquad \overline{\lambda}_2^n = \sup\{\lambda_2 \mid (\exists \lambda_1)\, \begin{pmatrix}\lambda_1\\\lambda_2\end{pmatrix} \in L^n\}.$$

For every $\varepsilon > 0$, we have

$$\lim_{n \to \infty} \Pr\left[\underline{\lambda}_1^n \geq \theta_1 - \Lambda\left(1 + \alpha\frac{|\xi|}{\pi}\right) - \varepsilon\right] = 1, \tag{20}$$

$$\lim_{n \to \infty} \Pr\left[\overline{\lambda}_1^n \leq \theta_1 + \Lambda\left(1 + \alpha\frac{|\xi|}{\pi}\right) + \varepsilon\right] = 1, \tag{21}$$

$$\lim_{n \to \infty} \Pr\left[\underline{\lambda}_2^n \geq \theta_2 - \alpha\frac{\Lambda}{\pi} - \varepsilon\right] = 1, \tag{22}$$

$$\lim_{n \to \infty} \Pr\left[\overline{\lambda}_2^n \leq \theta_2 + \alpha\frac{\Lambda}{\pi} + \varepsilon\right] = 1, \tag{23}$$

where $\alpha = (2/3.14\ldots)^{1/2}$. In addition, the bounds are tight (i.e., neither of the numbers $\Lambda(1 + \alpha|\xi|/\pi)$ and $\alpha\Lambda/\pi$ in (20)–(23) can be replaced by a smaller value).   □

Remark. Theorem 1 can be also restated in terms of bounds on the quantities of interest θ_1, θ_2, which are not consistently estimable, in terms of consistently estimable quantities Λ, ξ, π. For every $\varepsilon > 0$ we have

$$\lim_{n \to \infty} \Pr\left[\overline{\lambda}_1^n - \Lambda\left(1 + \alpha\frac{|\xi|}{\pi}\right) - \varepsilon \leq \theta_1 \leq \underline{\lambda}_1^n + \Lambda\left(1 + \alpha\frac{|\xi|}{\pi}\right) + \varepsilon\right] = 1,$$

$$\lim_{n \to \infty} \Pr\left[\overline{\lambda}_2^n - \alpha\frac{|\xi|}{\pi} - \varepsilon \leq \theta_2 \leq \underline{\lambda}_2^n + \alpha\frac{|\xi|}{\pi} + \varepsilon\right] = 1.$$

5 Conclusions

We have studied interval imprecision in the context of linear regression. Namely, when the interval imprecision is present only in the dependent variable, then we can derive consistently estimable bounds for the values of regression parameters. In general, the parameters themselves need not be consistently estimable from the observable interval-valued dependent variable and regressors, but— under certain stochastic assumptions on the widths of the intervals—are at least partially identified. The derived bounds on the identification region are tight.

References

1. Černý, M., Hladík, M., Rada, M.: On the possibilistic approach to linear regression models involving uncertain, indeterminate or interval data. Inf. Sci. **244**, 26–47 (2013)
2. Černý, M., Rada, M.: On the possibilistic approach to linear regression with rounded or interval-censored data. Measur. Sci. Rev. **11**, 34–40 (2011)
3. Černý, M., Rada, M., Sokol, O., Holý, V.: On the limit identification region for regression parameters in linear regression with interval-valued dependent variable. In: Pražák, P. (ed.) Proceedings of Mathematical Methods in Economics 2017 (MME 2017), Hradec Králové, Czech Republic, pp. 102–107 (2017)

4. Manski, C.: Partial Identification of Probability Distributions. Springer Series in Statistics. Springer, New York (2003). https://doi.org/10.1007/b97478
5. Nguyen, H.T., Kreinovich, V., Wu, B., Xiang, G.: Computing Statistics under Interval and Fuzzy Uncertainty. Studies in Computational Intelligence, vol. 393. Springer, Heidelberg (2012). https://doi.org/10.1007/978-3-642-24905-1
6. Rabinovich, S.G.: Measurement Errors and Uncertainties: Theory and Practice. Springer, New York (2005). https://doi.org/10.1007/0-387-29143-1
7. Stoye, J.: Partial identification of spread parameters. Quant. Econ. 1, 323–357 (2010)
8. Tamer, E.: Partial identification in econometrics. Annu. Rev. Econ. 2, 167–195 (2010)

State Estimation of a Dehydration Process by Interval Analysis

Carlos Collazos[1(✉)], César A. Collazos[2], Carlos Sánchez[1], Pedro Mariño[1],
Domingo A. Montaño[1], Iván Ruiz[1], Farid Meléndez-Pertruz[3],
Alejandra Rojas[1], and Adriana Maldonado-Franco[2]

[1] Universidad Manuela Beltrán, Bogotá D.C., Colombia
`carlos.collazos@docentes.umb.edu.co`
[2] Universidad Nacional de Colombia, Bogotá D.C., Colombia
[3] Universidad de la Costa, Barranquilla, Colombia
`http://www.umb.edu.co`

Abstract. This article presents a general methodology of state estimation by interval analysis in a dynamic system modeled by difference equations. The methodology is applied to a pineapple osmotic dehydration process, in order to predict the behavior of the process within a range of allowed perturbation. The paper presents simulations and validations.

Keywords: Physics model · Osmotic dehydratation
State estimation · Interval analysis

1 Introduction

When it comes to industrial processes, it is difficult to obtain a precise model for disturbances and noise that may interfere with these processes. This paper presents a methodology for state estimation, where the state equations for the process are known and the disturbances are limited through intervals. Interval algebra has diverse applications as shown in [1,2].

State estimation is fundamental for analysis, design, control and supervision of processes in engineering [3–6]. Specifically, state estimation methodology based on intervals has received a lot of attention in the last few years and literature about this subject shows a growing progress [7–12].

This work is organized in the following manner: Sect. 2 shows an approach to the problem statement and the process under study. Section 3 reviews the fundamentals of interval algebra, including the definition of interval, box, interval matrix and inclusion function. This section also presents the state estimation algorithm for solving differential equations according to [13]. Initially, the existence and uniqueness of the solution for the difference equations is verified, when the initial conditions belong to an interval vector. Afterwards, the solution is calculated through Taylor's expansion. Sections 4 and 5 present the state estimation of the studied process, with the interpretation of the obtained results. Finally, Sect. 6 finishes the work, highlighting a few future work perspectives.

© Springer Nature Switzerland AG 2018
J. C. Figueroa-García et al. (Eds.): WEA 2018, CCIS 915, pp. 66–77, 2018.
https://doi.org/10.1007/978-3-030-00350-0_6

2   Theoretical Framework

2.1   Problem Statement

The unknown state x for a dynamic system is defined by:

$$\dot{x}(t) = f(x(t)), y(t) = g(x(t)), x(0) \in [X_0] \tag{1}$$

where $x(t) \in R^n$ and $y(t) \in R^m$, and they denote, respectively, the state variables and the outputs of the system. Initial conditions $x(0)$ are supposed to belong to an initial "box" $[X_0]$. The concept of "box" will be described in Sect. 3. Time is $t \in [0, t_{max}]$. The functions f and g are real and can be differentiable in M, where M is an open set of R^n, such as $x(t) \in M$ for each $t \in [0, t_{max}]$. Besides, function f is at least k-times differentiable in the M domain. The output error is defined by:

$$v(t_i) = y(t_i) - y_m(t_i), i = 1, 2, \ldots, N. \tag{2}$$

We assume that $\underline{v(t)}$ and $\overline{v(t)}$ represent the lower and upper limit of acceptable output error, respectively. These limits correspond to a bounded noise. The integer number N is the total number of records. The interval arithmetics are used to calculate the guaranteed limits for the solution of Eq. 1 in the sampling times $\{t_1, t_2, \ldots, t_N\}$. Even though the studied process is a continuous dynamic system, Eq. 2 indicates that the problem statement is applicable for a discrete system, which is governed by difference Equations [4].

2.2   Studied Process (Osmotic Dehydration of Pineapple)

The osmotic dehydration process has highly complex dynamics, which implies that there are a great variety of models and experimental procedures for different kinds of fruits and foods [14–17]. Independent of the chosen model, some authors coincide that the most significant variables of the process are identified with the food concentration and the concentration of the solution where the food is immersed in [18,19]. Pineapple is a completely heterogeneous, highly watery and porous food, that when immersed in solutions with high concentration of soluble solids (sugar), provokes two simultaneous upstream main flows. The first flow corresponds to a transfer of soluble solids (sugar) from the solution to the food. The second one is flow of water from the food that goes highly concentrated to the solution. A third secondary and negligible flow of aroma, vitamins and minerals happens, which is less intense, and occurs from the fruit to the solution. The mass transfer mechanisms that are present in the osmotic dehydration at atmospheric pressure and room temperature are mainly discussion (Fick's laws of diffusion). These mechanisms are originated by the concentration differences between the food and the osmotic solution where the fruit is immersed in [18–20]. Figure 1 shows the previously described flows that occur during the osmotic dehydration.

The sugar concentrations found in the osmotic solution and the fruit are registered by refractometers and reported in refraction indexes or Degrees Brix.

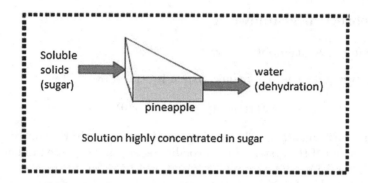

Fig. 1. Mass transfer process between solution and fruit

Degrees Brix can be understood as a percentage from 0 to 1 or a mass fraction, that provides the sugar mass contained in the mass of each analyzed component (solution and fruit). The model that was studied in this paper was extracted from [18] and it considers three state variables: concentration in fruit, concentration in tank 1 solution and volume that enters tank 1 from tank 2. The dehydration plant and its operation is described in [18–20]. Figure 2 shows the process.

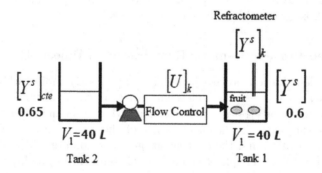

Fig. 2. Pineapple osmotic dehydration process diagram

The model of [18] assumes that there is a perfect mix in tank 1, where the flow is perfectly controlled and the values for concentration in fruit and in tank 1 obey ideally to mass balances. The process is modeled in a discrete manner with a sample time of ΔT. The model is represented by difference equations, as indicated below:

– Variation of sugar concentration for the solution:

$$[Y^S]_{k+1} = [Y^S]_k - B[C]_k[X^S]_k \Delta T + ([Y^S]_{cte} - [Y^S]_k)\frac{[U]_k \Delta T}{[V]_k} \tag{3}$$

- Variation of sugar concentration for the food:

$$[X^S]_{k+1} = [C]_k[X^S]_k\Delta T + \frac{[U]_k[X^S]_k\Delta T}{[V]_k} \tag{4}$$

where:
- $[V]_k$ is the variation of tank 1 volume:

$$[V]_{k+1} = [V]_k + [U]_k\Delta T \tag{5}$$

- $[C]_k$ is the specific rate of sugar concentration in food:

$$[C]_k = \mu\frac{[Y^S]_k}{K_{YS} + [Y^S]_k} \tag{6}$$

- B is a dimentionless proportion factor between the concentration variation of
  the solution and that of the food. This parameter is calculated using the final
  (subindex f) and initial (subindex o) values of the concentrations in solution
  and food during an experimental process:

$$B = \frac{[Y^S]_f - [Y^S]_o}{[X^S]_f - [X^S]_o} \tag{7}$$

- μ is the maximum change rate in sugar growth for the food. It is represented
  by:

$$\mu = \frac{\ln(\frac{[X^S]_f}{[X^S]_o})}{t_f - t_o} \tag{8}$$

- $K_{YS} = 0.65$ (gr. of sugar/gr. of osmotic solution in tank 1) is the saturation
  constant for sugar concentration in tank 1.

The raw material associated to the presented model is pineapple (*ananas comosus* in the cayena lisa variety) in a geometric shape (eighths of slice of 1 cm of thickness without any previous treatment).

The attributes of the osmotic solution for each tank were:

- Tank 2: Constant. $[Y^S]_{cte} = 0.65°\,Brix.$
- Tank 1: Reference. $[Y^S]_{ref} = 0.6°\,Brix.$

The process was simulated for a constant lineal entry flow: $[U2]_k$: (0 to 2.09) L/min for 180 min. The calculation of the kinetic parameter $[C]_k$ and the kinetic constants μ and B are assumed as known and are reported in Table 1.

Table 1. Kinetic constants for the experiment

μ (L/min)	B
0.0007	0.27

3   Methodology

3.1   Interval Analysis Fundamentals

At first, interval analysis was a response to explain quantification errors that occurred when real numbers were represented rationally in computers and the technique was extended to validated numerics [31]. According to [31], an interval $[u] = [\underline{u}, \overline{u}]$, is a closed and connected subset of R, denoted by IR. Two intervals $[u]$ and $[v]$ are equal, if and only if their inferior and superior limits are the same. Arithmetic operations between two intervals $[u]$ and $[v]$, can be defined by:

$$\circ \in \{+, -, \times, \div\}, [u] \circ [v] = \{x \circ y | [u], y \in [v]\} \tag{9}$$

The interval vector (or box) $[X]$ is a vector with interval components and it is equivalent to the cartesian product of scalar intervals:

$$[X] = [x_1] \times [x_2] \times ... \times [x_n] \tag{10}$$

The vector set of real n-dimensional intervals is denoted by IR^n. A matrix interval is a matrix where its components are intervals. The set of $n \times m$ real interval matrices is denoted by $IR^{n \times m}$. The classic operations for interval vectors or interval matrices are direct extensions of the same operations of point vectors [31].

The operations for punctual vectors can be extended to become classical operations for interval vectors [22]. This way, if $f : R^n \to R^m$, the range of function f in an interval vector $[u]$, is given by:

$$f([u]) = \{f(x) | x \in [u]\} \tag{11}$$

The interval function $[f]$ of IR^n to IR^m is a function of the inclusion of f if:

$$\forall [u] \in IR^n, f([u]) \subseteq [f]([u]) \tag{12}$$

An inclusion function of f can be obtained through the substitution of each occurrence of a real variable for its corresponding interval. Said function is called natural inclusion function. In practice, the inclusion function is not unique and it depends on the syntax of f [31].

3.2   Inversion Set

Consider the problem of determining a solution set for the unknowns u, defined by:

$$S = \{u \in U/\phi(u) \in [y]\} = \phi^{-1}([y]) \cap U \tag{13}$$

where $[y]$ is known a priori, U is a search set for u and ϕ of an invertible non-linear function, which is not necessarily in the classical sense. [23] includes the calculation of the reciprocal image of ϕ and that is known as a set inversion problem that can be solved using the SIVIA (Set Inversion Via Interval Analysis) algorithm. SIVIA as proposed in [9] is a recursive algorithm that goes through all the searching space so it does not lose any solution. This algorithm makes it possible to derive a guaranteed enclosure of the solution of set S, that meets: S is factible, enough to prove that $\phi([u]) \subseteq [y]$. Conversely, if it can be proven that $\phi([u]) \cap [y] = 0$, then the box $[u]$ is non-viable. On the contrary, there is no conclusion and the box $[u]$ is said to be undetermined. If the box is undetermined, the box is bisected and tried again until its size reaches a threshold precision, specified for $\epsilon > 0$. This criterion assures that SIVIA finishes after a limited number of iterations.

3.3 State Estimation

State estimation refers to the integration of Eq. 1. Thus, the goal is to estimate the state of vector x in the sampling times $\{t_1, t_2, \ldots, t_N\}$, which correspond to the times of output measurements. The box $[x(t_j)]$ is denoted as $[x_j]$, where t_j represents the sampling time, $j = 1, 2, \ldots, N$ and x_j represents the solution of (1) at t_j. For models like the one presented in (1), the sets are characterized by not being convex and there could even be several disconected components. Interval analysis consists of enclosing said sets in interval vectors that do not overlap and the usual inconvenient is obtaining wider solution interval vectors each time. This in known as the Wrapping Effect. This way, the wrapping effect yields poor results. The poverty brought by the big width of the set can be reduced through the use of a higher-order k for the Taylor expansion and through the use of mean value forms and matrices of pre-conditioning [13,24].

3.4 Prediction and Correction

Prediction aims at calculating the accessibility fixed for the state vector, while the correction stage keeps only the parts of the accessibility set that are consistent with the measurements and the error limits defined by Eq. 2. It is assumed that $[X_j]$ is a box that is guaranteed to contain x_j at t_j. The exterior aproximation of the predicted set $[X_{j+1}^+]$ is defined as the validated solution of the difference equation at t_{j+1}. The set $[X_{j+1}^+]$ is calculated using the EMV algorithm (extenden mean value), defined in [24]. The set is guaranteed to contain the state at t_{j+1}. At t_{j+1}, a "measurement vector", y_{j+1}, is obtained and it corresponds to the upper and lower limits for measurement noise.

$$[y_{j+1}] = [y_{j+1} - \underline{v_{j+1}}, y_{j+1} - \overline{v_{j+1}}] \tag{14}$$

Then, the set $[g]^{-1}([y_{j+1}])$ is calculated. This evaluation is obtained by the SIVIA algorithm. The expected solution at the sampling time t_{j+1} is finally given by $[x_{j+1}] = [X_{j+1}^+] \cap [g]^{-1}([y_{j+1}])$. The procedure for the state estimation is summarized in the following algorithm: For $j = 0$ to $j = N - 1$ do:

- Prediction step: compute $[X_{j+1}^+]$ using EMV algorithm.
- Correction step: calculate $[x_{j+1}]$ so that

$$[x_{j+1}] = [X_{j+1}^+] \cap [g]^{-1}([y_{j+1}])$$

3.5   Extended Mean Value (EMV)

The most efficient methods to solve state estimation for dynamic systems are based on Taylor's expansions [24]. These methods consist of two parts: the first part verifies the existence and uniqueness of the solution, using the fixed point theorem and the Picard-Lindelf operator. At a time t_{j+1}, a box, *a priori* $[\tilde{x}_j]$, that contains all the solutions that correspond to all the possible trajectories between t_j and t_{j+1} is obtained. In the second part, the solution at t_{j+1} is calculated using Taylor's expansion, in the term that remains is $[\tilde{x}_j]$. However, in practice, the set $[\tilde{x}_j]$ often doesn't contain the true solution [25]. Therefore, the used technique consists of inflating this set until the next inclusion is verified with the following expression:

$$[x_i] + hf([\tilde{x}_i]) \subseteq [\tilde{x}_i] \tag{15}$$

where h indicates the integration stage and $[x_j]$ is the first solution. This method is summarized in the Enclosure algorithm, which was developed by [26]. The inputs are $[x_j]$ and $\alpha > 0$ and the output is $[\tilde{x}_j]$:

$$[x_j] = [\tilde{x}_j]$$
$$\text{While } ([x_j] + hf([\tilde{x}_j])) \subseteq [\tilde{x}_j] \text{ do:}$$
$$[\tilde{x}_j] = inflate([\tilde{x}_j], \alpha)$$

The function inflate for an interval vector $[u] = [\underline{u_1}, \overline{u_1}], \ldots, [\underline{u_n}, \overline{u_n}]$, operates as follows:

$$[(1 - \alpha)\underline{u_1}, (1 + \alpha)\overline{u_1}], \ldots, [(1 - \alpha)\underline{u_n}, (1 + \alpha)\overline{u_n}]$$

Precision depends of the α coefficient. If the set $[\tilde{x}_j]$ satisfies the inclusion presented in Eq. 15, then the inclusion $x(t) \in [\tilde{x}_j]$ is maintained for all $t \in [t_j, t_{j+1}]$. The solution x_{j+1} of the differential equation given in Eq. 1 at t_{j+1} is guaranteed, in the interval vector $[x_{j+1}]$ and it is given by the Taylor expansion [31]:

$$[x_{j+1}] = [x_j] + \sum_{i=1}^{k-1} h^i f^{[i]}([x_j]) + h^k f^{[k]}([\tilde{x}_j]) \tag{16}$$

where k denotes the end of the Taylor expansion and the $f^{[i]}$ coefficients are the Taylor coefficients of the $x(t)$ solution, which are obtained in a recursive form by:

$$f^{[1]} = f, f^{[i]} = \frac{1}{i} \frac{\partial f^{[i-1]}}{\partial x} f, i \geq 2 \tag{17}$$

The application of the inflate function in the set $[\tilde{x}_1]$ leads to increase of its width. The poor quality introduced by the wider set can be reduced through the use of a higher order k for the Taylor expansion in Eq. 17. But the width of the solution always increases, even for higher orders. To sort this obstacle, Rihm [27] proposes evaluating (17) through the extended mean value algorithm, based on mean value forms and pre-conditioning matrices. This algorithm is used to solve the differential equation given in (1). The inputs for this algorithm are $[\tilde{x}_j]$, $[x_j]$, $\hat{x}_j$, $[v_j]$, p_j, A_j, h and the outputs are $[\tilde{x}_{j+1}]$, $\hat{x}_{j+1}$,$[v_{j+1}]$, $[p_{j+1}]$, A_{j+1}. The variable $\hat{x}_j$ is the mean point of a certain interval v_j. The initial conditions may be provided by $p_0 = 0$, $q_0 = 0$ and $v_0 = x_0$. Up next, the sequence of the algorithm is presented:

1. $[v_{j+1}] = \hat{x}_j + \sum_{i=1}^{k-1} h^i f^{[i]}(\hat{x}_j) + h^k f^{[k]}([\tilde{x}_j])$
2. $[S_j] = I + \sum_{i=1}^{k-1} J(f^{[i]}; [x_j]) h^i$
3. $[q_{j+1}] = ([S_j]A_j)[P_j] + [S_j]([v_j] - \hat{x}_j))$
4. $[x_{j+1}] = [v_{j+1}] + [x_{j+1}]$
5. $A_{j+1} = m([S_j]A_j)$
6. $[p_{j+1}] = A_{j+1}^{-1}([S_j]A_j)[p_j] + (A_{j+1}^{-1}[S_j])([v_j] - \hat{x}_j)$
7. $\hat{x}_{j+1} = m([v_{j+1}])$

In the previous algorithm, I represents the identity matrix (with the same dimension of the state vector). $J(f^{[i]}; [x_j])$ is the Jacobian matrix of the Taylor coefficient, $f^{[i]}$, which is evaluated over $[x_j]$. The variables $\hat{x}_j$ and $[v_j]$ are calculated in the state $(t_j - 1)$.

4   Results

The state estimation algorithm is applied to the pineapple dehydration model. The analysis is taken to simulation level. Noise R is delimited for the state variables $[Y^S]$, $[X^S]$ and $[V]$ respectively, as follows:

$$R = \begin{bmatrix} -0.05 & 0.05 \\ -0.05 & 0.05 \\ -0.05 & 0.05 \end{bmatrix} \tag{18}$$

The initial conditions for the state variables $[Y^S]$, $[X^S]$ and $[V]$, are given by:

$$x(0) = \begin{bmatrix} 0.135 & 0.145 \\ 0.600 & 0.610 \\ 40.45 & 40.55 \end{bmatrix} \tag{19}$$

The results of the prediction are calculated for the state variables and the specific rate of sugar concentration in the food, which is a function of the state variables. In Figs. 3, 4, 5 and 6, the dotted lines present the simulated values and solid lines show the model reconstruction. The obtained results for the state variables display that the uncertainty is adequately controlled by the estimation algorithm, in spite of the fixed noise, which is in sync with the experimental conditions of the process. The estimation of the specific concentration rate is a close approximation to the model data. This proves the method's efficiency, based on the higher order of the Taylor expansion, to solve state equations through center forms and pre-conditioning matrices.

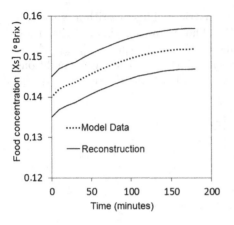

Fig. 3. State estimation and model data for variation of sugar concentration in food

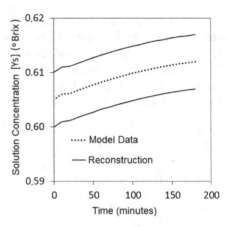

Fig. 4. State estimation and model data for variation of sugar concentration in solution

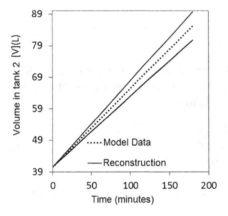

Fig. 5. State estimation and model data for variation of volume in tank 2

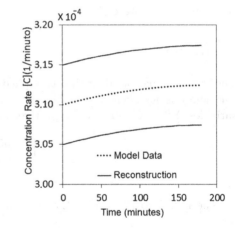

Fig. 6. State estimation and model data for sugar concentration rate in food

5 Discussion

The state estimation methodology complement the probabilistic methods, where noises and disturbances are assumed as random variables and the problem of state estimation is solved through the election and optimization of adequate criteria [28]. However, in practice, it is often complicated to make a characterization of the random variables that model noise and disturbances, making it difficult to evaluate proposed stochastic hypothesis. This way, the estimation by intervals method offers an alternative approach that is based on the fact that the dynamic system is limited to a defined uncertainty, having a state estimation in an enclosed error context. This approach allows characterizing the values of the state vector, which are consistent with the model structure and the defined error limits. It is important to highlight that when the dynamic system is governed by non-linear differential equations, it is fundamental to linearize the model and afterwards, applying the estimation algorithms presented in this work.

6 Conclusions

State estimation algorithms were applied to a fruit dehydration process, where it was necessary to know beforehand the operation ranges of the process. The used state estimation algorithms allowed for the process to be manipulated so that the necessary state variables were monitored, in order to rebuild the process based on interval analysis.

The SIVIA and EMV algorithms were experimentally validated, which allowed for the definition of an adequate operation zone for the plant. State estimation led to a solution that is in sync with the system's response, which is based on the dynamics of the process' model.

State estimation is highly dependent of limited error. If the error is not bound in the proper intervals, the reconstruction of the state variable may be wrong, for when the prediction is made. The bounded noise allows finding important relationships between input and output variables of the process.

In the future, interval analysis may allow using control techniques based on state estimation, that may be able to complement traditional methods of automatic control. The methodology used in this work is applicable to real processes such as those shown in [29–31] and may be used for failure detection and diagnostics. It is possible to determine reliable intervals for the correct functioning of the system, just as the precision of the regions. This has a direct relationship with the level of uncertainty and the plant's instrumentation.

References

1. Burgos, M., González, A., Vallejo, M., Izquierdo, C.: Selección económica de equipo utilizando matemáticas de intervalos. Información Tecnológica **9**(5), 311–316 (1998)
2. Campos, P., Valdés, H.: Optimización global por intervalos: aplicación a problemas con parámetros inciertos. Información Tecnológica **17**(5), 67–74 (2006)
3. Zapata, G., Cardillo, J., Chacón, E.: Aportes metodológicos para el diseño de sistemas de supervisión de procesos contínuos. Información Tecnológica **22**(3), 97–114 (2011)
4. Jauberthie, C., Verdiere, N., Trave, L.: Fault detection and identification relying on set-membership identifiability. Annu. Rev. Control. **37**(1), 129–136 (2013)
5. Li, Q., Jauberthie, C., Denis, L., Cher, Z.: Guaranteed state and parameter estimation for nonlinear dynamical aerospace models. In: Informatics in Control, Automation and Robotics (ICINCO), Vienna, Austria (2014)

6. Ortega, F., Pérez, O., López, E.: Comparación del desempeño de estimadores de estado no lineales para determinar la concentración de biomasa y sustrato en un bioproceso. Información Tecnológica **26**(5), 35–44 (2015)
7. Kieffer, M., Jaulin, L., Walter, E.: Guaranteed recursive nonlinear state bounding using interval analysis. Int. J. Adapt. Control. Signal Process. **16**(3), 193–218 (2002)
8. Jaulin, L.: A nonlinear set membership approach for the localization and map building of underwater robots. IEEE Trans. Robot. **25**(1), 88–98 (2009)
9. Jaulin, L., Walter, E.: Set inversion via interval analysis for nonlinear bounded-error estimation. Automatica **294**, 1053–1064 (1993)
10. Paşca, I.: Formally verified conditions for regularity of interval matrices. In: Autexier, S., et al. (eds.) CICM 2010. LNCS (LNAI), vol. 6167, pp. 219–233. Springer, Heidelberg (2010). https://doi.org/10.1007/978-3-642-14128-7_19
11. Rauh, A., Auer, E.: Modeling, Design, and Simulation of Systems with Uncertainties. Springer, Berlin (2011). https://doi.org/10.1007/978-3-642-15956-5
12. Jauberthie, C., Chanthery, E.: Optimal input design for a nonlinear dynamical uncertain aerospace system. In: IFAC Symposium on Nonlinear Control Systems, Toulouse, France (2013)
13. Nedialkov, N., Jackson, K.R.: A new perspective on the wrapping effect in interval methods for initial value problems for ordinary differential equations. In: Kulisch, U., Lohner, R., Facius, A. (eds.) Perspectives on Enclosure Methods, pp. 219–263. Springer, Vienna (2001). https://doi.org/10.1007/978-3-7091-6282-8_13
14. Arreola, S., Rosas, M.: Aplicación de vacío en la deshidratación osmótica de higos (ficus carica). Información Tecnológica **18**(2), 43–48 (2007)
15. Arballo, J.: Modelado y simulación de la deshidratación combinada osmótica-microondas de frutihortícolas. Ph.D. thesis in Engineering, Universidad de La Plata, Argentina (2013)
16. García, A.: Análisis comparativo de la cinética de deshidratación osmótica y por flujo de aire caliente de la piña (ananas comosus, variedad cayena lisa). Revista Ciencias Técnicas Agropecuarias **22**(1), 62–69 (2013)
17. García, M., Alvis, A., García, C.: Evaluación de los pretratamientos de deshidratación osmótica y microondas en la obtención de hojuelas de mango (Tommy Atkins). Información Tecnológica **26**(5), 63–70 (2015)
18. Jaller, S., Vargas, S.: Comparación de la transferencia de materia en los procesos de deshidratación osmótica a presión atmosférica y con impregnación de vacío en la piña cayena lisa (ananás comosus l. meer) a través de un modelo matemático. Undergraduate thesis for Agroindustrial Production Engineering, Universidad de La Sabana, Chía, Colombia (2000)
19. González, G.: Viabilidad de la piña colombiana var. cayena lisa, para su industrialización combinando operaciones de impregnación a vacío, deshidtratación cayena lisa (ananás comosus l. meer). Ph.D. thesis, Universidad Politécnica de Valencia, Valencia, Spain (2000)
20. Wullner, B.: Instrumentación y control de un deshidratador osmótico a vacío. Undergraduate thesis for Agroindustrial Production Engineering, Universidad de La Sabana, Chía, Colombia (1998)
21. Moore, R.: Automatic error analysis in digital computation. Technical report LMSD-48421, Lockheed Missiles and Space Co., Palo Alto, CA (1959)
22. Moore, R.E.: Interval Analysis. Prentice Hall, New Jersey (1966)
23. Jaulin, L., Walter, E.: Set inversion via interval analysis for nonlinear bounded-error estimation. Automatica **29**(4), 1053–1064 (1993)

24. Nedialkov, N., Jackson, K., Pryce, J.: An effective high-order interval method for validating existence and uniqueness of the solution of an IVP for an ODE. Reliab. Comput. **7**, 449–465 (2001)
25. Milanese, M., Norton, J., Piet-Lahanier, H., Walter, E.: Bounding Approaches to System Identification. Plenum, New York (1996)
26. Lohner, R.: Enclosing the solutions of ordinary initial and boundary value problems. Wiley-Teubner, Stuttgart, pp. 255–286 (1987)
27. Rihm, R.: Interval methods for initial value problems in ODEs. In: Herzberger, J. (ed.) Topics in Validated Computations: Proceedings of the IMACS-GAMM International Workshop on Validated Computations, University of Oldenburg. Elsevier Studies in Computational Mathematics. Elsevier, Amsterdam, New York (1994)
28. Walter, E., Pronzato, L.: Identification de modles paramtriques partir de donnes exprimentales. Masson, Montreal (1994)
29. Castellanos, H.E., Collazos, C.A., Farfán, J.C., Meléndez-Pertuz, F.: Diseño y Construcción de un Canal Hidráulico de Pendiente Variable. Información Tecnológica **28**(6), 103–114 (2017). https://doi.org/10.4067/S0718-07642017000600012. Accessed 20 July 2018
30. Collazos, C.A., Castellanos, H.E., Burbano, A.M., Cardona, J.A., Cuervo, J.A., Maldonado-Franco, A.: Semi-mechanistic modelling of an osmotic dehydration process. WSEAS Trans. Syst. **16**, 27–35 (2017). E-ISSN 2224-2678
31. Duarte, J., Garcá J., Jiménez, J., Sanjuan, M.E., Bula, A., González, J.: Autoignition control in spark-ignition engines using internal model control structure. J. Energy Resour. Technol. **139**(2) (2016)

A Note About the (x, y) Coordinates
of the Centroid of a Fuzzy Set

Juan Carlos Figueroa-García[1]([⊠]) (iD), Eduyn Ramiro López-Santana[1],
and Carlos Franco-Franco[2]

[1] Universidad Distrital Francisco José de Caldas, Bogotá, Colombia
{jcfigueroag,erlopezs}@udistrital.edu.co
[2] Universidad del Rosario, Bogotá, Colombia
carlosa.franco@urosario.edu.co

Abstract. This paper presents some considerations about the centroid
of a fuzzy set, where the y-coordinate (or vertical centroid) is defined
and discussed. An interesting fact about the y-centroid is analyzed using
some results for Gaussian, triangular, and non-convex fuzzy sets. Some
considerations about the obtained results are provided and some recommendations are given.

Keywords: Fuzzy numbers · Vertical centroid · Fuzzy distance

1 Introduction and Motivation

Fuzzy sets deal with non-probabilistic uncertainty where statistical information
is absent or incomplete, and it has been applied mostly in engineering problems.
As in probability theory and inferential statistics where averages and variances
are widely used as order statistics of a population, fuzzy sets use the centroid as
central tendency of a fuzzy granule.

This way, many works have been devoted to compute the centroid of a fuzzy
set (see Carlsson and Fullér [1], Klir and Folger [9], Klir and Yuan [10], Wu and
Mendel [15] and Mendel and Wu [11], Yager [16], Figueroa-García and Pachon-
Neira [7,8], Figueroa-García, Chalco-Cano and Román-Flores [5]).

Now, an interesting property of any function (or area between functions) is
that we can compute its moments over its axis X, Y and determine its generalized
centroid. Of course, some functions make easier its computation while others are
more complex. This property can be extended to fuzzy sets in order to locate
the coordinates of its centroid in the x, y axis using the same concepts of the
moments of a function.

This paper focuses on the vertical centroid of a fuzzy set. The paper is divided
into seven sections. Section 1 introduces the topic. In Sect. 2, some basics on fuzzy
sets/numbers are provided; in Sect. 3, a definition of the vertical centroid of a
fuzzy set is presented. Section 4 presents the concept of the (x, y) coordinates
of the centroid of a fuzzy set; Sect. 5 presents how to compute the Minkowski

© Springer Nature Switzerland AG 2018
J. C. Figueroa-García et al. (Eds.): WEA 2018, CCIS 915, pp. 78–88, 2018.
https://doi.org/10.1007/978-3-030-00350-0_7

metric between the centroids of two fuzzy sets; Sect. 6 presents some interesting results for fuzzy sets/numbers, and Sect. 7 presents the concluding remarks of the study.

2 Basics of Fuzzy Sets/Numbers

Let $\mathcal{P}(X)$ be the class of all crisp sets, $\mathcal{F}(X)$ is the class of all fuzzy sets, $\mathcal{F}_1(X)$ is the class of all convex fuzzy sets, and $I = [0, 1]$ be the set of values in the unit interval. A fuzzy set namely A is characterized by a membership function $\mu_A : X \to I$ defined over a universe of discourse $x \in X$. Thus, a fuzzy set A is the set of ordered pairs $x \in X$ and its membership degree, $\mu_A(x)$, i.e.,

$$A = \{(x, \mu_A(x)) \mid x \in X\}. \tag{1}$$

Let us denote $\mathcal{F}_1(\mathbb{R})$ as the class of all fuzzy numbers, then a fuzzy number is defined as follows:

Definition 1. *Let $A : \mathbb{R} \to I$ be a fuzzy subset of the reals. Then $A \in \mathcal{F}_1(\mathbb{R})$ is a Fuzzy Number (FN) iff there exists a closed interval $[x_l, x_r] \neq \emptyset$ with a membership function $\mu_A(x)$ such that:*

$$\mu_A(x) = \begin{cases} c(x) & \text{for } x \in [c_l, c_r], \\ l(x) & \text{for } x \in [-\infty, x_l], \\ r(x) & \text{for } x \in [x_r, \infty], \end{cases} \tag{2}$$

where $c(x) = 1$ for $x \in [c_l, c_r]$, $l : (-\infty, x_l) \to I$ is monotonic non-decreasing, continuous from the right, i.e. $l(x) = 0$ for $x < x_l$; $l : (x_r, \infty) \to I$ is monotonic non-increasing, continuous from the left, i.e. $r(x) = 0$ for $x > x_r$.

The α-*cut* of a set $A \in \mathcal{F}_1(\mathbb{R})$, $^\alpha A$ is the set of values with a membership degree equal or greatest than α, this is:

$$^\alpha A = \{x \mid \mu_A(x) \geqslant \alpha\} \ \forall \ x \in X, \tag{3}$$

$$^\alpha A = \left[\inf_x {}^\alpha\mu_A(x), \ \sup_x {}^\alpha\mu_A(x) \right] = \left[\check{A}_\alpha, \hat{A}_\alpha \right]. \tag{4}$$

It is clear that the centroid $c_x(A)$ of any symmetric fuzzy set is the same no matter its variance is. Also $c_x(A)$ changes as its skewness does. Now, an interesting question about the centroid of a fuzzy set is: where is it located at?. Since $c_x(A)$ of a symmetric fuzzy set does not change, the question about how non-symmetric shapes affect $c_x(A)$, is open. A not so widely analyzed imprecision measure is the vertical centroid (or y-centroid) of a fuzzy set which can help to understand how the shape of A locates $c_x(A)$. Next sections will provide some definitions about its y-centroid and its properties.

3 The Vertical Centroid of a Fuzzy Set

We start by using the concept of the *moment* of the area defined over two points a, b (see Protter and Morrey-Jr. [12]).

Definition 2. *Let $f : X \to \mathbb{R}$ and $g : X \to \mathbb{R}$ two continuous functions over X where $f(x) \geqslant g(x) \; \forall \; x \in X$. The area Λ under the region bounded by $f(x)$ and $g(x)$ over the interval $[a, b] \in \mathbb{R}$ is:*

$$\Lambda = \int_a^b [f(x) - g(x)] \, dx \tag{5}$$

and the x, y moments M_x, M_y of the region bounded by $f(x)$ and $g(x)$ are:

$$M_x = \frac{1}{\Lambda} \int_a^b x * [f(x) - g(x)] \, dx, \tag{6}$$

$$M_y = \frac{1}{\Lambda} \int_a^b \frac{1}{2} \left[f(x)^2 - g(x)^2 \right] \, dx. \tag{7}$$

The area Λ and the moments M_x, M_y of the region bounded by $f(x)$ and $g(x)$ are shown in Fig. 1.

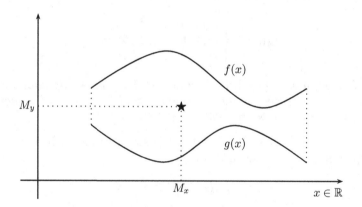

Fig. 1. Moments M_x and M_y of the area between $f(x)$ and $g(x)$

Note that $f(x) = \mu_A(x)$ and $g(x) = 0$ for any fuzzy set, so the total area of the fuzzy set A is:

$$\Lambda_A = \int_x \mu_A(x) dx. \tag{8}$$

And the horizontal centroid (or x-centroid) of a fuzzy set namely $c_x(A)$ corresponds to the moment M_x and classical centroid of A (see Carlsson and Fullér [1], Wu and Mendel [15], and Mendel and Wu [11]):

$$c_x(A) = \frac{1}{\Lambda_A} \int_x x * \mu_A(x) \, dx. \tag{9}$$

A fuzzy set $A : X \to I$ is a bidimensional measure and its horizontal centroid is a measure of central tendency of A which fulfills $c_x : A \to X$. Now, the vertical centroid of A can be defined as the vertical center of gravity of A, as shown as follows:

Definition 3. *Let $A \in \mathcal{F}(X)$ be a fuzzy set, then the vertical centroid $c_y(A)$ of A is a function $c_y : A \to I$ defined as follows:*

$$c_y(A) = \frac{1}{A_A} \int_x \frac{1}{2} \mu_A(x)^2 \, dx. \tag{10}$$

Now, if we consider that the y-coordinate of any fuzzy set is $f(x) = \mu_A(x)$ and $\mu_A(x) \geqslant 0 \ \forall \ x \in X$ which implies that $g(x) = 0$, then Eq. (7) reduces to:

$$f(x)^2 - g(x)^2 = \mu_A(x)^2 - 0 = \mu_A(x)^2.$$

Also c_y seems to be very similar to c_x, the only difference lies in how they are measured. While c_x is multiplied by $x \in X$, c_y is multiplied by $\mu_A \in [0, 1]$ which makes the difference.

Definition 4. *Let $A \in \mathcal{F}_1(\mathbb{R})$ be a fuzzy number, and $^\alpha A = \left[\check{A}_\alpha, \hat{A}_\alpha \right]$ be its α-cut, $\alpha \in [0, 1]$. The vertical centroid $c_y(A)$ of A is as follows:*

$$c_y(A) = \frac{1}{A_A} \int_I \alpha * \left(\hat{A}_\alpha - \check{A}_\alpha \right) d\alpha, \tag{11}$$

which is equivalent to:

$$c_y(A) = \frac{1}{A_A} \int_x \frac{1}{2} \mu_A(x)^2 \, dx. \tag{12}$$

4 (x, y) Coordinates of the Centroid of a Fuzzy Set

The main idea behind c_x and c_y comes from real-valued integration and the mass center of a granule, so we compute $c_A(x, y)$ using classical integration (in the Lebesgue sense). Thus, Definition 3 is the y-mass center of $\mu_A(x)$, and it can be easily computed for well known membership functions. If A is a non-convex fuzzy set, then numerical integration is required.

Now, as we can compute the (x, y) coordinates of the centroid of A then we can define $c(A)$ as follows:

Definition 5. *Let $A \in \mathcal{F}(X)$ be a fuzzy set, $c_x(A) \in X$ be its x-centroid, and $c_y(A) \in [0, 1]$ be its y-centroid. The (x, y) coordinate representation of $c(A)$ namely $c_A(x, y)$ is*

$$c_A : A \to \mathbb{R} \times I \tag{13}$$

where $x = c_x(A)$ and $y = c_y(A)$.

Now, Proposition 1 shows that $c_y(A)$ attaches its maximum value if and only if A is an interval.

Proposition 1. *Let A be a fuzzy set with unitary membership function I_A e.g.*
$\mu_A(x) = 1 \, \forall \, x \in X$, $B \in \mathcal{F}(X)$ be a fuzzy set where $B \subseteq I_A$. Then $c_y(A) = 0.5$
and $c_y(A) \geqslant c_y(B)$.

Proof. It is easy to prove that $c_y(A)$ is 0.5 since:

$$c_y(A) = \frac{1}{2} \frac{\int_x \mu_A(x)^2 \, dx}{\Lambda_A} = \frac{1}{2} \frac{\int_x 1^2 \, dx}{|X|} = \frac{1}{2} \frac{|X|}{|X|} = \frac{1}{2},$$

now, it is clear that:

$$B \subseteq I_A \implies \mu_A(x) \geqslant \mu_B(x) \, \forall \, x \in X,$$

so we have that:

$$\int_x \mu_A(x)^2 \, dx \geqslant \int_x \mu_B(x)^2 \, dx \implies |X| \geqslant \int_x \mu_B(x)^2 \, dx,$$

which leads to the following inequality:

$$\int_x \mu_B(x)^2 \, dx \leqslant \int_x \mu_B(x) \, dx \int_x \mu_B(x) \, dx,$$

$$\int_x \mu_B(x)^2 \, dx \leqslant \Lambda_B \Lambda_B, \tag{14}$$

so by monotonicity we have that:

$$\frac{\int_x \mu_B(x)^2 \, dx}{\Lambda_B} \leqslant 1 \leqslant \Lambda_B \tag{15}$$

by multiplying by $1/2$ and rearranging we have

$$\frac{\Lambda_B}{2} \geqslant \frac{1}{2} \geqslant \frac{1}{2} \frac{\int_x \mu_B(x)^2 \, dx}{\Lambda_B}, \tag{16}$$

now as $c_y(A) = 1/2$ then it reduces to:

$$\frac{\Lambda_B}{2} \geqslant c_y(A) \geqslant c_y(B) \tag{17}$$

and the proof is concluded.   □

5   Minkowski Centroid-Distance Between Two FNs

The p-order Minkowski metric (a.k.a. d_p distance/metric) between two objects
A, B in the Euclidean space with coordinates (x_1, y_1) and (x_2, y_2) is:

$$d_p(A, B) = \left(|x_1 - x_2|^p + |y_1 - y_2|^p \right)^{1/p}.$$

Now, as $c_A(x, y)$ and $c_B(x, y)$ are composed by coordinates $(c_x(A), c_y(A))$
and $(c_x(B), c_y(B))$, then we can define the d_p distance between the centroids of
two fuzzy sets A, B as follows.

Definition 6. *Let $A \in \mathcal{F}(\mathbb{R})$ and $B \in \mathcal{F}(\mathbb{R})$ be fuzzy sets; $c_A \in \mathbb{R} \times I$, $c_B \in \mathbb{R} \times I$ be its centroids. The centroid-based distance $d_p(c_A, c_B)$ between A, B is:*

$$d_p(A, B) = \left(|c_x(A) - c_x(B)|^p + |c_y(A) - c_y(B)|^p \right)^{1/p}. \tag{18}$$

6   Obtained Results

6.1   Convex Fuzzy Sets

This example focuses on the y-centroid of some **convex fuzzy sets** since they are among the most used in practical applications (see Definition 4). For instance, the y-centroid of a Gaussian fuzzy set $G(c, m)$ with center m and spread m (see Fig. 2) is as follows:

$$c_y(A) = \frac{\sqrt{\pi}}{2\sqrt{2\pi}}$$

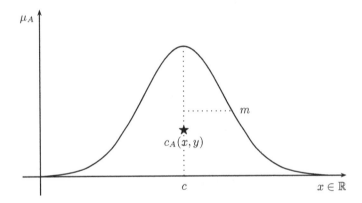

Fig. 2. Gaussian fuzzy number A

So its coordinates are:

$$c_A(x, y) = \left(c, \frac{\sqrt{\pi}}{2\sqrt{2\pi}} \right)$$

The y-centroid of a triangular fuzzy set $T(\check{a}, \bar{a}, \hat{a})$ with parameters $\check{a}, \bar{a},$ and $\hat{a}$ (see Fig. 3) is:

$$c_y(A) = \frac{1}{3}$$

So its coordinates are:

$$c_A(x, y) = \left(\frac{\check{a} + \bar{a} + \hat{a}}{3}, \frac{1}{3} \right)$$

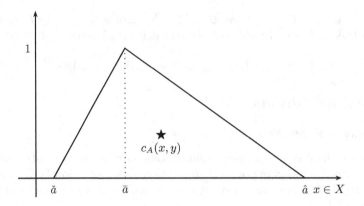

Fig. 3. Triangular fuzzy set/number $\tilde{A}$

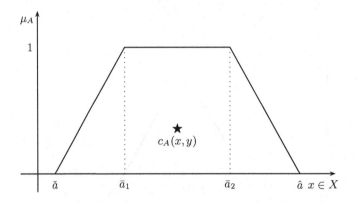

Fig. 4. Trapezoidal fuzzy set/number $\tilde{A}$

The y-centroid of a trapezoidal fuzzy set $Tr(\check{a}, \bar{a}_1, \bar{a}_2, \hat{a})$ with parameters $\check{a}, \bar{a}_1, \bar{a}_2$, and $\hat{a}$ (see Fig. 4) is:

$$a = \bar{a}_2 - \bar{a}_1, \tag{19}$$

$$b = \hat{a} - \check{a}, \tag{20}$$

$$c = \bar{a}_1 - \check{a}, \tag{21}$$

$$c_y(A) = \frac{2a + b}{3(a + b)}. \tag{22}$$

So its coordinates are:

$$c_A(x, y) = \left(\frac{2ac + a^2 + cb + ab + b^2}{3(a + b)}, \frac{2a + b}{3(a + b)} \right).$$

6.2   Non-convex Fuzzy Set

In this example (see Fig. 5) we compute $c_x(A)$ and $c_y(A)$ (see Definition 3) of a **non-convex fuzzy set** defined as follows:

$$\mu_A = \max\left(\frac{4}{5}G(25, 8), G(50, 8), \frac{1}{2}G(75, 8)\right).$$

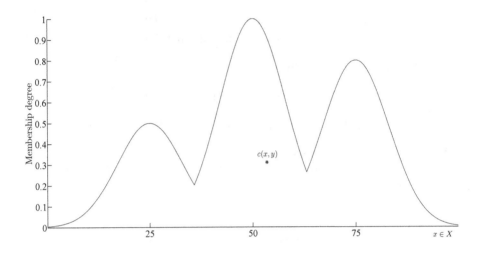

Fig. 5. Non-convex fuzzy set A

Then, we computed $c_x(A)$ and $c_y(A)$ using Eqs. (9) and (10) whose results are:

$$c_x(A) = 53.435, \tag{23}$$
$$c_y(A) = 0.3107. \tag{24}$$

So the coordinates of $c_A(x, y)$ are:

$$c_A(x, y) = (53.435, 0.3107).$$

6.3   Computing the Distance Between Two Fuzzy Sets

In this example, we compute the centroid-based distance as shown in Definition 6 and Eq. (18). To do so, we first compute the centroids of the following two fuzzy sets:

$$\mu_A(x) = T(1, 5, 13), \tag{25}$$
$$\mu_B(x) = T(11.5, 3) \tag{26}$$

whose centroids are:

$$c_x(A) = 6.3333, c_y(A) = 0.3333, \tag{27}$$
$$c_A(x,y) = (6.3333, 0.3333), \tag{28}$$
$$c_x(B) = 11.5, c_y(B) = 0.3535, \tag{29}$$
$$c_B(x,y) = (11.5, 0.3535). \tag{30}$$

So the d_1 distance is computed as follows:

$$d_1(A,B) = \big(|c_x(A) - c_x(B)| + |c_y(A) - c_y(B)|\big)$$
$$= |6.3333 - 11.5| + |0.3333 - 0.3535| = 5.1868 \tag{31}$$

And the distance d_2 is as follows

$$d_2(A,B) = \big(|c_x(A) - c_x(B)|^2 + |c_y(A) - c_y(B)|^2\big)^{1/2}$$
$$= \big(|6.3333 - 11.5|^2 + |0.3333 - 0.3535|^2\big)^{1/2} = 5.1667 \tag{32}$$

The obtained results are shown in Fig. 6. Note that $d_p(A,B)$ measures how far $c_A(x,y)$ and $c_B(x,y)$ using both coordinates, and how $d_p(A,B)$ decreases as $p \to \infty$.

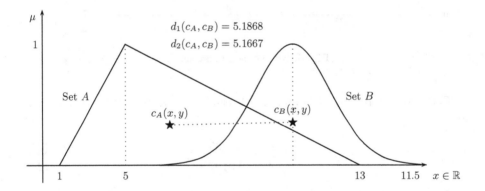

Fig. 6. Centroid-based distance between two sets A, B, $d_p(c_A, c_B)$

7   Concluding Remarks

We have provided some interesting results about $c_A(x,y)$. We presented a definition of the y-centroid of some well known fuzzy sets e.g. Gaussian, triangular, trapezoidal, and non-convex fuzzy sets. We also have shown that an interval shaped fuzzy set contains the higher possible y-centroid.

Note that for intervals, triangular, and Gaussian fuzzy sets its y-centroids are constants while for trapezoidal fuzzy sets c_y depend on its parameters. An easy way to compute $c_y(A)$ for any non-convex fuzzy set (intuitionistic, non-normalized, etc.) is presented as well.

Also we have provided a definition of the Minkowski centroid-based distance $d_p(A,B)$ between two fuzzy sets A, B as shown in Definition 6. Our definition is based on concepts of center of mass (see Protter and Morrey-Jr. [12]) and the classical definition of the centroid of a fuzzy set provided by Carlsson and Fullér [1], and Chiao [2,3].

The distance $d_p(A,B)$ involves $c_x(A)$ and $c_y(B)$, but x-coordinates are which most contribute to $d_p(A,B)$ while y-coordinates have a smaller impact over $d_p(A,B)$. For some popular same-shaped fuzzy sets (intervals, triangular, and Gaussian), the distance $|c_y(A) - c_y(B)|^p = 0$. This is possible one of the most important reasons for which practitioners do not pay attention to $c_y(A)$.

7.1 Further Topics

The application of our proposal to decision making problems, including fuzzy differential equations, fuzzy linear programming, among others, appears as an interesting field to be covered in the future. Also some extensions to Interval Type-2 fuzzy sets are promissory fields to be covered (see Figueroa-García, Chalco-Cano and Román-Flores [4,5], Juan Carlos Figueroa-García, Melgarejo-Rey and Hernández-Pérez [6], and Salazar-Morales et al. [13,14]).

References

1. Carlsson, C., Fullér, R.: On possibilistic mean value and variance of fuzzy numbers. Fuzzy Sets Syst. **122**(1), 315–326 (2001)
2. Chiao, K.P.: A new ranking approach for general interval type-2 fuzzy sets using extended alpha cuts representation. In: International Conference on Intelligent Systems and Knowledge Engineering, vol. 1, pp. 594–597. IEEE (2015)
3. Chiao, K.P.: Ranking type-2 fuzzy sets using parametric graded mean integration representation. In: International Conference on Machine Learning and Cybernetics, vol. 1, pp. 606–611. IEEE (2016)
4. Figueroa-García, J.C., Chalco-Cano, Y., Román-Flores, H.: Distance measures for interval type-2 fuzzy numbers. Discrete Appl. Math. **197**(1), 93–102 (2015). https://doi.org/10.1016/j.dam.2014.11.016
5. Figueroa-García, J.C., Chalco-Cano, Y., Román-Flores, H.: Yager index and ranking for interval type-2 fuzzy numbers. IEEE Trans. Fuzzy Syst. (1), 1–9 (2018, in press). https://doi.org/10.1109/TFUZZ.2017.2788884
6. Figueroa-García, J.C., Melgarejo-Rey, M.A., Hernández-Pérez, G.: Representation of the Minkowski metric as a fuzzy set. Optim. Lett. (2018, in press). https://doi.org/10.1007/s11590-018-1290-6
7. Figueroa-García, J.C., Pachon-Neira, D.: On ordering words using the centroid and Yager index of an interval type-2 fuzzy number. In: Proceedings of the Workshop on Engineering Applications, WEA 2015, vol. 1, pp. 1–6. IEEE (2015)
8. Figueroa-García, J.C., Pachon-Neira, D.: A comparison between the centroid and the Yager index rank for type reduction of an interval type-2 fuzzy number. Revista Ingeniería Universidad Distrital **2**, 225–234 (2016)

9. Klir, G.J., Folger, T.A.: Fuzzy Sets, Uncertainty and Information. Prentice Hall, Englewood Cliffs (1992)
10. Klir, G.J., Yuan, B.: Fuzzy Sets and Fuzzy Logic: Theory and Applications. Prentice Hall, Englewood Cliffs (1995)
11. Mendel, J.M., Wu, D.: Cardinality, fuzziness, variance and skewness of interval type-2 fuzzy sets. In: Proceedings of FOCI 2007, pp. 375–382. IEEE (2007)
12. Protter, M.H., Morrey-Jr., C.B.: College Calculus with Analytic Geometry. Addison-Wesley, Reading (1970)
13. Salazar-Morales, O., Serrano-Devia, J.H., Soriano-Mendez, J.J.: Centroid of an interval type-2 fuzzy set: continuous vs. discrete. Revista Ingeniería 16(2), 1–9 (2011)
14. Salazar-Morales, O., Serrano-Devia, J.H., Soriano-Mendez, J.J.: A short note on the centroid of an interval type-2 fuzzy set. In: Proceedings of 2012 Workshop on Engineering Applications (WEA), pp. 1–6. IEEE (2012)
15. Wu, D., Mendel, J.M.: A comparative study of ranking methods, similarity measures and uncertainty measures for interval type-2 fuzzy sets. Inf. Sci. 179(1), 1169–1192 (2009)
16. Yager, R.: A procedure for ordering fuzzy subsets of the unit interval. Inf. Sci. 24(1), 143–161 (1981)

Control of a Permanent Magnet Synchronous Generator Using a Neuro-Fuzzy System

Helbert Espitia[1]($\boxtimes$), Guzmán Díaz[2], and Susana Díaz[2]

[1] Universidad Distrital Francisco José de Caldas, Bogotá, Colombia
heespitiac@udistrital.edu.co
[2] Universidad de Oviedo, Oviedo, Spain
{guzman,sirene}@uniovi.es

Abstract. This document shows a neuro-fuzzy control system to regulate the velocity of a permanent magnet synchronous generator. This scheme comes up with two neuro-fuzzy systems where the first identifies the dynamics of the plant; the second is employed for control purposes. Subsequently, the performed training is examined to different reference values.

Keywords: Control · Neuro-fuzzy · Generator

1 Introduction

Distributed generation systems are a remarkable alternative for energy use. Considering energy transformation, many applications of distributed generation employ permanent magnet synchronous generators (PMSG). Both energy demands and the increasing associated costs require new systems for economic and no disruptive energy generation. Distributed generation (DG) has become an appealing system for energy supply [1]. DG also allows to supply the constant demands of energy, the improvement the reliability to preventing failures, and to enhance energy quality through sophisticated control schemes [2]. In addition, many DG applications employ synchronous permanent magnet generators, whereby, this is to be considered when designing control strategies in a DG system [3,4].

Meanwhile, neuro-fuzzy systems appear as a remarkable control alternative in highly complex systems which is given by non-linearities, parameter variation, and saturations, among others [5]. For proper employment of strategies in neuro-fuzzy control systems, it is necessary a prior plant identification, after control optimization is made using this model. Consequently, this document performs the identification and control for a permanent magnet synchronous generator. Such identification uses data reported in [6] and the controller training is made by Dynamic Backpropagation, including different reference values.

© Springer Nature Switzerland AG 2018
J. C. Figueroa-García et al. (Eds.): WEA 2018, CCIS 915, pp. 89–101, 2018.
https://doi.org/10.1007/978-3-030-00350-0_8

2   Permanent Magnet Synchronous Generator

In generation processes, a key component is the transformation mechanism from mechanical to electric power; this process can be carried out using different generator alternatives; however, permanent magnet synchronous generator is widely employed for eolian power and micro-turbines, among others [3,4].

PMSG model is derived from the referent for mobile-synchronous of two stages $d - q$, where axis q is $90°$ ahead of axis d with respect to the direction of rotation [7,8]. The equations for coordinates $d - q$ are:

$$\frac{di_d}{dt} = \frac{1}{L_d}v_d - \frac{R}{L_d}i_d + \frac{L_q}{L_d}pw_r i_q \tag{1}$$

$$\frac{di_q}{dt} = \frac{1}{L_q}v_q - \frac{R}{L_q}i_q - \frac{L_d}{L_q}pw_r i_d - \frac{\lambda pw_r}{L_q} \tag{2}$$

$$T_e = 1.5p[\lambda i_q + (L_d - L_q)i_d i_q] \tag{3}$$

where L_q, L_d are the inductances in axis q and d, R resistance of the stator, i_q, i_d currents in axis q and d; v_q, v_d voltages in axis q and d, w_r angular velocity of the rotor, λ amplitude of the flux induced by the permanent magnets, p number of pole pairs, and T_e electromagnetic torque. The equations of the mechanical system are:

$$\frac{dw_r}{dt} = \frac{1}{J}(T_e - Fw_r - T_m) \tag{4}$$

$$\frac{d\theta}{dt} = w_r \tag{5}$$

where J is the inertia of rotor, F viscous friction of rotor, θ rotor angular position, and T_m mechanical torque. Using $\gamma = 2\pi/3$, the current conversions form dq to abc axis is given by (6) and the voltage conversions form abc to dq by (7).

$$\begin{bmatrix} i_a \\ i_b \\ i_c \end{bmatrix} = \begin{bmatrix} \cos(\theta) & -\sin(\theta) \\ \cos(\theta - \gamma) & -\sin(\theta - \gamma) \\ \cos(\theta + \gamma) & -\sin(\theta + \gamma) \end{bmatrix} \begin{bmatrix} i_d \\ i_q \end{bmatrix} \tag{6}$$

$$\begin{bmatrix} v_d \\ v_q \end{bmatrix} = \frac{2}{3} \begin{bmatrix} \cos(\theta) & \cos(\theta - \gamma) & \cos(\theta + \gamma) \\ -\sin(\theta) & -\sin(\theta - \gamma) & -\sin(\theta + \gamma) \end{bmatrix} \begin{bmatrix} v_a \\ v_b \\ v_c \end{bmatrix} \tag{7}$$

The implemented scheme for PSMG data (input-output) is shown in Fig. 1, where the input of the generator (torque) receives a random signal obtaining diverse output behaviors (angular velocity).

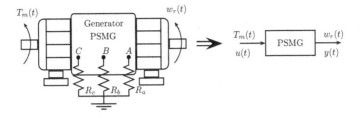

Fig. 1. Scheme for obtain PSMG input-output data.

3   Neuro-Fuzzy Control System

The neuro-fuzzy control system is proposed as an alternative to identify and control dynamic systems, using its capacity as approximator for general functions [5]. A fuzzy system allows a preliminary architecture for the structure of a plant estimator and controller; this also allows to deal with the difficulty that neuronal networks present to establish this structure together with parameter initialization [5]. Furthermore, plant identification is made using Backpropagation algorithm. Moreover, for controller training, Dynamic Backpropagation algorithm is employed, this algorithm integrate the fuzzy plant model together with the controller.

3.1   Neuro-Fuzzy Control System Architecture

This architecture uses two neuro-fuzzy systems: one for the controller and the second for the plant model. Under this scheme, a first step is to identify the plant, then, training control is performed to achieve the system output according to the reference. Figure 2 shows the scheme of a neuro-fuzzy control system.

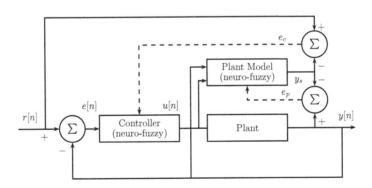

Fig. 2. Neuro-fuzzy control system.

As shown in Fig. 3 for the plant model, $u[n]$ is the input signal; likewise, the output signal is $y_s[n]$. Consequently, the structure obtained is:

$$y_s[n] = f_p(y[n-1], y[n-2], ..., y[n-p+1], u[n], u[n-1], ..., u[n-q+1], H_p) \quad (8)$$

Similarly, controller input corresponds to error signal $e[n]$, while the output is the control action $u[n]$. Then the general equation is stated as:

$$u[n] = f_c(e[n], e[n-1], ..., e[n-m+1], u[n-1], u[n-2], ..., u[n-q+1], H_c) \quad (9)$$

In these equations, p represents the output delays, q input delays, m error delays, H_p the plant estimator parameters, and H_c controller parameters. Typically, the number of delays employed increases along with the order of the plant. Figure 3 represents an example of the scheme employed to identification and control.

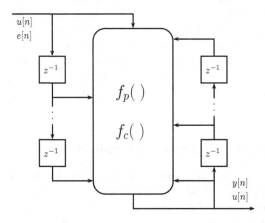

Fig. 3. Example of neuro-fuzzy structure for plant identification and control.

3.2   Plant Identification Scheme

An approach for PMSG system model consists of a neuro-fuzzy structure able to perform the same function [9]. Adaptation or training for parameters is made as:

$$H_p(k+1) = H_p(k) - \eta \frac{dJ_p(k)}{dH_p(k)} \quad (10)$$

where J_p corresponds to the adjustment function defined as:

$$J_p = \frac{1}{2}(y[n] - y_s[n])^2 \quad (11)$$

the gradient of J_p for parameter adjustment is:

$$\frac{dJ_p}{dH_p} = \frac{dJ_p}{dy_s[n]} \frac{dy_s[n]}{dH_p} \quad (12)$$

3.3   Controller Architecture

In this case, controller input corresponds to error variable $e[n]$, and the output to the action control $u[n]$. The Dynamic Backpropagation algorithm is employed for control training. Parameter adaptation is made as:

$$H_c(k+1) = H_c(k) - \eta \frac{dJ_c(k)}{dH_c(k)} \tag{13}$$

where J_c is the fitness function defined as:

$$J_c = \frac{1}{2} \left(r[n] - y_s[n] \right)^2 \tag{14}$$

with this approach, the variation of J_c in function of parameters is:

$$\frac{dJ_c}{dH_c} = \frac{dJ_c}{dy_s[n]} \frac{dy_s[n]}{dH_c} \tag{15}$$

4   Neuro-Fuzzy Scheme for Plant Identification

Gaussian sets are used for neuro-fuzzy identification, an example is shown in Fig. 4. This architecture is similar to the employed in radial neuronal networks; a related work using a neuro-fuzzy systems is presented in [10].

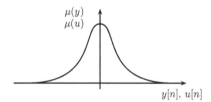

Fig. 4. Gaussian fuzzy set.

Equation (16) shows the input-output expression using the product as t-norm, also using fuzzy Gaussian sets. Consequently, the equations associated with the inference process are:

$$f_p(w) = \sum_{l=1}^{Q} y_l \left[\prod_{r=1}^{P} \exp \left(-\left(\frac{w_r - \delta_{rl}}{\rho_{rl}} \right)^2 \right) \right] \tag{16}$$

where,

$$z_l = \prod_{r=1}^{P} \exp \left(-\left(\frac{w_r - \delta_{rl}}{\rho_{rl}} \right)^2 \right) \tag{17}$$

$$f_p = \sum_{l=1}^{Q} y_l z_l \tag{18}$$

Here, Q is the number of fuzzy rules, P is the number inputs in the system, y_l is the respective actuator, w_r is the data system input; finally, δ_{rl} and ρ_{rl} correspond to the center for the standard deviation of the Gaussian sets in the respective antecedent. The set of parameters corresponds to $H_p = h_{rl} \in \{y_l, \delta_{rl}, \rho_{rl}\}$.

4.1   Training for the Plant Estimator

Taking into account the Backpropagation algorithm for a neuro-fuzzy system, and employing the gradient descent method to determine system parameters, it is seeks to minimize the error function:

$$J_p = \frac{1}{2}[y[n] - f_p(w[n])]^2 \tag{19}$$

For a time n, $w[n]$ corresponds to the system input data, $y[n]$ corresponds to the actual output data. These data define the respective pairs for training input-output. The error derivatives are calculated to parameter training:

$$y_l[k+1] = y_l[k] - \alpha \frac{dJ_p}{dy_l}\Big|_n \tag{20}$$

$$\delta_{rl}[k+1] = \delta_{rl}[k] - \alpha \frac{dJ_p}{d\delta_{rl}}\Big|_n \tag{21}$$

$$\rho_{rl}[k+1] = \rho_{rl}[k] - \alpha \frac{dJ_p}{d\sigma_{rl}}\Big|_n \tag{22}$$

Thus, for parameter updating the equations are:

$$y_l[k+1] = y_l[k] - \alpha(f_p - y)z_l \tag{23}$$

$$\delta_{rl}[k+1] = \delta_{rl}[k] - \alpha(f_p - y)y_l[k]z_l\frac{2(w_r[n] - \delta_{rl}[k])}{(\rho_{rl}[k])^2} \tag{24}$$

$$\rho_{rl}[k+a] = \rho_{rl}[k] - \alpha(f_p - y)y_l[k]z_l\frac{2(w_r[n] - \delta_{rl}[k])^2}{(\rho_{rl}[k])^3} \tag{25}$$

Figure 5 represents a neuro-fuzzy system. The first layer has Gaussian functions which are used for the calculations of z_l. Second layer determines the product of consequents y_l and the value of z_l. Finally, the third layer determines the inference output $f_p(w)$. The steps for parameters adaptation algorithm of a neuro-fuzzy system are:

1. Determine the neuro-fuzzy system by establishing Q, P and parameters $y_l[0]$, $\delta_{rl}[0]$ and $\rho_{rl}[0]$, which correspond to the initial setup.
2. Calculate the outputs to each layer using a pair of input-output $(w[n], y[n])$, $n = 1, 2, \ldots$ in the k-th training stage, $k = 0, 1, 2, \ldots$.
3. Update the parameters $y_l[k+1]$, $\delta_{rl}[k+1]$ and $\rho_{rl}[k+1]$, where α corresponds to learning rate.

4. Return to step 2 with $k = k + 1$ until J_p, be less than a ε defined, or when k equals a definite number.
5. Return to step 2 with $n = n + 1$, namely, update the parameters using the next input-output pair $(w[n + 1], y[n + 1])$.

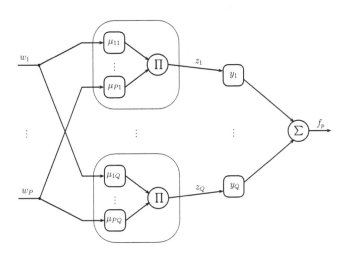

Fig. 5. Neuro-fuzzy system used for identification.

The previous algorithm is defined for a stage in which each element of the training group is employed only once; the parameters are then updated using function $J_p[n]$ which depends on a single training pair in time. Initial parameters can also be determined in accordance with the expert linguistic rules, or be chosen in a such a way that the corresponding set membership functions evenly cover the input-output space [11].

5   Architecture of the Neuro-Fuzzy Controller System

Fuzzy control system employs the fuzzy sets shown in Fig. 6. Particularly, Fig. 6a presents a fuzzy sigmoid set for modeling positive values of the universe of discourse; in contrast, Fig. 6b represents negative values for error $e[n]$ and the control action $u[n]$.

It is also considered the fuzzy sets in Fig. 6, as well as the controller general structure given by Eq. (9), the Fig. 7 shows the proposed fuzzy controller. Controller output can be calculated as:

$$u[n] = \sum_{i=1}^{M} \sum_{j=1}^{N} v_{ij} \mu_{ij}(x_i) \tag{26}$$

For the implementation case is taken $M = 5$ and $N = 2$; additionally, $x_i \in \{u[n-1], u[n-2], e[n], e[n-1], e[n-2], \}$. In this way each input x_i can define a function f_i as follows:

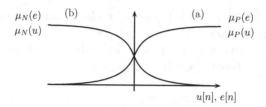

Fig. 6. Sigmoid fuzzy sets.

$$f_i = \sum_{j=1}^{2} v_{ij}\mu_{ij}(x_i) = v_{i1}\mu_{i1}(x_i) + v_{i2}\mu_{i2}(x_i) \tag{27}$$

On the other hand, the membership function $\mu_{ij}(x_i)$ is:

$$\mu_{ij}(x_i) = \frac{1}{1 + e^{-\sigma_{ij}(x_i - \gamma_{ij})}} = \left(1 + e^{-\sigma_{ij}(x_i - \gamma_{ij})}\right)^{-1} \tag{28}$$

The set of controller parameters corresponds to $H_c = h_{ij} \in \{v_{ij}, \sigma_{ij}, \gamma_{ij}\}$.

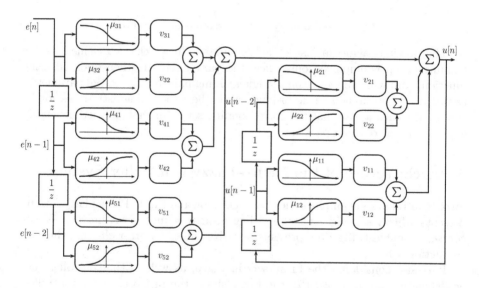

Fig. 7. Neuro-fuzzy system used for control.

5.1   Controller Training

To establish the controller training equations the performance function is:

$$J_c = \frac{1}{2}\left(r[n] - y_s[n]\right)^2 \tag{29}$$

The equation for error is $e[n] = r[n] - y_s[n]$; meanwhile, the equation for the fuzzy model plant corresponds to:

$$y_s[n] = f_p(y_s[n-1], y_s[n-2], u[n], u[n-1], u[n-2]) \tag{30}$$

for practical a manipulation $w_r \in \{y_s[n-1], y_s[n-2], u[n], u[n-1], u[n-2]\}$. Taking into account the architecture for the controller (Fig. 7), and the expressions to f_i (Eq. 27), the controller dynamics is given by:

$$u[n] = f_1(u[n-1]) + f_2(u[n-2]) + f_3(e[n]) + f_4(e[n-1]) + f_5(e[n-2]) \tag{31}$$

The variation of the plant in function of the controller parameters is:

$$\frac{dy_s[n]}{dH_c} = \frac{d}{dH_c} f_p(y_s[n-1], y_s[n-2], u[n], u[n-1], u[n-2]) \tag{32}$$

The respective variation of error $e[n]$ for the controller parameter H_c is:

$$\frac{de[n]}{dH_c} = -\frac{dy_s[n]}{dH_c} \tag{33}$$

The derivative of y_s respect to controller parameters H_c is:

$$\frac{dy_s}{dH_c} = y_1 \sum_{r=1}^{P} P_{r1} \frac{dw_r}{dH_c} + y_2 \sum_{r=1}^{P} P_{r2} \frac{dw_r}{dH_c} + y_3 \sum_{r=1}^{P} P_{r3} \frac{dw_r}{dH_c} + \ldots \tag{34}$$

reorganizing:

$$\frac{dy_s}{dH_c} = \left(\sum_{l=1}^{Q} y_l P_{1l}\right) \frac{dw_1}{dH_c} + \left(\sum_{l=1}^{Q} y_l P_{2l}\right) \frac{dw_2}{dH_c} + \left(\sum_{l=1}^{Q} y_l P_{3l}\right) \frac{dw_3}{dH_c} + \ldots \tag{35}$$

where:

$$P_{rl} = \frac{d\mu_{rl}(w_r)}{dw_r} \prod_{\substack{k=1 \\ k \neq r}}^{P} \mu_{kl}(w_k) \tag{36}$$

and

$$\frac{d\mu_{rl}(w_r)}{dw_r} = -2e^{-\left(\frac{w_r - \delta_{rl}}{\rho_{rl}}\right)^2} \frac{w_r - \delta_{rl}}{\rho_{rl}^2} \tag{37}$$

Using C_r from Eq. (38) allows to establish Eq. (40).

$$C_r = \sum_{l=1}^{Q} y_l P_{rl} \tag{38}$$

Likewise, the variation of the control action $u[n]$ respect to h_{ij} is:

$$\frac{du[n]}{dh_{ij}} = \frac{df_1(e[n])}{dh_{ij}} + \frac{df_2(e[n-1])}{dh_{ij}} + \frac{df_3(e[n-2])}{dh_{ij}} + \frac{df_4(u[n-1])}{dh_{ij}} + \frac{df_5(u[n-2])}{dh_{ij}}$$

As shown, the gradient parameters need to be calculated in function of the plant and the controller as well. The equations for training parameters are:

$$\frac{de[n]}{dh_{ij}} = -\frac{dy_s}{dh_{ij}} \tag{39}$$

$$\frac{dy_s[n]}{dh_{ij}} = C_1\frac{dw_1}{dh_{ij}} + C_2\frac{dw_2}{dh_{ij}} + C_3\frac{dw_3}{dh_{ij}} + C_4\frac{dw_4}{dh_{ij}} + C_5\frac{dw_5}{dh_{ij}} \tag{40}$$

$$\frac{du[n]}{dh_{ij}} = \frac{df_1(x_1)}{dh_{ij}} + \frac{df_2(x_2)}{dh_{ij}} + \frac{df_3(x_3)}{dh_{ij}} + \frac{df_4(x_4)}{dh_{ij}} + \frac{df_5(x_5)}{dh_{ij}} \tag{41}$$

In (41) using $l = 1, 2, .., 5$ and considering Eq. (27), if $l \neq i$ then:

$$\frac{df_l(x_l)}{dh_{ij}} = \left[\frac{d}{dx_l}(v_{l1}\mu_{l1}(x_l)) + \frac{d}{dx_l}(v_{l2}\mu_{l2}(x_l))\right]\frac{dx_l}{dh_{ij}} \tag{42}$$

Additionally, if $l = i$ then:

$$\frac{df_i(x_i)}{dh_{i1}} = F_{h_{i1}} + \left(K_{h_{i1}} + \frac{d}{dx_i}(v_{i2}\mu_{i2}(x_i))\right)\frac{dx_i}{dh_{i1}} \tag{43}$$

$$\frac{df_i(x_i)}{dh_{i2}} = F_{h_{i2}} + \left(\frac{d}{dx_i}(v_{i1}\mu_{i1}(x_i)) + K_{h_{i2}}\right)\frac{dx_i}{dh_{i2}} \tag{44}$$

where:

$$F_{v_{ij}} = \left(1 + e^{-\sigma_{ij}(x_i - \gamma_{ij})}\right)^{-1} \tag{45}$$

$$F_{\sigma_{ij}} = -v_{ij}\left(1 + e^{-\sigma_{ij}(x_i - \gamma_{ij})}\right)^{-2}e^{-\sigma_{ij}(x_i - \gamma_{ij})}(\gamma_{ij} - x_i) \tag{46}$$

$$F_{\gamma_{ij}} = -v_{ij}\left(1 + e^{-\sigma_{ij}(x_i - \gamma_{ij})}\right)^{-2}e^{-\sigma_{ij}(x_i - \gamma_{ij})}\sigma_{ij} \tag{47}$$

$$K_{v_{ij}} = v_{ij}\left(1 + e^{-\sigma_{ij}(x_i - \gamma_{ij})}\right)^{-2}e^{-\sigma_{ij}(x_i - \gamma_{ij})}\sigma_{ij} \tag{48}$$

$$K_{\sigma_{ij}} = v_{ij}\left(1 + e^{-\sigma_{ij}(x_i - \gamma_{ij})}\right)^{-2}e^{-\sigma_{ij}(x_i - \gamma_{ij})}\sigma_{ij} \tag{49}$$

$$K_{\gamma_{ij}} = v_{ij}\left(1 + e^{-\sigma_{ij}(x_i - \gamma_{ij})}\right)^{-2}e^{-\sigma_{ij}(x_i - \gamma_{ij})}\sigma_{ij} \tag{50}$$

Taking α as the learning rate, the equations for parameters updating are:

$$v_{ij}[k+1] = v_{ij}[k] - \alpha\frac{de[n]}{dv_{ij}} \tag{51}$$

$$\sigma_{ij}[k+1] = \sigma_{ij}[k] - \alpha\frac{de[n]}{d\sigma_{ij}} \tag{52}$$

$$\gamma_{ij}[k+1] = \gamma_{ij}[k] - \alpha\frac{de[n]}{d\gamma_{ij}} \tag{53}$$

6   Neuro-Fuzzy Control for a Permanent Magnet Synchronous Generator

Control system implementation requires data shown in Fig. 8(a), which respectively corresponds to input $u[n]$ and output $y[n]$ for a permanent magnet synchronous generator, as previously considered in [6]. These data allow the identification of a dynamic model through the use of a neuro-fuzzy system. The results obtained for the plant identification appears in Fig. 8(b).

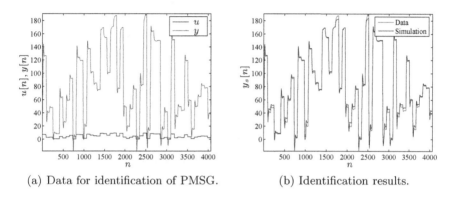

(a) Data for identification of PMSG.   (b) Identification results.

Fig. 8. Data for identification of PMSG dynamic model and identification results.

Furthermore, considering different reference values $r \in \{160, 120, 80, 40\}$ takes place the training of the neuro-fuzzy controller; in that way, the results are shown in Figs. 9(a), (b) and 10. Figure 9(a) exhibits the output after the optimization process. Subsequently, Fig. 9(b) shows the value of control signal; finally, Fig. 10 displays the values of the objective function.

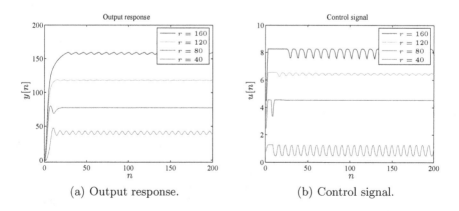

(a) Output response.   (b) Control signal.

Fig. 9. Output response $y[n]$ and control signal $u[n]$.

In Figs. 9(a) and (b) it is observable different behaviors in the system for the reference values considered prevailing an oscillatory behavior in steady state. In the same way, Fig. 10 also displays different behaviors in the algorithm convergence during the training process.

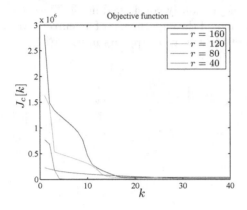

Fig. 10. Convergence for objective function J_c.

7   Conclusions

This document displayed the implementation of a neuro-fuzzy system to velocity control for a permanent magnet synchronous generator. Fuzzy systems allow the establishment of a structure to both the identification of the plant and controller. In these systems, the parameters are first optimized for plant identification and later for the controller adjustment.

The references here considered show different behaviors in both output signal and the convergence for controller training. In this way it is important the data used for plant identification.

Acknowledging the existence of different behaviors for the references considered, this control system can be accompanied including a real time adaptive scheme for controller training.

References

1. Dugan, R., McDermott, T., Ball, G.: Planning for distributed generation. IEEE Ind. Appl. Mag. **7**, 80–88 (2001)
2. Piagi, P., Lasseter, R.: Microgrid: a conceptual solution. In: Proceedings of the Power Electronics Specialists Conference, vol. 6, pp. 4285–4290 (2004)
3. Chen, J., Wu, H., Sun, M., Jiang, W., Cai, L., Guo, C.: Modeling and simulation of directly driven wind turbine with permanent magnet synchronous generator. In: IEEE Innovative Smart Grid Technologies-Asia (ISGT Asia) (2012)

4. Patil, k., Mehta, B.: Modeling and simulation of variable speed wind turbine with direct drive permanent magnet synchronous generator. In: International Conference on Green Computing Communication and Electrical Engineering (ICGCCEE) (2014)
5. Nguyen, H., Prasad, N., Walker, C., Walker, E.: A First Course in Fuzzy and Neural Control. Chapman & Hall/CRC, London (2003)
6. Espitia, H., González, G.: Identification of a permanent magnet synchronous generator using neuronal networks. In: IEEE Workshop on Engineering Applications (WEA), pp. 1–5 (2015)
7. Patil, K., Mehta, B.: Modeling and control of variable speed wind turbine with permanent magnet synchronous generator. In: International Conference on Advances in Green Energy (ICAGE), 17–18 December 2014 (2014)
8. Yin, M., Li, G., Zhou, M., Zhao, C.: Modeling of the wind turbine with a permanent magnet synchronous generator for integration. In: IEEE Power Engineering Society General Meeting, pp. 1–6 (2007)
9. Li, Y., Zhao, X., Jiao, L.: A nonlinear system identification approach based on neuro-fuzzy Networks. In: Proceedings of ICSP (2000)
10. Morales, L.: Estudio y evaluación del método de defuzificación basado en relaciones booleanas (DBR) aplicado a las redes neuro-difusas, para la identificación de sistemas no lineales. Proyecto de grado en Ingeniería Electrónica, Universidad Distrital Francisco José de Caldas (2009)
11. Wang, L.: A Course in Fuzzy Systems and Control. Prentice Hall, Englewood Cliffs (1997)

A Fuzzy Linear Fractional Programming Approach to Design of Distribution Networks

Eduyn López-Santana[1]([⊠]) [iD], Carlos Franco[2] [iD],
and Juan Carlos Figueroa-García[1] [iD]

[1] Universidad Distrital Francisco José de Caldas, Bogotá, Colombia
{erlopezs,jcfigueroag}@udistrital.edu.co
[2] Universidad del Rosario, Bogotá, Colombia
carlosa.franco@urosario.edu.co

Abstract. This paper studies the distribution network design problem considering the uncertain information in the demand, capacities, costs and prices in a multi-product environment and multiple periods. We consider a fractional objective function that consist in maximize the ratio between total profit and total cost. We use a model that integrates a facility location problem with a distribution network problem with fuzzy constraints, technological coefficients, and costs. To solve the problem, we use a method that transform the fuzzy linear fractional programming model in an equivalent multi-objective linear fractional programming problem to calculate the upper, middle and lower bounds of the original problem.

Keywords: Fuzzy linear fractional programming
Linear fractional programming · Distribution network · Fuzzy sets

1 Introduction

The distribution network design (DND) problem seeks to meet the demand for a set of customers using a set of available resources from a set of warehouses and supply these warehouses from a set of available factories. The problem consists in selecting the best raw according the distance, time, costs of freight, among other aspects, [1].

In general, the literature about this problem assumes that the information of costs, capacities and demands are known and deterministic, however, the uncertainty of the information is a real-world feature in many situations and consider it could be help to deal with better decisions [2].

In this paper, we study the DNP problem considering the uncertainty in the costs, prices, capacities and demand. In addition, we consider the maximization of the ratio between profits and costs as the objective function. Thus, we have a fuzzy linear fractional programming (FLFP) problem and to solve we use an equivalent multi-objective linear fractional programming problem to calculate the upper, middle and lower bounds of the FLFP problem.

The reminder of this paper is organized as follows: Sect. 2 presents a background and the problem statement. Section 3 describe a brief description of FLFP model.

© Springer Nature Switzerland AG 2018
J. C. Figueroa-García et al. (Eds.): WEA 2018, CCIS 915, pp. 102–113, 2018.
https://doi.org/10.1007/978-3-030-00350-0_9

Section 4 state the FLFP model to DND and an example is presented in Sect. 5. Finally, Sect. 6 shows the conclusions and states some research lines for future works.

2 Background and Problem Statement

In the DND problem is given a set of possible locations of production factories and warehouses (or distribution centers) with production and storage capacities, respectively. Then, the problem consists in to determine the best location of a given number of factories and warehouses to meet the demand of a set of customers maximizing the ration between the profits and costs associated with the opening factories and warehouses and the distribution of products from factories to end customer's sites. On the other hand, it determines how many products should be and store in factories and warehouses, respectively. In most the problems studied are assumed to be the information of costs, profits, capacities, and demands are known and deterministic. We consider that this information is imprecise and could be modeled as triangular fuzzy numbers.

The DNP problem has been widely studied in the literature [3–7]. This seeks how to set up a distribution network that consists of an integrated system of localization and distribution considering different facilities (stages) like factories, warehouses, centers of consumption and multiple products and periods Within a planning horizon. in a distribution network, warehouses act as intermediary nodes between suppliers and their points of sale, therefore in these you can store products in inventory to supply future demands.

Similar problems have been analyzed in works such as [8–12]. The simplest methods address the problem of logistical networks where the parameters used in the model are deterministic and it is possible to formulate problems of whole linear programming, given the conditions of opening of plants and warehouses. A solution method for the discrete DC-based problem was published in 2007 [3], in the problem the configuration of the network is made for emerging markets or new markets. To use the DC technique Programming, is reformulated a linear problem and then, it solves multiple linear problems until you get the right solution.

López-Santana et al. [1] developed a model that involves multiple products and demand under uncertainty for the DND problem. They propose a fuzzy linear programming model to solve the problem. There are several models have been proposed for optimization under uncertainty and a variety of algorithms have been developed and used successfully in many applications [13–16].

Similar problems with demand under uncertainty have been worked by [17] in which the demand has a stochastic behavior described by a probability density function and solved with stochastic programming. Bread and Nagi [18] use an approximation by stochastic programming and a solution heuristic for this problem.

Finally there are models that involve uncertainty by using fuzzy logic given the difficulty of programming stochastic, by applying fuzzy sets and numbers to handle uncertainty in some parameters of a linear programming model [19].

3 Fuzzy Linear Fractional Programming (FLFP)

We consider a linear fractional programming model with fuzzy constraints and fuzzy objective function based in [19]. The FLFP problem may be written as:

$$\max \widetilde{Z} = \frac{\sum \widetilde{c}_j x_j + \widetilde{\alpha}_j}{\sum \widetilde{d}_j x_j + \widetilde{\beta}_j} \tag{1}$$

Subject to

$$\sum \widetilde{a}_{ij} x_j \leq \widetilde{b}_i, \ i = 1, 2, \ldots, m, \tag{2}$$

$$x_j \geq 0, j = 1, 2, \ldots, n. \tag{3}$$

We assume that, $\widetilde{c}, \widetilde{\alpha}, \widetilde{d}, \widetilde{\beta}, \widetilde{a}$, and $\widetilde{b}$ are triangular fuzzy numbers. Let $r \in (0, 1]$ be the grade of satisfaction associated with the fuzzy constraints of the problem. According with [19], the fuzzy constraints (2) are to be understood with respect to the ranking relation. Thus, for $r \in (0, 1]$, the feasible set of the FLFP problem can be described as $S_r = \left\{ x | x \in R^n, x > 0, \sum a_{ijr}^L x_{jr} \leq b_{ir}^L, \sum a_{ijr}^M x_{jr} \leq b_{ir}^M, \sum a_{ijr}^U x_{jr} \leq b_{ir}^U, \forall i, j \right\}$.

Then, a vector $x \in S_r$ is called r–feasible solution of FLFP problem and is an optimal solution of the FLFP problem, if there does not exist any $x \in S_r$, such that $\widetilde{Z}(x^*) \leq_r \widetilde{Z}(x)$.

Let x be the acceptable optimal solution of the FLFP problem. Then the corresponding objective value $\widetilde{Z}(x) = [Z^L(x), Z^M(x), Z^U(x)]$ is called acceptable optimal value of the FLFP problem. The method proposed by [19] are stated as follows:

1. Formulate the real-life problem as a FLFP problem as (1) to (3). We assume that all fuzzy numbers are triangular. Any triangular fuzzy numbers can be represented by $\widetilde{a}_{ij} = \left(s_{ij}, l_{ij}, r_{ij} \right)$, $\widetilde{b} = (t_i, u_i, v_i)$, $\widetilde{c}_j = \left(k_j, m_j, n_j \right)$, $\widetilde{d}_j = \left(f_j, g_j, p_j \right)$, $\widetilde{\alpha}_j = \left(q_{j1}, q_{j2}, q_{j3} \right)$, $\widetilde{\beta}_j = \left(r_{j1}, r_{j2}, r_{j3} \right)$ for all i, j. Then the problem obtained in Step 1 may be written as:

$$\max \widetilde{Z} = \frac{\sum \left(k_j, m_j n_j \right) x_j + \left(q_{j1}, q_{j2}, q_{j3} \right)}{\sum \left(f_j, g_j, p_j \right) x_j + \left(r_{j1}, r_{j2}, r_{j3} \right)} \tag{4}$$

Subject to

$$\sum \left(s_{ij}, l_{ij}, r_{ij} \right) x_j \leq (t_i, u_i, v_i), \ i = 1, 2 \ldots, m, \tag{5}$$

$$x_j \geq 0, j = 1, 2, \ldots, n. \tag{6}$$

2. To transform both the objective function and constraints into its equivalent crisp problem (a crisp problem could be stated as a mathematical programming model without the fuzzy information). Then the problem may be written as follows:

$$\max \frac{\sum k_j x_j + q_1,\ \sum (m_j - k_j) x_j + (q_2 - q_1),\ \sum (n_j + k_j) x_j + (q_1 + q_3)}{\sum f_j x_j + r_1,\ \sum (g_j - f_j) x_j + (r_2 - r_1),\ \sum (p_j + f_j) x_j + (r_1 + r_3)} \quad (7)$$

Subject to

$$\sum s_{ij} x_j \leq t_i,\ i = 1, 2 \ldots, m, \quad (8)$$

$$\sum (l_{ij} - s_{ij}) x_j \leq (u_i - t_i),\ i = 1, 2, \ldots, m, \quad (9)$$

$$\sum (r_{ij} + s_{ij}) x_j \leq (v_i + t_i),\ i = 1, 2, \ldots, m, \quad (10)$$

$$x_j \geq 0,\ j = 1, 2, \ldots \ldots, n. \quad (11)$$

3. The FLFP problem is reduced into an equivalent tri-objective programming (TOP) problem as:

$$\max \left\{ \frac{\sum k_j x_j + q_1}{\sum f_j x_j + r_1}, \frac{\sum (m_j - k_j) x_j + (q_2 - q_1)}{\sum (g_j - f_j) x_j + (r_2 - r_1)}, \frac{\sum (n_j + k_j) x_j + (q_1 + q_3)}{\sum (p_j + f_j) x_j + (r_1 + r_3)} \right\} \quad (12)$$

Subject to constrains (8) to (11).
4. Formulate the following model for obtaining lower bounds $Z^L(x), Z^M(x)$ and $Z^U(x)$ of the objective value as follows:

$$(\text{LFP}) \max Z^L = \frac{\sum k_j x_j + q_1}{\sum f_j x_j + r_1} \quad (13)$$

$$(\text{MFP}) \max Z^M = \frac{\sum (m_j - k_j) x_j + (q_2 - q_1)}{\sum (g_j - f_j) x_j + (r_2 - r_1)} \quad (14)$$

$$(\text{UFP}) \max Z^U = \frac{\sum (n_j + k_j) x_j + (q_1 + q_3)}{\sum (p_j + f_j) x_j + (r_1 + r_3)} \quad (15)$$

5. The above problems (LFP), (MFP), (UFP) are crisp linear fractional programming problem subject to constrains (8) to (11), which can be solved by transformation of Charnes and Cooper [20] that consists in given a linear fraction as:

$$\max z = \frac{\sum c_j x_j + \alpha}{\sum d_j x_j + \beta} \quad (16)$$

Subject to

$$\sum a_{ij} x_j \leq b_i,\ i = 1, 2, \ldots, m, \quad (17)$$

$$x_j \geq 0,\ j = 1, 2, \ldots, n. \quad (18)$$

The transformation $x_j' = tx_j$ and $\sum d_j x_j + \beta = t$, with a variable $t \geq 0$ transform the problem in a linear programming model as:

$$\max z = \sum c_j x_j' + \alpha t \tag{19}$$

Subject to

$$\sum a_{ij} x_j' - b_i t \leq 0, i = 1, 2, \ldots, m, \tag{20}$$

$$\sum d_j x_j' + \beta t = 1 \tag{21}$$

$$x_j \geq 0, j = 1, 2, \ldots, n. \tag{22}$$
$$t \geq 0$$

This equivalent linear programming model is solved with traditional methods.
6. The solutions could be stated and obtain the optimal solutions of $\tilde{Z} = (Z^L, Z^M, Z^U)$.

4 A FFLP Model to Design Distribution Networks

Our model for the DND problem is based on [1] where a dedicated system to manufacturing of different products for which is considered some possible locations of your production factories and a series of distribution centers where your products will be stored before being transported to the final customers. On the other hand, you should evaluate the type of technology for factory, which has different consumptions and costs. Also, in the warehouse it is necessary to select the most appropriate technology that ensures adequate storage, since the products must be subject to certain conditions of storage. As main assumption of this problem consists in defining as initial condition the selected factories and stores since the model proposed by [1] use binary variables, but our approach does not consider this feature.

The sets are defined as follows:

- L is the product set, indexed in $l = 1 \ldots L$
- I is the set of factories, indexed in $i = 1 \ldots I$
- J is the set of warehouses, indexed in $j = 1 \ldots J$
- K Is the set of sale points, Indexed in $k = 1 \ldots K$
- P is the type of technology of each factory, Indexed in $p = 1 \ldots P$
- Q is the type of technology of each store, indexed in $q = 1 \ldots Q$
- T is the set of periods, indexed in $t = 1 \ldots T$

The parameters are stated as follows:

- M_{ipt}: Maximum capacity matrix (available hours) for the factory i with technology p in the period t.
- V_{jqt}: Maximum Capacity matrix (Available hours) for the distribution center j with technology q in the period t.

- r_{lp}: portion of technology consuming the product lp roduced in a factory with one of the technology p (in hours per unit of product).
- s_{lq}: portion of technology consuming the product l stored in a distribution center with one of the technology q (in hours per unit of product).
- g_{ip}: fixed cost associated with factory opening i with the type of technology p.
- f_{jq}: fixed cost associated with the opening of the distribution center j with the type of technology q.
- c_{ijlp}: Unit cost associated with product type l produced and shipped from a factory i with a technology Q to a distribution center j.
- b_{jklq}: Unit cost associated with product type l stored and shipped from the distribution center j with a technology q to a point of demand k.
- h_{jl}: unit cost of inventory for the product l in the Warehouse j.
- ρ_l: Unit profit associated with a product type l.
- D_{klt}: demand for a point of sale k of the type of product l in the period t.

The decision variables are:

- X_{ijlpt}: Quantity in units shipped from the factory i with technology p to the warehouse j of the product l in period t.
- Y_{jklqt}: Quantity in units shipped from warehouse j with technology q to the point of sale k of the product l in the period t.
- W_{jlt}: Inventory at the end of the period t of the product l in the Warehouse j.

The linear fractional programming model is stated as follows:

$$\max Z = \frac{\mathcal{J}}{\mathcal{C}} \tag{23}$$

$$\mathcal{J} = \sum_{t \in T} \sum_{j \in J} \sum_{k \in K} \sum_{l \in L} \sum_{q \in Q} \rho_l Y_{jklqt} \tag{24}$$

$$\mathcal{C} = \sum_{t \in T} \sum_{i \in I} \sum_{j \in J} \sum_{l \in L} \sum_{p \in P} c_{ijlp} X_{ijlpt} + \sum_{t \in T} \sum_{j \in J} \sum_{k \in K} \sum_{l \in L} \sum_{q \in Q} b_{jklq} Y_{jklqt}$$
$$+ \sum_{t \in T} \sum_{j \in J} \sum_{l \in L} h_{jl} W_{jlt} + \sum_{i \in I} \sum_{p \in P} g_{ip} + \sum_{j \in Q} \sum_{q \in Q} f_{jq} \tag{25}$$

subject to:

$$\sum_{j \in J} \sum_{l \in L} r_{lp} * X_{ijlpt} \leq M_{ip} \quad \forall i \in I, \forall p \in P, \forall t \in T \tag{26}$$

$$\sum_{k \in K} \sum_{l \in L} s_{lq} * Y_{jklqt} \leq V_{jqt} \quad \forall j \in J; \forall q \in Q; \forall t \in T \tag{27}$$

$$W_{jlt} = W_{j,l,t-1} + \sum_{i \in I} \sum_{p \in P} X_{ijlpt} - \sum_{k \in K} \sum_{q \in Q} Y_{jklqt} \quad \forall j \in J; \forall l \in L; \forall t \in T \tag{28}$$

$$W_{jlt} = W_{j,l0} + \sum_{i \in I} \sum_{p \in P} X_{ijlpt} - \sum_{k \in K} \sum_{q \in Q} Y_{jklqt} \quad \forall j \in J; \forall l \in L; t = 1 \tag{29}$$

$$\sum_{j \in J} \sum_{q \in Q} Y_{jklqt} \leq D_{klt} \quad \forall k \in K; \forall l \in L; \forall t \in T \tag{30}$$

$$\begin{aligned}
X_{ijlpt} &\geq 0 \quad \forall i \in I; \forall j \in J; \forall l \in L; \forall p \in P; \forall t \in T \\
Y_{jklqt} &\geq 0 \quad \forall j \in J; \forall k \in K; \forall l \in L; \forall q \in Q; \forall t \in T \\
W_{jlt} &\geq 0 \quad \forall j \in J; \forall l \in L; \forall t \in T
\end{aligned} \tag{31}$$

The objective function (23) seeks to maximize the ration between the profit (24) and the total costs (25) of the distribution network. The constraints (26) and (27) refer to the fulfillment of the capacity of factories and distribution centers in each of the periods, respectively. Constraints (28) are product balance and inventories in each distribution center, for each product and each period. Constraints (29) are special case of (28) when $t = 1$, then this consider the initial inventory denoted by $W_{j,l0}$. Constraints (30) ensure that the demand for each customer, product and each period must meet. Constraints (31) refers to the nature of the decision variables.

For the model described in (23) to (31), all parameters are modeled as triangular fuzzy numbers in similar way of the parameters defined in Sect. 3. To solve the problem, we apply the steps defined in Sect. 3 to obtain the optimal lower bounds $Z^L(x), Z^M(x)$ and $Z^U(x)$.

5   Example of Application

The following example is presented to show the application of the proposed model and the solution approach. We consider 5 factories, 4 warehouses, 4 customers, 4 and 3 types of technology for factories and warehouses, respectively, 5 planning horizon periods. A single Type of product (although it can be extended to multiple products). The information of the parameters is described in the Tables 1, 2, 3, 4, 5, 6 and 7. The facility is taken the capacity as constant throughout the planning horizon. In addition, the profit is $\rho_{1t} = (100, 200, 250)$ for periods in the planning horizon.

Table 1. Consumption portion of technology (Hours/unit)

Factory				Store			
l,p	r_{lp}^M	r_{lp}^L	r_{lp}^U	l,q	s_{lq}^M	s_{lq}^L	s_{lq}^U
1, 1	0.969085	0.7462	1.15321	1, 1	0.918330	0.78058	1.02853
1, 2	0.389046	0.34625	0.50576	1, 2	0.913122	0.74876	1.08662
1, 3	0.858348	0.65234	1.04718	1, 3	0.994356	0.74577	1.13357
1, 4	0.928971	0.74318	1.11477				

Table 2. Capacities and fixed costs of stores

j, q	V_{jq}^M	V_{jq}^L	V_{jq}^U	f_{jq}^M	f_{jq}^L	f_{jq}^U
1, 1	4500	3735	5625	3650000	3029500	4015000
2, 1	3825	2677.5	4245.75	5600000	4480000	6160000
3, 1	4005	2963.7	4405.5	5600000	4424000	6552000
4, 1	4140	3270.6	5216.4	3400000	2958000	3978000
1, 2	3735	2950.65	4108.5	4300000	3569000	4988000
2, 2	4140	2898	4968	4200000	3276000	5166000
3, 2	3915	3484.35	4580.55	5150000	4532000	5716500
4, 2	3825	3327.75	4590	3650000	2591500	4343500
1, 3	4725	3543.75	5292	4450000	3827000	5740500
2, 3	4185	2971.35	4938.3	4900000	3724000	6125000
3, 3	4545	3636	5726.7	4800000	3792000	5568000

Table 3. Capacity and fixed cost of factories

i, p	M_{ip}^M	M_{ip}^L	M_{ip}^U	g_{ip}^M	g_{ip}^L	g_{ip}^U
1, 1	2000	1460	2500	3090000	2193900	3615300
2, 1	2800	2184	3388	3060000	2601000	3916800
3, 1	2250	2025	2812.5	3480000	2610000	4036800
4, 1	2475	2153.25	2846.25	3480000	2888400	4489200
5, 1	3000	2100	3810	3000000	2490000	3750000
1, 2	2000	1700	2400	2850000	2451000	3192000
2, 2	2175	1653	2414.25	3180000	2226000	3847800
3, 2	2125	1827.5	2741.25	2850000	2536500	3192000
4, 2	2400	1896	3048	3360000	2956800	4368000
5, 2	2275	1774.5	2752.75	3030000	2393700	3393600
1, 3	2225	1780	2692.25	3000000	2340000	3570000
2, 3	2000	1540	2360	3330000	2331000	3796200
3, 3	2675	1872.5	3263.5	3540000	2761200	4566600
4, 3	2250	1980	2902.5	3450000	2794500	4450500
5, 3	2900	2523	3451	3360000	2788800	4368000
1, 4	2200	1760	2596	3120000	2776800	3525600
2, 4	2975	2380	3599.75	2880000	2476800	3571200
3, 4	2475	2004.75	2747.25	3510000	2843100	4457700
4, 4	2900	2552	3654	2880000	2448000	3283200
5, 4	2225	1691	2536.5	3570000	2570400	4533900

Table 4. Cost of shipping from factory to warehouse

i,j,l	c^M_{ijlp}				c^L_{ijlp}				c^U_{ijlp}			
	1	2	3	4	1	2	3	4	1	2	3	4
1, 1, 1	47	59	48	57	40.42	44.25	38.88	49.59	55.93	74.93	55.68	74.1
2, 1, 1	47	50	55	34	39.01	40	47.3	28.9	59.69	55.5	61.05	39.44
3, 1, 1	50	57	38	41	41.5	49.59	33.44	32.39	57	69.54	42.56	47.15
4, 1, 1	29	41	27	59	25.23	32.8	21.87	43.66	37.7	52.48	30.24	65.49
5, 1, 1	43	49	39	56	35.26	43.12	30.03	39.2	53.75	55.86	47.97	68.32
1, 2, 1	31	40	55	55	26.35	31.2	44	47.85	37.2	52	60.5	62.15
2, 2, 1	35	27	30	35	30.8	19.44	24.9	26.6	44.45	34.56	38.7	45.15
3, 2, 1	55	53	43	57	42.35	47.17	31.82	42.18	64.35	60.42	49.02	73.53
4, 2, 1	39	44	37	37	28.86	38.72	31.08	32.56	45.63	49.28	46.62	46.62
5, 2, 1	38	41	43	32	30.78	33.62	34.83	25.6	49.4	52.07	48.16	38.4
1, 3, 1	25	46	58	53	21.5	34.96	49.3	39.22	29.75	57.5	66.7	58.3
2, 1, 3	46	43	43	39	40.94	38.27	36.98	30.42	55.66	54.18	49.88	46.02
3, 3, 1	60	33	52	35	42	27.39	38.48	27.3	69	37.95	58.24	40.95
4, 1, 3	57	44	55	45	41.61	31.24	40.15	40.05	70.11	48.4	69.85	56.25
5, 1, 3	50	26	39	40	44	23.14	31.2	33.6	56	31.98	43.68	47.2
1, 4, 1	52	43	58	31	36.92	36.98	46.98	26.66	62.92	48.16	73.08	35.65
2, 4, 1	33	35	56	52	24.09	30.45	50.4	39	36.96	39.55	69.44	58.24
3, 4, 1	59	55	27	44	43.07	48.95	22.68	31.24	70.21	65.45	32.67	56.76
4, 4, 1	30	40	48	25	21.6	33.2	34.56	18.5	35.1	47.2	60.96	30.75
5, 4, 1	47	30	54	27	33.37	23.1	48.6	20.25	61.1	38.1	59.4	29.97

Table 5. Cost of shipping from warehouse to client

j,k,l	t^M_{jkl}			t^L_{jkl}			t^U_{jkl}		
	1	2	3	1	2	3	1	2	3
1, 1, 1	27	23	27	21.87	20.24	20.25	30.78	25.53	34.02
2, 1, 1	38	25	40	30.4	21.75	28	41.8	31	46.8
3, 1, 1	44	46	33	36.08	40.48	27.72	50.6	59.34	39.93
4, 1, 1	20	36	32	15	27.36	28.48	24.2	43.92	36.8
1, 2, 1	21	26	38	18.27	18.98	26.98	27.3	33.28	45.98
2, 2, 1	42	46	39	33.18	33.12	30.03	54.6	58.88	47.97
3, 2, 1	28	23	24	23.8	18.86	20.88	35.56	29.67	30.24
4, 2, 1	37	46	32	28.86	32.66	23.68	44.4	58.42	36.48
1, 3, 1	40	37	23	35.6	27.75	20.47	45.6	45.88	28.52
2, 1, 3	36	27	45	27.36	22.68	31.5	39.6	33.75	52.65
3, 3, 1	22	41	27	17.6	29.52	19.17	24.42	51.25	34.29
4, 1, 3	48	25	25	39.84	20	18	54.72	31.25	27.75
1, 4, 1	36	38	40	25.92	27.36	35.2	42.84	44.46	47.6
2, 4, 1	42	36	46	37.38	25.2	37.26	52.92	42.12	57.5
3, 4, 1	30	22	46	25.5	17.38	41.4	33.6	27.06	51.06
4, 4, 1	36	47	36	29.16	40.42	27	42.48	52.17	44.64

Table 6. Demand in the planning horizon

k, l, t	D_{klt}^M	D_{klt}^L	D_{klt}^U	k, l, t	D_{klt}^M	D_{klt}^L	D_{klt}^U
1, 1, 1	931	765	1210	3, 1, 3	1149	989	1498
2, 1, 1	987	832	1273	4, 1, 3	1468	1367	1772
3, 1, 1	806	666	1175	1, 1, 4	1933	1831	2158
4, 1, 1	830	699	1200	2, 1, 4	1115	941	1401
1, 1, 2	1155	1001	1379	3, 1, 4	1089	947	1457
2, 1, 2	1270	1121	1525	4, 1, 4	1110	967	1436
3, 1, 2	760	572	1055	1, 1, 5	2287	2148	2582
4, 1, 2	1052	909	1363	2, 1, 5	2425	2240	2686
1, 1, 3	1323	1191	1582	3, 1, 5	951	771	1270
2, 1, 3	1670	1484	2040	4, 1, 5	1572	1390	1873

Table 7. Cost of inventory

j, l	h_{jl}^M	h_{jl}^L	h_{jl}^U
1, 1	11	9.02	12.65
2, 1	10	8.4	11.9
3, 1	10	8	11.7
4, 1	11	9.79	12.32

This problem was executed in Xpress-MP .8.4 on Windows 10 64-bit, with a processor Intel i5 3337 (2 × 1.8 GHz) y 6 GB of RAM. Figure 1 shows the result of the membership function of $\widetilde{Z}(x)$. The fuzzy optimal solution is $\widetilde{Z} = (Z^L, Z^M, Z^u) = (0.37382, 0.75764, 0.93456)$. This result gives a lower bound of the fuzzy optimal solutions for the DND problem and helps the decision makers to involve the uncertain information.

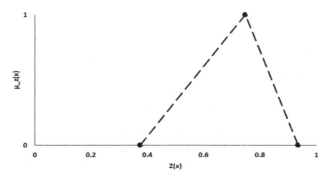

Fig. 1. Membership function of $\widetilde{Z}(x)$

6 Conclusions

This paper reviews the DND problem under uncertain information of costs, profits, capacities and demands. We consider a fractional objective function and solve the fuzzy linear fractional objective function with a method to transform the problem in an equivalent multi-objective linear fractional programming to obtain a lower bound of the fuzzy optimal solution. In addition, our proposed approach is easy to implement than other iterative methods that solve the similar problems in the literature.

This work generates possible futures as extended the approach to multi-objective linear fractional programming. Moreover, it is possible to apply the approach in real-world instances and compare with another approach likes stochastic programming.

Acknowledgments. We thank Fair Isaac Corporation (FICO) for providing us with Xpress-MP licenses under the Academic Partner Program subscribed with Universidad Distrital Francisco Jose de Caldas (Colombia).

References

1. Lopez-Santana, E., Méndez, G., Franco, C.: Diseño de cadenas de distribución con demanda bajo incertidumbre: una aproximación de programación lineal difusa. Ingeniería **18**, 68–84 (2013)
2. Shen, Z.-J.M., Daskin, M.S.: Trade-offs between customer service and cost in integrated supply chain design. Manuf. Serv. Oper. Manag. **7**, 188–207 (2005)
3. Nam, N.C., Le An, T.H., Tao, P.D.: A branch and bound algorithm based on DC programming and DCA for strategic capacity planning in supply chain design for a new market opportunity. In: Waldmann, K.-H., Stocker, U.M. (eds.) Operations Research Proceedings 2006. Operations Research Proceedings, vol. 2006, pp. 515–520. Springer, Heidelberg (2007). https://doi.org/10.1007/978-3-540-69995-8_82
4. Yin, Y., Kaku, I., Tang, J., Zhu, J.: Supply chain design using decision analysis. In: Yin, Y., Kaku, I., Tang, J., Zhu, J. (eds.) Data Mining. Decision Engineering, pp. 121–132. Springer, London (2011). https://doi.org/10.1007/978-1-84996-338-1_7
5. Velásquez, R., Teresa Melo, M., Nickel, S.: An LP-based heuristic approach for strategic supply chain design. In: Haasis, H.-D., Kopfer, H., Schönberger, J. (eds.) Operations Research Proceedings 2005. Operations Research Proceedings, vol. 2006, pp. 167–172. Springer, Heidelberg (2006). https://doi.org/10.1007/978-3-540-69995-8_82
6. Seidel, T.: Rapid supply chain design by integrating modelling methods. In: Parry, G., Graves, A. (eds.) Build To Order, pp. 277–295. Springer, London (2008). https://doi.org/10.1007/978-1-84800-225-8_16
7. Liao, S.-H., Hsieh, C.-L.: Integrated location-inventory retail supply chain design: a multi-objective evolutionary approach. In: Deb, K., et al. (eds.) SEAL 2010. LNCS, vol. 6457, pp. 533–542. Springer, Heidelberg (2010). https://doi.org/10.1007/978-3-642-17298-4_57
8. Yan, H., Yu, Z., Edwin Cheng, T.C.: A strategic model for supply chain design with logical constraints: formulation and solution. Comput. Oper. Res. **30**, 2135–2155 (2003)
9. Hammami, R., Frein, Y., Hadj-Alouane, A.B.: A strategic-tactical model for the supply chain design in the delocalization context: mathematical formulation and a case study. Int. J. Prod. Econ. **122**, 351–365 (2009)

10. Talluri, S., Baker, R.C.: A multi-phase mathematical programming approach for effective supply chain design. Eur. J. Oper. Res. **141**, 544–558 (2002)
11. Beamon, B.M.: Supply chain design and analysis. Int. J. Prod. Econ. **55**, 281–294 (1998)
12. Jayaraman, V., Ross, A.: A simulated annealing methodology to distribution network design and management. Eur. J. Oper. Res. **144**, 629–645 (2003)
13. Sahinidis, N.V.: Optimization under uncertainty: state-of-the-art and opportunities. In: Computers and Chemical Engineering, pp. 971–983 (2004)
14. Singh, A.R., Jain, R., Mishra, P.K.: Capacities-based supply chain network design considering demand uncertainty using two-stage stochastic programming. Int. J. Adv. Manuf. Technol. **69**, 1–8 (2013)
15. Selim, H., Ozkarahan, I.: A supply chain distribution network design model: an interactive fuzzy goal programming-based solution approach. Int. J. Adv. Manuf. Technol. **36**, 401–418 (2008)
16. Rao, K.N., Subbaiah, K.V., Singh, G.V.P.: Design of supply chain in fuzzy environment. J. Ind. Eng. Int. **9**, 1–11 (2013)
17. Georgiadis, M.C., Tsiakis, P., Longinidis, P., Sofioglou, M.K.: Optimal design of supply chain networks under uncertain transient demand variations. Omega **39**, 254–272 (2011)
18. Pan, F., Nagi, R.: Robust supply chain design under uncertain demand in agile manufacturing. Comput. Oper. Res. **37**, 668–683 (2010)
19. Das, S.K., Edalatpanah, S.A., Mandal, T.: A proposed model for solving fuzzy linear fractional programming problem: numerical point of view. J. Comput. Sci. **25**, 367–375 (2018)
20. Charnes, A., Cooper, W.W.: Programming with linear fractional functionals. Naval Res. Logist. Quart. **9**, 181–186 (1962)

Methods for Generating Contexts Based on Similarity Relations to Multigranulation

Dianne Arias[1] , Yaima Filiberto[1(✉)] , and Rafael Bello[2]

[1] Department of Computer Science, University of Camagüey, Camagüey, Cuba
{dianne.arias,yaima.filiberto}@reduc.edu.cu
[2] Department of Computer Science, University of Las Villas, Santa Clara, Cuba
rbellop@uclv.edu.cu

Abstract. Multigranulation is a new approach to the Rough Set Theory, where several separability relationships are used to obtain different granulations of the universe. The Multigranulation starts from the existence of different contexts or subsets of features to characterize the objects of the universe. This approach has been used to develop various learning techniques. It is usually part of the existence of these contexts. In this paper, a method for the generation of contexts from the construction of similarity relations is proposed. The proposed method has been tested in improving the efficiency of the k-NN method, using different data.

Keywords: Multigranulation · Contexts
Similarity relations

1 Introduction

The complete process of extracting knowledge from databases is known as KDD (Knowledge Discovery in Databases). This process includes various stages, ranging from the obtention of data to the application of the knowledge acquired in decision-making. Among those stages, there is what can be considered as the core of the KDD process and that consists in the extraction of knowledge from the data. This phase is crucial for obtaining appropriate results, and depends on the automated learning algorithm that is applied.

Machine Learning is a branch of Artificial Intelligence, whose objective is to develop techniques that allow creating programs that can learn in a similar way to what humans have done, that is, to learn by themselves; able to generalize behaviors from information stored in the form of examples [30]. It is, therefore, a process of induction of knowledge. Usually the examples are described by a set of features.

One of the most recent theories used for data analysis and construction of learning techniques is the Rough Set Theory (RST) [32,34]. RST has been used

© Springer Nature Switzerland AG 2018
J. C. Figueroa-García et al. (Eds.): WEA 2018, CCIS 915, pp. 114–123, 2018.
https://doi.org/10.1007/978-3-030-00350-0_10

to develop methods for the uncovering of rules [11,18,27,28,31,37,41] and the selection of attributes [8,10,12,35,44,45], among other problems of knowledge discovery. With this theory it is possible to treat both quantitative and qualitative data, and in particular it is useful to deal with the uncertainty caused by inconsistencies in the information; the inconsistency describes a situation in which there are two or more conflicting values to be assigned to a variable [4,33]. Among the advantages of the RST for data analysis is that it is based only on the original data and does not need any external information; no assumption about the data is necessary [40].

An important issue in the RST is the selection of feature (attributes) based on the concept of reduction. A reduct is a minimal set of attributes that preserves the partition of the universe and therefore the ability to perform classifications [25]. The use of reducts in the selection and reduction of feature has been studied by different authors, among them [1–3,6,7,17,23–25,32,43].

The RST is defined from a decision system $SD = (U, A \bigcup d)$, where U denotes the universe of objects, A is the set of predictive features and d the decision feature, and a relationship of separability. In classical RST, a relation of equivalence is used as a relation of separability, which makes it applicable when the domain of the feature is discrete. When there are continuous feature, two alternatives have usually been followed: discretize the data or use an extension of the theory. In the first case, the original information system is transformed into another one where the classical approach is applicable [38,39]. In the second case, the classic approach of the RST is extended by accepting that objects that are not inseparable but sufficiently close or similar can be grouped in the same class [42]; that is, a relation of similarity is used instead of an equivalence relation. Any subset of features $A_i \subseteq A$ allows to build an equivalence relation; however, it does not happen the same with the construction of the appropriate similarity relationship for an application domain. In [14,15] a method for constructing similarity relations is proposed.

Another extension of the RST is to use more than one separability relationship to perform the granulation of the universe, which is known as multigranulation [29,36]. In this case, from the set of predictive features A, two or more subsets A_1, ..., A_k, $A_i \subseteq A$, are formed of feature that allow defining the separability relation. These subsets of features are called contexts [22]. Based on this multigranulation approach, different techniques for the discovery of knowledge have been formulated.

Sometimes it is natural to define contexts from the application domain. In other cases it is not, which becomes a problem to solve to apply the techniques based on multigranulation. In this paper, a method for constructing contexts based on the technique for the construction of relations of similarity proposed in [14,15] is proposed.

2   Multigranulation in the Rough Set Theory

The granulation of the universe based on a simple granulation may be insufficient in some application domains. Based on this consideration, Qian et al. [36]

introduced multigranulation in the rough ensemble theory (MGRS) to apply more broadly the rough sets theory in practical applications, in the lower/upper approximations they are approximated by granular structures induced by multiple binary relations.

In Fig. 1 of the author Qian in [36], the bias region is the lower approximation of a set X obtained by a single granulation $P \bigcup Q$, which is expressed by the equivalence classes in the quotient set $U/(P \bigcup Q)$, and the shaded region is the lower approximation of X induced by two granulations $P + Q$, which is characterized by the equivalence classes in the quotient set U/P and the quotient set U/Q together.

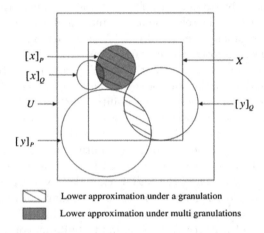

Lower approximation under a granulation
Lower approximation under multi granulations

Fig. 1. Difference between Pawlaks rough set model and MGRS.

From the point of view of the applications of the RST, the multigranulation in the RST is very desirable in many real applications, such as analysis of data from multiple sources, discovery of knowledge to from data with large dimensions and distributive information systems.

Since Qian in 2006 proposed multigranulation in the RST, the theoretical framework has been widely enriched, and many extensions of these models have been proposed and studied.

RS approaches based on multigranulation start from the existence of different granulations determined by the relationships $A_1, A_2, \ldots, A_m \subseteq A$. In all the papers of $RS + MG$ it is assumed that there are those A_i. But it is not clear who the A_i are. A variant is that each A_i is contexts (subsets of features) that can be clearly identified by the experts in the domain of application, this case is the least common and depends on the domain of application. Another variant would be to build them. This variant is more general, and in addition, it is very appropriate especially for domains with many predictive features. In the following section we propose a method with this purpose.

3   Method of Constructing Contexts in RS for the Case of Multigranulation

Be a decision system $DS = (U, A \cup d)$, where the domain of the feature in A and the domain of the decision feature d can be discrete or continuous values, from which the number of contexts is 30% of the total features of the dataset, then the amount of feature by context are compute in a random way, and the weight of the features that constitute each context is calculated with the weight calculation method $PSO + RST$ [13] and delete the features with a low weight until get the number of the feature generate by a random way. Finally the equal contexts are eliminated. Following the algorithm is described.

Algorithm 1. Pseudocode for PSO+RST+MG algorithm

---

1. Calculate the weights of features using PSO+RST method.
2. Generate set of contexts
   $$C = \{C_1 \dots C_{nc}\} | nc = (n * 30/100)$$
3. For each context:
   Calculate the number of feature randomly
   $$N_a = rand(n - 1) + 2$$
   Select the subset A_c with the N_a feture with the greatest weight
   $$C_i = \{A_c | A_c \subset A\}$$
4. Select of different context
   $$\forall C_i, C_j | C_i, C_j \exists C \wedge C_i \neq C_j$$

To evaluate the quality of the constructed contexts, the $k - NN$ method is used. The purpose is to show how using the contexts allows to increase the accuracy of the method.

Once these contexts are obtained with the weights calculated as described in the Algorithm 2, where the contexts C_i are used to make $k - NN$ assemblies as shown in the $Knn + PSO + RST + MG$ algorithm, where each object is classified taking into account each context and the final value of the classification is the statistical mode of classification value by context.

Algorithm 2. Pseudocode for k-NN+PSO+RST+MG algorithm

---

1. For each C_i
   Evaluate C_i using K-nn
2. For each object O_j calculate the class for each C_i using K-nn
   $$Cl = Cl_{ij}, Cl_{ij}, .., Cl_{nm}$$
3. Assign the statistical mode of the Cl set as the value of the object class O_j

---

Where n and m is number of features and objects respectively.
Then Fig. 2 shows graphically the result once applied the proposed method.

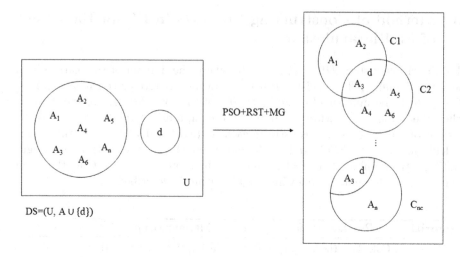

Fig. 2. PSO + RST + MG method

The method for calculating the weights is the *PSO + RST* that is shown below.

PSO + RST Algorithm:

Step 1: Initialize a population of particles with random positions and velocities in a D-dimensional space.

Step 2: For each particle, evaluate the quality measure of similarity using expression 1, in *D* Variables.

$$\max \rightarrow \left\{ \frac{\sum\limits_{\forall X \epsilon U} \varphi(x)}{|U|} \right\} \tag{1}$$

Step 3: Compare the quality measure of the current similarity of each particle with the quality measure of the similarity of its previous best position *pBest*. If the current value is better than *pBest*, then assign to *pBest* the current value, and $P_i = X_i$, that is, the current location becomes the best one so far.

Step 4: Identify the particle in the neighborhood with the greatest value for the quality of similarity measure and assign its index to the variable *g* and assign the best value of the quality measure of similarity to *m*.

Step 5: Adjust the speed and position of the particle according to Eqs. 2 and 3 (for each dimension)

$$\vartheta_i(t+1) = \alpha * \vartheta_i(t) + U(0, \varphi 1)(pBest(t) - x_i)$$
$$+ U(0, \varphi 2(gBest(t) - x_i) \tag{2}$$
$$x_i(t+1) = x_i(t)\vartheta_i(t+1) \tag{3}$$

Table 1. Datasets

Datasets	Instances	Feature	Contexts	Features average X contexts
Car	392	7	4	5
Schizo	104	14	4	6
Soybean-small	47	35	10	24
Hepatitis	155	19	5	15
Dermatology	358	34	8	18
Lung-cancer	32	56	16	25
Biomed	194	8	4	5
Analcaa-bankruptcy	50	6	3	4
Sponge	76	45	11	22
Tae	15	5	2	4

Step 6: Verify if the stop criterion is met (maximum number of iterations or if it takes five iterations without improving the quality measure of the global similarity (m)), if not, go to **Step 2:**.

4   Experimental Setup

We will apply the proposed methods to some datasets from the UCI Machine Learning repository (cars, schizo, soybean-small, hepatitis, Dermatology, lung-cancer, biomed, analcaa-bankruptcy, sponge, tae). The description of these datasets appears in Table 1.

The training and test sets were obtained, for the first 75% of the cases and for the second 25%, in a completely randomized way. Following this principle of random selection, the process was repeated ten times and ten training sets and ten test sets were obtained for each data set, in order to apply cross validation [9] for a better validation from the results. The comparative study of the results was performed using classification accuracy measure [26].

The parameters used in the experimentation, for the $PSO + RST + MG$ method were: TB = 33, NI = 100, ce1 = ce2 = 2 and the values of e1 and e2 for the function of similarity between attributes and for the function of similarity for the decision attribute were 0.74–0.94 and 1.0. The stop condition is: when 100 iterations are reached or when in five iterations the fitness value does not improve (measure quality similarity quality).

It is used as a $k - NN$ [46] classifier with $k = 1$ to make a comparison of the results obtained after the creation of the contexts of the proposed method $PSO + RST + MG$ with Bagging [5], Random Subspace [19] and AdaBoostM1 [16], which are ensembles that use the k-NN as the base algorithm, implemented

Table 2. Experimental setup for k-NN with $k = 1$

Dataset	AdaBoostM1	RandomSubSpace	Bagging	PSO+RST+MG
Car	73.98⊖	78.82⊖	73.99⊖	80.9⊕
Schizo	59.45⊖	60.45⊖	58.64⊖	66.2⊕
Soybean-small	100⊙	97.5⊖	100⊙	100⊙
Hepatitis	80.71⊖	82.63⊖	80.75⊖	82.7⊕
Dermatology	92.99⊖	95.25⊖	92.71⊖	96.4⊕
Lung-cancer	65⊖	68.33⊖	68.33⊖	74.8⊕
Biomed	89.71⊙	90.76⊖	89.71⊖	100⊕
Analcaa-bankruptcy	84⊖	86⊖	88⊖	92⊕
Sponge	92.32⊖	94.82⊖	93.57⊖	96.1⊕
Tae	61.67⊖	59.71⊖	62.33⊖	63.3⊕

Table 3. Average rankings of the algorithms (Friedman)

Algorithm	Ranking
AdaBoostM1	3.45
RandomSubSpace	2.55
Bagging	2.9
PSO + RST + MG	1.1

in the WEKA[1] tool and using the $k - NN$ as a classifier, in all cases. Table 2 shows the experimental results of the comparison between the algorithms.

In order to compare the results, a multiple comparison test is used to find the best algorithm. In Table 3 the results of the Friedman statistical test are shown. There can be observed that the best ranking is obtained by our proposal. Thus, ⊕ indicates that the accuracy is significantly better when $PSO + RST + MG$ method is used, ⊖ signifies that the accuracy is significantly worse and ⊙ signifies that there is no significant differences. Also the Iman-Davenport test was used [21]. The resulting p-value = 0.000012128664 $< \alpha$ (with 3 and 27° of freedom) indicates that there are indeed significant performance differences in the group.

There is a set of methods to increase the power of multiple test; they are called sequential methods, or post-hoc tests. In this case it was decided to use Holm [20] test to find algorithms significantly higher. $PSO + RST + MG$ - as the control method- conduct to pair wise comparisons between the control method and all others, and determine the degree of rejection of the null hypothesis. The results reported in Table 4 reject all null hypotheses whose p-value is lower than 0.05, hence confirming the superiority of the control method.

---

[1] Open source tool. Available under public licenses GNU in http://www.cs.waikato. ac.nz/ml/weka/.

Table 4. Post Hoc comparison Table for $\alpha = 0.05$ (FRIEDMAN)

i	Algorithm	$z = (R_0 - R_i)/SE$	p	Holm
3	AdaBoostM1	4.070319	0.000	Reject
2	Bagging	3.117691	0.002	Reject
1	RandomSubSpace	2.511474	0.012	Reject

5 Conclusion

In this work, a new method of generating contexts for multigranulation is proposed, this is based on the extended Rough Set Theory. The number of contexts for a decision system depends on the number of features of the decision system, the subset of features in each context is selected according to the weighs of the features. The weighs are computed using the method $PSO + RST$, proposed before by the authors. The contexts obtained were evaluated as ensembles using the $k - NN$ method as the base classifier; and these results are compared respect other methods, with positive results.

References

1. Bello, R., Nowe, A., Caballero, Y., Gómez, Y., Vrancx, P.: A model based on ant colony system and rough set theory to feature selection. In: Proceedings of the 7th Annual Conference on Genetic and Evolutionary Computation, pp. 275–276. ACM (2005)
2. Bello, R., Nowe, A., Gomezd, Y., Caballero, Y.: Using ACO and rough set theory to feature selection. WSEAS Trans. Inf. Sci. Appl. **2**(5), 512–517 (2005)
3. Bello, R., Puris, A., Falcón, R., Gómez, Y.: Feature selection through dynamic mesh optimization. In: Ruiz-Shulcloper, J., Kropatsch, W.G. (eds.) CIARP 2008. LNCS, vol. 5197, pp. 348–355. Springer, Heidelberg (2008). https://doi.org/10.1007/978-3-540-85920-8_43
4. Bosc, P., Prade, H.: Fuzzy set and possibility theory-based treatment of flexible queries and uncertain or imprecise databases. In: Uncertainty Management in Information Systems: From Needs to Solutions, p. 285 (1997)
5. Breiman, L.: Bagging predictors. Mach. Learn. **24**(2), 123–140 (1996)
6. Caballero, Y.: Aplicación de la teoría de los conjuntos aproximados en el preprocesamiento de los conjuntos de entrenamiento para algoritmos de aprendizaje automatizado. Departamento de Ciencias de la Computación, Santa Clara, Universidad Central "Marta Abreu" de la Villas (2007)
7. Carlin, U.S., Komorowski, J., Øhrn, A.: Rough set analysis of medical datasets and a case of patients with suspected acute appendicitis. In: Proceedings of Workshop on Intelligent Data Analysis in Medicine and Pharmacology. Citeseer (1998)
8. Degang, C., Changzhong, W., Qinghua, H.: A new approach to attribute reduction of consistent and inconsistent covering decision systems with covering rough sets. Inf. Sci. **177**(17), 3500–3518 (2007)
9. Demšar, J.: Statistical comparisons of classifiers over multiple data sets. J. Mach. Learn. Res. **7**(Jan), 1–30 (2006)

10. Düntsch, I., Gediga, G.: Rough set data analysis. In: Encyclopedia of Computer Science and Technology, vol. 43, no. 28, pp. 281–301 (2000)
11. Fan, Y.-N., Tseng, T.-L.B., Chern, C.-C., Huang, C.-C.: Rule induction based on an incremental rough set. Expert Syst. Appl. **36**(9), 11439–11450 (2009)
12. Fazayeli, F., Wang, L., Mandziuk, J.: Feature selection based on the rough set theory and expectation-maximization clustering algorithm. In: Chan, C.-C., Grzymala-Busse, J.W., Ziarko, W.P. (eds.) RSCTC 2008. LNCS (LNAI), vol. 5306, pp. 272–282. Springer, Heidelberg (2008). https://doi.org/10.1007/978-3-540-88425-5_28
13. Filiberto, Y.: Métodos de aprendizaje para dominios con datos mezclados basados en la teoría de los conjuntos aproximados extendida. Universidad Central de Las Villas (2012)
14. Yaima, F., Rafael, B., Yaile, C., Rafael, L.: Using PSO and RST to predict the resistant capacity of connections in composite structures. In: González, J.R., Pelta, D.A., Cruz, C., Terrazas, G., Krasnogor, N. (eds.) Nature Inspired Cooperative Strategies for Optimization (NICSO 2010), pp. 359–370. Springer, Heidelberg (2010). https://doi.org/10.1007/978-3-642-12538-6_30
15. Filiberto, Y., Caballero, Y., Larrua, R., Bello, R.: A method to build similarity relations into extended rough set theory. In: 2010 10th International Conference on Intelligent Systems Design and Applications (ISDA), pp. 1314–1319. IEEE (2010)
16. Freund, Y., Schapire, R.E.: Experiments with a new boosting algorithm. In: 13th International Conference on Machine Learning (1996)
17. Gomez, Y., Bello, R., Puris, A., García, M.M., Nowe, A.: Two step swarm intelligence to solve the feature selection problem. J. UCS **14**(15), 2582–2596 (2008)
18. Grzymala-Busse, J.W., Siddhaye, S.: Rough set approaches to rule induction from incomplete data. In: Proceedings of the IPMU, vol. 2, pp. 923–930 (2004)
19. Ho, T.K.: The random subspace method for constructing decision forests. IEEE Trans. Pattern Anal. Mach. Intell. **20**(8), 832–844 (1998)
20. Holm, S.: A simple sequentially rejective multiple test procedure. Scand. J. Stat. 65–70 (1979)
21. Iman, R.L., Davenport, J.M.: Approximations of the critical region of the Fbietkan statistic. Commun. Stat.-Theory Methods **9**(6), 571–595 (1980)
22. Intan, R., Mukaidono, M.: Multi-rough sets based on multi-contexts of attributes. In: Wang, G., Liu, Q., Yao, Y., Skowron, A. (eds.) RSFDGrC 2003. LNCS (LNAI), vol. 2639, pp. 279–282. Springer, Heidelberg (2003). https://doi.org/10.1007/3-540-39205-X_38
23. Jensen, R., Shen, Q.: Finding rough set reducts with ant colony optimization. In: Proceedings of the 2003 UK Workshop on Computational Intelligence, vol. 1, pp. 15–22 (2003)
24. Kohavi, R., Frasca B.: Useful feature subsets and rough set reducts. In: Third International Workshop on Rough Sets and Soft Computing, pp. 310–317 (1994)
25. Komorowski, J., Pawlak, Z., Polkowski, L., Skowron, A.: Rough sets: a tutorial. In: Rough Fuzzy Hybridization: A New Trend in Decision-making, pp. 3–98 (1999)
26. Kuncheva, L.I.: Combining Pattern Classifiers: Methods and Algorithms. Wiley, Hoboken (2004)
27. Lee, S., Propes, N., Zhang, G., Zhao, Y., Vachtsevanos, G.: Rough set feature selection and diagnostic rule generation for industrial applications. In: Alpigini, J.J., Peters, J.F., Skowron, A., Zhong, N. (eds.) RSCTC 2002. LNCS (LNAI), vol. 2475, pp. 568–571. Springer, Heidelberg (2002). https://doi.org/10.1007/3-540-45813-1_75

28. Li, P., Wang, X., Guan, Y.: Question classification with incremental rule learning algorithm based on rough set. J. Electron. Inf. Technol. **30**(5), 1127–1130 (2008)
29. Lin, G., Liang, J., Qian, Y.: Multigranulation rough sets: from partition to covering. Inf. Sci. **241**, 101–118 (2013)
30. Mitchell, T.: Machine learning, ed. science/engineering/math, portland (1997)
31. Øhrn, A., Komorowski, J., Skowron, A., Synak, P.: The design and implementation of a knowledge discovery toolkit based on rough sets-the rosetta system (1998)
32. Pal, S.K., Skowron, A.: Rough-Fuzzy Hybridization: A New Trend in Decision Making. Springer, New York (1999)
33. Parsons, S.: Current approaches to handling imperfect information in data and knowledge bases. IEEE Trans. Knowl. Data Eng. **8**(3), 353–372 (1996)
34. Pawlak, Z.: Rough sets. Int. J. Parallel Program. **11**(5), 341–356 (1982)
35. Pawlak, Z., Grzymala-Busse, J., Slowinski, R., Ziarko, W.: Rough sets. Commun. ACM **38**(11), 88–95 (1995)
36. Qian, Y., Liang, J., Yao, Y., Dang, C.: MGRS: a multi-granulation rough set. Inf. Sci. **180**(6), 949–970 (2010)
37. Sabu, M.K., Raju, G: Rule induction using rough set theory. an application in agriculture. In: 2011 International Conference on Computer, Communication and Electrical Technology (ICCCET), pp. 45–49. IEEE (2011)
38. Son, N.H., Hoa, N.S.: An application of discretization methods in control. In: Proceedings of the Workshop on Robotics, Intelligent Control and Decision Support Systems, pp. 47–52 (1999)
39. Son, N.H., Hoa, N.S.: Discretization of real value attributes for control problems. In: Workshop on Robotics, Intelligent Control and Decision Support Systems, PJWSTK, pp. 47–52 (1999)
40. Tay, F.E.H., Shen, L.: Economic and financial prediction using rough sets model. Eur. J. Oper. Res. **141**(3), 641–659 (2002)
41. Teoh, H.J., Cheng, C.-H., Chu, H.-H., Chen, J.-S.: Fuzzy time series model based on probabilistic approach and rough set rule induction for empirical research in stock markets. Data Knowl. Eng. **67**(1), 103–117 (2008)
42. Vanderpooten, D.: Similarity relation as a basis for rough approximations. Adv. Mach. Intell. Soft Comput. **4**, 17–33 (1997)
43. Wang, X., Yang, J., Teng, X., Xia, W., Jensen, R.: Feature selection based on rough sets and particle swarm optimization. Pattern Recognit. Lett. **28**(4), 459–471 (2007)
44. Wang, Y., Ma, L.: Feature selection for medical dataset using rough set theory. In: Proceedings of the 3rd WSEAS International Conference on Computer Engineering and Applications, pp. 68–72. World Scientific and Engineering Academy and Society (WSEAS) (2009)
45. Yao, Y.Y., Zhong, N.: An analysis of quantitative measures associated with rules. In: Zhong, N., Zhou, L. (eds.) PAKDD 1999. LNCS (LNAI), vol. 1574, pp. 479–488. Springer, Heidelberg (1999). https://doi.org/10.1007/3-540-48912-6_64
46. Zaldívar, J.M.: Estudio e incorporación de nuevas funcionalidades al k-NN workshop v1. 0. Computación. Camagüey, Universidad de Camagüey (2008)

Price Prediction with CNN and Limit Order Book Data

Jaime Niño[1]([✉]), Andrés Arévalo[1], Diego Leon[2], German Hernandez[1], and Javier Sandoval[2]

[1] Universidad Nacional de Colombia, Bogotá, Colombia
{jhninop,ararevalom,gjhernandezp}@unal.edu.co
[2] Universidad Externado de Colombia, Bogotá, Colombia
{diego.leon,javier.sandova}@uexternado.edu.col

Abstract. This work introduces how to use Limit Order Book Data (LOB) and transaction data for short-term forecasting of stock prices. LOB registers all trade intentions from market participants, as a result, it contains more market information that could enhance predictions. We will be using Deep Convolutional Neural Networks (CNN), which are good at pattern recognition on images. In order to accomplish the proposed task we will make an image-like representation of LOB and transaction data, which will feed up into the CNN, therefore it can recognize hidden patterns to classify Financial Time Series (FTS) in short-term periods. Data enclose information from 11 NYSE instruments, including stocks, ETF and ADR. We will present step by step methodology for encoding financial time series into an image-like representation. Results present an impressive performance, 74.15% in Directional Accuracy (DA).

Keywords: Short-term forecasting · Deep Learning
Convolutional Neural Networks · Limit Order Book
Pattern recognition

1 Introduction

In recent years developments in telecommunications, information technology and computer science have helped to transform Finance into a highly sophisticated scientific discipline capable to analyze huge flows of real time data. Large datasets and nonlinearities, data noisiness and complexity make Machine Learning (ML) techniques very appropriated to handle FTS analysis. As a result, vast number of literature reports Machine Learning applications for price prediction [5,7,10–12]. Works include Artificial Neural Networks, Support Vector Machines and Deep Learning. For this work, we use a Convolutional Neural Network to predict price movements. We will be working with both LOB and transaction (tick) data. As mentioned before, LOB data contains all traders intentions to negotiate an asset at a particular price and quantity at certain time t. LOB information is

© Springer Nature Switzerland AG 2018
J. C. Figueroa-García et al. (Eds.): WEA 2018, CCIS 915, pp. 124–135, 2018.
https://doi.org/10.1007/978-3-030-00350-0_11

richer than transaction data, which only records prices and quantities exchanged at certain time t. In order to use CNN, we represent both LOB and tick data as images. Results are very competitive when compare to other DL approaches reported in [2,4,8,13,16], with the advantage of using the same trained model for different assets.

This paper continues as follows: section two gives a brief summary of CNN, section three explains how LOB and tick data are transformed into images, section four explains full methodology from data acquisition up to image data classification, section five shows results and section six gives final remarks, conclusions, and further work opportunities.

2   Convolutional Neural Networks (CNN)

CNN are one type of network topology, widely used to applied Deep Learning (DL) principles. They have been used for Image Processing and Classification task. A CNN is a variation of a Multilayer Perceptron, which means that it is a feed-forward network, however, it requires less processing when compared to a MLP, due to the mechanism used to process input data. One of its main characteristic is to be space invariant, that is due to the convolution operator that transforms data inputs.

CNN are biological inspired, trying to emulate what happens in mammal's Visual Cortex, where neural cells are specialized to distinguish particular features. Building blocks of a CNN architecture are in charge of doing this feature detection by activating or de-activating a set of neurons. Since market agents decisions are mostly made from visual analysis of order changes in the LOB, we expect that a CNN based algorithm can learn patterns in order to help trigger trading decisions. In fact, [14,15] shown that a visual dictionary could be constructed from LOB data and that dictionary has predicting capabilities.

The two main build blocks of a CNN are the convolution layer and the pooling layer, which in conjunction with a dense layer, complete a CNN.

Convolution Layer. It is in charge of applying convolution operator to the input matrix, in other words it applies a kernel to filter data input. Depending on the parameters used, it can reduce or maintain input's dimensionality. The reason to convolve is to identify edges. That means to identify or separate features that later on can be used to construct more complex representations in deeper layers.

Pooling Layer. It is a local operator, that takes convolution output and maps subregions into a single number. The pooling operator can extract the max value of the mapped subregion (Max pooling) or the average value of the mapped subregion (Average Pooling). In other words, it gets subsamples out of the Convolution Layer.

Dense Layer. Finally, the deeper convolutional layer is connected to a dense layer (fully connected), from which network obtains its outputs. As mentioned before, the CNN topology may have one or more dense layers.

3 Limit Order Book and Tick Data Transformation

3.1 Definitions

Limit Order Book. Order Book Data records market agents buy/sell intentions. It includes a time-stamp, quantity and price to buy/sell. This data is known as Limit Order Book (LOB). Formally, an order $x = (p, q, t, s)$ sent at time t_x with price p_x, quantity q_x (number of shares) and side s_x (buy/sell), is a commitment to buy/sell up to q_x units of an asset at price p_x. Orders are sorted by quoted price p and arrival time t. Sell orders have larger prices than buy orders. [6,9,14] Some other useful concepts include [9,14]:

- Spread size is the difference between the best sell and buy price.
- Bid price is the highest price among all active buy orders at time t. Conversely, Ask price is the lowest price among all active sell orders at time t. Both are called best quotes.
- An LOB $L(t)$ is the set of all active orders at time t.

Dynamics of LOB are complex [6,9], since it reflects interactions among market agents with a different point of views and different trading strategies. For a particular time t, LOB concepts are illustrated on Fig. 1.

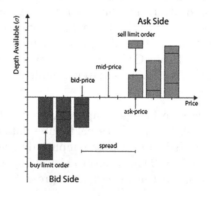

Fig. 1. LOB snapshot, taken from [9]

When all recorded intentions are joined, they can be seen as an Image Fig. 2. On this image representation, y-axis represent prices, the x-axis is time and each point is a quantity willing to be traded. The darker the color the most quantity q at certain price p. In [15], authors used this graphic representation to cluster LOB-Patterns in order to build a classifier. Based on this work, LOB data can be seen as a list of tuples (prices-quantities) where agents expect to negotiate. Numerically, this representation can be seen as a multivariate FTS[1].

LOB Representation. For a set of successive timestamps, LOB data can be represented as a matrix-like object, where column labels are timestamps, row labels are prices and the content of each cell is the number of shares to bid/ask. Each cell contains a quantity q, with subindex side s, time t and price line p. Order side could be either ask a or bid b. Because there are order imbalances, price lines subindex are k for the ask side and j for the bid side.

Table 1. LOB matrix representation

	t_0	$t_1 \dots t_n$	
$AskPrice_k$	q_{a0_k}	$\dots \dots$	q_{an_k}
$AskPrice_{k-1}$	$q_{a0_{k-1}}$	$\dots \dots$	$q_{an_{k-1}}$
$\dots$	$\dots$	$\dots \dots \dots$	
$AskPrice_0$	q_{a0_0}	$\dots \dots$	q_{an_0}
$BidPrice_0$	q_{b0_0}	$\dots \dots$	q_{bn_0}
$\dots$	$\dots$	$\dots \dots \dots$	
$BidPrice_{j-1}$	$q_{b0_{j-1}}$	$\dots \dots$	$q_{bn_{j-1}}$
$BidPrice_j$	q_{b0_j}	$\dots \dots$	q_{bn_j}

Normalizing each q_{sti} between 0–255, will produce a LOB gray scale image. However, there is a lot more information in LOB data. Because each order is recorded individually and sorted by arrival time, it is possible to aggregate volumes at the same price. By doing so you can get how many different orders (quotes) are placed at the same price. Formally, for each unique price p adds all quantities q_k, where $q = [q_1, q_2, \dots q_m]$, being m the last entered order at price p.

This information is very important because is different to have many distinct agents interested at one particular price that just a few ones. However this fact, under real market conditions, goes hand in hand with how much volume (quantity) of the asset is available at that particular price p. In other words, it is important to have some sense of the distribution. It is different to have a lot volume concentrated in just one participant that distributed across many. To introduce this information in our representation, we used $max_{p_k}(q)$, for each unique price p at line k, signaling a sense of the volume distribution.

As a result, we will represent LOB data in a 4-channel representation, which can be seen as a RGBA image, where:

- R channel is only used for ask volumes q_a, 0 otherwise.
- G channel is only used for bid volumes q_b, 0 otherwise.

---

[1] Some considerations should be done, particularly related to the dimensionality of the FTS.

- B channel is only used to represent total number of placed orders at a unique price p.
- A channel is only used to represent volume distribution for a unique price p, taking $max_{p_k}(q)$.

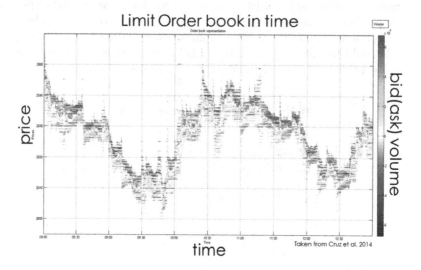

Fig. 2. LOB as Image, taken from [15] (Color figure online)

Tick Data. Tick data records transactions, that is prices and quantities exchanged for a particular asset. Formally, a transaction occurs when at time t the bid price equals the ask price. At this point, a transaction $T = (p, q, t)$ occurs, where p_T is the price, q_T is the shares quantity exchanged and t_T is the transaction time-stamp [14]. Tick data is a univariate time series[2].

Tick Data Graphical Representation. As mentioned before, tick data is the most widely used data when modeling FTS. This is because is easier to obtain. LOB data is more difficult to get and usually cost a lot, not just in money terms but also in storage terms. Transactions are heavily influenced by the intentions recorded in the LOB, but they do not have the richness of LOB. Nevertheless, we expect, that in conjunction with the LOB, to yield better results. In other to homogenize inputs, it is necessary to transform tick data into a matrix-like representation. In [18], authors show a step by step methodology that transforms univariate time series into an image representation. This transformation is called Grammian Angular Field (GAF), which consists of the following steps[3]:

- Time series normalization between $[-1, 1]$

---

[2] Bivariate if volumes are included.
[3] For full details please refer to [18].

– Time series is converted from Cartesian to Polar coordinates

$$\phi = arccos(x_t); r = \frac{t_i}{N}, t_i \in N \tag{1}$$

– GAF matrix deduction, defined as:

$$\begin{bmatrix} <x_1, x_1> & \ldots & <x_1, x_n> \\ <x_2, x_1> & \ldots & <x_2, x_n> \\ \vdots & \ddots & \vdots \\ <x_n, x_1> & \ldots & <x_n, x_n> \end{bmatrix},$$

where $<x, y>= x \cdot y - \sqrt{I - x^2} \cdot \sqrt{I - y^2}$.

Authors in [18] used for non-Financial Time Series. In this paper, we apply the same general steps in order to obtain a graphical version of the tick data, as illustrated in Table 2.

Table 2. Original tick data vs image representation of tick data

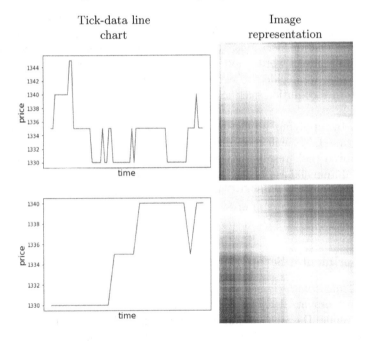

One advantage of this transformation is that marks peaks of the input signal, based on intensity levels Table 2. This is useful for pattern recognition because it helps to differentiate price variances within the original signal. On the other hand, the transformed input can be rolled back to the original signal [18]. We expect that on this new space, patterns could be easier to identify since CNN's learning capabilities have been proven good in frequency spaces. In fact, in a previous work we show how a wavelet transformation improve results over a pure time-space approach [2][4]. Next section will give step by step explanation for our experiment.

4   Classifying Financial Time Series with CNN

4.1   Why a CNN for FTS Classification

- Firstly, DL models have demonstrated a greater effectiveness in both classification and prediction tasks. Its superiority is due to the fact that they are able to learn useful representations from raw data, avoiding the local minimum issue of ANNs, by learning in a layered way using a combination of supervised and unsupervised learning to adjust weights W.
- Secondly, DL applications in computational finance are limited [3,4,8,17,19] and as long as it goes to our knowledge, there is no publication applying CNN to FTS using LOB data for short-term periods forecasting.
- Thirdly, CNN are good for pattern recognition, real traders have told us that they try to identify patterns by following buy/sell intentions in a numeric form. In a previous work, [14] identified volume barriers patterns to translate them into trading decisions and [15] identified visual patterns and cluster them into a bag of words model to predict market movements. As a result of these works, we decided to extend them and use a more suitable technique for pattern recognition such as CNN on image-like representation of market data.
- Finally, by applying input space change (from time to a frequency), we expect that CNN will recognize patterns more effective, indeed authors in [2] improved their results by using wavelets to represent high frequency data of several financial assets [1]. Even tough our images are not natural ones, we expect that CNN's layers are capable to distinguish simple frequency changes (edges) at lower layers in order to identify more complex patterns at deeper ones.

4.2   Experimental Setup

- Data acquisition: Original dataset is compose of LOB and transaction data for 11 instruments listed on NYSE, from Dec 24, 2015 to Apr 27, 2017, from EDGX venue. Dataset includes information from US stocks (AIG, C, MSFT, FB), ETF (SPY) ADR (EC, CIB, AVAL, AVH, RBS, DB). 4,371,945 LOB files transformed into 1,491,240 image like representation, including LOB and tick data totaling 6.2 GB in disk. For training and testing purposes we use a dataset containing 350,000 and 35,000 images respectively.[5]

---

[4] We used other DL topologies.
[5] Data provided by DataDrivenMarket Corporation.

- Data preparation: For each stock, data normalization was conducted, taking into account some considerations which include handling of no orders at some price levels in LOB data, some liquidity constrains and event of LOB. Details are given in the next subsection.
- Data transformation: For each stock both LOB data and tick data are transformed to an image-like representation, following the methodology previously explained.
- CNN modeling: We chose a base CNN architecture. We trained and test it with transformed data.
- CNN comparison again other DL topologies: We compare results achieved results obtained in this work against others, which have been used for similar problems (Short-term forecasting) but different Deep Learning topologies (RNN, LSTM, Multilayer Perceptron, DBN).

Following paragraphs will provide further details of our experimental setup.

4.3   Data Preparation

Data Normalization. For each stock, prices, volumes (quantities) and a number of orders at the same price were normalized between (0–1). Given the fact that LOB data may have price levels with no demand /offer, minimum values were reduced by a small factor so that minimum values had a small value above zero. Data normalization by stock facilitates magnitude equilibrium across all stock data, regardless their nominal prices or volumes.

Handling of LOB events. We took an event-based approach, that is to analyze a fixed number of LOB events (10 in this case). Each event is record at 5 s interval. This means that the LOB matrix explained in Sect. 2 Table 1, was partitioned into fixed segments of 10. We use the same window to create the corresponding image for tick data. Figure 3 illustrates procedure described above.

Handling of LOB Deepness. Given deepness asymmetry between buy and sell sides, we decided to work with LOB data of 5 lines depth for each book side. Prices start from the best quotes (down/up) side depending (bid/ask).

Additional Considerations. It is important to note the following:

- Prices with no volume will have a 0 value. This value will be always different for the lowest volume after normalization, as mentioned before.
- For modeling purposes, we resize each image to be 10 width and 40 height.

Prices	TimeStamps							
	0	1	...	9	10	...	n-1	n
AskPrice$_k$	qa_(0,k)	qa_(1,k)	...	qa_(9,k)	qa_(10,k)	...	qa_(n-1,k)	qa_(n,k)
AskPrice$_{k-1}$	qa_(0,k-1)	qa_(1,k-1)	...	qa_(9,k-1)	qa_(10,k-1)	...	qa_(n-1,k-1	qa_(n,k-1)
...	...	...	...	...	...	...	...	...
AskPrice$_1$	qa_(0,1)	qa_(1,1)	...	qa_(9,1)	qa_(10,1)	...	qa_(n-1,1)	qa_(n,1)
AskPrice$_0$	qa_(0,0)	qa_(1,0)	...	qa_(9,0)	qa_(10,0)	...	qa_(n-1,0)	qa_(n,0)
BidPrice$_0$	qb_(0,0)	qb_(1,0)	...	qb_(9,0)	qb_(10,0)	...	qb_(n-1,0)	qb_(n,0)
BidPrice$_1$	qb_(0,1)	qb_(1,1)	...	qb_(9,1)	qb_(10,1)	...	qb_(n-1,1)	qb_(n,1)
...	...	...	...	...	...	...	...	...
BidPrice$_{j-1}$	qb_(0,j-1)	qb_(1,j-1)	...	qb_(9,j-1)	qb_(10,j-1)	...	qb_(n-1,j-1	qb_(n,j-1)
BidPrice$_j$	qb_(0,j)	qb_(1,j)	...	qb_(9,j)	qb_(10,j)	...	qb_(n-1,j)	qb_(n,j)

Input$_0$ Input$_1$

Input$_{n-11}$ Input$_{n-10}$

Fig. 3. LOB Events

4.4 CNN Modeling

Data Input. Four channel images are used, one for LOB data another for tick data. A five dimensional tensor is used for data input, with size $[n, 2, 10, 40, 4]$. The first dimension is the number of samples, second one the number of images categories (LOB/tick) an the other three, image dimensions (Width, Height, Channels) (Fig. 4).

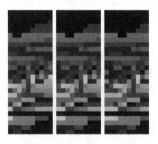

Fig. 4. LOB data images

Data Labeling. Data will be classified in three different classes as shown on Table 3. Classes exhibit unbalance, which could be adjusted by reducing the interval that determines flat movements.

Table 3. Three class rules

Price direction	Rule	Class
Upward movement (27.92%)	Last tick price above 0.015% vs last tick of the previous window	0
Downward movement (27.75%)	Last tick price below −0.015% vs last tick of the previous window	1
Flat movements (44.32%)	Otherwise	2

CNN Architecture. We use a standard CNN architecture, which consists of (Input + Conv + Pool + Conv + Pool + Dense + Dropout), input images' size is 10 X 40. Experiments include both LOB and tick data. We used TensorFlow.

Special considerations for training size included dropout at 40% and batch size at 100. The dataset was split into 90%for training, 10% for testing.

5 Results

5.1 Model Comparison Against Other DL Topologies

The CNNs were used to classify the three target classes (Up, Down, Flat). Table 4 shows the proposed model performance (74.15%). As observed on Table 4, proposed model is very competitive against similar works, with the advantage that one model runs for several assets. Metrics are displayed on Table 5

Table 4. Comparison against other DL topologies

DL topology	Classes	Data used	Directional accuracy
Multilayer Perceptron [2]	2	1-Stock, tick data	66%
Deep Belief Network [13]	2	1-Stock, LOB + Tick data	57%
Deep Neural Network + Wavelet [1]	2	19 stocks, Tick data, one model per stock	[64%–72%]
Proposed Model (CNN)	3	**12-stocks, LOB + Tick data**	**74.15%**

Table 5. Metrics at different steps

Metric	Step			
	150,000	300,000	450,000	600,000
Accuracy	73.89%	73.99%	74.05%	**74.15%**
Mean class accuracy	74.73%	74.70%	74.72%	**74.90%**
MSE	0.642	0.640	0.634	**0.629**
True positives	8495	8438	8440	**8501**
False positives	2576	2508	2468	**2497**
False negatives	2399	2456	2454	**2393**

6 Conclusion and Future Research

CNN for FTS prediction purpose worked well. DA shows that results are very competitive, in fact, better than other approaches tested before [2,13,15]. As expected, performance improves when both LOB and tick data is used in conjunction, and the main reason is simple: there is more market information. Image-like representation is useful and even could be extended, that is it is possible to have more channels in the original input image (matrix).

Perceived advantages

- One network for multiple assets. It is not usually the case, given the fact that each asset has it owns dynamics. Image-like representation homogenize inputs, resulting in an image representing market information, finding patterns across all image set, regardless the asset.
- Lifetime of trained model. In financial applications frequent retraining is the norm. This approach extends the lifetime of the trained model due to the time invariance fact associated with images.

Perceived disadvantages

- It is a data intensive technique. As there are more images for training, results will improve.
- Preprocessing could be tricky. There are a lot of details to take into account when transforming raw data.

It is necessary to perform out of sample test, to check DA with unseen data, as well as possible re-training periods. For FTS it is necessary to re-train models frequently given the fact that Financial Markets exhibit trends in both long and short periods of times. Moreover, it is necessary to test different flat intervals. We think that there are a lot of possibilities for improvement, including a combination with other topologies such as (LSTM and CNN), and to code more information in more channels, for example, technical information, time among others.

References

1. Arévalo, A., Nino, J., León, D., Hernandez, G., Sandoval, J.: Deep learning and wavelets for high-frequency price forecasting. In: Shi, Y., et al. (eds.) ICCS 2018. LNCS, vol. 10861, pp. 385–399. Springer, Cham (2018). https://doi.org/10.1007/978-3-319-93701-4_29
2. Arévalo, A., Niño, J., Hernández, G., Sandoval, J.: High-frequency trading strategy based on deep neural networks. In: Huang, D.-S., Han, K., Hussain, A. (eds.) ICIC 2016. LNCS (LNAI), vol. 9773, pp. 424–436. Springer, Cham (2016). https://doi.org/10.1007/978-3-319-42297-8_40
3. Arnold, L., Rebecchi, S., Chevallier, S., Paugam-Moisy, H.: An introduction to deep learning. In: ESANN (2011). https://www.elen.ucl.ac.be/Proceedings/esann/esannpdf/es2011-4.pdf

4. Chao, J., Shen, F., Zhao, J.: Forecasting exchange rate with deep belief networks. In: The 2011 International Joint Conference on Neural Networks, pp. 1259–1266. IEEE, July 2011. http://ieeexplore.ieee.org/articleDetails.jsp?arnumber=6033368ieeexplore.ieee.org/xpls/abs_all.jsp?arnumber=6033368

5. Chen, M., et al.: Data, information, and knowledge in visualization. IEEE Comput. Graph. Appl. **29**(1), 12–19 (2009)

6. Cont, R., Stoikov, S., Talreja, R.: A stochastic model for order book dynamics. Oper. Res. **58**, 549–563 (2010)

7. De Goijer, J., Hyndman, R.: 25 years of time series forecasting. J. Forecast. **22**, 443–473 (2006)

8. Ding, X., Zhang, Y., Liu, T., Duan, J.: Deep learning for event-driven stock prediction. In: Proceedings of the Twenty-Fourth International Joint Conference on Artificial Intelligence (ICJAI) (2015). http://ijcai.org/papers15/Papers/IJCAI15-329.pdf

9. Gould, M.D., Porter, M.A., Williams, S., McDonald, M., Fenn, D.J., Howison, S.D.: Limit order books. Quant. Finance **13**, 42 (2010)

10. Hamid, S., Habib, A.: Financial forecasting with neura networks. Acad. Account. Financ. Stud. J. **18**, 37–56 (2014)

11. Huang, G., Huang, G.B., Song, S., You, K.: Trends in extreme learning machines: a review. Neural Netw. **61**, 32–48 (2015)

12. Längkvist, M., Karlsson, L., Loutfi, A.: A review of unsupervised feature learning and deep learning for time-series modeling. Pattern Recognit. Lett. **42**, 11–24 (2014). http://www.sciencedirect.com/science/article/pii/S0167865514000221

13. Niño-Peña, J.H., Hernández-Pérez, G.J.: Price direction prediction on high frequency data using deep belief networks. In: Figueroa-García, J.C., López-Santana, E.R., Ferro-Escobar, R. (eds.) WEA 2016. CCIS, vol. 657, pp. 74–83. Springer, Cham (2016). https://doi.org/10.1007/978-3-319-50880-1_7

14. Sandoval, J.: Empirical Shape Function of the Limit-Order Books of the USD/COP Spot Market. In: ODEON, no. 7 (2013). https://ssrn.com/abstract=2408087

15. Sandoval, J., Nino, J., Hernandez, G., Cruz, A.: Detecting informative patterns in financial market trends based on visual analysis. Procedia Comput. Sci. **80**, 752–761 (2016). http://www.sciencedirect.com/science/article/pii/S1877050916308407. International Conference on Computational Science 2016, ICCS 2016, 6–8 June 2016, San Diego, California, USA

16. Shen, F., Chao, J., Zhao, J.: Forecasting exchange rate using deep belief networks and conjugate gradient method. Neurocomput. **167**(C), 243–253 (2015). https://doi.org/10.1016/j.neucom.2015.04.071

17. Takeuchi, L., Lee, Y.: Applying Deep Learning to Enhance Momentum Trading Strategies in Stocks (2013)

18. Wang, Z., Oates, T.: Encoding Time Series as Images for Visual Inspection and Classification Using Tiled Convolutional Neural Networks (2015). https://pdfs.semanticscholar.org/32e7/b2ddc781b571fa023c205753a803565543e7.pdf

19. Yeh, S., Wang, C., Tsai, M.: Corporate Default Prediction via Deep Learning (2014). http://teacher.utaipei.edu.tw/~cjwang/slides/ISF2014.pdf

Feature Group Selection Using MKL Penalized with ℓ_1-norm and SVM as Base Learner

Henry Jhoán Areiza-Laverde⬡, Gloria M. Díaz⬡,
and Andrés Eduardo Castro-Ospina$^{(\boxtimes)}$⬡

Grupo de Investigación Automática, Electrónica y Ciencias Computacionales,
Instituto Tecnológico Metropolitano, Medellín, Colombia
henryareiza135582@correo.itm.edu.co, {gloriadiaz,andrescastro}@itm.edu.co

Abstract. Objective feature selection is an important component in the machine learning framework, which has addressed problems like computational burden increasing and unnecessary high-dimensional representations. Most of feature selection techniques only perform individual feature evaluations and ignore the structural relationships between features of the same nature, causing relations to break and harming the algorithm performance. In this paper a feature group selection technique is proposed with the aim of objectively identify the relevance that a feature group carries out in a classification task. The proposed method uses Multiple Kernel Learning with a penalization rule based on the ℓ_1-norm and a Support Vector Machine as base learner. Performance evaluation is carried out using two binarized configurations of the freely available MFEAT dataset. It provides six different feature groups allowing to develop multiple feature group analysis. The experimental results show that the implemented methodology is stable in the identification of the relevance of each feature group during all experiments, what allows to outperform the classification accuracy of state-of-the-art methods.

Keywords: Multiple Kernel Learning · Multimodality
Feature selection · Group LASSO · Sparsity

1 Introduction

Large data increasing of last decades has raised the emergence of many challenges nowadays, making the use of computational systems to be strictly necessary to process the huge amount of available information in open access datasets. In this scenario, machine learning techniques have been implemented to design different approaches that take advantage of this wide information quantity and perform tasks as regression, classification, automatic detection, among others [23].

H. J. Areiza-Laverde—Supported by Colciencias and the Instituto Tecnológico Metropolitano.

© Springer Nature Switzerland AG 2018
J. C. Figueroa-García et al. (Eds.): WEA 2018, CCIS 915, pp. 136–147, 2018.
https://doi.org/10.1007/978-3-030-00350-0_12

Although machine learning techniques allow to process large amounts of information, they have also faced some issues that must be solved to improve the algorithms performance and reduce the computational burden. One of the most relevant problem is the dimensional reduction of the feature representation space, which is directly related to model overfitting. Therefore, different techniques have been developed to make an objective feature selection, these techniques can be applied as a preprocessing step, like a wrapping method based on the algorithm performance or can be embedded into the main algorithm [13,16].

Some recent approaches have studied the possibility to adapt classic feature selection techniques with the purpose of select or remove complete feature groups, instead to eliminate features one by one, this is namely feature group selection [16,22]. Feature group selection has many advantages in data processing, especially when there is a lot of information to solve a specific problem using computational methods, for example, to solve multimodal problems, i.e., when there is information coming from different sources [4], since each source can be perceived as a feature group, this type of strategies are also known as multi-view learning. The use of multiple sources can lead to a performance enhancement because the algorithms can obtain many information about the problem at hand, nevertheless, it is necessary to identify the most useful information and avoid unnecessary data that could represent an increase in cost from the financial until the computational side.

Some of the most simple feature group selection techniques are based on a user defined threshold. In this type of methods, the machine learning algorithm is trained with each feature group to eliminate the groups that have a lower performance than a predefined selection threshold [24]. Other methods perform a more detailed feature analysis and select the feature groups based on a penalization value embedding in the algorithm, it allows the machine learning algorithm to automatically select the most relevant feature groups or simply assign a weight to each group, which is associated to the effect they have in the overall performance [19]. Other more specific feature group selection techniques are methodologies with strategies like forward-addition and backward-elimination [18], correlation among feature stream analysis [22] and analysis based on graphs and subgraphs [8]. These strategies have centered their efforts in maintain the intra-groups relationships, because a fundamental issue in all these methods is to achieve the ability to treat the whole feature groups like individual data representations instead of sums of individual features.

On the other hand, one methodology that has gained popularity in classification tasks over the last decades is the Multiple Kernel Learning (MKL), this machine learning strategy has showed to be very useful since it can achieve a high performance in classification tasks and one of its most important property is the capability of incorporate information of different sources within a single algorithm, evaluating in an independent way each source contribution on classification task [11]. Some works have suggested to use this property to apply embedded feature selection, and can be expanded to feature group selection owing to a whole feature group creates a single Kernel matrix that measures non-linear similarities on data [9,11].

This work presents a theoretical and experimental study about the use of MKL penalized with ℓ_1-norm using a Support Vector Machine (SVM) as base learner to apply embedded feature group selection on a classification task, the results show that the implemented methodology is stable during all experiments and allows to improve the classification accuracy regarding to results in some state-of-the-art classification methods. The document is organized as follows: Sect. 2 describes the theoretical foundations of the implemented methods to develop the proposed methodology. In Sect. 3 the dataset used and the experimental setup of the performed tests are presented, providing details about the algorithm parameters configuration. In Sect. 4 the achieved results are presented and a detailed analysis of these is made regarding related state-of-the-art methods. Finally, Sect. 5 presents the conclusions and possibilities for future work that can be developed as a continuation of this research work.

2 Theoretical Framework

2.1 Support Vector Machines

Support Vector Machines are discriminative classifiers proposed for binary classification problems and are based on the structural risks minimization theory. The main property of an SVM is its categorization as a wide margin classifier [3]. Given a dataset with N independent and identically distributed training samples $\{(x_i, y_i)\}_{i=1}^{N}$ where x_i is a D-dimensional input vector and $y \in \{-1, +1\}$ is the labels vector of dimension N, the SVM basically finds the discriminative line with maximal margin M that better separates the samples in the feature space. The classification function is given by the expression in Eq. (1).

$$f(x) = \langle w, x \rangle + b \tag{1}$$

where w is the vector of weights corresponding to the coefficients for each sample x_i, b is the hyperplane separation bias term and the $\langle \cdot, \cdot \rangle$ operator represents the dot product between two vectors.

As shown in Fig. 1, it must be fulfilled that $f(x) = 1$ in $+1$ region, $f(x) = -1$ in -1 region and $f(x) = 0$ over the decision boundary. Samples enclosed by ovals are called *support vectors*. Given a scalar value r, and since w is orthogonal with the decision boundary, it is possible to demonstrate that r and M correspond to Eqs. (2) and (3), respectively.

$$r = \frac{2}{\|w\|^2} \tag{2}$$

$$M = \|rw\| = \frac{2}{\|w\|^2}\|w\|$$

$$M = \frac{2}{\|w\|} \tag{3}$$

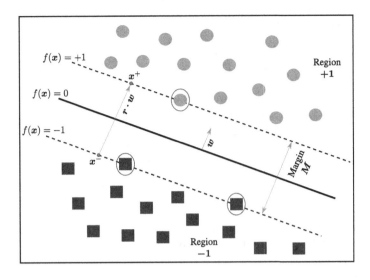

Fig. 1. Representation of a dataset separated by an SVM

In this way, the SVM maximizes M, which is equivalent to minimize $\|w\|$, this is the primal optimization problem of the SVM and is expressed in Eq. (4).

$$w^* = \min_w \quad \frac{1}{2}\|w\|_2^2 + C\sum_{i=1}^{N}\xi_i \tag{4}$$
$$s.t. \quad y_i(\langle w, x \rangle + b) \geq 1 - \xi_i$$

where C is a regularization parameter and ξ is the vector of slack variables, it is known as *soft margin representation* of the SVM.

The main method to solve this quadratic optimization problem with restrictions is through Lagrange Multipliers to obtain the expression in Eq. (5), namely *dual function* of the SVM.

$$\max_{0 \leq \alpha \leq C} \quad \sum_{i=1}^{N}\alpha_i - \frac{1}{2}\sum_{i=1}^{N}\sum_{j=1}^{N}\alpha_i\alpha_j y_i y_j \langle x_i, x_j \rangle \tag{5}$$
$$s.t. \quad \sum_{i=1}^{N}\alpha_i y_i = 0$$

where α is the dual variables vector and the classification function is given by the Eq. (6).

$$f(x) = \sum_{i=1}^{N}\alpha_i y_i \langle x_i, x \rangle + b \tag{6}$$

2.2   Kernels and MKL

In the dual function of the SVM (Eq. (5)) an important term appears: $\langle x_i, x_j \rangle$, this term is the Kernel function and is expressed as $K(x_i, x_j)$, where $K : \mathbb{R}^D \times \mathbb{R}^D \longrightarrow \mathbb{R}$. The Kernel function is defined as a non-linear similarity measure and it can be raised in different ways, the most common Kernel functions are presented in Eqs. (7), (8) and (9).

$$K_{Linear}(x_i, x_j) = \langle x_i, x_j \rangle \tag{7}$$

$$K_{Polynomial}(x_i, x_j) = (\langle x_i, x_j \rangle + 1)^q, \quad q \in \mathbb{N} \tag{8}$$

$$K_{Gaussian}(x_i, x_j) = \exp\left(\frac{-\|x_i - x_j\|_2^2}{\sigma^2}\right), \quad \sigma > 0 \tag{9}$$

The Kernel function is fundamental to the SVM performance, at this point is where the MKL shows to be very useful, since this methodology basically establish that multiple linear or non linear combinations of Kernels can be used instead of one single Kernel, as in Eq. (10).

$$K_\eta(x_i, x_j) = f_\eta\left(\{K_m(x_i^m, x_j^m)\}_{m=1}^P\right) \tag{10}$$

The combination function $f_\eta : \mathbb{R}^P \to \mathbb{R}$ is composed by P feature representations (feature groups) of training samples. The great advantage of this formulation is that each feature representation is independent and they can be provided by different sources, varying the acquisition and composition nature or the number of features in each representation. The combination function f_η can be defined as in Eq. (11).

$$f_\eta = K_\eta(x_i, x_j) = \sum_{m=1}^P \eta_m K_m(x_i^m, x_j^m) \tag{11}$$

where η_m represents the weight assigned to each Kernel function K_m, which is equivalent to assign a weight to each feature representation or feature group.

It is possible to apply a penalization to each Kernel weight, enabling that the algorithm could determine the relevance of each feature group based in the value assigned to each Kernel weight, providing a straightforward interpretation of results [11]. The most common penalization methods used in this type of problems are the ℓ_1-norm and ℓ_2-norm [9,10].

2.3   MKL-Based Feature Group Selection

MKL algorithms are frequently raised with the optimization problem presented in Eq. (12) [25].

$$\min_{\mathcal{H}_\eta} \quad \frac{1}{2}\|\mathcal{H}_\eta\|^2 + \zeta \sum_{i=1}^N \mathcal{L}(y_i, f(x_i)) \tag{12}$$

where $\mathcal{L}(\cdot)$ is a loss function regularized by the parameter ζ, and $\mathcal{H}_\eta$ is a Kernel function parametrized by η, this Kernel function corresponds to the Eq. (13).

$$\mathcal{H}_\eta = K(\cdot, \cdot, \eta) = \sum_{j=1}^{P} \eta_j K_j(\cdot, \cdot) \tag{13}$$

A well known function in the literature and specially practical to this problem is the *Hinge loss function*, which can be used as $\mathcal{L}(\cdot)$ and is defined in Eq. (14).

$$\mathcal{L}(y, f(x)) = (1 - yf(x))_+ \tag{14}$$

When the *Hinge loss function* is implemented, the dual representation of MKL problem can be computed using Lagrange Multipliers to obtain the Eq. (15).

$$\min_{\eta \in \Delta} \max_{\alpha \in \mathcal{Q}} \mathbf{1}^\top \alpha - \frac{1}{2}(\alpha \circ y)^\top \left(\sum_{j=1}^{P} \eta_j K_j \right) (\alpha \circ y) \tag{15}$$

where Δ is the domain of η and $\mathcal{Q}$ is the domain of α. $\mathbf{1}$ is a vector with all components equal to one and $\circ$ define the Hadamard (element wise) product between two vectors. $\mathcal{Q}$ is usually defined as in Eq. (16).

$$\mathcal{Q} = \{\alpha \in \mathbb{R}^N : \alpha^\top y = 0, 0 \leq \alpha \leq \zeta\} \tag{16}$$

It is clear how $\mathcal{Q}$ is equivalent with the Lagrange coefficient constraints of the SVM. The most interesting analysis arises when determining the Δ domain, because when $\eta \in \Delta$, it correspond to a simplex condition, i.e., this domain corresponds to the Eq. (17).

$$\Delta = \left\{ \eta \in \mathbb{R}_+^P : \sum_{j=1}^{P} \eta_j = 1, \eta_j \geq 0 \right\} \tag{17}$$

This Δ constraint is known as the ℓ_1-norm of the Kernel weights, this convex sum can be solved using the Least Absolute Shrinkage and Selection Operator (LASSO) [21], since it allows to minimize the sum of squares residual restricted to the sum of the coefficients being equal to a constant. The main property of LASSO method is in its constraint nature, because this method produces coefficients exactly equal to zero, allowing a simultaneous variable elimination during the training task, this is known as a *sparse method*. In this way, the MKL algorithm penalized by ℓ_1-norm and solved by the group LASSO method, allows to compute the Kernels relevance based on the weights η, which is equivalent to determine the relevance of the feature groups associated to each Kernel.

3   Experimental Setup

Details of implemented tools and methods parametrization are presented below, describing the algorithm configuration used during experiments.

3.1 Benchmark Dataset

In this work the *Multiple Features Dataset* (MFEAT) was used, this dataset is freely available online on the UCI Machine Learning Repository [7]. The MFEAT dataset contains six different feature groups of handwritten digits since '0' to '9' corresponding to ten classes, this dataset composition allows to develop multiple feature group studies specially. Each feature group was extracted from 2000 samples, corresponding to 200 samples per class. The feature groups are conformed as follows:

- *Fac*: 216 profile correlations
- *Fou*: 76 Fourier coefficients of the character shapes
- *Kar*: 64 Karhunen-Loève coefficients
- *Mor*: 6 morphological features
- *Pix*: 240 pixel averages in 2×3 windows
- *Zer*: 47 Zernike moments

Aiming to evaluate the individual relevance of each feature group in MFEAT, the number of classes was binarized since the SVM classifier is designed only for binary classification problems, therefore, two configurations of the MFEAT dataset were used. The first configuration was constructed by grouping the smaller digits (0–4) in one unique class, and the larger digits (5–9) in another class, this dataset configuration was called MFEAT-SL. The second dataset configuration was constructed grouping the even digits in one unique class, and the odd digits in a second class, this dataset configuration was called MFEAT-EO. This dataset configurations were designed taking as reference the work presented in [11].

3.2 Test Design

After the datasets were binarized, the tests were performed associating a weighted Gaussian Kernel to each feature group, all the Kernels were computed with the same parameter $\sigma = 10$, besides, the regularization parameter of the SVM was assigned with the value $C = 5$, both values were empirically tuned based on the achieved classification accuracy. Although it was sought to obtain a high classification performance, the greatest interest of the tests was focused on objectively determine the relevance of each feature group for the classification task. In this sense, it was achieved by identifying in detail the behavior of η_i weights associated to each Kernel.

For the tests development, the MKL Toolbox provided by [11] was used, a normalization of both data and Kernels was applied, in addition, *eps* was set to 0.001, this is a proper parameter of the Toolbox to determine when a weight η_i must be set to zero. Additionally, the Mosek tool was used as solver [17], this tool is free to use only for research and educational purposes.

To obtain a suitable validation of the feature group relevance computed by the method, a seventh feature group was added to the dataset, namely as *Rand*, which contains normalized random values. This last feature group was added waiting for the algorithm to being able to identify it as a weak feature group and assign it a very low relevance, i.e., a Kernel weight equal to zero. Seven tests were performed over each database configurations in total, identifying and manually eliminating the least relevant feature group in each of the test, and re-training the algorithm in the next test with one less group until only the most relevant feature group of all was hold. Cross-validation using K-folds with $k = 30$ was applied during each test, it was used to avoid model overfitting.

4   Results and Discussion

The test results are divided in two stages, the first stage corresponds to tests carried out on MFEAT-SL and the second stage corresponds to tests performed on MFEAT-EO. Table 1 contains the summary of results obtained by applying the seven tests corresponding to the MFEAT-SL dataset configuration, in these results is initially highlighted how the method identifies the random values group (Rand) in the first test, assigning it a relevance equal to zero, which means that the method is quite sensitive to this data type that does not provide useful information for the classification task. Another important detail is the stability that the method presents regarding the relevance assigned to each feature group through each test, even from the first test it was possible to clearly see the order in which the less relevant feature groups would be eliminated. Moreover, it is noteworthy that the classification performance with respect to accuracy was minimally affected when less relevant feature groups were removed, thus, a considerable feature space reduction was achieved and consequently a processing time reduction was reached maintaining a suitable accuracy performance.

Table 1. Relevance and performance results on MFEAT-SL

Trial number	Accuracy (%)	Feature group relevance (η_i)						
		Fac	Pix	Fou	Mor	Kar	Zer	Rand
Test 1	99.34 ± 1.24	**0.441**	0.356	0.076	0.064	0.048	0.015	0.000
Test 2	$\mathbf{99.41 \pm 0.93}$	**0.439**	0.358	0.076	0.064	0.048	0.015	—
Test 3	99.36 ± 0.94	**0.442**	0.359	0.079	0.067	0.053	—	—
Test 4	99.34 ± 0.95	**0.434**	0.403	0.093	0.070	—	—	—
Test 5	99.05 ± 1.66	**0.474**	0.412	0.114	—	—	—	—
Test 6	98.96 ± 1.24	**0.503**	0.497	—	—	—	—	—
Test 7	98.64 ± 1.51	**1.000**	—	—	—	—	—	—
Ranking	—	**1**	2	3	4	5	6	7

Regarding Table 2, where the results obtained by applying the seven tests corresponding to the MFEAT-EO dataset configuration are presented, the results show a similar behavior that the ones described in Table 1, showing that the method straight away identifies the random data feature group (Rand) assigning it a relevance equal to zero. Moreover, results remain consistent regarding the assigned relevance of each feature group and accuracy performance throughout the tests. The results presented in Table 2 provide a more interesting detail, in this case the best accuracy performance is obtained when only two feature groups are used to train the algorithm (Fac and Pix), which highlights the fact that the proposed method not only can reduce the large amount of features, but also, the overall performance of the classifier can be improved reducing the number of feature groups, thus achieving a double benefit and an enormous utility for the implemented application.

Table 2. Relevance and performance results on MFEAT-EO

Trial number	Accuracy (%)	Feature group relevance (η_i)						
		Fac	Pix	Fou	Mor	Kar	Zer	Rand
Test 1	99.41 ± 1.01	**0.676**	0.161	0.102	0.056	0.003	0.002	0.000
Test 2	99.41 ± 0.93	**0.676**	0.161	0.102	0.056	0.003	0.002	—
Test 3	99.34 ± 0.95	**0.671**	0.167	0.102	0.057	0.003	—	—
Test 4	99.39 ± 1.02	**0.669**	0.167	0.105	0.059	—	—	—
Test 5	99.44 ± 1.09	**0.677**	0.219	0.104	—	—	—	—
Test 6	**99.51 ± 0.82**	0.748	0.252	—	—	—	—	—
Test 7	99.46 ± 0.83	**1.000**	—	—	—	—	—	—
Ranking	—	**1**	2	3	4	5	6	7

It should be noted that accuracy measures presented in Tables 1 and 2 show their respective standard deviation, this deviation is produced when apply the Cross-validation using 30-folds. Standard deviation of the feature group relevance values was always less than 1.2%, whereby it was not showed in tables, this small variation of feature group relevance shows the great method stability again.

Regarding other state-of-the-art methods, the only work that can be directly compared with this one, is presented in [11], their classification accuracy over MFEAT-SL using a nonlinear MKL classification algorithm was 98.64 ± 0.25% using only four feature groups (Fou, Kar, Pix and Zer) and 98.82 ± 0.2 using the six feature groups, and over MFEAT-EO the classification accuracy using a localized MKL classification algorithm was 98.94±0.29% using only four feature groups (Fou, Kar, Pix and Zer) and 99.24±0.18 using the six feature groups, this results show that the methodology proposed in this paper not only outperforms all the results in [11], but it also prove that the elimination of irrelevant feature groups is useful to improve the classification accuracy as it is shown in the results obtained over MFEAT-EO.

Several studies have been developed over the MFEAT dataset, but most of them have implemented different dataset configurations in their tests. Although those studies are not directly comparable with the results of this work, their classification accuracies can be taken as a reference point to analyze the proposed method performance regarding classification accuracy showing its effectiveness. Some works have implemented the six feature groups and all the classes in MFEAT, e.g., in [12] a Self-organising fuzzy logic classifier was proposed achieving 93.66% in classification accuracy, [20] propose a classification method based in Multi-View Laplacian Eigenmap (MV-LEM) attaining 94.6% in classification accuracy and in [1] the ensemble learning method namely Learn++ with a multilayer perceptron classifier as base learner was used, obtaining 97.71% in classification accuracy as best result.

Other proposals have used a reduced feature group number, e.g., [14] use a linear regression classification method over a single feature group (Fou), their best result is $81.5 \pm 2.85\%$ in classification accuracy, in [15] the ensemble learning method namely Global Mapping Block with a Bayesian network classifier as base learner over five feature groups (Fac, Fou, Kar, Mor and Zer) is used and they achieve $97.7 \pm 0.6\%$ in classification accuracy and in [5] MKL with a Bayesian classification method is implemented over four feature groups (Fou, Kar, Pix and Zer), their best result is $97.8 \pm 1\%$ in classification accuracy.

Finally, other authors use all the feature groups but apply one by one feature selection methods, e.g., [6] use a multilayer perceptron classifier and apply a genetic-algorithm-based feature selection technique keeping 233 relevant features and achieving 98.38% in classification accuracy in their best results, and in [2] a Random Forest classifier and a ranking-based feature selection technique was used achieving 98.89% in classification accuracy keeping only 147 relevant features.

5   Conclusions

In this work an experimental analysis which sought to identify objectively the individual feature groups relevance in a classification task was presented. The proposed method consisted in the use of MKL over an SVM, applying a sparse penalty by means of the ℓ_1-norm to restrict the weights assigned to the Kernels computed per feature group, given that this weights represent the relevance that each feature group has for the classification task. Obtained results show that proposed method is consistent along experiments and correctly evaluates the feature groups relevance, even allowing in some cases the accuracy performance to be improved while considerably reducing the excessive use of data provided by different feature groups, additionally, the method allows to improve the accuracy performance regarding other state-of-the-art classification methods and the achieved results have an straightforward interpretability and are fully replicable and reproducible.

As future work it should be implement auto-tuning methods to select the best Kernel types and the Kernel parameters to be associated to feature groups, besides, to propose a strategy that allow the method to automatically eliminate the less relevant feature group by means of a threshold applied to the Kernel weights and extend the base learner to a multi-class SVM model.

References

1. Brahim, A.B., Khanchel, R., Limam, M.: Robust ensemble based algorithms for multi-source data classification. Int. J. Comput. Inf. Syst. Ind. Manag. Appl. **4**, 420–427 (2012)
2. Cilia, N.D., De Stefano, C., Fontanella, F., di Freca, A.S.: A ranking-based feature selection approach for handwritten character recognition. Pattern Recognit. Lett. (2018)
3. Cristianini, N., Shawe-Taylor, J.: An introduction to Support Vector Machines and Other Kernel-based Learning Methods. Cambridge University Press, Cambridge (2000)
4. Culache, O., Obadă, D.R.: Multimodality as a premise for inducing online flow on a brand website: a social semiotic approach. Procedia-Soc. Behav. Sci. **149**, 261–268 (2014)
5. Damoulas, T., Girolami, M.A.: Pattern recognition with a Bayesian Kernel combination machine. Pattern Recognit. Lett. **30**(1), 46–54 (2009)
6. De Stefano, C., Fontanella, F., Marrocco, C., Di Freca, A.S.: A GA-based feature selection approach with an application to handwritten character recognition. Pattern Recognit. Lett. **35**, 130–141 (2014)
7. Dheeru, D., Karra Taniskidou, E., Duin, R.: UCI machine learning repository - multiple features data set (2017). https://archive.ics.uci.edu/ml/datasets/Multiple+Features
8. Dhifli, W., Aridhi, S., Nguifo, E.M.: MR-SimLab: scalable subgraph selection with label similarity for big data. Inf. Syst. **69**, 155–163 (2017)
9. Foresti, L., Tuia, D., Timonin, V., Kanevski, M.F.: Time series input selection using multiple Kernel learning. In: ESANN, pp. 123–128 (2010)
10. Gönen, G.B., Gönen, M., Gürgen, F.: Probabilistic and discriminative group-wise feature selection methods for credit risk analysis. Expert Syst. Appl. **39**(14), 11709–11717 (2012)
11. Gönen, M., Alpaydın, E.: Multiple Kernel learning algorithms. J. Mach. Learn. Res. **12**(Jul), 2211–2268 (2011)
12. Gu, X., Angelov, P.P.: Self-organising fuzzy logic classifier. Inf. Sci. **447**, 36–51 (2018)
13. Hernández-Muriel, J.A., Álvarez-Meza, A.M., Echeverry-Correa, J.D., Orozco-Gutierrez, A.A., Álvarez-López, M.A.: Feature relevance estimation for vibration-based condition monitoring of an internal combustion engine. Tecno Lóg. **20**, 159–174 (2017). http://www.scielo.org.co/scielo.php?script=sciarttext&pid=S0123-77992017000200011&nrm=iso
14. Koç, M., Barkana, A.: Application of linear regression classification to low-dimensional datasets. Neurocomputing **131**, 331–335 (2014)
15. Kyunghoon, K.: Approaches to the design of machine learning system. Ph.D. thesis, Escuela de Graduados de la Universidad Nacional de Seúl (2016)
16. Li, J., Cheng, K., Wang, S., Morstatter, F., Trevino, R.P., Tang, J., Liu, H.: Feature selection: a data perspective. ACM Comput. Surv. (CSUR) **50**(6), 94 (2017)
17. Mosek, A.: The mosek optimization software. **54**(2-1), 5 (2010). http://www.mosek.com
18. Raza, H., Cecotti, H., Prasad, G.: Optimising frequency band selection with forward-addition and backward-elimination algorithms in EEG-based brain-computer interfaces. In: 2015 International Joint Conference on Neural Networks (IJCNN), pp. 1–7. IEEE (2015)

19. Subrahmanya, N., Shin, Y.C.: Automated sensor selection and fusion for monitoring and diagnostics of plunge grinding. J. Manuf. Sci. Eng. **130**(3), 031014 (2008)
20. Symons, C.T., Arel, I.: Multi-view budgeted learning under label and feature constraints using label-guided graph-based regularization. In: International Conference on Machine Learning, Workshop on Combining Learning Strategies to Reduce Label Cost. Citeseer (2011)
21. Tibshirani, R.: Regression shrinkage and selection via the lasso. J. R. Stat. Soc. Ser. B (Methodol.) **58**, 267–288 (1996)
22. Wang, J., Wang, M., Li, P., Liu, L., Zhao, Z., Hu, X., Wu, X.: Online feature selection with group structure analysis. IEEE Trans. Knowl. Data Eng. **27**(11), 3029–3041 (2015)
23. Witten, I.H., Frank, E., Hall, M.A., Pal, C.J.: Data Mining: Practical Machine Learning Tools and Techniques. Morgan Kaufmann, Burlington (2016)
24. Xiang, S., Yang, T., Ye, J.: Simultaneous feature and feature group selection through hard thresholding. In: Proceedings of the 20th ACM SIGKDD International Conference on Knowledge Discovery and Data Mining, pp. 532–541. ACM (2014)
25. Xu, Z., Jin, R., Yang, H., King, I., Lyu, M.R.: Simple and efficient multiple Kernel learning by group lasso. In: Proceedings of the 27th International Conference on Machine Learning (ICML 2010), pp. 1175–1182. Citeseer (2010)

Voice Pathology Detection Using Artificial Neural Networks and Support Vector Machines Powered by a Multicriteria Optimization Algorithm

Henry Jhoán Areiza-Laverde[1] (ID), Andrés Eduardo Castro-Ospina[1(✉)] (ID),
and Diego Hernán Peluffo-Ordóñez[2]

[1] Grupo de Investigación Automática, Electrónica y Ciencias Computacionales,
Instituto Tecnológico Metropolitano, Medellín, Colombia
andrescastro@itm.edu.co
[2] SDAS Research Group, Yachay Tech, Urcuquí, Ecuador
www.sdas-group.com

Abstract. Computer-aided diagnosis (CAD) systems have allowed to enhance the performance of conventional, medical diagnosis procedures in different scenarios. Particularly, in the context of voice pathology detection, the use of machine learning algorithms has proved to be a promising and suitable alternative. This work proposes the implementation of two well known classification algorithms, namely artificial neural networks (ANN) and support vector machines (SVM), optimized by particle swarm optimization (PSO) algorithm, aimed at classifying voice signals between healthy and pathologic ones. Three different configurations of the *Saarbrucken voice database* (SVD) are used. The effect of using balanced and unbalanced versions of this dataset is proved as well as the usefulness of the considered optimization algorithm to improve the final performance outcomes. Also, proposed approach is comparable with state-of-the-art methods.

Keywords: Voice pathology · Computer-aided diagnosis
Optimization · Classification

1 Introduction

Today, computer-aided diagnosis (CAD) systems are increasingly gaining importance due mainly to the technological advances. Indeed, last decades have allowed the medicine to take a new level of precision, enabling the most modern CAD systems to be sufficiently reliable to be taken into account in real medicine applications [8, 20]. CAD systems offer support to experts in different areas of research, it allows to make decisions with a high confidence level reaching reliable and true

H.J. Areiza-Laverde—This work is carried out under grants provided by Programa Nacional de Jóvenes Investigadores e Innovadores – COLCIENCIAS – Announcement 775 of 2017.

diagnoses being a very important issue when dealing with diseases, whose timely and appropriate treatment may drastically affect the patients' life [5,19].

Since the incursion of engineering in medicine, a lot of works have been developed while different specialized areas of medicine have emerged. For instance, the use of medical images to develop CAD systems is currently one of the most relevant methods on research [23,26]. Likewise, there are many works that propose CAD systems to use signals and time series to support the diagnoses made by the specialists in medicine [1,12]. A specific area that uses the information contained in signals measured from the human body, is the area that studies the human voice signals, this type of signals are widely used for voice recognition tasks, which are useful at present [4,9]. Within the medicine area, there are also research approaches in which CAD systems based on the human voice are proposed, this type of systems are used to determine if a person presents a type of voice pathology, furthermore, it can be used to classify between different voice diseases that a patient could present [15,25].

In recent years, there has been an exponential growth of the amount of data that is available to the scientific community from all research areas, thus, the medical area has not been unaware of this trend, the number of datasets available to perform research works in medicine has increased considerably [7,13]. This large increase in data has focused the interest of new research works towards the implementation of analysis and diagnostic support techniques using computational tools to improve the performance and efficiency of the proposed methods. One of the areas that has been contributing significantly to solve this need, is the use of machine learning methods to develop automatic systems [29].

Some recent works have developed different methods to detect voice pathologies obtaining a variety of results regarding the performance of the classifiers designed in each proposal. This research works has implemented balanced [2,3,11,17] and unbalanced [14,18] datasets versions showing that the use of unbalanced data causes a considerable reduction in the performance of classification algorithm. Other works aim to take advantage of the huge information of some datasets and use alternative signals to the speech like electroglottography (EGG) signals [16] or recordings of complete sentences instead of only vowels pronounced in different intonations [24], and also try to apply a very recent technique known as Deep Learning [10].

In this work, the implementation of two different and well known machine learning algorithms, namely artificial neural networks (ANN) and support vector machines (SVM), optimized by particle swarm optimization (PSO) algorithm is proposed to classify voice signals from a public dataset into healthy and pathological subjects. Obtained results show the effect of using balanced and unbalanced data as well as the usefulness of the considered optimization algorithm to improve the final performance outcomes. Furthermore, achieved results with the proposed approach are comparable with state-of-the-art methods.

The rest of this paper is organized as follows: Sect. 2 describes the dataset used, the features generation techniques implemented and the machine learning algorithms used in this work. Section 3 presents the experimental setup of the developed tests, providing details about the configuration and selected parameters of the algorithms. In Sect. 4 the obtained results are presented and a detailed analysis of these is made regarding related works of the state of the art. Finally, Sect. 5 presents the conclusions and possibilities for future work that can be developed as a continuation of this research work.

2   Materials and Methods

2.1   Benchmark Dataset

In this work was used a German open access dataset called "Saarbrucken voice database" (SVD) [6]. Consisting of a total of 2225 sessions, of which 1356 correspond to pathological subjects and the remaining 869 correspond to healthy people, the database is conformed both with examples of male and female voices. Each of the sessions is made up as follows:

- Recordings of vowels [i, a, u] in four different intonations [neutral, high, low, ascending-descending]
- Recordings of the sentence "Guten Morgen, wie geht is Ihnen?", which in English translates "Good morning, how are you?"

On doing so, each session contains 13 different recordings, although some of them are incomplete or simply some of the recordings were excluded due to quality issues. Recordings of the vowels also contain the EGG signals, which were also used for this study. All recordings were taken with a sampling frequency of 50 kHz and a resolution of 16 bits.

2.2   Feature Generation

With the aim of generating a discriminative representation from the data at hand, three different types of features were generated from each signal, namely common signal features, acoustic features and noise features. Such generation was done over both the speech signal and the EGG signals, achieving two feature vectors, which were concatenated to form a single feature vector.

Common Signal Features: This type of features are widely used for different kind of signals, are based on the time information and also on the frequency information of the signal [10,11,27], the latter generally by means of Fourier transform. The main purpose of generating common signal features is because of their outstanding representation of each signal with a low computational cost, also since they are well known and are easy to implement [22]. The features generated at this stage are:

- Fundamental frequency.
- Mean frequency.
- Median value of signal.
- Standard deviation.

- Variance.
- Smallest element in signal.
- Largest element in signal.
- Maximum to minimum difference.
- Peak magnitude to RMS ratio.
- Root mean square level.
- Root sum of squares level.
- Period of sequence.

Acoustic Features: These features seeks specific information of the human voice signals, in comparison with the previous features, acoustic features are implemented only for voice signals, specially for voice recognition tasks and in some cases for pathology detection [11,14,29]. Specifically, at this stage the Mel-Frequency-Cepstral Coefficients (MFCC) were extracted from each signal of the database [30], such coefficients are widely used in the state-of-the-art, given that they provide information that takes advantage of the main components of a human voice signal, ignoring environmental and frequency factors with low importance or which prevents a correct generation of features. The MFCC were computed from the signals by using the following parameters, the configuration used by [14] was mainly taken into account:

- Analysis frame duration $AFD = 40$ ms.
- Analysis frame shift: $AFS = 20$ ms.
- Preemphasis coefficient: $PC = 0.97$.
- Number of filterbank channels: $NFC = 30$.
- Number of cepstral coefficients: $NCC = 10$
- Cepstral sine lifter parameter: $CSLP = 22$.
- Lower frequency limit: $LFL = 300$ Hz.
- Upper frequency limit: $UFL = 3400$ Hz.

Aiming to obtain the most relevant information of the MFCC and considering the huge amount of generated data, from each Cepstral Coefficient, the following measures were extracted: Median value, Standard deviation, Variance, Smallest element, Largest element, Maximum to minimum difference, Peak magnitude to RMS ratio, Root mean square level and Root sum of squares level. Finally, a total of 90 acoustic features are obtained for each signal.

Noise-Based Features: Some related studies have been developed under the assumption that voice signals that present pathologies contain more noise than the voice signals belonging to healthy people [14,29], therefore, allowing some measures of noise in the signals to be good descriptors to be able to identify when a person has any speech pathology. In this study, three noise measurements which synthesize the proportion of noise that is present in each signal were implemented. The measures generated were the ratio of signal to noise (SNR), which measures the relationship between the power of the fundamental content and the power of the entire non-harmonic content of the signal. The second measure was the total harmonic distortion (THD), which is measured from the fundamental frequency and the first five harmonics of the signal. The last noise-based-feature was the signal to noise and distortion ratio (SINAD), which measures the power ratio between all harmonics and the noise content in the signal.

2.3   Considered Classifiers

As a result of the feature generation stage, a matrix representation of the data corresponding to the speech and EGG signals was obtained, this new representation of the data allows to train two well known classifiers for machine learning tasks due to their high performance and excellent ability to generate nonlinear decision boundaries, namely, artificial neural network [21] and a support vector machine [28], whose basic configurations are explained below:

Artificial Neural Network – ANN: It was intended that the architecture implemented for the neural network to be simple to minimize the computational cost in the classification task, so that the predictions made by the classifier were both accurate and fast. From this criterion, it was decided to implement a fully connected neural network architecture with a single hidden layer [21]. The number of neurons in the input layer is defined by the number of features extracted from the signals, and the number of neurons in the hidden layer was selected through an architecture analysis of the neural network, evaluating its classification performance from a single neuron to 100 neurons in the hidden layer, the results of this network architecture selection test can be seen in Sect. 3.

Support Vector Machine – SVM: Considering that the results when using an SVM depend directly on the selected kernel and its parameters, the tests were performed using three different kernels, the first one being the linear kernel which is the one with the lowest computational cost, but at the same time, it does not allow the estimation of complex decision boundaries to perform the classification task [28]. The second kernel used was the polynomial kernel, which slightly increases the computational cost in exchange for being able to obtain more complex decision boundaries that better fit to the data. The last kernel used is of the most implemented in classification tasks because it allows to obtain decision boundaries that fit adequately to the training data, thus obtaining an accuracy generally higher than the previous kernels, this is the Gaussian or Radial Basis Function (RBF) kernel. The mathematical definition of the implemented kernels is as follows:

$$K_{Linear}(x_i, x_j) = \langle x_i, x_j \rangle$$
$$K_{Polynomial}(x_i, x_j) = (\langle x_i, x_j \rangle + 1)^q, \quad q \in \mathbb{N}$$
$$K_{Gaussian}(x_i, x_j) = \exp\left(\frac{-|x_i - x_j|_2^2}{2\sigma^2}\right), \quad \sigma > 0$$

where $\langle \cdot, \cdot \rangle$ represents the dot product between two vectors.

2.4   Validation and Optimization

K-Fold Cross-Validation: In classification tasks, it is very important to be able to correctly evaluate the obtained results, ensuring that the classifier generalizes adequately predictions on unknown examples. Considering this, different methods and evaluation measures has been proposed allowing to make a rigorous analysis of the performance of the learning algorithm. One of the most well-known evaluation methods used in the state of the art is K-Fold Cross-Validation. This method consists on dividing the entire database into K evaluation subsets, thus training K times the considered classifier so that in each training a subgroup (Fold) is excluded from the database, and used at the end of the training stage as a test set, after executing the K-Fold Cross-Validation evaluation method, a prediction is obtained for each example contained in the database, so that it can be evaluated with any performance measure to verify that the results are not overfitted to the database at hand.

Particle Swarm Optimization (PSO): Both neural networks and SVMs have input parameters that must be selected by the user that directly affect the result of the classification, an improperly selected parameter can lead the classifier to not fit well the data or get overfitted. To avoid the manually selection and tuning of these parameters, one of the most used and broadly known optimization algorithm in the state of the art is the PSO, which is widely implemented because it uses stochastic a cooperative methods to find the optimal working point of the function to be optimized, which in this case corresponds to the classifier performance. Furthermore, we choose to use the PSO algorithm since is generally able to find a global optimum because it is less likely than other algorithms to fall into local optimum.

3   Experimental Setup

3.1   Preprocessing

A preprocessing step was performed over each one of the signals of the database, aiming to suppress atypical values of the signals and enhance the feature generation step by making it more efficient. At preprocessing stage, as a first step the original sample frequency was reduced from 50 kHz to 25 kHz, it is a common practice in this type of studies aiming to simplify the computational processing demand and to bring near the data to the normal human speech frequency at same time [14]. Then, a 5th-order median filter was applied on each signal, allowing to attenuate atypical values contained on the signal due to the effect of instruments used to acquire such signals and environmental noise perturbations.

3.2   Dataset Configuration

For this work, the complete database was not used because the results obtained by [14] were mainly taken into account, this work showed that the best vowel to perform a classification between healthy and pathological subjects is the vowel 'a' in neutral intonation, so it was decided to use for this analysis only such vowel with neutral intonation, but unlike the aforementioned work, it was decided to use the signals of the sentence "Guten Morgen, wie geht is Ihnen?" and the EGG signal to obtain more information from each example.

Only the sessions corresponding to subjects older than 18 years were selected from the database, by selecting only the 'a' vowel in neutral intonation a total of 1333 examples of pathological subjects and 668 healthy subjects were downloaded, these were used to create the first configuration matrix (X_1) of dimensions 2001×210, where the rows correspond to the number of examples and the columns correspond to the concatenated characteristics of the speech and EGG signals. Additionally, the sessions corresponding to the sentence "Guten Morgen, wie geht is Ihnen?" of subjects older than 18 years were also downloaded, in this way, 1333 examples of subjects with pathologies and 615 healthy subjects were used to create the second configuration matrix (X_2) of dimensions 1948×105, this matrix has half of the features than the first one, because the EGG signals corresponding to the sentences are not found in the original database. Taking advantage of the large number of examples, in the sentences dataset was decided to take the 615 examples of healthy subjects and the 615 longest files regarding the duration of the recording of the pathological subjects, with the purpose of working with a balanced dataset allowing to compare the obtained results with other works that also implement a balanced version of the benchmark dataset, in this way, the third configuration matrix (X_3) of dimensions 1230×105 was created.

3.3   Artificial Neural Network

The ANNs architecture consists of three layers of fully connected network type, each dataset $(X_1, X_2$ and $X_3)$ has its own ANN architecture. The test to select the number of neurons of the hidden layer was carried out changing the number of neurons between 1 and 100, this range was selected because architectural tests showed that after 100 neurons in the hidden layer, all the ANNs suffered from overfitting, thus decreasing the overall performance and increasing the computational burden. A 20-Fold Cross-Validation was applied, with a fixed regularization parameter $\lambda = 0.5$ and 300 as the maximum number of iterations. The results of the architectural analyzes are shown in Fig. 1, obtaining finally 80, 57 and 30 as the best numbers of neurons in the hidden layer for X_1, X_2 and X_3, respectively.

Once the ANN architectures are defined, it was used the PSO algorithm to optimize both the number of iterations to fit the ANN and the regularization parameter λ. A total of 100 particles were used with a maximum of 50 iterations in addition to a 20-Fold Cross-Validation algorithm applied to avoid the overfitting issue. The results of this final test for the ANN classifier are shown in Table 1.

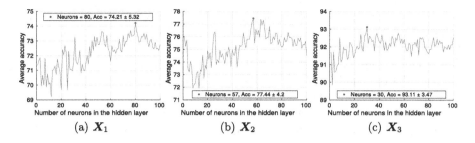

Fig. 1. Analysis for setting the number of neurons in the hidden layer

3.4 SVM

The tests for the SVM classifier were performed in the same way as in the neural network, where the PSO algorithm was employed to optimize the regularization parameter C and the kernel parameters used in the SVM, 100 particles were used and a maximum of 50 iterations with a 20-Fold Cross-Validation obtaining the results shown in Table 2.

4 Results and Discussion

The results shown in Table 1 demonstrate how the PSO algorithm not only improved the overall performance of the ANN designed for each database, but also significantly reduced the number of iterations required to train each classifier. The achieved performance improvement can be noticed when comparing the final classification results respect to those obtained in the architecture analysis shown in Sect. 3. In addition to calculating the algorithm accuracy, other evaluation measures were calculated in Table 1 to obtain more information about the behavior and performance of the classification algorithm.

Table 1. Classification results of ANN

Dataset	Average accuracy	Standard deviation	Sensitivity	Specificity	Geometric mean	Optimal parameters	
						Iterations	λ
X_1	76.06 %	3.34 %	84.85 %	58.53 %	70.47 %	31	10.4131
X_2	79.63 %	4.44 %	87.77 %	61.95 %	73.74 %	49	5.8104
X_3	93.27 %	2.32 %	95.61 %	90.89 %	93.22 %	264	2.1403

The results shown in Table 2 demonstrate how the classification accuracy over each configurations of the dataset can vary considerably depending on the selected kernel. The final performance results allow to identify that polynomial Kernel adjusts X_1 and X_3 in a better way, while the Gaussian Kernel shows better performance in X_2. In addition, when analyzing the results presented in Tables 1 and 2, it is possible to determine that the ANN is the classifier that shows a better performance over the three database configurations, regarding that both classifiers (ANN and SVM) were configured in simple ways looking for a low computational cost during training step. Furthermore, The results show that third dataset configuration matrix (X_3) highly improves the results over the other two, the main reason of that is the use of a balanced version of the dataset, it show that the SVD dataset contain several samples that contains recording fails and quality errors, this analysis is supported by the results presented in the state-of-the-art methods.

Table 2. Classification results of SVM

Dataset	Kernel	Average accuracy	Standard deviation	Sensitivity	Specificity	Geometric mean	Optimal parameters	
							C	Kernel param.
X_1	Linear	74.76 %	**3.66** %	84.62 %	55.09 %	68.28 %	8.194	—
	Polynomial	**75.36** %	4.11 %	**85.60** %	54.94 %	68.58 %	0.442	q = 2
	Gaussian	75.32 %	4.02 %	84.92 %	**56.14** %	**69.05** %	10.830	$\sigma = 24.647$
X_2	Linear	77.83 %	3.75 %	**87.02** %	57.89 %	70.97 %	16.031	—
	Polynomial	77.70 %	**3.62** %	86.42 %	58.86 %	71.32 %	0.253	q = 3
	Gaussian	**78.51** %	4.45 %	86.20 %	**61.79** %	**72.98** %	8.398	$\sigma = 9.899$
X_3	Linear	92.47 %	**2.87** %	96.10 %	88.78 %	92.37 %	1.351	—
	Polynomial	**92.77** %	2.99 %	95.94 %	**89.59** %	**92.71** %	3.958	q = 1
	Gaussian	92.62 %	4.37 %	**96.42** %	88.78 %	92.52 %	12.151	$\sigma = 39.281$

In some recent works the SVD dataset has been implemented in different ways and configurations, obtaining a variety of results regarding the performance of the classifiers designed in each proposal. The results of those works have allowed to deduct that this dataset is composed by several samples with corrupted information and incomplete recordings. Therefore, the research works developed around the SVD dataset has implemented balanced versions of this, for example, the works that have used the 'a' vowel in normal intonation are: [17] obtaining 93.2% ± 0.01% of accuracy with 262 healthy and 244 pathologic samples, [2] obtaining 98.94% of accuracy with 266 healthy and 263 pathologic samples, [3] obtaining 99.68% of accuracy with 262 healthy and 244 pathologic samples and [11] obtaining 100.0% of accuracy with 705 healthy and 705 pathologic samples. Besides, a work that have implemented a very recent technique known as Deep Learning used a balanced version of the dataset with 583 healthy and 583 pathologic samples obtained 71.36% of classification accuracy [10].

Some other works, try to take advantage of the huge information of the dataset and implement the alternative signals to the speech, in [16] uses the EGG signals of the 'a' vowel in normal intonation achieving 99.87% of accuracy with approximately 400 samples of the dataset. On the other hand, in [24] uses the sentence "Guten Morgen, wie geht is Ihnen?" pronounced by 632 healthy and 101 pathologic subjects, obtaining 67.2% of sensibility and 70.3% of specificity, showing that the use of unbalanced data causes a considerable reduction in the performance of classification algorithm. Only two works have used the complete dataset in the experiments, [14] achieved 67.0% of accuracy when using only the 'a' vowel in normal intonation making the base line of studies in this dataset, and in [18] were implemented all the useful samples corresponding to the 'a' vowel in normal intonation of the SVD, obtaining 94.7% ± 0.21% of accuracy in their best results, the features generated were based on vocal tract area irregularity and applying PCA to reduce the number of features implemented for the classification task.

Although the classification accuracies in all these state-of-the-art methods are not directly comparable with the achieved results of this work, given that they use different database configurations and change the number of examples used for the classification task, all those results can be taken as reference points to prove the great change in accuracy when change the number of examples, showing that the SVD database represent a great challenge regarding the sessions acquisition quality.

5   Conclusion

In this work a voice pathology detection framework was presented, three different configurations of the SVD dataset was designed to apply two well known classifiers (ANN and SVM) to detect pathologies in voice signals. This is the first work that uses a optimization algorithm (PSO) to automatically tune the parameters of the classifiers aiming to achieve the best performance. Three different dataset configurations and the use of different classifiers allowed to identify the benefit of using the optimization algorithm to enhance the classification results and reveal that the SVD dataset contain several samples that represent a challenge mainly because it contains recording fails and quality errors, showing the best results over the third dataset configuration matrix (X_3) because it was balanced allowing to avoid some fail examples from the original dataset. Besides, the results show that the use of a complete sentence pronounced by the subjects could be more relevant to the classification task, since the use of the sentence "Guten Morgen, wie geht is Ihnen?" achieved best performance in all the experiments. As future work, the use of new descriptors will be taken into account and a feature selection algorithm will be implemented to reduce the dimension of the representation space.

Acknowledgments. This work was partially supported by the grants provided by Programa Nacional de Jóvenes Investigadores e Innovadores – COLCIENCIAS – Announcement 775 of 2017 and the support for Instituto Tecnológico Metropolitano from Medellin-Colombia.
Also, authors specially thank the support given by the SDAS Research Group.

References

1. Acharya, U.R., Fujita, H., Oh, S.L., Hagiwara, Y., Tan, J.H., Adam, M.: Application of deep convolutional neural network for automated detection of myocardial infarction using ecg signals. Inf. Sci. **415**, 190–198 (2017)
2. Al-nasheri, A., Muhammad, G., Alsulaiman, M., Ali, Z.: Investigation of voice pathology detection and classification on different frequency regions using correlation functions. J. Voice **31**(1), 3–15 (2017)
3. Al-nasheri, A., et al.: An investigation of multidimensional voice program parameters in three different databases for voice pathology detection and classification. J. Voice **31**(1), 113–e9 (2017)
4. Ali, F.: Voice recognition anatomy, processing, uses and application in C (2017)
5. AlZubaidi, A.K., Sideseq, F.B., Faeq, A., Basil, M.: Computer aided diagnosis in digital pathology application: review and perspective approach in lung cancer classification. In: 2017 Annual Conference on New Trends in Information & Communications Technology Applications (NTICT), pp. 219–224. IEEE (2017)
6. Barry, W., Pützer, M.: Saarbrucken voice database. Institute of Phonetics, Universität des Saarlandes (2007). http://www.stimmdatenbank.coli.uni-saarland.de
7. Béranger, J.: Big Data and Ethics: The Medical Datasphere. Elsevier, New York City (2016)
8. Castro-Ospina, A., Castro-Hoyos, C., Peluffo-Ordonez, D., Castellanos-Dominguez, G.: Novel heuristic search for ventricular arrhythmia detection using normalized cut clustering. In: 2013 35th Annual International Conference of the IEEE Engineering in Medicine and Biology Society (EMBC), pp. 7076–7079. IEEE (2013)
9. Chiu, C.C., et al.: State-of-the-art speech recognition with sequence-to-sequence models. arXiv preprint arXiv:1712.01769 (2017)
10. Harar, P., Alonso-Hernandezy, J.B., Mekyska, J., Galaz, Z., Burget, R., Smekal, Z.: Voice pathology detection using deep learning: a preliminary study. In: 2017 International Conference and Workshop on Bioinspired Intelligence (IWOBI), pp. 1–4. IEEE (2017)
11. Hemmerling, D., Skalski, A., Gajda, J.: Voice data mining for laryngeal pathology assessment. Comput. Biol. Med. **69**, 270–276 (2016)
12. Ibrahim, S., Djemal, R., Alsuwailem, A.: Electroencephalography (EEG) signal processing for epilepsy and autism spectrum disorder diagnosis. Biocybern. Biomed. Eng. **38**(1), 16–26 (2018)
13. Lytras, M.D., Papadopoulou, P.: Applying Big Data Analytics in Bioinformatics and Medicine. IGI Global, Pennsylvania (2017)
14. Martínez, D., Lleida, E., Ortega, A., Miguel, A., Villalba, J.: Voice pathology detection on the Saarbrücken voice database with calibration and fusion of scores using MultiFocal toolkit. In: Torre Toledano, D., et al. (eds.) IberSPEECH 2012. CCIS, vol. 328, pp. 99–109. Springer, Heidelberg (2012). https://doi.org/10.1007/978-3-642-35292-8_11
15. Mendoza, L., Peña, J., Muñoz-Bedoya, L., Velandia-Villamizar, H.: Speech subvocal signal processing using packet wavelet and neuronal network. TecnoLógicas, 655–667 (2013). https://doi.org/10.22430/22565337.371
16. Muhammad, G., Alhamid, M.F., Hossain, M.S., Almogren, A.S., Vasilakos, A.V.: Enhanced living by assessing voice pathology using a co-occurrence matrix. Sensors **17**(2), 267 (2017)
17. Muhammad, G., et al.: Voice pathology detection using interlaced derivative pattern on glottal source excitation. Biomed. Signal Process. Control **31**, 156–164 (2017)

18. Muhammad, G., et al.: Automatic voice pathology detection and classification using vocal tract area irregularity. Biocybern. Biomed. Eng. **36**(2), 309–317 (2016)
19. Orozco-Naranjo, A.J., Muñoz-Gutiérrez, P.A.: Detection of pathological and normal heartbeat using wavelet packet, support vector machines and multilayer perceptron. Tecno Lógicas **31**, 73–91 (2013)
20. Parascandolo, P., Cesario, L., Vosilla, L., Viano, G.: Computer aided diagnosis: state-of-the-art and application to musculoskeletal diseases. In: Magnenat-Thalmann, N., Ratib, O., Choi, H.F. (eds.) 3D Multiscale Physiological Human, pp. 277–296. Springer, London (2014). https://doi.org/10.1007/978-1-4471-6275-9_12
21. Schalkoff, R.J.: Artificial Neural Networks, vol. 1. McGraw-Hill, New York (1997)
22. Schilling, R.J., Harris, S.L.: Fundamentals of Digital Signal Processing Using MATLAB. Cengage Learning, Boston (2011)
23. Semmlow, J.L., Griffel, B.: Biosignal and Medical Image Processing. CRC Press, Boca Raton (2014)
24. Shinohara, S., et al.: Multilingual evaluation of voice disability index using pitch rate. ASTESJ **2**(3), 765–772 (2017)
25. Shriberg, L.D., et al.: A diagnostic marker to discriminate childhood apraxia of speech from speech delay: II. Validity studies of the pause marker. J. Speech Lang. Hear. Res. **60**(4), S1118–S1134 (2017)
26. Summers, R.M.: Deep learning and computer-aided diagnosis for medical image processing: a personal perspective. In: Lu, L., Zheng, Y., Carneiro, G., Yang, L. (eds.) Deep Learning and Convolutional Neural Networks for Medical Image Computing. ACVPR, pp. 3–10. Springer, Cham (2017). https://doi.org/10.1007/978-3-319-42999-1_1
27. von Tscharner, V.: Time-frequency and principal-component methods for the analysis of emgs recorded during a mildly fatiguing exercise on a cycle ergometer. J. Electromyogr. Kinesiol. **12**(6), 479–492 (2002)
28. Vapnik, V.N.: The Nature of Statistical Learning Theory. Springer, Heidelberg (1999). https://doi.org/10.1007/978-1-4757-3264-1
29. Verde, L., De Pietro, G., Sannino, G.: Voice disorder identification by using machine learning techniques. IEEE Access **6**, 16246–16255 (2018)
30. Wojcicki, K.: HTK MFCC MATLAB. MATLAB Central File Exchange (2011)

Automatic Visual Classification of Parking Lot Spaces: A Comparison Between BoF and CNN Approaches

Jhon Edison Goez Mora$^{(\boxtimes)}$ iD, Juan Camilo Londoño Lopera iD, and Diego Alberto Patiño Cortes iD

Universidad Nacional de Colombia - Medellín Campus, Medellín, Colombia
{jegoez,jclondonol,dapatinoco}@unal.edu.co

Abstract. Computer vision has a wide and diverse range of applications nowadays. A particular one is automatic detection of parking lot occupancy, where a computer has to identify whether a parking lot space is empty or occupied. As in any visual classification problem, detecting parking lot spaces relies on the existence of a representative visual dataset. This problem of binary classification is commonly approached using features with adequate level of invariance to changes in illumination or rotation, that allow feeding these features into classifiers such as the SVM. Most used approaches are based on the use of convolutional neural networks, some times based on pre-trained models which in general have quite high performance. however several of these methods are tested with common experiments that do not take into account the variations that occur when training with different combinations of angles, lighting variations, and weather types. That is why in this paper we present a comparison between two approaches to solve the problem of parking lot classification with two methods: Convolutional Neural Networks and Bag of Features. In this paper we show how to use the standard Bag-of-features model to learn a visual dictionary, and use it to classify empty and occupied spaces. Results are compared with CNN approaches, emphasizing on accuracy, sensitivity analysis, and execution time.

Keywords: Images processing · Invariance · Parking lot
Convolutional Neural Networks · Bag of features

1 Introduction

One common application of computer vision is automatic surveillance. In this area, a camera, in most cases fixed in an environment which is desired to be a lookout in search of particular objects, persons, threats among other visual objects. A particular case of automatic surveillance is parking lot occupancy automatic detection; where a computer has to identify whether a parking lot space is empty or occupied.

© Springer Nature Switzerland AG 2018
J. C. Figueroa-García et al. (Eds.): WEA 2018, CCIS 915, pp. 160–170, 2018.
https://doi.org/10.1007/978-3-030-00350-0_14

Parking lot spaces classification relies on the existence of a representative visual dataset as any visual classification problem. Recent papers focused on the same problem has successfully used the PKLot dataset [6] created in the Federal University of Parana and the Pontifical Catholic University of Parana.

This problem of binary classification is commonly approached using extractors of characteristics that have properties of invariance to changes of illumination or rotation that can later be fed into classifiers such as the SVM (support vector machines). the most common solutions are based on the use of CNN (convolutional neural networks) either based on pre-trained models, sometimes modified for reducing training time. However, several of these methods are tested with common experiments that do not take into account variations that occur when training and testing with different combinations of sets doing an comparing them at running times, accuracy and precision. That is the reason why in this paper we present a comparison between two approaches to solve the problem of parking lot classification: Convolutional Neural Networks and BoF (Bag of Features). Is fine-tuned the VGG16 CNN and compared our own results against several state-of-the-art results. Later, is used Bag-of-features model to learn a dictionary of visual words and used it to classify empty and occupied spaces. The results were compared emphasizing accuracy, sensitivity analysis, and time performance. This comparison also theorizes some of the reasons why both approaches fails on false positives and false negatives.

This document is organized as follows: In Sect. 2 it's present a short review of several approaches to solving the problem of parking lots classification. Sections 3 and 4 describe the general approach we used to solve the binary classification problem. Section 5 shows the results of applying our approach and the one that uses neural networks with various combinations and tests to each method. Finally, the Sect. 6 provides some remarks about this work and present some discussion and future work.

2   Previous Work

A still open discussion in computer vision is to determinate whether the algorithms of parameters selection or the hand selection of features are suitable for a visual classification problem. The algorithms of parameters selection solve the problem to create an informative set of feature adequate. They have proved to obtain good results but require a large data set in order to train the models. On the other way, hand selection of features are fast and also achieve good results. However, it takes time to design an optimal set of feature to a specific problem. In this short review, it's present some examples of both approaches and highlights some of their advantages and weaknesses.

Several studies on the stated problem based on hand selection of features can be found in recent literature [2,8,9]. In those works, authors use a wide variety of feature sets of which a large proportion exploits the color of information of the images through several color spaces. As an example in [4] used the HSV color space and establish as features the histogram of the hue (H) channel. This channel was selected because of its invariance to rotation and low computational cost. In [1] the authors used the LUV color space. The magnitude of the gradient of the image that indicates the intensity of the change in color space at each point and six channels of quantified gradient as the features for determining the parking lot availability. In [12] only the a* and b* from La*b* color space were used because of their invariance to illumination. All these works use classic classifiers such as SVM or KNN (k-nearest neighbors) to determinate the state of the parking lot with successful results of about 90% of accuracy.

There are also some studies in literature based on Deep Learning and CNN aiming to solve the problem of classifying empty/occupied parking lot spaces. Within this approach, the use of pre-trained models is recurrent. As an example in [3] used LeNet-5 model, and AlexNet model. quoting the reference has two convolutional layers followed by max pooling and two fully connected layers. The first layer (conv1) takes a $224 \times 224 \times 3$ input from the original image. Layers conv2 and fc4 have a reduced number of filters and neurons to better suit a binary classification task without over-fitting. Within fc5, the last Gaussian RBF (radial basis function) layer is replaced with a classical inner product layer acting like a 2-way soft max classifier. They also stated that the detection of free spaces is still an open problem because in most cases the developed solution only fits specific environments and are very difficult to generalize. These models are the base for the construction of a less complex net which could Achieve a more robust solution to changes in lighting and perspective.

In [13] the authors used the VggNet model that is designed to recognize over 1000 classes. The model was fine-tuned to solve the binary problem of the identifies free/occupied parking spaces. In addition, they develop an application for smartphones in order to inform users of the availability of parking spaces. In [5] the authors develop own model of CNN. Unlike other related works, discrimination was made in the tests by the type of climate present in the PKLot Dataset. Better performance is obtained in comparison with the original PKLot paper [6]. In most of the related studies with CNN approaches, the authors argued to have better results than the methods that use other classifiers like SVM.

Finally, found two alternative methods [7,10]: In [7] the parking spaces are presented as a set of surfaces to build a 3d cube for later training a set of weak classifiers that are later merged and ponder to solve the problem. On the other side, in [10] surveillance cameras were used to obtain a binary map of the parking space. As features for classification, they used local entropy average and the standard deviation of the average of the local entropy. The reason for this choice is because they related the state of the parking spaces with the local entropy Which is quantified from the uniformity of the grayscale values of the region.

3   Materials and Methods

3.1   Dataset

For testing and validation of the proposed methods for development of the solution is used the PkLot dataset. PKLot is a robust parking lot occupancy dataset that has visual information about three different parking lots with several camera angles, the images are taken at different day hours, and different weather conditions. PKLot image acquisition was done in two parking lots. One of them uses two cameras with different angles but in different periods of time as shown in the Fig. 1(a) and (b). The other parking lot is bigger, an has a different point of view. The images were taken during a period of 30 days excluding the nocturnal hours arguing the low quality obtained during this hours. PkLot images are classified into three types of weather: sunny, cloudy, and rainy. it's were taken in a range of 8 to 25 days. Every single image were segmented by parking spaces and labeled by the availability of spaces. Table 1 show the distribution and the total segmented images for testing with the proposed methods, additionally, the dataset provides the completely segmented images of the three parking lots for all the days and hours in which the test was made and rotates the parking spaces so that they are left with an orientation of 0 or 90 degrees depending on the angle that has the camera for the parking lot. Based on these images is make the training and testing process for the classification of the parking space.

(a) Parking 04 rainy.   (b) Paking 05 sunny.

(c) Parking PUC cloudy.

Fig. 1. Pklot Dataset

3.2   Methods

For the solution of the parking spaces problem, were implemented two methods in order of compared his performance. The first one is CNN, technique that has already implemented in solving this kind of problem. The second one is the method of Bag of Features, an alternative algorithm to the mentioned in the state of art.

Table 1. PKLot Dataset

Parking lot	Weather condition	Occupied spaces	Empty spaces
UFPR04	Sunny	32166	26334
(28 parking spaces)	Cloudy	11608	27779
	Rainy	2351	5607
UFPR05	Sunny	57584	42306
(45 parking spaces)	Cloudy	33764	23202
	Rainy	6078	2851
PUCPR	Sunny	96762	111672
(100 parking spaces)	Cloudy	42363	90417
	Rainy	55104	27951

Convolutional Neural Networks. This method is based on the principle of operating of the visual cortex of a biological brain, due to its characteristics poses an advantage for image processing and especially for the comparison process, previously observed the modification of networks such as AlexNet, LeNet and VggNet To work the classification of parking spaces. In this paper, the network Vgg16 is used. That aims to classify 1000 different classes but is modified to become a binary problem (busy, empty) see Fig. 2(a). And a fine-tuning is made modifying the weights of the last layer of the neural network for the specific task of sorting the parking spaces.

Bag of Features. The method consists of creating a set of parking spaces descriptors that will be used as the source of information of a classifier. These descriptors are extracted from the points of interest in the image, such as color changes, corners, edges, among others. Use is made of the SIFT algorithm to extract both the keypoints and the characteristics. These characteristics are extracted for each image resulting in a vector of dimension n x 128 (n is the number of keypoints found in all the images).

With vector of visual words, it's performed a clustering by the method of Euclidean distance for converting the number of clusters selected in the dictionary of visual words. Once the representative points are obtained, it takes new images from the parking lots for compared the "visual words" to the dictionary and so the word recurrence histogram is formed for each image supplied. The histogram has a number of bings equal to the number of clusters. The process described above is done for each class separately, occupied and empty. Later this information is used for the training of an SVM classifier. This process described in the scheme of the Fig. 2(b).

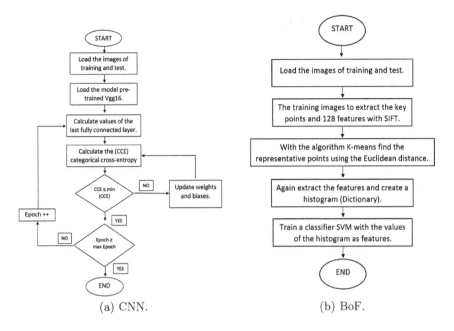

(a) CNN.   (b) BoF.

Fig. 2. Flowchart

4   Methodology

To applicate, the CNN is used the python library Theano to evaluate mathematical expressions and the API Keras, also, is used the pre-trained model Vgg16 and the algorithm of Vgg16 [5] is loaded to do the fine tune of the classes. This algorithm used the categorical cross-entropy as a metric for error minimization and the Adam optimizer to reduce the learning rate during the epochs.The results were compared with the works of the state of art, valid his performance to use as a comparison criterion with the BoF method.

For the Bag of features method, it's use 10000 images that combine all weather types and all the parking lots. Then an iterative algorithm is performed to finding the number of clusterings where is presented best performance. The results of this test determined that the number of clusters more adequate was K = 800 that obtained a performance of 92.04%. The classifier SVM implemented was the Toolbox Balu [11], where is used a Radial Basis Kernel.

With the number of clusters obtained, the tests performed as follows: both methods are exposed to three types of test, one discriminated by the type of parking, climate types are combined and proved to be successful. In the second one test are combined to types of parking and tested the performance of the methods related to climatic variations. Finally is develop an integration of all types of climate and parking using 50% of the images as training and 50% for testing.

5   Experiments and Results

For the compilation used a computer with the next characteristics:

- RAM: 30 GB
- CPU: 8 Cores
- GPU: 8 GB
- HD: SSD

Several experiments are done to test the algorithms. in the first place, the all data base is divided into 70% of the images for doing the training and 30% to do the testing. The Table 2 show the accuracy, precision, and recall obtained for the methods. The better results were for the algorithm CNN. tested in the parking lot PUCPR, with an accuracy, precision, and recall of over 99%. For another side with the results of the BoF method, gets an percents that varies a lot with the type of parking. The worst results are in the parking UFPR04 and the best in the PUCPR which has a fairly high top view that favors the classification.

Table 2. Results of CNN/BoF with all type of weather and parking 70 for train and 30 to test

Parking Lot	Accuracy		Precision		Recall	
	– CNN –	– BoF –	– CNN –	– BoF –	– CNN –	– BoF –
UFPR04 (28 parking spaces)	99.39	76.82	99.60	63.62	99.32	93.11
UFPR05 (45 parking spaces)	99.11	80.84	98.59	63.09	99.24	86.86
PUCPR (100 parking spaces)	99.77	92.04	99.74	92.10	99.84	93.11
All (173 parking spaces)	99.55	85.77	99.46	79.51	99.65	92.11

After performing the test with the total set of images, tests develop discriminated between types of parking and the types of weather. This to find the situations where the algorithms do the task with better performance identifying the invariance versus some changes and identifying the images that represent a challenge.

It trained with each set of parking lots and with the total set of all types of climate, and each trained group is tested with the same training set and with the other parking spaces. Table 3 show the results of the Convolutional Neural Network where obviously the best results are presented when testing with the same set of training and especially when testing with all the set of images. On the other way where there is a considerable decrease in accuracy, it is due to the variations in the parking UFPR04 and UFPR05 that is the same but have very different observation points and angles. The results of the test with the UFPR04 and train with UFPR05 was 94.11%. Also, a possible over-training observed when training with all the images and testing with the parking UFPR05 with an accuracy of 82.2%.

The same proof is made with BoF, the results show a considerable difference with the CNN, the accuracy, and the precision are very low. In the training with the UFPR05 and testing in UFPR04 a precision of 65% and a precision of 38% is presented. This indicates that this parking lot as a reference for training is not very adequate and the alternative method does not achieve a good performance with the small information that is obtained from the parking lot UFPR05.

Table 3. Testing on different parking lot on all type of weathers

Training	Testing	CNN		BoF	
		Accuracy	precision	Accuracy	precision
UFPR04	UFPR04	99.15	99.95	95.26	92.28
	UFPR05	99.68	94.21	90.35	78.63
	PUCPR	97.28	96.74	85.32	77.83
	All	98.05	97.94	88.18	80.67
UFPR05	UFPR04	94.11	98.06	65.10	38.72
	UFPR05	98.98	99.81	89.91	75.95
	PUCPR	93.24	94.89	75.19	57.58
	All	94.77	96.44	76.93	57.09
PUCPR	UFPR04	96.72	98.97	71.63	52.63
	UFPR05	90.37	77.71	77.52	51.91
	PUCPR	99.78	99.92	91.95	91.07
	All	97.11	95.55	85.34	77.07

For the proof with CNN, the same configuration is taken with the training set but for the test is analyzed with each of the types of weather presented in the dataset. This determines with which parking lot presents a better invariance in the face of weather changes and which of the types weather represents a challenge. However it is not a big difference and the precision remains above 90%. the results are observed in the Table 4. For the BoF method, show that the results in accuracy drop considerably obtaining an average of 83.9%.

Once obtained the results with a set of training determined by the three types of parking, we proceed to perform the same tests using the type of climate for the training. For the first experiment with CNN of Table 5, it is obtained that the results of the exactitude stay quite high when training with the weathers and test with each parking lot. the average of the results is 98%, with the best ones being those that were performed with the training of Cloudy tested with each type of parking lot.

The BoF presents on average an accuracy of 81.5%. the type of cloudy weather generates very low precision performance reaching 36% this indicates that many of the parking spaces that were full were identified as empty. While training with the rainy type generates high results over 96% as seen in the

Table 4. Testing different parking lots on different weathers

Training	Testing	CNN		BoF	
		Accuracy	precision	Accuracy	precision
UFPR04	Cloudy	98.99	99.02	86.63	80.62
	Rainy	96.67	95.97	89.51	80.48
	Sunny	97.80	97.71	88.72	80.61
UFPR05	Cloudy	97.67	99.45	71.09	54.27
	Rainy	92.51	98.45	82.29	56.74
	Sunny	93.62	93.73	79.54	61.08
PUCPR	Cloudy	97.39	96.38	84.18	77.73
	Rainy	98.89	98.08	88.19	77.44
	Sunny	96.41	94.39	85.23	76.30

Table 5. Testing on different weathers on different parking lots

Training	Testing	CNN		BoF	
		Accuracy	precision	Accuracy	precision
Cloudy	UFPR04	98.51	99.73	63.86	36.88
	UFPR05	99.10	98.52	76.63	48.52
	PUCPR	99.59	99.70	87.91	79.72
	All	99.29	99.45	81.54	65.83
Rainy	UFPR04	98.73	99.62	75.15	97.93
	UFPR05	98.35	96.39	67.01	98.03
	PUCPR	99.55	99.33	87.13	96.77
	All	99.20	98.89	80.43	97.11
Sunny	UFPR04	98.57	99.88	86.66	84.22
	UFPR05	98.65	99.37	88.29	87.50
	PUCPR	99.67	99.88	92.54	93.27
	All	99.29	99.75	90.59	90.71

Table 5. This method presents some difficulty in recognizing the parking spaces of the different parking lots using only one type of whether to train.

For the last test, the training and test are climate type. With this it is verified which method presents a better invariance to the changes of illumination, brightness and other effects that generate the three types of climate captured in the dataset. In Table 6 observed how distributing the training of the CNN with the types of climate the best results are obtained among all the tests carried out. The average is 99% in accuracy and precision, considering that comparisons are made with rainy days and tested on sunny days these results are quite good and check the effectiveness of the network in the face of changes present by lighting

Table 6. Testing on different weathers on all parking lots

Training	Testing	CNN		BoF	
		Accuracy	precision	Accuracy	precision
Cloudy	Cloudy	99.76	99.84	80.65	69.46
	Rainy	99.44	99.61	84.63	60.63
	Sunny	98.99	99.14	81.58	65.53
Rainy	Cloudy	99.56	99.49	83.40	97.37
	Rainy	99.69	99.61	85.71	96.83
	Sunny	98.80	98.25	77.24	97.18
Sunny	Cloudy	99.51	99.88	90.66	90.93
	Rainy	99.28	99.65	90.16	86.85
	Sunny	99.12	99.70	90.79	91.41

and the previously mentioned factors. In the case of BoF, a result similar to that of the network is obtained, on average an accuracy of 85% is given and at the 87% precision these being the best results as see in Table 6.

6 Conclusions

In each of the proposed methods, there is a small decrease in performance when tested in a different parking lot of which it was trained. however, the results show an improvement in both methods when are trained with the set of the weathers, because despite not having information about variations in lighting it contains information on all types of angle an distances in the PKlot.

The convolutional neuronal network presents a better overall performance against the BoF method; Although the computational cost for training is high, it is a procedure that is performed only in the initial stage, so it is considered that the most appropriate method to implement it is the CNN.

Considering the results obtained in this work, we propose, as future work, to perform practical tests in a real parking lot where a comparison can be made to determine if the computational cost and the execution time inherent to the of the CNN method justifies its implementation by the performance achieved and its advantages over the BoF alternative method.

References

1. Ahrnbom, M., Aström, K., Nilsson, M.: Fast classification of empty and occupied parking spaces using integral channel features. In: Conference on Computer Vision and Pattern Recognition Workshops (2016)
2. Amato, G., Carrara, F., Falchi, F., Gennaro, C., Meghini, C., Vairo, C.: Deep learning for decentralized parking lot occupancy detection. Expert. Syst. Appl. **72**, 327–334 (2017)

3. Amato, G., Carrara, F., Falchi, F., Gennaro, C., Vairo, C.: Car parking occupancy detection using smart camera networks and deep learning. In: IEEE Symposium on Computers and Communication (2016)
4. Baroffio, L., Bondi, L., Cesana, M., Redondi, A.E., Tagliasacchi, M.: A visual sensor network for parking lot occupancy detection in smart cities. In: 2nd World Forum on Internet of Things (WF-IoT) (2015)
5. Cazamias, J., Marek, M.: Parking space classification using convoluional neural networks (2016)
6. De Almeida, P.R.L., Oliveira, L.S., Britto, A.S., Silva, E.J., Koerich, A.L.: PKLot- a robust dataset for parking lot classification. Expert. Syst. Appl. **42**, 4937–4949 (2015)
7. Huang, C.C., Vu, H.T., Chen, Y.R.: A multiclass boosting approach for integrating weak classifiers in parking space detection. In: 2015 IEEE International Conference on Consumer Electronics - Taiwan, ICCE-TW 2015, vol. 8215, no. c, pp. 314–315 (2015)
8. Huang, C.-C., Vu, H.T.: Vacant parking space detection based on a multi-layer inference framework. IEEE Trans. Circuits Syst. Video Technol. **8215**(c), 1598–1610 (2016)
9. Ichihashi, H., Katada, T., Fujiyoshi, M., Notsu, A., Honda, K.: Improvement in the performance of camera based vehicle detector for parking lot. In: IEEE International Conference on Fuzzy Systems (2010)
10. Mateus, P.A., Maldonado, E.O., Nino, C.L.: Surveillance and management of parking spaces using computer vision. In: 2015 20th Symposium on Signal Processing, Images and Computer Vision, STSIVA 2015 - Conference Proceedings (2015)
11. Mery, D.: BALU: a Matlab toolbox for computer vision, pattern recognition and image processing (2011). http://dmery.ing.puc.cl/index.php/balu
12. True, N.: Vacant Parking Space Detection in Static Images (2007)
13. Valipour, S., Siam, M., Stroulia, E., Jagersand, M.: Neural networks, parking stall vacancy indicator system based on deep convolutional (2016)

On the Use of Neuroevolutive Methods as Support Tools for Diagnosing Appendicitis and Tuberculosis

Alvaro David Orjuela-Cañón[1]($\boxtimes$), Hugo Fernando Posada-Quintero[2],
Cesar Hernando Valencia[3], and Leonardo Mendoza[4]

[1] Universidad Antonio Nariño, Bogotá D.C., Colombia
alvorjuela@uan.edu.co
[2] University of Connecticut, Storrs, CT, USA
[3] Universidad Santo Tomás, Bucaramanga, Colombia
[4] Universidade Estadual do Rio de Janeiro, Rio de Janeiro, Brazil

Abstract. Artificial neural networks are being used in diagnosis support systems to detect different kind of diseases. As the design of multilayer perceptron is an open question, the present work shows a comparison between a traditional empirical way and neuroevolution method to find the best architecture to solve the disease detection problem. Tuberculosis and appendicitis databases were employed to test both proposals. Results show that neuroevolution offers a good alternative for the tuberculosis problem but there is lacks of performance in the appendicitis one.

Keywords: Neuroevolution · Artificial neural networks
Diagnosis support systems · Tuberculosis · Appendicitis

1 Introduction

Nowadays with the increasing volume in data, different fields have been advantage beneficiaries with the advances of the computational intelligence. More techniques and methods are employed in big data, knowledge extraction and support of decision making in diverse applications. One example of this can be encountered in medical purposes, where a better management of data, faster performance and improvement of the level of accuracy detection in diseases have made evident [1].

Different proposals from the computational intelligence have been employed to support problems in medical and biomedical applications. Learning systems as artificial neural networks (ANN) are commonly used in different applications such as image analysis and pattern recognition, biochemical analysis, drug design and diagnostic systems mainly [2–4]. In this last field, ANN have been used as support assistance for diagnosis of appendicitis in patients presenting with acute right iliac fossa [5], and comparisons with traditional medical models as the decision trees also have been implemented [6, 7]. Exploring different proposals of these learning systems, a database from 801 patients was applied to distinct proposals of ANN as radial basis function, multilayer network and probabilistic networks with results that reached rates of 99% in

© Springer Nature Switzerland AG 2018
J. C. Figueroa-García et al. (Eds.): WEA 2018, CCIS 915, pp. 171–181, 2018.
https://doi.org/10.1007/978-3-030-00350-0_15

accuracy [8]. Other study to regard is related with analysis of data from a rural location, based on information collected in a period of 12 months from 156 patients, which also employed an ANN [9]. For the tuberculosis case, ANN have been widely used in diagnosis support systems. Proposals with different input information have been exposed, having results with sensitivity values upper than 80%, reaching rates of 100% in some cases. For specificity, results have been less satisfactory, with registered values that have dropped to 40%, in the worst case [10–13]. All those results show differences according to available information used in each study. Some studies just used a couple of variables, and a very few cases used all medical data of patients. It also depends on the quality of the information system used for such studies.

Neuroevolution of augmenting topologies (NEAT) is a technique to evolve ANN based on genetic algorithms. It was proposed in the beginning of the present millennium and is based on modifications of the weights and structure of the network synapses. Meanwhile the balance between the fitness of the evolved solutions and their diversity is maintained, crossover among topologies is developed, applying speciation [14–16].

Present work establishes a comparison between two different techniques to obtain the best architecture of an ANN to solve the disease detection problem in diagnosis support systems for tuberculosis and appendicitis. First technique is based on a traditional empirical mode to find the number of nodes in the hidden layer of a multilayer perceptron (MLP), which consists in to modify the number of nodes and test the network performance. Second method is based on NEAT technique to find the nodes and connections to solve the mentioned problems.

2   Methodology

Two databases were used for our comparison due to its similarities in number of examples, proportion of positive cases and number of variables to be considered. Both databases are detailed in this section. Then, aspects about the implementation of the ANN for disease detection will be explained.

2.1   Databases

First database was obtained from the TB Program at Hospital Santa Clara (HSC) in Bogotá D.C. - Colombia. Information from people under suspicion of pulmonary tuberculosis in the period from January 2008 to March 2011 was considered. The Ethics and Research Committee of the HSC approved this study. An informed consent was not needed because all data were obtained in a retrospective and anonymous mode. Only data from subjects with confirmed diagnostic were considered (using culture and individuals that finished the anti-TB therapy). At the end, information of 105 subjects was used: 83 subjects (79%) with TB confirmed and 22 subjects (21%) that were determined without the disease using diagnosis of exclusion. Confirmation of the TB cases was achieved using a culture test. For TB negative cases, tests did not have a positive culture test, other disease was found meanwhile the treatment, and as mentioned, a diagnosis of exclusion was used.

Features were extracted from different information. A first examination of signs and symptoms was performed by medical personnel, and a clinical suspicion diagnosis was determined. This variable was represented in an input variable named "Clinical information", which takes a "1" value when just the medical report was considered, and "0" when other test result or additional information lead the subject to start the treatment. Other included variables were extracted from sex, age, homeless, diabetes status, and HIV (human immunodeficiency virus)/AIDS (acquired immunodeficiency syndrome) status. This last was determined using the study of clinical suggestion and confirming the status with exams, but without complementary information as CD4 cell or viral load. All variables were coded with zeros and ones according to negative or positive presence, respectively (Table 1). Age variable was maintained as numeric, with its original information, and a normalization given by the maximum value was achieved. This procedure was developed to avoid saturation of values in the synaptic weights of network and to avoid a wrong representation of the information in training.

Table 1. Variables used in the Tuberculosis diagnostic problem.

Variable		Quantity
Sex	Male	72 (69%)
	Female	33 (31%)
Age	Mean + std	40.8 + 17.7
Clinical information	Yes	30 (29%)
	No	75 (71%)
HIV/AIDS	Yes	28 (27%)
	No	77 (73%)
Homeless	Yes	33 (27%)
	No	72 (72%)
Diabetes	Yes	2 (2%)
	No	103 (98%)

Second database represents seven medical measures with information from laboratory tests to confirm the diagnosis of appendicitis [17]. A total of 106 patients admitted to the emergency room during a three-month in 1980 and a six-month period of 1981–1982 were included with 85 with confirmed diagnostic by biopsy analysis with a histologic examination of the removed appendix. The age range was from two to 81 years with a mean age of 25. Fifty-five patients were males and 51 were females [18].

Variables were extracted from information from temperature and an admission blood sample. Then, total white count, manual differential count, cytochemical differential, and C-reactive protein quantity were taken into account. All values were real and then when normalized to be in the interval [0–1], according with the previous works reported in [17, 18]. Information about these variables can be seen in Table 2, where 'Yes' means subjects with confirmed disease.

Table 2. Variables used in the appendicitis diagnostic problem.

Variable		Mean + std
Temperature (°F)	Yes	100.2 + 1.4
	No	99.2 + 1.1
Total White Blood Count (WBC)	Yes	13.8 + 3.7
	No	9.2 + 4.8
Neutrophils count (%)	Yes	79.9 + 8.0
	No	68.3 + 11.4
Neutrophils count (x10^9/L)	Yes	11.0 + 3.3
	No	6.6 + 4.5
Manual differential count (%)	Yes	16.7 + 14.3
	No	8.3 + 10.6
Manual differential count (x10^9/L)	Yes	2.2 + 2.1
	No	0.7 + 0.8
C-reactive proteins	Yes	4.0 + 4.3
	No	2.2 + 4.4

2.2   Models Determination

For estimating the statistical error and generalization of the models, using the explained dataset, cross-validation technique was employed [19]. In this case, the dataset was divided into three sets ensuring that data from people without and with the disease are equitable distributed. This is performed to assess the generalization of the trained model, preserving a portion of data that was not used in training. Table 3 shows these sets and the number of its members.

Commonly, one hidden layer and one output layer are enough to solve classification problems, regardless of the type of input variable [20]. The ANN used in this work had an input layer composed of seven units, each one for each variable, and one output layer composed just of one neuron. Values of +1 and −1 were used to represent if input data corresponds to a patient with TB or not, respectively. Neurons in the hidden layer were established in an experimental way, testing from two to ten neurons. All neurons had a hyperbolic tangent function as activation function.

Between different algorithms to train the ANN, resilient backpropagation was used because its speed and low computational cost [21]. In training, also a cross-validation strategy was considered. In each case, training was performed with two sets (see Table 3) and results for validation were computed with the left out set, maximizing the classification rate between TB and no disease. To avoid overfitting, an early stopping procedure was implemented. Performances of the obtained models were evaluated using sensitivity and specificity. The different trainings were performed employing MATLAB 2017a (The MathWorks, Inc, Natrick, MA) through its Neural Networks Toolbox [22].

Table 3. Dataset division for training and validation.

Fold	Tuberculosis			Appendicitis		
	Positive	Negative	Total	Positive	Negative	Total
1	28	7	35	29	7	36
2	28	7	35	28	7	35
3	27	8	35	28	7	35
Total	83	22	105	85	21	106

In the development of the NEAT approach, a proposal begins with a network in a similar way that a MLP feed-forward network of only input neurons and output neurons. As evolution progresses through discrete steps, the complexity of the network grows, inserting more nodes into a connection between input-output path and creating new connections within the actual nodes. For this, parameters of the network are represented into a phenotype of genetic algorithms, encoding the schemes that means every connection and neuron in an explicit representation. In this way, the NEAT method attempt simultaneously the learned weights and an appropriate topology for the MLP.

For this case, a cross-validation was used and 100 initializations were implemented to compute statistical measures of the results and to see the coherence between them. Fitness computation was based in the error given by the distance of the output from the correct answer summed for all patterns included in the training set. The resulting number was squared to give more proportionally more fitness the closer a network was to a solution [14]. First generation was formed by networks without hidden nodes with one output and a number of inputs according with the number of variables in each database. Also, a node with bias information was settled as one. There were connections corresponding with these initial nodes, representing the genes in each genome, and each connection with a random weight.

One hundred runs were developed by each fold considered in the database for training. Each run was composed by 200 as maximum number of generation for a generational loop, and the population size was of 150. The population with best results was save as more representative of each run. Finally, the results were collected to study the generalization of the network in front of new patterns taken from the fold left out. The NEAT tool for Matlab © was employed to developed the experiments [16].

3 Results

First, results with comparison for both databases when the NEAT method was applied are presented. Then, results for each disease are shown in terms of sensitivity and specificity. Figures 1 and 2 show the results for the three used folds, visualizing the average of nodes in the hidden layer found by the NEAT method. It is possible to see that the tuberculosis detection, architectures between two and six nodes were obtained to do the classification. Meanwhile, the Appendicitis problem shows that between ten and twelve nodes, in mean, are necessary to perform the classification.

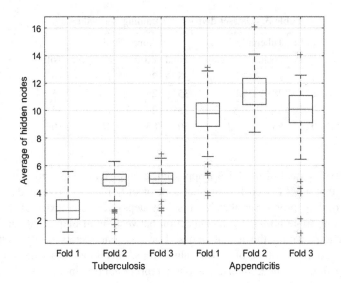

Fig. 1. Results for average of number of hidden nodes found for the NEAT method in both databases.

Other comparison can be visualized in the number of connections in the hidden layer (Fig. 2), where the appendicitis problem seems to be more difficult to classify. This can be indicated by the higher numbers for nodes and connections, compared with the tuberculosis case.

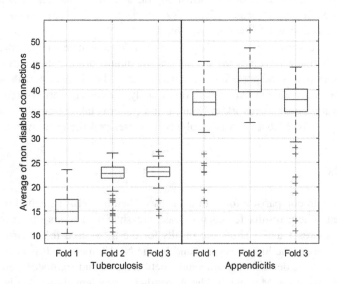

Fig. 2. Results for average of disabled connections found for the NEAT method in both databases.

Neuroevolution results were compared with the empirical method to find the number of nodes in the hidden layer in a MLP between two and ten, according as mentioned before. The best values of each fold were taken into account to compute the comparative results. Table 4 resumes these corresponding results. For this, the best value in each fold was taken into account and mean and standard deviation were computed for these measures. In empirical cases, the model to detect appendicitis had three nodes in the hidden layer for all folds. The model to detect tuberculosis had two, five and nine nodes in the hidden layer, respectively.

Figures 3 and 4 show the ROC curve for the used folds. It is possible to see that best results were reached with the empirical method (Fig. 4). Therefore, the NEAT method reached comparable results for the detection (Fig. 3). In a similar way, Figs. 5 and 6 show the results for appendicitis detection, allowing to observe similarities in both methods, but with best results for the empirical one (Table 4).

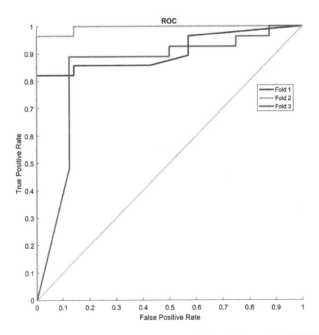

Fig. 3. ROC curve for three folds in the tuberculosis problem using NEAT method.

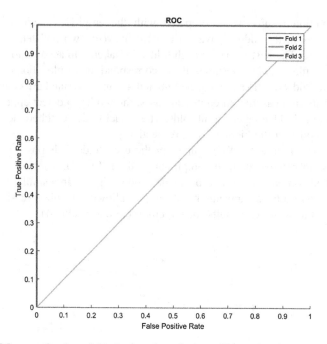

Fig. 4. ROC curve for three folds in the tuberculosis problem using the empirical method.

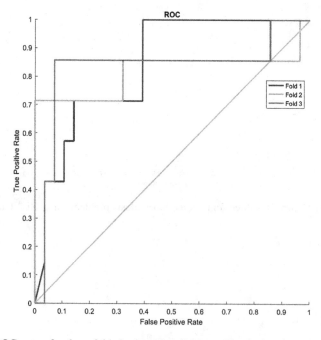

Fig. 5. ROC curve for three folds in the appendicitis problem using the NEAT method.

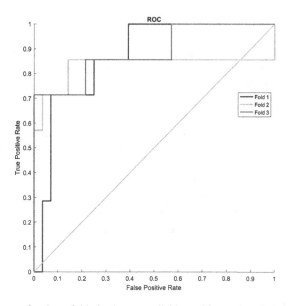

Fig. 6. ROC curve for three folds in the appendicitis problem using the empirical method.

Table 4. Comparison results for both employed techniques.

Measure (%)	Tuberculosis		Appendicitis	
	Neuro-evolution	Empirical	Neuro-evolution	Empirical
Sensitivity	88.09 + 7.43	96.42 + 3.57	91.86 + 11.03	96.51 + 3.44
Specificity	90.47 + 8.24	100 + 0	68.45 + 5.15	71.43 + 0

4   Discussion

First observation is given by the complexity of models for both diseases. Tuberculosis diagnosis problem come from an easier problem compared with the appendicitis problem, this can be seen according with the number of hidden nodes and the connections in the network when NEAT method was used (Figs. 1 and 2). There is possible to note that tuberculosis problem can be solve with between three and six nodes, while appendicitis problem needs between ten and twelve nodes in mean to detect the disease.

After the comparison with the empirical technique, it is possible to observe that the results are equivalent for the tuberculosis detection (Table 4). NEAT offers best results for this particular problem, finding a better sensitivity and specificity. At the same time a smaller architecture also is found. This because the results are for architectures between three and six nodes in the NEAT method compared with three, five or nine nodes for the empirical way. This, in terms of number of connections is more efficient because for NEAT method this number can be in the interval 15 to 25 in mean. Instead the model with six nodes in the hidden layer for the empirical method produces around 50 connections.

In the case of appendicitis detection, the values for sensitivity and specificity were not so good. It is notable the results for the specificity when the empirical way was implemented, but sensitivity was not well succeeded as in reported works, where reached rates of 89% [18] and 97% [9]. However, the results are comparable and the scope of this work was to compare two different methods to obtain ANN architectures. In this case, a NEAT method offered comparable results as regards to measures of sensitivity and specificity, and size of the architecture related with nodes and connections.

Differences in the results can be explained by the type of used variables. For the tuberculosis case, most of variables are binary inputs, manifesting existence or absence of the variable. Meanwhile the used variables in the appendicitis problem were all real, making more difficult the classification. In spite of ANN can be deal with any type of input variable, for the present case, this could manifest a problem. This supposes a future work to do by the light of these results.

5   Conclusions

Two methods to obtain networks architectures were compared for the disease detection problem. A neuroevolution of augmenting topologies and traditional empirical way were employed to detect diseases based on different input variables. Results show that for tuberculosis case, the NEAT method offered better results and for appendicitis case the results are comparable in terms of sensitivity and specificity, but for architecture size represent a bigger network.

Acknowledgment. Authors thank the Universidad Antonio Nariño under project 2016207, University of Connecticut, Universidad Santo Tomas and Universidade Estadual do Rio de Janeiro for the support and financial assistance in this work. Also, the Hospital Santa Clara and Carlos Awad for making available the database related with tuberculosis.

References

1. Kalantari, A., Kamsin, A., Shamshirband, S., Gani, A., Alinejad-Rokny, H., Chronopoulos, A.T.: Computational intelligence approaches for classification of medical data: state-of-the-art, future challenges and research directions. Neurocomputing **276**, 2–22 (2017)
2. Amato, F., López, A., Peña-Méndez, E.M., Vavnhara, P., Hampl, A., Havel, J.: Artificial neural networks in medical diagnosis (2013)
3. Amato, F., González-Hernández, J.L., Havel, J.: Artificial neural networks combined with experimental design: a soft approach for chemical kinetics. Talanta **93**, 72–78 (2012)
4. Seera, M., Lim, C.P.: A hybrid intelligent system for medical data classification. Expert Syst. Appl. **41**, 2239–2249 (2014)
5. Prabhudesai, S.G., Gould, S., Rekhraj, S., Tekkis, P.P., Glazer, G., Ziprin, P.: Artificial neural networks: useful aid in diagnosing acute appendicitis. World J. Surg. **32**, 305–309 (2008)

6. Huang, R., Lee, S., Lai, C., Hsiao, Y., Ting, H.: Acute effects of obstructive sleep apnea on autonomic nervous system, arterial stiffness and heart rate in newly diagnosed untreated patients. Sleep Med. **14**, e27 (2013)

7. Ting, H.-W., Wu, J.-T., Chan, C.-L., Lin, S.-L., Chen, M.-H.: Decision model for acute appendicitis treatment with decision tree technology - a modification of the alvarado scoring system. J. Chin. Med. Assoc. **73**, 401–406 (2010)

8. Park, S.Y., Kim, S.M.: Acute appendicitis diagnosis using artificial neural networks. Technol. Health Care **23**, S559–S565 (2015)

9. Yoldaş, Ö., Tez, M., Karaca, T.: Artificial neural networks in the diagnosis of acute appendicitis. Am. J. Emerg. Med. **30**, 1245–1247 (2012)

10. Santos, A.M., Pereira, B.B., Seixas, J.M., Mello, F.C.Q., Kritski, A.L.: Neural networks: an application for predicting smear negative pulmonary tuberculosis. In: Auget, J.L., Balakrishnan, N., Mesbah, M., Molenberghs, G. (eds.) Advances in Statistical Methods for the Health Sciences, pp. 275–287. Springer, Boston (2007)

11. El-Solh, A.A., Hsiao, C.-B., Goodnough, S., Serghani, J., Grant, B.J.B.: Predicting active pulmonary tuberculosis using an artificial neural network. Chest J. **116**, 968–973 (1999)

12. Elveren, E., Yumuvak, N.: Tuberculosis disease diagnosis using artificial neural network trained with genetic algorithm. J. Med. Syst. **35**, 329–332 (2011)

13. Er, O., Temurtas, F., Tanrikulu, A.Ç.: Tuberculosis disease diagnosis using artificial neural networks. J. Med. Syst. **34**, 299–302 (2010)

14. Stanley, K.O., Miikkulainen, R.: Evolving neural networks through augmenting topologies. Evol. Comput. **10**, 99–127 (2002)

15. Floreano, D., Dürr, P., Mattiussi, C.: Neuroevolution: from architectures to learning. Evol. Intell. **1**, 47–62 (2008)

16. Miikkulainen, R.: Neuroevolution. In: Encyclopedia of Machine Learning. Springer, New York (2010)

17. Marchand, A., Van Lente, F., Galen, R.S.: The assessment of laboratory tests in the diagnosis of acute appendicitis. Am. J. Clin. Pathol. **80**, 369–374 (1983)

18. Weiss, S.M., Kapouleas, I.: An empirical comparison of pattern recognition, neural nets and machine learning classification methods. Read. Mach. Learn. 177–183 (1990)

19. Kohavi, R.: A Study of Cross-Validation and Bootstrap for Accuracy Estimation and Model Selection. Presented at the (1995)

20. Haykin, S.: Neural Networks and Learning Machines. Prentice Hall, Upper Saddle River (2009)

21. Riedmiller, M., Braun, H.: A direct adaptive method for faster backpropagation learning: the RPROP algorithm. In: 1993 IEEE International Conference on Neural Networks, pp. 586–591 (1993)

22. Beale, M.H., Hagan, M.T., Demuth, H.B.: Neural network toolbox getting started guide R2011b (2011)

An Algebraic Model to Formalize Sentences and Their Context: Use Case Scenario of the Spanish Language

Edgardo Samuel Barraza Verdesoto[1]([✉]), Edwin Rivas Trujillo[2],
Víctor Hugo Medina García[2], and Duván Cardona Sánchez[3]

[1] University of Seville, Seville, Spain
edgbarver@alum.us.es
[2] University Distrital Francisco José de Caldas, Bogotá, Colombia
erivas@udistrital.edu.co, victorhmedina@gmail.com
[3] University Pontificia Javeriana, Bogotá, Colombia
cardonaduvan@javeriana.edu.co

Abstract. This paper introduces a model based on set theory and modern algebra that formalizes sentences and their context. The model aims at dividing sentences in cores which will be mapped into sets of an algebraic space; some of these cores have a type of context called *strictly linguistic context*. These sets along with an operation form *algebraic structures* are capable to generate new members starting from the elements mapped. In Addition, the model defines a function that can restore part or the whole of the original sentence from these sets by guaranteeing its structure and meaning. All of these processes can be used for several applications, but our main interest is the dynamic creation of small theories such as microtheories; this could be accomplished through queries that compare contexts and activate the restoring of sentences. The use case scenario has been limited to the Spanish language.

Keywords: Algebraic structure · Abelian group · Context
Nominal phrases · Verbal cores · Small theories

1 Introduction

The study of the *context*, its formalization and its influence on language production, decision making, automatic reasoning, among others, have been studied by many disciplines: pragmatics [15], neuroscience [7,14,21], psycholinguistics [2], and computer science [5,8,9,12,13,18,20]. All of them have delivered models to answer questions like "what is the context?" or "how to use it?," sometimes from different points of view. Our main goal is to model a sentence and one type of context named *strictly linguistic context* [17,23] which is contained inside of the sentences and provides the environment necessary to understand their message.

Building ontologies [11] for large amounts of data is a task that can involve applications such as *Text2Onto* [6] or *OntoLearn*[22] which are capable to convert

© Springer Nature Switzerland AG 2018
J. C. Figueroa-García et al. (Eds.): WEA 2018, CCIS 915, pp. 182–193, 2018.
https://doi.org/10.1007/978-3-030-00350-0_16

texts into ontologies. The *microtheories* [12] are another alternative; they are small theories that can coexist with others that they contradict them [16] because each one of them requires a different *context* to complete its semantics. The common trend is to build theories based on a whole text, and to store them in a monolithic knowledge base. The novelty of our approach is the organization of a text in modules that can be selected, manipulated, matched, etc., conveniently, and without losing of its meaning, through operations created in the context of algebraic structures. Hence, Ontologies, theories or small theories could be built dynamically from sections of the text or by linking part of several texts. This paper introduces some objects that can drive the dynamic creation of small theories. One of these objects, called *nominal cores*, is an expression without verbs, but with meaning; they are embedded in the sentences and contain *strictly linguistic context*. The *nominal cores* could be a starting point to compare topics or to establish relationships inside the same sentence, among different sentences, or even with other texts. Although the study of these elements is part of our research, this paper will only present a *formalization of sentences based on these cores*.

The document will be organized as follow, the first section will introduce the model by explaining its components and roles. The second section will analyze a heuristic for the Spanish language that is capable of dissociating texts in *verbal and nominal cores* to fill the sets of the model. In the third section, the results of experiments will be also exposed. Finally, conclusions will be drawn on the overall work and future work will be discussed.

2 A View of the Model

In this section, the basics of the the algebraic model will be defined. The exposition will contain an explanation of basic concepts, and some axioms, definitions, and theorems required to formalize the model will be introduced. The use case scenario discussed in this model includes only the sentences in the Spanish language, therefore, some concepts and processes will be aimed at that context.

2.1 The Context of a Sentence

The context involved in the sentences belongs to an explicit category named *strictly linguistic context* [17,23] which is the set of all factors that accompany a word by affecting its interpretation, its consistency, and its meaning [1]. *Nominal phrases* are *sequence of words* that contain this type of context [10,19].

2.2 Sets and Processes

A general view of the model is shown in Fig. 1. The dynamic of the system starts with a process called *dissociation* that divides a sentence into linguistic categories using a parser [3]. Subsequently, a set of *heuristics* re-processes the

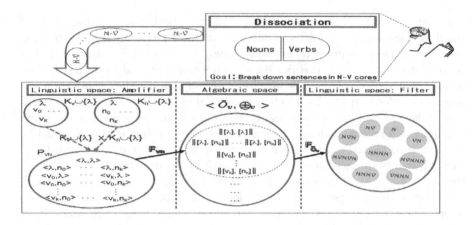

Fig. 1. Processes and sets of the model

parser's output to obtain two types of clusters *nominal cores* and *verbal cores*; these will be defined latter.

Each time a *nominal core* or a *verbal core* is generated, it is inserted into a set K_n or K_v respectively. As soon as the sentence has been processed entirely, the *Cartesian Product* $K_v \bigcup \{\lambda\} \times K_n \bigcup \{\lambda\}$ takes place, and new elements are added inside of P_{vn}. These processes are repeated for each sentence in a text. Table 1 illustrates the result of all these processes carry out over the sentence: *"Toda clase de establecimientos comerciales podremos encontrar en las calles Velásquez y Tetúan"*. For this implementation, all sentences are expected with a verb starting the expression, and the verb v_0 is missing. Formally, the sets and their elements are defined as follows:

Table 1. Cores and Cartesian product of a sentence

Word	Category
Toda, clase, de, establecimientos, comerciales	n_0:nominal-core (pron, n, p, n, adj)
podremos, encontrar	v_1:verbal-core (v, v)
en, las, calles, Velásquez, y, Tetúan	n_1:nominal-core (p, a, n, N, c, N)
Cartesian Product	
$<\lambda, \lambda>$, $<\lambda, n_0>$, $<\lambda, n_1>$	$<v_1, \lambda>$, $<v_1, n_0>$, $<v_1, n_1>$

Axiom 1. *There is* the empty sequence of words (null) *and it will be denoted* λ.

Definition 1 (The set K_n). *Let us denote K_n the set that contains **nominal cores**. In this model, a cluster of words that contains a **nominal phrase** will be named **nominal core**.*

Definition 2 (The set K_v). *Let us denote K_v the set that contains **verbal cores** which are non-null **sequences of words** belonging to a sentence which does not contain nouns, and contain at least one verb; they express an action, an existence, an achievement, or a state.*

Definition 3 (The set P_{vn}). *Let P_{vn} be the Cartesian product $K_v \bigcup \{\lambda\} \times K_n \bigcup \{\lambda\}$.*

2.3   The Algebraic Space

The set P_{vn} contains elements that are not good candidates for representing in whole or in part the original sentence, e.g., the couple $<v_1, n_0>$ in Table 1 reproduce: *podemos encontrar toda clase de establecimientos comerciales*, which does not correspond with any part of the original sentence and, what is even worse is that the meaning could be changed. Hence, P_{vn} should be mapped to other *space* where the *cores* can be manipulated without loosing its consistency regard to the original sentence. One set and one mapping will be defined for this purpose.

Definition 4 (The set $\bar{O}_v$). *Let us denote $\bar{O}_v$ as the set of all couples of sequences in the form:*

$$[\![X]\!] = [\![[v_0 : v_1 : \cdots : v_k], [n_0 : n_1 : \cdots : n_k]]\!]$$

Each v_i belongs to $K_v \bigcup \{\lambda\}$, each n_i belongs to $K_n \bigcup \{\lambda\}$, and i is an index indicates the order how the element was dissociated from the sentence. The following combinations are possible: $[\![[v], [n]]\!]$; $[\![[v], [\lambda]]\!]$; $[\![[\lambda], [n]]\!]$; or $[\![[\lambda], [\lambda]]\!]$.

The notation $[\![X_i]\!]$ will be introduced to refer to a member of $\bar{O}_v$. Additionally, $[\![X_{a/b}]\!]$, where $a < b$, means that a member has λ elements before the subscript a and after the subscript b in both components; the notation $[\![[V_{a/b}], [N_{c/d}]]\!]$ or $[\![[v_{a/b}], [n_{c/d}]]\!]$ specifies the same in each component of a member. In addition, the expression $[\![[v_i], [n_j]]\!]$ means that the couple has one member with an only element in each component, each one in two different positions.

*On the other hand, an expression $\lambda_{a/b}$ means that there are λ-**elements** between the positions **a** and **b**, both included. Additionally, if an element such as λ_k appears, this means that the λ-element exist in the k position. A couple of sequences with only λ-elements can be modelled as $[\![[\lambda_{0/\infty}], [\lambda_{0/\infty}]]\!]$ and it will be called Γ.*

Definition 5 (Function F_{vn}). *Let us define F_{vn} the injective function that maps a subset of pairs $<v_i, n_i> \in P_{vn}$ in pairs $[\![[v_i], [n_i]]\!] \in \bar{O}_v$.*

Figure 2 shows an implementation of the F_{vn} function applied to a sentence. The left box is a subset of P_{vn} and the right box correspond to the range of the mapping in $\bar{O}_v$; the superscript indicates the cardinality of the sets. The subsets of P_{vn} must accomplish the following characteristics:

1. All members must have **strictly linguistic context**. Hence, the set does not contain elements of type $<v_i, \lambda>$, but elements such as $<\lambda, n_i>$ can be accepted.
2. Elements of type $<v_i, n_j>$ must to have the same subscript $(i = j)$. The same subscript means that the *verbal core* is found immediately before of the *nominal core* in the sentence.

p_λ:$<\lambda, \lambda>$	$P_{vn}{}^7$: Subset of Cartesian product	e_λ:$[\lambda][\lambda]$	$\bar{O}_v{}^7$: Mapping
p_0:$<\lambda, n_0$: La marcha>		e_0:$[\lambda][n_0]$	
p_1:$<\mathcal{V}_1$: *programada*, n_1:para el próximo 26 de marzo>		e_1:$[\lambda:\mathcal{V}_1][\lambda:n_1]$	
p_2:$<\mathcal{V}_2$:,*que ha sido denominado*, n_2:día nacional>		e_2:$[\lambda:\lambda_1:\mathcal{V}_2][\lambda:\lambda:n_2]$	
p_3:$<\lambda, n_3$:por la vida>		e_3:$[\lambda:\lambda:\lambda:\lambda][\lambda:\lambda:\lambda:n_3]$	
p_4:$<\lambda, n_4$:,la Paz y la justicia>		e_4:$[\lambda:\lambda:\lambda:\lambda][\lambda:\lambda:\lambda:\lambda:n_4]$	
p_5:$<\mathcal{V}_5$:,*recibía*, n_5:críticas>		e_5:$[\lambda:\lambda:\lambda:\lambda:\lambda:\mathcal{V}_5][\lambda:\lambda:\lambda:\lambda:\lambda:n_5]$	
p_6:$<\lambda, n_6$:ayer de parte de dos miembros del partido ARENA: Alfredo Cristiani y Jorge Velado>		e_6:$[\lambda:\lambda:\lambda:\lambda:\lambda:\lambda][\lambda:\lambda:\lambda:\lambda:\lambda:\lambda:n_6]$	

Fig. 2. The figure shows the mapping of a sentence into the algebraic space

2.4   The Algebraic Structure

An algebraic structure composed by a set that has *closure* under an operation will be introduced. The **closure** property is convenient because the operation can generate new members in $\bar{O}_v$ without connection to the subset of the P_{vn}.

Definition 6 (Operation $\oplus_v$). *By natural way, a binary operation $\oplus_v$ for couples belonging to $\bar{O}_v$ and its functionality will be defined. The subscripts used have the following order relation:* $0 < i < j < k < m$.

*Positional and Dual. The operation is **dual** and **positional**. **Dual** means that if two members belonging to $\bar{O}_v$ are operated, the operation occurs in **verbal** **vector** and **nominal** component separately. **Positional** means that if and only if two operands have the same subscript, they can be operated. For example:*

$$[[\lambda_0 : v_1 : \lambda_2], [\lambda_0 : n_1 : \lambda_2]] \oplus_v [[\lambda_0 : \lambda_1 : v_2], [\lambda_0 : \lambda_1 : n_2]]$$
$$\Rightarrow [[\lambda_0 : v_1 : v_2], [\lambda_0 : n_1 : n_2]]$$

Gamma Cases. An operation between λ_i and x_i, with x_i characterizing a verbal core or a nominal core, will produce x_i. Hence, an operation between $[X_i]$ and Γ behaves as follows:

$$[X_i] \oplus_v \Gamma = \Gamma \oplus_v [X_i] = [X_i]$$

Null Cases. If two members of $\bar{O}_v$ are operated and they have elements in their components with the same subscript, the result of the operation in this position is λ. The following cases are possible:

1. $[\![X_{i/k}]\!] \oplus_v [\![X_{j/m}]\!] = [\![[v_{i/j-1} : \lambda_{j/k} : v_{k+1/m}], [n_{i/j-1} : \lambda_{j/k} : n_{k+1/m}]]\!]$

2. $[\![X_{i/j}]\!] \oplus_v [\![X_{i/j}]\!] = [\![[\lambda_{0/j}], [\lambda_{0/j}]]\!] = [\![[\lambda_{0/\infty}], [\lambda_{0/\infty}]]\!] = \Gamma$

Abelian Group $<\bar{O}_v \ \oplus_v>$. The set $\bar{O}_v$ along with the binary operation $\oplus_v$ form an *Abelian Group structure finite* and *no cyclic*, its means that the set for $\bar{O}_v$ is closed under the operation $\oplus_v$, that it is *associative*, that the *neutral and symmetrical elements* exist, and that it is *commutative*. The proof will not be presented in this paper due their extension, instead, the contribution of each property to the model will be explained.

Firstly, The *closure property* guarantees that an operation between two members of $\bar{O}_v$ always yields a member of $\bar{O}_v$. In this model, the operation will generate new members in $\bar{O}_v$ by reducing or expanding the *context* in the couples. Secondly, the *Associative property* states that the result of several operations executed sequentially is not affected by the order of their execution two-by-two, and, thus, their products will contain the same *context* and the same *meaning*. Thirdly, *Abelian groups* are endowed with a *symmetrical element* providing richness to the operations, e.g., it is possible to delete or replace cores inside of vectors due the *symmetrical element*. Furthermore, if the *neutral element* does not exist, the *symmetrical* either. The *symmetrical element* of a member of $<\bar{O}_v$ is itself and the *neutral element* is Γ. Finally, *Commutativity property* states that if two elements of the set $\bar{O}_v$ are operated, the final *context* and *meaning* will be the same.

2.5 Restoring Sentences

The Spanish language has been classified as a language with a **SVO** structure (*Subject-Verb-Object*) [4]. The **S** and **O** are cores closely related with nominal categories, whereas the **V** core is associated to verbal categories. Hence, for simplicity and without loss of generality, the **SVO** structure can be seen as a *NVN* sequence where N corresponds to a sequence of *nominal cores* and V corresponds to an *verbal core*. In this subsection, a function capable of restoring *well-formed sentences* structurally from the *algebraic space* will be defined.

Definition 7 (Well-formed Spanish sentences structurally [WFSSS]). *Let us denote **WFSSS** the sequences **NVN** or any of these variants: **N**, **NV**, **VN**, and **NVN**. Some examples of this type of sequence are: NVNV, NVN-VNVN, VNVNVN, etc.*

Definition 8 (Function $F_{\bar{O}_v}$). *Let $F_{\bar{O}_v}$ be a function that maps members of $\bar{O}_v$ into **WFSSS**. Table 2 shows the mapping. The blank space will be represented by the symbol ƀ.*

Table 2. Function $F_{\bar{O}_v}$

$[\![X]\!]$	$F_{\bar{O}_v}([\![X]\!])$
$[\![\lambda_{0/m}][N_{0/m}]\!]$	$\lambda_0 bn_0 b \cdots b\lambda_m bn_m$
$[\![V_{0/m}][\lambda_{0/m}]\!]$	$\lambda_0 b\lambda_1 b \cdots b\lambda_m$
$[\![V_{i/m}], [N_{i/m}]\!]$	$v_i bn_i \cdots v_j bn_j \cdots v_m bn_m$
$[\![\lambda_{i/j} : V_{j+1/m}], [N_{i/m}]\!]$	$\lambda_i bn_i b\lambda_{i+1} bn_{i+1} \cdots v_{j+1} bn_{j+1} \cdots v_m bn_m$
Special cases	
$[\![\lambda_{i/j} : V_{j+1/k}], [N_{i/k-1} : \lambda_k]\!]$	$\lambda_i bn_i b\lambda_{i+1} bn_{i+1} \cdots bv_{j+1} bn_{j+1} \cdots bv_k b\lambda_k$
$[\![V_{i/k}], [N_{i/k-1} : \lambda_k]\!]$	$v_i bn_i b \cdots bv_k b\lambda_k$

Theorem 1. *All expressions in the set* $\bar{\Theta}$ *are* **WFSSS**.

Proof. If an expression in Spanish language meets Definition 7 then it is considered **WFSSS**. Table 3 shows the structure of a sentence by applying the function $F_{\bar{O}_v}$. Each one of these possibilities meets the requirements of a **WFSSS**. Q.E.D.

Table 3. Structure of a sentence by applying the $F_{\bar{O}_v}$ mapping

$F_{\bar{O}_v}([\![X]\!])$	Sentence structure	Type
$\lambda_0 bn_0 b \cdots b\lambda_m bn_m$	$n_0 \; n_1 \; \cdots \; n_m$	N
$\lambda_0 b\lambda_1 b \cdots b\lambda_m$	λ	*null*
$v_i bn_i \cdots v_j bn_j \cdots v_m bn_m$	$v_i \; n_i \; \cdots \; v_j \; n_j \; \cdots \; v_m \; n_m$	**VNVN**
$\lambda_i bn_i b\lambda_{i+1} bn_{i+1} \cdots v_{j+1} bn_{j+1} \cdots v_m bn_m$	$n_i \; n_{i+1} \; \cdots \; v_{j+1} \; n_{j+1} \; \cdots \; v_m \; n_m$	**NVNVN**
Special cases		
$\lambda_i bn_i b\lambda_{i+1} bn_{i+1} \cdots bv_{j+1} bn_{j+1} \cdots bv_k b\lambda_k$	$n_i \; n_{i+1} \; \cdots \; v_{j+1} \; n_{j+1} \; \cdots \; v_k$	**NVNV**
$v_i bn_i b \cdots bv_k b\lambda_k$	$v_i \; n_i \; \cdots \; v_k$	**VNV**

Hence, an implementation of the function $F_{\bar{O}_v}$ can rebuild well-formed sentence structurally from the *algebraic space*.

2.6 Semantics and Sub-groups

The meaning of a sentence generated by $F_{\bar{O}_v}$ must be secured, but this function $F_{\bar{O}_v}$ can not guarantee it completely, e.g., if the elements e_1 and e_4 in Fig. 2 are operated to generate a new member, the result will be:

$$[\![v_1], [n_1]\!] \oplus_v [\![\lambda_4], [n_4]\!] = [\![v_1 : \lambda_{2/4}], [n_1 : \lambda_{2/3} : n_4]\!]$$

Now, by applying $F_{\bar{O}_v}$, the sentence generated would be: *"programada para el próximo 26 de marzo la Paz y la justicia"* whose meaning is confusing, although it is syntactically correct.

The problem can be solved by dividing the set $\bar{O}_v$ in sub-groups and establishing a hierarchy among them through mappings. Figure 3 shows a possible

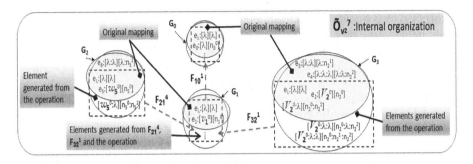

Fig. 3. A sentence mapping with the organizations inside of the set $\bar{O}_v$

reorganization in $\bar{O}_v$. The mapping among sets works in a cascade way from the core selected toward the root. Each function inserts λ-elements to the left hand for each member mapped, thenceforth, the operation $\oplus_v$ is applied between the mapped element and a *key-element* which is the only verb belonging to the codomain and that we will call **head-v**. Additionally, the only elements mapped are those embedded in the dashed box. For example, if the function $F_{21}^4(e_5)$ is applied the procedure would be the following:

$$e_5 = [\![[v_5{}^0],[n_5{}^0]]\!] \Rightarrow e_5^{21} = [\![[\lambda_{0/3}:v_5^{21}],[\lambda_{0/3}:n_5^{21}]]\!]$$
$$\Rightarrow e_5^{21} \oplus_v e_{1-k} = [\![[v_1{}^0:\lambda_{1/3}:v_5^{21}],[n_1{}^0:\lambda_{1/3}:n_5^{21}]]\!]$$
$$\Rightarrow (e_5^{21} \oplus_v e_1)^{10} \oplus_v e_{0-k} = [\![[\lambda:(v_1{}^0)^{10}:\lambda_{2/4}:(v_5^{21})^{10}],[n_0:(n_1{}^0)^1:\lambda_{2/4}:(n_5^{21})^{10}]]\!]$$

The superscript over the functions means the number of λ-elements to insert, and the superscript over the e_i-elements indicates the function that mapped them. The final result would be: *"La marcha programada, para el próximo 26 de marzo, recibía críticas"*. It is noteworthy that all source text of the sentences must be consistent, this is convenient because if a sentence is restored, it is also consistent.

3   Implementing the Model

The implementation has been focused on finding the limits of the cores and to build the algebraic space. First of all, a framework was built with a layered architecture which was instantiated to process texts in Spanish language. The most relevant framework layers are following: *recognition of the language, planning,* and *reaction*. The first one was designed to identify the language of the text and to divide it in sentences which will be sent to the next layer one by one. The second one chooses the applications that should be executed to dissociate a sentence and to initialize the sets of the model. The last one executes the applications chosen by the planner. The framework also has a main module for control and instantiation of the layers.

The *reaction* layer executes several *heuristics* to process only texts in the Spanish language; it was divided in three phases. In the first phase, each sentence is processed by a *linguistic tool*, commanded by the parser **VISL** [3][1]. The second phase, named *classifier*, receives from the parser output a very extensive word-classification for compacting in a new set of categories more reduced. In the third phase, called *packer*, are created the *cores*, this process involves a loop where neighboring words (or clusters) are operated for packing them in an only one class of the following: *nominal cores*, *determinants*, and *verbal cores*. The *cores* are saved in a database by creating the sets of the model.

A *verbal core* category introduces a *sequence of cores* that ends where a new *verbal core* starts or when the sentence ends. The *verbal cores* are used to establish hierarchies among subgroups where each one of them has a *verbal core* as their *head-v* (see Subsect. 2.6). The hierarchy among subgroups depends on the characteristics of the *head-v* which are as follows: *main verbal-core* (**main-v**), *subordinated verbal-core* (**subord-w**), and *optional verbal-core* (**opt-V**). The **main-v**-subgroups are arranged in a vector which is ordered by the *head-v*-subscripts; the vector is the **root** of the hierarchy and any other category or subcategory will be subordinated to any one of its elements.

The **opt-V** subcategory introduces a *sequence of cores* that is considered optional, i.e., if a subgroup contains a *head-v* with the **opt-V** subcategory, its information is considered no essential to the restoring sentence process. The **opt-V** category scope in a sentence ends where a new *verbal core* with category **subord-w** or **main-v** starts.

The **subord-w** class introduces a *sequence of cores* subordinated with regard to the immediately following **main-v**-subcategory in the sentence. Additional, If several **subord-w** groups appear before the **main-v** group, they will form a **subord-w**-vector subordinated. The combination **subord-w** + **main-v** is grouped as a special unit because where all information embedded inside of them is essential to its meaning.

The *determinants* separates 2 *nominal cores* or, introduces a *nominal-core sequence* after a *verbal core*. As well as the *verbal cores*, they have a subclassification: *preposition determinant* (**prep-d**), *conjunction determinant* (**conj-d**), *disjunction determinant* (**comma-d**), and *optional determinant* (**opt-d**). The (**prep-d**) and (**opt-d**) introduce a *nominal-cores sequence*, but the sequence introduced by the second one is optional (see **opt-V** above). The (**conj-d**) is a *determinant* that suggests to combine the *nominal-cores sequence* introduced by it with the previous *nominal-cores sequence* for understanding. On the other hand, the **comma-d** determinant suggests separation, i.e., the *nominal core* introduced starts a new sub-sentence inside of the sentence. The sub-sentence ends when a new (**conj-d**) or a (**opt-d**) starts, or the sentence ends. An example of this implementation is shown in the Sect. 2.6. The group G_2 is subordinated with regard to G_1, and the group G_3 contains optional information.

---

[1] The parser **VISL**, from the *University of Southern Denmark* has been used in this work under the permission of this institution.

3.1   Results of the Sentence Dissociation and Generation of the Sets

The *dissociation* and *generation of the sets* processes were tested with three types of corpora: Entertainment, Tourism, and News. Table 4 shows the statistics of the creation of the subsets belonging to the *Cartesian-product* which will be mapped to the *algebraic space* and their errors in the process. The $<v, n>$ column represents the number of subgroups that are created in the *algebraic space* without regard their type inside of the hierarchy neither the sentence where it comes from. The second and third columns show two types of *nominal cores*; the first one is the set whose subject is explicit inside of the core, while in the second one corresponds to an anaphoric subject. The analysis of the implementation is focuses on terms of three types of errors that can occurs in the execution of the layers, these errors are following: *parsing error*, *compacting error*, and *false-positive error*.

Table 4. Statistics related to the creation of cores

	Subsets of VxN			Type of errors in cores				Total Sentences
	$<v,n>$	$<n,\lambda>$		% S-CP	Parser Error	Compact Error	False Positives	%FP	
		Subject	Anaph						
Entertainment_1	76	47	173	89%	4	15	17	5%	332
Entertainment_2	15	12	31	89%	1	0	6	9%	65
Tourism_1	143	28	144	97%	3	2	5	2%	325
Tourism_2	57	16	53	98%	2	0	0	0%	128
Tourism_3	54	6	62	98%	1	0	2	2%	125
News_1	40	23	43	97%	0	1	2	2%	109
News_2	24	7	26	89%	2	0	5	8%	64
News_3	49	16	43	93%	2	1	5	4%	116

The *parsing error* is generated by the *syntactic parser* when it does not classify adequately the words in the sentence, its errors were minimal because this tool is very powerful and it has been tested exhaustively. The *compacting error* is associated with the effectiveness of the *classifier* heuristic, the heuristic can be influenced by the *parsing error*. The *false-positive error* represents the errors occurred in the *dissociation process* and the *generation of sets*, and it is the type of error more significative. The generation of cores depend on the *parsing* and the *classifier* processes. The measure of the *false-positive error* is lightly superior with regard to the previous errors which shows a great success in the heuristic. The worst case scenario occurs in a small corpus and it is a 9% error, this little loss of sentences is not enough significative to compromise the main idea of the text, because the rest of the sentences can support it fully. In general, the *dissociation process* and the *generation of the sets* delivered good results.

4   Conclusions and Future Work

The main goal underlying this research is to generate a space where query-answer processes will be performed in natural language, and the decision-making could be carried out by creating small theories based on sentences restored from several sources along with the query sentence. Our approach would produce a reduction in the performance in the selecting and the decision. Firstly, because the searching is improved by making possible the creation of nets both inside of a sentence and among sentences (hierarchies), and even among texts. Secondly, although there are several tools to convert texts into theories or ontologies, the process of restoring sentences would reduce the number of those sentences suitable to form a small theory with regard to a query; this contributes to tasks such as the building of the theory which could be created dynamically, and the performance of decision-making process.

This paper introduces two main processes that could be useful for generating of small theories free of inconsistencies. The use case scenarios was the sentences in in the Spanish language. The first process divides sentences in cores for mapping them into an *algebraic space* where they can be manipulated and re-processed; an implementation was made with good results. The other process refers to the restoring of the whole or part of a sentence by mapping elements from the algebraic space to a linguistic space by ensuring syntactically well-formed sentences structurally, and the meanings can be guaranteed with some rearrangements of the sets in the algebraic space. Regarding future works on this line, the anaphora could be implemented to establish links between cores of different sentences.

Summarizing, a new model based on mathematical foundations with an opened use was introduced, and an implementation of the *dissociation and generation of the sets* was presented with good results. The repository generated contains several sets that form *Abelian groups*. Finally, A rearrangement of the groups for the Spanish language was suggested which guarantee the structure and the meaning of the sentences restored from the algebraic space. This approach might have several applications in fields such as search engines because the information is saved in its original format (text), and the decision regarding a topic would be generated by satisfying small theories created dynamically through the interaction between the repository and the queries.

References

1. Arroyo Cantón, C., Berlato Rodríguez, P.: La comunicación: Lengua castellana y Literatura. Oxford University Press, España (2012)
2. Bazire, M., Brézillon, P.: Understanding context before using it. In: Dey, A., Kokinov, B., Leake, D., Turner, R. (eds.) CONTEXT 2005. LNCS (LNAI), vol. 3554, pp. 29–40. Springer, Heidelberg (2005). https://doi.org/10.1007/11508373_3
3. Bick, E.: A constraint grammar-based parser for Spanish. In: TIL (2006)
4. Boeree, G.: Basic language structures (2017). http://webspace.ship.edu/cgboer/basiclangstruct.html

5. Buvac, S., Mason, I.A.: Propositional logic of context. In: AAAI, pp. 412–419 (1993)
6. Cimiano, P., Völker, J.: Text2Onto - a framework for ontology learning and data-driven change discovery. In: Montoyo, A., Muñoz, R., Métais, E. (eds.) NLDB 2005. LNCS, vol. 3513, pp. 227–238. Springer, Heidelberg (2005). https://doi.org/10.1007/11428817_21
7. Conway, M., Pleydell-Pearce, C.: The construction of autobiographical memories in the self memory system. Psychol. Rev. **107**(2), 261–288 (2000)
8. Costanza, P., Hirschfeld, R.: Language constructs for context-oriented programming: an overview of contextL. In: Proceedings of the 2005 Symposium on Dynamic Languages, pp. 1–10, New York (2005)
9. Ghidini, C., Giunchiglia, F.: Local models semantics, or contextual reasoning = locality + compatibility. Artif. Intell. **127**(2), 221–259 (2001). https://doi.org/10.1016/S0004-3702(01)00064-9
10. González Calvo, J.M.: Los conceptos de proposición, oración y enunciado. La frase nominal. Servicios de Gestión y Comunicación S.L, Liceus (2006)
11. Gruber, T.R.: Toward principles for the design of ontologies used for knowledge sharing. Int. J. Hum.-Comput. Stud. **43**(5–6), 907–928 (1995). https://doi.org/10.1006/ijhc.1995.1081
12. Guha, R.: Contexts: a formalization and some applications. Ph.D. thesis, Stanford University, Stanford, CA, USA (1992)
13. Haase, P., et al.: D3.1.1 context languages - state of the art. Technical report D3.1.1, Universität Karlsruhe (TH) (2006)
14. Havel, I.M.: Strategies of Remembrance: From Pindar to Hölderlin, Chap. 2. Cambridge Scholars (2009)
15. Kecskes, I.: The paradox of communications. Socio-cognitive approach to pragmatics. Inf. Control, 52–55 (2010)
16. Lenat, D.B., Guha, R.V.: Building Large Knowledge-Based Systems; Representation and Inference in the CYC Project. Addison-Wesley Longman Publishing Co., Inc. (1989)
17. Luna Traill, E., Vigueras Avila, A., Baez Pinal, G.E.: Diccionario básico de lingüística. UNAM (2005)
18. McCarthy, J.: Notes on formalizing context. In: Proceedings of the 13th International Joint Conference on Artifical Intelligence, pp. 555–560, San Francisco, CA, USA (1993)
19. Montealegre, R.: La comprension del texto: sentido y significado. Revista Latinoamericana de Psicología **36**(2), 243–255 (2004)
20. Salvaneschi, G., Ghezzi, C., Pradella, M.: Context-oriented programming: a software engineering perspective. J. Syst. Softw. **85**(8), 1801–1817 (2012). https://doi.org/10.1016/j.jss.2012.03.024
21. Tulving, E.: Episodic and semantic memory. In: Tulving, E., Donaldson, W. (eds.) Organization of Memory, pp. 381–403. Academic Press, New York (1972)
22. Velardi, P., Faralli, S., Navigli, R.: Ontolearn reloaded: a graph-based algorithm for taxonomy induction. Comput. Linguist. **39**(3), 665–707 (2013). http://dblp.uni-trier.de/db/journals/coling/coling39.html#VelardiFN13
23. Vivaldi, G.M., Sánchez, A.: Curso de Redacción. Thomson Eds, Paraninfo S.A. (2000)

Application of the AdaBoost.RT Algorithm for the Prediction of the COLCAP Stock Index

Laura Reyes Fajardo[✉] and Andrés Gaona Barrera

Universidad Distrital Francisco José de Caldas, Bogotá, Colombia
lmreyesf@correo.udistrital.edu.co

Abstract. AdaBoost is an Artificial Intelligence algorithm widely used in classification problems with outstanding results in low complexity models. In this article, the prediction of the COLCAP series is carried out through the AdaBoost.RT algorithm with self-adaptive φ. Firstly, the COLCAP index time series is analyzed in order to verify its stationarity by the unit root test. Exogenous information is used based on five time series of financial character, which were selected after performing a grey relational analysis and principal component analysis. To find optimal values of the algorithm, the variation of each value was executed. The results show that it is possible to predict the COLCAP index through AdaBoost using 48 weak classifiers resulting in MAPE = 1.247% and RMSE = 17.87. With a less complex model that uses two weak apprentices the results were MAPE = 1.403% and RMSE = 22.56.

Keywords: AdaBoost · COLCAP · Boosting · Forecasting

1 Introduction

The analysis and financial time series forecasting has been studied through classical econometric or statistical models. There are linear methods such as Box-Jenkins, Kallman Filters, ARIMA, segmented regression or non-linear methods such as False Neighbors nearby, Taken's Theorem; that in spite of having a strong statistical support has not shown a high effectiveness in the prediction of the future values of the stock market [1,2]. Classic statistical methods do not integrate the uncertainty inherent in financial time series into their models, which in many cases are not explicitly represented [3,4]. Models based on computational intelligence for the financial time series forecasting, such as neural networks or fuzzy systems, include within the structure of the model, the ability to deal with noisy or vagueness in information and in the Neural Networks case, can determine non-linear relationships between the output and the inputs [5,6].

However, Neural Networks present drawbacks such as local convergence of learning algorithms, selection of an optimal architecture for the prediction model

© Springer Nature Switzerland AG 2018
J. C. Figueroa-García et al. (Eds.): WEA 2018, CCIS 915, pp. 194–205, 2018.
https://doi.org/10.1007/978-3-030-00350-0_17

and slow training speed, which restrict their development in practice [7]. A computational model not explored in the prediction of financial series and that partially solves the disadvantages of Neural Networks, is the AdaBoost algorithm. AdaBoost is a Boosting method widely used in classification problems, which has demonstrated its efficiency and good generalization results in this type of problems [8,9]. However, its applicability to regression problems has been limited because the original algorithm was not designed to be used in continuous output spaces. Some approximations in regression problems are presented in [10,11].

This work develops a methodology based on the AdaBoost algorithm for a time series forecasting. The time series chosen for analysis is the COLCAP series, which is the main index of the Colombian stock market and which reflects the variations of the 20 most liquid stocks on the Colombian Stock Exchange [12]. COLCAP has been previously modeled using a neural network in [13] and through the GARCH statistical model [14]. The methodology presented is divided into three phases: input analysis, where the series is studied and the input characteristics necessary for the AdaBoost model are chosen. In the second phase, the training process of a strong classifier is developed using the AdaBoost.RT algorithm, where AdaBoost.RT's own parameters are performed, such as the weight of the samples, the adjustment weight of the mean square error and the adaptability factor. In the third phase, the effectiveness of the algorithm is quantified using the MAPE, RMSE and the correlation factor indicators.

This document is organized into six sections: in Sect. 2 the AdaBoost.RT explanation is presented. The prediction methodology with AdaBoost together with the description of the experiments carried out is described in Sect. 3. Section 4 shows the results of the prediction made for the use of AdaBoost, highlighting the strong returns of the best approximation based on the MAPE, RMSE and the complexity of the regressor indicators. Finally; Sects. 5 and 6 concludes on the discussion of the experiences and results.

2 AdaBoost.RT

Originally, the AdaBoost algorithm was developed to solve binary classification problems [15] and the algorithm was extended to multi-class algorithms [16]. AdaBoost has been widely used to solve classification problems and showed to have decent performance in these type of problems [8,9,17]. Its breakthrough lies on including a distribution of the training database and there are several methods to do this. The way in which the training database distribution is updated depends on the Boosting method that is being used. The original method is based on boosting with filters, but it needs a large amount of training data, which in most cases is not possible. There are multiple versions of AdaBoost that are differentiated according to the way that the training data is redistributed [16].

Due to AdaBoost's popularity in classification problems, the algorithm was extended to regression problems with the AdaBoost.R algorithm, where the regression problem is reduced to a binary classification problem. However, this extension has two inconvenients. Firstly, each example in the regression sample is expanded into multiple classification examples and then the number of Boosting iterations is linearly increased. Secondly, the iteration error function changes and even this function differs between samples of the same iteration [15]. Afterwards, several methods have been proposed to reduce the regression problem into a classification problem, where the AdaBoost.RT is highlighted due to its performance and it is easier to implement than AdaBoost.R [18].

Algorithm 1. AdaBoost.RT Algorithm

Inputs   : Sequence of m examples
$(x_1, y_1), (x_2, y_2), \cdots, (x_m, y_m)$ *where* $y \in \mathbb{R}$;
Weak Learner Algorithm;
Integer T ;   // Number of algorithm itertions
Threshold φ $(0 < \varphi < 1)$;   // Demarcate correct samples

Initialize: $D_t(i) = \dfrac{1}{m}$ $\forall i$;   // Probability Distribution Function

while $t \leq T$ **do**

Train the Weak learner, providing D_t;
Build the regression model: $f_t(x) \rightarrow y$
Calculate the Absolute Relative Error (ARE) for each training sample

$$ARE(i) = \frac{f_t(x_i) - y_i}{y_i}$$

Calculate the $f_t(x)$ error rate:

$$\varepsilon_t = \sum_{i:ARE_t(i) > \varphi} D_t(i)$$

Set $\beta_t = \varepsilon_t^n$;   // n=1,2,3 (Linear, square or cubic)
Update the distribution D_t

$$D_{t+1}(i) = \frac{D_t(i)}{Z_t} * \begin{cases} \beta_t & \text{if } ARE_t(i) \leq \varphi \\ 1, & otherwise \end{cases}$$

end
Output : Calculate the Strong Learner

$$SL(x) = \frac{\sum^T \left\{ \left(\log \dfrac{1}{\beta_t} \right) f_t(x) \right\}}{\sum^T \left(\log \dfrac{1}{\beta_t} \right)}$$

The AdaBoost.RT algorithm with self-adaptative φ modifies the AdaBoost.RT algorithm (described in Algorithm 1) to change the value of φ into a self-adaptive one according to the evolution of the models error through every iteration. The value of φ will increase, while the error rate (ε_t) of the current iteration remains higher than the error rate of the previous iteration (ε_{t-1}). If the error (ε_t) is smaller than (ε_{t-1}), the value of φ will decrease.

3   Methodology

To assess the performance and effectiveness of the AdaBoost.RT algorithm in the prediction of financial series compared with feed-forward neural network predictors, the COLCAP time series is selected due to its relevance in the Colombian stock market. COLCAP is the main index in the Colombian stock exchange since it represents the variation of the 20 stocks with more liquidity and serves as a reference point for national and international investors alike [14]. For this work, the COLCAP sequence is studied between January 4 of 2008 and December 16 of 2016 [19]. The behavior of the COLCAP serie in the interest period is shown in Fig. 1.

For the analysis and prediction of the COLCAP index, three phases are proposed for the development of this work which include the input analysis, the predictor's modelling and the assessment of the results, as shown in Fig. 2

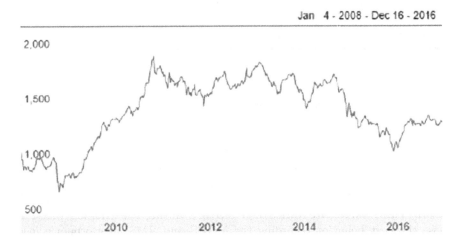

Fig. 1. COLCAP stock from January 4, 2008 to December 16, 2016 [20]

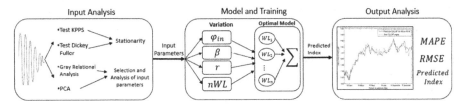

Fig. 2. Methodology

3.1   Input Analysis

In this phase, the stationary component analysis is carried out for the COLCAP series and the input parameters are chosen for the forecasting model.

Stationary Test. The search of trends and stationary components is executed to verify the stationarity of the COLCAP series, since their presence requires its elimination. For the long-term trend analysis, the KPSS (Kwiatkowski-Phillips-Schmidt-Shin) test is used where the null hypothesis of stationarity is sought involving a trend against the alternative of unit root [21]. To discard unit roots, the Augmented Dickey Fuller test is used [21].

Characteristics Selection. The COLCAP forecasting is made using series exogenous information, so the behavior of other actions in the Colombian stock market and the economic indicator of the exchange rate between the dollar and the peso. Therefore, is developed a history log of the stocks that have been a part of COLCAP since it began to be quoted, assessing the rebalancing and restructuration that are included in the estimations of the indexs [12]. Afterwards, a grey relational analysis is put in place to determine the influence of the chosen features with the time series, where the influence can be divided into: Marked, Relatively Marked, Noticeable, Relevant or Negligible [22] and Principal Component Analysis (PCA) that offers the variance percentage of each series [23].

3.2   Predictor Modelling and Training

Crossed validation is used to divide the sample data into training subset going from January 4, 2008 to December 14, 2015 and a subset for testing the year-based prediction from December 16, 2015 to December 16, 2016. The parameters used for training and validation of the AdaBoost.RT algorithm are shown in Table 1. Since the initial synchronization values (φ_{in}, r and β) are unknown a-priori. These values are varied and assessed during the training phase to choose the best behavior regarding the MAPE and RMSE performance metrics explained in the Output Analysis section.

Variation of the Weight Update on Correct Samples β_t. As seen in Algorithm 1, the update of the sample distribution D_i depends on the β_t factor, by calculating ε_t^n where $n = 1$, 2 or 3 (linear, quadratic or cubic) and where ε is the error of the weak learner from iteration t. In the literature, it is is not defined the most effective update method. Therefore, tests were carried out for each case where the initial value of $\varphi = 0.2$ and $r = 0.5$ remain constant according to the conclusions presented in [24].

Variation of φ Initial Value. The main advantage of the AdaBoost.RT algorithm is based on the adaptability of φ depending on the RMSE error in each iteration t, but the initial value of this parameter is not considered. In [24], it

Table 1. Parameters of AdaBoost.RT algorithm with self-adaptative φ

Parameter	Value
Weak learner algorithm	Perceptron
Number of weak learners (nWL)	1–50
Assessment criteria	$MAPE, RMSE$, Prediction
$\varphi_{initial}$	0.1–0.5
r	$0.3, 0.5, 0.7$
$\beta = error^n$	$n = 1, 2, 3$

is recommended that φ is initialized between 0.2 and 0.4, since a value higher than 0.4 turns the algorithm into unstable. Hence, the initial value of φ will be varied to find the optimal one for the COLCAP forecast.

Variation of r Parameter. The last parameter that can be varied and that depends on the problem is r, an adjustment factor of RMSE exchange rate used to update the weights on the samples of AdaBoost.RT algorithm. In [24], it is suggested that r = 0.5 but it is indicated that it can be selected depending on the application.

3.3   Output Analysis

A qualitative and quantitative assessment is established from the obtained predictors AdaBoost.RT, considering the performance metrics and the complexity of the resulting models. The performance metrics are calculated using MAPE and RMSE, additionally, the Pearson correlation coefficient is considered when the predictions are compared both for AdaBoost and neural networks, since it is an index that can be used to measure the relation degree between two variables. Finally, the complexity of the model is assessed through the number of weak classifiers.

$$RMSE = \sqrt{\frac{1}{m} \sum_{i=1}^{m} (\hat{y}_i - y_i)^2} \tag{1}$$

$$MAPE = \sqrt{\frac{100}{m} \sum_{i=1}^{m} \frac{|\hat{y}_i - y_i|}{|\hat{y}_i|}} \tag{2}$$

4   Results and Analysis

4.1   Input Analysis

When applying the KPSS test to the series, the stationary hypothesis was rejected, which indicates that the time series does not have long-term trends and leads to the need to apply another unit root test to discard the presence of unit roots in the time series. The Augmented Dickey Fuller test rejected the unit root hypothesis and the rejection of the presence of trends with the KPSS test, conclude that the COLCAP series is stationary.

To determine the input characteristics of the model, a history log of the stocks that have been included in the COLCAP index since its quotation began. In this time period, the index suffered 36 rebalancing operations and 8 restructurations constituted by 46 stocks that have had different percentages on each rebalancing operation. To visualize the frequency of stocks showing up in the index, a histogram of stock appearance in the COLCAP index in the chosen timeslot was made. Only 7 stocks have been a part of the index between 33 and 36 occasions.

Analyzing the total percentage of the stocks included in the calculation of the index more than 32 times, can be seen that the stocks of ECOPETROL and PFBCOLOM bring in together 29.06% of the COLCAP index in the chosen timeslot. It was also observed that ISA, EXITO, ISAGEN and CORFICOLCF had a constant contribution but not that relevant. Although BVC was a stock present in more than 90% of the index's quotation, its contribution was lower than 0.5% so is not considered for the prediction of the index. The CORFI-COLCF stock was not quoted in the market during two timeslots, in which the rebalancing and restructuration operations of COLCAP were made. This renders the CORFICOLCF time series discontinuous, affecting the accuracy of the model, so it was also discarded.

Therefore, the stocks chosen for the prediction of the index due to their permanence and importance in its calculation are: ECOPETROL, PFBCOLOM, ISA, ÉXITO and ISAGEN. Additionally, keeping in mind that COLCAP is the most significant economic index in Colombian economy [13], it was decided to include the exchange rate of the Colombian peso (COP) in terms of the dollar (USD). Each series used as an input parameter has the same size than the COLCAP series (2184 samples).

Table 2. Grey relational and principal componentes analysis

Stock	Grey relational ratio	Influence	Variance(%)
PFCOLOMB	**0.866**	Marked	18.02
EXITO	**0.822**	Marked	19.81
ISA	**0.742**	Relatively marked	14.39
ECOPETROL	**0.742**	Relatively marked	17.51
ISAGEN	**0.653**	Notable	11.71
USD	**0.555**	Relevant	18.56

Gray relational analysis was carried out to determine the relationship between each of the input parameters with the COLCAP series, presented in

Table 2 (Grey Relational Ratio and Influence). It can be seen that none of the parameters has a negligible influence, therefore, we proceed to make principal component analysis to determine the percentage of variance of each of the input parameters.

Based on the principal component analysis, presented in Table 2 (Variance), it was seen that ÉXITO is the parameter with the largest variance percentage with approximately 20% and the one that has the lowest variance is ISAGEN with 11%. It can be stated that the variance share of the parameters is in a close range and that no parameter is negligible, which is why the prediction is carried out with the parameters ECOPETROL, ISA, PFCOLOMB, ÉXITO, ISAGEN and USD.

4.2   AdaBoost.RT Predictor Results

After analyzing the results from the variations of parameters β, φ_{in} and r, it was determined that the best model was obtained with $\beta = error$, $\varphi_{in} = 0.4$ and $r = 0.5$ (Fig. 3).

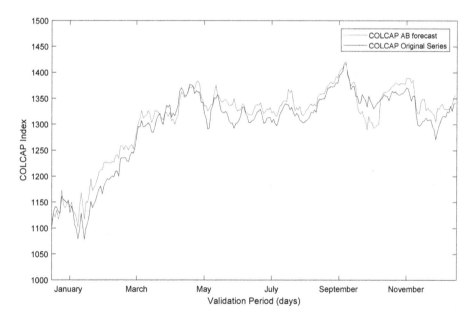

Fig. 3. Comparison between original series and forecast with the best AdaBoost model (48 WL)

Based on the results of the variation of the weights from the correct samples β_t, the best performance for this problem was seen in the linear case ($n = 1$), although the models designed with other types of updates (quadratic and cubic)

Table 3. Performance parameters of the prediction models

Model	MAPE	RMSE	Correlation coefficient	Complexity
AdaBoost2	1.403%	22.56	0.84	2 WL
AdaBoost14	1.353%	20.54	0.89	14 WL
AdaBoost48	1.247%	17.87	0.99	48 WL

have prediction errors lower than 2%. The biggest difference among the update methods lies in the number of weak learners of the model.

The variation of the initial value of φ has no marked influence in the mean error of the models when varying the number of weak learners. In terms of the results, the best joint model was obtained with $\varphi_{in} = 0.4$ and an error of 1.247%. As in the previous case, the other models do not show errors above 2%.

The overall variation of r has no marked influence in the mean error of the models when varying the number of weak apprentices. Furthermore, the results in the variation of the parameter r show no relation between such parameter and the performance of the models.

5   Discussion

The results obtained showed the need to implement the proposed variation since the search space is not simple and it is not possible to establish a priori the parameters (β, φ_{in}, r) of the algorithm as a unique and particular condition at the moment of initializing AdaBoost. Furthermore, the variation of the initial value of the limiting factor of correct samples (φ_{in}) leads to lower error in the model with 48 weak learners. Additionally, an error higher by only 0.15% was detected and it reduces the model to only two weak learners. This also happened with the variation of the adjustment factor r, where the number of weak learners can be reduced from 48 to 14 with an increase in error of 0.1%.

The AdaBoost.RT algorithm with self-adaptive φ considers that the best model has the lowest error even if it has the highest complexity given that the complexity is not a selection criteria. In case it is necessary to implement a model in physical system or a simple model with good performance, the model with two weak learners can be chosen as the best one since it does not imply a significant reduction in performance (lower than 0.2%). However, the comparison of the level of complexity is directly made between the number of neurons in the hidden layer and the number of weak apprentices with a network that has 6 input neurons, 1 output neuron and the synapses that come with it. Therefore, the model with 14 weak apprentices is less complex than the neural network with 8 neurons. Currently, the only parameter to determine the stronger learner is based on the prediction error and, according to the previous discussion, it is necessary to include a parameter related to the complexity of the model (nWL) in the selection process of the best strong learner.

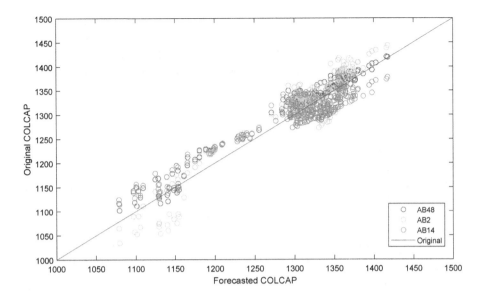

Fig. 4. Dispersion diagram of the AdaBoost forecasts and the original series

In Fig. 4, the dispersion diagram of the COLCAP series estimated through the differents AdaBoost models can be seen. According to the parameters shown in Table 3, the best AdaBoost model is AB48, because has the best performance in each indicator except in Complexity, but it can be seen that MAPE and RMSE are slightly lower than the model with only two WL.

6   Conclusions

The AdaBoost.RT algorithm with self-adaptive φ is an Artificial Intelligence model capable of satisfyingly solving prediction problems for the time series, such as the one presented in this work for the COLCAP series with a MAPE of 1.247%.

The selection parameter of the stronger learner must not be based solely on the MAPE of the model. It must include the complexity in order to have both, a low complexity model with good performance as seen in the models with 48 and 2 weak apprentices in which the complexity is very different, yet their index values are similar.

The performance of the AdaBoost model relies on the algorithm parameters (β, φ_{in}, r), since it is not possible to establish them a priori. Therefore, it is necessary to design an autonomous method for parameter selection so that it is not necessary to perform "trial and error" experiments to find the optimal value for problem solving. Instead, the problem's characteristics must be used to find the optimal value which would require an automatic tuning mechanism of the algorithm's parameters.

Within the experimentation on how to generate the model, abrupt changes were identified in the strong classifier since the self-adaptive φ method only takes into account the error from the current iteration. Therefore, a self-adaptive method should be implemented that includes the current error and its gradient so that it considers the error of consecutive iterations.

References

1. Susruth, M.: Financial forecasting: an empirical study on box - Jenkins methodology with reference to the Indian stock market. **10**(2), 115–123 (2017)
2. Huck, N., Guegan, D.: On the use of nearest neighbors in finance. Finance **26**, 67–86 (2007)
3. Meade, N.: A comparison of the accuracy of short term foreign exchange forecasting methods. Int. J. Forecast. **18**(1), 67–83 (2002)
4. Mahfoud, S., Mani, G., Reigel, S.: Nonlinear versus linear techniques for selecting individual stocks. In: Decision Technologies for Financial Engineering, pp. 65–75 (1997)
5. Chen, A.S., Leung, M.T., Daouk, H.: Application of neural networks to an emerging financial market: forecasting and trading the Taiwan stock index. Comput. Oper. Res. **30**(6), 901–923 (2003)
6. Kodogiannis, V., Lolis, A.: Forecasting financial time series using neural network and fuzzy system-based techniques. Neural Comput. Appl. **11**, 90–102 (2002)
7. Liu, S., Jingwen, X., Zhao, J., Xie, X., Zhang, W.: Efficiency enhancement of a process-based rainfall-runoff model using a new modified AdaBoost.RT technique. Appl. Soft Comput. J. **23**, 521–529 (2014)
8. Alfaro, E., García, N., Gámez, M., Elizondo, D.: Bankruptcy forecasting: an empirical comparison of AdaBoost and neural networks. Decis. Support. Syst. **45**(1), 110–122 (2008)
9. Wen, J., Zhang, X., Xu, Y., Li, Z., Liu, L.: Comparison of AdaBoost and logistic regression for detecting colorectal cancer patients with synchronous liver metastasis. In: 2nd International Conference on Biomedical and Pharmaceutical Engineering, ICBPE 2009 - Conference Proceedings (2009)
10. Liu, H., Tian, H., Li, Y., Zhang, L.: Comparison of four Adaboost algorithm based artificial neural networks in wind speed predictions. Energy Convers. Manag. **92**, 67–81 (2015)
11. Hu, G.-S., Zhu, F.-F., Zhang, Y.-C., Yu, J.-L.: Study of integrating AdaBoost and weight support vector regression model. In: 2009 International Conference on Artificial Intelligence and Computational Intelligence, pp. 258–262 (2009)
12. de Colombia, B.V.: Metodología para el cálculo del íncide COLCAP. Technical report, Bolsa de Valores de Colombia, Bogotá (2016)
13. Perdomo, G.A.V., Sepúlveda, J.M.: Diseño y Evaluación de un Modelo de Pronóstico para el Índice COLCAP mediante Filtros de señal y Redes Neuronales Artificiales. In: Encuentro Internacional de Investigadores en Administración, number c, pp. 625–643 (2011)
14. Espinosa Acuña, O.A., Vaca González, P.A.: Fitting the classical and Bayesian GARCH models with student-t innovations to COLCAP index. In: Simposio Internacional de Estadística 2015, (c) (2015)
15. Freund, Y., Schapire, R.E.: A decision theoretic generalization of on-line learning and an application to boosting. Comput. Syst. Sci. **57**, 119–139 (1997)

16. Schapire, R.E.: Explaining AdaBoost. In: Schölkopf, B., Luo, Z., Vovk, V. (eds.) Empirical Inference, pp. 37–52. Springer, Heidelberg (2013). https://doi.org/10. 1007/978-3-642-41136-6_5
17. Wang, Y., Han, P., Xiaoguang, L., Renbiao, W., Huang, J.: The performance comparison of Adaboost and SVM applied to SAR ATR. CIE Int. Conf. Radar Proc. **00**, 1–4 (2007)
18. Solomatine, D.P., Shrestha, D.L.: AdaBoost.RT: a boosting algorithm for regression problems. In: 2004 IEEE International Joint Conference on Neural Networks (IEEE Cat. No.04CH37541), vol. 2, pp. 1163–1168 (2004)
19. Autorregulador del Mercado de Valores de Colombia: Todo lo que un Inversionista debe saber sobre los nuevos Índices de la Bolsa de Valores de Colombia
20. de Colombia, B.V.: Índices bursátiles en línea
21. Brockwell, P.J., Davis, R.A.: Introduction to Time Series and Forecasting, 2nd Edn (2002)
22. Sallehuddin, R., Shamsuddin, S.M.H., Hashim, S.Z.M.: Application of grey relational analysis for multivariate time series. In: 2008 Eighth International Conference on Intelligent Systems Design and Applications, pp. 432–437 (2008)
23. Rencher, A.C.: Methods of Multivariate Analysis, 2nd edn (2002)
24. Tian, H.X., Mao, Z.Z.: An ensemble ELM based on modified AdaBoost. RT algorithm for predicting the temperature of molten steel in ladle furnace. IEEE Trans. Autom. Sci. Eng. **7**(1), 73–80 (2010)

Prototype of a Recommendation System Based on Multi-agents in the Analysis of Movies Dataset

Andres Ballén[(✉)], Nancy Gelvez[(✉)], and Helbert Espitia

Universidad Distrital Francisco José de Caldas, Bogotá, Colombia
adballend@correo.udistrital.edu.co,
{nygelvezg,heespitiac}@udistrital.edu.co

Abstract. In this paper is made a proposal of a recommendation system based on multi-agents, showing the architecture designed, the server used for the development of the multi-agent system, as well as the communication between necessary agents to carry out a tour recommended. The implemented proposal allows to make suggestions to users about movies. By means of neural networks it is determined if the proposed route for the user is correct or if it is necessary to improve the suggestion for following recommendations. In order to generate the recommendations, the free dataset of MovieLens was used, where a database was created to allow the analysis of them; and also to obtain a response to new recommendations for users.

Keywords: JSON · Multi-agent · Agent · System
Neuronal network · Recommendation · SPADE

1 Introduction

The use of information has created a new stigma on how to analyze data from individuals, through the implementation of recommender systems, it has been developed a new way to publicize relevant elements to users. Recommender systems are filtering technology that can predict items that may be of interest to users. These systems use technology that helps users to find items of interest, such as books, movies, songs, etc. [1].

Multi-agent systems are the union of several intelligent agents that interact in a shared environment coordinating actions. These agents interact with each other allowing to have goals and motivations for a response [2]. Smart Python Agent Development Environment (SPADE) free platform systems, developed at the Polytechnic University of Valencia, allow to develop multi-agent systems through its platform, also allowing interaction and communication between agents to reach a common goal.

Multi-agent recommender systems are able to solve problems when a large amount of data are used. The paper [3] shows these issues also representing the

© Springer Nature Switzerland AG 2018
J. C. Figueroa-García et al. (Eds.): WEA 2018, CCIS 915, pp. 206–217, 2018.
https://doi.org/10.1007/978-3-030-00350-0_18

idea of improving the experience of students with an effective learning model, which through recommendation system improves the learning experience of people. This encourages the improvement of human-system relation when recommending items or documents.

In this document, the implementation of a prototype of a recommender system based on multi-agent, developed using platform exposed SPADE, using neural networks to make a suggestion shaped the path about films that may be pleasing to the user. For recommendation system the MovieLens dataset is used, these data help to obtain general information for a recommendation to the user with the prototype. Throughout the document are shown the document class diagrams and databases used, in addition to the visualization of the neural network created and the output obtained.

2   Framework

2.1   Neural Networks

One branch of artificial intelligence widely applied by the scientific community is that corresponding to artificial neural networks (ANNs), describing them as those networks that consist of information elements whose local interactions depend on the behavior of the entire system [4].

The main purpose of the neural systems is to centralize the control of biological functions, some of them are in charge of energy supply; the neuronal system is connected to metabolism, cardiovascular control and breathing. However, when discussing the subject of neural computation it only takes into account the sensory and motor functions, as well as an internal process that is suggested to be called "thought" [5].

One definition of neural network is like a massively parallel distributed processing that has a natural tendency to store empirical knowledge and make it available for use [6]. Two important aspects are:

1. Knowledge is acquired by the network through a learning process.
2. Interneuronical connections, known as synaptic weights are used to store knowledge.

An artificial neural network is the one that simulates the inputs, weights and output of an activation function [7] where each input is assigned a weight that is subsequently added to use the activation function; in this way the neurons have the ability for pattern recognition [8].

There are several types of neural networks that can be classified as forward or backward. In networks, going forward means that the signals move forward, but in self-recurrent networks connections can go back. A clear example of classification of neural networks is given by the number, as these can be monolayer or multilayer [9]. Moreover, an example of a multilayer neural network is shown in Fig. 1.

The development of new information technologies is now a trend that allows people play all these phases of thoughts of artificial neural networks. However,

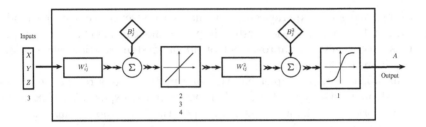

Fig. 1. Neural network multilayer.

the implementation of artificial sensory functions to make the machines can see and hear is possible to create a new extension to a new learning technique on computers.

Currently, many projects on neural networks can be found; for example, the USB memory Movidius, which is designed by Intel has the ability to run a neural network by simply connecting the USB to a computer [10]. Moreover, Deep Mind, which is another company of software, opened a training platform for building neural networks in a practical and efficient way for the development of this technology [11]. These projects are in addition to new business practices to offer autonomous driving vehicles by the use of neural networks together.

2.2 Intelligent Agent

An agent is a computer system that demonstrates that is able to perceive its environment with the help of sensors and acting on such environment through effectors. A rational ideal agent should make every effort to maximize the performance of its shares, based on the evidence provided by its sensors and knowledge. An agent is autonomous as long as its actions and choices depend more on its own experience that the knowledge about the environment introduced by the programmer [12]. Figure 2 shows the diagram reference SPADE agent.

2.3 Multiagent

The multi-agent system is a collection of multiple autonomous agents (intelligent), each acting toward their goals while all interacting in a shared environment and can possibly communicate and coordinate their actions.

Set of autonomous, usually heterogeneous and potentially independent agents, working together for solving a problem. A multi-agent system consists of distributed nodes or elements of an artificial intelligence system, where the conduct of these results produces a result of an intelligent whole system.

A multi-agent system is a computer system composed of multiple agents that interact with other, each agent has its own goals and motivations and success of the interaction requiring cooperation, coordination and negotiation among them [5]. The example of multiagent system is shown in Fig. 3.

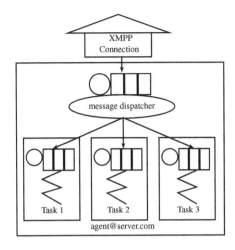

Fig. 2. Diagram of a reference SPADE agent [13].

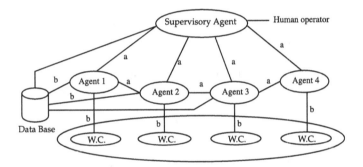

Fig. 3. Modeling of a multiagent [14].

2.4 SPADE

Smart Python Multi-agent Development Environment (SPADE) is a free plat-form multi-agent systems, developed in Python and based on XMPP instant messaging technology developed in 2005 at the Polytechnic University of Valen-cia [13]. The platform was born as a proof of concept to test the technology of instant messaging as the transport protocol for intelligent agents. Since then, the project has continued to grow and adding new features taking advantage of the flexibility of instant messaging protocol based on XML, and the number of extensions developed for it which are usable within the framework of multi-agent systems. The SPADE platform is based on a set of standards, the most noteworthy FIPA and XMPP/Jabber [13], this model is shown in Fig. 4.

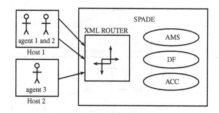

Fig. 4. Model of the SPADE platform [13].

2.5   Recommendation System

According to [1] "A recommender system is a filtering technology personalized information used to predict whether a particular user likes a particular item (problem prediction), or to identify a set of N items that may be of interest to certain users (problem recommendation top-N)".

Considering [15] "Recommender systems are a series of mechanisms and techniques applied to information retrieval to try to solve the problem of data overload on the Internet. These help users to choose the objects that may be useful or of interest; these objects can be any type, such as books, movies, songs, websites, blogs, etc".

In these definitions it can be seen that a recommendation system is a set of tools and techniques used to retrieve information to try to predict the solution to a problem of recommendation.

Recommender systems are characterized by liken relevant user information, but are distinguished as follows:

- Frequency of use: The systems are targeted for extended and long lasting use.
- Representation needs: These systems are expressed in the form of questions to analyze information from user profiles.
- Objective: The recommendation systems eliminate information that is not important according to user profiles.
- Social Scope: The relationship with the user is important to analyze the tastes and preferences in the system.

Recommendation Techniques. Recommender systems user profile contrast with the necessary features for accurate recommendation where there are three filtering techniques that identify the type of system that can be used:

1. Explicit Feedback: For explicit feedback, through a survey process the user gives a rating of content. This feedback accurately allows meet user preferences allowing to give a rating of content.
2. Implicit Feedback: The implicit feedback evaluates, without user intervention, possible options for recommendation, whether through movies, web articles, books, TV shows, and others. These events allow us to analyze and understand the tastes and preferences of the user.

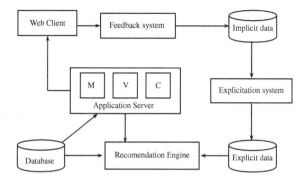

Fig. 5. Model recommendation system for e-books [16].

3   Prototype

For the development of this prototype a multi-agent architecture is implemented as seen in the Fig. 6. This project is developed with this architecture due to the need to cover in a different way the process of recommendation of elements for a person, thus, this system is created allowing the choice of the different agents that exist in the prototype. In this case, the system agent, the verification officer, and the feedback agent, are responsible for analyzing the users' qualifications to verify if the route was liked. Aditionally the recommendation and the search agent, have as objective the search for accurate information to reach the objective of the recommendation. This was the reason why this type of multi-agent system was developed, due to the need of another solution for this problem.

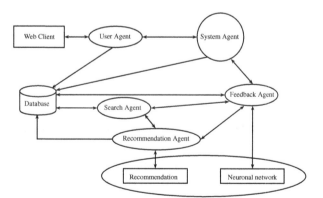

Fig. 6. System diagram.

The user agent is in charge of entering the system to ask for a recommendation from the user. In the SPADE development platform, the intelligent agent is appointed with an ID, and the IP address of the machine that is working, in this case "usuario@127.0.0.1". These data allow to know the user required to make the recommendation and the name of the agent that reaches the system. Once the recommendation user agent obtains a JSON file format, it is show the output determined by the system.

System agent is responsible for handling all connected entities and handles the references of all agents besides communication system; moreover, the proper functioning of this is generated as a recommendation. The agent of the system is type-reactive that has the function of obtaining the identifier of the user that requires a recommended route. Through the stimulus this agent contributes to the interaction of the other agents in their environment.

The search agent is the one responsible for obtaining the necessary parameters to make a recommendation to a user. The agent of recommendation is reactive with a module of consultation that allows the data-analysis obtained by the search agent, it processes the information reaching the measurement to conclude with the recommended route for the user. This agent processes the data of the user agent verifying new coincidences regarding the tastes and preferences of other users, delivering a response of the recommendation in a file with JSON format.

The feedback agent is a learning entity composed of a self-teaching module and formed by a neural network, where by having the interaction of the movies user ratings; this network allows to feedback their learning to improve their behavior. This agent reads the ratings provided by the user in a list of recommendations. All data are presented with a score of 1 to 5, where 1 represents the lowest value and 5 the highest. These results verify that the recommending agent has made recommendations to a user, managing corrections and repairs to improve further recommendations. These architectures of the main agents of this prototype can be seen in Fig. 7.

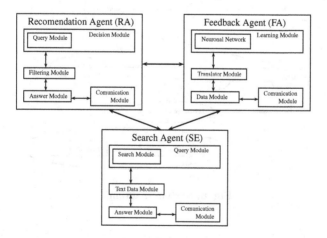

Fig. 7. Agent architecture.

Communication is a vital importance part in the system; thus, the entities of this multiagent system communicate each other using the XMPP communication protocol. Through a type of ontology, conversation identifier, shipping address and content, these agents can interact with each other. This type of communication allows to engage the predetermined behavior of each agent to solve incoming problems. Figure 8 shows the relations of three of the most important agents of the prototype, whose communication allows to identify a possible recommendation.

This prototype multi-agent system was created with the MovieLens dataset [17]. Using this information allowed to analyze the qualifications that users of that platform have given to films that have been watched, which has been helpful when testing the system. The system is designed with intelligent agents to communicate with the environment, where the primary objective is the recommendation for a user. The operation of the system is the arrival of a new user agent, which can stimulate the system, creating a request to the system agent, allowing the creation of the recommendation to the user.

In Fig. 8 is observed the system database design, where movie data tables and user ratings are taken from MovieLens dataset. These data obtained from this source served to meet the qualifications that users of the platform have and which are useful for analyzing the behavior of the system when a recommendation is created.

To check whether a route satisfies the recommendations for a user, a neural network that identifies the time that a user has watched the film, as well as the valuation given to it was created. This network verifies data and verifies whether the recommendation given by the system is relevant to the tastes of a user. In Fig. 9 the design of the neural network with two inputs and one output is shown. All data are analyzed by the network, giving a score from 1 to 5 in response to analysis.

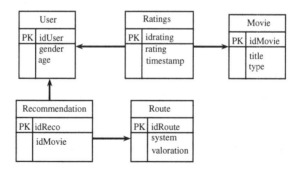

Fig. 8. Diagram database.

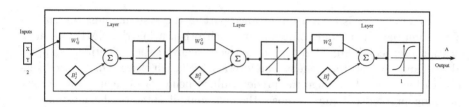

Fig. 9. Neural network diagram.

4 Results

To design and train the neural network were considered different activation functions. In all cases, the neural network has three different layers of customization. In the first case, the network configuration with two first layers using *logsig*, and the last with *satlin*. In the second case, the two first layers configuration with *logsig*, and the third *purelin* as activation function was performed. In the third case of a layer configuration, it was performed with *purelin*, followed by two layers of *logsig*. For the final case is used in the first layer a *logsig* activation function, the second is *satlin* and the third function is *purelin*.

The training process is performed 10 times for each case, the stats of data obtained during this development are in Table 1, where is shown the maximum and minimum value obtained, in addition to the mean and standard deviation. This table shows the best performance value in each case considered, case 4 is chosen for handling the neural network in the recommendation system (best minimum value). The record of training process (best run) for each network configuration is shown in Fig. 10.

Table 1. Neural network training results.

Case	Max	Min	Mean	Standard deviation
1	1,8205E-06	7,8464E-17	4,52E-07	7,62215E-07
2	3,8011	1,1961E-09	5,53E-01	1,33040547
3	0,64175	5,3245E-08	1,60E-01	0,32087485
4	0,0010988	2,8237E-20	3,67E-04	0,00063346

Cases 2 and 3 show the worst configurations that can be performed for the neural network considering de minimum value. It is also considered that case 1 is a valid option for testing with that configuration because it has a better average value than the other 3 cases.

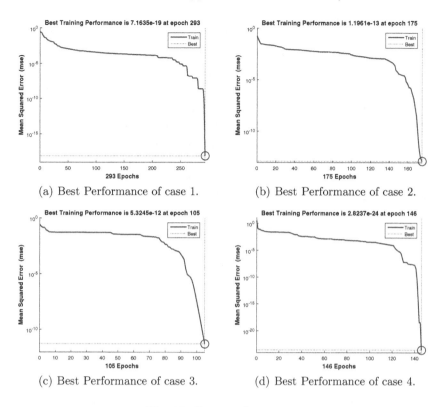

(a) Best Performance of case 1.

(b) Best Performance of case 2.

(c) Best Performance of case 3.

(d) Best Performance of case 4.

Fig. 10. Cases performance.

After completing the tests of the neural network, the recommender system test was performed with MovieLens dataset and a random user who allow to check the recommendation. To be connected with the system is used a web server enabling communication of another web service, obtaining the result of the request made. Table 2 shows a summary of the recommendation for the user test, which obtains identifiers, movie name and path identifier created by the system.

These data are obtained from the table ratings database where Table 3 shows the decoding result obtained by the agent system feedback. This path identifier give the recommendation and the score associated. In this case the assessment provided by the system is 4 points.

Table 2. Decoding the recommendation file.

User ID	Recomendation ID	Movie Id	Movie name
1	121	7153	Lord of the Rings
1	121	1080	Monty Python's Life of Bryan (1979)
1	121	6874	Kill Bill: Vol 1 (2003)
1	121	356	Forrest Gump (1994)
1	121	4973	Amelie Poulain
1	121	593	Silence of the Lambs
1	121	318	Beautiful Mind
1	121	16	Wall-E
1	121	1213	Godfather
1	121	5418	Casino (1995)

Table 3. Decoding output feedback agent.

Recommendation ID	Route ID	System valoration
121	12	4

5   Conclusions

From the analysis of the information obtained using the dataset, it is possible to create a recommender system based on multi-agent, which allows tours to movie recommendations. These recommendations are based on the ratings of MovieLens users platform. Based on data analysis, intelligent agents interact for response to request a route to a user. This route, as shown in Fig. 10(d), consists of 10 films which are tested to verify if they can be ideal to the tastes of users.

This test allowed to know the importance of managing large volumes of data, for the recommendation algorithm used in the system had to be efficient to respond to the request; however, to obtain the output data has not been verified if the recommendation is consistent with users requirements, because the web server cannot connect to the primary server that has provided the information.

The stats of the neural network training enabled to analyze the performance obtained for the considered cases, choosing the configuration of case 4 to implement the system, also the case 1 is an option to be considered. Additionally cases 2 and 3 are with poor performance on tests.

Use of multi-agent system through the SPADE platform makes possible to analyze the prerequisites for creating this system using the communication protocol XMPP for the communications among agents. This development is satisfactory and is expected to be use in recommendation systems on various topics like arts and historical collections.

References

1. Resnick, P., Varian, H.R.: Recommender systems. Commun. ACM. **40**, 56–58 (1997). https://doi.org/10.1145/245108.245121
2. Zapata, L.F.: Sistemas Multiagente. Foundations 142 (2010)
3. Brigui-Chtioui, I., Caillou, P., Negre, E.: Intelligent digital learning: agent-based recommender system. In: Proceedings of 9th International Conference on Machine Learning and Computing, pp. 71–76 (2017). https://doi.org/10.1145/3055635. 3056592
4. Hilera, J., José Martínez Hernando, V.: Redes neuronales artificiales : fundamentos, modelos y aplicaciones / J.R. Hilera González, V.J. Martínez Hernando, Madrid (1995). (PDF Download Available)
5. Matich, D.J.: Redes Neuronales: Conceptos Básicos y Aplicaciones. Historia Santiago **55** (2001)
6. Kubat, M.: Neural networks: a comprehensive foundation by Simon Haykin, Macmillan, 1994, ISBN 0-02-352781-7. Knowl. Eng. Rev. **13**(4), S0269888998214044 (1999)
7. Arrieta, J., Torres, J., Velásquez, H.: Predicciones de modelos econométricos y redes neuronales: el caso de la acción de SURAMINV. Semest. Económico **12**, 95–109 (2009)
8. Pérez, F., Fernández, H.: Las redes neuronales y la evaluación del riesgo de crédito. Rev. Ing. Univ. Medellín. **6**, 77–91 (2007)
9. Heaton, J.: Introduction to Neural Networks with Java. Heat Transfer Research Inc., Navasota (2008)
10. Raya, A.: Intel presenta la Inteligencia Artificial en una memoria USB. http:// omicrono.elespanol.com/2017/07/inteligencia- artificial-en-una-memoria-usb/
11. Deepmind: Open sourcing Sonnet - a new library for constructing neural networks. https://deepmind.com/blog/open-sourcing-sonnet/
12. Russel, S., Norvig, P.: Inteligencia Artificial. Prentice hall, Madrid (2004)
13. Gregori, M., Cámara, J., Bada, G.: A jabber-based multi-agent system platform. In: Proceedings of fifth International Joint Conference on Autonomous agents multiagent System, pp. 1282–1284 (2006). https://doi.org/10.1145/1160633.1160866
14. Botía, J.A.: Modelado de un Sistema Multi-Agente mediante la aplicación de la metodología INGENIAS con el Ingenias Development Kit (2007)
15. Ricci, F., Rokach, L., Shapira, B.: Introduction to recommender systems handbook. In: Ricci, F., Rokach, L., Shapira, B., Kantor, P.B. (eds.) Recommender Systems Handbook, pp. 1–35. Springer, Boston (2011). https://doi.org/10.1007/978-0-387-85820-3_1
16. Nunez-valdéz, E.R., et al.: Plataforma de recomendación de contenidos para libros electrónicos inteligentes basada en el comportamiento de los usuarios. Ventana Inforática. **14**, 25–40 (2012)
17. Maxwell, F., Konstan, J.: The movielens datasets: history and context. ACM Trans. Interact. Intell. Syst. **5**, 19 (2016). https://doi.org/10.1145/2827872

A Game Theory Approach for Intrusion Prevention Systems

Julián Francisco Mojica Sánchez[1], Octavio José Salcedo Parra[1,2(✉)], and Lewys Correa Sánchez[2]

[1] Department of Systems and Industrial Engineering, Faculty of Engineering, Universidad Nacional de Colombia, Bogotá D.C., Colombia
{jfmojicas, ojsalcedop}@unal.edu.co
[2] Faculty of Engineering, Intelligent Internet Research Group, Universidad Distrital "Francisco José de Caldas", Bogotá D.C., Colombia
osalcedo@udistrital.edu.co,
lcorreas@correo.udistrital.edu.co

Abstract. This document evaluates works related to game theory applied to IPS (Intrusion Prevention System) in networks and proposes a game theory model that allows optimize expenditure of resources in detection of intrusions in networks.

Keywords: Intrusion prevention system · Game theory · Vulnerabilities

1 Introduction

The internet of things every day is being introduced more into our daily lives due to the access that people have both to internet and new technology, with the increase of everyday devices connected to the internet also increases the amount of sensitive information transmitted wirelessly [1].

The increment of devices connected to Internet and the sharing of a big amount of sensitive information and the intrinsic vulnerabilities of wireless communications, made the infrastructure of the Internet of Things networks a point of interest for criminals. For that reason it is necessary to ensure the privacy, available and integrity of this information through security adaptive mechanisms to different types of attacks [2].

The simplicity required in the Internet devices of the thing makes impossible the implementation of internally security systems in these. Because the creation of devices has been increasing to a greater extent than the development in network security with IOT devices, these devices have become a gateway to networks for attackers. Among the different attacks suffered by Wi-Fi networks connected to IOT devices we have: low password exploitation, reverse engineering hardware, remote code execution, man in the middle and hidden monitoring functions. The most common use of remotely controlling IOT devices by cybercriminals is DoS, due it is easy to achieve if the devices have not been configured with basic security measures and allows them to obtain money by preventing access to a server or website [3].

© Springer Nature Switzerland AG 2018
J. C. Figueroa-García et al. (Eds.): WEA 2018, CCIS 915, pp. 218–229, 2018.
https://doi.org/10.1007/978-3-030-00350-0_19

The sensitivity of information and the failures in the security of wireless networks have led the research community to undertake research and development efforts simultaneously in new IOT devices and security mechanisms for wireless networks. An important point is the need for real-time processing and reaction to attacks because IOT devices transmit information constantly [4].

In this document, a model based on game theory will be created to establish the intrusion detection criteria of an IPS (Intrusion Prevention System) for networks, based on the review of previously developed related works.

2 Related Works

In 2016 Wang, Du, Yang, Zhu, Shen and Zhang propose an attack-defense game model for detecting malicious nodes in Embedded Sensor Networks (ESN) using a repeated game approach, where they define the function of rewards that attackers and defenders will receive for their actions [5]. To solve errors and absences in detection use a game tree model. They show that the game model does not have a pure Nash equilibrium but mixed strategy, where the nodes are changing due to the strategies of attackers and defenders so that they are in dynamic equilibrium, where limited resources are used and provided Security protection at the same. Finally, they perform simulations where they show that with the proposed model they can reduce energy consumption by 50% compared to the existing model All Monitor (AM) and improve the detection rate from 10% to 15% compared to the existing model Cluster Head (CH).

In 2013 Manshaei, Zhu, Alpcan, Bacar and Hubaux carry out a review of the investigations in privacy and security in communication and computer networks that have a game theory approach [6]. In their content they have a section of Intrusion Detection Systems where they present the different works found in the review of the literature; the way in which the IDS are configured; Networked IDS, where different IDSs operate in the network independently and the security of each subsystem that they individually protect depends on the performance of the other IDS; Collaborative Intrusion Detection System Networks, in this case in the network operate different IDS in collaborative way, that is, they share the knowledge of the new attacks they detect, but the system can be compromised if the control of an IDS is taken by an attacker and finally the response to intrusions, where they expose an intrusion response system based on Stackelberg stochastic game called Response and Recovery Engine (RRE).

3 Game Theory Models

The prevention of intrusions can be understood as an attack scenario - defense, in which the person in charge of the security of the network decides whether it is necessary or not to put in operation the system of prevention of intrusions, because this operation has a cost that would not be necessary if the network is not being attacked.

The defender has two strategies (U_D): defend or not defend and in the case of the attacker (U_A): attack or not attack. The realization of these strategies has rewards and costs that will determine the way the two actors act. These costs and rewards are defined below:

- Cost of starting the IPS Cm
- Average loss when the system is attacked Ci
- Cost to attack by the attacker Ca
- Cost of not attacking by the attacker Cw
- Payment to the defender for taking an action strategy defensive Ui
- Payment to the attacker for taking an action strategy offensive Ua

Now you can understand that the reward of the attackers Pa is equal to average losses when the system is attacked, that is:

$$P_a = C_i \tag{1}$$

It is necessary to define when it is profitable for the attacker to carry out the attack:

$$C_w < P_a - C_a \tag{2}$$

The above equation means that the attacker will perform an attack when its reward minus the cost of attacking greater than the cost of not attacking.

On the other hand, the attacker will not make an attack when the cost of starting the IPS is much lower than the loss average when the system is attacked, because in this case surely the defender would have started the IPS, therefore this will be in operation and the attack will be detected and the attacker isolated from the network.

From this it is possible to define the reward matrix as:

$$\begin{bmatrix} P_a - C_a, \ U_i - C_i & -U_a, \ U_i - C_m \\ C_w, \ U_i & C_w, \ U_i - C_m \end{bmatrix}$$

Where the columns correspond to the strategies of the defender, that is, not defend and defend; and the rows do reference to the attacker's strategies, that is, attack and not attack.

They determine that there is no pure Nash equilibrium, therefore they analyze if the game model is in mixed Nash equilibrium.

Analyzing the mixed Nash equilibrium for the game they found the probability that the attacker attacks σ and the probability that the defender defends δ.

From Eq. (10) it is possible to find δ

$$\delta = \frac{P_a - C_a - C_w}{P_a - C_a + U_a} \tag{3}$$

From Eq. (11) it is possible to find σ

$$\sigma = \frac{C_m}{C_i} \tag{4}$$

With these rewards depending on the probability of taking the strategy of attacking and defending, they found the rewards of not attacking and defending as $(1 - \sigma)$ and $(1 - \delta)$ respectively. Therefore, the strategies of the attackers under a mixed Nash equilibrium are:

$$(\delta, 1 - \delta) = \left(\frac{P_a - C_a - C_w}{P_a - C_a + U_a}, \frac{U_a + C_w}{P_a - C_a + U_a} \right) \tag{5}$$

$$(\sigma, 1 - \sigma) = \left(\frac{C_m}{C_i}, \frac{C_i - C_m}{C_i} \right) \tag{6}$$

To analyze the Nash equilibrium by mixed strategy, it is possible to start assuming that the probability of attacking *sigma* is high, so that $C_m \gg C_i$, that is, the attack occurs when it is not profitable to start the IPS, which makes the defense probability low.

In case the probability of defense is high, it means that the IPS has probably been launched because the losses to be attacked are greater than the cost of having the IPS in operation, that is, $C_m \gg C_i$ which indicates that the attack probability must be low.

In conclusion, the probabilities of attack and defense are inversely proportional and the system will be in mixed Nash equilibrium when:

$$\sigma = \delta \tag{7}$$

Now Manshaei [6] explains a two-player Bayesian game, a defense node and a malicious or regular one. The malicious node can choose between attacking and not attacking, while the defense node can choose between monitoring and not monitoring. The security of the defender is quantifiable according to the property that protects w, therefore, when there is a security failure the damage is represented by $-w$. Then the payoff matrix is presented:

$$\begin{bmatrix} (1 - \alpha)w - C_a, (2\alpha - 1)w - C_m & w - C_a, -w \\ 0, \beta w - C_m & 0, 0 \end{bmatrix}$$

In this matrix the columns represent the behaviors of the defender (monitor and not monitor) and the rows attacker behaviors (attack and not attack), C_a and C_m are costs of attacking and monitoring, α and β are the detection rate and the false alarm rate of the IDS respectively and μ_0 the probability that a player is malicious.

Finally they show that when $\mu_0 < \frac{(1+\beta)w + Cm}{(2\alpha + \beta - 1)w}$ the game supports a strategy of pure balance (attack if it is malicious, do not attack if it is regular), do not monitor, μ_0 and when $\mu_0 > \frac{(1+\beta)w + Cm}{(2\alpha + \beta - 1)w}$ the game does not have a pure strategy.

4 Proposed Model

From the model described by Manshaei and establishing that the two players are intruder and defender, since the intruder is ready to carry out the attack because has done a vulnerability study and has planned the different strategies to follow in order to enter authorized to the network, the time when no attack represents a C_w cost (waiting cost) because the network can change and the investment mentioned above both of time and of resources can be lost. Therefore, the payment matrix is:

$$\begin{bmatrix} (1-\alpha)w - C_a, (2\alpha-1)w - C_m & w - C_a, -w \\ -C_w, -\beta w - C_m & -C_w, 0 \end{bmatrix}$$

The following explains each of the possible scenarios and the respective payments for the intruder and the defender:

- When the intruder attacks and the defender monitors: Reward of the attacker, the times the system fails of detection for the good that protects less the cost to attack; the defender's reward, the times the system works less the times it fails for the good that protects, all this except the cost of monitoring.
- When the intruder attacks and the defender does not monitor: the reward of the attacker, the good that one wants to obtain minus the cost of attacking; the defender's reward, in this case is the loss of good.
- When the intruder does not attack and the defender monitors: reward of the attacker, in this case it is the loss for waiting to perform the attack; the reward of defender, false alarm rate degrades the good and its It also has the cost of monitoring.
- When the intruder does not attack and the defender does not monitor: reward of the attacker, in this case it is the loss wait to perform the attack; the reward of the defender, in this case it is null since it does not spend on monitoring and it is not attacked.

Depending on the strategy that the other actor takes and the respective payments they obtain, it is possible to determine if there is a Nash equilibrium.

When the defender does not monitor, the attacker has two possible strategies: Attack, with gain $w - C_a$; and do not attack, where he gets $-C_w$, therefore you will always choose to attack.

When the defender also monitors the attacker can choose between attacking and not attacking, assuming a detection rate greater than 90%, attacking would lose the cost of attacking, while not attacking would lose the cost of waiting.

Generally the deployment of an attack to take control of the network or the information it contains is more expensive than carrying out a recognition and learning of the network and its vulnerabilities, therefore the attacker will choose not to attack.

$$-C_w > -C_a$$

Now it is necessary to fix the behavior of the attacker and analyze the possible strategies that the defender will perform.

First, when the attacker decides to attack and assuming a detection rate greater than 90%.

$$(2\alpha - 1)w - C_m > -w$$

This means that the defender will choose to monitor.
Second, when the attacker decides not to attack

$$-\beta w - C_m < 0$$

Then, the defender will always choose not to monitor.

After analyzing the different strategies, it is clear that in neither scenario will both actors be satisfied with their reward. Which prevents that pure Nash equilibrium exists in the proposed game.

5   Model Evaluation

Because there is no point in the rewards matrix in which both the defender and the attacker feel comfortable with the situation, it is necessary to determine if the model is in mixed Nash equilibrium, for this the probability that the attacker attack σ and the probability that the defender defends δ.

The mixed strategy of the attacker is:

$$U_A = [(1 - \alpha)w - C_a]\delta\sigma + [w - C_a](1 - \delta)\sigma + (-C_w)\delta(1 - \sigma) + (-C_w)(1 - \delta)(1 - \sigma) \tag{8}$$

The mixed strategy of the defender is

$$U_I = [(2\alpha - 1)w - C_m]\delta\sigma + (-w)(1 - \delta)\sigma + [-\beta_w - C_m]\delta(1 - \sigma) \tag{9}$$

Using the extreme value method to solve the strategy of the Nash mixed model, the equations are derived (17) and (18) regarding δ and σ respectively and are equal to zero.

$$\frac{\partial U_A}{\partial \sigma} = -\delta\alpha w + w - C_a + C_w = 0 \tag{10}$$

$$\frac{\partial U_I}{\partial \sigma} = 2\sigma\alpha w - \beta w - C_m + \sigma\beta_w = 0 \tag{11}$$

From the Eq. (19) its possible find δ:

$$\delta = \frac{w - C_a + C_w}{w\alpha} \tag{12}$$

From the Eq. (20) its possible find σ:

$$\sigma = \frac{\beta w + C_m}{2\alpha w + \beta_w} \tag{13}$$

To analyze the Nash equilibrium by mixed strategy, you can start assuming that the probability of attacking δ be high, for this to be $Cm \gg 2\alpha w$, this means that the attacker could attack comfortably when the goods that protects the defender are not so valuable to him, which is why I will not have activated the IPS. In the case where you come from protect are valuable the defense probability will increase and the probability of attack will decrease.

Therefore, it is found again that the probabilities of attack and defense are inversely proportional and the system will be in mixed Nash equilibrium when:

$$\delta = \sigma \tag{14}$$

Additionally, in case the probability of defense be high, this situation occurs when the cost of waiting for attacker is greater than the cost of attacking, that is, when it is more profitable for the attacker to effect his attack than to follow waiting for the right moment.

Below is presented a graphical function analysis that defines the probability that the attacker attacks vs the cost of monitoring under certain parameters.

Initially, the good that seeks to protect (w) was set up as 100 and the cost of monitoring varied from 0 to 100 per 1, this was established because it is illogical to use more resources protecting a good than the value for the defender. The alpha value was also set at 95% and different beta values were used to analyze the behavior of the probability that the attacker attacks based on the false alarm rate, this behavior is presented in Fig. 1.

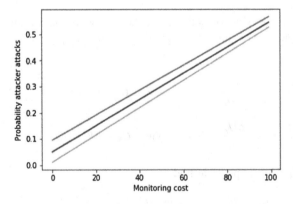

Fig. 1. Probability attacker attacks vs monitoring cost with: w = 100, alpha = 95%, beta = 20% (red), beta = 10% (blue) and beta = 2% (green) (Color figure online)

When analyzing Fig. 1 it can be observed that by decreasing the false alarm rate (beta) the probability of the attacker attacking is diminished, which is because if the IPS is more efficient the attacker will tend not to carry out an attack until you are sure that it will not be detected.

Second, w = 100 and beta = 2% were set to observe the behavior of the probability of the attacker attacking with different values of detection rate, this can be seen in Fig. 2.

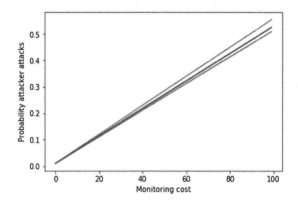

Fig. 2. Probability attacker attacks vs monitoring cost with: w = 100, beta = 2%, alpha = 98% (red), alpha = 95% (blue) and alpha = 90% (green) (Color figure online)

Figure 2 shows that by decreasing the detection rate the probability that the attacker will attack will be greater, this happens in the same way as in the previous case, because if the system becomes less efficient it will be more profitable for the attacker to make an attack, therefore, the probability that the attacker will attack will increase.

Third, alpha = 98%, beta = 2% was set and the value of w was varied to analyze how the probability that the attacker attacks with respect to the variation of the cost of the desired good is affected. opt to make the attack. Said analysis was carried out starting from Fig. 3.

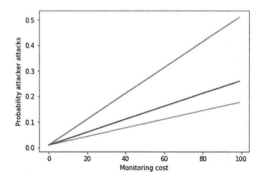

Fig. 3. Probability attacker attacks vs monitoring cost with: alpha = 98%, beta = 2%, w = 100 (red), w = 200 (blue) and w = 300 (green) (Color figure online)

Figure 3 shows that increasing the cost of the good that the attacker wants to obtain, the likelihood that the attacker attacks is reduced, this seems to go against the logic but it is because if the good is much more valuable than the cost of monitoring, the defender will always want to protect said good by starting the IPS and therefore it will be more complex for the attacker to violate the security of the system.

Below is a graphical function analysis that defines the probability that the defender defends vs the cost of attack under certain parameters.

In a similar way to the previous case we started by initially establishing the good that we want to protect w as 100 and varying the cost of attack from 0 to 100 every 1, this was defined in that way because it was assumed that the attacker has an idea of how Valuable is the good that you expect to obtain when making an attack and is not willing to spend more than the value of said good.

The value of alpha was also set at 95% and different values of C_w were used to analyze the behavior of the probability that the defender defends with respect to the cost of waiting to carry out the attack, this behavior is presented in Fig. 4.

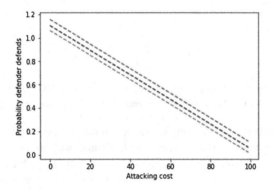

Fig. 4. Probability defender defends vs attacking cost with: w = 100, alpha = 95%, Cw = 10 (red), Cw = 5 (blue) and Cw = 1 (green) (Color figure online)

Figure 4 shows that by decreasing the value of the waiting cost to carry out the attack, the probability that the defender defends will also decrease. This is because the attacker is so clear about the vulnerabilities of the network that it is very cheap for him to wait for the attack, therefore the defender must activate the IPS as soon as possible to correct the failures in network security.

Second, $w = 100$ and $C_w = 10$ were set to observe the behavior of the probability that the defender defends with different values of detection rate, this can be seen in Fig. 5.

When looking at Fig. 5 it is understood that when the detection rate of the IPS decreases the probability that the defender defends increases, this behavior is due to the fact that when the IPS is less efficient the defender must have it active for a longer time in order to detect the intrusions and therefore the probability that the defender defends will be greater.

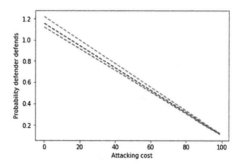

Fig. 5. Probability defender defends vs attacking cost with: w = 100, Cw = 10, alpha = 98% (red), alpha = 95% (blue) and alpha = 90% (green) (Color figure online)

Finally *alpha* = 98% and C_w = 10 were set to see how the cost of the good that protects the defender impacts the probability that the defender defends, this was done by variations in w and can be seen in Fig. 6.

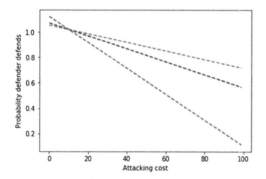

Fig. 6. Probability defender defends vs attacking cost with: alpha = 98%, Cw = 10, w = 100 (red), w = 200 (blue) and w = 300 (green) (Color figure online)

6   Discussion

The presented model is based on the model described by Manshaei [6] but this does not have a pure Nash equilibrium because in this new model it is defined that there are two players: a defender and an attacker, while in the presented by Manshaei it is possible that the attacker is not malicious in which there is a pure balance and is not to attack and not monitor.

Regarding the model presented by Wang [5] the same conclusion was reached that the system will be in equilibrium when the probability of attacking:

$$\sigma = \frac{\beta w + C_m}{2\alpha w + \beta w} \qquad (15)$$

Equal to the probability of defending:

$$\delta = \frac{w - C_a + C_w}{w\alpha} \qquad (16)$$

And in case these are not equal the model is regulated to over time until you reach this balance even though you in this case the detection rate and false are taken into account IPS alarms, which is raised in the model described by Manshaei [6] and makes the model closer to reality.

The analysis of the probability functions that the attacker attacks and that the defender defends allows to obtain a clearer view of the decisions that the players of this game can take and the reasons to act in a certain way.

7   Conclusions

- This model of game theory adds a new feature to intrusion prevention systems, where you can evaluate how complex it is to perform a vulnerability analysis on the network that is defending itself. Because if it is much less expensive to perform the analysis than the attack, it will be more profitable for the attackers to launch their attack plan and therefore the IPS must be in operation to prevent such attacks and avoid loss of information, money and reputation.
- The proposed model is regulated over time until reaching the equilibrium point at which the probability of attacking σ is equal to the probability of defending δ.

$$\sigma = \frac{\beta w + C_m}{2\alpha w + \beta w} = \frac{w - C_a + C_w}{w\alpha} = \delta$$

- Decreasing the false alarm rate (beta) the probability of the attacker attacking is diminished.
- Decreasing the detection rate the probability that the attacker will attack will be greater.
- Increasing the cost of the good that the attacker wants to obtain, the likelihood that the attacker attacks is reduced.
- Decreasing the value of the waiting cost to carry out the attack, the probability that the defender defends will also decrease.
- When the detection rate of the IPS decreases the probability that the defender defends increases.
- When the cost of the good that the defender protects increases, the probability that the defender defends also increases.

References

1. Michaels, S., Akkaya, K., Selcuk Uluagac, A.: Inducing data loss in Zigbee networks via join/association handshake spoofing. In: 2016 IEEE Conference on Communications and Network Security (CNS), Philadelphia, PA, pp. 401–405 (2016). https://doi.org/10.1109/cns. 2016.7860527
2. Sforzin, A., Marmol, F.G., Conti, M., Bohli, J.M.: RPiDS: raspberry Pi IDS - a fruitful intrusion detection system for IoT. In: Proceedings - 13th IEEE International Conference on Ubiquitous Intelligence and Computing, 13th IEEE International Conference on Advanced and Trusted Computing, 16th IEEE International Conference on Scalable Computing and Communications, pp. 440–448 (2017). https://doi.org/10.1109/UIC-ATC-ScalCom-CBDCom-IoPSmartWorld.2016.0080
3. Sharma, P.K., Moon, S.Y., Moon, D., Park, J.H.: DFA-AD: a distributed framework architecture for the detection of advanced persistent threats. Clust. Comput. **20**(1), 597–609 (2017). https://doi.org/10.1007/s10586-016-0716-0
4. Chen, J., Chen, C.: Design of complex event-processing IDS in internet of things. In: Proceedings - 2014 6th International Conference on Measuring Technology and Mechatronics Automation, ICMTMA 2014, pp. 226–229 (2014). https://doi.org/10.1109/ICMTMA.2014. 57
5. Wang, K., Du, M., Yang, D., Zhu, C., Shen, J., Zhang, Y.: Game-theory-based active defense for intrusion detection in cyber-physical embedded systems. ACM Trans. Embed. Comput. Syst. **16**(1), 121 (2016). https://doi.org/10.1145/2886100
6. Manshaei, M.M.H., Zhu, Q., Alpcan, T., Bacar, T., Hubaux, J.-P.: Game theory meets network security and privacy. ACM Comput. **45** (2013). https://doi.org/10.1145/2480741. 2480742

Simulation Systems

A Simulation Model for the Attention to Users in Emergency Situations in the City of Bogotá

German Mendez-Giraldo[1(✉)] , Eduyn López-Santana[1(✉)] ,
and Carolina Suarez-Roldan[2]

[1] Universidad Distrital Francisco José de Caldas, Bogota, Colombia
{gmendez, erlopezs}@udistrital.edu.co
[2] Universidad Cooperativa de Colombia, Bogota, Colombia
carolina.suarez@campusucc.edu.co

Abstract. A simulation model is presented for the attention to users in emergency situations in Bogota. This system is vital importance for the development, security and stability of the city. The simulation process begins with an intelligence model that allows acquiring the knowledge of complex process of attention of users and understanding relationships among resources which attend emergencies. This system is managed by Emergency Regulatory Center (ERC) assigned to the District Health Secretary. Within the results achieved, it is possible to obtain an improvement in measures of performance such as average time in the system and the average time blocked which show an inadequate level service because they are result of excessive time in waiting calls and the subsequent system exit. Different scenarios were proposed in order to increase reception capacity of the incidents in the activation system's phase, which is equivalent to increase the technicians auxiliaries of regulatory medical (TARM) and of the regulatory doctor (RD).

Keywords: Attention of users · Emergencies · Simulation

1 Introduction

The International Labor Organization [1] states that the service of public urgencies (SPU) deals of exceptional situations that occur in society and stand a threat for life. The institutions that provide this service have common characteristics such as rescuing people who need external help, protection of property to avoid destruction or damage, and on the other hand, periods of quiet work interrupted by periods of great psychological stress and physical activity. These organizations, called dispatch agencies, are responsible for responding to citizens' requests through the allocation of resources or mobile units such as ambulances, police cars, and fire trucks, among others.

The creation of Unique Number of Security and Emergencies (UNSE) is justified by low level of coverage in the Capital District, in 2015 of 779,087 calls only 281,140 were served with dispatches of resources, which is equivalent to 36%. The most frequent incident was calls from the residence with 24.5% and followed by calls of incidents on public roads with 25.6% [2]. The agencies that are part of UNSE are the

© Springer Nature Switzerland AG 2018
J. C. Figueroa-García et al. (Eds.): WEA 2018, CCIS 915, pp. 233–245, 2018.
https://doi.org/10.1007/978-3-030-00350-0_20

Emergency Prevention and Assistance Fund (EPAF); the ERC, the Unit of Fire Department, the Mobility Secretary and the Metropolitan Police.

For the presented model, the data was taken from the ERC, as proposed by the World Health Organization (WHO), emergency is considered as a pathology whose evolution is slow and not necessarily fatal and that must be attended in a maximum of six hours, to avoid major complications and the urgency as that urgent situation that puts in immediate danger the life of the patient or the function of an organ. Likewise this study realized refers to emergencies type 1 or 2 where one or two operative entities are worked and where they have two hours to attend the request (level 1) at maximum or in the case of level 2 up to eight hours; that is to say that they are not considered disasters or great calamities that are classified as level 3, 4 and 5 emergencies; also last two categories receive international cooperation but are less frequent. For example, Bogota's emergencies in 2015 reached just over 280,000 incidents in level 1 and 2 and those in level 3 and 4 only reached a little over 30,000. The above reasons motivate us to work emergencies type 1 and 2.

The rest of the paper is organized as follows: Sect. 2 presents a background and states the problem. Section 3 shows the simulation model with the validation process. Section 4 presents some results over a set of scenarios. Finally, Sect. 5 concludes this work and state some lines as future works.

2 Background and Problem Statement

One of the factors that most affect the performance of this emergency system is economic resources allocation [3, 4], with more resources, it increasing incidents prevention such as traffic accidents or home emergencies are improved, also response time is also improved [4]. In contrast, the budget for the Federal Emergency Management Agency of the USA in 2016 was 13.900 million dollars while for the National Unit for Disaster Risk Management which is a similar agency in Colombia for same year this was only 26.7 million dollars. Likewise, the amount of ambulance or emergency service vehicles is approximately 35% less, in terms of ambulances per inhabitant compared with London [5]. Another aspect to consider is the coverage of this service when population increase; for example, Bogota has presented a greater growth compared to other regions of Colombia, in 2010 Colombia had a projected population of 45.5 million people, for 2015 of 48.2 million and in 2020 of 50.9 million; while in Bogota had an estimated population of 7.4 million in 2010, 7.9 million in 2015 and 8.4 million for 2020 [6]. In accordance with above, it is observed that in the city of Bogotá demand of telephone calls requesting attention to incidents has increased by 82% for period from 2010 to 2015, but in the same period it had a percentage decrease in dispatch of operating center by 5% [2].

2.1 Literature Review

Over last few years, citizens have expressed dissatisfaction with the response times of emergency and in general with emergency services; the WHO indicates that there is one ambulance for every 25 thousand inhabitants; nevertheless, in Bogota there is a service vehicle for every 90,000 people. Another cause of discomfort is failure to dispatch sufficient resources when they are required; approximately these situations represent 30% of the incidents handled by the ERC [5]. It is clear that quantity and quality of resources along with response time are key factors in the survival of people, that is, deaths that are not direct result of primary damages are result of delay in rescue [7, 8]. The time that elapses between moment of the accident and treatment time of the shock is what is known as the Golden Hour [9] and should be as lower as possible [9].

The application of quantitative techniques, especially of the simulation, for health services improvement has had an increasing acceptance, not just to evaluate the performance estimating real population coverage; but also, to use resources adequately, i.e., to reduce population waiting because ambulances are busy [10, 11]; or increasing the speed to attend to emergency requests and provide transportation between home care to hospitals through the simulation of discrete events, [12]. Simulation has also been used to evaluate the efficiency of emergency call centers in France [13], or to calculate sizing of the ambulance fleet and the location of the base station thereof in order to increase the survival probability of patients [14]. In addition, it is used to calculate time to rapid response to medical emergencies as function of fleet size and ambulances location [15].

2.2 Methodology

In addition to the basic methodology of simulation, it was necessary to implement a procedure for knowledge acquisition in order to understand how the ERC serves its users. Firstly, we describe briefly the traditional simulation methodology, which has the following stages: (1) Definition of the system, where the object of the system, the main components and processes are defined, as well as the restrictions, environment and main resources. (2) Definition of the problem, determine one or more performance measures and other indicators that show system results. (3) Collection and processing of information. This stage, in detail, is explaining later due to system complexity. (4) Model formulation which the endogenous and exogenous variables, the functional relationships and the parameters are established, as well as the randomness treatment required, balancing the accuracy and reliability of the model versus its complexity. (5) Translation of the model to a programming language that in this case is used one of specific purpose. (6) Validation to verify that simulation model does represent the real system under study. (7) Experimentation, where different scenarios are established to improve the performance measures, in other words, it consists in analyzing different solution alternatives. (8) Interpretation, stage necessary to study other impacts of different alternatives or scenarios, and after that make the best decision.

Activation phase in ERC's Operational Center uses a protocol; this is an instrument which contains the most frequent types of incidents, their conceptual definition, a questionnaire that must be used with user to find level of incident priority (high, medium or low), The purpose of this protocol is to standardize information request; as pertinent and complete it, as possible. Another aspect to take into account are the resources, these are located in strategic points that are defined in four zones in which the city is divided (North 1, 2 and South 1, 2). But the most important understands how the system runs; Fig. 1 shows the functional model in which it is observed how the regulatory physician is responsible for the medical decisions that are taken to care of patients. He analyzes incidents and their priority assigned before and he acts corresponding its importance level.

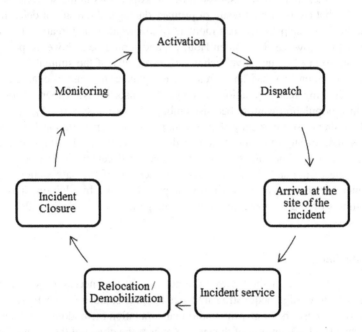

Fig. 1. Model of emergency attention type 1 and 2.

Activation: Starts from the moment the incident arrives at the Operative Center and is initially attended by the Medical Regulation Assistant Technician (MRAT) or the Psychologist depending on incident. He is responsible for receiving, updating and/or validating the incidents information in the system. After that, the MRAT consults with RD the type of incident, priority and medical indications. According to priority, if it is high or medium incidents are sent to the Dispatch phase and if priority is low, incidents are attended and closed in this phase.

Dispatch: Dispatcher first responds to high priority incidents, he register the incident's data, and the analysis of RD to assess the need to allocate resources according to the patient's clinical status and defines the type and amount of resource needed. Dispatcher is in charge of verifying the availability of the mobile units, at the same time registering the resource(s) to the incident and communicating to the mobile the assigned incident, its place and priority.

Arrival at the Site of the Incident: It is the time between ambulances begin displacement and arrive at incident's site reporting the time of arrival to Dispatcher. In this phase is identified if incident is failed (the resource is sent but not used on the site due to a false alarm, address dose not exists or patient was not found, or the patient was carried by other means or incident was canceled) or not failed (the resource was used in the incident's scene or site). In the case of failed incidents, the Dispatcher closes the incident and releases the resources in system.

Incident Service: It is the medical care of incidents on site. When ambulance has a doctor, the decisions are made at the site of incident; these medical determinations must be reported by the Mobile to the Dispatcher. On the other hand, if the ambulance does not have doctor, the Dispatcher presents incident's information to the RD who is in Operating Center, to receive the medical indications and to define if the incident requires transferring to a hospital. Subsequently, the Dispatcher explains to ambulance's personnel the decisions and orientations of the RD. Those incidents that do not require transfer to hospital are closed and changed the state of the resource in the system by the Dispatcher; while incidents which need transferring to hospital, personnel report to Dispatcher the departure time from the incident's site.

Relocation/Demobilization: This stage starts when the Mobile leaves with the patient from the incident site and arriving to the hospital or in general to the Healthcare Institution (HI). It is possible that ambulance is retained or not, depending on whether the patient is immediately received or he should wait.

Incident Closure: At the moment in which the hospital receives the patient, personnel report departure time from the hospital to the Dispatcher, who is responsible for making the closure and changing the state of the resource in the system.

Monitoring: The follow-up of the incidents is carried out in parallel with the development of the previous stages; frequency of each time a monitoring call must be made is defined by the priority of the incident. The other follow-up is done in the dispatching stages until the incident is closed in system; it is a monitoring between ambulance's personnel and the Dispatcher and its frequency depends of priority too.

3   Proposed Model

Table 1 lists the variables that are identified in each of the phases of the methodology and that constitute a main part of the simulation model.

Arrival information of incidents, 201,508 data were analyzed, corresponding to 94.6% of all registers for selected year; while for variables associated with dispatch, 189,483 data were taken corresponding to 92.4% of the available data. It was found incidents considered as failed near to 59.303 corresponding to 37.4% and real incidents about 99.306 which correspond to the remaining 62.6%. Main incidents were: Traffic accidents, common sick, unconscious by respiratory failures, respiratory distress, injured, missing persons, cerebral event convulsions, gastrointestinal symptoms, accidents on the way, chest pains, gynecology-obstetrics, suicide attempts, abuses, mental disorders, sexual violence, natural death, natural death on public road, rescues and burns.

All these incidents were represented by random variables as well as their corresponding priorities (high, medium or low). On the other hand, there were several combined incidents that arise in same case. A variable of special interest was area in which incident happens; it can be north and south, each of them has own resources but

Table 1. Variables used in the model

Activity	Variables
Activation	Demand of the incident
	Time in which you enter the incidents in the system
	Time to validate the incident data
	Priority of incidents
	Medical attention time of the incidents that do not require dispatch
	Type of server that attended the incident that does not require dispatch
Dispatch	Time in which the incident enters Dispatch (by type of incident)
	The time in which recourse to incidents is assigned (Dispatch time)
	The type and amount of resource that is assigned by type of incident
	The medical attention time of the incident in the dispatch area
	Type of server that attended the incident with the user online by type of incident
	Time of beginning and/or dispatch of the displacement of the resource to the site of the incident
	Incidents that are in dispatch and that do not require recourse by type of incidents
Monitoring	Prioritization of incidents to follow up
	Frequency of follow-up calls by type of incident
	Time of follow-up calls by type of incident
	Update the type of incident and its priority
Arrival at the site of the incident	Time of arrival of the resource to the incident site
	Recognition time of the scene of the incident
	Resources that were not used per incident
	Causes of resources not used in the incident
Incident service	Emergencies that installed the stabilization and classification module (MEC)
	Time in which the crew of the mobile reports the data of the patient of the incident to the Dispatch area
	Time in which the Regular Doctor determine how the incident will be treated
	Attendance time of the resource at the incident site
	Incidents that require transfer to an IPS
	Start time of displacement of the resource from the incident site to the IPS
	Incidents that request more resources from incident site resources

(*continued*)

Table 1. (*continued*)

Activity	Variables
	Time in which the resources are requested from the mobiles to the dispatch area (type of incidents)
	Type and amount of resources requested by the mobile phones that are on the site (type of incident)
	Type and amount of resource that is assigned in the dispatch area against the requirement of mobile
	Time when requested resources arrive from the motives of the incident
Relocation/demobilization and incident closure	Time of arrival of the resource to the hospital unit per incident
	Number of follow-up calls in the transfer of the patient to the hospital unit by type of incident
	Time of recourse in the hospital unit per incident
	Exit time of the hospital unit resource per incident
	Time of arrival of the resource to the base
	Number of follow-up calls for the mobile phone that is withheld in the hospital unit by type of incident
	Time of demobilization of resources in the area of impact in emergencies
	Time of closure of incidents
	Type of closure of the incident

if it is required can share them between areas. The historical values taken as measures of performance (in minutes) are: Time of dispatch of resource (TDR), time of arrival at place of the incident (TAS), time of attention at the place of the incident (TAI), time of arrival at the hospital (TAH), and time of retention of the resource in the hospital (TRH), these data are listed in Table 2.

Table 2. Real system performance measurement

Performance measure	TDR	TAS	TAI	TAH	TRH
Real data	16830	13332	8021	6469	6741
Out of control points	2354	312	355	378	830
Average	5.97	13.43	31.47	18.62	81.62
Standard deviation	6.46	9.09	16.16	11.39	91.11

Likewise, these incidents have resources associated to attend them; these include mobile units belonging with each geographical area. The main resources are: Basic ambulances team (BAT), medical ambulance team (MAT), psychiatric ambulance (PSIQ), rapid response vehicle (motorcycles) and command team (ECOM). There are also human resources such as dispatchers, medical regulation technician auxiliaries

(MRTA), psychologists and regulatory doctors (RD), each one with specific functions within the process of attention of incidents. The analyzed system had similar resources both northern and southern areas as follows: 20 BAT, 7 MAT, 1 PSIQ, 1 ECOM, 3 MARTA and 1 RD.

Finally, there are some aspects that affected data homogeneity, then it was necessary grouping according their patterns to guarantee different probability density functions, increasing complexity of modeling. The most important factors were: Month, day and time of occurrence of the incident, the availability of non-human resources, the experience of officials, variables associated with traffic of the city, location of the incident place, location of the HI, availability of beds, among others. It is important to mention that secondary transfers and the activities of the follow-up phase of the Operating Center were not contemplated in the simulation model due to complexity and little information available. The model was developed in a specific simulation language; the preliminary version was made in ProModel® 4.2 and was updated to the ProModel® version 7.0. Since the input analysis showed that the north and south zones are statistically identical, their modeling was developed separately.

3.1   Validation

The validation of the results of the simulation model is done by comparing real and simulated mean and deviation, analysis is made for each of the output variables mentioned before: TDR, TAS, TAI, TAH, and HRT. The simulation model was executed with the following run parameters: Run length of 720 h, number of replicas equal to 38 and warm-up time of 50 h, in Fig. 2 and in Table 3. The results of this validation process according with a confidence level of 95% let to accept the simulation model.

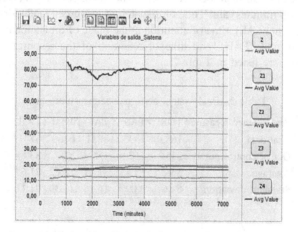

Fig. 2. Results of the model run.

Table 3. Results of the validation process.

Performance measure	TDR	TAS	TAI	TAH	TRH
Real average	5.97	13.43	31.47	18.62	81.62
Simulated average	6.98	12.71	25.95	17.8	79.5
Real standard deviation	6.46	9.09	16.16	11.39	91.11
Simulated standard deviation	6.557	7.535	10.275	9.946	47.729

4 Experimentation

Given that simulation model is statistically accepted, main results are as follow: Of the total incidents that the operational center receives, 96% corresponds to urgencies, being the traffic accident (30.85%), unconscious and/or respiratory arrest (13.06%) and respiratory difficulty (11.13%), the main three types of incident. On the other hand the remaining 4% belongs to emergency incidents where the most frequent are the traffic accident (63.64%), the structural fire (14.32%) and intoxication (6.82%). Another aspect is the failing incidents with a value of 38%, in which they represent unfavorable situations for the attention system; false alarms, not found patient, canceled, among others, are main causes. The remaining 62% of the incidents are true; of which, 17% corresponds to valuation without transfer at hospital and the remaining 83% belongs to valuation with primary transfer due to the severity of the patient. The utilization percentages of resources are as follow: TARM with 98% and RD with 90% are currently having a fairly high utilization, which may be symptoms of possible bottlenecks in the system.

4.1 Scenarios

For the design of scenarios, we consider just northern zone. The main system conditions were studied such as: Inputs, average times in the system and waiting, and a variable that indicates the blockage, in other words the number of incidents that are not attended to immediately, all information in Table 4. The most important resources are also analyzed (see Table 5), and finally, the different performance measures are showed for each scenario in Table 6. The scenarios were simulated with 38 replicas and a warm time of 50 h and a run time of 720 h. The proposed scenarios were as follows:

- Scenario 0: Actual situations
- Scenario 1: Increase a MRTA in each of the zones
- Scenario 2: Increase a MRTA and an one RD in each of the zones
- Scenario 3: Increase one MRTA and two RD in each zone
- Scenario 4: Increase two MRTA and one RD in each zone
- Scenario 5: Increase two MRTA and two RD in each zone.

4.2 Results

As shown in Table 4, as the MRTA and RD resources are increased, the number of incidents in the system and the blocking times are decreased. Both variables indicate

Table 4. Results of service system indicators for different scenarios

Scenario	Statistical	Total entries	Current qty in system	Avg. time in system (min)	Avg. time waiting (min)	Avg. time in operation (min)	Avg. time blocked (min)
0	Average	7944.78	708.83	976.72	2.99	66.94	906.79
	Std. dev.	81.25	95.15	135.69	0.04	1.07	135.74
1	Average	7924.72	486.11	727.61	3.17	67.79	656.65
	Std. dev.	96.84	111.60	134.81	0.04	0.97	135.16
2	Average	7882.83	40.94	106.26	5.28	70.23	30.75
	Std. dev.	83.97	10.96	7.70	0.17	1.13	7.49
3	Average	7901.50	33.61	98.41	6.40	70.02	22.00
	Std. dev.	95.41	8.29	5.60	0.22	0.86	5.24
4	Average	7887.11	42.22	103.40	5.48	70.01	27.91
	Std. dev.	65.32	13.02	11.59	0.10	0.65	11.35
5	Average	7899.56	36.39	100.63	6.81	70.13	23.70
	Std. dev.	95.69	13.64	7.47	0.28	0.85	6.73

Table 5. Percentage of use of the main resources in each scenario

Scenario	Statistical	BAT	MAT	PSIQ	ECOM	MARTA	RD
0	Average	45.76	88.54	39.8	29.74	99.97	93.84
	Std. dev.	1.2	0.34	1.71	1.74	0.14	0.29
1	Average	52.36	88.90	60.82	69.57	99.97	99.56
	Std. dev.	1.16	0.24	2.17	2.43	0.12	0.10
2	Average	52.37	88.39	38.61	31.61	86.88	79.99
	Std. dev.	1.40	0.29	1.75	2.57	1.98	2.15
3	Average	53.35	87.87	38.26	31.56	83.07	67.70
	Std. dev.	1.18	0.28	2.23	1.83	2.62	3.02
4	Average	52.13	88.12	38.63	32.19	80.85	82.56
	Std. dev.	0.95	0.26	2.66	1.90	2.71	2.22
5	Average	52.62	87.76	38.20	32.19	76.14	72.43
	Std. dev.	1.67	0.28	2.54	1.96	3.55	3.84

low compliance with adequate service levels. Clearly, in real situation, calls do not accumulate and therefore are lost, for that it is necessary an immediate attention and greater agility of system with more operators are required. It is important to note that scenario 4 in theory is good, where these indicators are improved, as well as the average waiting times of the incidents with and low cost. However, scenario 5 is even better because there is a better possibility of growth of service demands.

Table 5 shows utilization of resources MRTA and RD. In the current scenario as in the first three, a level of utilization in these resources of more than 90%, this is risky, because the model does not contemplate possible capacity losses. The best scenario in

Table 6. Performance measures for each scenario

Scenario	Statistical	TDR	TAS	TAI	TAH	TRH
0	Average	7.26	12.79	25.98	17.88	80.48
	Std. dev.	0.1	0.16	0.27	0.25	1.03
1	Average	7.33	12.79	26.10	17.89	80.31
	Std. dev.	0.01	0.14	0.17	0.23	1.03
2	Average	7.58	12.82	25.95	17.84	80.02
	Std. dev.	0.13	0.11	0.21	0.16	1.03
3	Average	7.64	12.78	25.99	17.86	79.34
	Std. dev.	0.13	0.10	0.25	0.24	0.97
4	Average	7.54	12.84	25.87	17.88	79.76
	Std. dev.	0.10	0.11	0.18	0.24	0.87
5	Average	7.67	12.81	26.04	17.86	79.99
	Std. dev.	0.13	0.11	0.16	0.22	1.23

this case would be 5 with the best use of these two resources. Also in the same Table is evidenced that the potential neck of the bottle are the ambulances with medical service (MAT), since in some scenarios they reach levels higher than 80%. The basic ambulances have idle capacity, but it is worth mentioning that in simulation model, preventive and corrective maintenance programs of these vehicles were not contemplated. Since these resources are now available, they are sufficient and should be adjustment to balance the service.

Table 6 shows how these performance measures are regulated by the system and is due to the elimination of calls that wait and therefore are not improved by the increase of resources since the system is stable itself. If we want to improve the system, we have to make structural changes.

5 Conclusions

The present research offers the design of a simulation model that represents the operation of the subsystems that works in the attention to the users. The model allows to evaluate the system performance and helps for the decision-making process. The results show a high number of calls waiting as well as a large time in the system. In real process, this indicates that many calls are failed and the emergency's service has not made. The critical variable of the system is the retention time of resource in hospital, with an average of 80.48 min; In terms of ambulance travel times, it is determined that arrival time at hospital is greater, than arrival time at the incident place, the first one is 17.88 and the second one is on average of 12.79 min. It is very difficult to reduce these displacement times, because both depend of incidents' places and hospital location. About the sending time has increased respect to previous years going from 7.26 to 25.98 min on average.

The arrivals or unsatisfied demand were identified in the system, which has already been confirmed and analyzed by previous investigations; it was characterized by waiting times of resources and unoccupied locations of system. These were improved both in scenarios 4 and 5 in which waiting time of the total calls of the system was reduced by about 90%.

6 Future Works

It is identified that it is necessary to increase the reception capacity of incidents in the activation phase, which is equivalent to increasing in two TARMs for each of the zones. It is also identified that RD is a limited resource that generates damming and waiting for incidents. Therefore, it is proposed to increase one RD in each of the zones, with them it can be attended efficiently even with an increase of 10% of the incidents, without affecting the waiting times of the incident within the system. With bigger increments it is necessary to increase to two RD. The other resources, although seem sufficient, are not; if the demand for services increases, ambulances with medical services should be expanded, since they are at the limit of their level of occupation.

Acknowledgements. Authors would like to thank the Emergency Department of the city of Bogotá, with the participation of all those officials who collaborated with the development of the research, information and all the support received by the experts of the Operative Center.

References

1. Londres, G.S.: Reseñas críticas. Rev. Int. Del Trab. **122**(1) (2003)
2. CRUE. Boletín de Estadísticas dela CRUE (2016). http://www.saludcapital.gov.co/DPYS/Paginas/BoletinEstadistico.aspx?RootFolder=%2FDPYS%2FCodificacin%2FBolet%C3%ADn%20Estad%C3%ADstico%202015%2FCRUE&FolderCTID=0x01200072E42472F12B304C9832E81B706B5458&View={5ABBE625-B30A-46FE-84A7-C406EE8398DE}
3. Haddow, G., Bullock, J., Coppola, D.P.: Introduction to Emergency Management. Butterworth-Heinemann, Oxford (2017)
4. Saghafian, S., Austin, G., Traub, S.J.: Operations research/management contributions to emergency department patient flow optimization: review and research prospects. IIE Trans. Healthc. Syst. Eng. **5**(2), 101–123 (2015)
5. Huertas, J.A., Barrera, O.D., Velasco, N.M. Amaya C.A. (2008). Evaluación del despacho de ambulancias del Centro Regulador de Urgencias y Emergencias de Bogotá (C.R.U.E.). http://dspace.uniandes.edu.co/xmlui/bitstream/handle/1992/1122/H%202008%2024.pdf?sequence=1
6. Departamento Administrativo Nacional de Estadística DANE. Estudios demográficos del DANE revelan que la población colombiana entre el 2005 y 2010 crecerá a una tasa media anual de 1.18%, lo que significa que al terminar el quinquenio Colombia tendrá una población de 45.508.205 (2005). https://www.dane.gov.co/files/BoletinProyecciones.pdf
7. Fiedrich, F., Gehbauer, F., Rickers, U.: Optimized resource allocation for emergency response after earthquake disasters. Saf. Sci. **35**(3), 41–57 (2000)
8. Chou, J.S., Tsai, C.F., Chen, Z.Y., Sun, M.H.: Biological-based genetic algorithms for optimized disaster response resource allocation. Comput. Ind. Eng. **74**, 52–67 (2014)
9. Rogers, F.B., Rittenhouse, K.J., Gross, B.W.: The golden hour in trauma: dogma or medical folklore? Injury **46**(4), 525–527 (2015)

10. Ünlüyurt, T., Tunçer, Y.: Estimating the performance of emergency medical service location models via discrete event simulation. Comput. Ind. Eng. **102**, 467–475 (2016)
11. Pinto, L.R., Silva, P.M.S., Young, T.P.: A generic method to develop simulation models for ambulance systems. Simul. Model. Pract. Theory **51**, 170–183 (2015)
12. Kergosien, Y., Bélanger, V., Soriano, P., Gendreau, M., Ruiz, A.: A generic and flexible simulation-based analysis tool for EMS management. Int. J. Prod. Res. **53**(24), 7299–7316 (2015)
13. Lamine, E., Fontanili, F., Di Mascolo, M., Pingaud, H.: Improving the management of an emergency call service by combining process mining and discrete event simulation approaches. In: Camarinha-Matos, L.M., Bénaben, F., Picard, W. (eds.) PRO-VE 2015. IAICT, vol. 463, pp. 535–546. Springer, Cham (2015). https://doi.org/10.1007/978-3-319-24141-8_50
14. McCormack, R., Coates, G.: A simulation model to enable the optimization of ambulance fleet allocation and base station location for increased patient survival. Eur. J. Oper. Res. **247**(1), 294–309 (2015)
15. Zaffar, M.A., Rajagopalan, H.K., Saydam, C., Mayorga, M., Sharer, E.: Coverage, survivability or response time: a comparative study of performance statistics used in ambulance location models via simulation–optimization. Operations Res. Health Care **11**, 1–12 (2016)

Hybrid Simulation and GA for a Flexible Flow Shop Problem with Variable Processors and Re-entrant Flow

German Mendez-Giraldo[1]($\boxtimes$), Lindsay Alvarez-Pomar[1]($\boxtimes$),
and Carlos Franco[2]

[1] Universidad Distrital Francisco José de Caldas, Bogotá, Colombia
{gmendez,lalvarez}@udistrital.edu.co
[2] Universidad del Rosario, Bogotá, Colombia
carlosa.franco@urosario.edu.co

Abstract. The problem of FFSP (Flexible Flow Shop Problem) has been sufficiently investigated due to its importance for production programming and control, although many of the solution methods have been based on GA (Genetic Algorithm) and simulation, these techniques have been used in deterministic environments and under specific conditions of the problem, that is, complying with restrictions given in the Graham notation. In this paper we describe an application of these techniques to solve a very particular case where manual work stations and equipment with different degrees of efficiency, technological restrictions, recirculation process are used. The nesting of the GA is used within a simulation process. It is showed that the method proposed in adjustment and efficiency is better compared with other heuristics, in addition to the benefits of using different techniques in series to solve problems of real manufacturing environments.

Keywords: Flexible workshop programming · Genetic algorithm
Simulation · Parallel machines · Process re-entry

1 Introduction

The problem of flexible flow programming better known as FFSP (Flexible Flow Shop Problem) is a particular problem which derives from a more general problem called workshop programming FSP (Flow Shop Scheduling) in which an operation is allowed to be performed by a machine chosen from a finite subset of machines. This results in two chained problems. The first is the assigning of each operation to a machine, and the second problem is to define the sequence; that is, the order of operations in the machines. FFSP provides a more realistic approach, but the combination of the assignment problem and its subsequent sequencing against what happens in the classic FSP makes it a hard NP-problem [1]. In particular, it is assumed that the FFSP work with serial stages and a number of identical machines that are located in parallel in each stage, however this model is not reflecting the real conditions of the system since it works with a manual operation in where the operators work with different speeds, giving rise to a case where there are machine problems in parallel with different

© Springer Nature Switzerland AG 2018
J. C. Figueroa-García et al. (Eds.): WEA 2018, CCIS 915, pp. 246–256, 2018.
https://doi.org/10.1007/978-3-030-00350-0_21

processing speeds, they have a speed v_i and the processing time p_{ij} that reflects the time it takes to process a job j in machine i. Subsequently in the next stage there is a baking process where there are also different efficiencies.

In the third stage, recourse should be done in order to use again the operators who performed the tasks in the first station, becoming a model of recirculation that obeys to problems of the flexible shop type in which a job visits a work center more than once. The objective function proposed in this model is the Makespan (C_{max}) and it is defined as the completion time of the last job that leaves the system. Given the complexity of the system it is observed that it is neither a pure FFSP nor a system of machines in parallel, it also presents a recirculation process. It is concluded that the best representation technique a modified FFSP.

2 Background and Problem Statement

2.1 Literature Review

In the case of the FFSP there are multiple approaches to address its solution, although not as extensive as in the case of the problems of the Job-Shop type that are more complex in nature than the first ones, among which stand out the colony of ants [2], genetic algorithms [3, 4] and simulation among others [5]. However, the techniques are varied and multiple, then a small sample that validates the afore mentioned is related. Authors such as Hong and Wang, modify the Palmer algorithm used in FFSP with two work centers, incorporating for this the fuzzy logic rules where the process times vary from center to center and that is based on the Longest process time (LPT), with these modifications, the assignment based on Fuzzy Rules is improved and then sequencing with Palme's rules, in this way they ensure that the problem is approached in a better way to reality [6]. There are also reviewed heuristic techniques based on the algorithms of Sriskandarajah & Sethi used for two work centers, modifying them using the Gupta algorithm to extend their use to more work centers. The authors seek to improve the efficiency of this algorithm in large numbers of works; however its largest instance is for 8 tasks [7].

Many other works use genetic algorithms (GA) in a simple or complex way to solve the problems of the FFSP as the problem of sequencing based on LPT rules for the selection of the machines, then compare their efficiency with the Workload Approximation (WLA) heuristic which reuses efficient small scales of work [8]. A little more complete is the comparison of different heuristic dispatch techniques such as FIFO, SPT, LPT, SDD by using the programming procedure of the bottleneck SBP (Shifting-Bottleneck-Procedure), for this a GA is used and the results show that the techniques SPT and SDD are substantially better than FIFO and LPT individually evacuated, but when evaluating with the GA the LPT and the SPT generate better (minimum) values for the Makespan and the maximum delay [9]. A proprietary and slave genetic algorithm (Master-slave genetic algorithm) technique is proposed to solve FFJS problems with flexible resources in which resource selection and sequencing are worked simultaneously to avoid a double GA. Its ability function is to minimize the maximum early and late deliveries, being superior to manually worked heuristics [10]. As well as this modification to GA is the work in which the hybridization of GA techniques with simulated annealing using variable and adaptive genetic operators, where the probabilities of cross-over and of mutation change compared to the results obtained between two successive populations. This method when compared to conventional GAs gives a better performance [11].

Most of these works are based on optimization techniques in static environments, without considering the conditions of uncertainty and complexity of production plants. Some of the conditions are not always considered as breakdowns of the machines, stochastic processing times, and change in delivery dates, difficulties with materials among many others. All of these conditions increasing the gap between the theoretical models and those that actually occur in real operations given by the uncertainty. Although these techniques have demonstrated their theoretical value, they are fare from reality where complexity increases in both the number of tasks and machines and stochastic aspects are introduced, which generates variability. The results are not efficient, that is why a nested model of two tools is proposed. Both have demonstrated their value for FJSSP (Flexible Job Shop Scheduling Problem), first the simulation as a representation technique and second, the genetic algorithms for finding solutions.

2.2   Proposed Model

The FFSP was raised in the 1990s [12] as a modification of the traditional problems of the Flow Shop [1], this problem FJSSP can be formulated as follows: Let the set W of n tasks $W = \{W_1, W_2, \cdots W_n\}$, which can be executed by a set of m identical serial machines $M = \{M_1, M_2, \cdots M_m\}$. Each task $W_i = (1 \leq i \leq n)$ consists of a sequence of n_i operations; $O_{ij} = (j = 1, 2, \ldots, n_i)$. Each route has to be executed in order to complete each task. The execution of operation j of task W_i requires a resource from a set of available machines. The assignment of the operation O_{ij} to machine $M_q \in M (1 \leq q \leq Q)$ implies the occupation of the latter during the process time denoted by p_{ijq}. The problem consists in determining a sequence of assignment of the operations to all the machines with the objective of minimizing the Makespan denoted by C_{max}, which is subject to a set of constraints: (i) the precedence of the operations in each task must be respected (ii) once the machine starts processing an operation it cannot be interrupted and each machine can process at maximum one operation at a time; (iii) all machines are available at time zero. Solving the FJSSP is traduce into assigning a machine for each operation and deciding the sequence or order of operations on each machine. This is that each operation is assigned to a certain machine; the problem of flexible workshop programming could be represented in this case as a workshop programming problem (JSP).

2.3   Modification of the Model

For real manufacturing environments are assumed changes in each period t, where $t = (1, 2, \ldots T)$ and T represents the programming period. In this case for each t there is a set W of task of different types. The tasks can be assimilated as production orders of product type k where $k = (1, 2, \ldots, K)$. This set W has a number of jobs n that change randomly with each period t, likewise the type of products k also varies in each period

t. The number of jobs and the type of products are random variables with f.d.p. known and independent. In the particular case, all W jobs require processing of the same sequence of operations by three stations each with different resources (operators and/or machines) denoted by M_z where $z = (1, 2, 3)$ is the number of resources that varies from process to process, but remains constant for the complete simulation process. Each resource has a different efficiency for each stage when executing the different type of product. Then we have an efficiency vector Γ denoted by $\Gamma = \{\Gamma_{M_z}\}$ that becomes an array of random variables with known and independent probability density functions.

This efficiency affects the execution of the processing times that are now denoted by a random variable p_{ijkM_z} which represents the processing time of operation i for job j of product type k and is executed in the resource M_z. The problem also involves determining the allocation of resources and defining the operational sequence for each random instance. The objective is to minimize the makespan C_{max}, which is subject to a set of restrictions: (i) the precedence of the operations in each task must be respected being the same; (ii) once a unit of a stage begins to process an operation, it cannot be interrupted, and each unit can process one operation at a time; (iii) all resources are available at time zero. There is an operational sequence composed of three processes, the first and the third are manual and they should use the same resources and the second is a baking process that has different technologies and therefore different processing times. It is necessary to have a resources assignment for the type of operation to be executed, in other words a set $M = \{W_i, E_k, W_l'\}$ where W_i represents the workers of the stage i that execute the operations O_{ij} while E_i refers to the set of resources that they process in the stage k executing the operations O_{kj} and finally W_l' are the workers of the station l executing the operations O_{lj}. Both equipment and operators have different efficiency, then an efficiency vector Γ denoted by $\Gamma = \left\{\Gamma_{W_i}, \Gamma_{E_k}, \Gamma_{W_l'}\right\}$. On the other hand, the process time denoted by p_{ijk} now also becomes a random variable.

3 Proposed Model

This model conceptually can be seen as the integration of two different and complementary techniques, simulation and the GA, see Fig. 1. When there is a scheduling problem, different modules or stages must be considered for their solution [13, 14], these are: first the selection of the order of processing and second, the selection of productive means to use. The novelty of the research consists in the development of a module that performs the simulation in which the measure of aptitude is the Makespan and after that, it feeds the AG. Additionally, a stage for the generation of representative problems is proposed, which is executed in the simulation module and allows understanding the phenomena that occur in these flexible job shop environments with parallel processors and recirculation processes.

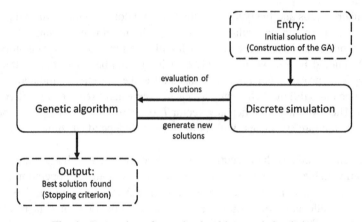

Fig. 1. Integration of genetic algorithms and simulation

When using GA in a problem, is very important to define the genetic structure of individuals, in particular it is recognized that flexible job shop scheduling problem is characterized by requiring information of the sequence to be scheduled, and selection of the technologies (manpower and machines) to be used. It is also important to decide the aptitude measure that is intended to be evaluated in order to select the best production program. See Fig. 2.

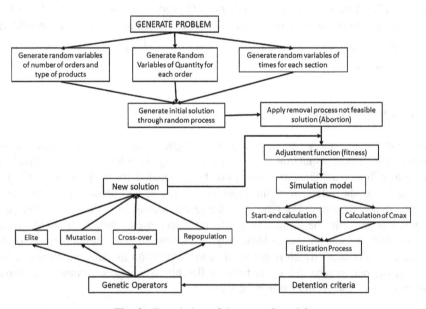

Fig. 2. Description of the general model

The parameters used in the development of the GA are: (1) Size of the population in this case of 100 individuals; (2) number of chromosomes that make up each individual, in our case equal to three chromosomes. First represents the order of processing, the second is used to define the operator resource used and the third chromosome is used to define the oven resource; (3) number of populations to be generated, in this problem it is a parameter that is modified according to convergence criteria; and (4) Genetic operators, these are: elitization where is taken the 20% of the best solutions, cross-over of 20% of the population to obtain another 20% of individuals and repopulation of 40% in order to obtain new solutions.

3.1   Description of the System

Within the modeling process it is required to simplify the production system that has three major tasks, the first is the design of the piece, which requires several operations as defined in the upper part of Fig. 3, the second is the Baking process in which the foundry takes place. The third process is polishing, but this requires to be done by the same operator who developed the design process, this is the reason to consider a re-entrance process system. As it can be deduced, in this case all the products go through the same sequence of operations that makes it of the job shop type, but with the particularity that both the workers as well as the ovens have different efficiencies for each type of product, see Table 1. On the other hand, it is a manufacturing system under request (make to order), each patient defines the design of the piece for this reason, production system cannot have inventories; in addition, because they are sometimes necessary for emergency surgeries therefore, products require the least possible delay. These characteristics are the reason why the production plan needs to be carried out in the shortest time possible; therefore, the main measure of performance to be used in the AG is the Makespan. Finally, ovens used as well as the operators involved in the process have different degrees of efficiency which makes it a flexible job shop problem.

Table 1. Sample values of the process times given in minutes

Product type	Modeling		Baked		Polished	
	Mean	Deviation	Mean	Deviation	Mean	Deviation
I	180	11.5	75	8.7	70	5.8
II	205	8.7	105	8.7	75	5.8
III	220	11.5	135	8.7	80	5.8
IV	225	8.7	165	8.7	70	5.8

The biweekly demand does not present trends or seasonal cycles and when the orders are analyzed, understanding these as the different orders to be manufactured from the same specific product reference, it was found that it is a random variable with parameters of average and deviation of orders biweekly equal to 48.6 and deviation of 2.88 orders. The participation by type on average corresponds to 35%, 30%, 25% and

10% for each type I to IV. On the other hand, Table 2 shows the different operators' efficiency when processing different types of products. For the baking process the ovens' time correspond to the technical conditions of this equipment.

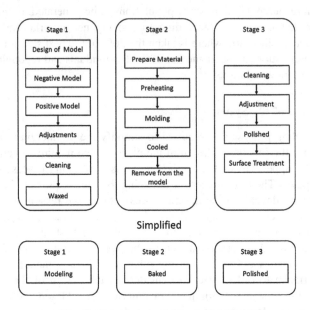

Fig. 3. Description of the general model

Table 2. Percentages of efficiency for different resources

Resource	Efficiency of the resource by type of product family in %			
	Type I	Type II	Type III	Type IV
Operator 1	86	106	114	85
Operator 2	96	118	101	114
Operator 3	102	89	98	90
Operator 4	98	82	83	80
Operator 5	91	87	100	92
Operator 6	90	93	112	113
Oven 1	96	90	103	106
Oven 2	84	102	91	113
Oven 3	109	92	102	91

3.2 Validation and Analysis of Results

For validation analysis, number of orders per fortnight was analyzed as well as the composition of the different types of product. These analyses are presented in Table 3.

It is concluded that both the number of orders and the simulated types each year are valid. Likewise, the data of a quarter was taken to compare the times in the different processes for each of different kind of products, these analyses are summarized and presented in Table 4.

Table 3. Validation test of the demand variable

		Average	Desv.	P(T ≤ t)	C. V.	Hypothesis
Orders processed	Real	48.95	3.071	0.11	2.07	Accept
	Simulated	50	0			
Product type I	Real	23.04	2.578	0.70	2.02	Accept
	Simulated	22.79	1.793			
Product type II	Real	12.16	1.372	0.48	2.01	Accept
	Simulated	12.45	1.444			
Product type III	Real	9.62	0.969	0.00	2.01	Accept
	Simulated	10.83	0.916			
Product type IV	Real	4.12	0.679	0.33	2.01	Accept
	Simulated	3.91	0.775			

Table 4. Mean difference test of the times by process and product

Product	Process	Real	Simulated	P(Z ≤ z)	C. V.	Hypothesis
Type I	Modeling	180.4	179.16	0.47	1.96	Accept
Type II		203.8	204.55	0.68	1.96	Accept
Type III		217.5	220.7	0.2	1.96	Accept
Type IV		226.5	225.64	0.8	1.96	Accept
Type I	Baked	74.8	74.37	0.7	1.96	Accept
Type II		104.5	104.55	0.99	1.96	Accept
Type III		134.8	135.52	0.48	1.96	Accept
Type IV		163	165.64	0.34	1.96	Accept
Type I	Polished	70.4	69.58	0.29	1.96	Accept
Type II		74.9	74.7	0.83	1.96	Accept
Type III		80.2	80.35	0.89	1.96	Accept
Type IV		68.8	70.42	0.38	1.96	Accept

Once data validation is used in the simulation and GA modules, the runs were carried out, to compare the results of FCFS and SPT heuristic rules with output of nested simulation and GA model. The measure of performance used was Makespan and 24 fortnights were run with 50 orders each one. The acceptance values are presented in Table 5 and in Fig. 4.

On average, results of FCFS Rule are almost the same as the SPT, in this instance of 30 runs the value for the first rule is 6727.4 min versus 6752.2 min of the SPT rule;

in any case the GA is better with an average of 4745.3 min that represents an average saving of 29.5%.

Table 5. Values of the FIFO-SPT Rules versus AG

Run	FCFS	SPT	GA	Run	FCFS	SPT	GA
1	6644.2	6630.1	4913.5	16	6113.3	6796.1	4670.4
2	6644.2	6630.1	4155.0	17	6434.3	6813.7	4614.1
3	8156.5	5048.6	4781.9	18	7641.9	5484.7	4506.5
4	5760.8	7202.0	4613.0	19	6144.8	5918.1	4839.1
5	7742.2	7408.1	4893.3	20	6723.0	7109.2	4758.8
6	6665.1	7138.8	4657.7	21	6524.2	6249.4	4620.9
7	7160.1	6227.4	4496.9	22	6884.1	6066.5	4869.0
8	6933.7	6218.5	4809.2	23	6383.1	7299.9	4796.2
9	6780.6	7551.0	4632.7	24	6788.6	7566.1	4732.5
10	7183.0	8037.2	4901.1	25	5787.0	6076.4	4878.6
11	5535.7	6800.0	4819.1	26	7222.0	7537.3	4977.0
12	7216.4	7238.0	4552.7	27	6064.9	6891.0	4940.8
13	7752.5	7588.8	5058.0	28	6497.2	7176.5	5100.4
14	6924.2	6452.9	4763.0	29	5959.5	6109.8	4715.3
15	7315.1	6243.1	4445.0	30	6240.7	7056.6	4846.6

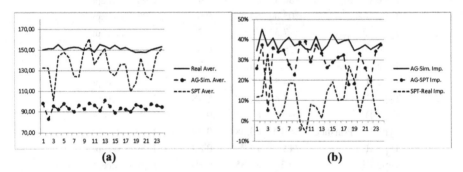

Fig. 4. (a) Comparison of FCFS and SPT heuristics versus simulation, (b) improvement percentage

4   Conclusions

As mentioned, there is a set of difficulties in the conventional process of scheduling such as generation of sequences not always adequate due to the variability of the system and because it is a non-polynomial problem, which causes increasing of computational execution. The GA has showed its value for production scheduling, but the novelty is the use of simulation module to track the programming, since it allows evaluating the performance of system by entry parameters generation for system and its subsequent execution of productive schedule. The quality of output will depend both input analysis as the validation of simulation's and GA's modules.

The fact of improving the solution by crossing three individuals through the exchange of complete chromosomes is highlighted, in this particular case, this crossing guarantees better results in measures of fitness function and execution time, allowing with less population to achieve good sequences of operation. This can be a new field of research in order to test in other instances and cases within the production scheduling.

It is highlighted the differences on performance, when using the combined heuristic SPT-FCFS rules, and use of GA. Since there is a significant improvement of the combined heuristic versus the actual performance of the system, but this is less than when GA is used. This is explained because the heuristic only analyzes the jobs' arrivals and shorter processing times of them, while the GA, in addition to analyzing these factors, takes efficiencies both operator and oven in order to be chosen.

The results of nested simulation and GA in addition to finding a better sequence of jobs, also allow manufacturing decision maker to level the use of operators and ovens, which avoids recharging the work to those workers of better performance, in contrast with real system. Likewise, the use of the ovens is improved, which allows for additional activities, and to be carried out maintenance in a better way.

References

1. Pinedo, M.L.: Scheduling: Theory, Algorithms, and Systems. Springer, Heidelberg (2016)
2. Sioud, A., Gagné, C., Gravel, M.: An ant colony optimization for solving a hybrid flexible flowshop. In: Proceedings of the Companion Publication of the 2014 Annual Conference on Genetic and Evolutionary Computation, pp. 17–18. ACM, July 2014
3. Sukkerd, W., Wuttipornpun, T.: Hybrid genetic algorithm and tabu search for finite capacity material requirement planning system in flexible flow shop with assembly operations. Comput. Ind. Eng. **97**, 157–169 (2016)
4. Zandieh, M., Hashemi, A.R.: Group scheduling in hybrid flexible flowshop with sequence-dependent setup times and random breakdowns via integrating genetic algorithm and simulation. Int. J. Ind. Syst. Eng. **21**(3), 377–394 (2015)
5. Xu, Y., Tan, W.: The modeling and simulation of flow shop scheduling problem based on adaptive genetic algorithm. RISTI (Revista Iberica de Sistemas e Tecnologias de Informacao) (17A), 25–41 (2016)
6. Hong, T., Wang, T.: A heuristic Palmer-based fuzzy flexible flow-shop scheduling algorithm. In: Fuzzy Systems Conference Proceedings 1999, vol. 3, pp. 1493–1497 (1999)
7. Hong, T., Wang, C., Wang, S.: A heuristic Gupta-based flexible flow-shop scheduling algorithm. In: 2000 IEEE International Conference on Systems, Man, and Cybernetics, vol. 1, pp. 319–322 (2000)
8. Wang, L., Dawei, L.: A scheduling algorithm for flexible flow shop problem. In: Proceedings of the 4th World Congress on Intelligent Control and Automation 2002, vol. 4, pp. 3106–3108 (2002)
9. Vásquez, J.A., Salhi, A.: Performance of single stage representation genetic algorithms in scheduling flexible flow shops. In: Proceedings of the 2005 IEEE Congress on Evolutionary Computation 2005, vol. 2, pp. 1364–1371 (2005)

10. Fenghe, J., Yaping, F.: Master-slave genetic algorithm for flow shop scheduling with resource flexibility. In: 2010 IEEE International Conference on Advanced Management Science (ICAMS), vol. 1, pp. 341–346 (2010)
11. Gao, H., Feng, B., Zhu, L.: An improved genetic algorithm for flow shop sequencing. In: International Conference on Neural Networks and Brain 2005, vol. 1, pp. 521–524 (2005)
12. Brucker, P., Schile, R.: Job-shop scheduling with multi-purpose machines. Computing **45**, 369–375 (1990)
13. de Freitas Rodrigues, R., Dourado, M.C., Szwarcfiter, J.L.: Scheduling problem with multi-purpose parallel machines. Discret. Appl. Math. **164**, 313–319 (2014)
14. Lowndes, V., Berry, S.: Appendix C: what to simulate to evaluate production planning and control methods in small manufacturing firm's. In: Berry, S., Lowndes, V., Trovati, M. (eds.) Guide to Computational Modelling for Decision Processes. SFMA, pp. 377–379. Springer, Cham (2017). https://doi.org/10.1007/978-3-319-55417-4_18

Evaluating the Supply Chain Design of Fresh Food on Food Security and Logistics

Javier Orjuela-Castro[1,2(✉)] and Wilson Adarme-Jaimes[2]

[1] Faculty of Engineering, Universidad Distrital Francisco José de Caldas,
Bogotá, Colombia
jaorjuelac@unal.edu.co
[2] Faculty of Engineering, Universidad Nacional de Colombia, Bogotá, Colombia
wadarmej@unal.edu.co

Abstract. The fresh fruit and vegetables sector is competitive and dynamic, with uncertainties related to supply and quality. These uncertainties generate challenges in food safety and food security issues for developing countries. Researchers have studied the supply chains (SCs) of perishable products from different perspectives of modeling. However, there are few studies that contemplate the dynamics and Supply Chain Design (SCD). This paper present a model based on system dynamics for SCs of fresh foods. The model evaluates different SCD and their impact on food security and logistics. Unlike the studies found in the literature, the model includes the loss derived from the life cycle of the food and from logistic operations. From the application of the model to three SCs of fresh fruits in Colombia, it was found that a combination of the design structures is required to achieve performance measures for food security and performance of logistics.

Keywords: Supply chain design · Fresh food · Food security
Logistics

1 Introduction

The Supply Chains of Food (SCF) consist of networks covering production, processing, distribution and even elimination [1]. They are very different from other SCs [2], because in the SCF there is a continuous change from the time it leaves the cultivator until the food reaches the consumer; there is variation of product quality that changes with time, even under optimum distribution conditions [3, 4]. The perishable nature of food generates losses; an estimated one-third of world production is wasted or damaged [5], placing food safety at risk.

Food security means sufficient and stable food supply availability and the ability to acquire or access food timely and permanently in reasonable quantity and quality [6]. FAO argues that food must be available at all times and that people must have access to it. The concept of availability is related to non-food scarcity, the conditions of sufficiency, stability and sustainability of the aggregate supply [7]. The global growth of food consumption presents several problems of supply and distribution in the cities of developing countries [8]. There are many factors that influence consumer perceptions

© Springer Nature Switzerland AG 2018
J. C. Figueroa-García et al. (Eds.): WEA 2018, CCIS 915, pp. 257–269, 2018.
https://doi.org/10.1007/978-3-030-00350-0_22

of food safety hazards and influence buying behavior [9]. Food security and food safety has been studied under different approaches: assessing consumer demand and food safety from the perception of risk, quality and price and its relation to food choice [10] and studied the ways in which small-scale fruit and vegetable producers in Kenya and India face increased food safety demand from their major export markets [11].

Regarding the analysis of food security with dynamic models, the food security has been studied taking into account the growth of food consumption, the production, the market, the price and budgets [12]. These results show that availability and access are the main limitations of consumption and food security. Also, others studies shows the complexity of the socio-ecological food system in food security, using a feedback perspective [13]. A system dynamics analysis concerning the vulnerability and resilience of food systems in developed countries is proposed by [14]. They discuss the differences in food systems between less developed and highly developed countries. Others studies structure the Food Supply and Distribution Systems (FSDS) methodology to evaluate food problems in urban environments, under a systemic approach, as a tool to define food policies [15]. A study of food SCs (SCF) should consider biophysical and organoleptic characteristics, shelf life, production time, transport conditions and storage. In this sense, the infrastructure of roads and food demand related to food security in a metropolis is analyzed and evaluated by [19], also analyze the dynamics of intermodal transport in the fruit chain, look at the influence of external integration on the logistic performance of the Mango SC [20] and study the losses derived from storage and transport in the mango chain [21]. There are no studies evaluating the flexible and resilient structure in CSF. From the context above, there is a clear need to evaluate the impact of the type of structure on the performance of CSF and food safety. This research determines how the SCF structure affects food safety and food security, using a model based on system dynamics. The model differs from those found in the literature, determining the dynamic impact of the structure of the perishable food chain and logistics, on food safety and food security.

2 Theoretical Overview

2.1 Some Characteristics of Perishable Foods

Perishable foods have specific characteristics due to their life cycle [26]. After the slaughter process, animal meat decays until it is no longer suitable for consumption [27, 28]. The elements of the fruit and vegetables life cycle suggested by [29] demonstrate the importance of the postharvest. In post-harvest, climactic fruits such as mango continue to mature as they continue their breathing process [30]. Non-climacteric fruits decompose at a faster rate; this is the case of blackberry and strawberry [31]. Both types of fruits begin a process of decay after harvest, changing their physical-chemical and organoleptic characteristics: loosing weight, firmness, external color, pH, acidity and soluble solids content [32]. Consumers demand better sensory properties, greater variety and food safety [16]. Therefore, it is essential that at the time of harvesting of fruits or vegetables, each fruit have a suitable level of maturity, depending on whether it is climacteric or not. In order to delay the process of post-harvest decay of climacteric fruit, modified or controlled atmospheres are used which reduce the rate of respiration [33]. In fresh foods, on the other hand, refrigeration is used to avoid loss of liquid and decay due to fungal or bacterial contamination [19] as well as correct packaging [21].

The deterioration of quality of perishable foods is commonly modeled with exponential functions that represent the process of birth-death. An effort to model the life cycle of foods is found in [34]. Also, others studies include functions of quality decay over time, using a differential equation to determine activation energy and temperature, which include first-order equations for the case of decay of food quality [35].

With regard to logistics in SC, different studies consider models whose objective is to minimize SC costs in terms of inventories for SCs of products with deterioration, taking into account the functions of decay over time [36, 37]. In relation to FSC, also it is consider functions of decaying quality through a mixed-integer linear programming model for production and distribution decisions that allows a calculation of costs of a FSC [38]. Others research proposes a multi-objective vehicle routing problem (VRP) model that minimizes distribution costs and maximizes the freshness of delivered food [39]. They examined the trade-offs between the distribution scenarios and cost-freshness trade-off.

2.2 Structure of the Supply Chains

This article evaluates different types of SC structures and combinations of these. The Lean structure targets low cost [40], focusing on the basic processes and eliminating all that does not generate value [41]. The Lean SC (SCL) is used for functional products with low variety and predictable demand such as processed foods [42]. These foods with long life cycles generate competition, resulting in low margins. A guide for the construction of an SCL can be found in [43] and for its implementation in [44].

The Agile SC structure focuses on rapid reconfiguration and responsiveness [45]. This structure is used for products with innovative and volatile demand, creating the need to be able to respond quickly [45]. It must understand and respond to an unpredictable and oscillating flow of demand [40], perishable products must have rapid and regular flows. The structure combines coverage and responsiveness [46].

The flexible structure is directed towards the ability to respond to changes without increasing operations, cost and without delay in response time [47]. Thus, this allows an increase in security and stability without sacrificing efficiency. Flexibility applies to labor costs, equipment technology and transportation, as a response to changes in the market, demand or prices [47]. Flexible SCs require a network that can adapt quickly to changes, for which the SC actors must be aligned and integrated [48]. Regarding flexibility in SCFs is considered inherently inflexible as quality reduces flexibility [49]. However, the seasonality of some fruits generates the need for flexibility in sowing. Agro-industries require the capacity to process all types of fruits. The flexibility of suppliers and industry are contemplated principles of flexibility in others studies [47].

The responsive SC structure, also called the "Sensitive Supply Chain" or "Continuous Replenishment", combines the characteristics of the agile and lean SCs. This structure is defined how a network of companies with rapid response ability and cost effectiveness. The operation of a responsive chain requires collaboration or integration of different actors [46], an evaluation of the effects of integration in fruit chains can be observed in [20].

3 Dynamic Hypothesis

The dynamic hypothesis considered is: "the flexible SC structure will improve the FSC's logistic performance, with special emphasis on producers and agribusiness, which will result in improved food safety and food security as availability and access increase". Thus, the causal loop diagram (CLD) represents the dynamic behavior of the factors influencing food flows and food security and safety, as illustrated in Fig. 1. There are two cycles of feedback, food security as well as food flows, which are described below:

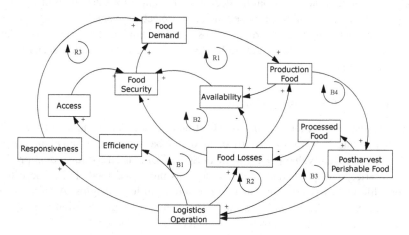

Fig. 1. CLD for represents the dynamic of food flows, food safety and food security.

Food Security and Safety: This cycle comprises three aspects related with the FSC, such as availability, food supply and food losses. They are affected by three feedback loops. _Availability_: First, the food production is determined by demand, which is connected with the food availability affecting food security, creating the reinforcing loop **R1**: Food Demand (FD) – Food Production (FP) – Availability (A) – Food Security (FS) – FP. The food production affects the inventories and logistics operation performance along SC. This situation comprises food losses caused by delays of logistical operation (e.g. transport and storage) that affect the food availability creating a balancing cycle **B3**: FD – FP – Postharvest Perishable Food (PPF) – Logistics Operations (LO) – Food Losses (FL) – A – FS – FD. _Access_: represents the dynamic behavior related with logistics operation performance that affects access to food supply. The cycle creates the balancing loop **B1**: FD – FP – PPF – LO - Efficiency (E) – Access (AC) – FS – FD. _Losses_: comprises two auto-balancing cycles. For fresh foods **B2**: FD – FP – PPF – LO – FL – SF – FD and for processed foods **B4**: FP – PPF - Processed Food (PF) – FL – FP.

Cycles of Food Production Rate and Logistical Operation: This cycle represents the interaction between production and logistical operation. Comprised by two cycles of reinforcement. The interaction among these activities is reflecting in the responsiveness, which impact on food demand, as represented in reinforcing loop. *Losses* **R2**: FP – FPF – LO – FL – FP and the cycle. *Responsiveness*: **R3**: FD – FP – PPF – LO – Responsiveness (R) – FD.

4 Dynamic Model for Perishable Food Chains

4.1 Stock and Flow Diagram

The proposed stock and flow diagram allows the analysis of the dynamics of a generic FSC considering the commercial relations between the agents and production flows through the different states. The simulation model represents downstream food flows and information associated with upstream orders. A simplified model structure is presented in Fig. 2; it includes the echelons of farmer, wholesaler of fresh and processed food, retailer of fresh and processed food as well as the consumer.

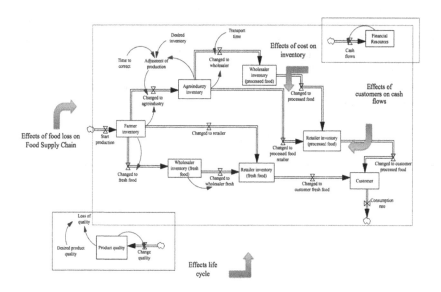

Fig. 2. Simplified model structure. (Color figure online)

The model of logistics and fresh FSC was made based on different structures [17–25], it can be considered multi-objective and multilevel or multi-echelon. The designed model includes losses derived from food handling practices, such as packing changes, damage from each actor's loading and unloading, as a constant flow output (blue box in simplified model structure). By being a dynamic model, it is possible to calculate the losses from storage and transport over time by including the Eq. (1) proposed by [35]:

$$Q_t = Q_0 + f_0(Q) = Q_0 - kt, \tag{1}$$

Where Q_t is the quality at the time t, Q_0 at the time of harvest and the first order function $\partial Q / \partial t = k$ is the decay rate of quality, k is the reaction rate Ae $(-E/RT)$, dependent on the temperature T, gas constant R and the activation energy E. When the order reaction is zero f_0 (Q) $= -kt$ and have order 1 is represented by Eq. (2).

$$f_1(Q) = e^{-kt} \tag{2}$$

The quality decay function has an exponential component, the quality Q_t at the time t can be written as Q_0 and the quality loss function represented by Eq. (3):

$$Q_t = Q_0 f_1(Q) = Q_0 e^{-kt} \tag{3}$$

4.2   Performance Measures

The performance measures are suggested, in accordance with the purpose of this research, and presented in Table 1. Food security will be measured as a result of availability and access. The availability is influenced directly by the logistic and processing operations times, but also the loss of food and quality of food throughout the chain. Access would also depend on the income of the population, but this factor is not contemplated in the model. Another factor that influences food security in the model is the logistics operation. If the inventory level is too high and too much is transported, more losses are generated.

Table 1. Performance measures.

					Measures of Performance			
	Supply time				Inventory Cost			Inventory Level
Availability	Transformation Process time				Transport Cost	Logistics Operation Efficiency		Amount of Food Transported
	Delivery Compliance		Access		Preparation Cost			Warehouse Storage Time
Quality	Losses by Inventory				Acquisition Cost			Transportation Time
	Losses By Transport				Cost of Decay			

4.3   Case of Study

In order to evaluate the hypothesis and validate the designed model, three chains of highly perishable fruits were selected: blackberry, strawberry and lulo. From these a survey was developed for the agents of each supply chain. The survey included logistical variables associated with procurement, inventory, transportation and distribution, as well as variables of trade, forms and frequency of negotiation. By means of non-probabilistic snowball sampling, 72 producers, 152 retailers (marketplaces and shopkeepers), 12 agroindustry, 28 wholesalers, 7 hypermarkets and 25 transporters were surveyed.

The fruits are sown in the department of Cundinamarca and sold in Bogotá, the capital of Colombia, which has a population of 7,000,000 inhabitants. Once harvested the fruits are transported from the farms in non-refrigerated vehicles of average capacity, between 3 and 10 tons, during a time of between one and three hours depending on the location of the farms. Fruits are sold mainly to wholesalers in "Corabastos", the most important market place in the country; occasionally agroindustries buy fresh fruit directly from the farmers. The fruits are sold from Corabastos to the retailers (e.g. hypermarkets); the agribusiness also buys from Corabastos. On the farms, fruits are packed in wooden boxes (blackberry) or plastic baskets (strawberry and lulo). In Corabastos they are sold in wooden boxes, cartons or plastic bags, resulting in a change of packaging. Fruits are supplied to Corabastos every day, but retailers usually buy two or three times per week. Agroindustry sells its processed fruits directly to retailers.

The stock-and-flow diagram integrates the chains of the three fruits in order to simulate the flexible chain. Five simulations were carried out for each integration scenario, each simulation uses a different seed value. The simulation time was 3,650 days, 10 years. To evaluate the effect of the long-term structure change, a DT = 0.25 was used. With the purpose of establishing the structure of the FSC fruits, scenarios were created. A first scenario models the current chain; the others simulate the other six structures. Table 2 shows the variables used and the change in each scenario.

Table 2. Proposed scenarios structure.

Variables	Chains	Current chain	Agile	Responsiveness	Lean	Flexible	Flexible/ agile	Flexible/ lean
Adjustment of production	Blackberry	1	1.19	0.81	0.81	1.19	1.19	1.19
	Strawberry		1.15	0.85	0.85	1.15	1.15	1.15
	Lulo		1.29	0.71	0.71	1.29	1.29	1.29
Type of vehicles farmer	All	2	1	1	3	2	2	2
Type of vehicles wholesaler		2	1	1	3	2	1	3
Use of the machines		1	1.5	1.5	0.5	1	1	1
Order processing farmer		1	0.5	0.5	2	0.5	0.5	0.5
Order processing wholesaler		1	0.5	0.5	2	0.5	0.5	2

The change of the production yield was made assuming normal distribution. The capacities of the vehicles change according to the structure: type 1 is 1 ton, type 2 is 5 tons and type 3 is 10 tons. For the current supply chain the machines work 2 shifts and change to 0.5 shifts or to 1.5 shifts. The order processing time also changes. For the current structure processing time 1 is assumed (representing 100%). For the other structures the time changes, increasing and decreasing in comparison to that percentage. The changes in these parameters were made based on the characteristics of each structure as shown in Table 3.

Table 3. Units of performance measure.

Measure		Units
Quality	Biophysical and organoleptic characteristics	Color, brix, pH, %acidity and texture on the shell
	Average losses of fruit, per warehouse and per transport	$\frac{Fruits\ Losses}{Total\ Fruits} \times 100\%$
Logistics operations	Average fruit inventory	$tons/day$
	Amount of average fruit transported	$tons/day$
Responsiveness	Storage time	
	Transport time	Días
	Fullfillment of demand	$\frac{Fruit\ sales}{Fruit\ demand} \times 100\%$
Efficiency	Costs: logistics, acquisition, production and loss	Colombian pesos

5   Simulation Results

The results are presented according to the performance measures, in order to establish the level of impact that the change structures have on food security. Runs for seven scenarios were carried out. The averages obtained from the simulations are presented with the changes of the 5 seeds; the tables show the 10-year run.

5.1   Food Security

Availability: Table 4 shows the results for the three fruit chains. The compliance of demand and lead-time are also shown. It was observed that the performance measures of the Agile and Flexible supply chains are very good especially in fresh fruit, this was one of the reasons that led to simulation the combined structures. These results show the structures with the best level of demand compliance for fresh fruit: Flexible-Agile (FA) and Flexible-Lean (FL). While the structure for fruit changes depending on the fruit, the best performance measure has been highlighted in grey.

Table 4. Demand fulfillment and lead-time for the simulation scenarios.

	Blackberry (%)		Strawberry (%)		Lulo (%)		Lead Time (day)		
	Fresh	Pulp	Fresh	Pulp	Fresh	Pulp	C1	C2	C3
Current	42.27%	15.88%	83.24%	10.07%	83.02%	19.06%	0.79	0.52	1.12
Agile	42.34%	15.38%	83.24%	11.85%	82.88%	18.53%	0.55	0.29	0.68
Responsiveness	42.34%	15.38%	66.57%	21.47%	82.88%	18.53%	0.55	0.29	0.68
Lean	42.17%	16.08%	83.24%	8.31%	66.53%	15.40%	1.27	0.98	1.99
Flexible	42.34%	15.38%	83.24%	11.85%	82.88%	18.53%	0.58	0.31	0.7
Flexible - Agile	45.24%	15.38%	83.24%	11.85%	82.88%	18.53%	0.57	0.31	0.7
Flexible - Lean	45.24%	15.38%	83.24%	11.83%	82.88%	18.54%	0.6	0.31	1.33

Quality: The loss of quality was measured by losses in inventory and transportation. The structures that had the largest losses of inventory were the current and the agile structures, while the ones with the least losses were the Lean and Responsive ones. The flexible-agile and flexible-lean had average losses. Regarding losses during transportation, the chains that presented the biggest losses were the Lean and Flexible chains. The one with least losses were the Agile and Responsive ones. The combined chains had average losses. The results show that the quality losses due to inventory and transport, different combinations must be used. The quantities lost in transport are inversely related to those lost in inventories, for example less inventory is lost with the Lean structure but the loss during transport is significant. The case of the agile structure is the reverse, the inventory loss is higher but the losses during transport are low. This shows the need to study the trade-offs of this issue, possibly through a multi-objective approach.

5.2 Logistic Operations

Results are reported for logistic operations, the changes of these performance measures in relation to the performance of the current chain are presented. For this reason the changes are presented as percentages, if the value is negative it means that it has decreased in relation to the current chain, if the value is positive it means that it has increased.

Inventory Level: The Table 5 shows the results of the simulation of fresh strawberry and strawberry pulp. The results show the largest decrease of inventory per actor and for the chain is indicated in grey, the largest average inventory is indicated in blue. The performance depends on the interest of the agents of the chain, if their strategy is a rapid response to the market a greater inventory (grey) is required. However, if a cost reduction is prioritized, a smaller inventory (blue) is required. Note that for all actors as well as for the chain the structure to select is the same. Except in the case of the fresh fruit retailer of strawberry.

Table 5. Improvement of inventory strawberry (percentage over current).

	Strawberry Fresh					Strawberry Pulp			
	Farmer	Agroindustry	Wholesaler	Retailer	Chain	Agroindustry	Wholesaler	Retailer	Chain
Agile	34.03%	11.46%	56.99%	1.59%	26.02%	20.68%	20.32%	18.83%	19.94%
Responsive	-16.00%	-31.77%	-67.45%	-20.18%	-33.85%	-23.24%	-23.74%	-25.47%	-24.15%
Lean	-29.90%	-18.43%	-70.28%	-11.64%	-32.56%	-29.93%	2.36%	-36.57%	-21.38%
Flexible	50.77%	19.71%	82.64%	1.72%	38.71%	30.15%	29.59%	28.06%	29.27%
Flexible - Agile	47.55%	-6.57%	45.71%	0.08%	21.69%	-2.48%	-2.99%	-3.02%	-2.83%
Flexible - Lean	20.87%	1.28%	12.36%	-9.92%	6.15%	0.22%	31.95%	-8.51%	7.89%

Amount of Food Transported: There should be a change of transport towards the structure that was able to transport more food, as illustrated in Table 6. This table shows that the best performance (more transport) for the fresh fruit chain is the Flexible structure, although for the producer-wholesaler segment the best is Flexible-Lean and for the wholesale-retailer segment the agile structure is the best one. The result for processed fruit is different.

Table 6. Improvement of transport strawberry (percentage over current).

	Strawberry Fresh			Strawberry Pulp		
	Farmer	Wholesaler	Chain	Agroindustry	Wholesaler	Chain
Agile	44.51%	0.03%	44.54%	-2.83%	-2.98%	-5.81%
Responsive	-44.83%	0.01%	-44.82%	-2.57%	-3.11%	-5.68%
Lean	-47.21%	0.02%	-47.19%	3.28%	-27.08%	-23.79%
Flexible	44.61%	-0.02%	44.59%	-2.52%	-2.59%	-5.11%
Flexible-Agile	45.80%	-1.26%	44.54%	-2.83%	-3.11%	-5.94%
Flexible- Lean	45.94%	-1.80%	44.14%	-2.31%	-50.54%	-52.85%

6   Conclusions

The model surpasses the models previously presented by other authors through including equations of loss of quality, associated with the life cycle of fresh food and the logistics operations of a supply chain. This model, using a multi-product, multi-level and multi-chain approach, can be used in order to evaluate several foods produced, processed and marketed by different agents of several food chains.

References

1. Yu, M., Nagurney, A.: Competitive food supply chain networks with application to fresh produce. Eur. J. Oper. Res. **224**(2), 273–282 (2013)
2. Zanoni, S., Zavanella, L.: Chilled or frozen? Decision strategies for sustainable food supply chains. Int. J. Prod. Econ. **140**(2), 731–736 (2012)
3. Sloof, M., Tijskens, L.M.M., Wilkinson, E.C.: Concepts for modeling the quality of perishable products. Trends Food Sci. Technol. **7**(5), 165–171 (1996)
4. Zhang, G., Habenicht, W., Spieß, W.: Improving the structure of deep frozen and chilled food chain with tabu search procedure. J. Food Eng. **60**(1), 67–79 (2003)
5. FAO. http://www.fao.org/docrep/016/i2697s/i2697s.pdf. Accessed 02 Mar 2015
6. Luning, A., Devlieghere, F.: Safety in the Agri-Food Chain. Wageningen, Wageningen Academic (2006)
7. Machado, A.: El mercado de tierras en Colombia: una alternativa viable. Una visión renovada sobre la reforma agraria en Colombia (1999)
8. Argenti, O., Marocchino, C.: Abastecimiento y distribución de alimentos en las ciudades de los países en desarrollo y de los países en transición. FAO (2007)
9. Yeung, M., Morris, J.: Food safety risk: consumer perception and purchase behavior. Br. Food J. **103**(3), 170–187 (2001)
10. Grunert, G.: Food quality and safety: consumer perception and demand. Eur. Rev. Agric. Econ. **32**(3), 369–391 (2005)
11. Narrod, C., Roy, D., Okello, J., Avendaño, B., Rich, K., Thorat, A.: Public–private partnerships and collective action in high value fruit and vegetable supply chains. Food Policy **34**(1), 8–15 (2009)
12. Ayenew, M., Kopainsky, B.: Food insecurity in Ethiopia: population, food production and market. In: 32nd International Conference of the System Dynamics Society, Delft, The Netherlands (2014)
13. Gerber, A.: Food security as an outcome of food systems. In: 32nd International Conference of the System Dynamics Society, Delft, The Netherlands, pp. 20–24 (2014)
14. Stave, A., Kopainsky, B.: Dynamic thinking about food system vulnerabilities in highly developed countries: issues and initial analytic structure for building resilience. In: 32nd International Conference of the System Dynamics Society, Delft, The Netherlands, pp. 20–24 (2014)
15. Armendàriz, V., Armenia, S., Atzori, S., Romano, A.: Analyzing food supply and distribution systems using complex systems methodologies. In: Proceedings in Food System Dynamics, Cambridge, USA, pp. 36–58 (2015)
16. Aramyan, L., Ondersteijn, C., Van Kooten, O., Lansink, A.: Performance indicators in agri-food production chains. In: Ondersteijn, C.J.M., Wijnands, J.H.M., Huirne, R.B.M., van Kooten, O. (eds.) Quantifying the Agri-food Supply Chain, pp. 47–64. Springer, Dordrecht (2006)
17. Orjuela, C., Javier, A.: Modelo logístico basado en dinámica de sistemas para la cadena lactea de la sabana de Bogotá. Thesis Maestría en Investigación Operativa y Estadística. Universidad Tecnológica de Pereira (2005)
18. Herrera, M.M., Orjuela-Castro, J.A.: Perspective of traceability in the food supply chain: an approach from system dynamics. Ingeniería **19**(2), 63–84 (2014)
19. Orjuela-Castro, J.A., Casilimas, W., Herrera, M.: Impact analysis of transport capacity and food safety in Bogota. In: Engineering Applications-International Congress on Engineering (WEA), pp. 1–7. IEEE-Xplore, Bogotá (2015)

20. Orjuela-Castro, J.A., Ruiz-Romero, A., Caicedo-Otavo, A.: External integration mechanisms effect on the logistics performance of fruit supply chains. A system dynamics approach. Rev. Colomb. Cien. Hortícolas **10**(2), 311–322 (2016)

21. Orjuela-Castro, J.A., Herrera-Ramírez, M.M., Adarme-Jaimes, W.: Warehousing and transportation logistics of mango in Colombia: a system dynamics model. Rev. Fac. Ing. **26**(44), 71–84 (2017)

22. Orjuela-Castro, J.A., Diaz Gamez, G.L., Bernal Celemín, M.P.: Model for logistics capacity in the perishable food supply chain. In: Figueroa-García, J.C., López-Santana, E.R., Villa-Ramírez, J.L., Ferro-Escobar, R. (eds.) WEA 2017. CCIS, vol. 742, pp. 225–237. Springer, Cham (2017). https://doi.org/10.1007/978-3-319-66963-2_21

23. Orjuela-Castro, J.A., Adarme-Jaimes, W.: Dynamic impact of the structure of the supply chain of perishable foods on logistics performance and food security. J. Ind. Eng. Manag. **10** (4), 687–710 (2017)

24. Herrera-Ramirez, M.M., Orjuela-Castro, J., Sandoval-Cruz, H.: Modelado dinámico y estrategico de la cadena agroindustrial de frutas. Universidad Piloto de Colombia, Bogotá (2017)

25. Orjuela-Castro, J.A., Morales-Aguilar, F.S., Mejía-Flórez, L.F.: Which is the best supply chain for perishable fruits, lean or agile? Rev. Colomb. Cienc. Hotícolas **11**(2), 294–305 (2017)

26. Kilcast, D., Subramaniam, P.: The stability and shelf-life of food. CRC Press, Cambridge (2000)

27. Poli, M., Parisi, G., Scappini, F., Zampacavallo, G.: Fish welfare and quality as affected by pre-slaughter and slaughter management. Aquac. Int. **13**(1), 29–49 (2005)

28. Ferguson, M., Warner, D.: Have we underestimated the impact of pre-slaughter stress on meat quality in ruminants? Meat Sci. **80**(1), 12–19 (2008)

29. Aked, J.: Fruits and Vegetables. En the stability and shelf life of food. CRC press, Cambridge (2000)

30. Singh, Z., Singh, K., Sane, A., Nath, P.: Mango-postharvest biology and biotechnology. Crit. Rev. Plant Sci. **32**(4), 217–236 (2013)

31. Tosun, I., Ustun, S., Tekguler, B.: Physical and chemical changes during ripening of blackberry fruits. Sci. Agricola **65**(1), 87–90 (2008)

32. Kader, A., Rolle, S.: The role of post-harvest management in assuring the quality and safety of horticultural produce, vol. 152. Food & Agriculture Organization, Rome (2004)

33. Orjuela-Castro, J., Pinilla, L., Rincón, R.: Aplicación de la tecnología de atmósfera controlada para la conservación de la granadilla. Ingeniería **7**(2), 45–53 (2001)

34. Blackburn, C.: Modelling shelf-life. In: The Stability and Shelf-Life of Food, pp. 65–78. CRC press, Cambridge (2000)

35. Labuza, P.: Application of chemical kinetics to deterioration of foods. J. Chem. Educ. **64**(4), 348–358 (1984)

36. Rau, H., Wu, Y., Wee, M.: Integrated inventory model for deteriorating items under a multi-echelon supply chain environment. Int. J. Prod. Econ. **86**(2), 155–168 (2003)

37. Wang, K., Lin, Y., Jonas, C.: Optimizing inventory policy for products with time-sensitive deteriorating rates in a multi-echelon supply chain. Int. J. Prod. Econ. **130**(1), 66–76 (2011)

38. Rong, A., Akkerman, R., Grunow, M.: An optimization approach for managing fresh food quality throughout the supply chain. Int. J. Prod. Econ. **131**(1), 421–429 (2011)

39. Amorim, P., Almada-Lobo, B.: The impact of food perishability issues in the vehicle routing problem. Comput. Ind. Eng. **67**, 223–233 (2014)

40. Harrison, A., Van Hoek, R.: Logistics Management and Strategy, 3rd edn. Pearson, Harlow (2008)

41. Naylor, J.B., Naim, M.M., Berry, D.: Leagility: integrating the lean and agile manufacturing paradigms in the total supply chain. Int. J. Prod. Econ. **62**, 107–118 (1999)
42. Lee, H.: Aligning supply chain strategies with product uncertainties. Calif. Manag. Rev. Repr. Ser. **44**, 105–119 (2002)
43. Srinivasan, M.M.: Building Lean Supply Chain with the Theory of Constraints. McGraw Hill, New York (2012)
44. Myerson, P.: Lean Supply Chain and Logistics Management. McGraw Hill, New York (2012)
45. Manson Jones, R., Towill, D.R.: Total cycle time compression and the agile supply chain. Int. J. Prod. Econ. **62**, 61–73 (1999)
46. Gattorna, J.: Dynamic Supply Chain, vol. 3. Pearson Education Ltd., Edingurgh (2015)
47. Simchi-Levi, D., Schmidt, W., Wei, Y.: From superstores to factory fires: managing unpredictable supply-chain disruptions. Harv. Bus. Rev. **92**, 96–101 (2014)
48. Stevenson, M., Spring, M.: Flexibility from a supply chain perspective: definition and review. Int. J. Oper. Prod. Manag. **27**(7), 685–713 (2007)
49. Van der Vorst, J.G., Van Dijk, S.J., Beulens, A.J.: Supply chain design in the food industry. Int. J. Logist. Manag. **12**(2), 73–85 (2001)

System Dynamics Modelling of Photovoltaic Power Generation Investment Decisions

Lindsay Alvarez-Pomar$^{(\boxtimes)}$ ⓘ, Edward Ricaurte-Montoya ⓘ,
and Ernesto Gomez-Vargas ⓘ

Universidad Distrital Francisco José de Caldas, Bogotá, Colombia
{lalvarez, egomez}@udistrital.edu.co,
edward.ricaurte741@gmail.com

Abstract. Most countries aim at the generation of electric power through renewable sources. The most developed countries have made great investments pursuing this goal. Photovoltaic energy is one of the options available even to domestic users. However, costs, radiation conditions and average household energy consumption won't make it a good option everywhere. In this article a model based on system dynamics is proposed, studying the viability of the use of photovoltaic systems at home. In the article, the Colombian case is reviewed 90% of the energy in Colombia is generated through hydroelectric plants and due to its high climate dependence, in times of drought the country is forced to import energy. We figured the number of photovoltaic systems necessary to avoid this importation and calculated the investment required by Colombian households to fulfill their energy needs.

Keywords: Electric power · Solar panels · Renewable energy
Demand · Imports · Consumption

1 Introduction

The demand for energy increases to support the growth of economies, per capita income and in general, the needs of the population, becoming a resource of great importance and therefore a concern for many countries. It is projected that the total energy consumption in the world will grow from 549 trillion BTUs in 2012 to 815 trillion BTUs in 2040, which represents an increase of 48% (U.S. Energy Information Administration (EIA), 2016).

This is an interesting occurrence in terms of global demand, since most of the growth of the world's energy consumption will occur in countries that are not part of the Organization for Economic Cooperation and Development (OECD). An increase of 71% is expected between 2012 and 2040, compared to an 18% increase for the OECD member countries. Between 2007 and 2012, non-OECD countries accounted for 57% of total energy consumption in the world, but by 2040, almost two-thirds of the world's primary energy will be consumed in economies that are not members of the OECD (US Energy Information Administration (EIA), 2016). Energy consumption is usually proportional to economic growth.

© Springer Nature Switzerland AG 2018
J. C. Figueroa-García et al. (Eds.): WEA 2018, CCIS 915, pp. 270–279, 2018.
https://doi.org/10.1007/978-3-030-00350-0_23

The richer the country the higher the energy demand [1]. All around the world, the events in the energy sector are placing more and more emphasis on renewable energies, because it is possible to reduce not only the impacts of climate change, but also the use of dispensable fossil fuels. More importance is being given to development strategies and the application of the principles of environmental transformation [2].

Currently, one of the renewable energy alternatives is solar photovoltaic systems, where solar radiation is captured in photovoltaic cells to generate electricity. This is achieved by panels with cells containing silicon (a semiconductor that is easily excited by light) thus producing a direct current which is then transferred to a bank of batteries where it is stored and derived to the inverter and finally transformed into alternating current (12 volts) [3].

The feasibility of implementing photovoltaic systems in Bogotá, Colombia will be determined through system dynamics, given that the solar generation capacity increased 26% in 2015, especially due to a reduction in the cost of production and the photovoltaic revolution that is taken place in Latin America, led by countries such as Chile 2015 where more than 362 MW and 873 MW are under construction and planning.

Green Tech Media (GMT), points out that Latin America was the region that showed the highest growth in solar energy in 2014, generating 625 MW, which is equivalent to a growth of 370% in relation to the previous year [4].

The cost of production of solar energy has become cheaper, approaching the costs of gas and coal. The primal factor in the reduction of the costs of production is mainly the decrease in the cost of solar panels, which, according to the International Renewable Energy Agency (IRENA), has been reduced by 80% since 2010 and it is expected to continue decreasing until it becomes one of the cheapest choices by 2040. Also, an important factor, are the new policies, implemented by the International Energy Agency (IEA).

2 Power Generation Analysis and Power Generation in Colombia

In Colombia, one of the main problems in the implementation solar technology is the frequent changes in climate. The average daily multiannual radiation is only 4.5 kWh/m^2. La Guajira could be the best area for this solar resource with a radiation close to 6 kWh/m^2 [5]. In [6], the development of solar energy in Colombia until 2008 is presented, emphasizing the need to formulate a program of development based on FENR (New and Renewable Sources of Energy). This program must integrate three essential elements: policy, capacity for development and project development. Only a coherent program can ensure the expansion of the FENR in the country and the use of its resources.

The difficulty in taking conventional electric power to geographically distant sectors, has encouraged the installation of photovoltaic panels, in some rural areas of regions such as Cundinamarca [5]. Of the 78,000 solar panels installed in Colombia, which produce around 6 MW, 57% are used in rural areas, and 43% for communication towers and traffic signage. It also highlights the importance that Silicon production has both in the execution of the projects and especially in the costs of the facilities. This production is instrumental in the development of photovoltaic solar energy. The capacity of production of silicon for photovoltaic panels would provide greater control and autonomy in the sector [7].

On the other hand, other variables have been taken into account in order to model the power sector using system dynamics. An approach has been used to model changes in energy intensity in the residential sector in Iran using simulation. They are trying to introduce some policies to make a constant improvement of energy intensity in the future [8]. Additionally, the city of Santa Fe, Argentina, is analyzed by system dynamics models that highlight the behavior of energy efficiency, which is directly affected by the production of renewable energy and state policies. An increase in energy efficiency will produce a drop in consumption and price, and together with the use of renewable energy they will make the energy model sustainable [9].

In general, a causal diagram is show in Fig. 1, using aggregated variables and their relationship, in order to be used as a base to model the dynamics of electrical power consumption.

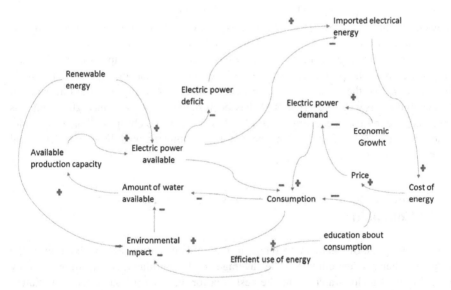

Fig. 1. Causal diagram of electrical power consumption. **Source:** The authors

The situation of the energy sector in Colombia is not the best, due to the crisis at the end of 2015 and in the first months of 2016, caused mainly by the decrease in the capacity of electric supply caused by El Niño, combined with the lack of forecasts by the Colombian government.

El Niño caused droughts throughout the country affecting the levels of hydro-electric dams, thus decreasing their production capacity. The power plants that produce electricity using gas, thermoelectric power plants, were forced to compensate for the increased demand. All this caused a deficit in the production of energy in the country.

On the supply side, the most serious problems are related to: (i) lack of incentives to substitute energy from the interconnected system for alternative energies (including sugarcane bagasse or the incorporation of wind power, despite Law 1715 of 2014); and (ii) lack of vigilance-control in the use of resources from the "Reliability Charge" paid to thermoelectric power plants [10].

This is how the increasingly depleted reserves of traditional sources of energy, such as fossil fuels, have revealed the need for alternative solutions to energy production, taking value from sources of energy that are more environmentally friendly, in such a way that they reduce the environmental impact [11].

Although the Colombian State Law 1715 of 2014 promotes the use of renewable resources, alternatives of high quality and efficiency that support the energy demand, it is important to consider the great benefits of further diversifying energy production, keeping in mind the great potential of both the country and the region, both for environmental and economic reasons. In certain cases, not only pollution could be reduced, but also periods of price increase would be less frequent [11] Reducing costs and decreasing energy imports could also result.

It is interesting to analyze the economic viability of roof mounted photovoltaic systems in urban areas, comparing their total investment cost with the cost of the energy that is currently being imported and the government subsidies to the different economic strata.

2.1 Photovoltaic Systems

The efficiency of conversion of solar radiation into electrical energy is the most critical point for the photovoltaic industry, being an aspect of competitiveness, since, by increasing the efficiency per unit area, the same amount of kWh is generated in a smaller area. In addition, performance depends, among many other factors, on the ambient temperature and the wind speed. Table 1 shows the efficiency of commercially available modules.

Table 1. Efficiency of commercially available modules. NREL. 2010, solar technologies market Report

Technology	Efficiency
Monocrystalline silicon	14%
Silicio multicristalino	14%
CdTe	11%
Amorphous silicon	6%
CIGS	11%

Inverter. The inverter is the element that interconnects the electricity production of the solar panels with the electrical system (distribution network or island with the network). In addition, the inverter must regulate the current and voltage for the system to work at the maximum power point.

Maintenance. Normal maintenance consists of cleaning the glass panels from time to time. You can learn how to keep the batteries (dry or gel) and monitor the good condition of the system. Most equipment, such as regulators or inverters, have status or performance indicators [16].

Total Cost. For international systems, the total costs of a photovoltaic system in June 2011 ranged between US $ 3,300/kWp and US $ 5,800/kWp for ceiling mounting systems. In Colombia, the cost is 16.5 USD/Wp on average. That is, up to three times more than what it costs internationally [17].

In the proposed model, we consider the behavior of the costs of the panels in other countries (see Fig. 2), taken into account the average annual reduction of 7.7% (during the years 2010 to 2014 31% reduction).

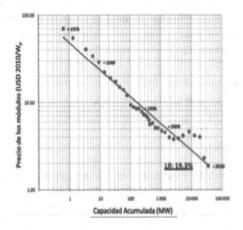

Fig. 2. Drop in costs for PV modules (1976–2010). International Energy Agency.

3   Data

Electric power generation in Colombia was 55,965.6 GWh in 2009, 2.9% higher than in 2008 (54,395 GWh). This positive evolution can be explained by the increase in demand and exportation of electricity to Ecuador and Venezuela; hydraulic generation decreased 11% because of El Niño and in 2014 the variation compared to 2013 was only 0.8% (see Table 2) [12, 13].

Electric power generation in Colombia was 55,965.6 GWh in 2009, 2.9% higher than the registered in 2008 (54,395 GWh). This positive evolution was due to the increase in demand and exportation of electricity to Ecuador and Venezuela; hydraulic generation decreased 11% because of the El Niño phenomenon and for 2014 its variation compared to 2013 was only 0.8% (see Table 2) [12, 13].

As part of the prospective modeling, the UPME (Unidad de Planeación Minero energética) found that between 4,208 and 6,675 MW of expansion are required for the next decade, highlighting Scenario 12 with a total of 4900 MW and with the greatest resilience, understood as the ability to adapt to events of hydrological extremes, good

Table 2. Energy Power generated in Colombia 2008–2015.

Year	Generated power (GWh)
2008	54395
2009	55965
2010	56897
2011	58616
2012	59990
2013	62197
2014	64327
2015	66548

behavior in terms of low generation costs, lower capital requirements and one of the lowest greenhouse gas emission [14]. On the other hand, the projection demand for electric power was based on the data of the Ministerio de Minas y Energia of Colombia, who has projected for a high, medium and low scenario for the next 15 years.

The total energy imported since 2003 amounts to 361 GWh corresponding to exchanges with Ecuador and Venezuela at a total cost of USD 18,713.3 thousand [13], as shows Table 3.

Table 3. Imported power in Colombia 2007–2015.

Year	Imported power (GWh)	Power cost
2007	38.4	1336
2008	37.5	2309.4
2009	20.8	1118.3
2012	6.5	243.2
2013	28.5	1682.5
2014	46.9	2935.7
2015	45.2	4658.9

The Congress of the Republic, through different laws, in particular the Tax Reforms and the last two Development Plans, has been modifying the validity and use of the sources of government funds created with specific destination for the normalization of networks (PRONE), energization of Interconnected Rural Areas (FAER) and non-Interconnected (FAZNI) and coverage of the consumption of users located in special zones (FOES) [15].

According to the above, and to determine the average annual investment value by the Government, the money destined for the FOES (subsidies) and the Solidarity Fund for Subsidies and Redistribution of Income (FSSRI) was taken into account, as well as the items that will apply from the budget of the Ministry of Mines and Energy - 2016.

4 Proposed Model

A system dynamic model was developed using IThink tool to simulate the power sector in Colombia on a planning horizon of 14 years (see Fig. 3). Given the average consumption of 1,700 kWh per year of energy per home, it was identified that panels of 2 kW are needed, given that in Colombia they can generate from 2500 to 3000 kWh per year depending on the geographical location where they are installed. [18].

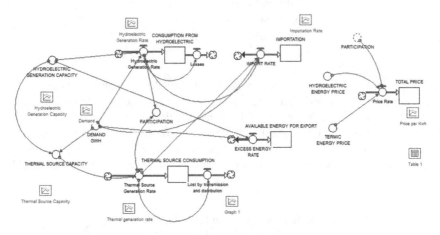

Fig. 3. System dynamic model of electrical power consumption in Colombia

Taking into account the annual variability, it is known that this is not inherent in the random behavior of the incidence of solar radiation in many regions of the world. For this reason, it is a general feature that is not specific of a geographic area or a given climate regime [19]. It does not exceed 11%.

To determine the amount of photovoltaic systems needed to supply the amount of energy imported into the country, a trial and error test was carried out, resulting in a total of 11'226.892 units which is equivalent to 1'403.361 panels approximately, taking into account that its useful life is 25 years and the companies that produce these systems guarantee its operation for a period of 10 years. The cost per system amounts to US $ 5639 according to quotes made with domestic suppliers.

5 Estimated Results

The total power generated through photovoltaic systems exceeds the amount of energy imported after 11 years, as shows in Fig. 4.

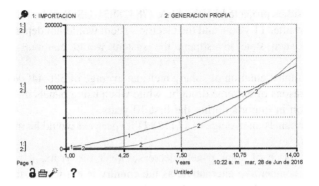

Fig. 4. Imported energy behavior vs energy generated through photovoltaic systems

The total investment required for the proposed photovoltaic system amounts to US $ 27,429,454,521.68 with an average annual investment rate of US $ 3,064,984,633.35 and an investment return of US $ 712.6, corresponding to the average cost of current electricity consumption. If the investment of the government funds is taken into account, it is concluded that the highest investment per household is US $ 350.71, and its behavior over time decreases (Fig. 5) given the reduction in the price of the panels.

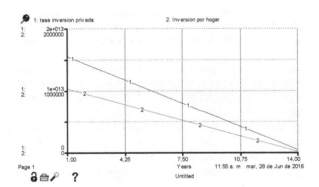

Fig. 5. Investment behavior needed to implement photovoltaic systems vs. investment per household

6   Conclusions

In this paper, we evaluate the technical and economic feasibility of the massive use of solar panels in Colombia using the theory of system dynamics and researching on photovoltaic power generation. We identify the main variables that affect solar energy generation and the impact of investment performance on power generation.

With the total investment projected by the state (78428851 USD) and by the private sector (41103214 USD) (based on information from the Ministry of Mines and Energy MinMinas) in 10 years the photovoltaic generation would have a participation of 9, 82% of the country's total energy generation.

With the subsidies projected by the State (78428851 USD) it would be possible to surpass the import after 11 years, and the electric system would not depend on imported energy. Without such state investment the system would continue to depend on importation.

Without the implementation of solar panels, an average of 386.44GWh-year would be imported in seasons of extreme drought, while when using panels there is a 39.14% observed reduction in imports during the first 10 years.

Without solar panels an average of 111738 USD per year would be imported during the first 10 years.

Although the price of solar panels decreases over the years, it remains a very expensive and uncompetitive alternative, as the country is not willing to invest in this sector. However, an even more detailed study by region, (where the type of system is more specifically established according to solar radiation conditions) should be conducted. As costs decrease there will be more incentives to implement interconnected photovoltaic systems.

References

1. DocPlayer Homepage. http://docplayer.es/18845088-Tendencias-recientes-de-la-oferta-y-demanda-de-energia-en-colombia.html. Accessed 19 July 2018
2. Blumberga, D., Dzene, I., Rošā, M., Davidsen, P., Moxnes, E.: System dynamic analysis for development of renewable energy resources in country. In: Proceedings of the 29th International Conference of the System Dynamics Society, Washington, USA, pp 24–28 (2011)
3. Dspace Homepage. https://www.dspace.espol.edu.ec/bitstream/123456789/16003/1/PROYE CTO%20DE%20IMPLEMENTACION%20DE%20PANELES%20SOLARES%20EN%20 HACIENDAS%20ALEJADAS%20DE%20LA%20FUENTE%20DE%20ENERGIA%20C ONVENCIONAL%E2%80%9D.doc. Accessed 19 July 2018
4. La primerísima homepage. http://www.radiolaprimerisima.com/noticias/192404/energia-solar-rompe-record-en-paises-de-america-latina. Accessed 19 July 2018
5. UPME-IDEAM. Atlas de Radiación Solar de Colombia. IDEAM, Bogotá (2005)
6. Rodríguez Murcia, H.: Desarrollo de la energía solar en Colombia y sus perspectivas. Revista de ingeniería **28**(1), 83–89 (2008)
7. Dinámica de sistemas Homepage. http://dinamica-de-sistemas.com/revista/1206k.htm. Accessed 19 July 2018
8. Jamshidi, M.M.: An Analysis of Residential Energy Intensity in Iran, A System Dynamics Approach. Sharif University of Technology Faculty of Computer Engineering, Tehran (2007)
9. Portillo, R., Tymoschuk, A.R.: Modelo Dinámico para el Estudio de la Situación Energética en la Ciudad de Santa Fe. I Congreso Argentino de Dinámica de Sistemas, III Congreso Brasileño de Dinámica de Sistemas y X Congreso Latinoamericano de Dinámica de Sistemas (2012)
10. Clavijo, S., Vera, A., Cuéllar, E.: La crisis energética de Colombia (2015–2016). Comentario Económico del Día – ANIF (2016)
11. Laumayer Homepage. https://laumayer.com/novedades-y-publicaciones/noticias/colombia-energias-limpias-renovables-o-alternativas/. Accessed 20 July 2018

12. Informes anuales Homepage. http://informesanuales.xm.com.co/2014/SitePages/operacion/
    2-4-Generaci%C3%B3n-del-SIN.aspx. Accessed 20 July 2018
13. XM S.A Homepage. http://www.xm.com.co/Pages/DescripciondelSistemaElectricoColom
    biano.aspx. Accessed 20 July 2018
14. UPME Homepage. http://www.upme.gov.co/Comunicados/2016/Comunicado_UPME_No02-
    2016.pdf. Accessed 20 July 2018
15. SIEL Homepage. http://www.siel.gov.co/LinkClick.aspx?fileticket=L9AASwJjMz8=. Acce-
    ssed 20 July 2018
16. Cooperación Alemana, GIZ.: Fomentando el uso de fuentes renovables de energía en el
    Salvador, 1st edn. Consejo Nacional de Energía, Salvador (2013)
17. Ortiz, J.D.: Viabilidad técnico-económica de un sistema fotovoltaico de pequeña escala.
    Revista Visión Electrónica 7(1), 103–107 (2013)
18. América Fotovoltaica Homepage. http://www.americafotovoltaica.com. Accessed 20 July
    2018
19. Hernández, J., Sáenz, E., Vallejo, W.A.: Estudio del recurso solar en la ciudad de Bogotá
    para el diseño de sistemas fotovoltaicos interconectados residenciales. Revista Colombiana
    de Física 42(2), 161–165 (2010)

A Goal-Seeking System Dynamics Methodology for Hospital Bed Capacity Planning

Sebastián Jaén$^{(\boxtimes)}$

Industrial Engineering Department, Universidad de Antioquia, Medellín, Colombia
jjaen@udea.edu.co

Abstract. Patient flow is at the core of hospital healthcare planners, managers and medical staff faced with the challenge of providing quality service. If patient flow is constrained at a downstream level, the hospital occupancy rises as well as the risk for adverse events and infections among patients. In this paper we introduce a methodology that both models patient flow in a hospital setting and determines the required downstream bed capacity that matches a desired target of hospital occupancy rate. The model uses a fundamental mode of dynamic behaviour known as goal-seeking that bridges the gap between the desired and the actual state of the system. Using the data provided by Hospital León XIII, an acute third level hospital in Medellín, Colombia, we illustrate a practical application of this methodology. The results let us conclude that the use of a goal-seeking structure withing the system dynamics (SD) modelling, enhances the reach of the SD methodology for dealing with the hospital bed capacity planning problem.

Keywords: Hospital bed capacity planning · Patient discharge
Patient flow · Hospital occupancy rate · System dynamics
Goal-seeking

1 Introduction

After the law 100 was passed in 1993, it changed the way health care was conceived and practiced in Colombia. A new model, for-profit insurance-based, replaced the former National Health System marking the end to a subsidies to supply approach, and the beginning of a subsidies to demand approach [1]. The reform brought autonomy to public and private hospitals and shifted their hierarchical relationship with health authorities, to a contract-based relationship with the insurance companies. This new arrangement has shown incentives for efficiency and quality, along with considerable increases in coverage [4]. However, the system still has many challenges. The accessibility and quality of the service are far from being universal. Hospitals operate facing cash-flow problems partly due to a set of regulatory adverse incentives generated by a for-profit insurance health care industry that delays or impedes billing [9].

© Springer Nature Switzerland AG 2018
J. C. Figueroa-García et al. (Eds.): WEA 2018, CCIS 915, pp. 280–291, 2018.
https://doi.org/10.1007/978-3-030-00350-0_24

In this scenario of limited cash-flow and an increasing demand for health care services, Colombian hospitals are being pressured to both reducing costs and fulfill a high quality standard of patient care. The hospital capacity, in terms of beds and patient discharge, is at the core hospital operations issues for hospital staff to manage and a public health concern. Since the practice of operational research methods has become more common in health care institutions worldwide, including Colombia [3], in this paper we present a system dynamics (SD) approach [8] to assess the problem of hospital bed capacity planning [10] considering the flow of patients and a given target hospital occupancy rate.

The model uses the data provided by Hospital León XIII, a large acute third level hospital in Medellín, Colombia. The research presents a methodology for modelling the hospital patient flow and its causal influence between the emergency department (ED) and the downstream wards. As a result, this research provides an aggregate SD model-methodology that incorporates a goal-seeking structure able to estimate the number of beds that the hospital wards need for identifying and unclogging bottlenecks, increase inpatient discharge, and adjust the level of occupancy rate to its desired target.

Traditional SD approaches aid the bed planning capacity problem by performing a successive process of scenario testing [15,18,25]. This process can be tedious, subjective, hardly exhaustive and in some cases impossible, if the number of values to determine is large. The advantage of using a goal-seeking structure as an integral feature allows the model itself to determine the required number of beds, while the amount of values to be found does not delay the process. Thus, this aids bed capacity planning without omitting its main sources of complexities in terms of variability and non-linearities (delays and feedbacks).

2   Background: System Dynamics as an Operational Research Tool for Assessing the Flow of Patients and Determining Bed Capacity

In recent time, most of the SD health care applications use it as a tool for visualizing and conceptualizing a problematic situation in a aggregated system [3]. In several works, SD is introduced as a methodology to guide policy makers, hospital managers and researchers for suggesting pathways of policy and the system redesign [11,19,26,27]. This confinement to this niche of strategic problems was strongly supported by the idea that the use of SD, commonly perceived as a deterministic methodology, is inadequate for modelling complex stochastic systems to the operational level [14,17]. However, recent SD literature [6,13,18,23] has been moving towards the analysis of hospital operational and tactic problems usually managed by the discrete event simulation (DES) and stochastic approaches as Markovian models [5,15,17]. The reason of this transition might be due to DES models do not generally attempt to determine the causes for variability in service rates [23]. They accept that service distributions exist and attempt to determine the best way to manage demand within the context [23]. However, from a system-wide perspective, the context is subject to be changed, re-designed, providing ample opportunities for improvement beyond the addition of servers and the minimization of service rates. Also, there is an increased awareness that health systems are complex and dynamic in nature, where SD is shown as an alternative for eliciting such behaviours [6].

The benefits of using SD as a tool for strategic planning in the health care systems are a recurrent topic in old and recent publications [11, 12, 19, 26]. One of the first works [19], evaluated the use of SD as a tool for planning and managing policies in health care. The authors found that SD approach allowed a relatively rapid modelling that clarifies in a generally intuitive manner the complexities of the system. Wolstenholme [26], also used the SD methodology for planning health care policies at a strategic level. However, this work finds that flow oriented policies have more leverage than stock oriented ones. This contribution is among the first addressing the problem of hospitals in terms of the link between the flow of patients and the number of health care facilities or beds. A similar approach is taken by the work of increasing demand in Nottingham, England [2]. The use of SD helps then identifying the system bottle-necks and its possible future behaviour if remaining with no intervention. This work has inspired a recent similar application [24] where SD makes visible a possible future in the Canadian health care system. Also, Lane and Husemann [11] focused in addressing the flow of acute patients through the UK health care system. In their approach, they acknowledge the pertinence of the SD methodology for mapping the flow of patients in a way that the client can understand it and become an active partner in the process of policy making. Also, they exposed the role of patient discharge as a condition that allows throughput.

Specifically to the operational problem of patients flow within hospitals, a system-wide approach seems to be a useful perspective as well. Proudlove, Black and Fletcher [16] remark that for streaming the flow of patients, hospitals must view the problem in terms of an interdependent system rather than individual departments. Marshall, Vasilakis and El-Darzi [14], point out that patient flow can be seen as the interaction of staff, patients and facilities. Proudlove, Black and Fletcher [16] noticed the complexity of the flow of patients caused by the interaction of several factors. Vanderby and Carter [23], acknowledged the need of a broad view of the hospital as a complete system when studying the flow of patients. As example, their work represents a novel approach to modelling patient flows in the hospital maintaining the quantitative foundation and industrial application of SD [8].

In this case, the authors provide a Paretian approach to limit the scope of the model by focusing on the seven primarily services which capture 69% of ED admissions. The second one element involves the concept of length of stay (LoS). Vanderby and Carter [23] show how, given the purpose of the model, the creation of stocks of homogeneous patients affected by the average LoS of the cohort in a given stage of their treatment can be an alternative and useful outcome that provides trust to the stakeholders and acceptance of the modells outputs. Demir, Lebcir and Adeyemi [6] present a different approach by defining LoS as the clinical needs and regulations related to treat patients. However, the model also implements the industrial use of SD. In a recent work [18], the quantitative SD approach to the bed capacity planning was implemented by studying the Irish healthcare system. It simulates the dynamics of the elderly inpatient pathways through the system identifying the bed blockages in post-acute services and, finding, through several simulations and scenarios the required amount of beds for temporarily unclogging the inpatient flow.

The present paper rests on several of the main modelling strategies mentioned in the former review. However, its approach tries to simplify the process of bed planning by adding a goal-seeking structure in the model. Traditional SD approaches aide the bed planning capacity problem by performing a successive process of scenario testing [15, 18, 25]. This process can be tedious, subjective, hardly exhaustive, and in some cases impossible, if the number of values to determine is large. At last, the required number of beds can be inferred accordingly with the simulation results. Then, a new round of scenario testing is performed to evaluate the robustness of the chosen values. The use of a goal-seeking formulation (GSF), can overcome some of the main limitations and enhances the potential of the SD methodology for addressing the bed capacity planning problem [10]. The aid of a GSF diverts the model to determine by itself the required number of beds to guaranty the inpatient flow, while the amount of values to be found does not delay the process. This suggests that it is proposed a methodology that makes a more efficient use of SD for bed capacity planning.

3   Model Equations

In the Hospital Leon XIII, the flow of patients begins with their arrive to the emergency department (ED). For the purpose of the model the ED was subdivided in three states (stocks) representing where the patient is in the process of being attended in the ED area. Figure 1 illustrates the hospital flows and stocks structure.

The admission to the ED is performed in the ED_A. There, the decision about the patient discharge or hospitalization, based on its medical condition, is made. If the patient is discharged it abandons the ED_A and enters ED_R where it has to wait until the paperwork and billing process is done. If the patient needs to be hospitalized it abandons the ED_A and enters ED_W, where it has to wait for an available bed in the hospitalization area H.

However, patients in the ED_W do not wait for any available bed, but one in an specific ward, of w wards, according with their medical condition. For this reason the model establishes that patients in ED_{Wi}, demand an available bed in the i ward.

The first equation corresponds to ED_A (Eq. 1). It is measured in patients, and the flows connected to it are: patients admitted, $a(t)$, discharged, $d(t)$, and referred to be hospitalized, $h(t)$. All of these flows are measured in patients per hour. In Eq. 2 the flow $a(t)$ uses the GRAPH function [21], and it returns the value of the number of patients admitted (a_j) at each Δt during the time horizon $t_o - t$. In Eqs. 3 and 4, $d(t)$ and $h(t)$ depend on the proportion of patients

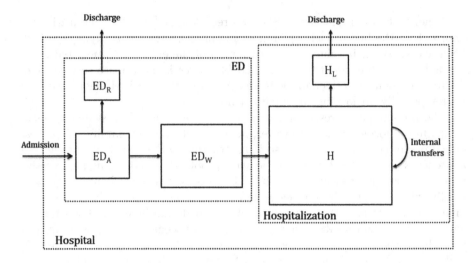

Fig. 1. Hospital flows and stocks structure.

to be discharged d_{ED}, and the ED_{ALoS}, which is the period of time between the moment of the patient admission and the decision about its discharge or hospitalization.

$$ED_A(t) = \int_{t_o}^{t} \big[a(t) - (d(t) + h(t))\big]dt + ED_A(t_o) \tag{1}$$

$$a(t) = GRAPH(t, t_o, \Delta t, \{a_{t_0}, a_2, ..., a_t\}) \tag{2}$$

$$d(t) = ED_A(t)d_{ED}/ED_{ALoS} \tag{3}$$

$$h(t) = ED_A(t)(1 - d_{ED})/ED_{ALoS} \tag{4}$$

The flow $d(t)$ is the incoming flow for the stock ED_R. The out flowing flow is the amount of patients discharged $l(t)$. The GRAPH function in Eq. 6 returns the l_j proportions of patients to be discharged per hour, which varies with the hour of the day.

$$ED_R(t) = \int_{t_o}^{t} (d(t) - l(t))dt + ED_R(t_o) \tag{5}$$

$$l(t) = ED_R(t)GRAPH(t, t_o, \Delta t, \{l_1, l_2, ..., l_{24}\}) \tag{6}$$

The sum of all w $ED_W(t)_i$ stocks correspond to the stock $ED_W(t)$. The inflow of each ED_{Wi} is $h^*(t)_i$ which is obtained by multiplying $h(t)$ and the proportion dH_i, which is the proportion of $h(t)$ patients demanding a bed in a given ward i.

$$ED_W(t) = \sum_{i=1}^{w} \left[\int_{t_0}^{t} (h^*(t)_i - r^*(t)_i)dt + ED_W(t_0)_i \right] \tag{7}$$

$$h^*(t)_i = h(t)dH_i, where \sum_{i=1}^{w} dH_i = 1 \tag{8}$$

The out flowing flow of each ED_{Wi} is $r^*(t)_i$. It corresponds to the number of patients obtaining an available bed in the ward H_i. The flow $r^*(t)_i$ depends on the number of patients in ED_{Wi}, and the available number of beds in the ward H_i, B_i. Additionally, it is considered a period of time r_{LOS}, in the process of transferring patients from ED_{Wi} to the ward H_i.

$$r^*(t_i) = MIN(ED_w(t)_i; B(t_i))/r_{LoS} \tag{9}$$

$B(t)_i$ is the available number of beds in the ward H_i, and is determined by Eq. 10, where β_i corresponds to the installed capacity of beds in the ward i, and $H(t)_i$ is the number of patients lying in bed, in the same ward.

$$B(t)_i = \beta_i - H(t)_i \tag{10}$$

The sum of all w $H(t)_i$ stocks corresponds to the stock $H(t)$, which is the number of hospitalized patients lying in bed. The inflows of each $H(t)_i$ are $r^*(t)_i$ and $t_{in}(t)_i$, where it corresponds to the incoming inpatients arriving to ward i due to the internal transfers. The outflows $t_{out}(t)_i$, and $dis(t)_i$, correspond to the inpatients to be transferred out and discharged from ward i, respectively.

$$H(t) = \sum_{i=1}^{w} \left[\int_{t_0}^{t} (r^*(t)_i - t_{out}(t)_i + t_{in}(t)_i - dis(t)_i)dt + H(t_0)_i \right] \tag{11}$$

The incoming patients transferred to ward i, $t_{in}(t)_i$ is the sum of all the outgoing patients from the w wards. The transition matrix T contains the proportion of patients transferred from ward i to ward j.

$$t_{in}(t)_i = \sum_{i=1}^{w} t_{out}(t)_j T_{ij}, where \sum_{i=1}^{w} T_{ij} = 1 \tag{12}$$

The time for a patient to be discharged or transferred from ward i depends on the ward lenght of stay, h_{LoS_i}. The percentage k_i determines the ratio of patients to be either discharged or transferred from a given ward i.

$$t_{out}(t)_i = H(t)_i ki/h_{LoS}i \tag{13}$$
$$dis(t)_i = H(t)_i(1 - ki)/h_{LoS}i \tag{14}$$

The outflow of patients discharged $dis(t)_i$ is accumulated in the stock of inpatients waiting to be released from the hospital $H_L(t)$. The flow of patients per hour released from the hospital is $hl(t)$, which varies according to the hour of the day.

$$H_L(t) = \sum_{i=1}^{w} \left[\int_{t_0}^{t} (dis(t)_i - hl(t)_i) dt + H_L(t_0)_i \right] \tag{15}$$

$$hl(t)_i = H_L(t)_i GRAPH(t, t_0, \Delta t, \{hl_1, hl_2, ..., hl_{24}\}) \tag{16}$$

Finally, the model incorporates the goal-seeking structure which is a result of a first-order negative feedback system. It is a self-correcting mechanism, that once is incorporated into the model, it forces the system to correct the deviations from the set goal [21]. The implementation in the model is attained by redefining β_i, which now is the number of beds required to match demand in terms of the gap between the current $(O(t)_i)$ and the desired (T_i) occupancy rate in the ward i.

$$\beta(t)_i = \int_{t_0}^{t} \left(\frac{\beta(t)_i (O(t)_i - T_i)}{AT} \right) dt + \beta(t_0)_i \tag{17}$$

The T_i values are defined by the hospital policies. The adjustment time (AT), determines how fast the response of the model should be to the narrow the gap and reach the desired target T_i.

4   Validation

The process of validation was guided by the tests performed on the model structure, behaviour and policies [7, 21]. The validation of the structure (components, relations, limits and dimensional consistency) was performed in a workshop where the model was presented and discussed with a group of the hospital staff members. The validation of the behaviour was performed on 51 output variables representing the state of the system in a given moment.

One group of variables (25) corresponds to the average occupancy rate per ward during the simulated year 2017. The summary results of the overall test of goodness of fit and statistical analysis between the actual (A) and the simulated (S) results are the following: R^2 0.99945, MAE -0.00203, X_S Mean 0.934, X_A Mean 0.931, S_S 0.5154, S_A 0.05143 and MSE 1.8608E-05. These results illustrate that the model is able to reproduce the average occupancy rate per ward.

The second group of variables corresponds to the two main output variables of the model: ED and hospitalization discharge of inpatients per hour. The first variable represents the number of inpatients discharged from the ED, and the second variable, is the sum of the number of inpatients discharged from the 25 different hospital wards. The measures of goodness of fit on these variables were performed on these variables according to the test suggested by Sterman [20, 21]. A graphical comparison between the actual and the simulated discharge rate of patients from the ED (ED_R in the model) and hospitalization, is depicted in Figs. 2 and 3.

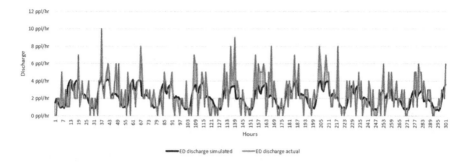

Fig. 2. Graphical comparison between simulated and actual ED discharge.

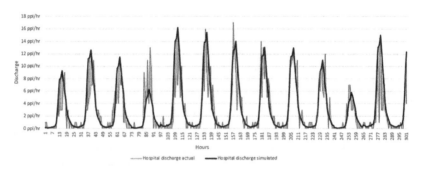

Fig. 3. Graphical comparison between simulated and actual hospital discharge.

The model simulates 8,640 h (1 year) of which Figs. 2 and 3 only illustrate 300. The comparisons show how the model is able to recreate the overall trend of the ED and hospital discharge behaviour. The summary results of the overall test of goodness of fit and statistical test for both output variables are presented in Table 1.

In Table 1, UM, US and UC reflect the fraction of the mean-square-error (MSE) due to bias, unequal variance, and unequal covariance, respectively [22]. In both cases, the majority of the error is concentrated in unequal covariation UC, while UM and US are small. This indicates that the point-by-point values of the simulated and actual series not match even though the model does a good job at capturing the average value and dominant trends in the actual data [20]. A large UC indicates the presence of noise or cyclical data not captured by the model, however, this error is unsystematic and is not considered a criteria for rejecting the model [20].

5   Results: Required Bed Capacity

After determining that the model is valid and able to reproduce observed data, Eq. 17 incorporates the goal-seeking formulation. For the purpose of illustrating the use of the model-methodology, the chosen target for each ward was 85% [10].

Table 1. Summary statistics for assessing simulated fit to actual data.

R^2 ED discharge: Sim vs Actual	0.555	R^2 Hosp. discharge: Sim vs Actual	0.79
MAE ED discharge: Sim vs Actual	1.379	MAE Hosp. discharge: Sim vs Actual	1.73
X_S Mean	2.674	X_S Mean	3.5
X_A Mean	2.607	X_A Mean	3.18
S_S Mean	1.216	S_S Mean	4.28
S_A Mean	2.146	S_A Mean	4.18
MSE ED discharge	3.20	MSE Hosp. discharge	7.83
UM	0.00141	UM	0.013
US	0.27093	US	0.001
UC	0.72766	UC	0.985
Sum	1	Sum	1

The demand variable is the main source of variability in the model. The correlation time derived from the demand variable is 7 days and could be used as the value for the AT parameter. A larger AT value delays the adjustment of the hospital occupancy rate.

Figure 4 depicts the simulation of the hospital average occupancy rate per hour and the accumulative average occupancy rate in the year. The simulation shows how from the initial value of 0.97, the model reaches the target given the implemented changes in the number of beds per ward shown in Table 2.

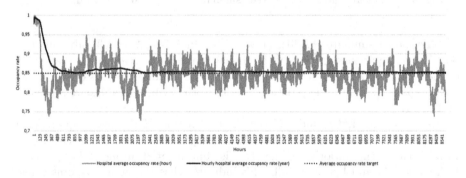

Fig. 4. Hospital average occupancy rate after determining bed capacity.

According to Table 2, the results illustrate that the main hospital bottlenecks are located in following wards: Orthopedics, general surgery and internal medicine. Also, the model makes evident the leftover capacity in the especial care unit and hematology. On average, the hospital bed capacity should increase up to 7.3% if 15% of the capacity is spared to attend contingencies and jumps in demand.

Table 2. Required number of beds after matching the target.

Ward	Initial	Required	% Change
General	29	31.24	8
Pediatrics	20	21.29	6
Internal medicine	30	33.39	11
Transplants	31	33.52	8
Nephrology	31	32.42	5
Internal medicine	30	32.8	9
Internal medicine	30	32.04	7
Internal medicine	29	33.18	**14***
Internal medicine	31	33.78	9
Neurology	26	28.54	10
Internal medicine	24	26.08	9
Hematology	21	19.68	−6
Internal medicine	26	28.41	9
Internal medicine	26	25.02	−4
General surgery	18	20.62	**15***
General surgery	31	35.17	**13***
Orthopedics	30	34.88	**16***
Orthopedics	33	35.54	8
Surgical neurology	32	35.66	11
Urology	29	30.9	7
Especial care unit	30	29.53	−2
Especial care unit	12	10.74	**−11***
Intensive care unit	10	9.95	−0.465
Intensive care unit	12	12.51	4
Intensive care unit	10	10.57	6
Sum	**631**	**677.42**	**7.3**

6   Conclusions

This paper has introduced a different approach to the use of SD as a tool for assessing the problem of bed capacity in hospitals. The implementation of a goal-seeking formulation within a SD model, enhances the potential of the SD methodology and provides new pathways for future research. Also, this approach offers an alternative to current approaches where bed planning is performed under several assumptions that ignore important aspects of reality. By handling the problem under a SD methodology, the analysis is able to introduce delays and feedbacks, which are key in understanding hospital complexity.

Given the process of validation on the output variables, the analysis shows that the modelling captures the average value and dominant trends in the actual data. However, the point-by-point values do not match. The output of the ED_R is especially inaccurate in this regard if compared with the H_L output. This result may be due to the fact that the ED is closer to demand than the hospitalization area, and thus it is influenced by it. Further modelling is necessary to incorporate these sources of variability in the model.

The approach can be adapted to any different hospital structure regardless of the number of wards. It is susceptible to the size of the time horizon of the model. Even though the model reaches the target after 855 periods of 8,640 (Fig. 4), the solution is more reliable if it has been tested under several scenarios of change in demand, especially if it has a seasonal component.

The results shown in Table 2 demonstrate how given a demand and a desired target, the León XIII hospital needs to increment its bed capacity by 7.3%. The methodology also reveals which wards are more demanded and congested, giving managerial staff ample opportunities to improve patient flow there.

The GSF was implemented to determine the required bed capacity to reach a desired target. However, under the same principle, it can be adapted to determine the required LoS in each ward in order to fulfill the same objective. This is especially important since such as Rashwan, Abo-Hamad and Arisha [18] acknowledge that increases in bed capacity are not a long-term solution for patient overcrowding.

References

1. Abadia, C.E., Oviedo, D.G.: Bureaucratic itineraries in Colombia. A theoretical and methodological tool to assess managed-care health care systems. Soc. Sci. Med. **68**(6), 1153–1160 (2009)
2. Brailsford, S.C., Harper, P.R., Patel, B., Pitt, M.: An analysis of the academic literature on simulation and modelling in health care. J. Simul. **3**(3), 130–140 (2009)
3. Brailsford, S., Vissers, J.: OR in healthcare: a European perspective. Eur. J. Oper. Res. **212**(2), 223–234 (2011)
4. Castano, R., Mills, A.: The consequences of hospital autonomization in Colombia: a transaction cost economics analysis. Health Policy Plan. **28**(2), 157–164 (2013)
5. Côté, M.J., Stein, W.E.: A stochastic model for a visit to the doctor's office. Math. Comput. Model. **45**(3–4), 309–323 (2007)
6. Demir, E., Lebcir, R., Adeyemi, S.: Modelling length of stay and patient flows: methodological case studies from the UK neonatal care services. J. Oper. Res. Soc. **65**(4), 532–545 (2013)
7. Forrester, J.W., Senge, P.M.: Test for building confidence in system dynamics models. TIMS Stud. Manag. Sci. **14**, 209–228 (1980)
8. Forrester, J.W.: Industrial Dynamics. Wiley, New York (1961)
9. Glassman, A.L., Escobar, M.L., Giuffrida, A., Giedion, U.: From Few to Many (2009)
10. Green, L.V.: Capacity planning and management in hospitals. In: Brandeau, M.L., Sainfort, F., Pierskalla, W.P. (eds.) Operations Research and Health Care, pp. 15–41. Kluwer Academic Publishers, Boston (2005)

11. Lane, D.C., Husemann, E.: System dynamics mapping of acute patient flows. J. Oper. Res. Soc. **59**(2), 213–224 (2007)
12. Lane, D.C.: Diagramming conventions in system dynamics. Oper. Res. Soc. **51**, 241–245 (2000)
13. Maliapen, M., Dangerfield, B.C.: A system dynamics-based simulation study for managing clinical governance and pathways in a hospital. J. Oper. Res. Soc. **61**(2), 255–264 (2009)
14. Marshall, A., Vasilakis, C., El-Darzi, E.: Length of stay-based patient flow models: recent developments and future directions. Health Care Manag. Sci. **8**(3), 213–20 (2005)
15. Patrick, J., Nelson, K., Lane, D.: A simulation model for capacity planning in community care. J. Simul. **9**(2), 111–120 (2014)
16. Proudlove, N.C., Black, S., Fletcher, A.: OR and the challenge to improve the NHS: modelling for insight and improvement in in-patient flows. J. Oper. Res. Soc. **58**, 145–158 (2006)
17. Qin, S., Thompson, C., Bogomolov, T., Ward, D., Hakendorf, P.: Hospital occupancy and discharge strategies - a simulation based study. Intern. Med. J. **47**, 894–899 (2017)
18. Rashwan, W., Abo-Hamad, W., Arisha, A.: A system dynamics view of the acute bed blockage problem in the Irish healthcare system. Eur. J. Oper. Res. **247**(1), 276–293 (2015)
19. Royston, G., Dost, A., Townshend, J., Turner, H.: Using system dynamics to help develop and implement policies and programmes in health care in England. Syst. Dyn. Rev. **15**(3), 293–313 (1999)
20. Sterman, J.D.: Appropriate summary statistics for evaluating the historical fit of system dynamics models. Dynamica **10**(II), 51–66 (1984)
21. Sterman, J.D.: Business Dynamics (2006)
22. Theil, H.: Applied Economics Forecasting. North Holland Publishing Company, Amsterdan (1966)
23. Vanderby, S., Carter, M.W.: An evaluation of the applicability of system dynamics to patient flow modelling. J. Oper. Res. Soc. **61**(11), 1572–1581 (2009)
24. Vanderby, S.A., Carter, M.W., Latham, T., Feindel, C.: Modelling the future of the Canadian cardiac surgery workforce using system dynamics. J. Oper. Res. Soc. **65**(9), 1325–1335 (2013)
25. Wang, J., Li, J., Howard, P.K.: A system model of work flow in the patient room of hospital emergency department. Health Care Manag. Sci. **16**(4), 341–51 (2013)
26. Wolstenholme, E.: A patient flow perspective of U.K. health services: exploring the case for new intermediate care initiatives. Syst. Dyn. Rev. **15**(3), 253–271 (1999)
27. Wong, H.J., Morra, D., Wu, R.C., Caesar, M., Abrams, H.: Using system dynamics principles for conceptual modelling of publicly funded hospitals. J. Oper. Res. Soc. **63**(1), 79–88 (2011)

Dynamic Performance of the Agricultural Sector Under Conditions of Climate Change and Armed Post-conflict

Olga Rosana Romero[1,3][✉], Gerard Olivar[2], and Carmine Bianchi[1,3]

[1] Faculty of Natural Sciences and Engineering, Jorge Tadeo Lozano University,
Bogotá, Colombia
olgar.romeroq@utadeo.edu.co
[2] Department of Electrical and Electronics Engineering and Computer Sciences,
National University of Colombia, Manizales, Colombia
golivart@unal.edu.co
[3] Department of Political Sciences and International Relations,
University of Palermo, Palermo, Italy
carmine.bianchi@unipa.it

Abstract. The agricultural sector is a strategic source for the sustenance of the population worldwide, however, given the lack of a favourable environment that guarantees its sustainability and growth, this sector is exposed to multiple conflicts and needs, which affect its performance and even causing desertion of the producer. In this research, we model and analyse the agricultural sector of the potato in the Colombian context, which in addition to being a strategic food to respond to food crisis, represents the needs of the agricultural sector, where about 90% of producers are classified as small because of their low participation in land tenure and where, in addition to the low level of technology, the situation of armed conflict and climate change which negatively impacts their results. This paper deals with the simulation of the agricultural sector of the potato, projecting its results for the post-armed conflict where an improvement in its performance is expected, however it is contrasted with the conditions of climate change to determine the real impact in the sector. Since previous studies address the problem separately, here we propose a dynamic and comprehensive analysis with scope on the production, the intermediation for the marketing of the product and its financial performance, which allows us to understand the real impact on the performance of the sector.

Keywords: Agricultural sector of the potato
Dynamic performance management · Climate change · Post conflict
System dynamics

1 Introduction

The rural area in Colombia represents 94% of the extension of the national territory [1], where about 24% of the population lives, being the scenario of multiple problems that affect the country, such as the armed conflict of more than five decades, the presence of

© Springer Nature Switzerland AG 2018
J. C. Figueroa-García et al. (Eds.): WEA 2018, CCIS 915, pp. 292–304, 2018.
https://doi.org/10.1007/978-3-030-00350-0_25

illicit crops and social inequality; proof of this is that 0.4% of the agricultural producer units own 41.1% of the total rural area registered by the National Administrative Department of Statistics DANE [1], that is, it is the property or responsibility of a single natural or legal producer. The concentration of land, leads to inequality factors, where for Colombia in the rural area, 41.4% of the population lives in poverty and 18% in extreme poverty [2].

These factors deteriorate with the unproductive, where about 36 million hectares are dedicated to livestock production and could have agricultural or forestry use, generating speculation in prices and a greater concentration of land and wealth. In Colombia, of the total rural area, only 6.3% is destined to crops, that is, approximately 7.12 million hectares have agricultural vocation (compared to 113 million total rural hectares), and whose production meets the food needs about 70% of the total Colombian population [3], mostly from small and medium-sized farmers.

According to the Food and Agriculture Organization FAO [4], the world needs to produce at least 50% more food for 9 billion people estimated for the year 2050, considering aspects such as climate change that can affect crop yields up to 25% [5], and increase the volatility of prices that can lead to higher rates of poverty, malnutrition and school dropout, among other factors, and given the background of the agricultural sector in Colombia, the world food safety concern is relevant.

Climate change generates direct impacts on crops and plants, given its incidence on rainfall and temperature, aspects that are not unrelated to potato cultivation, which can generally reduce yields on cultivated areas as result of the rise in temperature, thermal and water stress, shorter growth seasons and the presence of pests, among other aspects.

The FAO and the Colombian Ministry of Agriculture through the Institute of Hydrology, Meteorology and Environmental Studies IDEAM [6], using the AquaCrop model, have simulated the productivity of the potato crop under the scenario of variability and climate change in the areas of Cundinamarca and Boyacá, based on the Special Report on Emissions Scenarios (SRES) prepared by the Intergovernmental Panel on Climate Change (IPCC), projecting a decrease in the yield of tuberous production, which oscillates between −2% up to −50%, varying in each semester and according to the location.

The yields in crops, particularly potatoes, have been the subject of research, seeking to counteract the difficulties generated by climate change, studying levels of irrigation, soil type and territorial effects, such as Woli and Hoogenboom [7], Adabi and Moradi [8], Dua and Sharma [9], Raymundo and Asseng [10], Deguchi and Iwama [11], Kleinwechter and Gastelo [12].

For its part, the Colombian National Planning Department DNP [13], indicates that after the signing of the peace treaty and as a result of the post-conflict, Colombia may perceive significant results in the economic dividends, due to the extrapolation of the analysis carried out over 36 countries that have ended their armed conflicts, of which 18 are similar to the Colombian case. Among other benefits, the per capita GDP growth is estimated at 71%, the investment rate would go from 29% to 35%, higher foreign investment up to 176%, and an increase of up to 75% in exports.

Several authors address the sectorial impact and the quantification of the benefits after the post-conflict, such as Santa Maria, Rojas and Hernández [14], Álvarez and Rettberg [15], Ibañez and Velásquez [16] Authors such as Hewitt and Gantiva [17], Bell and Méndez [18] and Llosa and Casas [19] study the repercussions of the armed conflict on the mental health of the population and its possible effects during the post-conflict.

Several studies have been carried out separately in terms of climatic change and armed post-conflict, and it is in the interest of this work first to analyse the predicted effects together, since on the one hand it is stated that climate change decreases the yield of crops and in turn the post-conflict generates benefits in the productivity of the sector, and second to integrally simulate the dynamic performance of the sector through a multidimensional measurement that covers the incidence on variables such as crop yield, costs, tons harvested, the sale price among others.

2 Dynamic Performance Management

Dynamic performance management of resources to achieve higher returns is a complex task, even more when the decision maker is confronted with scenarios where the dynamic interaction of the elements of a system is intertwined with external and internal factors, generating difficulty to identify and predict relationships (Fig. 1).

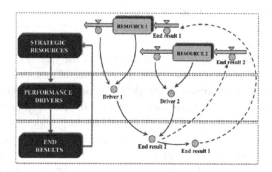

Fig. 1. General structure of dynamic performance management (DPM) [20]

This is how System Dynamics (SD) has been complemented with Dynamic Performance Management (DPM) to support the decision maker in the measurement of performance management and strategy design [20].

Dynamic performance management is approached from three complementary views, an objective, an instrumental, and a subjective [20]. The objective view defines the object of performance management, the instrumental view defines how to affect the object, and the subjective view defines who is responsible for carrying out the activities to achieve the desired impact. The instrumental vision allows us to understand how the allocation of strategic resources affects performance and these in turn influencing the final results [21].

On the other hand, the sustainable growth of organizations is analysed through the institutional and inter-institutional levels. This paper studies the agricultural sector of the potato, through the inter-institutional perspective, whose system is composed by producers in different sizes and contributing through the yield of their crop to the supply that is commercialized in the market. The strategic resources are represented in planted areas, harvested tons, product supply, price variation, and financial benefit. These all affect the performance drivers, such as the yield achieved in the crop, the level of intermediation for the commercialization of the product, the price differences between periods, and the financial gross margin ratio, generating changes in the final results of sowing, harvest, price and financial profit (Fig. 2).

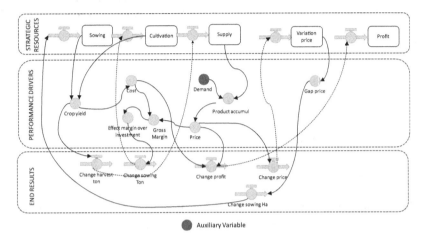

Fig. 2. DPM of the supply of the agricultural sector of the potato

Starting from the analysis of the causal relationships, we model the potato agricultural sector taking into account the effect of climatic change, and post-conflict, through three macro processes: production, market and intermediation and financial performance, allowing the simulation of the system and the valuation of its performance with the multidimensional measurement of the variables of interest, in this case the yield, the cost of production, the financial benefit, the harvested hectares and tons sown, results that in a particular way have an impact on the producers (institutional level), the aggregation to the agricultural sector (inter-institutional level) and therefore customers.

3   Modelling the System

Identified the strategic resources, the performance drivers and the final results, in this session the agricultural sector is modelled, considering the effects of climate change and post-conflict.

3.1   Causal Loop Diagram

Through causal loop diagrams, the relationships of the system are presented, associated with the loops of financial performance, market and intermediation, and production. These feedbacks influenced by external factors such as climate change and the post-conflict. The feedback loops are presented in the Fig. 3.

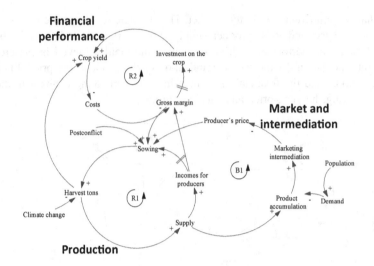

Fig. 3. Causal diagram of the agricultural sector of the potato

The dynamic behaviour of the system and its effects are analysed through the feedback loops explained below:

Production
The reinforcing feedback loop R1 is given by the behaviour of the sowing that allows to obtain the harvest that will be offered in the market, generating the income of the producer, however additional elements such as the post-conflict situation positively encourage the process of sowing due to an environment with more favourable characteristics for the development of the rural sector, but in the face of the climate change situation and the high dependence on rainfall on the crop, the tons harvested decrease.

Market and Intermediation
Once the harvest is obtained, the product is offered to the market with a natural condition in the sector and is the accumulation of product at certain times of the year, generating an environment encouraging the proliferation of intermediaries for the retailing of the product, with a direct effect on the price paid to the producer, which ends up affecting the next sowing decision. This is a balancing loop, represented as B1.

Financial Performance
The yield of production (tons obtained per hectare sown), impacts the production costs, which in turn determines the economic benefit perceived by the producer and that allows to improve the level of investment on the crop in order to improve the yield in the next period. The reinforcement loop R2 seeks the increase of the producer's profits with the effect of oscillation due to the delays that occur in the decision making process and the time required by the crop.

Given the interest of understanding the possible impacts of climate change and the post-conflict on the performance of the potato agricultural sector, the objective is to test the hypotheses defined in Subsect. 4.4.

3.2   Stock and Flow Diagram

The stock and flow diagram associated with the feedback loops and the processes described in the dynamic management of performance, is presented in the Fig. 4.

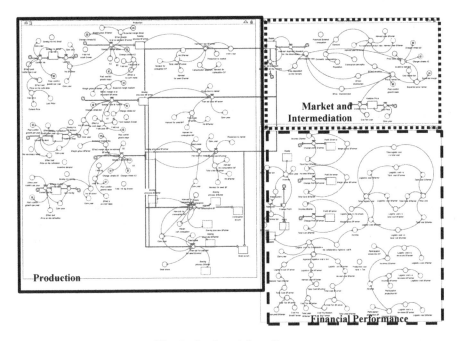

Fig. 4. Stock and flow diagram

Production

This sector represents the production in different phases of the crop until harvest, according to the type of producer, its size and the performance associated with its characteristics. The type of producer (i) is given by its size, where i, is 1 = small, 2 = medium and 3 = large. The equations of the strategic resources in this sector are given by:

- Hectares cultivated by each producer type i according to their size:

$$HS_i(t) = HS_i(t - dt) + (RHC_i - RLH_i)dt \quad \forall i = 1, 2, 3 \tag{1}$$

- Tons cultivated by each producer type i according to their size:

$$TS_i(t) = TS_i(t - dt) + (RTS_i - RH_i - RSS_i - RSC_i)dt \quad \forall i = 1, 2, 3 \tag{2}$$

Market and Intermediation
This sector represents the relationship between supply and demand which determines the accumulation of the product in the market, affecting the sale price, which is also sensitive to the level of intermediation and production costs. The equations of the strategic resources in this sector are given by:

- Supply of the Product (SP):

$$SP(t) = SP(t - dt) + \left(\sum_{i=1}^{n} RTH_i - RHI - RHF \right) dt \quad \text{where } i = 1, 2, 3 \quad (3)$$

- Price Variation (VP):

$$VP(t) = VP(t - dt) + (RCP - RLP)dt \quad (4)$$

Financial Performance
This sector represents the behaviour of the revenues, general costs, logistics and financial margin resulting from production and demand served, which affects the performance of the next production. The equations of the strategic resources in this sector are given by:

- Total Profit

$$PF(t) = PF(t - dt) + (RPF)dt \quad (5)$$

- Profit for each producer type i (PF_i):

$$PF_i(t) = PF_i(t - dt) + (RPF_i)dt \quad \forall i = 1, 2, 3 \quad (6)$$

3.3   Verification and Validation of the Model

Verification
The logical behaviour of the model is verified through the simulation of the variables of total cost, total yield, supply, price and sowing. For the case of the cost of the product, an inverse relationship is presented in the Fig. 5, dependent on the yield of the crop.

Regarding the sowing process (Fig. 6), the producer makes decisions based on the price perceived in the previous harvest, presenting a delay associated with the flow of information, to subsequently influence the physical process of cultivated hectares.

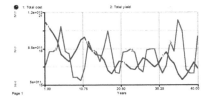 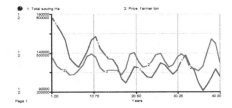

Fig. 5. Verification of the cost and yield of the crop

Fig. 6. Verification of the price and sowing

Validation

The validation process is carried out through the analysis of mean absolute percentage error (MAPE), comparing the historical data of time series between 17 and 24 years and the data obtained through the simulation of the dependent variables of the model, such as hectares harvested, tons produced, price and cost, reported by FAO [22].

In the case of hectares planted, the mean absolute percentage error is 14.61%, on the tonnes produced it is 13.52%, on the price and the cost the absolute average percentage error it is 20.14% and 20.33%, respectively, showing acceptable behaviour that adequately represents the system (Figs. 7 and 8).

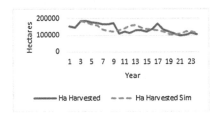 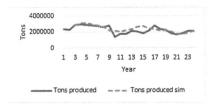

Fig. 7. Validation harvested hectares

Fig. 8. Validation tons produced

4   Results

The results of the model were analysed through the simulation of scenarios on climate change and post-conflict, to jointly determine how they affect the performance of the sector.

4.1   Climate Change Scenarios

The possible effects of rainfall on variations in product yields under climate change scenarios are projected by the Food and Agriculture Organization of the United Nations [23], based on these studies, in this research we consider the following scenarios (Table 1):

Table 1. Climate change scenarios

Scenario	Description
E1	Baseline scenario, without additional considerations of climate change
E2	Scenario considering climate change in a very heterogeneous world with continuous increase of the global population; with regionally oriented, fragmented and slow economic growth (according to FAO A2)

4.2 Post-conflict Scenarios

According to the National Planning Department (DNP) [13], after the armed conflict experienced by Colombia for approximately 50 years, and as a result of the peace treaty, a significant improvement in the performance of the national economy is expected, particularly in the performance of the agriculture sector. Based on the above, the following scenarios are considered in the model (Table 2):

Table 2. Post-conflict scenarios

Scenario	Description
P1	Baseline scenario, without affectation of the post conflict
P2	A scenario that considers the post-conflict based on an analysis of 38 countries that have experienced peace processes and extrapolating these results to the national reality

Given the interest of studying the performance of the system including the predicted effects by climate change and by the armed post-conflict in Colombia, we start from the premise that the system does not present mechanisms of associativity and collaboration, being producers dependent of the intermediation for commercialization of their products and subject to the accumulation of production in certain periods due to the effect of climatic precipitations in the absence of technification in the irrigation systems. The simulation considers 18 years, as aggregate planning of the production (yearly), in order to identify the behaviour towards the medium-long term.

4.3 Multidimensional Analysis

In order to determine the performance of the system and the development of the sector, it is analysed from 3 dimensions, cost, yield of the crop and financial margin perceived, with the different combinations of the proposed scenarios (Fig. 9).

The highest costs of the product are projected in the scenarios where post-conflict is not considered, with estimated yields between 16.84 and 17.37 tons per hectare planted and with the financial gross margin perceived by the producer decreased in conditions of climate change due to the concentration of the product and decrease in crop yields. When considering the system in post-conflict conditions, the performance measures of cost, yield and gross financial margin improve, however when analyzing the post-conflict scenario with climate change it shows a financial margin of 18.6%, that is, an

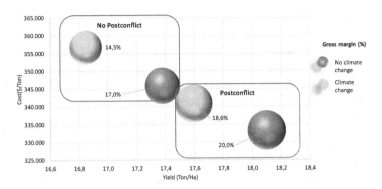

Fig. 9. Multidimensional analysis of the performance of the agricultural sector

increase of 1.6% compared to to the base scenario (not post-conflict and without changes in climate change), which highlights the need to develop actions that intensify the performance of the sector and its producers to a greater extent.

4.4 Hypothesis Testing

To contrast the hypotheses proposed, the statistical software SPSS was used, analysing the results of crop yield, cost per tonne produced and gross financial margin with the model applied for the evaluation of the effect of climate change and post conflict armed in the agricultural sector, particularly the potato. Null hypotheses and the alternative hypothesis are shown below:

Contrast Hypothesis

H_0 = Despite a more favourable environment in the agricultural sector after the armed conflict, climate change conditions, particularly in the potato sector, does not allow a significant improvement in the performance of the tons produced[1], the cost performance of the product[2] and the performance of the financial rewards perceived by the producer[3].

H_1 = Despite a more favourable environment in the agricultural sector after the armed conflict, climate change conditions, particularly in the potato sector, does allow a significant improvement in the performance of the tons produced, the cost performance of the product and the performance of the financial rewards perceived by the producer.

- With a significance level $\alpha = 0.05$ $F \sim F_{0,05;1;78} = 3,96 > F_c = 1.02^1$, $F \sim F_{0,05;1;78} = 3,96 > F_c = 0.293^2$, $F_{0,05;1;78} = 3,96 > F_c = 2.53^3$
- Decision: To accept the null hypothesis.
  Conclusion: The expected positive effect of the post-conflict in the agricultural sector of the potato is counteracted by climate change, without a significant improvement over the yields produced, in the cost performance of the product and in the performance of the financial rewards perceived by the producer.

5 Conclusions

The agricultural sector in Colombia must face a new panorama, which encompasses social, economic and environmental factors, with great potential at the level of its own development and contribution to the resolution of global problems, such as food shortages. Potatoes are one of the most widely consumed foods in the world and easily accessible to the poorest, being a key product to meet the increasingly growing food needs, where the agricultural producer is the central axis to achieve this purpose, however, the reality of the sector shows a great dispersion in the favourable conditions for the farmer, where the small-sized producer predominates, sensitive to both market and environmental variations, given the low level of investment and technification constraining sustainable growth.

Among the multiple factors that surround the potato sector, the effects of climate change and the condition of armed post-conflict are analysed simultaneously, with the expectation of opposite behaviours, where climate change threatens to reduce the yield of the crop, and after the armed post-conflict a growth of the sector is projected, as a consequence of a lesser desertion of the field, greater investment, better social conditions and a greater presence of the state. When analysing the conjugation of these factors and after the multidimensional evaluation of the performance of the producers and the sector, it is observed that the actions that are unleashed at the level of the armed post-conflict represent an important contribution on the development of the sector, however it is counteracted by the effect of climate change, indicating that for a true boom in the sector, strategies with specific focus should be developed, obeying a central development plan.

The multidimensional analysis reveals the most adverse situation for the sector, which is presented under a scenario of armed conflict and with climatic change, with a fall in crop yield of 0.6 tons per cultivated hectare, a decrease of 14.6% on the gross financial margin, a growth of 2.1% of the hectares planted as a result of the low yield of the crop and an increase in the cost per ton of 3.17%, which impacts the consumer price. The best performance scenario is presented as a post-conflict armed situation without climate change, with an increase of 3 percentage points of the financial gross margin, a greater yield of 0.8 tons per hectare planted, a 6.5% decrease in cost per ton, plus conservation of cultivated hectares.

When analysing the scenario with the highest probability of occurrence, presence of climatic change and armed post-conflict conditions, it shows a slight rebound in the variables of interest, 1.2% increase in crop yield, a 1.4% decrease in the cost per ton, an increase of 1.3 percentage points in the gross financial margin, plus stability in the hectares planted. Although this scenario shows a better behaviour in contrast to the scenario without climate change and armed conflict, the results show a fairly moderate growth when compared with countries such as China, India and the United States, reaching unfavourable deviations for Colombia. For example, higher product prices between 50% and 65% and lower yield in tons harvested per hectare up to 15%, that is, low performance persists in comparison with other markets, highlighting the need to promote actions of both the public and private sectors, which leverage real development of producers and the sector in general, making it more competitive and with the faculty of addressing challenges of greater globality, even surpassing the national context.

References

1. National Administrative Department of Statistics (DANE), National Agricultural Census 2014, Bogotá (2014)
2. National Administrative Department of Statistics (DANE), Monetary and Multidimensional Poverty: Main results 2014, Bogotá (2015)
3. Agricultural Society of Colombia, Situation and perspectives of agriculture in Colombia, Bogotá (2016)
4. Food and Agriculture Organization of the United Nations: FAO's work on climate change. FAO (2015)
5. International Food Policy Research Institute IFPRI: Climate change, Washington, D.C. (2009)
6. Food and Agriculture Organization of the United Nations - Ministry of Agriculture: Use of the AquaCrop model to estimate yields for potato cultivation in the departments of Cundinamarca and Boyacá. FAO, Bogotá (2013)
7. Woli, P., Hoogenboom, G.: Simulating weather effects on potato yield, nitrate leaching, and profit margin in the US Pacific Northwest. Agric. Water Manag. **201**, 177–187 (2018)
8. Adavi, Z., Moradi, R., Tadayon, M., Mansouri, H.: Assessment of potato response to climate change and adaptation strategies. Scientia Hortic. **228**, 91–102 (2018)
9. Dua, V., Sharma, J.: Forecasting impact of climate change on potato productivity in west Bengal and adaptation strategies. Indian J. Hortic. **74**(4), 533–540 (2017)
10. Raymundo, R., et al.: Performance of the SUBSTOR-potato model across contrasting growing conditions. Field Crops Research **202**, 57–76 (2017)
11. Deguchi, T., Iwama, K., Haverkort, A.: Actual and potential yield levels of potato in different production systems of Japan. Potato Res. **59**(3), 207–225 (2016)
12. Kleinwechter, U., Gastelo, M., Ritchie, J., Nelson, G., Asseng, S.: Simulating cultivar variations in potato yields for contrasting environments. Agric. Syst. **145**, 51–63 (2016)
13. National Planning Department (DPN): Economic dividend for peace, Bogotá (2015)
14. Santa Maria, M., Rojas, N., Hernández, G.: Economic growth and armed conflict in Colombia, Bogotá (2013)
15. Alvárez, S., Rettberg, A.: Quantifying the economic effects of conflict: an exploration of the costs and the studies on the costs of the colombian armed conflict. Colomb. Int. **67**, 14–37 (2008)
16. Ibáñez A., Velásquez A.: The Impact of Forced Displacement in Colombia: Socio-Economic Conditions of the Displaced Population, Linkage to Labor Markets and Public Policies. Series Social Policies. CEPAL, Santiago de Chile (2008)
17. Hewitt, N., et al.: Psychological effects on children and adolescents exposed to armed conflict in a rural area of Colombia. Acta Colomb. de Psicol. **17**, 79–89 (2014)
18. Bell, V., Méndez, F., Martínez, C., Palma, P., Bosch, M.: Characteristics of the colombian armed conflict and the mental health of civilians living in active conflict zones. Confl. Health **6**(1), 1–8 (2012)
19. Llosa, A., Casas, G., Thomas, H., Mairal, A., Grais, R., Moro, M.: Short and longer-term psychological consequences of operation cast lead: documentation from a mental health program in the Gaza Strip. Confl. Health **6**(1), 1–10 (2012)

20. Bianchi, C.: Enhancing performance management and sustainable organizational growth through system-dynamics modelling. In: Grösser, S., Zeier, R. (eds.) Systemic Management for Intelligent Organizations: Concepts, Models-Based Approaches and Applications, pp. 143–161. Springer, Berlin, Heidelberg (2012). https://doi.org/10.1007/978-3-642-29244-6_8

21. Cosenz, F.: Supporting start-up business model design through system dynamics modelling. Manag. Decis. **55**(1), 57–80 (2017)

22. Food and Agriculture Organization (FAO). http://www.fao.org/faostat/en/#data/QC/visualize. Accessed 17 Sept 2017

23. Food and Agriculture Organization of the United Nations (FAO): Use of the AquaCrop model to estimate agricultural yields in Colombia. FAO, Bogotá D.C. (2013)

Mathematical Modeling and Computational Simulation of the Diffusive Behavior of Adenocarcinoma Biomarker Particles

Esteban Vallejo[1]($\boxtimes$), Gustavo Suárez[1], William Torres[1], and Adolfo Uribe[2]

[1] Mathematics Group (GMAT), Universidad Pontificia Bolivariana,
Cir.1 #70-01, 050031 Medellín, Colombia
{esteban.vallejomo,gustavo.suarez,william.torres}@upb.edu.co
[2] Video-Endoscopy Unit, Clínica las Américas,
Dg. 75B #2A-80/140, 050025 Medellín, Colombia
adolfouribeobesidad@gmail.com

Abstract. Colorectal adenocarcinoma is one of the carcinogenic diseases that most affects the health of the world population. This disease is manifested biologically by the segregation of biomarker substances in the human system. This paper presents the development of a numerical-mathematical model for the study of the diffuse behavior of particles segregated by this type of cancer. Flow conditions, characteristics and properties of the diffusive medium are determined, and the study domain is defined. A mathematical description is elaborated to represent the behavior of the phenomenon by means of constitutive laws of the biosystem. A numerical-computational algorithm is constructed that makes possible the analysis of the different behavioral conditions; in this paper one of the multiples settings is showed. The computational implementation is done using Taylor series defined by finite differences with a refinement of the grid that can be controlled by the user. In addition, a structural element is incorporated with which it is intended to evaluate the level of concentration in the structure-substance contact zone. As a platform for the implementation of the algorithm, Matlab program is used. The results have been plotted by surface curves. Concentration levels are obtained at three points of interest, including concentrations at the structure-substance contact point, with concentration values of $1 * 10^{-6} \frac{kg}{m^3}$. The research is oriented in the search of an alternative that allows the detection of colorectal cancer in its early phase.

Keywords: Colorectal adenocarcinoma · Mathematical modeling
Numerical algorithm · Simulation · Diffusive behavior

Supported by Universidad Pontificia Bolivariana.

J. C. Figueroa-García et al. (Eds.): WEA 2018, CCIS 915, pp. 305–316, 2018.
https://doi.org/10.1007/978-3-030-00350-0_26

1   Introduction

Worldwide, colorectal cancer (CRC) is one of the most frequently diagnosed degenerative diseases in the population [22,25]. Despite the fact that some countries have improved their preventive systems for the detection of the disease, a high morbidity and mortality rate persists due to late detection factors. [9,28,30,34]. In Colombia, for the year 2012, the CRC ranked fourth (7.8%) in the estimated number of cases of incidence, being also the third cause of death (8.5%) associated with cancer for both sexes. Globally, however, the CRC ranked third (9.7%) in the estimated number of incident cases and fourth (8.5%) in the estimated number of death cases [31].

A great problem once the disease is presented, is the low probability of discovering at an early stage the substances that indicate the appearance of adenocarcinoma, a condition that, if solved, would allow the application of more effective treatments, less invasive procedures and reduce the harmful advance of cancer development [2,4,6,9,10,18,22,25,26,28–30,34]. It is due to this that biomarkers and biosensors are being developed that allow CCR early detection.

Several research groups have developed mathematical modeling and computational simulations specifically to predict the growth of the advanced middle stage tumor, as well as to study the generation of metastases during different periods of the disease in the patient [1,3,7,12,15,20,21,23,24,33].

Also, the propagation of malignant cells in the blood is being studied modeling the events of intravasation [2,4,6,22,28], which is why mathematical modeling and computational simulation of the diffusive behavior is necessary.

CRCs generally develop as a result of neoplastic progression from adenomas into adenocarcinomas, which are defined as neoplasia derived from the lining of the gut. It is widely accepted that this transformation is triggered by the accumulation of both genetic and epigenetic alterations. The progression from an adenoma to carcinoma may take decades, which provides a window of opportunity for early CRC detection. Mass screening would therefore greatly contribute to the early diagnosis and timely treatment of CRC [16].

On account of that it is known that CRC develops from the accumulation of genetic and epigenetic changes in the epithelial cells of the colon, molecular markers directed to genetic alterations in tumor tissues and peripheral blood have been evolved [17]. For this reason, the American Society of Clinical Oncology (ASCO) has been exploring several biochemical substances to determine CRC, such as: carcinoembryonic antigen, DNA ploidy, microsatellite instability (MSI/hMSH2 or hMLH1), CA 19-9, thymidine synthase, dihydropyrimidine dehydrogenase and thymidine phosphorylase, but several of these substances have been declared as markers that do not predict CRC early [2,25,28–30,34].

In the present paper, the diffusion of a particulate substance in the bloodstream is studied, leaving open the possibility of characterizing the particles in a specific way through the parameterization of their physical properties.

Through mathematical modeling and computational simulation, data are obtained that respond to different conditions of the domain of study, changes in boundary conditions, the presence or absence of geometric structures in the domain and variations in the parameters of the governing equation.

The results obtained in the disposition of the particles and the levels of concentration will be used to give continuity to the research of biosensors for the detection of colorectal cancer.

2   Materials and Methods

2.1   Mathematical Model

The diffusive behavior is produced by the Brownian movement of the biomarker particles through the blood fluid, establishing a concentration gradient between the two substances that come into contact. The mathematical model used corresponds to the first and second Fick's law.

The two-dimensional differential equation used to model the diffusion phenomenon transiently is defined as follows:

$$\frac{\partial C}{\partial t} = D_{AB} \nabla^2 C, \tag{1}$$

where D_{AB} is the diffusive coefficient of solute A in solvent B and C is the concentration $(\frac{kg}{m^3})$.

(1) It can also be presented as:

$$\frac{\partial C}{\partial t} = D_{AB} \left(\frac{\partial^2 C}{\partial x^2} + \frac{\partial^2 C}{\partial y^2} \right), \tag{2}$$

which is the diffusion equation in transient state for two dimensions.

The diffusive flow through a continuous and homogeneous medium can be described by the first law of Fick:

$$J = -D_{AB} \nabla C, \tag{3}$$

where J is the mass flow $(\frac{kg}{m^2 s})$ along the concentration gradient ∇C with a diffusion coefficient defined as the Constant $D_{AB}(\frac{m^2}{s})$. This equation could be used to establish the boundary conditions of the Ω domain.

2.2   Study Domain, Flow Condition and Properties of the Medium

Study Domain and Flow Condition: Cell-free circulating DNA (cfDNA) is defined as extracellular DNA present in the blood. The amount of circulating cfDNA in serum and plasma seems to be significantly higher in patients with tumors than in healthy controls, especially in those with advanced-stage tumors than in early-stage tumors. Several studies aimed at correlating rearrangements in matched tissue and plasma samples were conducted to confirm that circulating cfDNA analysis can be used as a diagnostic tool [27]. cfDNA can be detected in plasma or serum samples not only in patients suffering from

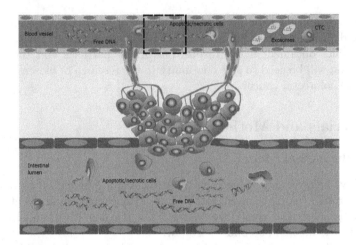

Fig. 1. Hypothesis for circulating free DNA development. The primary tumor releases cells into the bloodstream or intestinal lumen. In healthy individuals, apoptosis and necrosis are the main pathways linked to cell degradation and, consequentially, to DNA fragmentation. In cancer patients, in addition to the aforementioned necrosis and apoptosis, there would seem to be abnormal mechanisms of DNA degradation or secretion that increase levels and fragmentation of DNA. CTC: Circulating tumor cells. [5]. The broken line represents the portion of the blood vessel used for the present study.

cancer or other destructive diseases but also in healthy individuals. It has been suggested that cfDNA in healthy people is primarily of hematopoietic origin, nevertheless, cfDNA in cancer patients additionally results from apoptotic and necrotic processes characteristic of tumor cells with high cellular turnover. Both mechanisms simultaneously contribute to cfDNA production in cancer patients because the typical apoptotic low molecular weight DNA fragments as well as the high molecular weight DNA molecules characteristic of cell death processes has been detected in serum and plasma. Apoptosis results in DNA fragments of about 180 base pairs (bp) or corresponding multiples, while necrosis produces much larger fragments [5,11,13,27].

According to a study conducted by J. Xu et al., of a total of 70 individuals, 70 individuals, including healthy controls (N = 38) and CRC patients at stage I (N = 7), stage II (N = 10), stage III (N = 7) and stage IV (N = 8), the average concentration of cfDNA for both sexes, with an age range between 34 and 72 years is 4.38 ng/ml.

Genome instability, especially copy-number variation (CNV), is a hallmark of cancer and has been proved to have potential in clinical application. J. Xu et al. determined the diagnostic potential of chromosomal CNV at the arm level by whole-genome sequencing of CRC plasma samples (n = 32) and healthy controls (n = 38). Two methods including regular z score and trained Support Vector Machine (SVM) classifier were applied by them for detection of colorectal cancer and their results showed that the specificity of regular z score analysis for the detection of colorectal cancer was 86.8% (33/38), whereas its sensitivity was only 56.3% (18/32). Applying a trained SVM classifier (n = 40 in trained group) as the standard to detect colorectal cancer relevance ratio in the test samples (n = 30), a sensitivity of 91.7% (11/12) and a specificity 88.9% (16/18) were finally reached [32].

According to Jung et al., It was estimated that in colon cancer patients with tumor sizes of 100 g, about 3.3% of the tumor DNA is released into the blood-stream daily, Fig. 1 shows the behavior through a blood vessel and intestinal lumen [13].

Based in the J. Xu et al. results, the average concentration in MKS system is: $4.38 \, \text{ng/ml} \equiv 4.38 * 10^{-6} \, \text{kg/m}^3$.

In the present research, a piece of the blood vessel illustrated at Fig. 1 is studied in order to know how is the behavior and concentrations values of cfDNA. It is assumed a blood vessel diameter of $30 \, \mu\text{m}$, which is located in the mucous plexus of the colon [14]. In accordance with Martnez et al. results [19], the mass of a cell taken as reference is $3 \, \text{ng}$, thus, if tumour descripted by Jung have a mass of $100 \, \text{g}$, then $3.33 * 10^{10}$ cells are necessary to conform that tumor.

It is commonly accepted an average molecular weight of each base pair (bp) of DNA of $1.02 * 10^{-24} \, \text{kg}$ [8] and a cell contains $6 * 10^9$ bp. So, the amount of DNA present in the 100 g tumour can be calculated as:

$$6 * 10^9 \, \tfrac{\text{bp}}{\text{cell}} * 1.02 * 10^{-24} \, \tfrac{\text{kgDNA}}{\text{bp}} = 6.12 * 10^{-15} \, \tfrac{\text{kgDNA}}{\text{cell}}.$$
$$6.12 * 10^{-15} \, \tfrac{\text{kgDNA}}{\text{cell}} * 3.33 * 10^{10} \, \text{cell} = 2.0380 * 10^{-4} \, \text{kgDNA}.$$

If the release of cfDNA is assumed to be continuous during a day (86400 s) and about 3.3% of the tumor DNA is released into the bloodstream daily, then:

$$2.0380 * 10^{-4} \, kgDNA * 3.3\% * \tfrac{day}{86400 \, s} = 7.7840 * 10^{-11} \, \tfrac{\text{kgDNA}}{\text{s}}.$$

The circular base area of the blood vessel chosen is $7.068 * 10^{-10} \text{m}^2$, thus, diffussive flux $J = \frac{7.7840*10^{-11} \, \text{kg/s}}{7.068*10^{-10} \, \text{m}^2} = 0.1101 \tfrac{\text{kg}}{\text{ms}^2}$, which is the left boundary condition as is illustrated in Fig. 2.

Properties of the Medium: The diffusion coefficient D_{AB}, which relates the characteristics of the blood with the biomarker particles, allows defining the ease with which these are diffused in the bloodstream. The Einstein-Stokes equation (4) allows finding the value of this coefficient by relating characteristics of the two elements that interact and whose values can be consulted in Table 1.

$$D_{AB} = \frac{K_B T}{6 \pi \mu r} \tag{4}$$

Table 1. Properties of the medium.

Element	Type	Value	Description
r	Constant	$3.06 * 10^{-8}$ m	Particle radius
μ	Constant	$3.70 * 10^{-3}$ kg/ms	Blood viscocity
T	Constant	$311.15\,^{\circ}$K	Blood mean temperature
K_B	Constant	$1.3806504 * 10^{-23}$ kgm^2/Ks^2	Boltzmann constant
D_{AB}	Constant	$2.01 * 10^{-12}$ m^2/s	Coefficient of diffusion of the biomarker particles (A) in the blood (B)

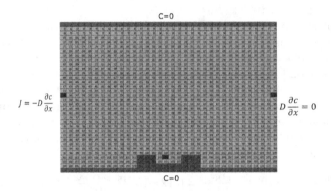

Fig. 2. Discretization of the domain by grid of 34×34 nodes dimensions.

2.3 Numerical Model

Domain Discretization: The blood vessel is represented by a longitudinal cut consisting of four borders defined as follows: two closed to represent the inner surface and two open borders for the transit of blood flow, Fig. 2.

It is possible to perform a discretization through a grid, as can be seen in Fig. 2, where a structural element is also added on the wall vascular inferior. For practical purposes, it is decided to use a grid of 34×34 nodes. In the same grid, it was decided to monitor for all time step of the simulation, 3 points of interest whose coordinates in terms of rows and columns of nodes in the grid are: $(17, 1)$, $(31, 17)$ and $(17, 34)$ and their real coordinates, according to dimensions of the section chosen to simulate are $P1 \approx (0, 1.5 * 10^{-5})$; $P2 \approx (1.4 * 10^{-5}, 2.6 * 10^{-6})$ and $P3 \approx (3 * 10^{-5}, 1.5 * 10^{-5})$.

Formulation of the Finite Difference Method: The Taylor series development centered at point a, of a concentration function C(x) is:

$$C(x) = C(a) + C'(a)\frac{(x-a)}{1!} + C''(a)\frac{(x-a)^2}{2!} + C'''(a)\frac{(x-a)^3}{3!} + \ldots \quad (5)$$

If $h = x - a$, then the previous expression is equal to

$$C(x) = C(a) + C'(a)\frac{h}{1!} + C''(a)\frac{h^2}{2!} + C'''(a)\frac{h^3}{3!} + \dots \tag{6}$$

It is convenient to rewrite the last expression in its alternative forms:

$$C(x + h) = C(x) + C'(x)h + C''(x)\frac{h^2}{2} + C'''(x)\frac{h^3}{6} + \dots \tag{7}$$

$$C(x - h) = C(x) - C'(x)h + C''(x)\frac{h^2}{2} - C'''(x)\frac{h^3}{6} + \dots \tag{8}$$

If h is small, the terms involving h^4, h^5 can be neglected. Actually, if all terms are ignored with h^2 and above, and solving (7) and (8), respectively, for $C'(x)$ The following approximations are obtained for the first derivative:

$$C'(x) \approx \frac{[C(x + h) - C(x)]}{h}. \tag{9}$$

$$C'(x) \approx \frac{[C(x) - C(x - h)]}{h}. \tag{10}$$

Subtracting (7) and (8) also yields:

$$C'(x) \approx \frac{[C(x + h) - C(x - h)]}{2h}. \tag{11}$$

On the other hand, if the terms with h^3 and above are ignored, then when adding (7) and (8) an approximation of the second derivative $C''(x)$ is obtained:

$$C''(x) \approx \frac{[C(x + h) - 2C(x) + C(x - h)]}{h^2}. \tag{12}$$

In particular, (9) is called forward difference, (10) is a difference backwards and both (11) and (12) are called central differences.

Using the implicit method for the solution of parabolic partial differential equations, and makes use of the Eqs. (11) and (12) to solve the system of equations in the subsequent iteration (k + 1) from the system solved in the previous iteration (k), the following numeric expression is obtained from (2):

$$\frac{1}{D_{AB}}\frac{C_{i,j}^{k+1} - C_{i,j}^k}{ht} = \frac{C_{i+1,j}^{k+1} - 2C_{i,j}^{k+1} + C_{i-1,j}^{k+1}}{hx^2} + \frac{C_{i,j+1}^{k+1} - 2C_{i,j}^{k+1} + C_{i,j-1}^{k+1}}{hy^2}. \tag{13}$$

After clearing the previous temporal component (k), we arrive at the equation:

$$-\frac{C_{i,j}^k}{D_{AB}ht} = \frac{C_{i+1,j}^{k+1} - 2C_{i,j}^{k+1} + C_{i-1,j}^{k+1}}{hx^2} + \frac{C_{i,j+1}^{k+1} - 2C_{i,j}^{k+1} + C_{i,j-1}^{k+1}}{hy^2} - \frac{C_{i,j}^{k+1}}{D_{AB}ht} \tag{14}$$

The Eq. (14) will then be the one that will allow to perform the numerical algorithm for the computational simulation of the diffusive behavior of colorectal adenocarcinoma indicator particles (cfDNA).

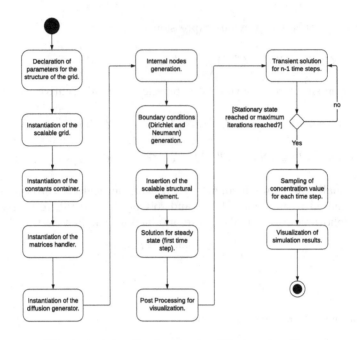

Fig. 3. Activity diagram for the diffusion algorithm.

2.4 Numerical Algorithm

Object-oriented programming using the Matlab software allows creating algorithms with reusable functions, considerably reducing the number of lines of code and establishing an organized structure for the implementation and maintenance of the algorithm. Figure 3 allows us to understand the different sequential activities performed by the numerical algorithm implemented. This algorithm, once defined the dimensions of the grid and the location of the elements contained in the domain, allows a mesh refinement that preserves the proportions of the object of study and its different components. The Fig. 3 also shows the strategy implemented with the implicit method, which requires a previous solution on which the subsequent iterations are based to calculate the solution for the next time step.

3   Results

In Fig. 4, section (a) shows the highest concentration values because the measurement point is located on the left border, where the diffusive flow originates and is at the highest intensity. During the first 4 seconds it presents a considerable growth, however in the later seconds there is a clear tendency to maintain the concentration in values close to $1 * 10^{-6} \frac{kg}{m^3}$ indicating that it approaches a stationary behavior as time progresses to 20 s of simulation.

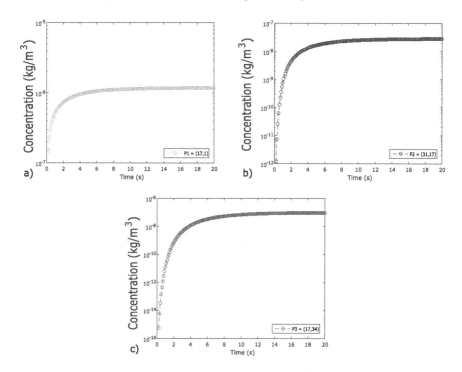

Fig. 4. Concentration for each control point in logarithmic scale.

Section (b) corresponds to the measurement point located on the surface of the hypothetical biosensor and describes the level of concentration that comes into contact with its surface with values that could be sufficient to emit a signal indicating the existence of the disease if the biosensor is also made with nanostructured material that allows a better capture of the particles, such as a graphene surface.

Section (c) represents the behavior of the particles at the exit of the study region, which of course starts with the lowest values because in the first seconds, the particles have not yet advanced sufficiently in their diffusive process. It is important to note that as in the other control points, approximately in the second 4, the accelerated increase in concentration levels begins to decrease, however, when overlaying the graphs (b) and (c) it is possible to notice that approximately in the second 5 the concentration values in the biosensor and in the output are equalized, this is due to the height at which the measuring point of the output is located, which registers values even higher than those registered by the measuring point located in the sensor surface. This indicates that the height plays an important role in the amount of concentration collected since as can be seen in Fig. 5, where the contour lines indicate that the distribution of particles is not completely uniform but correspond to the characteristic shape of the profile of blood velocity.

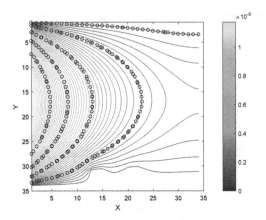

Fig. 5. Contour lines of behavior of cfDNA particles.

4   Conclusions

The concentration values found in the computational simulation are coherent with the scale of values obtained in other studies present in the references of this paper, which implies results that make sense from the behavior in situations presented in an experimental manner. The present study has a special relevance in the investigation of the early diagnosis of colorectal adenocarcinoma, since it can simulate different configurations in the study domain, allowing in a faster way to represent different boundary conditions and internal geometries in the study domain due to the construction of an algorithm capable of supporting different parameterizations. This investigation contributes to the incorporation of computational models to the study of the behavior of the biomarker particles of colorectal adenocarcinoma from the diffusion, later studies could incorporate convective components in the model, being able to simulate much more complex situations as possible turbulences in the behavior of the cfDNA through the blood.

References

1. Ašeris, V., Baronas, R., Kulys, J.: Computational modeling of bienzyme biosensor with different initial and boundary conditions. Informatica 24(4), 505–521 (2013)
2. Bupathi, M., Wu, C.: Biomarkers for immune therapy in colorectal cancer: mismatch-repair deficiency and others. J. Gastrointest. Oncol. 7(5), 713–720 (2016)
3. Couniot, N., Afzalian, A., Van Overstraeten-Schlögel, N., Francis, L.A., Flandre, D.: Capacitive biosensing of bacterial cells: analytical model and numerical simulations. Sens. Actuators B: Chem. 211, 428–438 (2015)
4. Cunningham, D., et al.: Colorectal cancer. Lancet 375(9719), 1030–1047 (2010)
5. De Maio, G., Rengucci, C., Zoli, W., Calistri, D.: Circulating and stool nucleic acid analysis for colorectal cancer diagnosis. World J. Gastroenterol. 20(4), 957–967 (2014)

6. Ferlay, J., et al.: Cancer incidence and mortality worldwide: sources, methods and major patterns in GLOBOCAN 2012. Int. J. Cancer **136**(5), E359–E386 (2015)
7. Ferreira, P., Baptista, M., Maria, S.D., Vaz, P., Di Maria, S., Vaz, P.: Cancer risk estimation in Digital Breast Tomosynthesis using GEANT4 Monte Carlo simulations and voxel phantoms. Phys. Med. **32**(5), 717–723 (2016)
8. Fonseca, J.C., Marques, J.C., Paiva, A.A., Freitas, A.M., Madeira, V.M., Jørgensen, S.E.: Nuclear DNA in the determination of weighing factors to estimate exergy from organisms biomass. Ecol. Model. **126**(2–3), 179–189 (2000)
9. Gonzalez-Pons, M., Cruz-Correa, M.: Colorectal cancer biomarkers: where are we now? BioMed Res. Int. **2015**, 14 p. (2015)
10. Hamm, A., et al.: Tumour-educated circulating monocytes are powerful candidate biomarkers for diagnosis and disease follow-up of colorectal cancer. Gut **65**(6), 990–1000 (2016)
11. Hao, T.B., et al.: Circulating cell-free DNA in serum as a biomarker for diagnosis and prognostic prediction of colorectal cancer. Br. J. Cancer **111**(8), 1482–1489 (2014)
12. Hushiarian, R., Yusof, N.A., Houshiarian, N., Abdullah, A.H., Ahmad, S.A.A.: Computer modeling to optimize the sensitivity of an optical DNA nanosensor. Sens. Actuators B: Chem. **207**(Part A), 716–723 (2015)
13. Jung, K., Fleischhacker, M., Rabien, A.: Cell-free DNA in the blood as a solid tumor biomarker-A critical appraisal of the literature. Clin. Chimica Acta **411**(21–22), 1611–1624 (2010)
14. Kachlik, D., Baca, V., Stingl, J.: The spatial arrangement of the human large intestinal wall blood circulation. J. Anat. **216**(3), 335–343 (2010)
15. Kang, G., et al.: Colorectal tumour simulation using agent based modelling and high performance computing. Future Gener. Comput. Syst. **67**, 397–408 (2017)
16. Lam, K., Pan, K., Linnekamp, J.F., Medema, J.P., Kandimalla, R.: DNA methylation based biomarkers in colorectal cancer: a systematic review. Biochim. et Biophys. Acta - Rev. Cancer **1866**(1), 106–120 (2016)
17. Lee, H.S., et al.: Circulating methylated septin 9 nucleic acid in the plasma of patients with gastrointestinal cancer in the stomach and colon. Transl. Oncol. **6**(3), 290–IN4 (2013)
18. Mahasneh, A., Al-shaheri, F., Jamal, E.: Molecular biomarkers for an early diagnosis, effective treatment and prognosis of colorectal cancer: current updates. Exp. Mol. Pathol. **102**(Mar), 475–483 (2017)
19. Martínez-Martín, D., et al.: Inertial picobalance reveals fast mass fluctuations in mammalian cells. Nature **550**(7677), 500–505 (2017)
20. Matsuzawa, F., Ohki, S.Y., Aikawa, S.I., Eto, M.: Computational simulation for interactions of nano-molecules: the phospho-pivot modeling algorithm for prediction of interactions between a phospho-protein and its receptor. Sci. Technol. Adv. Mater. **6**(5), 463–467 (2005)
21. Murmu, T., Adhikari, S.: Nonlocal mass nanosensors based on vibrating monolayer graphene sheets. Sens. Actuators B: Chem. **188**, 1319–1327 (2013)
22. O'Connell, J.B., Maggard, M.A., Ko, C.Y.: Colon cancer survival rates with the new American Joint Committee on Cancer sixth edition staging. J. Natl. Cancer Inst. **96**(19), 1420–1425 (2004)
23. Petrauskas, K., Baronas, R.: Computational modelling of biosensors with an outer perforated membrane. Nonlinear Anal.: Model. Control **14**(1), 85–102 (2009)
24. Podduturi, V.P., Magaña, I.B., O'Neal, D.P., Derosa, P.A.: Simulation of transport and extravasation of nanoparticles in tumors which exhibit enhanced permeability and retention effect. Comput. Methods Prog. Biomed. **112**(1), 58–68 (2013)

25. Prakash, S., Malhotra, M., Shao, W., Tomaro-Duchesneau, C., Abbasi, S.: Polymeric nanohybrids and functionalized carbon nanotubes as drug delivery carriers for cancer therapy. Adv. Drug Deliv. Rev. **63**(14–15), 1340–1351 (2011)

26. Sadreddini, S., et al.: Chitosan nanoparticles as a dual drug/siRNA delivery system for treatment of colorectal cancer. Immunol. Lett. **181**, 79–86 (2017)

27. Salvi, S., et al.: Cell-free DNA as a diagnostic marker for cancer: current insights. OncoTargets Ther. **9**, 6549–6559 (2016)

28. Teker, K.: Bioconjugated carbon nanotubes for targeting cancer biomarkers. Mater. Sci. Eng.: B **153**(1–3), 83–87 (2008)

29. Valle, L.: Recent discoveries in the genetics of familial colorectal cancer and polyposis. Clin. Gastroenterol. Hepatol. **15**(6), 809–819 (2017)

30. Wei, Q., et al.: IMP3 expression in biopsy specimens as a diagnostic biomarker for colorectal cancer. Hum. Pathol. **64**, 137–144 (2017)

31. World Health Organization: Estimated number of incident cases, both sexes, worldwide (top 10 cancer sites) in 2012 (2012)

32. Xu, J.F., et al.: A novel method to detect early colorectal cancer based on chromosome copy number variation in plasma. Cell. Physiol. Biochem. **45**(4), 1444–1454 (2018)

33. Yang, W., Lai, L.: Computational design of ligand-binding proteins. Curr. Opin. Struct. Biol. **45**, 67–68 (2017)

34. Zhang, B., et al.: A colon targeted drug delivery system based on alginate modificated graphene oxide for colorectal liver metastasis. Mater. Sci. Eng. C **79**, 185–190 (2017)

Langmuir–Hinshelwood Mechanism Implemented in FPGA

Luis Alejandro Caycedo Villalobos$^{(\boxtimes)}$ (iD)

Fundación Universitaria Los Libertadores, Bogotá, Colombia
lacaicedov@libertadores.edu.co
http://www.ulibertadores.edu.co/

Abstract. The use of numerical methods such as the Montecarlo model make possible development software for simulate heterogeneous catalytics processes in secuencial systems or multiprocessing-based architectures. The objective of this work is to develop an implementation proposal in FPGA logic devices as an alternative of the simulation for processes catalytics in a parallel way. By using purposed implementation, it is obtained the development of the processes in parallel of the mechanism of Langmuir-Hinshelwood in a FPGA hardware platform.

Keywords: Heterogeneous catalysis · Parallelizable model
Digital system · FPGA

1 Introduction

The present work has its origins in a hardware proposal to simulate the process of heterogeneous catalytic reaction by means of a parallel processing structure that allows to represent the interactions of the atoms of platinum (Pt) with the molecules of carbon monoxide (CO) and oxygen (O_2) through the mechanism of Langmuir-Hinshelwood. Develop and implement the parallel model on FPGA of the catalytic oxidation process of CO in a rectangular array of $N \times N$ that allows the study of the low dimensionality in the kinetics of the catalytic process in works in this area and achieving the development of new a tool. Next, the development of this work will be presented in each of the phases established, the conceptual development of the discretization of the mechanism and its implementation model of the hardware parallelization through FPGA, the validation of the implemented model and the data collection of processes of simulation for various partial pressure conditions for CO and O_2.

2 Kinetic Model of the Catalytic Reaction

The kinetic model of the catalytic reaction was taken from Rodríguez [1] in his study the low dimensionality of the catalytic reaction, the fundamental theoretical aspects are presented next.

© Springer Nature Switzerland AG 2018
J. C. Figueroa-García et al. (Eds.): WEA 2018, CCIS 915, pp. 317–327, 2018.
https://doi.org/10.1007/978-3-030-00350-0_27

2.1 Kinetic Equations of the Catalytics Processes

The development of the kinetic model that describes the mechanism of Langmuir-Hisnhelwood for an oxidation reaction of CO focuses on the crystalline structure of the catalytic surface, which for the particular case is that of platinum in the orientation [100], the structure of the surface corresponds to the type centered on the faces - FCC, with a neighborhood of order four that defines a structure type 5, a center and four neighbors. With FCC crystal structure, the surface can be modeled as a structure of size $N \times N$ and periodic border, the points of intersection of the net are modeled as solid spheres and each face of the crystal is formed by a center and four sites of net. This structure allows to use the discrete model of a surface where each active center available to perform the reaction corresponds to the intersection of the net of $N \times N$. The separation distance between each center corresponds to the network constant a that is proportional to the size of the centers of the net and their separation between nodes [4]. Within the structure of the surface and its model of net for $N \times N$, the kinetics of the reaction establishes elementary steps for the reaction on each active center, Ziff-Gulari-Barshad (ZGB) model [4], which describes the Langmuir-Hisnhelwood mechanism using the following kinetic equations:

$$Z + A \longrightarrow AZ \tag{1}$$

$$AZ \longrightarrow Z + A \tag{2}$$

$$2Z + B_2 \longrightarrow 2BZ \tag{3}$$

$$AZ + BZ \longrightarrow 2Z + AB \tag{4}$$

The Eq. 1 describes the adsorption on the surface of the adsorbate in the gas phase, 2 the desorption of the adsorbate on the surface, 3 the adsorption of the adsorbate that dissociates on the surface, and, 4 the catalytic reaction in the surface. In the previous equations Z is an active center on the catalytic surface, A corresponds to the dissociatless adsorbate and B_2 corresponds to the dissociated adsorbate. The particular kinetic equations for the Langmuir-Hisnhelwood mechanism were derive from the Eqs. 1, 2, 3 y 4 and, in function of the two precursors, *carbon monoxide* (CO) and *oxygen* (O_2) was described as follows:

$$CO_g + * \xrightarrow{k_1 p_{co}} CO_{ads} \tag{5}$$

The Eq. 5 corresponds to the adsorption phase of CO, here the CO_g corresponds to the carbon monoxide in the gas phase, $\{*\}$ the free places on the surface, CO_{ads} the carbon monoxide in the adsorption phase, k_1 the adsorption rate of carbon monoxide, p_{co} the partial pressure of CO_g.

$$CO_{ads} \xrightarrow{k_{-1}} CO_g + * \tag{6}$$

The Eq. 6 is the desorption phase of CO_{ads} CO_{ads} corresponds to the carbon monoxide in the adsorption phase, CO_g the carbon monoxide in the gas phase, $\{*\}$ the free places on the surface, $k-1$ the desorption rate of carbon monoxide.

$$O_{2g} + * \xrightarrow{k_2 p_{O2}} 2O_{ads} \tag{7}$$

The Eq. 7 is the adsorption phase of O_2 in the gas phase, O_{2g} corresponds to the oxygen in the gas phase, $\{*\}$ the free places on the surface, $2O_{ads}$ the oxygen in the adsorption phase, k_2 the oxygen adsorption rate, p_{o2} the partial pressure of O_{2g}.

$$2O_{ads} \xrightarrow{k_{-2}} O_{2g} + 2* \tag{8}$$

The Eq. 8 is the desorption of O_{ads} if the temperature of the process is different to $500\,\mathrm{K}$, $2O_{ads}$ corresponds to the oxygen in phase of assortment, O_{2g} to oxygen in the gas phase, $\{2*\}$ the free places on the surface, k_{-2} the rate of desorption of oxygen.

$$CO_{ads} + O_{ads} \xrightarrow{r} CO_2 + 2* \tag{9}$$

The Eq. 9 is the oxidation reaction of CO_{ads} on the platinum surface, CO_{ads} corresponds to the carbon monoxide in the adsorption phase, O_{ads} the oxygen in adsorption phase, CO_2 the carbon dioxide in the reaction phase, $\{2*\}$ the free places on the surface, r is the speed of the reaction.

The behavior of the adsorbates on the surface establishes a relationship between the empty active centers and the active centers with a particular type of adsorbates defined as a covering factor, $0 \leq \phi_x \leq 1$. The ligation equation describing the kinetics corresponds to $\phi_E + \phi_{CO} + \phi_o = 1$. Here ϕ_E is constant and represents the total of available active places. The kinetics of the adsorption process [3] is established by the law of velocities as follows:

$$\frac{d\phi_{CO}}{dt} = k_1 p_{CO}(\phi_E - \phi_{CO} - \phi_o) - k_{-1}\phi_{CO} - r\phi_{CO}\phi_O \tag{10}$$

$$\frac{d\phi_O}{dt} = k_2 p_{O2}(\phi_E - \phi_{CO} - \phi_o)^2 - k_{-2}\phi_O^2 - r\phi_{CO}\phi_O \tag{11}$$

The Eq. 10 corresponds to the variation of the coverage factor of CO_{ads}, where k_1 is the adsorption rate, p_{CO} is the partial pressure of the CO in phase of gas, k_{-1} is the desorption speed of CO and r is the reaction speed of CO with O. The Eq. 11 corresponds to the variation of the coverage factor of O_{ads}, where k_2 is the adsorption velocity of O, p_{O2} is the partial pressure of O in the gas phase, k_{-2} is the desorption speed of O and r is the reaction rate of CO with O.

2.2   Transition Probabilities of Kinetic Equations

The kinetic previous equations present a stochastic behavior determined by the phase in which the process is presented, in this section the probabilistic model used in the model for each phase of the process will be developed.

The dynamics of the catalytic reaction is conditioned by the probabilities of the occurrence of a process state for an active center and its neighborhood, therefore the probabilities of the process are modeled as $P(\alpha|\beta)$ and it is the probability of the state α, given the occurrence of the state β. By definition, given a probability space $(\Omega, F, \mathbf{P})$ and two events $\alpha, \beta \in F$ with $P(\beta) > 0$, the conditional probability of α given β is defined as:

$$P(\alpha|\beta) = \frac{P(\alpha \cap \beta)}{P(\beta)} \tag{12}$$

Where Ω is the sample space of the possible results of the process, F is σ-algebra, (Ω, F) is the measurable space, and $\mathbf{P}$ is a probability function that assigns a probability to every event fulfilling the axioms of Kolmogórov [3]. The probability space $(\Omega, F, \mathbf{P})$ for the model of the oxidation kinetics of CO corresponds to:

$$\Omega : \{*_{Hex}, *_{1x1}, CO_{ads}, O_{ads}, CO_2\} \tag{13}$$

$$\begin{aligned} F : \{\{*_{Hex}, CO_{ads}\}, \{*_{Hex}, CO_g\}, \{*_{Hex}, *_{1x1}\}, \\ \{*_{1x1}, *_{Hex}\}, \{*_{1x1}, CO_{ads}\}, \{*_{1x1}, CO_g\}, \\ \{*_{1x1}, O_{ads}\}, \{*_{1x1}, O_g\}, \{O_{ads}, CO_{ads}\}\} \end{aligned} \tag{14}$$

$$\begin{aligned} \mathbf{P} : \{P[1x1 \rightarrow Hex], P[Hex \rightarrow 1x1], P[CO_{ads}], \\ P[O_{ads}], P[CO_{des}], P[CO_{dif}], P[CO_2]\} \end{aligned} \tag{15}$$

The probability function $\mathbf{P}$ (15) defines a set of probabilities according to the phase of the catalytic reaction in which the process is found, where the probabilities $\{P[1x1 \rightarrow Hex], P[Hex \rightarrow 1x1], P[CO_{dif}]\}$ correspond to processes that are not defined by a kinetic equation. Its model is based on the particular characteristics of the surface and the corresponding adsorbate. Each of the $\{P[CO_{ads}], P[O_{ads}], P[CO_{des}], P[CO_2]\}$ probabilities is associated with a kinetic equation (5, 6, 7, 9), the general equation as a function of these probabilities is defined as:

$$\begin{aligned} P(\alpha|\beta) = p_1(\alpha)\delta_{\beta_1,\alpha_1+1}\delta_{\beta_2,\alpha_2} + p_2(\alpha)\delta_{\beta_1,\alpha_2} \\ + p_3(\alpha)\delta_{\beta_1,\alpha_1}\delta_{\beta_2,\alpha_2+2} + p_4(\alpha)\delta_{\beta_1,\alpha_1}\delta_{\beta_2,\alpha_2-2} \\ + p_5(\alpha)\delta_{\beta_1,\alpha_1-1}\delta_{\beta_2,\alpha_2-1} \end{aligned} \tag{16}$$

The probability p_4 is equal to zero for temperatures equal to or greater than $500\,\mathrm{K}$. The remaining probabilities are determined as follows:

$$p_1(\alpha) = \begin{cases} \overline{k_1}(m - \alpha_1 - \alpha_2), & \text{si } \alpha_1 + \alpha_2 < m, \\ 0, & \text{si } \alpha_1 + \alpha_2 \geq m, \end{cases} \tag{17}$$

$$p_2(\alpha) = \alpha_1 \overline{k_{-1}} \tag{18}$$

$$p_3(\alpha) = \begin{cases} \frac{1}{2}\overline{k_2}(m - \alpha_1 - \alpha_2)(m - 1 - \alpha_1 - \alpha_2) \end{cases} \tag{19}$$

$$p_4(\alpha) = \frac{1}{2}\alpha_2(\alpha_2 - 1)\overline{k_{-2}}, \tag{20}$$

$$p_5(\alpha) = \alpha_1\alpha_2\overline{r} \tag{21}$$

Where $\overline{k_1} = k_1 p_{CO}$, $\overline{k_{-1}} = k_{-1}$, $\overline{k_2} = \frac{m}{m-1}k_2 p_{o2}$, $\overline{r} = r$.

3 Simulation Using Cellular Automata

The simulation of the heterogeneous catalysis with the mechanism of Langmuir-Hisnhelwood carried out by Rodríguez [1] was based on the Monte-Carlo method for cellular automata and probabilistic transition rules. One option to this implementation is to use asynchronous blocks of cellular automata [6] as an efficient method of parallelization in its implementation. The main model corresponds to the asynchronous cellular automaton (ACA), from which the structure of synchronous blocks of cellular automata is derived.

3.1 Model of Cellular Automaton for the Oxidation of CO on Pt

The Langmuir-Hisnhelwood mechanism for heterogeneous catalysis is described by [3]. The simulation of the reaction by ACA is defined by $\aleph = (\mathbf{A}, \mathbf{X}, \Theta)$, where $\mathbf{A}$ are the possible states of the cell, $\mathbf{X}$ is the set of possible cells, Θ is the transition rules [6]. The possible cell states are defined by:

$$\mathbf{A} : \{*_{1x1}, *_{Hex}, CO_{ads}^{1x1}, CO_{ads}^{Hex}, O_{ads}^{1x1}, CO_{ads}^{Hex}\} \tag{22}$$

The set of possible cells $\mathbf{X} = \{(i,j) : i = 1, \ldots, M_i, \ j = 1, \ldots, M_j\}$ corresponds to the set of integer values that are coordinates of a discrete space of the catalytic surface. A cell is represented by the pair $(u, (i,j))$, where $u \in \mathbf{A}$ is the state of the cell, $(i,j) \in \mathbf{X}$ it is a coordinate of the cell. The next neighbors are determined by the function $\varphi(i,j) : \mathbf{X} \longrightarrow \mathbf{X}$, $\mathbf{T}(i,j)$ is the set of neighboring cells next to cell (i,j) that for the particular case is defined as $T_5(i,j) = (i-1,j), (i,j), (i+1,j), (i,j-1), (i,j+1)$.

4 Proposal for a Parallel Model of the Mechanism of Langmuir-Hinshelwood

The proposed parallelizable model is based on the geometry of the crystalline structure of the platinum - $pt[100]$ explained in the work of Rodríguez [1] where the net is an array of $N \times N$ cells and each center of the network corresponds to a free active center. In each active center is carried out the processes of the Langmuir-Hinshelwood mechanism described in 5, 6, 7, 8 and 9.

4.1 Parallel Model for N × N Active Centers

The model of the crystal structure centered on the faces for the platinum can be represented as a closed surface by means of an arrangement of N × N active centers and periodic limit, the developed proposal consist of an arrangement of an array of N × N and coordinates in two dimensions of the following way:

$$L^{N \times N} = \begin{pmatrix} (1,1) & (1,..) & (1, N-1) & (1,N) \\ (2,1) & (2,..) & (2, N-1) & (2,N) \\ (..,1) & (..,..) & (.., N-1) & (..,N) \\ (N-1,1) & (N-1,..) & (N-1, N-1) & (N-1,N) \\ (N,1) & (N,..) & (N, N-1) & (N,N) \end{pmatrix}$$

where (i, j) corresponds to an active center such that $1 \leq i \leq N, 1 \leq j \leq N$, and the neighborhood of the Von Neumann type corresponds to:

$$T_5 = \begin{pmatrix} (..,..) & (i-1,j) & (..,..) \\ (i,j-1) & (i,j) & (i,j+1) \\ (..,..) & (i+1,j) & (..,..) \end{pmatrix}$$

obtaining the arrangement $T_5 \subset L$. The limits of the L arrangement correspond to the periodic type where

$$L(periodic)^{N \times N} = \begin{pmatrix} (N,N) & (N,1) & (N,..) & (N,N-1) \\ (1,N) & (1,1) & (1,..) & (1,N-1) \\ (2,N) & (2,1) & (2,..) & (2,N-1) \\ (..,N) & (..,1) & (..,..) & (..,N-1) \\ (N-1,N) & (N-1,1) & (N-1,..) & (N-1,N-1) \\ (N,N) & (N,1) & (N,..) & (N,N-1) \end{pmatrix}$$

where the first row and the first column of $L(periodic)^{N \times N}$ correspond to the last row and the last column respectively, in this way it is obtained the periodic limit of $L^{N \times N}$. Now each active net center is associated with a unique net identifier from its coordinates in such a way that the $*(i, j)$ corresponds to the identifier $m = ((i-1)*N)+j)$ for $1 \leq i \leq N, 1 \leq j \leq N$. The generation of neighborhoods of the Von Neumann type for the arrangement $L_m^{N \times N}$ correspond to:

$$T_{5_m}(i,j) = \begin{pmatrix} \cdots & ((i-2)*N)+j & \cdots \\ (i-1)*N)+(j-1) & (i-1)*N)+j & (i-1)*N)+(j+1) \\ \cdots & ((i)*N+j) & \cdots \end{pmatrix}$$

4.2   Parallel Model of the Active Center

The parallelizable model of the active center is based on the 5-tuple $\{Q, \Sigma_\varepsilon, \delta, q_0, F\}$ where Q is the set of finite states, Σ_ε is the set of transition probabilities of states, $\delta : Q \times \Sigma_\varepsilon \longrightarrow P(Q)$ is the function transition, $q_0 \in Q$ is the start state and $F \subset Q$ is the set of end states. In the particular case for the active center (i, j) the 5-tuple corresponds to:

1. $Q : \{*_{1x1}, *_{Hex}, CO_{ads}^{1x1}, CO_{ads}^{Hex}, O_{ads}^{1x1}, CO_2\}$
2. $\Sigma_\varepsilon : \{p_{*_{1x1}}, p_{*_{Hex}}, pCO_{ads}, pCO_{des}, pO_{ads}, pCO_2\}$
3. $\delta : Q \times \Sigma_\varepsilon \longrightarrow P(Q)$
4. $q_0 : *_{Hex}$
5. $F : \{CO_2\}$

To define δ the transition matrix is established
   Additional to the transition matrix δ it is necessary to establish the diffusion matrix for the neighborhood $T_{5_m}(i, j)$ depending on the probabilities and the corresponding μ_i (Tables 1 and 2).

Table 1. Transition matrix for the probabilities of the catalytic process

State	p_{*1x1}	p_{*Hex}	pCO_{ads}	pCO_{des}	pO_{ads}	pCO_2
$*_{1x1}$		$*_{Hex}$	CO_{ads}^{1x1}		O_{ads}^{1x1}	
$*_{Hex}$	$*_{1x1}$		CO_{ads}^{Hex}			
CO_{ads}^{1x1}		CO_{ads}^{Hex}	CO_{ads}^{1x1}	CO_{ads}^{1x1}		
CO_{ads}^{Hex}	CO_{ads}^{1x1}	CO_{ads}^{Hex}	CO_{ads}^{Hex}	$*_{Hex}$		
O_{ads}^{1x1}						CO_2
CO_2						CO_2

Table 2. Von Neumann neighborhood diffusion matrix

Von Neumann neighborhood	μ_0	μ_1	μ_2	μ_3
$((i-2)*N)+j$	$CO_{(i,j)}$			
$((i-1)*N)+(j-1)$		$CO_{(i,j)}$		
$((i)*N)+j$			$CO_{(i,j)}$	
$((i-1)*N)+(j-1)$				$CO_{(i,j)}$

4.3   Proposed Model for Active Center

The Fig. 1 presents the functional architecture for an active center $*(i,j)$, the proposal focuses on the interaction it must have with its neighbors and the operations defined in the parallelizable model of the active center. The model combines the processes described in 5, 6, 7, 8, 9 and the spread over the surface of the CO_{ads} and the interaction with the Von Neumann neighborhood.

The fundamental states of the model correspond to the phase of the surface

$$\{*, CO_{ads}, O_{ads}, CO_2\} \tag{23}$$

and for the gas phase the defined states are

$$\{CO_g, O_g, CO_{des}, *_{1x1}, *Hex\} \tag{24}$$

In the Fig. 1 the states of the surface are represented in the block $\{R_1 R_0\}$ where to each state is assigned a binary value $*$: $\{00\}, CO$: $\{10\}, O$: $\{01\}, CO_2$: $\{11\}$, the value of R_1 is modified by the $input_x$ selected according to the probability of $p(x)$ obtained by the random number generator, that is, if $R_1 R_0$: $\{01\} \cup \{00\}$. If $R_1 R_0$: $\{10\} \cup \{11\}$ is written in the $input_x$ the value of R_1 according to the probability $p(x)$ obtained by the random number generator.

The gas phase block evaluates the state in $R_1 R_0$ in addition to the reconstruction phase of the surface $\{*_{1x1}, *Hex\}$, if it is in $*_{1x1}$ and $R_1 R_0$: $\{00\}$ it is possible to write in $R_1 R_0$: $\{01\}$ according to the probability $p(O_{ads})$, in the state $*Hex$ and $R_1 R_0$: $\{10\}$ it is possible to write in $R_1 R_0$: $\{00\}$ according to the probability $p(CO_{des})$, in the state $(*_{1x1}) \cup (*Hex)$ and $R_1 R_0$: $\{00\}$ it is possible to write in $R_1 R_0$: $\{10\}$ according to the probability $p(CO_{ads})$, in the state

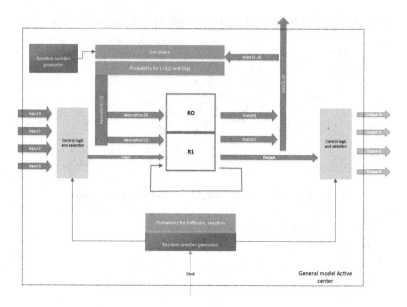

Fig. 1. Proposed model for active center

$*_{Hex} \cup R_1R_0 : \{10\}$ and the next four neighbors are in CO_{ads} the reconstruction of the surface and write $*1x1$, in state $*_1x1$ and probability $p(*_{Hex})$ is written $*_Hex$.

In the Fig. 1, the block *Random number generator* generates a random number between 0 and 1, R_1R_0 is a two-bit register, *Control logic and selection* performs the selection of the $input_x/output_x$ according to the value of the random number generator and the value in the register R_1R_0. The $input_x$ and the $output_x$ are connected to the neighbors for the Von Neumann neighborhood. The current status of the active center corresponds to the value of R_1R_0.

5   Results Implementation Proposed Parallel Model

The proposed parallelizable model was implemented on a board *DE2* with an Altera FPGA of the family *CycloneII* EP2C35F672C6N.

5.1   Simulation Results Using the Proposed Parallel Model

The results of the simulation of the heterogeneous catalysis using the proposed parallelizable model of the mechanism of Langmuir-Hinshelwood implemented on FPGA correspond to two classes, the first is the spatial-temporal evolution and the second is the response of the surface coverage in function of $\phi_{CO}, \phi_O, \phi_E$ and the Langmuir isotherm for the catalytic reaction.

For the first case, through the visualization module in a VGA Monitor for the 640×480 standard, shown in Fig. 2, it was possible to check the evolution,

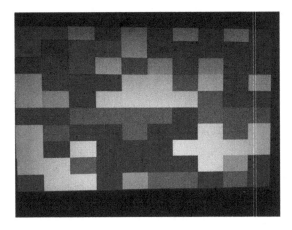

Fig. 2. Simulation image seen a the VGA 640×480 interface

adsorption, desorption, diffusion of CO_{ads} and the reaction by means of the representation in two dimensions of the catalytic surface. Each rectangle represents an active center (state of the *automata_catalysis* instance) and its corresponding color is explained as: red is CO_{ads}, blue is O_{ads}, green is CO_2 and white is a free active center. The Fig. 2 presents an image of how the simulation is seen by means of the proposed parallelizable model implemented in FPGA, the card is connected through an Arduino interface to a Matlab script, every change in the monitor is synchronized with each new value of $\phi_{CO}, \phi_O, \phi_E$ received.

In the second case, the partial covering behavior of the surface as a function of $\phi_{CO}, \phi_O, \phi_E$ is a graph constructed using the MATLAB script, the values taken from Rodríguez's work for the Sticking coefficient are $S_{CO} = 0.1$ and $S_O = 0.9$ and variation of the partial pressure $0.1 \leq y_{co} \leq 0.98$ [1].

In the Fig. 3 the results of the simulation are represented by the proposed parallel model, this model agrees with the results obtained in the works of Rodríguez [1] and Kovalyov [4], here the graph of the average value of ϕ_{CO} crosses the graph of the average value of ϕ_O in $y_{co} = 0.9$ where the oscillatory response reported in those jobs occurs.

In the Fig. 4 the behavior of ϕ_{CO} and ϕ_O on the surface is presented, the oscillatory behavior is typical at this point of the reaction and corresponds to the stability point from the point of view of the Langmuir Isotherm at the point of intersection between the curve of ϕ_{CO} and ϕ_O. The previous results are in line with the results obtained by Rodríguez [1].

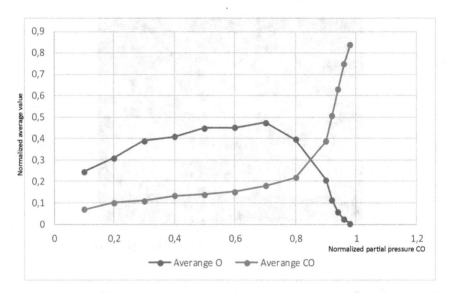

Fig. 3. Isotherm - Simulation results through the parallelizable proposal implemented in FPGA. Variable partial pressure $Sco = 0.01$, $So = 0.9$

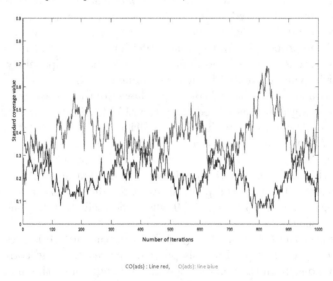

Fig. 4. Simulation results through the parallelizable proposal implemented in FPGA. Oscillations catalytic reaction. $Sco = 0.01$, $So = 0.9$

6   Conclusion

After the development of the parallelizable model proposed for the Heterogeneous catalytic process simulation using the mechanism of Langmuir-Hinshelwood, the following can be concluded:

- The field of implementation of parallel systems using platforms based on FPGA is a field that allows the development of hardware solutions as proposed, in the particular case it was possible to develop a proposal of a parallel model using simple logical operations and without the use of external memory.
- The results of the simulation of the heterogeneous catalytic reaction obtained by the proposed parallelizable model were compared with the results presented by Rodríguez and other authors, in such a way that it could be determined that the simulated reaction was consistent with that established in the experiments carried out. The cut-off point between phi_{CO} and phi_O corresponded to the value where the oscillations described in Rodríguez's work were presented.

References

1. Rodríguez, P., Diego, J.: Efecto de la baja dimensionalidad en la cinética de la oxidación catalítica del CO, Trabajo de grado para optar por el título de maestro en física, Director: Luis Demetrio López Carreño. Universidad Nacional de Colombia, departamento de física, año (2008)
2. Chopard, B., Droz, M.: Cellular Automata Modeling of Physical Systems. Cambridge University Press, Cambridge (1998). University of Geneva
3. Wu, X.-G., Kapral, R.: Catalytic CO oxidation on Pt surfaces: a lattice-gas cellualr automaton model. Grupo de física - química teórica. Departamento de química, Universidad de Toronto - Canada. Physica pp. 284–301, año (1992)
4. Kovalyov, E.V., Elokhin, V.I.: Statistical lattice model for the bimolecular reaction on dynamically changing surface of a body centered metal crystal. Kinetics ans Catalisis, 485–497 (2006)
5. Bandman, O.L., Kireeva, A.E.: Stochastic cellular automata simulation of oscillations an autowaves in reaction-diffusion systems. Numer. Anal. Appl. 8(3), 208–222 (2015). ISSN 1995-4239
6. Sharifulina, A., Elokhin, V.: Simulation of heterogeneous catalytic reaction by asynchronous cellular automata on multicomputer. In: Malyshkin, V. (ed.) PaCT 2011. LNCS, vol. 6873, pp. 204–209. Springer, Heidelberg (2011). https://doi.org/10.1007/978-3-642-23178-0_18. ISSN 0302-9743
7. Schiff, J.L.: Cellular Automata a Discrete View of the World. Wiley, Hoboken (2008). University of Auckland
8. Luenberger, D.G.: Introduction to Dynamic Systems, Theory, Models, and Applications. Wiley, New York (1979). Stanford University
9. Navarrete, G.: Introducción a las ecuaciones en diferencias. Fundación Universitaria Konrad Lorenz (2003)
10. Peralta, F.I., Duchén, G., Rubén, V.: Complejidad Lineal y Algoritmo de Berlekamp - Massey para la Construcción de Generadores de Secuencias Pseudoaleatorias, Instituto Politécnico Nacional, ESIME Unidad Culhuacan, Sección de estudios de Posgrado e Investigación, México D.F. México (2006)

Modeling the Traceability and Recovery Processes in the Closed-Loop Supply Chain and Their Effects

Milton M. Herrera[1,2(✉)], Lorena Vargas[3], and Daly Contento[3]

[1] Faculty of Economic Sciences, Universidad Militar Nueva Granada,
Bogotá, Colombia
[2] Università Degli Studi di Palermo, Palermo, Italy
miltonmauricio.herreraramirez@unipa.it
[3] Faculty of Engineering, Universidad Piloto de Colombia, Bogotá, Colombia
lorenavargasortiz@hotmail.com,
daly-contento@upc.edu.co

Abstract. The traceability and recovery plays a main role in the competitiveness of the food supply chain. The quality control of fruit manufacturing mainly depend of the traceability technologies used. In this sense, the quality control policies aimed at the traceability of products cause impact to production capacity and recovery. In the closed-loop supply chain (CLSC), wastes recovery and control in manufacturing contributes to improvement of the quality, as well as sustainable production. This article presents a dynamic behaviour analysis of production capacity, traceability and recovery on the peach-supply chain. Consequently, the study shows a simulation model based on system dynamics (SD) methodology. Results of simulation model explain why the delay in the waste recovery and traceability processes affect on the supply chain and its demand. The case of study is the peach supply chain, due partly to its great market potential for food industry.

Keywords: Traceability · Simulation · Closed-loop supply chain
Recovery

1 Introduction

The importance of the environment with respect to products and processes for sustainable manufacturing is increasingly recognized. One of the environmental problems that appear in the production processes is the waste of food, which is becoming a global problem; an important part of the cultivated food is not consumed in the last instance. According to the Food and Agriculture Organization (FAO), approximately one-third (by weight) of global food production is lost or wasted every year [1]. Such level of inefficiency has serious sustainability implications [2] increasingly important due to its impact economic, social and environmental impact [3], that food comes from agriculture and ends up as waste consumes energy during the life cycle stages [4]. The increase of waste in the food supply chain has involved new recovery processes, new quality standards and the need to generate additional control measures to avoid this waste [5].

© Springer Nature Switzerland AG 2018
J. C. Figueroa-García et al. (Eds.): WEA 2018, CCIS 915, pp. 328–339, 2018.
https://doi.org/10.1007/978-3-030-00350-0_28

The recovery processes modelling allows understanding the flows and resources such as information and material. Hence, CLSC management has emerged to address the waste recovery. In recent years, the formal modelling framework in CLSC has started to increase [6]. Different authors have measured sustainable supply chain management in a variety of ways [6–9]. Li et al. [10] examined the impact of corporate social responsibility on the sustainable supply chain through the perspective of governance policy and stakeholders. Also, Wang et al. [11] analysed the impact of subsidy policies on the development of the recycling and remanufacturing auto parts industry. This studies shown an active role of the investment incentives on recovery processes through industry policies. Despite the governance policy aimed at investment and competitiveness, the analysis of capacities in recovery and traceability to the sustainable supply chain management is needed. The traceability processes in CLSC allows measure the quality of products and their impact on customers. In this sense, the design of quality policies applied to improvement of supply chain allows increase the competitiveness of recovery industry, also mitigating food waste, positively impacting the three dimensions of sustainability (economic, social and environmental) [12].

The waste has a relationship with the processes of traceability and quality, which depend on the control instruments or the quality policies of the Colombian government, despite the fact that the government has been playing an important role in the promotion of waste recovery, the lack of waste control and traceability processes in the food supply chain limit the development in the recovery industry. The peach supply chain generated a significant amount of solid waste that reduces the quality of products and production capacity, according to the Ministry of Agriculture in the year 2017 Colombia produced 28,252 tons of peach, of which 8,729 were used for consumption national and only 4 tons were exported, this gives us as a result that only 31% of the total production is being consumed.

The insufficiency in the instruments of control for the industry affects the quality of the products and diminishes the capacity of competitiveness that have the products in the international market. This is evidenced in the production of the peach since in spite of having 69% of the available production, production that is not consumed nationally; the amount of imports is very high [13]. Figure 1 shows that peach is the fruit with the largest amount of imports in Colombia, presenting a market opportunity for national consumption and to grow competitively in the international market, therefore, it is necessary to improve the processes of control and traceability of waste to increase the quality of the internal product.

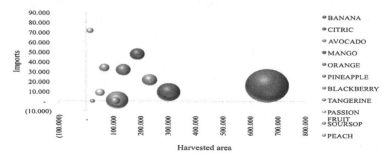

Fig. 1. Behavior of imported fruit vs. harvested area according to its production capacity

The simulation model provides experimental tools, which can be used to evaluate alternative sustainable policies. The SD methodology is one of the more practical ways of reproducing the behaviour of the system targets, as well as an adequate analysis tool [14, 15]. Among the different approaches available to assess the sustainable supply chain management problem [16, 17], SD methodology contribute to feedback modelling. Some studies have used SD modelling in reverse logistics and production recovery [11, 18]. Also, some researches on SD modelling in supply chain management focused on capacity planning of the remanufacturing networks and CLSC with recycling [19]. This study presents a SD model that allows understand the behaviour in the peach supply chain as from a closed-loop perspective. The propose of this modelling is support strategic decision based on better understand the impact of product quality and traceability time on the CLSC performance.

The rest of this paper is organized as follows. In the next section shows the literature review about CLSC management. The dynamic hypothesis and the simulation model are described in Sect. 3. The results of simulation model are analysed in Sect. 4. Finally, Sect. 5 presents the most relevant concluding remarks.

2 Literature Review

Food waste is described as waste or lost food products, which were initially intended for human consumption, except for those that were intended for animal feed (excluding pet food) [20]. The waste of food affects several sectors worldwide, one of them is the economic one, since within the factors they use to measure their growth is the environmental impact related to production, focusing on energy consumption and issues related to the climate change. Therefore, in any production process the energy used must be quantified to avoid excess production of fruits that will not be consumed properly and that their waste can drastically affect the environment [21].

The reduction of food waste is one of the main objectives established by the United Nations to achieve a more sustainable world by the year 2030. To realize this goal, three main areas of food waste generation have been identified: the deterioration of the product during logistics operations, by products of food processing and consumer perception of quality and safety [22]. The causes of food waste in the processing sector were classified as follows: losses resulting from processing operations and quality assurance, and products that do not meet the quality demands of the trade [23]. Other factors contributing to food waste included inventory control (where internal "sell-by dates" were reached), non- compliance of the packaging with market requirements, damages to packaging and product returns. Losses and waste in the food supply chain are inevitable; however, not irreducible [24].

One of the strategies that have been proposed for the reduction of food waste is the design of sustainable food supply chains, but due to the population increase it is increasingly difficult. Maintaining global food security requires more sustainable food production and a significant reduction of waste before and after harvest, therefore, it is important to evaluate each of the processes that are carried out to produce food. The fruit, one of the most important processes is the time of harvest where waste can be reduced along the supply chain, in order to increase the quality of the fruit.

Additionally, it is important to evaluate fruit maturity in time, predicting the possible date of harvest, enhancing agricultural practices and allowing the final product to arrive fresher and with higher quality to the consumer [25].

The search for sustainability depends on all the contributors to the food supply chains, including the agricultural and industrial sectors, as well as producers, retailers, final consumers [26], and government entities. The government intervention has a high degree of importance in the behaviors of the supply chains in the context of the sustainability of the environment and public health [27]. Thus, the design agricultural policy plays an important role to improve the food supply chain. In this sense, one of the policies that has been used for the reduction of food waste during primary production and the procedure is the reuse of food discarded directly as food or indirectly as animal feed [20].

Several studies show that the improper waste disposal constitutes a risk to human health [28]. The sustainable development is a dynamic process, which improving the quality of life [29]. The CLSC can improve the product life cycle through of the new traceability and design processes. Therefore, the CLSC design is needed. In this sense, more research is needed to investigate the decision making process in the complex and adaptive supply chain system [7, 30, 31]. Consequently, the cooperation among partnering companies in sustainable supply chain is needed. Several types of performance indicators used to assessment the quality and cooperation in supply chain. The traceability processes allow improving the quality on the supply chain [32]. Also, Bueno-Solano and Cedillo-Campos [33] studied the dynamic impact on global supply chain performance in term of security and efficient movement of goods.

In the case of supply chain management many studies have presented planning alternative [17], green marketing [34, 35], government intervention [36, 37], network design [38, 39] and collaboration capacity [40]. The supply chain management involve relationships between different disciplines: natural and social sciences, as well as the interdisciplinary nature evident from the variety of fields [31]. These relationships show the interaction between sustainability and supply chain through of the policies and operations analysis.

The supply chain management take into account three dimensions of sustainable development: economic, environmental and social [41]. Frostenson and Prenkert [42] analyzed the supply chain management in term of a complex network. This network perspective implied difficulties to control due to the structure of multiple supply chains. The complex interaction of supply chain involves various drivers as well as impacts on customers demand. Gupta and Palsule [8] defined supply chain as a set of practices that include environmental impact, value chain for each product, and product life cycle. In this sense, the product life cycle depend of the design, recycling and disposal activities. Fleury and Davies [43] assessed the lifecycle of the mining and metal sector as well as the recycling, reuse and remanufacture processes.

In the CLSC literature, several problematic aspects related to management and planning have been identified [44–46]. In this sense, Vlachos et al. [45] developed a simulation model for dynamic capacity planning of remanufacturing in CLSC. This study analyzed the recovery obligation imposed by government policies and the "green image" effect on customer demand. The SD methodology is used to model reverse logistics problems, which allows better understand the flow of used products [18].

Other studies shows the investment incentives effect on sustainable supply chain diffusion and planning in Chinese Industry [47, 48]. This paper developed a simulation model to better understand the delay effects of waste recovery and traceability processes on customer demand.

3 Model Structure

According to Sterman [49] four stages are used to develop SD model: the conceptualization of system, formulation, evaluation and implementation. This section presents model structure used the SD methodology. Section 3.1 maps a causal loop diagram (CLD) for represents the relationships among traceability and recovery capacities and their effects on quality control (conceptualization). Section 3.2 shows the stock-and-flow diagram used to assesses the closed-loop supply chain. The mathematical formulation of the model is presents in Sect. 3.3 (formulation).

3.1 Dynamic Hypothesis

To help determine the impact of traceability processes on the image and quality in peach supply chain, a dynamic hypothesis was utilized. The cyclical structures of feedback loops contribute to present the causal relationships of the variables that describe the behavior of dynamic hypothesis through CLD [33]. Figure 2 shows the dynamic hypothesis that describes the behavior of traceability and recovery capacities. The balancing loop (B1) presents quality image of customers, which depends on production and recovery capacities affecting the peach demand. The balancing loop (B2) shows the quality policy effects on improvement of traceability program and production capacities. The next balancing loop (B3) describes recovery capacity effect on quality image of customers. In the loops B2 and B3 represent the interaction relations between traceability and recovery policies in the manufacture of products based on fruits.

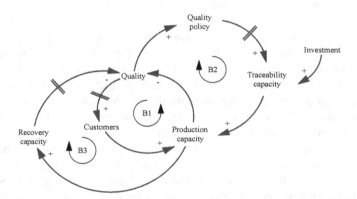

Fig. 2. CLD for represents the effects of traceability capacities and recovery and relationships with quality control.

3.2 Stock and Flow Diagram

For the model here proposed, three subsystems were identified. The first was the structure of customers demand; the second structure shows the peach supply chain, and finally the CLSC represented in the recovery capacity. This research used the stock-and-flow diagram as illustrated in Fig. 3. The dimensional structure of simulation model to each variable is also evaluated according to [50].

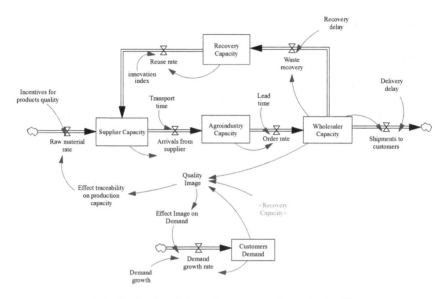

Fig. 3. Stock-and-flow diagram to evaluate the CLSC

The structure of supply chain depends on the number of intermediaries. So, waste also depends on the number of intermediaries [51], however this study shows the main intermediaries and their focus in recovery capacity. In this sense, the modeling was based on studies proposed by [15, 44, 52]. Although supply chain are considered complex systems, the structure proposed is a first basic model capable to measure the impact of recovery and traceability capacities.

3.3 Mathematical Model

The designed model includes changes in decision rules (policies) that affect the recovery capacity in the supply chain, which cause discrepancy. For the case of study, the discrepancy is the GAP between the desired capacity of recovery and the current capacity. The capacity of recovery is determine by the waste recovery rate. The waste recovery rate (WR) was calculated taking into account desired recovery capacity (DRC), wholesaler capacity (WC) and the time to recovery (TR), as shown in Eq. (1).

$$WR = (DRC - WC)/TR \qquad (1)$$

Other equations were used to find the provider's capacity, which is determined by subtracting the raw material rate minus arrivals from supplier. To find the agroindustry capacity subtract the supplier's arrivals minus the order rate, and to find the wholesaler capacity subtract the order rate minus the shipments to customers minus the waste recovery.

4   Results of Simulation Model

4.1   Quality Control

The proposed model takes into account the traceability effect on the quality perception due to the impact of the waste recovery delay. The product quality principally depends of the traceability processes, which plays a role important in waste recovery processes. Thus, the simulation experiment shows the low-and-high delay effect on waste recovery processes. Figure 4 shows the behavior of quality image that presented an increase of the perception on quality of customers demand due to the low delay in waste recovery processes (effect 2). In contrast, the high delay produces a decrease of the perception on quality of customers demand (effect 1). This confirms the importance of creating policies that make it possible to speed up the recovery of waste in the production chain, which in this way improves quality in relation to the end customer, and therefore the production process will also improve.

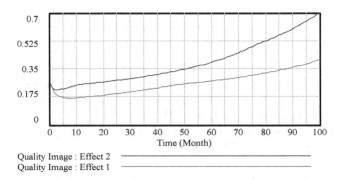

Fig. 4.   Behavior of quality control caused by delays in recovery processes

4.2   Traceability

The increase of traceability effect on production capacity is caused by low delay in waste recovery processes, which allows investment incentives in traceability technologies, as shows Fig. 5 (effect 2). Therefore, the traceability and recovery processes in CLSC involve effects on production capacity and investment policies. As in the previous analysis, the results show that with less delay in waste recovery, traceability is greater and this in turn has a positive influence on the proposed policies, since it encourages external investment that improves the process of production of the supply chain that is under study. This confirms the structure of CLD obtained by [32].

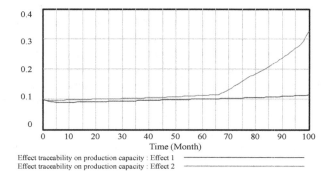

Fig. 5. Behavior of traceability effect on production capacity

4.3 Recovery Capacity

The delays in waste recovery processes affect to the capacity of remanufacturing in CLSC, as shown in Fig. 6. So, a lower recovery capacity is better to quality perception due the traceability processes. Results showed that the introduction of quality policy increased waste recovery and allows the expansion of peach supply chain. As from the foregoing that in order to optimize a supply chain it is important that all the processes involved, including the capacity for recovery, have an effective development time that does not delay the other processes that are intrinsically involved.

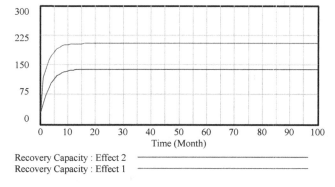

Fig. 6. Behavior of recovery capacity with changes in the recovery time

5 Concluding Remarks

Based on the simulation results, the quality perception plays a role important in supply chain capacities. As a result, this study showed the importance of the recovery and traceability processes that affect on quality perception. The developed model agrees with the work done by [32] where it indicates that the traceability processes allow to improve the quality in the supply chain and therefore improve the production capacity of the peach. Additional is established that a greater recovery of waste, creates the need to generate new quality standards and the need to control additional operations to avoid the increase of the waste generated by the supply chain of specific products, in this case of the peach [5]. An agreement is also reached with others studies where it is indicated that the quality of the product depends mainly on the processes of traceability, which performs an important role in waste recovery processes [15].

The developed model can be used to analyse the measure of the performance of the fruit supply chain in the terms of sustainable alternative policies, through the creation of policies that help to minimize the amount of food and to mitigate the impact In addition, this study can be useful for making policy decisions regarding the dynamics of CLSC. An extension of this study could find the impact of the traceability and recovery processes on the product price in CLSC. Finally, this document has a contribution to the model framework as well as to the CLSC design.

Acknowledgments. The authors would like to thank the anonymous reviewers for their helpful comments that helped improve the content of the paper. We would also like to acknowledge the comments of the Professor J. Orjuela.

References

1. FAOSTAT: Database of Country Indicators, Rome (2017)
2. Tostivint, C., de Veron, S., Jan, O., et al.: Measuring food waste in a dairy supply chain in Pakistan. J. Clean. Prod. **145**, 221–231 (2017). https://doi.org/10.1016/j.jclepro.2016.12.081
3. Hoolohan, C., McLachlan, C., Mander, S.: Trends and drivers of end-use energy demand and the implications for managing energy in food supply chains: synthesising insights from the social sciences. Sustain. Prod. Consum. **8**, 1–17 (2016). https://doi.org/10.1016/j.spc.2016.06.002
4. Abeliotis, K., Lasaridi, K., Costarelli, V., Chroni, C.: The implications of food waste generation on climate change: the case of Greece. Sustain. Prod. Consum. **3**, 8–14 (2015). https://doi.org/10.1016/j.spc.2015.06.006
5. Pandey, P.K., Cao, W., Biswas, S., Vaddella, V.: A new closed loop heating system for composting of green and food wastes. J. Clean. Prod. **133**, 1252–1259 (2016). https://doi.org/10.1016/j.jclepro.2016.05.114
6. Brandenburg, M., Govindan, K., Sarkis, J., Seuring, S.: Quantitative models for sustainable supply chain management: developments and directions. Eur. J. Oper. Res. **233**, 299–312 (2014). https://doi.org/10.1016/j.ejor.2013.09.032
7. Seuring, S., Müller, M.: From a literature review to a conceptual framework for sustainable supply chain management. J. Clean. Prod. **16**, 1699–1710 (2008). https://doi.org/10.1016/j.jclepro.2008.04.020

8. Gupta, S., Palsule-Desai, O.D.: Sustainable supply chain management: review and research opportunities. IIMB Manag. Rev. **23**, 234–245 (2011). https://doi.org/10.1016/j.iimb.2011. 09.002
9. Hassini, E., Surti, C., Searcy, C.: A literature review and a case study of sustainable supply chains with a focus on metrics. Int. J. Prod. Econ. **140**, 69–82 (2012). https://doi.org/10. 1016/j.ijpe.2012.01.042
10. Li, Y., Zhao, X., Shi, D., Li, X.: Governance of sustainable supply chains in the fast fashion industry. Eur. Manag. J. **32**, 823–836 (2014). https://doi.org/10.1016/j.emj.2014.03.001
11. Wang, Y., Chang, X., Chen, Z., et al.: Impact of subsidy policies on recycling and remanufacturing using system dynamics methodology: a case of auto parts in China. J. Clean. Prod. **74**, 161–171 (2014). https://doi.org/10.1016/j.jclepro.2014.03.023
12. Gokarn, S., Kuthambalayan, T.S.: Analysis of challenges inhibiting the reduction of waste in food supply chain. J. Clean. Prod. **168**, 595–604 (2017). https://doi.org/10.1016/j.jclepro. 2017.09.028
13. Ministerio de Agricultura y Desarrollo Rural (2018) Agronet
14. Vargas, J., Herrera, M.M.: Comparación de ténicas de modelamiento para el control de procesos: un enfoque de aprendizaje con dinámica de sistemas. Inventum **18**, 37–48 (2015)
15. Herrera-Ramírez, M.M., Orjuela-Castro, J., Sandoval-Cruz, H., Martínez-Vargas, M.A. Modelado dinámico y estratégico de la cadena agroindustrial de frutas. Universidad Piloto de Colombia, Bogotá D.C. (2017)
16. Azadi, M., Jafarian, M., Farzipoor Saen, R., Mirhedayatian, S.M.: A new fuzzy DEA model for evaluation of efficiency and effectiveness of suppliers in sustainable supply chain management context. Comput. Oper. Res. **54**, 274–285 (2014). https://doi.org/10.1016/j.cor. 2014.03.002
17. Mele, F.D., Guillen-Gosalbez, G., Jimenez, L., Bandoni, A.: Optimal planning of the sustainable supply chain for sugar and bioethanol production. Comput. Aided Chem. Eng. **27**, 597–602 (2009). https://doi.org/10.1016/S1570-7946(09)70320-7
18. Sterman, J.D.: Systems Thinking and Modeling for a Complex World. McGraw-Hill, Boston (2000)
19. Kumar, S., Nigmatullin, A.: A system dynamics analysis of food supply chains - case study with non-perishable products. Simul. Model. Pract. Theory **19**, 2151–2168 (2011). https:// doi.org/10.1016/j.simpat.2011.06.006
20. Redlingshöfer, B., Coudurier, B., Georget, M.: Quantifying food loss during primary production and processing in France. J. Clean. Prod. **164**, 703–714 (2017). https://doi.org/ 10.1016/j.jclepro.2017.06.173
21. Mangmeechai, A.: The environmental life cycle assessment of agricultural sector in Thailand: EIO-LCA approach. Environ. Qual. Manag. **26**, 47–56 (2017). https://doi.org/10. 1002/tqem.21503
22. Orjuela, J., Herrera, M., Casilimas, W.: Impact analysis of transport capacity and food safety in Bogota (2015). https://doi.org/10.1109/WEA.2015.7370138
23. Raak, N., Symmank, C., Zahn, S., et al.: Processing- and product-related causes for food waste and implications for the food supply chain. Waste Manag. **61**, 461–472 (2017). https:// doi.org/10.1016/j.wasman.2016.12.027
24. Irani, Z., Sharif, A.M., Lee, H., et al.: Managing food security through food waste and loss: small data to big data. Comput. Oper. Res., 1–17 (2017). https://doi.org/10.1016/j.cor.2017. 10.007
25. Li, B., Emr, N., Malling, E., Me, K.: Advances in non-destructive early assessment of fruit ripeness towards defining optimal time of harvest and yield prediction—a review. Plants **7**, 3 (2018). https://doi.org/10.3390/plants7010003

26. Magalhães, V.S.M., Ferreira, L.M.D., Silva, C.: An overview on the research status of the problem of food loss and waste along food supply chains. In: Proceedings of the International Conference on Computers and Industrial Engineering, CIE (2017)
27. Ding, H., Wang, L., Zheng, L.: Collaborative mechanism on profit allotment and public health for a sustainable supply chain. Eur. J. Oper. Res. **267**, 478–495 (2018). https://doi.org/10.1016/j.ejor.2017.11.057
28. Besiou, M., Georgiadis, P., Van Wassenhove, L.N.: Official recycling and scavengers: symbiotic or conflicting? Eur. J. Oper. Res. **218**, 563–576 (2012). https://doi.org/10.1016/j.ejor.2011.11.030
29. Diabat, A., Kannan, D., Mathiyazhagan, K.: Analysis of enablers for implementation of sustainable supply chain management - a textile case. J. Clean. Prod. **83**, 391–403 (2014). https://doi.org/10.1016/j.jclepro.2014.06.081
30. Wu, Z., Pagell, M.: Balancing priorities: decision-making in sustainable supply chain management. J. Oper. Manag. **29**, 577–590 (2011). https://doi.org/10.1016/j.jom.2010.10.001
31. Linton, J.D., Klassen, R., Jayaraman, V.: Sustainable supply chains: an introduction. J. Oper. Manag. **25**, 1075–1082 (2007). https://doi.org/10.1016/j.jom.2007.01.012
32. Herrera Ramírez, M.M., Orjuela Castro, J.A.: Perspectiva de trazabilidad en la cadena de suministros de frutas: un enfoque desde la dinámica de sistemas. Ingeniería **19**, 63–84 (2014)
33. Bueno-Solano, A., Cedillo-Campos, M.G.: Dynamic impact on global supply chains performance of disruptions propagation produced by terrorist acts. Transp. Res. Part E Logist. Transp. Rev. **61**, 1–12 (2014). https://doi.org/10.1016/j.tre.2013.09.005
34. Liu, S., Kasturiratne, D., Moizer, J.: A hub-and-spoke model for multi-dimensional integration of green marketing and sustainable supply chain management. Ind. Mark. Manag. **41**, 581–588 (2012). https://doi.org/10.1016/j.indmarman.2012.04.005
35. Brindley, C., Oxborrow, L.: Aligning the sustainable supply chain to green marketing needs: a case study. Ind. Mark. Manag. **43**, 45–55 (2014). https://doi.org/10.1016/j.indmarman.2013.08.003
36. Vermeulen, W.J.V., Kok, M.T.J.: Government interventions in sustainable supply chain governance: experience in Dutch front-running cases. Ecol. Econ. **83**, 183–196 (2012). https://doi.org/10.1016/j.ecolecon.2012.04.006
37. Zhang, H., Li, L., Zhou, P., et al.: Subsidy modes, waste cooking oil and biofuel: policy effectiveness and sustainable supply chains in China. Energy Policy **65**, 270–274 (2014). https://doi.org/10.1016/j.enpol.2013.10.009
38. Eskandarpour, M., Dejax, P., Miemczyk, J., Péton, O.: Sustainable supply chain network design: an optimization-oriented review. Omega (U.K.) **54**, 11–32 (2015). https://doi.org/10.1016/j.omega.2015.01.006
39. Chaabane, A., Ramudhin, A., Paquet, M.: Design of sustainable supply chains under the emission trading scheme. Int. J. Prod. Econ. **135**, 37–49 (2012). https://doi.org/10.1016/j.ijpe.2010.10.025
40. Van Hoof, B., Thiell, M.: Collaboration capacity for sustainable supply chain management: small and medium-sized enterprises in Mexico. J. Clean. Prod. **67**, 239–248 (2014). https://doi.org/10.1016/j.jclepro.2013.12.030
41. Beske, P., Land, A., Seuring, S.: Sustainable supply chain management practices and dynamic capabilities in the food industry: a critical analysis of the literature. Int. J. Prod. Econ. **152**, 131–143 (2014). https://doi.org/10.1016/j.ijpe.2013.12.026
42. Frostenson, M., Prenkert, F.: Sustainable supply chain management when focal firms are complex: a network perspective. J. Clean. Prod. **107**, 85–94 (2015). https://doi.org/10.1016/j.jclepro.2014.05.034

43. Fleury, A.M., Davies, B.: Sustainable supply chains-minerals and sustainable development, going beyond the mine. Resour. Policy **37**, 175–178 (2012). https://doi.org/10.1016/j.resourpol.2012.01.003
44. Georgiadis, P., Besiou, M.: Sustainability in electrical and electronic equipment closed-loop supply chains: a system dynamics approach. J. Clean. Prod. **16**, 1665–1678 (2008). https://doi.org/10.1016/j.jclepro.2008.04.019
45. Vlachos, D., Georgiadis, P., Iakovou, E.: A system dynamics model for dynamic capacity planning of remanufacturing in closed-loop supply chains. Comput. Oper. Res. **34**, 367–394 (2007). https://doi.org/10.1016/j.cor.2005.03.005
46. Savaskan, R.C., Bhattacharya, S., Van Wassenhove, L.N.: Closed-loop supply chain models with product remanufacturing. Manag. Sci. **50**, 239–252 (2004). https://doi.org/10.1287/mnsc.1030.0186
47. Tian, Y., Govindan, K., Zhu, Q.: A system dynamics model based on evolutionary game theory for green supply chain management diffusion among Chinese manufacturers. J. Clean. Prod. **80**, 96–105 (2014). https://doi.org/10.1016/j.jclepro.2014.05.076
48. Kuai, P., Li, W., Cheng, R., Cheng, G.: An application of system dynamics for evaluating planning alternatives to guide a green industrial transformation in a resource-based city. J. Clean. Prod. **104**, 403–412 (2015). https://doi.org/10.1016/j.jclepro.2015.05.042
49. Sterman, J.D.: Appropriate summary statistics for evaluating the historical fit of system dynamics models. Dynamica **10**, 51–66 (1984)
50. Sterman, J.D.: Business dynamics: Systems Thinking and Modeling for a Complex World. McGraw-Hill, New York City (2000)
51. Sachan, A., Sahay, B.S., Sharma, D.: Developing Indian grain supply chain cost model: a system dynamics approach. Int. J. Product. Perform. Manag. **54**, 187–205 (2005). https://doi.org/10.1108/17410400510584901
52. Orjuela-Castro, J., Herrera-Ramirez, M., Adarme-Jaimes, W.: Warehousing and transportation logistics of mango in Colombia: a system dynamics model. Rev. Fac. Ing. **26**, 71–85 (2017). https://doi.org/10.19053/01211129

A Markov-Monte Carlo Simulation Model to Support Urban Planning Decisions: A Case Study for Medellín, Colombia

Julián Andrés Castillo[1(✉)], Yony Fernando Ceballos[2],
and Elena Valentina Gutiérrez[2]

[1] Subsecretaría de Catastro, Secretaría de Gestión y Control Territorial,
Municipio de Medellín, Colombia
jandres.castillo@udea.edu.co
[2] Departamento de Ingeniería Industrial, Facultad de Ingeniería,
Universidad de Antioquia, Medellín, Colombia
{yony.ceballos,elena.gutierrez}@udea.edu.co

Abstract. The identification of properties and land destinations are key factors in urban planning decisions, especially in rapid-growing urbanized cities. This information is vital for cadaster matters, property taxes calculations, and therefore for the financial sustainability of a city. In this work we present a Markov-Monte Carlo simulation model to predict changes in land destinations. First, a Markov chain is established to identify the transition finite-state matrix of property destinations, and then a Monte Carlo simulation model is used to predict the changes. We present a case study for the city of Medellín, Colombia, using historical information from the cadaster office from 2004 to 2016. Results obtained allow identifying the urban areas with the larger number of changes. Moreover, these results provide support for urban planning decisions related to workforce sizing and visits sequences to the identified areas.

Keywords: Markov chains · Monte carlo simulation
Land destination · Urban planning

1 Introduction

In rapid-growing urbanized cities, the identification of properties and land destinations are key factors in urban planning decisions. The type of buildings and the use of land are input parameters for urban planning policies, they are used for property taxes calculations, and therefore they impact the financial sustainability of a given city [25]. Moreover, city growth is planned based on such information aiming to ensure access to basic services and dignified housing [13,27]. Thus, a proper identification and prediction of destination can support better urban planning decisions.

The city of Medellín (Colombia) is the second largest of the country with nearly 2.5 millions inhabitants [7], an urban area of 380.64 square kilometers,

© Springer Nature Switzerland AG 2018
J. C. Figueroa-García et al. (Eds.): WEA 2018, CCIS 915, pp. 340–351, 2018.
https://doi.org/10.1007/978-3-030-00350-0_29

and more than 960,000 registered properties [1]. The city uses a political division based on Agreement 64 of 2014, base for the territorial ordering plan (*Plan de Ordenamiento Territorial*, POT) [8], which defines 16 communes and five rural areas. In Medellín, properties and land destinations are classified by the cadastral office, known as Subsecretary of Cadastre (SSC), which uses an unique identifier for each property, known as cadastral registration, and assigns a code related to the land destination. Thereby, ten different codes are considered to classify land destinations. For example, if the destination is housing for people, the land use code is considered residential, if it is for product sales, is considered commercial, and so on for each of the ten destination types.

By law, the SSC must keep an updated report of properties and land destinations. In order to do so, an annual budget is assigned by the municipality council, and two key activities must be performed: first, SSC analysts identify which properties might present changes in their land destinations; second, once these properties are identified, SSC crews are assigned to visit them, and perform reviews that allow to confirm those changes. Currently, the first activity is completed by the interpolation of several data sets. However, the large volume of data, the interconnections between data sets, and the complexity to estimate changes of properties and land destinations, represent not only economic and financial challenges, but also computational difficulties. This problem faced by the SSC motivates an application of Markov-Monte Carlo simulation model to help the prediction of land use changes, and to support urban planning decisions in Medellín.

Similar problems have been studied in the literature using spatial approaches. In [21, 24, 28], authors develop an approximation with satellite images taking advantage of the characteristics of the LandSat TM images, and with the use of Markov chains, and even cellular automaton, they predict land use changes. Our study differs from previous described approaches in the use of quantitative and qualitative information of land destinations and not their geographical information. The use of alphanumeric data and not geographical information, provides an agile process instead of simulating over almost one million geographical data, which turns the present task into a complex process. The use of Markov Chains and Monte Carlo simulation (MCMC) allows simple approximations for more realistic statistical modeling. MCMC methods provide support to analyze complex problems using generic software. MCMC is essentially a Monte Carlo simulation integration using Markov chains for the extraction of required distributions samples, and the use of averages to approximate expectations. The Markov chain Monte Carlo draws these samples by executing an ingeniously constructed Markov chain for a long time [12]. MCMC emerged in the statistical physics literature, and it has been used since then for spatial statistics and image analysis. It has had a deep effect on Bayesian statistics, and most of the applications concur in the field of Bayesian inference [12].

The most common MCMC applications in the literature are the Metropolis-Hastings algorithm [3] and the Gibbs sampler [2]. Recently, the work of [29] focused their efforts on combining these two types of approximations to reach a solution in their work, and authors used a hybrid MCMC to model uncertainty. The work presented in [19] uses a binary MCMC procedure for forecasting large and small regional fires status on an annual basis. Other type of applications for MCMC are the Bayesian inference which in most cases requires approximating the posterior distribution by Markov chain Monte Carlo sampling [22]. Other studies use Subset Simulation, a Markov Chain Monte Carlo technique used to estimate rare event probabilities in physical models, more efficiently than Monte Carlo simulation. Subset Simulation is applied to estimate the probability of failure in nonlinear elasto-plastic finite element problems [14]. The literature shows that the MCMC method is vastly used in the literature and in this study, we use MCMC to predict the changes of properties and land destinations in Medellin, Colombia. To do so, we focus our approach in simulation and we use the idea of the Markov matrix to identify probabilities.

In this paper, we propose a Markov-Monte Carlo simulation model to predict changes in land destinations. First, a Markov chain is established to identify the transition finite-state matrix of property destinations, and then a Monte Carlo simulation model is used to predict the changes. We present a case study for the city of Medellín, Colombia, using historical information from the cadaster office from 2004 to 2016. The case study allows evidencing how the use of our approach helps to improve the use of the government funds in the local cadastre by optimizing the resources used in the field visits of the cadastre crews. The remainder of this paper is structured as follows. Section 2 presents the problem definition and the characteristics of the case study. Section 3 describes the Markov-Monte Carlo simulation model proposed. Section 4 presents the results of the case study. Finally, Sect. 5 summarizes the main findings and concludes the paper outlining future work opportunities.

2   Problem Definition

Colombian land registry regulations are based in the Law 14 of 1983 [5] and Resolution 70 of 2011 [16]. These laws define cadastre as the inventory or census, fully updated and classified, of properties belongings to the State and private individuals. The objective of this inventory is to achieve correct physical, legal, economic and fiscal identification of land destinations. By law, in Colombia cadastre must keep physical updated information, and part of this corresponds to the correct identification of properties and land destinations that are registered by cadastral changes in the data base as defined by the local guideline. Resolution 70 of 2011 defines a change in destination as a mutation on the property and defines cadastral destinations in Colombia in ten types, which are classified by the SSC in codes from 1 to 10, as follows:

1. Residential
2. Commercial and Services
3. Industrial
4. Government Properties
5. Road Networks

6. Miner
7. Recreational or Sports
8. Public Areas
9. Plain Land (lots)
10. Complementary

This classification is based on the main activity for which the property is used or destined, and it is used for the billing of property taxes of Medellín. In this paper, we use the word "*destinations*" instead of the words "*land use*", because the second one refers, in most of the literature, to the use of land as a territory or polygon. In this work, the use of land includes buildings as a whole where, the use of construction prevails over the territory, as defined by the local law of Medellín. The cadastral information of properties destination is used in the present work to identify and predict the changes of use or destination in the city, according to the commune in which the property is located. The city of Medellín presents an urban political division as shown in Fig. 1, which includes a numbering for the communes that goes from 1 to 16, where the center of the city is represented by the commune 10. Socioeconomic registers show that communes 11 and 14population with high economic capacity, while communes of the eastern and western periphery of the city present a population with lower economic capacity [7].

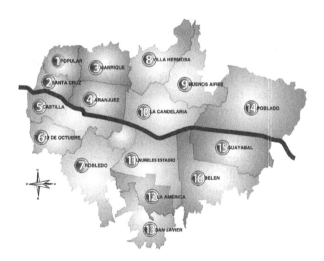

Fig. 1. Communes distribution in Medellín, Colombia

As mentioned previously, the SSC of Medellín must keep an updated report of properties and land destinations. For doing so, the SSC must use the resources assigned by the municipality council efficiently, in order to complete the two key activities of the process: data analysis for the estimation of land destination changes, and assignment and routing of crews to perform visits to those properties. Both activities, the data analysis and the property visit, use a set of components to determine whether a property presents a change in its destination or not. The components are: public services facilities, construction licenses granted, property sales and leases, and cadastral mutations.

The identification and update of properties and land destinations is a vital process for the financial sustainability of Medellín. According to Agreement 66 of 2017 [4], property values and therefore property taxes are calculated based on land destinations. Consequently, a structured method to identify changes in land destinations, can provide support to perform better properties identification, and to complete fair and equitable taxes calculations.

3   A Markov-Monte Carlo Simulation Model

To solve the problem described above, we first build a transition state matrix to identify land destinations. Then, we integrate the matrix within a Monte Carlo simulation model. Next we provide a description of each step.

3.1   Transition State Matrix

Based on the methodologies proposed by [10, 15], we build a hybrid model mixing Monte Carlo simulation with Markov chains to predict the use of a property for the year 2017, with the information of properties registered for the previous year. Based on the previous characterizations of land destinations and the historical information from the cadastral database from 2004 to 2016, we calculate the probability of properties destination changes. For each commune, and according to the average of the years between 2004 and 2016, we quantify the number of properties that changed, the relation between proprieties that do not change and those that changed in every commune using cumulative averages per year as shown on Eq. (1).

We create a matrix with the number of properties that change their use for each couple of years, starting with years 2004–2005 and ending in 2015–2016, for a total of 12 matrix that will form the basis for the probability change matrix. The matrix of Markov transition probabilities is built based on Eq. (1), where M is the resulting probability matrix, K including indexes i and j correspond to the data of the annualized partial change of used matrix, with their respective row positions m and column n, and P corresponds to the sum of properties identified during the process of destination changes.

$$M = \sum_{i=2004}^{2016} K(i,j) \Big/ \sum_{i=2004}^{2016} P(m,n) \tag{1}$$

After the calculation of the transition probabilities matrix, we find that states 5 and 6 are absorbent (Value $= 1$) and the other states are recurrent (Value > 0) and is shown in Table 1. To find the steady-state probabilities (no time dependent), we load in Matlab a custom-made function described in Algorithm 1.

Table 1. State transition matrix for the uses of the properties of Medellín

Use	1	2	3	4	5	6	7	8	9	10
1	0.99788	0.00133	0.00036	0.00028	0.00000	0.00000	0.00001	0.00001	0.00008	0.00005
2	0.00281	0.92835	0.00131	0.00043	0.00000	0.00000	0.00000	0.00000	0.00003	0.06707
3	0.01194	0.00780	0.89168	0.00041	0.00000	0.00000	0.00002	0.00002	0.00004	0.08809
4	0.00558	0.00999	0.00046	0.98362	0.00000	0.00000	0.00012	0.00000	0.00023	0.00000
5	0.00000	0.00000	0.00000	0.00000	1.00000	0.00000	0.00000	0.00000	0.00000	0.00000
6	0.00000	0.00000	0.00000	0.00000	0.00000	1.00000	0.00000	0.00000	0.00000	0.00000
7	0.00578	0.01156	0.00000	0.00000	0.00000	0.00000	0.98266	0.00000	0.00000	0.00000
8	0.15789	0.00000	0.00000	0.00000	0.00000	0.00000	0.00000	0.78947	0.05263	0.00000
9	0.11162	0.01223	0.00612	0.00612	0.00000	0.00000	0.00153	0.00000	0.85780	0.00459
10	0.00016	0.00006	0.00001	0.00000	0.00000	0.00000	0.00000	0.00000	0.00002	0.99976

Table 2. Variable codification and steady-state

Use	Variable	Steady-state
Residential	Res	0.1014
Commercial	Com	0.0025
Industrial	Ind	0.0005
Equipment	Equ	0.0018
Communication Roads	Via	0.0000
Miner	Min	0.0000
Recreational	Rec	0.0001
Public space	Esp	0.0000
Lots	Lot	0.0002
Complementary	Com	0.8935

The Algorithm is defined with the following notation: Q is the transition matrix of the Markov Chain. We use the algorithm of state space reduction to compute the stationary distributions of Q. P is a copy of Q in which the algorithm updates the values. Parameter $n8$ is the number of rows of Q, $n1$ and $n2$ are the indexes of the matrix. Values x and y are symbolic matrices with $n8$ rows and one column, while $n3$, $n4$, $n5$ and $n6$ are data updates for the array result called $y2$. Each of the uses is recorded as the variables in Table 2 and they are applied to identify the steady-states that are shown in the same table. The data of the variables corresponding to Roads and Mining are not taken into account, since they are absorbing states.

3.2   Simulation Model

We implemented the simulation model with a function. The simulation algorithm begins with two input parameters in the function which are: the commune (geographical location of the property) and the current use of the property.

Algorithm 1. Steady-state calculation

```
1: function STEADY-STATE(Q,ns)
2:     syms z, P ⟵ Q, [ ns ,ms ] ⟵ size(P), n ⟵ ns, n8 ⟵ n
3:     while n8 > 1 do
4:         if n1 < n8 - 1 then
5:             while n2 < n8 - 1 do
6:                 P(n1,n2) ⟵ P(n1,n2)+ P(n1,n8)*P(n8,n2)/(1-P(n8,n8))
7:                 n2 ⟵ n2+1
8:             end while
9:             n1 ⟵ n1+1
10:        else
11:            n8 ⟵ n8-1
12:        end if
13:    end while
14:    y ⟵ sym(ones(n,1)), n3 ⟵ 1
15:    if n3 < n then
16:        y ⟵ sym(ones(n,3))
17:        while n5 < n3 do
18:            x(n5) ⟵ y(n5)
19:            n3 v⟵ n3+1
20:        end while
21:        z ⟵ sum(x.*P(1:n3,n3+1)) / (sym(1)-P(n3+1,n3+1))
22:        y(n3+1) ⟵ z / (sym(1)+z)
23:        while n6 < n3 do
24:            x(n5) ⟵ y(n5)
25:            n3 v⟵ n3+1
26:        end while
27:        z ⟵ sum(x.*P(1:n3,n3+1)) / (sym(1)-P(n3+1,n3+1))
28:        y(n3+1) ⟵ z / (sym(1)+z)
29:    else
30:        y2 ⟵ y
31:    end if
32: end function
```

According to the commune, the probability of property change is defined using an uniform random variable. Such value is compared with the commune accumulated probability reference as "hit or miss" method [26]. If the random value is within the range of variation, the property is marked true, otherwise is marked false and its destination is preserved. If and only if the change is marked true, the algorithm proceeds to identify the use of the property. For doing so, it creates a new uniform random variable and compares it with the first state values in Table 1, that corresponds to the transition matrix. If the random value is found within the range, the property changes its destination, otherwise, it is compared against the accumulated probability of the second state. If the value is within the range, this property is marked as destination change towards this new use, and so on, until the function reach the last cumulative probability and determine the destination change.

The code metrics are provided by the embedded code analysis in Visual Studio 2015, where a method is created with a reference to the MsExcel file for the execution of the code analysis. The method generates the following results: Cyclomatic complexity index [20]: 18; Inheritance degree: 0; Class clusters: 2, and Code lines: 320. According to previous metrics, the method has a good performance to complete the algorithm, with a computing time of 322 min to process an instance with 961,000 properties, evaluated for 12 simulations. The method was implemented on a computer with a Intel Core i7 processor (32 GB in RAM) running under Windows 10 64-bit.

3.3   Verification of Convergence of the Model

In this work is important to evaluate the convergence of the model. This process is one of the most difficult steps in the modeling Markov-Monte Carlo simulation [29]. Several methods have been proposed in the literature: tracing the steps of the sample [17], the method of variance reduction [9], and the spectral analysis approach [23]. A detailed review and comparison of methods for verification of convergence can be found in [6,22]. Despite these convergence verification techniques, in general there is no guarantee that a Markov chain will explore the entire space of the target distribution in finite time [18]. Most of the existing convergence verification methods are based on the detection of non-convergence rather than convergence. In this work, we verify convergence empirically, by comparing whether the subsequent data inferred from the chain in the final result of the simulation are consistent. In the initial stage, a Markov chain may not reach steady state or equilibrium. It is often suggested that the first samples must be discarded and not used for subsequent statistical inference. There is no systematic and universal way to calculate the number of samples that should be discarded. The author in [11] suggests that in many cases discarding initial samples is sufficient. In this work, the first two samples are discarded and therefore, only the remaining 10 simulations were taken into consideration.

4   Results: Case Study

Results of the simulation are interpreted in a one-year time cycle, because each of the cumulative processes performed in this study were taken from annualized changes in use, therefore, results of the simulations correspond to annualized values. By carrying out 12 simulations, each of them corresponds to 12 cumulative years of cadastral changes, which will be used in the next cadastral update process for the city of Medellín. Table 3 shows the number of changes from the initial destination (code for the rows) to the final destination of the simulation process (code for the columns). Table 4 shows the amount of changes in use per commune.

Table 3 shows the number of destination changes as a result of the simulation process. As seen in Table 4, major changes were set in communes 14, 16 and 10. These communes required in year 2017, a larger assignment of workforce in order

Table 3. Total changes per destination

	1	2	3	4	5	6	7	8	9	10
1	606093	1763	465	370	0	0	0	0	11	13
2	876	84974	398	144	0	0	0	0	0	0
3	155	105	6798	3	0	0	0	0	0	0
4	137	274	17	2045	0	0	0	0	4	0
5	0	0	0	0	5249	0	0	0	0	0
6	0	0	0	0	0	2	0	0	0	0
7	0	3	0	0	0	0	69	0	191	0
8	490	0	0	0	0	0	0	981	0	2294
9	2352	261	142	130	0	0	0	0	15297	0
10	145	63	17	0	0	0	0	0	0	209485

Table 4. Total Properties with destination change

Commune	Residential	Commercial	Industrial	Government	Lots	Complementary
1	66	11	5	3	4	3
2	33	17	4	4	21	11
3	65	32	7	11	2	8
4	58	29	15	16	16	49
5	42	44	11	9	7	119
6	45	23	8	8	7	70
7	310	155	55	40	17	363
8	101	39	12	17	15	51
9	341	120	39	36	10	232
10	389	129	99	60	25	292
11	270	302	130	78	13	70
12	96	191	56	37	12	89
13	177	92	39	27	7	100
14	1044	536	376	164	19	322
15	199	256	28	11	12	63
16	313	373	110	96	12	209
50	82	12	4	1	2	1
60	210	54	17	5	0.0	128
70	61	7	6	3	0.0	10
80	119	33	12	12	1	113
90	134	14	6	9	4	4

to complete the visits to each of the properties, and to verify land destination changes. Table 5 shows the types of land destinations that presented the largest changes. As it can be seen, most of the third part of the changes occurs when the

Table 5. Changes showing percentage

Destination	Total changes	Percent
Residential	4155	38.39%
Commercial and Services	2469	22.81%
Industrial	1039	9.60%
Government properties	647	5.98%
Plain land (lots)	206	1.90%
Complementary	2307	21.32%
Total	10823	100.00%

new destination is Residential. Another high proportion of destination changes occur in the Commercial and Services type, with more than one fifth of the total changes. These two destination types (Residential and Commerce) are the main categories in which other properties tend to change. Not far behind is the Complementary destination, with another fifth of the changes, showing that parking and storage is the third new destination that emerges in this study. The rest of land destinations represent less than 18% of the changes as shown in Table 5.

5   Conclusions

In this work, we have presented a Markov-Monte Carlo simulation model to predict changes in land destinations in Medellín, Colombia. The model provides support to SSC, to keep up to date the inventory of the properties, and to minimize the gap between reality and the information stored in the cadastral database. The model first establishes a Markov chain to identify the transition finite-state matrix of property destinations. Then, a Monte Carlo simulation model is used to predict the changes. The model was evaluated with data from the cadaster office 2004 to 2016.

According to the results, communes 14, 16 and 10 are the ones with the largest destination changes. Furthermore, the model also allowed identifying the type of land destinations with the largest changes. More than one third of the changes occur when properties change to Residential use. Commercial and Service destination is the second land use with more than one fifth of the total changes, and the Complementary land use the third with another fifth of the total changes. These results were used by the SSC in 2017 and 2018, to assign and route crews to visit properties and verify changes in land destinations.

The information obtained from this simulation model is currently used for the capture of valuation information of the city properties, by the Medellín Real Estate Observatory "Observatorio Inmobiliario de Medellín" (OIME). The identification of land destinations by commune, provides a guide for the identification of future new constructions or demolitions. The capture of land destination changes affects directly the city treasury department, because land destinations are a fundamental part for the collection of property taxes.

Future work includes the expansion of the scope of the model, since the cadastral information presents a combination of Use and Type of land destinations, where the Type corresponds to a sub-use or sub-destination of the property. The aim is to obtain the current 83 categories used by the SSC, and to expand the spectrum of land destinations and be as specific as possible. It is estimated that this type of detailed approach can generate many absorbing states. This is due to the existence of land destinations that do not change over time in the cadastral database. Example of these cases include shopping centers, residential buildings or recreational parks.

Acknowledgments. The authors acknowledge the support from the Subsecretaría de Catastro of Medellín, for providing the necessary information for this study.

References

1. Berrio Marín, J.A.: Noventa Años De Historia De Catastro Medellín. In: Comité Permanente sobre el Catastro en Iberoamérica (CPCI) (ed.) IX Simposio sobre el Catastro en Iberoamérica, del Comité Permanente del Catastro en Iberoamérica (CPCI) y Celebración 90 años de Catastro Medellín, p. 36. Comité Permanente sobre el Catastro en Iberoamérica (CPCI), IX Simposio sobre el Catastro en Iberoamérica, del Comité Permanente del Catastro en Iberoamérica (CPCI) y Celebración 90 años de Catastro Medellín., Medellin, Colombia (2016). https://www.medellin.gov.co/irj/go/km/docs/pccdesign/medellin/Temas/Catastro/Publicaciones/SharedContent/Documentos/2016/IXSimposioCatastro/4M90AnosCatastroMedellinALBERTOBERRIOMARIN.pdf
2. Casella, G., George, E.I.: Explaining the Gibbs sampler. Am. Stat. **46**(3), 167–174 (1992)
3. Chib, S., Greenberg, E.: Understanding the metropolis-hastings algorithm. Am. Stat. **49**(4), 327–335 (1995)
4. Concejo de Medellín: Acuerdo 66 de 2017: Estatuto tributario (2017). https://www.medellin.gov.co/irj/go/km/docs/pccdesign/medellin/Temas/Hacienda/Normas/SharedContent/Documentos/2017/Acuerdo066de2017-Medellin.pdf
5. Congreso de Colombia: Ley 14 de 1983 (1983)
6. Cowles, M.K., Carlin, B.P.: Markov chain Monte Carlo convergence diagnostics: a comparative review. J. Am. Stat. Assoc. **91**(434), 883–904 (1996). http://links.jstor.org/sici?sici=0162-1459%28199606%2991%3A434%3C883%3AMCMCCD%3E2.0.CO%3B2-X
7. DANE: Series de Población, Reloj Estadistico. Technical report, Departamento Administrativo Nacional de Estadística (DANE) (2016). http://www.dane.gov.co/index.php/estadisticas-por-tema/demografia-y-poblacion/series-de-poblacion
8. DAP, D.A.d.P.: Acuerdo 48: Plan de ordenamiento territorial de Medellín POT - 2014 (2014). https://www.medellin.gov.co/irj/portal/ciudadanos?NavigationTarget=navurl://474b42d2a001a412ed3117d306a43135
9. Gelman, A., Rubin, D.B.: Inference from iterative simulation using multiple sequences. Stat. Sci. **7**(4), 457–511 (1992)

10. Geyer, C.J.: Markov chain monte carlo lecture notes. Course notes, Spring Quarter (1998)
11. Geyer, C.J.: Markov Chain Monte Carlo Lecture Notes (2005)
12. Gilks, W.R., Richardson, S., Spiegelhalter, D.: Markov Chain Monte Carlo in Practice. CRC Press, Boca Raton (1995)
13. Grant, J., Tsenkova, S.: New Urbanism and Smart Growth Movements. Elsevier (2012)
14. Green, D.K.: Efficient Markov chain Monte Carlo for combined subset simulation and nonlinear finite element analysis. Comput. Methods Appl. Mech. Eng. **313**, 337–361 (2017)
15. Hillier, F.S., Lieberman, G.J.: Introduction to Operations Research, 9th edn. McGraw-Hill, New York (2010)
16. IGAC: Resolución 070 De 2011 (2011)
17. Kass, R.E., Carlin, B.P., Gelman, A., Neal, R.M.: Markov chain Monte Carlo in practice: a roundtable discussion. Am. Stat. **52**(2), 93–100 (1998). http://www.tandfonline.com/doi/abs/10.1080/00031305.1998.10480547
18. Lee, H.K.H.: Bayesian methods: a social and behavioral sciences approach. Am. Stat. **62**(4), 356 (2008). http://www.tandfonline.com/doi/abs/10.1198/000313008X370915
19. Magnussen, S.: A Markov chain Monte Carlo approach to joint simulation of regional areas burned annually in canadian forest fires. Comput. Electron. Agric. **66**(2), 173–180 (2009)
20. McCabe, T.J.: A complexity measure. IEEE Trans. Softw. Eng. **4**, 308–320 (1976)
21. Muller, M.R., Middleton, J.: A Markov model of land-use change dynamics in the Niagara Region, Ontario, Canada. Landsc. Ecol. **9**(2), 151–157 (1994)
22. Peltonen, J., Venna, J., Kaski, S.: Visualizations for assessing convergence and mixing of Markov chain Monte Carlo simulations. Comput. Stat. Data Anal. **53**(12), 4453–4470 (2009)
23. Raftery, A.E., Lewis, S.: How many iterations in the Gibbs sampler? In: Bayesian Statistics, pp. 763–773 (1992)
24. Reveshty, M.A.: The assessment and predicting of land use changes to urban area using multi-temporal satellite imagery and gis: a case study on Zanjan, iran (1984–2011). J. Geogr. Inf. Syst. **3**(04), 298 (2011)
25. Schwarz, N., Flacke, J., Sliuzas, R.: Modelling the impacts of urban upgrading on population dynamics. Environ. Model. Softw. **78**, 150–162 (2016). http://dx.doi.org/10.1016/j.envsoft.2015.12.009
26. Sobol, I.: A Primer for the Monte Carlo Method. Taylor & Francis, London (1994). https://books.google.com.co/books?id=P5jWKfR91OkC
27. Wey, W.M., Hsu, J.: New urbanism and smart growth: toward achieving a smart National Taipei University District. Habitat Int. **42**, 164–174 (2014)
28. Xia, H., Liu, H., Zheng, C.: A Markov-Kalman model of land-use change prediction in XiuHe Basin, China. In: Bian, F., Xie, Y., Cui, X., Zeng, Y. (eds.) GRMSE 2013. CCIS, vol. 399, pp. 75–85. Springer, Heidelberg (2013). https://doi.org/10.1007/978-3-642-41908-9_8
29. Zhang, J., Tang, W.H., Zhang, L., Huang, H.: Characterising geotechnical model uncertainty by hybrid Markov chain Monte Carlo simulation. Comput. Geotech. **43**, 26–36 (2012)

A Coalitional Game for Achieving Emergent Cooperation in Ad Hoc Networks Through Sympathy and Commitment

Julian F. Latorre[1], Juan Pablo Ospina[1(✉)] [iD], and Jorge E. Ortiz[1,2]

[1] Research Group TLÖN, National University of Colombia, Bogotá, Colombia
{jflatorreo,jpospinalo,jeortizt}@unal.edu.co
[2] Computing Systems and Industrial Engineering Department,
National University of Colombia, Bogotá, Colombia

Abstract. Cooperation among nodes is fundamental for ad hoc networks. In such systems, there is no centralized control, and the network components require self-organize themselves to accomplish their individual and collective goals. These conditions make necessary include cooperation mechanisms during the network operation for improving the system capacity for solving problems through collective actions. In this article, socially inspired computing is used to propose a coalitional game based on the concepts of sympathy and commitment with the purpose of achieving emergent cooperation in ad hoc networks. The results show cooperation may emerge even in scenarios in which agents do not have a cooperative strategy, producing a better network performance and a suitable resources distribution.

Keywords: Ad hoc networks · Trust · Cooperation
Socially inpired computing

1 Introduction

A common requirement in ad hoc networks is to achieve cooperation among nodes, users, and applications to accomplish networking task like routing, resources sharing and security [9, 16]. Since nodes contribute with their resources, such as energy, memory, and processing for the system benefit, they should be able to use the resources provided by others to achieve their own goals. In this regard, it is essential to encourage nodes, users and applications to participate in networking tasks because higher cooperation means a better network performance [22]. Furthermore, there is another trend towards the automation of self-organizing networks in which users can be both, producers and consumers of resources. For example in ad hoc networks, energy grids, and sensor networks there is no a centralized controller or any other orchestration forms; instead, the system requires self-organizing mechanisms like cooperation to produce the necessary agreement among components to accomplish networking task [21, 23].

J. C. Figueroa-García et al. (Eds.): WEA 2018, CCIS 915, pp. 352–362, 2018.
https://doi.org/10.1007/978-3-030-00350-0_30

Additionally, before proposing any method to face the challenges related to cooperation mechanisms in ad hoc networks some natural questions arise: how to achieve a sustainable cooperation process? How to deal with selfish behaviors? Is the cooperation method effective? In this paper, we argue that some answers to these questions can be found in the computational models of sympathy and commitment. We conclude that cooperation may emerge even in scenarios in which agents do not have a cooperative strategy. Also, we show that it is possible to face some challenges related to ad hoc networks through socially inspired computing.

The rest of the paper is organized as follows. In Sect. 2 a brief introduction to ad hoc networks and cooperation models is presented. Section 3 describes models of sympathy and commitment. Section 4 presents the computational modeling of cooperative services through coalitional games. Section 5 shows the performance evaluation of the proposed model and compares it with previous results. Finally, Sect. 6 concludes the article.

2 Cooperation Models in Ad Hoc Networks

Ad hoc networks are self-organized computing systems formed by wireless mobile devices with limited resources. It can be seen as a set of autonomous components operating into a dynamic environment; each component operates based on the local information provided for its neighbors, and the system functionalities arise as an emergent behavior due to interactions among nodes, users and applications [21,23]. In such networks, cooperation process can be understood as a requirement to solve problems through collective actions, in which the accomplishment of the tasks depends on interaction and interoperation of unreliable and conflicting components. In the following section, we briefly review cooperation models and social dilemmas to put in context our model.

2.1 Cooperation Models

Cooperation models in ad hoc networks can be divided into two categories according to the method they use to produce collaborative behaviors: credit-based models and trust models. The first one is based on an economic incentive to promote interaction among network components. In such models, networking tasks are treated as services that can be charged to nodes, users, and applications through virtual currencies. Some representative proposals of these models are presented in [7,15]. On the other hand, models based on trust and reputation can work in decentralized environments and deal with free-riders and selfish nodes; if a node is not willing to cooperate, the affected nodes may deny cooperation in future interactions. Likewise, trust and reputation measures may be dynamic and evolve according to environmental conditions to produce groups of nodes according to their interests [9].

Furthermore, the conditions required to achieve cooperation in self-organized systems, have been widely studied by game theory. It studies models of conflict and cooperation between rational decision-makers in systems composed of co-dependent and interdependent components. In the context of the ad hoc networks, game theory has been used to deal with challenges related to resources distribution, information control, and selfish behaviors through no-cooperative games [1,17]. Besides, cooperation can emerge in scenarios in which agents do not have an initial cooperative strategy, making necessary to analyze the set of conditions in which a game may become cooperative, unviable or unprofitable [19]. For instance, Tit for Tat (TFT) provides a well-known framework to achieve emergent cooperation based on the past behavior of other players. However, even TFT can be defeated whether a large population of selfish nodes appears, or because of failures in message exchange [20,34]. A complete analysis of these proposals is presented in [3,4].

Similarly, cooperation patterns of living systems (biological, social, political and economical) have been analyzed for many disciplines like philosophy, social science, artificial intelligence, and mathematics in order to inspire new technological solutions for artificial systems [5,18]. Nevertheless, the majority of these proposals use an individual methodological approach and can be divided into five categories [36]: Middle Age Contractualism, Classic Prosperity Theory, Neo-classic Economy Theory, the Individualism associated to the Situational logic of Karl Popper and the Structuralism derived from James S. Coleman. All these approaches face several challenges to archive cooperation under uncertainty conditions in highly dynamic environments. In contrast, the empirical results of social sciences show that decision makers do not make rational decisions all the time, and the limited rational theory may explain and go forward to the incompatibility problems between methodological individualism and neo-classic paradigms. This approach gives an opportunity to build new cooperation models for artificial systems [2,35].

2.2 Social Dilemmas

Social dilemmas are situations in which individual rationality leads to collective irrationality, i.e., when a reasonable individual behavior leads to a situation in which everyone is worse off. There are many scenarios in which two agents need to deal with a situation of defecting or nor not each other in the presence of common goals in an uncertain environment [14]. Likewise, a group of agents facing a social dilemma may completely understand the situation, may appreciate how each of their actions contributes to a negative outcome, and still be unable to do anything to change the result. In this regard, social dilemmas are marked by at least one other outcome in which everyone is better off [6,8,12].

Also, groups of interest and communities are closely defined by their capacity to manage local resources and imparting justice for any subgroup that belongs to them [24,26]. There is a considerable part of rational theory related to social dilemmas that allow us to inspire mechanisms to rule resources and tasks distribution in artificial systems. What we can do is create scenarios in which justice may be familiar to all agents through a function that represents a set of rules to manage distribution and cooperation issues. Besides, the approaches based on methodological individualism face a significant challenge when decision-makers need to gather information to reveal the conditions of the environment [2]; the data could be socially spread but not useful because of it needs to be absorbed by agents. As a result, the limits in the capacity of an agent to obtain information are substantial barriers for its diffusion, setting complex scenarios in which meta-strategies are needed [33].

The following matrices outline a set of pay functions that are used for the most common negotiation and decision scenarios and in game theory [11]:

$$\begin{matrix} & L & R & \\ \begin{bmatrix} (3,3) & (0,5) \\ (5,0) & (1,2) \end{bmatrix} & & & \begin{matrix} U \\ D \end{matrix} \end{matrix} \Rightarrow \quad \text{Prisoner's Dilemma (PD)}$$

$$\begin{matrix} & L & R & \\ \begin{bmatrix} (3,3) & (2,2) \\ (2,2) & (1,1) \end{bmatrix} & & & \begin{matrix} U \\ D \end{matrix} \end{matrix} \Rightarrow \quad \text{Partial commitment matrix}$$

$$\begin{matrix} & L & R & \\ \begin{bmatrix} (3,3) & (2,2) \\ (2,5) & (1,1) \end{bmatrix} & & & \begin{matrix} U \\ D \end{matrix} \end{matrix} \Rightarrow \quad \text{Total commitment matrix}$$

$$\begin{matrix} & L & R & \\ \begin{bmatrix} (1,1) & (0,0) \\ (0,0) & (1,1) \end{bmatrix} & & & \begin{matrix} U \\ D \end{matrix} \end{matrix} \Rightarrow \quad \text{Coordination matrix}$$

3   An Axiomatic Approach for Sympathy and Commitment

In this article, we argue that is possible to produce emergent cooperation in an ad hoc network using sympathy and commitment links among the system components. This idea has an anthropological foundation that claims human beings are made with too much more than rational structures and shows that people could join to situations not only based on the idea of utility [28,30]. Likewise, it is necessary to identify the limits in the agent's capacity to produce groups according to their common interests and knowledge [29]. In the following sections, we present the concepts related we our model.

3.1   Sympathy and Commitment

On the one hand, sympathy among individuals supposes a previous meeting or at least an expectation of what others can do. On the other hand, commitment arises due to interactions among agents; this is a process in which each individual gets a common knowledge that allows identifying the group as a cooperative unit. Thus, if the agents need to generate any level of commitment in the system, a common idea about what may be reached through cooperation is required. In this regard, our aim is to try to configure a scenario in which all agents sympathize with each other and cooperate according to their needs [30].

3.2 Choice Rules and Axiom Rankings

According to Amartya Sen, three axioms about choice rules are presented [27]:

- *The symmetry preference axiom (SPA):* if everyone has the same welfare function, then any transfer from a richer man to a poorer man, which does not reverse the inequality, is always preferable.
- *The Weak Equity Axiom (WEA):* if person i is worse off than person j whenever i and j have the same income level, then no less income should be given to i than to j in the optimal solution of the pure distribution problem.
- *The Joint Transfer Axiom (JTA):* It is possible to specify a situation in which j is better off than k (the worst off person), and worse off than i, such that some transfer from i to j, even though combined with a simultaneous transfer from k to j, leads to a preferred state than in the absence of the two transfers.

4 A Coalitional Game Model for Achieving Emergent Cooperation

4.1 Coalitional Games

Game theory provides a mathematical framework to analyze models of conflict and cooperation among rational decision-makers. There are three basic structures used to model collective situation: coalitional games, extensive-form games, and strategic-form games. Coalitional games assume that all agents know what they want, the capacities of the coalition, and can dissolve the coalition if it is needed. However, some argue that coalitional games are related to the study of axioms of symmetry, equity, efficiency and other desirable properties that make easier the analytic modeling of a system [17]. Also, coalitional games involve the concept of weighting as a payment for the players that contribute in its coalition. In such scenarios, the works of Gillies [10] and Shapley [32] can be analyzed. They show that cooperative games can be used to model the set of interactions and environmental conditions that represent the behavior of a group regarding efficiency, symmetry, invariance, and independence [31].

4.2 Computational Modeling of Cooperative Services

To provide services using a coalition game, a coordinator agent needs to take the custody of a set of worker agents to perform the required tasks. Also, if it is not possible to complete tasks in a reasonable time, the coordinator will inform the node about the impossibility of providing the service, and starts a negotiation process to get new resources for the coalition. So, who made the request involves its resources in the negotiation represented in an agent or a pool of worker agents. When the negotiation ends, the new resources are assigned uniformly through the agents involved in the process.

Algorithm 1. Commitment and confidence verification scheme.

Input:
  At each tournament round, the complete set of players.
Output:
  The confidence and commitment temporal state set.

    procedure SETCONFIDENCE(g_{ij})
      if $profit >= 0$ **then**   ▷ a sympathetic rational goal...
        $c_j \leftarrow set\_c\_by\_r(j, True)$ ▷ Set confidence
        $c_i[j] \leftarrow True$ ▷ and commitment
      else
        $c_j \leftarrow set\_c\_by\_r(j, False)$ ▷ Unset confidence
        $c_i[j] \leftarrow c_j$ ▷ but respect commitment
      end if
    end procedure

    function SET_C_BY_R(j, p)
      if p **then**   ▷ ...the rational goal again...
        if j not in r_i **then**
          $r_i[j] \leftarrow True$ ▷ Get Commitment with j
          $c\_by\_r \leftarrow False$ ▷ but fool this time
        else
          $c\_by\_r \leftarrow r_i[j]$ ▷ Commitment already set
          $r_i[j] = True$ ▷ so, preserve the commitment
        end if
      else if j not in r_i **then**
        $r_i[j] \leftarrow False$ ▷ Don't commit with a cheater
        $c\_by\_r \leftarrow False$ ▷ in principle...
      else if j in r_i **then**
        $c\_by\_r \leftarrow r_i[j]$ ▷ Honor your word, but don't
        $r_i[j] \leftarrow False$ ▷ commit with a cheater
      end if
      return c_by_r
    end function

4.3 Proposed Algorithms for Sympathy and Commitment

The method mentioned above is made after setting the confidence levels as is shown in the Algorithm 1. This model requires a structure in which all agents can behave in a self-organizing manner and can interact with each other without restrictions. According to these conditions, an autonomous control structure is proposed. The idea is that each coalition can be divided into two layers with different kinds of agents; the first one will be in charge of specific or private functions in the nodes (worker agents); the second layer will be in charge of control functions related to the resources and task distribution (coordinator agents). Likewise, the core of the negotiation process is the confident scheme in which an agent can register, verify and modify the conditions of trust and commitment according to their interactions with others. The complete steps are presented below:

1. Each agent has two data structures that will be used to store the commitment and trust levels of other coalitions. In the first negotiation, these levels will be empty and filled according to the outcomes of each game.

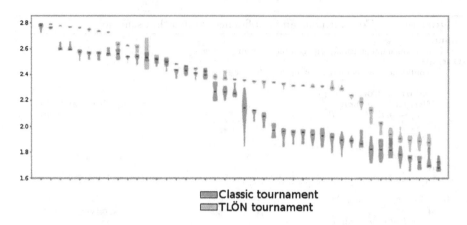

Fig. 1. Classic tournament vs. TLÖN coalitionist tournament.

2. The trust level of a coalition can be verified through the result of previous interactions (sympathy). If the coalition has not had any communication, the default trust will be false.

3. To establish or modify the trust level, the function $SetConfidence(g_{ij})$ is used. It takes as arguments the difference between the profits of a game and the unique identifier of the opponent.

4. If the profit is greater than or equal to zero, the coalition will establish a true temporal value for the trust associated with the opponent and will proceed to verify the commitment structures using the function $Set\_C\_by \_R \ (j,p)$. If there is no prior commitment, the new value of trust will be false, and the value of commitment will be true. If the commitment exists and is true, both will be maintained, and a cooperative strategy will be executed in the coalition tasks.

5. On the other hand, if the profit is negative (transfer of k to j being $G(k) <= G(j)$) and k is in worse conditions than j (being k a node belonging to the same coalition and there is a i node that replicates condition with k), the k agent will set a false time value for the trust associated with the opponent j and proceed to verify the commitment structures.

6. If the commitment is true and an inequality state is recognized, the commitment will be maintained, and trust will be true. On the other hand, if the state of inequality is not identified, or there is no prior commitment, the new value of trust will be false. If the commitment exists and is true, but the condition of inequality is not recognized, the value of the trust will become true, and commitment will be established as false. If the commitment is false, both trust and commitment will be maintained in the same value.

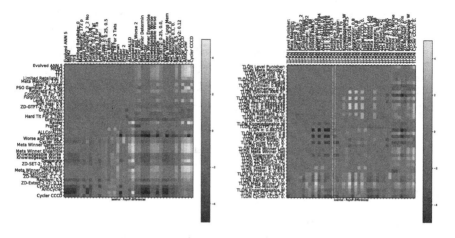

Fig. 2. Heat map for payment differences among 40 players. Classic tournament vs. TLÖN tournament.

5 Simulations and Results

The axiomatic framework presented above has been implemented in a multi-agent system written in Python, in which several wireless devices are emulated and interconnected through a virtual network interface provided by the B.A.T.M.A.N routing protocol [25]. Three initial scenarios were configured with classic nodes, pure coalitional nodes, and mixed nodes. For all cases, a random set of game strategies are uniformly selected according to Axelrod library [13], and each node to play a complete PD tournament of fixed length. The probability of applying a successful strategy is modeled as a random variable, which represents noisy matches or errors during the strategy execution. The three scenarios are described below.

5.1 Simulation Scenarios

Initially, in the first scenario, every coordinator node has a purely rational decision model (Classic Tournament). This scenario let us see differences between the decisions made by nodes with limited rationality and incomplete information and those in which pay-off matrix is fixed. The second scenario was called TLÖN tournament. In this case, the behavior of the coalitions is socially inspired and guided through the models of sympathy and commitment. In such scenarios, the coordinator nodes implement an abstract interface that allows them to define during runtime the payoff matrix and simulate a complete information game through the agent coordination. Finally, we create a mixed case in which rational and rational-limited agents were introduced to evaluate the effects of a coalitionist decision scheme into a classic game of rational agents. All scenarios were tested with populations from 10 to 1000 agents.

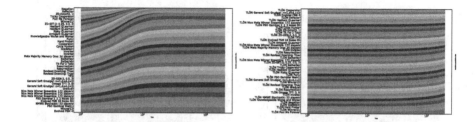

Fig. 3. Population dynamics of a classic and TLÖN tournament

5.2 Performance Evaluation

According to the conditions presented above, it is possible to see through the Axelrod-Python tool [13] that the average payoff received by the TLÖN scenario is higher than the most rational strategies provided by this library. Besides, it is possible to estimate an improvement in the system near to 30% as it shown in Fig. 1.

In the heat graphic presented in Fig. 2 it is possible to observe a fewer inequity between the payoff received by players in the coalition and the player with rational strategies. The most significant differences between dominant and dominated strategies could be mitigated by a pair Defector - Cooperator in which variations on the payoff falls from ±5 to almost 0. The same occurs with the majority of cooperator with strategies like TitForTat, Forgiver and Generous Tit for Tat, Pavlov, SoftMayority, FirmbutFair, and so on. A similar condition can be seen in Fig. 3 in which the changes in the population of coalitions are shown. The TLÖN tournament shows a greater duration of the different coalition. These conditions are a direct result of an equal resources distribution. Also, it improves the system sustainability and endurance of the cooperation processes.

6   Conclusions

In the future communications networks, cooperation will be a fundamental part of the network performance in environments in which there is no a centralized control or other orchestration forms. In this article, we have shown that it is possible to use coalitional games to achieve emergent cooperation in ad hoc networks. We used socially inspired computing to proposed a trust model based on the concepts of sympathy and commitment. Also, we configure scenarios in which all agents feel free to sympathize with each other and cooperate according to their needs. Our proposal introduces two different layers of agents in each node. First, a layer of workers in charge of performing specific tasks. Second, a layer of coordination in charge of distributing resources and tasks among the workers. The results show a better average payoff compare with pure rational strategies and a fair distribution of resources that improves the duration of the coalitions in the system.

References

1. Abdalzaher, M.S., Seddik, K., Elsabrouty, M., Muta, O., Furukawa, H., Abdel-Rahman, A.: Game theory meets wireless sensor networks security requirements and threats mitigation: a survey. Sensors **16**(7) (2016). https://doi.org/10.3390/s16071003, http://www.mdpi.com/1424-8220/16/7/1003
2. Arrow, K.J.: Methodological individualism and social knowledge. Am. Econ. Rev. **84**(2), 1–9 (1994)
3. Axelrod, R., Hamilton, W.D.: The evolution of cooperation. Science **211**(4489), 1390–1396 (1981)
4. Axelrod, R.M.: The Complexity of Cooperation: Agent-based Models of Competition and Collaboration. Princeton University Press, Princeton (1997)
5. Bentham, J.: The Rationale of Reward. John and H. L. Hunt (1825)
6. Berkes, F., Feeny, D., McCay, B.J., Acheson, J.M.: The benefits of the commons. Nature **340**, 91 (1989). https://doi.org/10.1038/340091a0
7. Buttyán, L., Hubaux, J.P.: Enforcing service availability in mobile ad-hoc wans. In: 2000 First Annual Workshop on Mobile and Ad Hoc Networking and Computing, MobiHOC, pp. 87–96. IEEE (2000)
8. Dawes, R.M.: Social dilemmas. Annu. Rev. Psychol. **31**(1), 169–193 (1980). https://doi.org/10.1146/annurev.ps.31.020180.001125
9. Fitzek, F.H., Katz, M.D.: Mobile Clouds: Exploiting Distributed Resources in Wireless, Mobile and Social Networks. Wiley, Hoboken (2013)
10. Gillies, D.B.: Some theorems on n-person games. Ph.D. thesis, Princeton University (1953)
11. Grossi, D., Turrini, P.: Dependence in games and dependence games. Auton. Agents Multi-Agent Syst. **25**(2), 284–312 (2012)
12. Hardin, G.: The tragedy of the commons. Science **162**(3859), 1243–1248 (1968). https://doi.org/10.1126/science.162.3859.1243
13. Knight, V., Campbell, O., Harper, M., eric-s-s, Janga, V.R., Campbell, J., Langner, K.M.: Axelrod-Python/Axelrod: v3.8.1, October 2017. https://doi.org/10.5281/zenodo.1010143
14. Kollock, P.: Social dilemmas: the anatomy of cooperation. Annu. Rev. Sociol. **24**(1), 183–214 (1998)
15. Marias, G.F., Georgiadis, P., Flitzanis, D., Mandalas, K.: Cooperation enforcement schemes for manets: a survey. Wirel. Commun. Mob. Comput. **6**(3), 319–332 (2006)
16. Mejia, M., Peña, N., Muñoz, J.L., Esparza, O., Alzate, M.A.: A game theoretic trust model for on-line distributed evolution of cooperation inmanets. J. Netw. Comput. Appl. **34**(1), 39–51 (2011)
17. Monsalve, S.: Teoría de juegos: ¿hacia dónde vamos?(60 años después de von neumann y morgenstern). Revista de economía institucional **4**(7) (2008)
18. von Neumann, J., Morgenstern, O.: Theory of Games and Economic Behavior (2007)
19. Nowak, M.A., Sasaki, A., Taylor, C., Fudenberg, D.: Emergence of cooperation and evolutionary stability in finite populations. Nature **428**(6983), 646–650 (2004)
20. Olejarz, J., Ghang, W., Nowak, M.A.: Indirect reciprocity with optional interactions and private information. Games **6**(4), 438–457 (2015)
21. Ospina, J.P., Ortiz, J.E.: Estimation of a growth factor to achieve scalable ad hoc networks. Ingeniería y Universidad **21**(1), 49–70 (2017)
22. Petruzzi, P.E., Busquets, D., Pitt, J.: A generic social capital framework for optimising self-organised collective action. In: 2015 IEEE 9th International Conference on Self-Adaptive and Self-Organizing Systems (SASO), pp. 21–30. IEEE (2015)

23. Qiu, T., Chen, N., Li, K., Qiao, D., Fu, Z.: Heterogeneous ad hoc networks: architectures, advances and challenges. Ad Hoc Netw. **55**, 143–152 (2017)
24. Rawls, J.: Teoría de la justicia. Filosofía Series, Fondo de Cultura Económica (1995)
25. Seither, D., König, A., Hollick, M.: Routing performance of wireless mesh networks: a practical evaluation of batman advanced. In: 2011 IEEE 36th Conference on Local Computer Networks (LCN), pp. 897–904. IEEE (2011)
26. Sen, A.: The Idea of Justice. Harvard University Press, Cambridge (2009)
27. Sen, A.: Rawls versus Bentham: an axiomatic examination of the pure distribution problem. Theory Decis. **4**(3–4), 301–309 (1974)
28. Sen, A.: Development as Freedom. Oxford Paperbacks, Oxford (2001)
29. Sen, A.K.: Rational fools: a critique of the behavioral foundations of economic theory. Philos. Public Aff. **6**(4), 317–344 (1977). https://doi.org/10.2307/2264946
30. Sen, A.K.: Collective Choice and Social Welfare, vol. 11. Elsevier, New York (2014)
31. Monsalve, S.: John Nash y la teoría de juegos. Lecturas Matemáticas **24**, 137–149 (2003)
32. Shapley, L.S.: A value for n-person games. Contrib. Theory Games **2**(28), 307–317 (1953)
33. Sherratt, T.N., Roberts, G.: The importance of phenotypic defectors in stabilizing reciprocal altruism. Behav. Ecol. **12**(3), 313–317 (2001). https://doi.org/10.1093/beheco/12.3.313
34. Sigmund, K.: The Calculus of Selfishness. Princeton University Press, Princeton (2010)
35. Simon, H.A.: The New Science of Management Decision. Prentice Hall PTR, Upper Saddle River (1977)
36. Udehn, L.: The changing face of methodological individualism. Annu. Rev. Sociol. **28**(1), 479–507 (2002). https://doi.org/10.1146/annurev.soc.28.110601.140938

Supporting the Natural Gas Supply Chain Public Policies Through Simulation Methods: A Dynamic Performance Management Approach

Mauricio Becerra Fernández[1,3]($\boxtimes$), Elsa Cristina González La Rotta[1], Federico Cosenz[2], and Isaac Dyner Rezonzew[3]

[1] Engineering Faculty, Catholic University of Colombia, Bogotá, Colombia
{mbecerra, ecgonzalez}@ucatolica.edu.co
[2] Department of Political Sciences and International Relations,
University of Palermo, Palermo, Italy
federico.cosenz@unipa.it
[3] Faculty of Natural Sciences and Engineering, Jorge Tadeo Lozano University,
Bogotá, Colombia
isaac.dynerr@utadeo.edu.co

Abstract. Natural gas is considered the transitional fuel par excellence between fossil and renewable sources, considering its low cost, greater efficiency and lesser impact on the environment. This is the reason why its demand levels have increased worldwide, requiring intervention of public and private stakeholders in order to meet these increments. The participation of diverse interconnected stakeholders (key actors) of the supplier-client form, constitutes a supply chain for natural gas, in which the effects of the application of public policy actions can be analysed in the time, using Dynamic Performance Management DPM methodology. The results of the model show the behaviour of the reserves, production and transport levels compared to scenarios that combine the implementation time of capacity expansion projects and supply reliability percentages, in which the national government can intervene, facilitating decision makers to identify the impact of the actions to be implemented, in the planning of policies aimed at guaranteeing the uninterrupted supply of this resource.

Keywords: Supply chain · Natural gas · Energy policies
Dynamic Performance Management · Systems dynamics · Modelling

1 Introduction

Natural gas is a fossil fuel demanded by different sectors, such as transport, industry, residential, commercial and electric power generation [1]. Its processing requires few stages from the source of extraction until delivery to the final consumer. It is transported safely and efficiently around the world, generating low environmental impact either in the form of liquefied natural gas (LNG) using methane tankers, or through various regions using pipelines. In the generation of conventional energy, natural gas is

© Springer Nature Switzerland AG 2018
J. C. Figueroa-García et al. (Eds.): WEA 2018, CCIS 915, pp. 363–376, 2018.
https://doi.org/10.1007/978-3-030-00350-0_31

one of the most efficient fossil fuels compared to other fuels, with a market share of at least 22% of fossil fuels, low costs of power plants, greater flexibility and speed in its construction. When natural gas is used for domestic heating, industrial heating, electricity generation and natural gas vehicles (NGV), produce on average 38% less CO_2 emissions than when using oil, coal, ACPM or gasoline, which contributes to reducing the greenhouse effects, especially in urban areas [2].

For the year 2016, 13276.3 million tons of oil equivalent were consumed in fuels (primary energy) in the whole world, of which 33.3% correspond to oil, 28.1% to coal, 24.1% to natural gas, 6.9% to hydroelectricity, 4.5% to nuclear energy and 3.2% to renewable sources. In the same year, 3542.9 million cubic feet of natural gas were consumed worldwide, of which, 27.3% correspond to North America, 4.9% to Central and South America, 29.1% to Europe and Eurasia, 14.5% to the Middle East, 3.9% to Africa and 20.4% to Asia (Pacific). Between 2005 and 2015, natural gas consumption increased worldwide by 2.3%. In contrast, the proven reserves of this resource rose to 6588.8 trillion cubic feet by the end of 2016, of which 6.0% correspond to North America, 4.1% to Central and South America, 30.4% to Europe and Eurasia, 42.5% to the Middle East, 7.6% to Africa and 9.4% to Asia (Pacific). Between 2006 and 2016, in the world these reserves grew by 17.9% [3].

Taking into account the low level of proven reserves, the decrease in national production levels, together with the current transport capacity and the increase in natural gas demand, it is considered of great importance to analyze the main actions in public policy, that allow generating the necessary capacity to guarantee long term uninterrupted supply of this energy resource of great importance for diverse public and private sectors. In the analysis of the effect of the application of public policies, it is found that methodology of Dynamic Performance Management (DPM) can contribute to the development of this research, given the possibility of involving both the public sector and the private sector, as well as, to identify the most relevant elements that affect the performance of the analyzed system. Based on the above and considering the characteristics of natural gas supply, the following are the most relevant and related research that apply DPM.

DPM is applied in educational institutions, Cosenz [4] provides tools that allow decision-makers to identify key performance drivers for the achievement of sustainable performance in the universities. On the other hand, Bianchi and Rua [5] research the capacity of the performance measures established by external institutions (government and inspection agencies) with respect to schools. Applying DPM methodology for decision-making in public institutions, Bianchi and Tomaselli [6] consider the lack of application of strategic planning in local public policy. Bianchi and Williams [7] show that DPM can strengthen the design of a set of measures aimed at improving results in terms of crime reduction. Another studiy using DPM as a support to decision making in programs for young people, Bianchi et al. [8] study how research grounded on a results-based approach, balance different objectives for stakeholders in the policy-making process. Cosenz and Noto [9] explore the causal relationships for the impact of corruption on the organizational performance.

In the approach to public management and business, Cosenz [10, 11] estudies how system dynamics modeling can be used to support public management, providing methodological support for the design of Business Models (BM). Regarding the application in small and medium enterprises (SMEs), Bianchi et al. [12] consider that systems dynamics methodology can add value to their performance management. Cosenz and Noto [13] analyze how SMEs are increasingly affected by the aforementioned crisis and the dynamic complexity. Applying DPM in the supply chain field, Ren et al. [14] propose an integrated, efficient and effective management system in the supply chains as a Dynamic Performance System.

Based on what has been discussed, this article uses Dynamic Performance Management approach, aiming to analyse the required capacity of the natural gas supply chain, in response to the demand, as well as to generate discussion regarding the policies that must be implemented to avoid shortages. The article is distributed as follows: in the methodology section the Dynamic Performance Management (DPM) framework is presented, then the application of the DPM in the natural gas supply chain for the Colombian case, based on system dynamics modelling. Finally, the results and conclusions of the model developed in front of different simulation scenarios are shown.

2 Research Methodology

The supply of natural gas involves public and private stakeholders, so DPM approach can contribute in the dynamic analysis of the interactions of these stakeholders, and how the applied policies can support a better effect on the reliability of the supply. In this section, it is worth noting the connection between the public and private sectors, as well as its contribution in the design of policies using the "instrumental" view of DPM methodology [15, 16].

The "instrumental" view defined the means to improve performance, in relation to a specific product. In this sense, it is necessary to identify the performance measures related to the final results and the respective drivers. To affect these drivers in each of the responsible areas, appropriate strategic resources that are systematically linked to each other must be built, maintained and deployed (Fig. 1). For Bianchi [16] within this methodology it is important to define the strategic resources, so that they can be modelled as material or immaterial resources available at a given time. Its dynamics depend on the corresponding input and output values that are obtained in the time of the results modelled as flows. Such flows are modelled as valves that decision makers can regulate through the incorporated policies, in order to influence the dynamics of each strategic resource and, therefore, through these, in the performance of the organization at the institutional and inter-institutional level.

On the other hand, performance drivers are a measure of factors that act in order to affect the final performance. These can be measured in relative terms, that is, as a relationship between the performance of the organization, perceived by the community or specific groups of users (customers) of the services or even competitors [16]. Finally, the elements considered in the DPM can be established by the combination and interaction of the levels (strategic resources, performance drivers, and end results) as shown in Fig. 1.

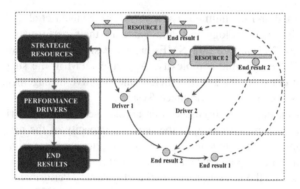

Fig. 1. The "instrumental" view of performance

3 Dynamic Performance Management in the Natural Gas Supply Chain

3.1 A Feedback View of Natural Gas Supply Chain

The hypothesis H_i considered for the construction of the model, is based on the proposals by Sterman [17] in the modelling of supply chains and Eker et al. [18] where the exploitation of natural gas is analysed by means of systems dynamics modelling.

- H_1: the margin of the players in the supply chain of natural gas and the unmet demand of the final consumer are affected by the implementation times of infrastructure projects and defined reliability percentages, guaranteeing the uninterrupted supply of the resource.

Figure 2 displays the main loops included in the model and we explain them below:

- *Transport supply*: the increase in demand for natural gas by the final consumption sectors (industrial, domestic, refineries, compressed vehicular natural gas, petrochemical, electric and residential), causes an increase in the need for natural gas to be transported, which after adjusting the current transport capacity with respect to the expected coverage to avoid shortages, generates the need for transport capacity and considering a delay for its construction.
- *Production supply*: the increase in the requirement of natural gas to transport, causes an increase in the need for natural gas to produce, which after the adjustment of the current production capacity with respect to the expected coverage to avoid shortage, generates the need for capacity of production and considering a delay for its construction.
- *Reserves supply*: the increase in the requirement of natural gas production, causes an increase in the need to develop natural gas reserves, which after the adjustment of the current generation capacity of reserves with respect to the expected coverage to avoid shortages, generates the need of capacity in the generation of these reserves and considering a delay for their development.

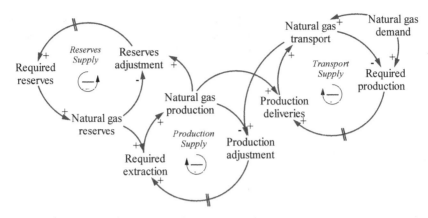

Fig. 2. Causal diagram for the natural gas supply model

3.2 Stock and Flow Diagram of the Natural Gas Supply Chain

The stock and flow diagram developed from the causal loop diagram (Fig. 2), combines the following modelling approaches and can be seen in Fig. 3.

- Sterman's approach [17] through the inventories replacement by adjusting the demanded requirements, comparing the current levels with the minimum levels of security to be maintained (supply reliability), which avoid the shortage in the supply of the products that flow into the chain considering the lead time of the supplier as a delay in the generation of capacity.
- Eker's approach [18] which presents the upstream exploitation as the life cycle of a natural gas field, analysing its states from the prospected resources, going through the development of reserves until the production stage.

Within the modelling of the supply chain of natural gas in Colombia, the main stakeholders that intervene in the supply are integrated [19].

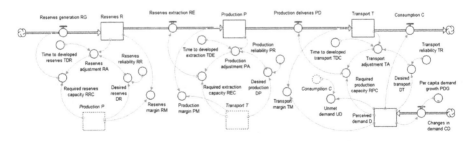

Fig. 3. Stock and flow diagram for the natural gas supply chain model

Within the design of the supply chain model, four interconnected stock variables are considered, which represent changes in the state of natural gas, from the generation of reserves to delivery to the final consumer. The demand for the previous link (player) in the chain, corresponds to the requirements of the following link, all this expressed in Giga Cubic Pipes [GCF]. The first stock corresponds to the reserves of natural gas (R), which represents the stocks of proved, probable and possible reserves, given by:

$$\frac{dR}{dt} = RG - RE \tag{1}$$

Where (RG) represents the generation flow of reserves, from the required capacity of these reserves (RRC):

$$RG = RRC \tag{2}$$

The reserve extraction (RE) flow is given by the required extraction capacity (REC):

$$RE = REC \tag{3}$$

The next stock in the chain is represented by the production of natural gas (P), the result of the treatment that the plants make to the natural gas extracted so that it can be transported to the final consumer, this is defined as follows:

$$\frac{dP}{dt} = RE - PD \tag{4}$$

Where (PD) represents the flow of production deliveries, which is given by the required production capacity (RPC):

$$PD = RPC \tag{5}$$

The next stock considered in the supply chain, corresponds to the transportation of natural gas (T) to the different consumption sectors, and is calculated by means of the following equation:

$$\frac{dT}{dt} = PD - C \tag{6}$$

Where (C) represents the consumption of natural gas in the country, which is equal to the total demand of the consumer sectors. The natural gas demand level (D) represents the national consumption of the resource and is calculated as follows:

$$\frac{dD}{dt} = CD \tag{7}$$

Where (CD) represents the changes in demand, which are given by the initial level of demand and the estimated per capita growth based on the population growth (PDG):

$$CD = D \times PDG \tag{8}$$

The required capacities in the natural gas supply chain is represented in a general form by the variable (Ci), which affects the inflows of the stocks (reserves, production and transport), are calculated by means of the following equations:

$$C_i = D_{i+1} + Ad_i \tag{9}$$

$$Ad_i = \frac{Dvd_{i+1} - Lv_i}{Dl_i} \tag{10}$$

$$Dvd_{i+1} = D_{i+1} \times (1 + Cp_i) \tag{11}$$

Where:

- i: sub-index indicating the key actors in the supply chain model (1 = reserve level, 2 = production level, 3 = transport level).
- D_{i+1}: demand level of the next key actor ($i + 1$).
- Ad_i: adjusted value of supply requirements of key actor i.
- Dl_i: time to make the adjustment to the demand in key actor i, given the delay in the generation of capacity.
- Lv_i: current level of key actor i.
- Dvd_{i+1}: desired values of demand by the next key actor ($i + 1$).
- CP_i: coverage percentage (reliability) of the key actor i.

The supply margins are presented as the supply and demand relationship, and are a performance indicator of the existing balance between the ability of the system to respond to the requirements of each link in the supply chain [20]. Therefore, the margins are calculated for the three stakeholders: transport (transport margin TM), production (production margin PM) and reserves (reserves margin RM).

$$TM = \frac{T}{D} \tag{12}$$

$$PM = \frac{P}{T} \tag{13}$$

$$RM = \frac{R}{P} \tag{14}$$

The main goal of the natural gas supply chain is to guarantee the uninterrupted supply of this resource, so that as a measure of performance in its management, unmet demand (UD) is calculated:

$$UD = D - C \tag{15}$$

3.3 Model Calibration and Validation

For the calibration and validation of the model, we use historical data for the stocks of reserves, production, transport and demand in Giga Cubic Feet. Data obtained from the main Colombian state institutions responsible for managing the supply of natural gas, called UPME (Mine Energy Planning Unit) and Ecopetrol (Colombian Petroleum Company). The calibration process consisted mainly of observing the behaviour of the stocks reserve, production, transport and demand, each one as a link in the natural gas supply chain. In the case of validation and based on the historical information, the values of the included parameters are shown in Table 1. The comparison made between these historical data and the simulated values for these variables are shown in Fig. 4.

Table 1. Data of the parameters used in calibration and validation

Supply chain link	Parameter	Measure unit	Value
Reserves	Reserves initial value	GCF	8044,491
	Time to developed reserves (TDR)	Year	20
	Reserves reliability (RR)	Dimensionless	0,15
Production	Production initial value	GCF	223,36
	Time to developed extraction (TDE)	Year	6
	Production reliability (PR)	Dimensionless	0,4
Transport	Transport initial value	GCF	238,52
	Time to developed transport (TDC)	Year	6
	Transport reliability (TR)	Dimensionless	0,3

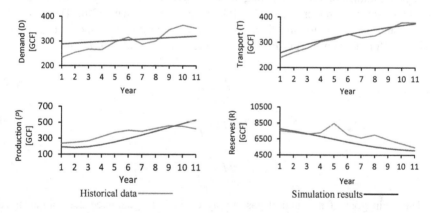

Fig. 4. Comparison between historical data and simulation results

3.4 Dynamic Performance Management Approach for the Natural Gas Supply Chain

Dynamic Performance Management (DPM) approach has been used in this article with the aim of analysing the effect of government interventions to guarantee the natural gas supply in the country, through the allocation of resources that, on the one hand, allow the acceleration in the implementation of infrastructure projects that increase the capacity of the stakeholders in the chain (required time for capacity development, *TDR*, *TDE* and *TDC*) and, on the other hand, increase the levels of reliability in the supply of the resource (*RR*, *PR* and *TR*). From this, the policy levers are defined for each link in the chain, in terms of reliability (percentage of security) and time for capacity development (required years for implementation).

Figure 5 shows the effect of the policy levers (diamond shapes) on the performance drivers (required capacities), which respond to the demanded levels in the client-supplier relationship, that is, the supplier responds to the supply requirements of the next key actor in the chain (customer), with the main purpose of guaranteeing the attention of the final consumer's demand (perceived demand), by advancing and transforming natural gas trough reserve levels, production and transportation of the supply chain (strategic resources).

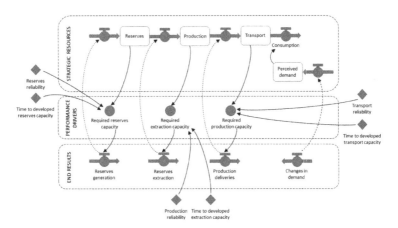

Fig. 5. The "instrumental" view of performance for the natural gas supply chain in Colombia

3.5 Scenarios Analysis in the Natural Gas Supply in Colombia

As mentioned previously, for the modelling the natural gas supply chain, Colombia is taken as a case study. Through the analysis of scenarios, the aim to observe the behaviour of the stock through the instrumental view of the DPM, as function of changes in the policy levers defined until the year 2050 (see Fig. 5). These changes are presented in three scenarios S1, S2, and S3 for the policy levers related to the development time of supply capacity in the chain stakeholders (*TDR*, *TDE*, and *TDC*) and for the policy levers related to the percentages of reliability or safety (*RR*, *PR* and *TR*). The proposed changes to these policy levers can be seen in Fig. 6.

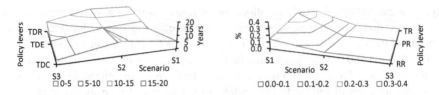

Fig. 6. Policy levers changes per scenarios for the natural gas supply chain model

The results for the strategic resources, show a stable demand for all the scenarios (considering that the objective of the supply chain is the uninterrupted supply). Natural gas levels show higher values in scenario S1, which is derived from higher reliability percentages. Scenario S2 shows shortages starting in 2032, due to the increase in response times in capacity development. By means of scenario S3, it is possible to meet demand with minors in strategic resources, maintaining low levels of reliability percentages and reducing capacity generation times (see Fig. 7).

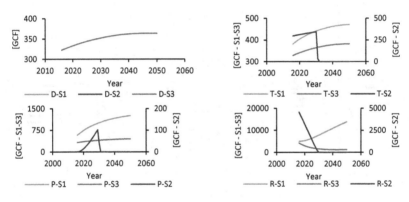

Fig. 7. Behavior of strategic resources in the natural gas supply chain model under three different scenarios

Performance drivers respond to the required supply levels based on the reliability percentages in scenarios S1 and S3, with lower values in scenario S3, given that capacity generation times are lower compared to the other scenarios. In scenario S2 the performance drivers of the *RRC* and *REC* respond to the shortage of the chain, on the other hand, the *RPC* performance driver given the raising the capacity requirements for the transport key actor, seeks to respond to the demand needs of the final consumers *D* (see Fig. 8).

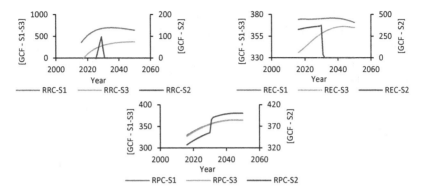

Fig. 8. Behavior of performance drivers in the natural gas supply chain model under three different scenarios

In the final results for scenarios S1 and S3, if the supply chain is observed backwards, that is, from the client to the suppliers, there is an increase in the discrepancy of transport, production and reserving stocks, effect widely studied in the supply chain models employing system dynamics, which is known as the bullwhip effect [21]. Scenario S1 shows a peak in the increase in the case of reserves *R*, given that initially reserves are not generated by the volume in which they are counted, but subsequently they fall by the configuration of the policy levers established for this scenario (see Fig. 9).

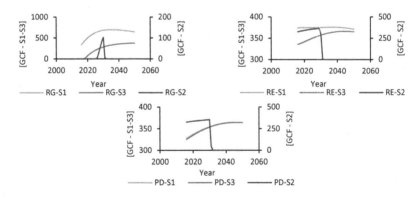

Fig. 9. Behavior of end results in the natural gas supply chain model under three different scenarios

As performance measures of the supply chain, the reserve, production and transport margins are initially calculated (Eqs. 12, 13 and 14), which, as mentioned, shows the behaviour of the relationship between supply and demand for each key actor involved in the chain. In scenario S2, there is a fall in the mentioned margins, which corresponds to the shortage given by higher values in the capacity generation times and low

percentages of reliability (see Fig. 6). In scenarios S1 and S3 there is no margin of
shortage or it equals zero, and it is noteworthy that in the case of scenario S1 for all the
stakeholders in the chain, a higher margin is observed than in scenario S3. Finally and
confirming the aforementioned, the unmet demand *UM* (Eq. 15) is presented in scenario S2, reaching 363 [GCF] from year 2032 (see Fig. 10).

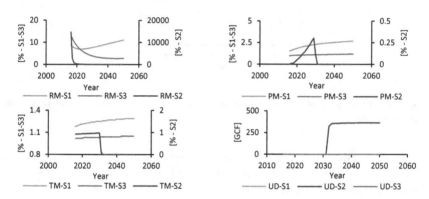

Fig. 10. Behavior of margins and unmet demand in the natural gas supply chain model under
three different scenarios

4   Conclusions and Future Work

Through the instrumental view of Dynamic Performance Management (DPM)
methodology, the most influential policy levers on performance drivers (requirements
in the generation of capacity of the stakeholders in the chain) are identified, allowing
the decision makers anticipate the effects of the resources allocation, by generating
infrastructure projects in the stakeholders (reserves, production and transport), for the
policies application that on the one hand, allow the attention of the demand and on the
other do not generate idle capacities in the supply system key actors.

We run three simulation scenarios to year 2050 that combine implementation times
(*TDR*, *TDE* and *TDC*) and reliability percentages as security stocks (*RR*, *PR* and *TR*),
scenarios that provide elements to the decision makers for the identification and pri-
oritization of policies, in each one of the stakeholders of the chain, which integrally
allows to improve the performance in the supply of natural gas. Therefore, it is considered that the regulator (national government) must set the mechanisms for the
integration of the stakeholders or organizations that are part of the supply chain of
natural gas, for the planning of the investment projects, the generation of infrastructure
in the various key actors, and the allocation of resources for the reduction of the
implementation times. This as confirmation of the hypothesis raised in this research,
related with the planning of the policies oriented to the improvement of the performance in the supply.

As future works, it is proposed to broaden the analysis of unused capacity in the
links of the chain, and incorporate the effects of prices on the generation of such

capacity in the natural gas supply chain, as well as the evaluation of already established policies by the national government to guarantee the uninterrupted supply.

References

1. Demirel, Y.: Energy: Production, Conversion, Storage, Conservation, and Coupling, 1st edn. Springer, London (2012). https://doi.org/10.1007/978-3-319-29650-0
2. International Gas Union and Eurogas. http://www.gasnaturally.eu/uploads/Modules/Publications/the-role-of-natural-gas-in-a-sustainable-energy-market-final.pdf. Accessed 21 Mar 2018
3. British Petroleum. http://www.bp.com/content/dam/bp/en/corporate/pdf/energy-economics/statistical-review-2017/bp-statistical-review-of-world-energy-2017-full-report.pdf. Accessed 15 Feb 2018
4. Cosenz, F.: A dynamic viewpoint to design performance management systems in academic institutions: theory and practice. Int. J. Public Adm. 37(13), 955–969 (2014)
5. Bianchi, C., Rua, R.S.S.: Applying dynamic performance management to detect behavioral distortions associated with the use of formal performance measurement systems in public schools: the case of Colombia. In: 39th APPAM Annual Fall Research Conference, pp. 1–25. APPAM, Chicago (2017)
6. Bianchi, C., Tomaselli, S.: A dynamic performance management approach to support local strategic planning. Int. Rev. Public Adm. 20(4), 370–385 (2015)
7. Bianchi, C., Williams, D.W.: Applying system dynamics modeling to foster a cause-and-effect perspective in dealing with behavioral distortions associated with a city's performance measurement programs. Public Perform. Manag. Rev. 38(3), 395–425 (2015)
8. Bianchi, C., Bovaird, T., Loeffler, E.: Applying a dynamic performance management framework to wicked issues: how coproduction helps to transform young people's services in Surrey County Council, UK. Int. J. Public Adm. 40(10), 833–846 (2017)
9. Cosenz, F., Noto, G.: A dynamic simulation approach to frame drivers and implications of corruption practices on firm performance. Eur. Manag. Rev. 11(3–4), 239–257 (2014)
10. Cosenz, F.: Supporting start-up business model design through system dynamics modelling. Manag. Decis. 55(1), 57–80 (2017)
11. Cosenz, F.: Supporting public sector management through simulation-based methods: a dynamic performance management approach. Int. Rev. Public Adm. 23(1), 1–17 (2018)
12. Bianchi, C., Cosenz, F., Marinković, M.: Designing dynamic performance management systems to foster SME competitiveness according to a sustainable development perspective: empirical evidences from a case-study. Int. J. Bus. Perform. Manag. 16(1), 84–108 (2015)
13. Cosenz, F., Noto, L.: Combining system dynamics modelling and management control systems to support strategic learning processes in SMEs: a dynamic performance management approach. J. Manag. Control 26(2), 225–248 (2015)
14. Ren, C., Chai, Y., Liu, Y.: Active performance management in supply chains. In: 2004 IEEE International Conference on Systems, Man and Cybernetics, pp. 6036–6041. IEEE, The Hague (2004)
15. Bianchi, C.: Improving performance and fostering accountability in the public sector through system dynamics modelling: from an 'external' to an 'internal' perspective. Syst. Res. Behav. Sci. 27(4), 361–384 (2010)

16. Bianchi, C.: Enhancing performance management and sustainable organizational growth through system-dynamics modelling. In: Grösser, N.S., Zeier, R. (eds.) Systemic Management for Intelligent Organizations: Concepts, Models-Based Approaches and Applications, pp. 143–161. Springer, Berlin, Heidelberg (2012). https://doi.org/10.1007/978-3-642-29244-6_8
17. Sterman, J.D.: Booms, busts, and beer. Understanding the dynamics of supply chains. In: The Handbook of Behavioral Operations Management: Social and Psychological Dynamics in Production and Service Settings, 1st edn. Oxford University Press, New York (2015)
18. Eker, S., Van Daalen, E.: Investigating the effects of uncertainties in the upstream gas sector. Int. J. Syst. Syst. Eng. 4(2), 99–139 (2013)
19. Mining and Energy Planning Unit of Colombia UPME. http://www1.upme.gov.co/Hidrocarburos/Estudios%202014-2016/Plan_Transitorio_Absatecimiento_Gas_Natural_Abril_2016.pdf. Accessed 22 Jan 2018
20. Redondo, J.M., Olivar, G., Ibarra-Vega, D., Dyner, I.: Modeling for the regional integration of electricity markets. Energy. Sustain. Dev. 43(1), 100–113 (2018)
21. Forrester, J.W.: Industrial dynamics. J. Oper. Res. Soc. 48(10), 1037–1041 (1997)

Modelling Collaborative Logistics Policies that Impact the Performance of the Agricultural Sector

Olga Rosana Romero[1,3(✉)], Gerard Olivar[2], and Carmine Bianchi[1,3]

[1] Faculty of Natural Sciences and Engineering,
Jorge Tadeo Lozano University, Bogotá, Colombia
olgar.romeroq@utadeo.edu.co
[2] Department of Electrical and Electronics Engineering and Computer Sciences,
National University of Colombia, Manizales, Colombia
golivart@unal.edu.co
[3] Department of Political Sciences and International Relations,
University of Palermo, Palermo, Italy
carmine.bianchi@unipa.it

Abstract. The performance of the agricultural sector is considered a fundamental factor for achieving sustainability of the most vulnerable population as well to meet the world's food needs. This is how countries like Colombia, recognize in their government plans the importance of the development of sector leveraged by infrastructures boosting their results, however, the instrumentation and design of public policies are a challenge for the governors given the dynamic complexity of the system. Through this research, we propose a model for the analysis of logistic public policies in the agricultural sector of the potato, where the collaboration through public-private partnerships (PPP) for the implementation of distribution centers act as an integrating axis among the producers, allowing the multidimensional measurement of its dynamic performance through simulating production, intermediation for its commercialization and financial results.

Keywords: Public policies · Collaborative logistics · Agricultural sector
Dynamic performance management · System dynamics

1 Introduction

Nearly 46% of humanity is located in rural areas [1], whose main activity is related to the agricultural sector, boosting the economy of developing countries and considered as a primary source for feeding the undernourished population, especially in those areas. Around the world, 37.7% of the total land is for agricultural activities, however, aspects such as climate change, degradation of natural resources and factors of violence, among others, affect farming capacity, risking the livelihood of 70% of the poor who live in rural areas and whose main source of income depends on the agricultural activity, plus also risking their ability to respond to the nutritional needs of the urban population.

These characteristics and their constant change must lead to the transformation and special attention of the value chains with higher efficiency demands, in a sector

© Springer Nature Switzerland AG 2018
J. C. Figueroa-García et al. (Eds.): WEA 2018, CCIS 915, pp. 377–389, 2018.
https://doi.org/10.1007/978-3-030-00350-0_32

dominated by the variability of the farmer's conditions, the inequity in land tenure and limited access to efficient infrastructure, which allows improving the conditions of the population and its competitiveness.

In this way, from the logistics networks point of view, the challenge arises first, balancing the variability of the conditions of supply and demand, second reducing the uncertainty in decision-making in a sector that requires both technical support to improve crop yields, and third implementing best practices for the conservation, storage and disposal of products that are mostly perishable, as is the case of potatoes, a key point of reference in this research and considered a fundamental product as an ancestral and cultural exponent of South America and that has served as a food base for the most vulnerable population in the world, given its nutritional and accessibility characteristics, occupying the fifth place of agricultural products of higher consumption worldwide [2].

The development of the rural sector is intimately related to the development of the agricultural producer, which comprises a set of elements to improve social, economic, and environmental dimensions, as well as technical quality of their production processes. In this research we evaluate performance multidimensionally through the production obtained, the costs per ton and the gross margin reached by the producer, among other variables such as the yield of the crop, the prices received and the harvested hectares, the foregoing based on what has been exposed by authors such as Vilches et al. [3], Naharro [4], David [5], Dwyer [6]. In the agricultural sector, like other types of supply chains, there are vertical and horizontal relationships, where alliances are considered a fundamental factor for productivity and competitiveness. This is exposed by authors such as Viera and Hartwich [7], Rojas [8], Kaplinsky [9] y Garza [10].

The approaches in the analysis of agricultural supply chains have a high tendency towards vertical collaboration models, understanding as vertical collaboration those that unite companies or entities in successive phases of the value chain, these are collaboration agreements between suppliers and customers [11]. According to Burgers [12] alliances between competitors are known as horizontal collaboration, where the entities involved operate in adjacent stages of the supply chain, cooperating with each other in processes prior to the natural competition that occurs in the market. Fernández et al. [13], present a model that allows to analyse the strategy of horizontal collaboration through a logistics operator, as the central axis of several clients with similar characteristics.

This work has the purpose of analysing the dynamic performance of the agricultural supply of potatoes in Colombia and the incidence of horizontal collaborative processes in distribution centers, which allow the formulation of public policies aimed at improving the performance of the rural sector and given its dynamic behaviour and continuous feedback, the proposed model is developed by using systems dynamics, considering the approach of various authors and their research proposals, which are analysed from the perspective of capacity planning in the supply chain, through private public partnerships and the encouragement level of the model by the State.

2   Dynamic Performance Management

The dynamics of both the public and private sectors, are addressed as a constant interaction in search of value creation and sustainable development, which as indicated by Bianchi [14], the identification of relationships contributes to the understanding of the systems, and also to its planning and control systems for improving the performance of the actors. Based on the methodology of dynamic performance management (DPM) and its instrumental vision, the causal relationships between the different levels of a system are analysed, considering the strategic resources, drivers of performance and final results, for its subsequent modelling, verification and validation.

In the case of the agricultural sector of the potato, three subsystems are considered, production, market and intermediation, and financial performance, where the strategic resources represent the stocks of the system's fundamental assets, such as sowing, harvesting, the supply and variation of the price received by the producer, and the profits obtained, which are affected by the final results, either as physical or information flows and that are driven by the yield of the crop, the relationship of intermediation for marketing, the accumulation of the product in the market, the variations in the price received and the gross financial margin obtained as a result of the year (Fig. 1).

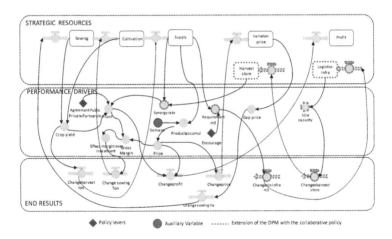

Fig. 1. Dynamic performance management chart of the supply of the agricultural sector of the potato

The integral analysis of these relationships, as well as the understanding of causality between the different factors, facilitates decision-making system intervention, being the outputs of the system the harvest and product supply in the market and being the main outcome the profitability of the producer.

Once the causal relationships among the strategic resources, performance drivers and final results have been understood, in order to measure the impact of public policies emphasized on collaborative logistics on the performance of the agricultural sector, measured multidimensionally as the product costs, tons produced, and financial performance we considered an expansion of the DPM, whose main strategic resource is the infrastructure of specialized distribution centers where producers converge and which allows them to adopt a central role not only as generators of the product, but as direct managers in its commercialization, decreasing the level of intermediation and balancing supply and demand, in the face of climate change conditions and with projections of the Colombian war post-conflict.

3 Modelling the System

In this section we present the modelling of horizontal logistics collaboration strategy through distribution centers, along with the verification and validation of the model.

3.1 Causal Loop Diagram Considering the Collaboration Strategy

The relationships are analysed through a causal diagram, where the interaction of production is identified with the development of the sector and how it depends on external aspects such as the weather, which can fragment the conditions of the producers and their associativity (Fig. 2).

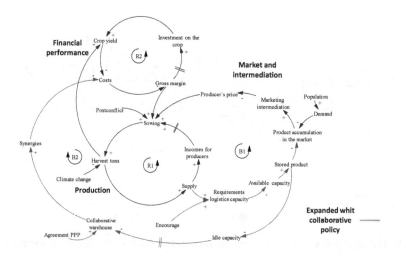

Fig. 2. Causal loop diagram

The dynamic behaviour of the system and its effects are analysed through the feedback loops as explained below.

Production Sector

The process of sowing and the subsequent harvest of the potato, generate the supply of the product in the market, volume that together with the price per ton will be the income of the producer. Likewise, production is affected by the effects of climate change and post-conflict conditions in the Colombian rural sector. The feedback flow of the production is evidenced in the reinforcing loop R1, generating an oscillation effect due to the delay in the decision of the producer to grow hectares according to the last income obtained.

Market and Intermediation

Although the supply determines the price of the product in the market, the interaction of collaborative infrastructures allows the supply to be balanced against the demanded product, which generates a competitive advantage for the producer, counter-mediating the marketing of the products in the market, as represented in the balancing feedback loop B1.

Financial Performance Sector

The production cost partially determines the producer's profits, which in turn contributes to the development and sustainability, being a differential factor for market competitiveness. Likewise, external factors such as climate change and internal factors such as the level of investment on the crop, impact performance, which in turn determines the cost of production and the profitability obtained. The feedback flow is evidenced in the reinforcing loop R2, seeking the increase in crop yield, with and oscillation effect.

Including Collaborative Policy, Synergies and Costs

When considering the strategy of collaboration between producers through distribution centers, the causal relationships are extended. The implementation of a collaborative public policy increases the synergies among the producers, counting on a physical platform that materializes the collaboration and economic benefits for the sector and its producers, represented in the balancing loop B2.

3.2   Stock and Flow Diagram

The stock and flow diagram for the sectors used in the validation of the behaviour of the model are shown in Fig. 3, where the production, the market and intermediation and the financial performance of the producers are considered.

Production Sector

In the stock and flow diagram we observe the variables: cultivated hectares (HS), cultivated tons (TS), tons used as seed (TSS), cultivation dedicated to self-consumption (SC) and exchange rates: current cultivated hectares (RHC), cultivated hectares of the previous period (RLH), rate of cultivated tons (RTS), rate of tons harvested per year (RTH), cultivation rate dedicated as seed (RSS) and rate of cultivation used for self-consumption (RSC). The main equations are given in the following way, where $i =$ type of producer by its size, $1 = small$, $2 = medium$ and $3 = large$, according to the amount of hectares sown, defined by the Agrocadenas Observatory of Colombia [15] and the National Administrative Department of Statistics (DANE) [16].

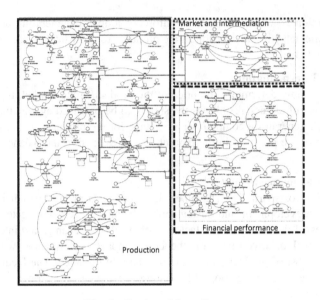

Fig. 3. Stock and flow diagram

- Hectares cultivated by each producer type i according to their size (HS):

$$\frac{dHS}{dt} = RHC_i - RLH_i \quad \forall i = 1, 2, 3 \tag{1}$$

- Tons cultivated by each producer type i according to their size (TS):

$$\frac{dTS}{dt} = RTS_i - RTH_i - RSS_i - RSC_i \ \forall i = 1, 2, 3 \tag{2}$$

Market and Intermediation

In this sector and according to the stock and flow diagram, the stocks are: supply (SP) and price variation (VP) and the exchange rates are: change of the harvest in the market through intermediaries (RHI), change of harvest in the market through the producer (RHF), current period price (RCP) and previous period price (RLP). Other significant variables in the sector are dependence on intermediation (DI), producer expectation price (EPP), product accumulation (PA), domestic demand (D), price received by the producer (PPP). The main equations of the sector are given by:

- Supply (SP)

$$\frac{dSP}{dt} = \sum_{i=1}^{n} RTH_i - RHI - RHF \quad \forall i = 1, 2, 3 \tag{3}$$

- Price variation (VP)

$$\frac{dVP}{dt} = RCP - RLP \quad \forall i = 1, 2, 3 \tag{4}$$

Financial Performance Sector

In the financial performance sector, there stock variables are total profits and profits by type of producer (PF) and the flow is change in received profits (RPF), and other relevant variables are: cost per ton produced (CTP), total costs (TC), income (IC), gross margin (MG).

- Total profits (PF):

$$\frac{dPF}{dt} = IC - TC \tag{5}$$

- Profits for each producer type i (PF_i):

$$\frac{dPF_i}{dt} = IC_i - TC_i \tag{6}$$

Extension of the Production Sector Including the Logistics Collaboration Structure

Given the interest for proposing collaborative policies in distribution centers, which allow the associativity of producers and the implementation of strategies that balance supply and demand, the development of collaborative infrastructures for the storage and distribution of the harvest is considered. The sector considers the available capacity and the development of warehouses, the unused capacity, as well as the associated agricultural production units, among others.

The expansion of the production sector considering the inclusion of the elements of the collaborative public policy, has the following stock variables: logistic infrastructure (WH), idle capacity (IDC), loss of stored harvest (LS); the flows are: change of new infrastructure (RNWH), return of infrastructure (RRWH) available capacity (RAC), capacity used (RUC), harvest received in the warehouse (RHS), harvest stored and dispatched (RHSS). Other relevant variables in the expansion of the sector are: relationship of synergies (SR), requirement of cubic meters for storage (SMR), capacity utilization (UC). The main equations are:

- Logistics infrastructure (WH):

$$\frac{dWH}{dt} = RNWH - RRWH \tag{7}$$

- Idle capacity (IDC):

$$\frac{dIDC}{dt} = RAC - RUC \tag{8}$$

- Loss of stored harvest (LS):

$$\frac{dLS}{dt} = RHS - RRHS \tag{9}$$

3.3   Model Verification and Validation

Model Verification

Through the verification process it is determid if the operational logic of the model corresponds with the logic of the design; for this, the behavior of the cost, the yield of the crop, the price received by the producer, the cultivated hectares and the supply were verified.

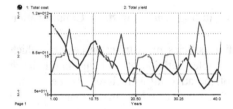

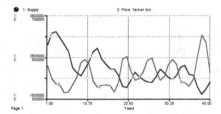

Fig. 4. Verification of the cost and yield of the crop

Fig. 5. Verification of the price and supply

The yield of the crop, that is, the amount of tons of product obtained per hectare planted, is closely related to the cost per ton harvested, representing an inverse relationship (Fig. 4), where the cost variable acts depending on the crop yield. The supply of product has an effect on the price received by the producer, because the accumulation of product, added to the level of intermediation, generates an imbalance with respect to demand, reflected in the growth or decrease in the price per ton (Fig. 5).

Model Validation

For the validation of the behaviour of the model, the analysis was performed on the variables that depend on the model and that define the behaviour of the system, such as hectares harvested, tons produced, price and cost, using the mean square error between historical data of a time series between 17 and 24 years, according to the historical information reported by FAO [17] (Figs. 6 and 7).

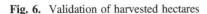

Fig. 6. Validation of harvested hectares   **Fig. 7.** Price validation

The absolute average percentage error obtained for the hectares planted was 14.61%, for the harvested tons and the per capita consumption was 13.52%, for the cost of the producer was 20.33%, and for the price of the producer 20.14%, representing acceptable deviations from the actual behaviour versus the simulated

4 Results

Given the interest of studying the performance of the system after the inclusion of collaborative logistics policies, where the distribution centers act as a central axis for the collection, storage and distribution of the product, balancing the demand and supply and impacting the level of intermediation commercial for the achievement of better results, measured in cost, crop yield and financial gross margin perceived by the producer, the evaluated strategies combine the implementation of public-private partnership for the administration and operation of the distribution centers and the encouragement level of the model by the State (Table 1):

Table 1. Strategies for the evaluation of the performance of the system

Strategic elements	Strategy			
	1 (S1)	2 (S2)	3 (S3)	4 (S4)
Public-private partnership <15 years	X		X	
Public-private partnership >15 years		X		X
Encourage with segmented participation <50% population	X	X		
Encourage non-segmented participation >50% population			X	X

The strategies are contrasted with the results obtained without implementing the collaborative logistics policy, represented as "E2P2 (No Policy)", but which considers the post-conflict situation and climate change, obeying the probable conditions that the system will face.

4.1 Multidimensional Analysis

The best performance of the system is observed in the multidimensional analysis, where the S4 strategy represents a private public alliance greater than 15 years and a moderate promotion of the collaborative model of the State towards the producer, that is to say that it congregates less than 50% of the total production, generating the lowest cost per ton produced ($315,713/ton), the highest yield (18.2 ton/ha) and the highest gross financial margin (24.8%) (Fig. 8).

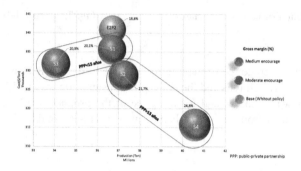

Fig. 8. Multidimensional analysis including the collaborative policy

Likewise, S4 strategy compared to the base scenario without policy inclusion (E2P2), shows a better performance in the system (Figs. 9 and 10).

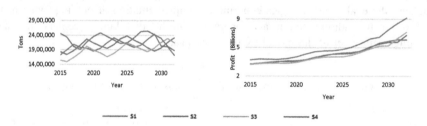

Fig. 9. Behavior of strategic resources: cultivation and profit under four different strategies

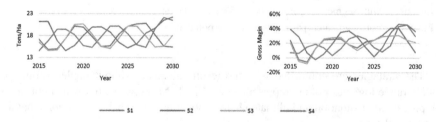

Fig. 10. Behavior of performance drivers: yield and gross margin under four different strategies

On the other hand, S2 strategy (public-private partnership greater than 15 years and medium encourage of the collaborative model from the State towards the producer) represents in its majority the second best projected performance, however, given the need to increase the development of the logistics infrastructure, it increases the risk of idle capacity, generating greater pressure on the system to increase its use, hence the importance of state intervention to accelerate the sustainable participation of producers under the collaborative model.

4.2 Hypothesis Testing

To make the contrast of the hypothesis, the statistical software SPSS was used, analysing the results of crop yield, cost per tonne produced and gross financial margin with the model applied for the evaluation of public policy of collaborative logistics in the agricultural sector, particularly the potato, through distribution centers. This analysis was carried out using a multivariate general linear model: The null hypotheses and the alternative hypothesis are shown below:

H_0 = The implementation of a public policy through collaborative distribution centers in the agricultural sector, particularly in the potato sector, does not influence the amount of tons produced[1], the cost of the product[2] and the financial profitability perceived by the producer[3].

H_1= The implementation of a public policy through collaborative distribution centers in the agricultural sector, particularly in the potato sector, influences the amount of tons produced, the cost of the product and the financial profitability perceived by the producer.

- With a level of significance α de 0.05 F $\sim$ $F_{0,05;1;78}$ = 3,96 < F_c = 13,67[1], $F_{0,05;1;78}$ = 3,96 < F_c = 7,92[2], $F_{0,05;1;78}$ = 3,96 < F_c = 7,96[3].
- **Decision:** Reject the null hypothesis.
- **Conclusion:** The implementation of a public policy through collaborative distribution centers in the agricultural sector, particularly in the potato sector, influences the amount of tons produced[1], the cost of the product[2] and the financial profitability perceived by the producer[3].

5 Conclusion

In this article the impact of horizontal logistics collaboration through distribution centers in the potato agricultural sector has been evaluated, which allows for the evaluation of public policy instruments and to improve their performance, the above using a multidimensional analysis of the variables associated with production, market, intermediation, and financial performance.

Public policy starts from the premise of the development of public private alliances, where the time agreed between the parties affects the performance of the sector and, according to the modelling, better results are obtained when public private alliances exceed 15 years, given the stability that exists, positively impacting the costs per ton. On the other hand, the promotion from the state towards the producer affects the level of commitment and interest of this actor, and where a moderate level of promotion leads to the best results, this for a sustainable coverage of the infrastructure of the collaborative warehouses and their permanent occupation. For the case of this work, it supposes a moderate level of promotion of the model reaching up to 50% of the productive population, which despite being counterintuitive, is accepted by the times required for the implementation of infrastructures, the sensitivity of idle capacity over financial performance and the uncertainty of crop yield associated with climate change, showing the need to open several distribution centers that gather, through an adequate logistics network, the productive, geographic and product distribution requirements, acting as decentralized physical nodes.

With the approach of the horizontal logistics collaboration between producers through the distribution centers, the financial margins are improved reaching an increase between 6 and 9 points, as the need for intermediation decreases and a better balance between supply and demand is achieved, where the synergies achieved allow economies of scale that favour the level of investment on the crop to obtain higher yields in the harvest.

On the other hand, the number of tons harvested show a growth of up to 11%, after the analysis with the assumption of implementation of the collaborative public policy, which is associated with a higher crop yield, where it would go from generating in average 17.6 tons/hectare to 18.2 tons/hectare, as a result of the higher profitability perceived by the producer that allows a better investment on the crop, as well as a more equitable price to offset the level of intermediation for its marketing, encouraging the decision of cultivation.

Production costs are positively impacted despite the generation of new costs related to the collaborative logistics of the distribution center, since the simulation does not suppose a subsidized model, that is, the producer must pay the access to the specialized infrastructure, compensated by the synergies achieved and whose benefits are mainly due to the balance reached between supply and demand, a decisive position for the management of prices and the commercialization of the product. The cost presents a decrease of up to 15.6%, allowing the producer a greater development and enabling it strategically for its growth and access to new markets, in a sustainable and profitable manner.

It is not possible to talk about rural development, without thinking about the development of the agricultural producer, therefore the actions generated for the intervention of the sector should be strategically focused on its competitiveness, guaranteeing the sustained rise of its economic, social and environmental realities, hence this work starts from the characterization of the producer and its performance over time, showing that collaborative relationships foster their development and therefore the associated environment, through a system based on productivity, to achieve greater competition that potentializes access to new markets and not a protectionist system that limits the development of the sector.

References

1. World Bank. http://data.worldbank.org/topic/agriculture-and-rural-development. Accessed 05 May 2016
2. Food and Agriculture Organization of the United Nations: Statistical Pocketbook: World food and agriculture. FAO, Rome (2015)
3. Vilches, A., Gil, D., Toscano, J., Macías, O.: Rural development and sustainability (2014). http://www.oei.es/decada/accion.php?accion=22. Accessed 21 Mar 2018
4. Naharro, M.: Rural development and sustainable development. The ethical sustainability. CIRIEC Public Soc. Coop. Econ. J. **55**, 7–42 (2006)
5. David, M.: Rural development in Latin America and the Caribbean: the construction of a new model? CEPAL-Alfaomega, Bogotá (2001)
6. Dwyer, J.: Review of Rural Development Instrument. University of Gloucestershire, London (2008)
7. Viera, L., Hartwich, F.: Approaching public-private partnership for agroindustrial research: a methodological framework, San José, Costa Rica (2002)
8. Rojas, M.: Productive alliances as an instrument of rural development in Colombia. In: Policies, Instruments and Experiences of Rural Development in Latin America and Europe. Ministry of Agriculture, Fisheries and Food of Spain, Madrid (2002)
9. Kaplinsky, R.: Spreading the gains from globalization: what can be learned from value chain analysis? Probl. Econ. Transit. **47**(2), 74–115 (2014)
10. Garza, F.: Public-private partnerships for research and development in agroindustrial chains: the situation in El Salvador. ISNAR, San José (2003)
11. Ariño, A.: Strategic alliances: options for the growth of the company. Financ. Strat. **236**, 40–51 (2007)
12. Burgers, W., Hill, C., Kim, C.: A theory of global strategic alliance: the case of the global auto industry. Strat. Manag. J. **14**(6), 419–432 (1993)
13. Fernández, M.B., La Rotta, E.C.G., Ramírez, M.M.H., Quiroga, O.R.R.: Collaborative planning capacities in distribution centers. In: Zhang, L., Song, X., Wu, Y. (eds.) AsiaSim/SCS AutumnSim - 2016. CCIS, vol. 643, pp. 622–632. Springer, Singapore (2016). https://doi.org/10.1007/978-981-10-2663-8_64
14. Bianchi, C.: Dynamic Performance Management. Springer, Heidelberg (2016). https://doi.org/10.1007/978-3-319-31845-5
15. Agrocadenas Observatory Colombia: The potato chain in Colombia, Bogotá (2005)
16. National Administrative Department of Statistics (DANE): National Agricultural Census 2014, Bogotá (2014)
17. Food and Agriculture Organization (FAO). http://www.fao.org/faostat/en/#data/QC/visualize. Accessed 17 Sept 2017

Software Engineering

Linear Temporal Logic Applied to Component-Based Software Architectural Models Specified Through ρ_{arq} Calculus

Oscar Javier Puentes$^{(\boxtimes)}$ and Henry Alberto Diosa

Research Group ARQUISOFT, Faculty of Engineering, Universidad Distrital
Francisco José de Caldas, Bogotá, Colombia
ojpuentesp@correo.udistrital.edu.co, hdiosa@udistrital.edu.co
http://arquisoft.udistrital.edu.co

Abstract. This paper reports a mechanism to incorporate Linear Temporal Logic (LTL) for a component-based software architectural configuration specified by the ρ_{arq}-calculus. This process was made through the translation of the system definition, structure and behavior, to Atomic Propositions Transition System (APTS), upon which, the verification of one property was performed using LTL. The PintArq software application was extended to support this mechanism. One example ilustrates the verification of responsiveness, a subtype of liveness property.

Keywords: ρ_{arq} calculus · Component-based software
Architectural execution flow · Linear temporal logic · Model checking

1 Introduction

On software architectures, a challenging area of growing interest has been to find mathematical tools that allow checking properties and quality aspects. There are some developments about formal methods [14], i.e., λ-calculus [4] for sequential processes, π-calculus [13,18] for concurrent processes, and recently, ρ-calculus [7] for object oriented paradigms [22]. ρ-calculus provides a foundation to model object oriented paradigm through Unified Modeling Language (UML) [12,16].

The ρ_{arq} calculus [9] was proposed to specify structural and behavioral aspects about component-based software architectures; furthermore, it's a tool to check desirable properties such as correctness [10]. Currently, a software application allows to visualize the software architectural execution flow specified by this calculus. This application receives a set of formulas as input and the software shows each stage of the execution [19].

The approach used in this project aims to apply (LTL) to specify properties and check models that satisfies them [3]. This work addresses on a subtype liveness property called "responsiveness".

At first, a conceptual frame is presented, then a translation method to Atomic Proposition Transition System using LTL operators is ilustrated, subsequently

© Springer Nature Switzerland AG 2018
J. C. Figueroa-García et al. (Eds.): WEA 2018, CCIS 915, pp. 393–405, 2018.
https://doi.org/10.1007/978-3-030-00350-0_33

an example is executed to show the checking process and by last, the new version of software application is described.

2   Conceptual Context

2.1 ρ_{arq} Calculus

ρ_{arq} calculus is an architectural description language (ADL) with formal notation to specify structural and dynamic aspects of component-based software architectures. Table 1 describes ρ_{arq}-calculus syntax. A more detailed description can be obtained in [9–11,19].

Table 1. Syntax of ρ_{arq} calculus. Source: [9,13,15,19–21]

SYMBOLS		MEANING
$x, y, z, \ldots$	variables	Variables only hold names.
$a, b, c, \ldots$	names	Names and variables are named references.
$u, v, w, \ldots ::= x \mid a$	references	
EXPRESSIONS		**INTERPRETATION**
$E, F, G ::=$	$\top$	**Null component** Component that doesn't execute any action.
$\mid$	$E \wedge F$	**Composition** It represents concurrent execution of E and F.
$\mid$	$E^{(int)}$	**Interior of component** E No observable part of E
$\mid$	$if(C_1 \cdots C_n)\ else\ G$	**Committed choice combinator** This representation of components with alternative executions in the $\rho_{arq} - Calculus$ is a derivation of the **Guarded Disjunction** proposed in the early extended versions of $\gamma - Calculus$ [20] [21] is a useful generalization of conventional conditional[1].
$\mid$	$x :: \overline{y}/E$	**Abstraction** It represents receiving a symbolic entity by means of x, it can replace $\overline{y}$ in E, as long as this entity is free in the scope of component E.
$\mid$	$x\overline{y}/E$	**Application** $x\overline{y}/E$ expresses sending $\overline{y}$ by means of x and continuing with the execution of E.
$\mid$	τ/E	**Internal reaction** It is represented with τ/E, this term doesn't have its explicit counterpart in the original $\rho - Calculus$. It might demand specifying many transitions as internal reactions to limit the quantity of observations [11].
$\mid$	$\exists w E$	**Declaration** $\exists w E$ introduces a reference w with scope E.
$\mid$	$x : \overline{y}/E$	**Replication** $x : \overline{y}/E$ can be expressed as: $x : \overline{y}/E \equiv x :: \overline{y}/E \wedge x : \overline{y}/E$ It produces a new abstraction, ready for reaction and it allows of replicating another when necessary.
$\mid$	$E^{\top}$	**E's succesful execution** Observable successful execution of E
$\mid$	$E^{\perp}$	**E's non succesful execution** Observable non succesful execution of E
$\mid$	$OSO(E)\ do\ F\ else\ G$	**On Success Of** If E executes with succes then it redirects to execute architectural expression F else it redirects to execute the architectural expression G.
$\mid$	$!OSO(E)\ do\ F\ else\ G$	**Replication of OSO rule** Consecutives observations of "On Succes Of " rule on the same component.
$\phi, \psi ::=$	$\top$	**Logical truth** Constraints as ϕ, ψ can resolve to true ($\top$).
$\mid$	$\perp$	**Logical false** Constraints as ϕ, ψ can resolve to false ($\perp$).
$\mid$	$x = y$	**Equational restriction** Constraints can correspond to equational constraints ($x = y$) with logical variables. The information about values of variables can be determined by means of equations that can be seen as constraints. The equations can be expressed as total information (i.e.: $x = a$) or partial information(i.e.: $x = y$); taking into account that the names are only values loaded to variables.
$\mid$	$\phi \wedge \psi$	**Conjunction of constraints** Constraints can correspond to conjunction ($\phi \wedge \psi$); the conjunction is congruent to constraints' composition. This leads to constraints that must be explicitly combined by means of reduction [15]:
$\mid$	$\exists \phi$	**Existential quantifier** The existential quantification over constraints is congruent to the variables declaration over constraints ($\exists x \phi$).

It uses structural congruence ($\equiv$) from ρ calculus, that holds for the least congruence (least logical relationship of equivalence) of the axioms and the reduction rules that represent the semantics (See Table 2). About new axioms showed on Table 2: *Observable replication*, it allows to do successive observations in the component execution and, *Observable Successful/Failure* that allows to do

Table 2. Structural congruence rules of ρ_{arq} calculus. Source: [9,15,19]

$(\alpha - conversión)$	Change of bounding references by free references
(ACI)	$\wedge$ It's associative, conmutative and satisfies $E \wedge \top \equiv E$
$(Interchange)$	$\exists x \exists y E \equiv \exists y \exists x E$
$(Scope)$	$\exists x\ E \wedge F \equiv \exists x (E \wedge F)\ \ if\ x \notin \mathcal{FV}(F)$
$(Equivalence\ of\ Constraints)$	$\phi \equiv \psi\ \ if\ \phi \Vdash_\Delta \psi\ y\ \mathcal{FV}(\phi) = \mathcal{FV}(\psi)$
$(Observable\ replication)$	$!OSO(E)\ do\ F\ else\ G \equiv OSO(E)\ do\ F\ else\ G \wedge !OSO(E)\ do\ F\ else\ G$
$(Observable\ Succesful/Failure)$	$[v/w]E^{(int)} \equiv \top \wedge if\ [\ (\top\ then\ E^\top),$ $(\top\ then\ E^\perp)\ ]$ $else\ (\top)$

replacements in a component inputs and execute it. A successful/failure observation can be represented by $(E^\top, E^\perp)$ respectively.

Calculus models behavior of component-based architectures through its operational semantic. So then, the calculus uses labeled transition systems (LTS) to show the evolution in the execution of the architecture through the operational semantic defined for this purpose. Additionally, it has a graphical notation based on stereotyped extension of UML 2.x that translates to calculus [9].

Table 3. Rewriting rules of ρ_{arq} calculus. Source: [9,15,19]

$(A_{\rho_{arq}})$	$\phi \wedge x : \overline{y}/E \wedge x'\overline{z}/F \longrightarrow \phi \wedge x : \overline{y}/E \wedge [\overline{z}/\overline{y}]E^{(int)} \wedge F\ \ si\ \phi \models_\Delta\ x = x',\ \mathcal{V}(\overline{z}) \cap \mathcal{BV}(E^{(int)}) = \emptyset$
$(C_{\rho_{arq}})$	$\phi_1 \wedge \phi_2 \longrightarrow \psi \qquad\qquad\qquad\qquad\qquad\qquad if\ \phi_1 \wedge \phi_2 \Vdash_\Delta \psi$
$(Comb_{\rho_{arq}})$	$\phi \wedge if\ (C_1)\ldots(C_n)\ else\ F\ fi \longrightarrow \begin{cases} E_k, & if\ \phi \models_\Delta\ \psi_k \\ F, & if\ \phi \models_\Delta\ \neg\psi_k\ \forall k = 1, 2, \ldots, n \end{cases}$
$Donde\ C_k ::= \exists \overline{x}(\psi_k\ Then\ E_k)\ ;\ k = 1, 2, \ldots, n$	
$(Ejec_\tau)$	
(a) $[OSO(E)\ do\ F\ else\ G] \wedge E^\top \longrightarrow F$, Because of succesful execution of E component	
(b) $[OSO(E)\ do\ F\ else\ G] \wedge E^\perp \longrightarrow G$, Because of non succesful execution of E component	

The rules at Table 3 specifying formally the progress in the execution of an architecture and they can be interpreted in this way:

- $A_{\rho_{arq}}$: *Application*, executes a concurrent combination of an abstraction with a replication that instances another application. This rule models remote procedures calls passing parameters within a component.
- $C_{\rho_{arq}}$: *Constraint combination* allows to combine restrictions with the purpose to extend or to simplify the rule set in the repository.
- $Comb_{\rho_{arq}}$: *Committed choice combinator* triggers the execution of an E_k component, if the context constraint is enough strong and it allows to deduce from ϕ, the guard ψ_k in the conditional. This rule chooses a component E_k within a group, as long as it holds the defined guard.
- $Ejec_\tau$: It sets the observational success/failure execution of a component. This is made with the purpose to represent a component as a black box, where the relevant part is the final behavior in its execution but not the internal processing, that is nos visible to an external observer.

2.2   Linear Temporal Logic

Linear Temporal Logic is built from the syntax and semantic described in CTL*
[8] with the constraint that it does not use quantifiers. Its formulas are uniquely
path-oriented and the representation does not generates a tree structure but one
unique path.

This logic has been used to model synchronous systems whose components
act step by step. This means, a transition progress in discrete time; the present
moment is defined as the actual state and the next moment is the successor.
The system is observable in 0, 1, 2, ... moments. A graphical representation over
some of the LTL operators is shown in Fig. 1.

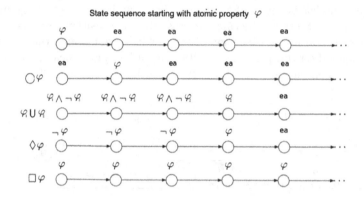

Fig. 1. Graphical representation of LTL operators. (Adapted from [3,8])

Syntax and Semantic to Check Temporal Properties. Syntax and semantic used to specify temporal properties of an software architectural model
described through calculus were based on [5] to specify properties in a reactive
system. A formula was built to specify LTL properties; this formula was composed by atomic propositions represented by $a_i \in AP$ where a_i is a state label
(or an alphabet **letter**) in the system, the basic boolean connectors $\land, \lor, \neg$ (*and,
or, not*), the basic temporal modalities $\bigcirc, \bigcup$ (*next, until*) and φ, φ_1, φ_2 which
are LTL formulas. Thus, a LTL formula can be expressed through Bakus-Naur
notation:

$$\varphi ::= true \,|\, a_i \,|\, \varphi_1 \land \varphi_2 \,|\, \neg\varphi \,|\, \bigcirc \varphi \,|\, \varphi_1 \bigcup \varphi_2$$

Rules of Logical Equivalence. The implication and double implication logical
connectors can be expressed through the basic operators ($\land, \lor$). Likewise, the
compound temporal modalities as $\Diamond$ (*eventually*), $\Box$ (*globally*), $\Diamond\Box$ (*eventually
forever*) and $\Box\Diamond$ (*infinitely often*) can be rewritten through the basic operators.
These rules are:

$$\varphi_1 \vee \varphi_2 = \neg(\neg\varphi_1 \wedge \neg\varphi_2) \qquad (1)$$

$$\varphi_1 \rightarrow \varphi_2 = \neg\varphi_1 \vee \varphi_2 \qquad (2)$$

$$\varphi_1 \leftrightarrow \varphi_2 = (\varphi_1 \rightarrow \varphi_2) \wedge (\varphi_2 \rightarrow \varphi_1) \qquad (3)$$

$$\Diamond\varphi = true \bigcup \varphi \qquad (4)$$

$$\Box\varphi = \neg\Diamond\neg\varphi \qquad (5)$$

$$\Box\Diamond\varphi = \Box(true \bigcup \varphi) \qquad (6)$$

$$\Diamond\Box\varphi = true \bigcup (\Box\varphi) \qquad (7)$$

2.3   Definitions

Some useful definitions were established by [3,5]:

- AP is the atomic proposition set of the system, it means: $AP = \{a_0, a_1, a_2, \dots, a_n\}$
- $\mathcal{P}(AP)$ is the power set over AP (set made up of all subsets over AP), it means:

$$\mathcal{P}(AP) = \{\{\}, \{a_0\}, \{a_1\}, \{a_2\}, \dots, \{a_n\}, \dots, \{a_0, a_1\}, \{a_0, a_2\}, \dots, \{a_0, \dots, a_n\} \dots \{a_1, a_2\} \dots\}$$

- A *word* is a sequence of elements over a set. For example: a *word* over AP would be $a_0 a_2$ or over $\mathcal{P}(AP)$ would be $\{a_0\}\{a_1\}\{a_0, a_1\}\{a_2\}$
- AP_{INF} is the infinite set composed by all *words* over the power set $\mathcal{P}(AP)$. For example:

$$AP_{INF} = \{\{a_0\}, \{a_0\}\{a_1\}, \{a_0\}\{a_1\}\{a_0\}, \{a_0\}\{a_1\}\{a_0, a_1\}, \{a_0\}\{a_1\}\{a_0, a_1\}\{a_0\}\{a_2\}\{a_0, a_2\} \dots\}$$

- A property defined over AP is a subset of AP_{INF}
- $Traces(a_i)$ is the path set which initial state is a_i. $Traces(a_i) \subseteq AP_{INF}$
- $Traces(ST)$ is the path set which all initial states in the transition system. $Traces(ST) \subseteq AP_{INF}$

With these definitions, an example of a property specification over a model can be expressed as: a_1 is always true.

This property can be represented as $\{A_0 A_1 A_2 \dots A_n \in AP_{INF}\}$ where each A_i contains $\{a_1\}$, in this case, a set of *words* that satisfies the property consists in: $\{\{a_1\}, \{a_1\}\{a_0, a_1\}, \{a_1\}\{a_1\}\{a_1, a_2\}, \{a_1\}\{a_0, a_1, a_2\}, \dots\}$. In this way, a formula specified in LTL describes subsets of AP_{INF}, it means that, a given formula LTL φ, can be associated with a *words* set identified with the expression $Words(\varphi)$ whose elements belong to the sequence of states reached in each transition. If φ is a LTL formula:

$\varphi \longrightarrow Words(\varphi) \subseteq AP_{INF}$; where $Words(\varphi)$ is the set that satisfies the formula:

φ: $Words(\varphi) = \{\sigma \in AP_{INF} \mid \sigma \text{ satisfies } \varphi\}$

Verification Rules. To determine if a word satisfies a formula, the next rules are applied:

With the word σ established: $Word \, \sigma : A_0 A_1 A_2 \dots A_n \in AP_{INF}$

- Each word in AP_{INF} satisfies *true*.

$$Words(true) = AP_{INF} \qquad (8)$$

- σ satisfies a_i, if $a_i \in A_0$.

$$Words(a_i) = \{A_0 A_1 A_2 \dots \mid a_i \in A_0\} \qquad (9)$$

– σ satisfies $\varphi_1 \wedge \varphi_2$, if σ satisfies φ_1 and σ satisfies φ_2.

$$Words(\varphi_1 \wedge \varphi_2) = Words(\varphi_1) \cap Words(\varphi_2) \tag{10}$$

– σ satisfies $\varphi_1 \vee \varphi_2$, if σ satisfies φ_1 or σ satisfies φ_2.

$$Words(\varphi_1 \vee \varphi_2) = Words(\varphi_1) \cup Words(\varphi_2) \tag{11}$$

– σ satisfies $\neg\varphi$, if σ not satisfies φ.

$$Words(\neg\varphi) = Words(\varphi)' \tag{12}$$

– σ satisfies $\bigcirc\varphi$, if $A_1 A_2 \ldots$ satisfies φ.

$$Words(\bigcirc\varphi) = \{A_0 A_1 A_2 \ldots \mid A_1, A_2 \in Words(\varphi)\} \tag{13}$$

– σ satisfies $\varphi_1 \bigcup \varphi_2$, there is j such as $A_j A_{j+1} \ldots$ satisfy φ_2 and for all $0 \leq i < j$ $A_i A_{i+1} \ldots$ satisfy φ_1.

$$Words(\varphi_1 \bigcup \varphi_2) = \{A_0 A_1 A_2 \ldots \mid \exists j. A_j A_{j+1} \ldots \in Words(\varphi_2)$$
$$\text{and } \forall 0 \leq i < j,\ A_i A_{i+1} \ldots \in Words(\varphi_1)\} \tag{14}$$

– σ satisfies $\Diamond\varphi = true \bigcup \varphi$, if there is a j such as $A_j A_{j+1} \ldots$ satisfies φ and for all $0 \leq i < j$ $A_i A_{i+1} \ldots$ satisfies $true$.

$$Words(\Diamond\varphi) = \{A_0 A_1 A_2 \ldots \mid \exists j. A_j A_{j+1} \ldots \in Words(\varphi)$$
$$\text{for } \forall 0 \leq i < j. A_i A_{i+1} \ldots \in Words(\varphi) \tag{15}$$

– σ satisfies $\Box\varphi = \neg\Diamond\neg\varphi$, for this case it decomposes in:
  1. σ satisfies $\Diamond\neg\varphi$, if there is a j such as $A_j A_{j+1} \ldots$ satisfies $\neg\varphi$
  2. σ satisfies $\neg\Diamond\neg\varphi$, if σ not satisfies $\Diamond\neg\varphi$.
  3. σ satisfies $\neg\Diamond\neg\varphi$, if for all j such as $A_j A_{j+1} \ldots$ satisfies φ

$$Words(\Box\varphi) = \{A_0 A_1 A_2 \ldots \mid \forall j. A_j A_{j+1} \ldots \in Words(\varphi) \tag{16}$$

3   The Method

The architectural configuration showed in the Fig. 2 was used to specify and verify the "responsiveness" property.

Formulas that specifies this configuration through the ρ_{arq}-calculus are:

$$E \overset{def}{=} [(p_E : x/xs_E)] \wedge \exists l_E[(r_E :: y/yl_E) \wedge (l_E :: i_E/E^{(int)})] \tag{17}$$

$$F \overset{def}{=} (p_F : z/zs_F) \wedge (p_{Fe} : w/ws_{Fe}) \tag{18}$$

$$M \overset{def}{=} \exists l_M[(r_M :: y/yl_M) \wedge (l_M :: i_M/M^{(int)})] \tag{19}$$

$$T \overset{def}{=} [(p_{Te} : n/ns_{Te})] \wedge \exists l_T[(r_T :: q/ql_T) \wedge (l_T :: i_T/T^{(int)})] \tag{20}$$

$$C_F E = r_E \overline{p_F} \tag{21}$$

$$C_F M = r_M \overline{p_{Fe}} \tag{22}$$

$$C_E T = r_T \overline{p_E} \tag{23}$$

$$C_E M = r_M \overline{p_E e} \tag{24}$$

$$C_T M = r_M \overline{p_T e} \tag{25}$$

The system's initial configuration is:

$$S = [F \wedge OSO(F) \ do \ C_F E \wedge E \ else \wedge C_F M \wedge M]$$
$$\wedge [OSO(E) \ do \ C_E T \wedge T \ else \ C_E M \wedge M] \tag{26}$$
$$\wedge [OSO(T) \ do \ T \ else \ C_T M \wedge M]$$

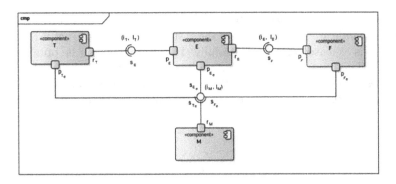

Fig. 2. Complex assembly of components. (Source [9])

3.1   APTS Generation

Atomic Propositions Transition System (APTS) represents the system states associated to atomic propositions. This model was generated by the architecture definition (components and connectors) and execution rules provided by the ρ_{arq}-calculus.

First Step: Identify the Source Components. Only they can start the execution. Each component inside the model represents a state: its execution (i.e. E). Transitions that they can take represent the successful or failure execution states (i.e. $E^\top$ and $E^\perp$ respectively), this behavior is shown in the Fig. 3.

Fig. 3. APTS representation of a component execution.

Second Step: Obtain Transitions Between States. It is done capturing system's behavior through evaluation of observation rules disposed in the formula. An observation rule is described as:

$$OSO(F)\, do\, [C_F E \wedge E]\, else\, [C_F M \wedge M] \tag{27}$$

From this rule it can be built links between states. If F executes successfully it communicates with E, else it links with M. In the arrival of new components, the first step is repeated and the APTS is developed until there are no more components to analyze.

Third Step: Close Process. In the moment to achieve end states (terminal states) they indicate a global state of the system. It proceeds to set if the system as a whole is executed or not successfully. This state only can be obtained from the terminal nodes whose execution represents one of the success or failure global final states. When it reaches one of these states, it connects again with the nodes that represent the source components for evaluating a new execution (Fig. 4).

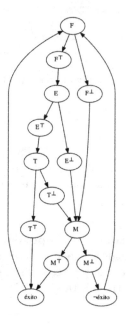

Fig. 4. Full APTS representation

3.2   Verification of a Temporal Property

Atomic properties were made up from the system states and the defined operators were used for this purpose. One property was specified in order to check if the system could fulfill it. For example (with previous APTS):

$$\varphi = F \rightarrow \Diamond(T^\top \vee M^\top) \tag{28}$$

This property defines if F executes, eventually in the future M or T will execute successfully.

A temporal property specifies paths (states sequences) that a transition system should expose (states that can be observable); these properties specify desired or allowable behavior expected from the system.

Formally, a property P is a subset of AP_{INF} where AP is the set of atomic propositions and AP_{INF} represents the words set that come from infinite words concatenation in $\mathcal{P}(AP)$. Therefore, a property is an infinite words set over

$\mathcal{P}(AP)$ [3] or in another way, if the execution of a program is a σ infinite states sequence, it is said that property P is true in σ if the sequences set defined by the program are contained in the property P [1].

One of these properties is named *liveness*. This property declares intuitively that "something good" eventually will happen or that a program eventually will reach a desired state [2,6,17]. Specifically, the *liveness* property shows one of the next behaviors: *Starvation freedom*, *Termination* and *Guaranteed service/Responsiveness*.

For this work was proposed the verification of the "Responsiveness" property, a subtype of liveness property. To check this property, the experiment proceeded from the simplest case until to reach the most complex case.

For $\varphi = F^\top \rightarrow \Diamond M^\top$

The following sets are by definition:

$$AP = \{F, F^\top, F^\perp, E, E^\top, E^\perp, T, T^\top, T^\perp, M, M^\top, M^\perp, success, failure\}$$
$$AP_{INF} = \{\{\}, \{F\}, \{F^\top\}, \{F^\perp\}, \{E\}, \{E^\top\}, \{E^\perp\}, \{T\}, \{T^\top\}, \{T^\perp\}, \{M\}, \{M^\top\}, \{M^\perp\}$$
$$, \{F\}\{F^\top\}, \{F\}\{F^\perp\}, \{F\}\{F^\top\}\{E\}, ...\}$$

The system complies the formula φ if:

$$Words(\varphi) = Words(F^\top \rightarrow \Diamond M^\top) \text{ and } Traces(TS) \cap Words(\varphi)$$

Applying the rules of composition, the formula can be expressed in subformulas that can be evaluated in the following sequence:

$$Words(\varphi) = Words(F^\top \rightarrow \Diamond M^\top); \qquad applying(2)$$
$$Words(\varphi) = Words(\neg F^\top \vee \Diamond M^\top); \qquad applying\ (11)$$
$$Words(\varphi) = Words(\neg F^\top) \cup Words(\Diamond M^\top); \quad applying(12)$$
$$Words(\varphi) = Words(F^\top)' \cup Words(\Diamond M^\top); \qquad applying(4)$$
$$Words(\varphi) = Words(F^\top)' \cup Words(true \bigcup M^\top)$$

the first terms set was described by extension:

$$Words(\varphi) = \{\{F\}, \{F\}\{F^\perp\}, \{F\}\{F^\perp\}\{M\}, \{F\}\{F^\perp\}\{M\}\{M^\top\},$$
$$\{F\}\{F^\perp\}\{M\}\{M^\top\}\{success\}, \{F\}\{F^\perp\}\{M\}\{M^\perp\},$$
$$\{F\}\{F^\perp\}\{M\}\{M^\perp\}\{\neg success\}\} \cup Words(true \bigcup M^\top); \qquad applying(14)$$
$$...$$

The process continues recursively until sets of states sequence that satisfy the specified property are found.

Likewise, the sequences that must be delimited inside the set of possible paths offered by the APTS must be filtered, therefore must be satisfied that $Traces(TS) \cap Words(\varphi)$, where $Traces(TS)$ is the set of possible paths in the transition system that are determined for the initial states in the system.

In this way, only paths that make true the temporal property for the APTS with the paths that begin with the initial states are filtered. The Fig. 5 shows the relationship between these elements; the intersection area represents the elements that satisfy the property.

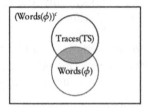

Fig. 5. Relationship between $Traces(TS)$ and $Words(\varphi)$ Source [5]

In this system it can be seen there are paths that move to successful execution of M ($M^\top$): $\{F\}\{F^\top\}\{E\}\{E^\top\}\{T\}\{T^\perp\}\{M\}\{M^\top\}$ and thus, property is satisfied for the system. On the other hand, a property that the system does not satisfy is the following: $\varphi =! (F \rightarrow \Diamond \neg success)$. It can be identified that not all paths lead to the successful execution and there is at least one path that flows towards an unwanted state of failure.

4   Results and Discussion

4.1   Mapping Architectural Specification to APTS

One of the worthy results in this job is the achieved method to map structural and behavioral architectural configurations using the ρ_{arq}-calculus to an ATPS that allows checking properties using LTL formulas. This effort is pertinent for academic communities that work and research about model checking possibilities. This result indicates that ρ_{arq}-calculus expressions are translatable to LTL formulas and the other properties could be analyzed.

4.2   PintArq Extension to Check LTL Properties

In the first version of the software, an architectural execution flow visualizer was achieved with the work described in [19] and it was named PintArq. It was built to support the method described in Sect. 3. To implement this solution, the software process development phases were carried out with their functional, structural an dynamic models that are completely documented and for free access in the ARQUISOFT Research Group portal. The prescriptive architecture of the application is illustrated in Fig. 6. This architecture is composed for the next modules:
Original modules:

Interpreter: It identifies structural elements and it transforms architectural expressions to UML component-configuration.

Rewriter: It obtains original expressions and rewrites them which represents reactions in the system.

Architect: It generates components and connectors from interpreted structural elements.

Drawer: It shows on screen, component-based architecture through an UML Component diagram (in SVG image format).

Transformer: It transforms architecture in an XMI file for exchange with other systems.

Modules added in this project:

APTS Generator: It creates the APTS based on the architecture (components and connectors) and initial calculus expressions.

Property Checker: It takes property provided for the user and identifies whether it is satisfied by the system. If property is not satisfied, it creates a counter-example path that represents this behavior.

Model checking viewer: It shows on screen, the generated APTS and the possible path in case the property is not satisfied.

To extend the PintArq tool with new possibilities to analyze software component-based architectures from model checking perspective is very interesting and it opens new research motivations to apply this proposal to real software architectures. Nowadays, the Pintarq tool must be extended to graphical modelling of real software systems or the tool could be extended with a models interchange module. This module should import real software component-based models and it should translate these models to ρ_{arq}-calculus. With this translation the software architect could use the analysis capabilities of PintArq tool.

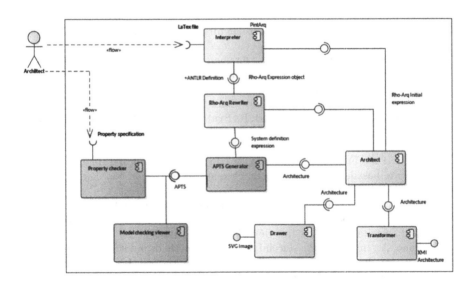

Fig. 6. PintArq's prescriptive architecture with additional components.

To obtain the detailed documentation about this project you can visit http:// arquisoft.udistrital.edu.co, option: "Proyectos finalizados".

5   Future Work

Several scenarios on which it can start or continue related work are:

1. Expand the scope of the mechanism to verify temporal properties as *Safety*, *Deadlock detection* or *Starvation freedom*.
2. Optimize the implementations to find the shortest path that the counterexample illustrate when the model does not satisfy the specified property.
3. Improve the implementation of the extension in PintArq to visualize the counterexample in the syntax of the formal ρ_{arq}-calculus and not in the LaTeX format.
4. Expand the analysis of possibilities to other temporal logics: Branch temporal logic, intuitionistic temporal logic and temporal multi-valued logic.

References

1. Alpern, B., Schneider, F.B.: Defining liveness. Inf. Process. Lett. **21**(4), 181–185 (1985)
2. Alpern, B., Schneider, F.B.: Recognizing safety and liveness. Distrib. Comput. **2**(3), 117–126 (1987)
3. Baier, C., Katoen, J.P.: Principles of Model Checking. MIT Press, London (2008)
4. Barendregt, H., Barendsen, E.: Introduction to lambda calculus. Nieuw archief voor wisenkunde **4**(Mar), 337–372 (2000). http://homepages.nyu.edu/~cb125/Lambda/barendregt.94.pdf
5. Biswas, S., Deka, J.K.: NPTEL: Computer Science and Engineering - Design Verification and Test of Digital VLSI Circuits (2014). http://nptel.ac.in/courses/106103116/19
6. Cheung, S.C., Giannakopoulou, D., Kramer, J.: Verification of liveness properties using compositional reachability analysis. In: Jazayeri, M., Schauer, H. (eds.) ESEC/SIGSOFT FSE -1997. LNCS, vol. 1301, pp. 227–243. Springer, Heidelberg (1997). https://doi.org/10.1007/3-540-63531-9_17
7. Cirstea, H., Kirchner, C.: ρ-Calculus. Its Syntax and Basic Properties, vol. 53, no. 9 (1998)
8. Clarke, E.: Model Checking. MIT Press, London (2000)
9. Diosa, H., Díaz Frías, J.F., Gaona, C.M.: Especificación formal de arquitecturas de software basadas en componentes: chequeo de corrección con cálculo rho-arq, no. 12 (2010)
10. Diosa, H.A., Díaz, J.F., Gaona C.M.: Cálculo para el modelado formal de arquitecturas de software basadas en componentes: cálculo ρ_{arq}. Revista Científica. Universidad Distrital Francisco José de Caldas, no. 12 (2010)
11. Bertolino, A., Inverardi, P., Muccini, H.: Formal methods in testing software architectures. In: Bernardo, M., Inverardi, P. (eds.) SFM 2003. LNCS, vol. 2804, pp. 122–147. Springer, Heidelberg (2003). https://doi.org/10.1007/978-3-540-39800-4_7
12. Micskei, Z., Waeselynck, H.: The many meanings of UML 2 sequence diagrams: a survey. Softw. Syst. Model. **10**(4), 489–514 (2010). https://doi.org/10.1007/s10270-010-0157-9
13. Milner, R.: Communicating and Mobile Systems: The Pi Calculus. Cambridge University Press, Cambridge (1999)

14. Montoya Serna, E.: Métodos formales e Ingeniería de Software. Revista Virtual Universidad Católica del Norte, no. 30, 1–26 (2011). http://revistavirtual.ucn.edu. co/index.php/RevistaUCN/article/view/62

15. Niehren, J., Müller, M.: Constraints for free in concurrent computation. In: Kanchanasut, K., Lévy, J.-J. (eds.) ACSC 1995. LNCS, vol. 1023, pp. 171–186. Springer, Heidelberg (1995). https://doi.org/10.1007/3-540-60688-2_43

16. Object Management Group: OMG Unified Modeling Language (OMG UML), version 2.5, March 2015

17. Owicki, S., Lamport, L.: Proving liveness properties of concurrent programs. ACM Trans. Program. Lang. Syst. **4**(3), 455–495 (1982)

18. Parrow, J.: An Introduction to the pi-Calculus (2001). http://homepages.nyu.edu/ ~cb125/Lambda/barendregt.94.pdf

19. Rico, J.A.: Representación visual de la ejecución de una arquitectura de software basada en componentes con especificación formal en cálculo ρarq (2015)

20. Smolka, G.: A calculus for higher-order concurrent constraint programming with deep guards. Technical report, Bundesminister für Forschung und Technologie (1994)

21. Smolka, G.: A Foundation for Higher-order Concurrent Constraint Programming. Tech. rep., Bundesminister für Forschung und Technologie (1994)

22. Wing, J.M.: FAQ on π-Calculus, pp. 1–8, December 2002

Design of App Based on Hl7 and IoT for Assistance PHD Health Programs

Sabrina Suárez Arrieta[1(✉)], Octavio José Salcedo Parra[1,2],
and Alberto Acosta López[1]

[1] Faculty of Engineering, Intelligent Internet Research Group, Universidad
Distrital "Francisco José de Caldas", Bogotá, D.C, Colombia
ssuareza@correo.udistrital.edu.co,
{osalcedo,aacosta}@udistrital.edu.co
[2] Department of Systems and Industrial Engineering, Faculty of Engineering,
Universidad Nacional de Colombia, Bogotá, D.C, Colombia
ojsalcedop@unal.edu.co

Abstract. The design of a communication architecture for different data management platforms is presented, between health entities through the HL7 standards, with the implementation of an application that allows the management of information, obtained from a device designed to the capture of vital signs in order to be used in different programs that seek to provide hospitalization services at home or days of medical care in areas of difficult access, allowing the control and monitoring of the signs captured to patients with different conditions.

Keywords: HL7 · Web service · IoT

1 Introduction

Different health entities in the country (especially EPS) currently provide a PHD home hospitalization service which is provided to different types of patients, which usually belong to one of the following categories; patients with sequelae of cerebrovascular accident, sequelae of spinal cord injuries or senile degenerative diseases; Chronic diseases such as EPOC, hypertension, degenerative arthritis, diabetes, SIDA or cancer; Pre-established pathologies that require the administration of medications intravenously or administration of parenteral nutrition; Complicated wounds, open abdomens in the process of healing; Articular replacements that require intravenous antibiotic management and pain management; Scheduled post-surgical patients that do not require permanent hospitalization.) [2].

The services that are usually provided to patients in the home hospitalization include:

- User communication with the Program 24 h a day.
- Assistance team made up of a doctor and a professional nurse who visits patients. Nursing assistant according to the level assigned by the program.
- Home therapies depending on the case, for the patient's training in their rehabilitation processes.

© Springer Nature Switzerland AG 2018
J. C. Figueroa-García et al. (Eds.): WEA 2018, CCIS 915, pp. 406–417, 2018.
https://doi.org/10.1007/978-3-030-00350-0_34

- Supply of medicines and surgical medical equipment.
- Phototherapy.
- Palliative care.
- Advice and nutritional support as the case may be.
- Taking of laboratories according to the case.
- Healing and wound management.
- Training the patient and his family to manage different types of catheters and stomata.
- Ambulance service in cases of medical emergency [1].

Although the services are quite complete, the patients do not have a record of their vital signs between the visits of the specialist staff, and it could be through a tool that allows the constant monitoring of their general health to expand the types of people to which can be provided with the PHD service; improving general attention through early detection of possible attacks and/or symptoms.

On the other hand, health brigades carried out by teams of volunteers throughout the country are becoming more frequent, reaching outlying areas where health services are scarce, and the registration and control of patients' medical records is poor unused. Only in departments like the Tolima at the beginning of 2015 an event was developed by the Health Brigade of the Colombian Air Force, 1904 people in need received timely attention due to the precarious conditions of the centers providing medical attention in the area [3].

HL7 (Health Level-7) is a set of protocols that allows to establish, through flexible standards, lines of work and methodologies, an effective and safe communication between different health entities, in addition, guarantees that the information that each health system it is transparent to the other [4]. In the work presented in this paper, the interoperability capabilities of the standard are used, proposing the design of an HL7 interface, which allows the management systems of the application developed during this paper to interoperate, for the management of the information collected in the provision of PHD services, with the current data management systems used in IPS (Providers of Health Services), EPS (Health Promoting Entities) and ARS (Subsidized Regime Administrators).

Another technology involved in the development of the project is the "IoT"; According to the Internet Business Solutions Group (IBSG) of Cisco, it is estimated that the term IoT "was born" sometime between 2008 and 2009, the concept was simple but powerful: if all the objects of our daily life were equipped with identifiers and wireless connectivity, these objects could communicate with others and be managed by computers, this way you could follow and tell everything, and greatly reduce waste, losses and costs. Provide computers to perceive the world and get all the information we need to make decisions [5]. Through this concept, the collection of the information provided by the constant readings of vital signs is achieved by means of a device that allows the measurement of these, for the patients who require it due to their corresponding condition, allowing a system of notifications both for the patient, as for the health professional in charge of the follow-up and attention of the case.

2 Work Carried Out

In several countries around the world there is currently a tendency to unify processes and information, in the same way we tend to seek support in technological solutions to achieve these objectives, which is seen around the world as well as a very marked globalization, is the search for interoperability between systems. This is why in a large number of countries (such as those belonging to the European Union, the US, and some Latin Americans, to a lesser extent, such as Brazil) [6] the hL7 protocol has already been implemented, which searches through information structures, the communication between the applications of different health entities, so that the information of the people, is always fed by the different services to which the patient can resort, and to the same extent there is a loss of null information.

There are multiple tools that currently offer free and customizable health services to the company since they are open source, for small and medium entities, they provide many of the services described in the methodology, supported by the security levels established by she. Among the companies most recognized today for providing this type of products are: Merge, which offers an installable product for the development in c# of an application that allows controlling the sending, storage and administration of information from medical records [13]. Companies like Bahmni offer their own framework for the installation and simple development of applications under the HL7 standards in the upper layers (Application, Presentation, Session and Transport).

Currently the use of the HL7 standard is widespread not only for its usefulness, but also for the ease of implementation thanks to the resources (libraries and controls) offered by some of the most commonly used frameworks and languages, such as .NET, Java, Ruby and JavaScript.

On the other hand, the advances made for the development with IoT in the field of medicine are remarkable, it has reached the development of architectures (most of them using Gateway gateways) that facilitate the interconnection of a series of sensors and actuators with the web world, as well as the design of protocols that allow these devices to comply with different performance specifications [7, 8]. In addition, the types of communication links necessary for the development of the device [9, 10] have been explored. Currently there is research in systems specifically related to medical and health applications, monitoring patients both in hospitals [11, 12].

We also find advances in less complex, open source developments available in public access repositories, which are able to communicate with applications automatically, saving the information obtained, according to the standard of HL7 for further processing, the portable meter [14]. And the project of vision, processing and storage of images in ultrasound [15], bring closer the possibility of providing effective care outside of a first level institution [16].

Among the architectures used among the works already described above we find:

1. IoT Technology for the Dynamic Content Adaptive eHealth Content Management Framework embedded in cloud architecture.

These systems produce and process exponentially increasing amounts of sensory data. In addition, they support real-time processing that requires a dynamically scalable and fault-tolerant architecture. Using cognitive services, the appropriate methods determine the appropriate overview of the system by providing adequate medical information from the sensory body data collected [17]. The underlying methodology uses correlation data between different factors, invoking the customizable eHealth cognitive content management system. The work of [17] demonstrates the corresponding socio-technical environment, the cognitive info communication methodologies applied and the related adaptive technological elements, represented in the following architecture (Fig. 1).

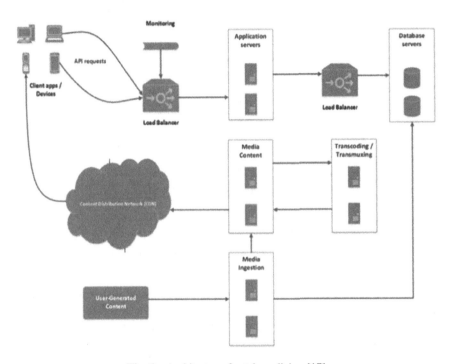

Fig. 1. Architecture for telemedicine [17].

This architecture offers stability and security at a high level, but does not take into account the security of the sensors and the vulnerabilities mentioned in [18], as devices without access, brute-force attacks on the architecture, data encryption, among others. Although there are ongoing standardization initiatives for the interoperability of IOT technology, there is no general solution for the entire sector at this time.

2. Architecture of an interoperable IoT platform Based on Micro-services.

It is based on the coexistence of heterogeneous systems supporting the Internet of Things, which shows an overview of the specific problems inherent in the IoT and the proposal of micro-services-based middleware architecture to connect heterogeneous IoT devices. Middleware functionality is achieved regardless of the size and complexity of a given device network, both from the aspect of the data model and from the aspect of connecting existing and newly created middleware components (Fig. 2).

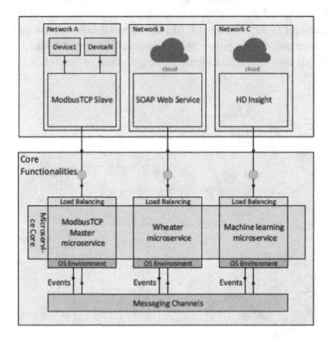

Fig. 2. Micro-services architecture [19]

In [19] we present an overview of the specific problems related to IoT and the proposal of a middleware architecture based on micro-services whose objective is to ensure cohesion between different types of devices, services and communication protocols, while maintaining the scalability of the system. In addition to the concepts provided, we describe the estimation of the regression model of process data flow processing based on different types of integration data source using the proposed architecture.

3. Secure IoT architecture for integrated intelligent service environments

In [20] the architecture is proposed (Fig. 3) to integrate several IoT services with each other, where user authentication is controlled through a service, using encryption and security keys. The identification of the user is done by obtaining the MAC, an ID generated by the system, the SIM number, and IMEI number among other features. For the communication of the services, an encrypted pin is used that travels throughout the network and is validated both in the application and in the Gateway that outputs the Internet. Although security is high in architecture, this quality attribute limits the interoperability of devices and limits the fact that all devices must be connected to the internet in order to validate whether they have access to the services or not. Not all devices that connect to the network have sufficient power to transmit and retransmit these messages.

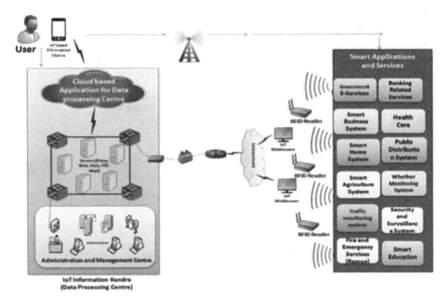

Fig. 3. Proposed architecture in [20]

4. Cisco

Cisco has proposed a framework (Framework) to ensure Internet of Things; this consists of four components which are: Authentication, authorization, network policies, secure analysis for visibility and control [21]. The authentication layer identifies the information of the IoT entity using X.509 certificates after establishing the trust relationship in the identification of the device and the connection of the device with the IoT infrastructure. The problem is that many devices do not have enough space to store the certificate, but they do not have the CPU power to execute the cryptographic operations that validate the certificates. The Framework authorization layer controls access outside of a device and only with authorization after authentication establishes a trust relationship between IoT devices to exchange information. The policy layer reinforced by teamwork consists of the elements that direct endpoint traffic securely over the infrastructure. The last layer defines the services that all the elements of the network infrastructure can participate to provide telemetry with the purpose of obtaining visibility.

3 Proposed Architecture

For the construction of the application, an SOA architecture is proposed, based on the construction of a web service that allows the communication between devices through the World Wide Web, through the transfer of files in XML and JSON format and based on the use of the HTTP, this service goes in favor of machine-to-machine interoperability over a network, looking for any application to be scalable (Fig. 4).

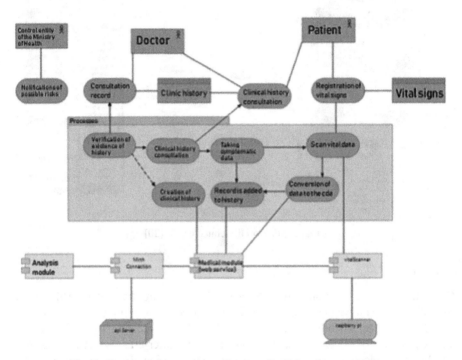

Fig. 4. Design architecture introduction viewpoint. Source: Authors

The basic actors of the system are represented through 3 main roles: the doctor (can be any other type of health specialist), the patient and an agency or control entity of the health secretary, each of these actors has permission to different services, the control agency of the secretary of health has access to a service of notification of risks which will allow diagnoses of problematic conditions that weigh on a whole population, on the other hand the services to which the patient accesses are the of the consultation of his own clinical history and the registration of his vital signs for the subsequent consignment in his clinical history. The consultation service is exclusively for the role of the doctor, he is the only one with the permissions to carry out a consultation in the web service.

To provide each of these services, business processes are performed, for the registration of a query (Fig. 5), starting from the event that is the consultation itself, verifying the existence of a clinical history (business object) and in if necessary, creation; later there is an aggregation to that clinical history of the symptomatic data, and then it is passed to another process that is the registration of the vital signs.

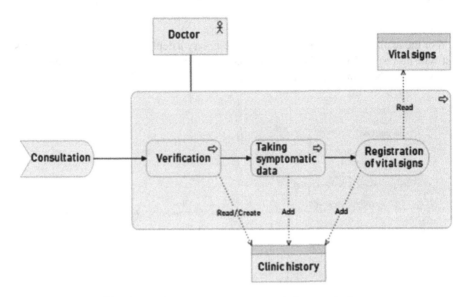

Fig. 5. Business process query record. Source: Authors

The business process of registering vital signs (Fig. 6) begins with the event of electing the option for taking vital signs.

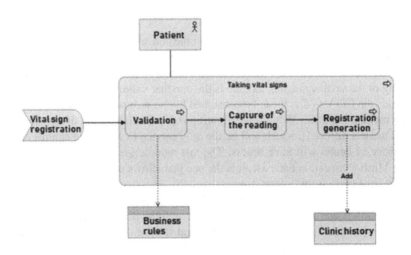

Fig. 6. Business process vital signs registry. Source: Authors

The patient participates in this business process and the first thing that is done is the validation that the business rules are being complied with (patient's condition, number of records taken per day, etc.), once the compliance of the patient is guaranteed. The business rules are made taking the vital signs, and immediately the record is drawn up that will be added to the clinical history.

For the realization of the processes, it is necessary a deployment by logical modules that will be responsible for implementation, in the diagram of structure of the application, we see how the different modules are integrated (Fig. 7).

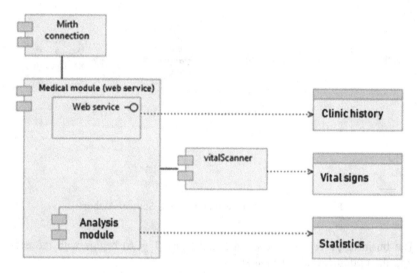

Fig. 7. Application structure. Source: Authors

The structure of the application is based on the construction of a web service which is the one that provides the services through the consumption of the information provided by other modules, the vital module Scanner is in charge of the execution of the taking of the vital signs, this module is the one that validates the business rules and later builds the CDA so that it can be consumed by the web service and later stored, the analysis module is the one that has the algorithms for the elaboration of statistics based on logic models diffuse [], which will be the only service to which the control entity of the ministry of health will have access. The last module is the one of the connection with the Mirth Connection database, it is the one that allows us through hl7 protocols to store and later consult the information.

The vital Scanner module is implemented in a raspberry pi device, which allows the control of takings and reading of vital signs through the different sensors described in previous works such as the vision, processing and storage of images in ultrasound [15] and the development of portable glucometer [16].

In general, we can guarantee that this architecture is not only intended to unify the information obtained from the different health entities, but also to use the information available in a research and reports module where the probable causes of the diseases are detected, investigated and controlled diseases of the general population, for the diagnosis of risk situations.

4 Architecture Comparison

The proposed architecture aims to solve several of the disadvantages found in the previously analyzed architectures; through the use of a middleware mechanism (raspberry) with a high level of processing and that supports the execution of software that allows applying the 4 components of the framework of the architecture proposed by cisco (Authentication, authorization, network policies, analysis secure for visibility and control), is intended to resolve the main weakness of the IoT Technology architecture for the Dynamic Content Adaptation eHealth Content Management Framework embedded in cloud architecture, with the proposed architecture when connecting the sensors to the middleware is responsible for ensuring the security of access to the data, configuring the sensors so that they simply display the information to a single device with the protocols defined for security.

The proposed architectural proposal is partially based on the architecture described above. Architecture of an interoperable IoT platform Based on Micro-services, since it seeks to ensure cohesion between different types of devices, services and communication protocols, while maintaining the scalability of the system, all through the use of middleware for communication between sensors.

It also uses the encryption of the information proposed in the Secure IoT Architecture for intelligent service integrated environments, through an element of the HL7 standard in version 3, which are the messages transmitted by XML, with Mirth Connection encryption, this guarantees the security of the information transmitted by the intelligent device.

5 Conclusions

1. Through the study and implementation of multiple architectures, we achieved the construction of a sufficiently robust to ensure security, interoperability and scalability.
2. Due to its modular pattern, the proposal allows the addition of new functionalities (different from those presented in this document), for the use of information for the generation of new studies and reports, starting from the data provided.
3. This architecture is scalable to any other type of sensor that wishes to be used, as sensor Nanos, since it is based on architectures that support the use of them.

References

1. Programa de Hospitalización Domiciliaria (PHD). http://www.colsanitas.com/portal/web/clinica-colombia/programa-de-hospitalizacion-domiciliaria-phd
2. Hospitalización en casa – FAMICARE. http://famicareclinicadia.com/hospitalizacion-en-casa.html
3. Brigada de Salud de la Fuerza Aérea Colombiana benefició a 1.904 Tolimenses – FAC. https://www.fac.mil.co/brigada-de-salud-de-la-fuerza-a%C3%A9rea-colombiana-benefici%C3%B3-1904-tolimenses
4. HL7 About us - HL7. http://www.hl7.org/
5. Jara, A.J., Zamora-Izquierdo, M.A., Skarmeta, A.F.: Interconnection framework for mHealth and remote monitoring based on the Internet of Things. IEEE J. Sel. Areas Commun. **31**(9), 47–65 (2013)
6. Guía de implementación HL7 para sistemas de notificación obligatoria en salud pública en Colombia. https://www.icesi.edu.co/revistas/index.php/sistemas_telematica/article/viewFile/1011/1036
7. Bassi, A., et al.: Enabling Things to Talk. Springer, Heidelberg (2013). https://doi.org/10.1007/978-3-642-40403-0
8. De Poorter, E., Moerman, I., Demeester, P.J.: Enabling direct connectivity between heterogeneous objects in the Internet of Things through a network-service-oriented architecture. Wirel. Commun. Netw. **2011**, 61 (2011). https://doi.org/10.1186/1687-1499-2011-61
9. Asensio, Á., Marco, Á., Blasco, R., Casas, R.: Protocol and architecture to bring things into Internet of Things. Int. J. Distrib. Sens. Netw. **10**, 158252 (2014)
10. Singh, S.K., Singh, M.P., Singh, D.K.: Routing protocols in wireless sensor networks–a survey. Int. J. Comput. Sci. Eng. Surv. (IJCSES) **1**, 63–83 (2010)
11. Architecture and Protocols for the Internet of Things: A Case Study. Department of Information Engineering, University of Padova, Padova, Italy. Consorzio Ferrara Ricerche (CFR), Ferrara, Italy
12. Rashwand, S., Misic, J.V.: Bridging between IEEE 802.15.6 and IEEE 802.11e for wireless healthcare networks. Ad Hoc Sens. Wirel. Netw. **26**, 303–337 (2015)
13. Contact page and general information of products offered by the company Merge. http://www.merge.com/Company.aspx
14. Page of the repository where the glucometer implementation is located. https://github.com/nebulabio/gluco
15. Page of the repository in which the Portable Ultrasound Project is located. https://hackaday.io/project/9281-murgen-open-source-ultrasound-imaging
16. Vignolo, J., Vacarezza, M., Álvarez, C., Sosa, A.: Niveles de atención, de prevención y atención primaria de la salud. Arch. Med. Interna **33**, 7–11 (2011)
17. Garai, Á., Attila, A., Péntek, I.: Cognitive telemedicine IoT technology for dynamically adaptive eHealth content management reference framework embedded in cloud architecture. In: 7th IEEE International Conference on Cognitive Infocommunications, pp. 187–192 (2016)
18. Giaretta, A., Balasubramaniam, S., Conti, M.: Security vulnerabilities and countermeasures for target localization in bio-nanothings communication networks. IEEE Trans. Inf. Forensics Secur. **11**(4), 665–676 (2016)

19. Vresk, T., Cavrak, I.: Architecture of an interoperable IoT platform based on microservices. In: 2016 39th International Convention on Information and Communication Technology, Electronics and Microelectronics (MIPRO), pp. 1196–1201 (2016)
20. Jerald, V., Rabara, A., Premila, D.: Secure IoT architecture for integrated smart services environment. In: IEEE International Conference on Computing for Sustainable Global Development, pp. 800–805 (2016)
21. Securing the Internet of Things: A Proposed Framework. http://www.cisco.com/c/en/us/about/security-center/secure-iot-proposed-framework.html

NeuroEHR: Open Source Telehealth System for the Management of Clinical Data, EEG and Remote Diagnosis of Epilepsy

Edward Molina$^{(\boxtimes)}$ ⓘ, Ricardo Salazar-Cabrera$^{(\boxtimes)}$ ⓘ,
and Diego M. López$^{(\boxtimes)}$ ⓘ

Telematics Engineering Group, University of Cauca, Popayán, Colombia
{eamolina, ricardosalazarc, dmlopez}@unicauca.edu.co

Abstract. Problem: A number of technologies has been developed aiming at improving the availability, opportunity, difficulty of access or efficiency of epilepsy diagnosis based on Electroencephalogram (EEG) data. However, these approaches are not all based on open technologies, neither are they integrated into Electronic Health Record information (EHR) systems to support continuity of care. Objective: To develop an open source EHR system for the management of patient's information, encounter scheduling, remote registration, and subsequent analysis of EEG data. Methods: The analysis, design, and implementation of the system followed the Scrum framework. The implementation was based on an open source platform for EHR systems named OpenMRS. Results: NeuroEHR supports the provision of Tele-EEG services, integrates patient's clinical information, and EEG data captured remotely from an EEG device, stores the data in an EEG repository, and allows a neurologist to provide a diagnosis based on clinical and EEG data. Conclusions: The NeuroEHR system is currently being used in the context of the NeuroMoTIC project, in which a pediatric EEG data set is being created and annotated, and some Artificial Intelligence algorithms are being tested to support a telehealth service for the diagnosis of epilepsy.

Keywords: Electronic health record system · Telehealth · Epilepsy diagnosis
Tele-EEG · EEG

1 Introduction

Currently in the world there are more than 450 million people with mental and neurological disorders, of which 80% are in low and middle income countries (LMIC) [1]. The main neurological and mental problems identified by the World Health Organization (WHO) are: depression, psychosis, epilepsy, developmental disorders, behavioral disorders, and dementia. It is estimated that approximately 20% of boys and girls suffer from any of these conditions [2]. In Colombia, the Neurological Institute estimates the prevalence of epilepsy at 2%, with only 30% of the population controlled [3]. In turn, a study by Vélez et al. revealed that the highest prevalence of epilepsy is found in children, affecting 71% of the population suffering the disease. Moreover, children below 6 years of age account for 28% of the cases [4].

© Springer Nature Switzerland AG 2018
J. C. Figueroa-García et al. (Eds.): WEA 2018, CCIS 915, pp. 418–430, 2018.
https://doi.org/10.1007/978-3-030-00350-0_35

One of the biggest obstacles in the early detection of neurological disorders, such as epilepsy, is the low availability of specialized professionals. In Colombia, for example, the total number of neurologists in 2011 was only 231 [5]. This small number of specialist affects the diagnosis of the disease, especially because of the complexity of the clinical test used in the diagnosis. The most common test to confirm an epilepsy case is the Electroencephalogram (EEG), which is a transitory signal, obtained placing electrodes on the scalp for recording brain electric activity. Considering that a typical EEG recording lasts 20–30 min (not including patient's preparation time) and the ambulatory EEG, also called video EEG, which takes from 24 to 48 h; the time invested by a specialist to read an EEG is very high.

Another important problem, especially in low and middle income countries, is the poor efficiency of health services, especially in rural areas. According to Colombian Clinical Practice Guidelines (CPG) for the diagnosis and treatment of epilepsy [3], all children, youth, and adults who present suspicious crises, such as seizure, should be treated urgently by a specialist within the next two weeks. However, in Colombia, the mean elapsed time since a seizure event occurs and the case is diagnosed is 4 months. This is especially critical for rural population, because specialized medical services are usually only provided in capital cities, so the patients requires several trips to receive diagnosis and treatment.

In response to the need for improving efficiency of epilepsy diagnosis services in rural areas, Tele-EEG services are a cost-effective alternative. In this direction, the state of the art analysis, presented in the following section, provides scientific evidence of the improvement in the availability, opportunity or efficiency in the diagnosis of epilepsy supported by EEG. However, these approaches are not all based on open technologies, neither are they integrated into Electronic Health Record (EHR) information systems to support continuity of care.

The objective of this paper is to describe the development of NeuroEHR, an open source EHR system for the management of patient information, encounter scheduling, remote registration, and subsequent analysis of EEG tests. NeuroEHR allows the provision of epilepsy diagnosis services in remote rural areas, therefore improving opportunity and access to diagnosis services. It is designed to operate in a Tele-EEG environment, in which one or several technicians (specialized medical staff) perform EEG exams on patients in the same or different geographical locations, record the patient's clinical information and EEG data, and provide an open source EHR service in which one or several neurologists can remotely read the EEG test to support EEG diagnosis and decision making.

In the following sections, the related previous works are described; the analysis, design, and implementation phases of the development process are presented; and finally, a case study in pediatric EEG analysis in Colombia using the NeuroEHR system is described, followed by the discussions and conclusions.

2 Related Works

Campos et al. described the implementation and evaluation of a real-time ambulatory consultation service based video-EEG [6]. The authors demonstrated an improvement in the opportunity of the diagnosis, treatment and immediacy of care, and accessibility to the electronic health records; concluding also that the Tele-EEG system had a positive impact on patient's opinion. The main gap of the proposed system is the need of a wide bandwidth Internet connection for sending online videos, which is not the case in most rural areas in LMIC. Also, it's not supported on open platforms and standards.

Celi et al. created the Mobile Clinical Information System – MOCA [7]. It is an open source Android platform used to collect patient's information through a mobile client. The system is integrated with OpenMRS, an open source EHR platform which has been used in many low and middle income countries. The software allows the transmission to a central server of clinical data, including EEG, audio or video files, using a cell phone. The specialist receives the data, enabling real time diagnosis. The main drawback with this work is that it does not provide an EEG repository within the system, for its further review by the specialist. The system was further adapted, and a mobile EEG tele-monitoring system was developed, but its clinical relevance was not demonstrated because it was not supported on professional EEG devices [8].

Townsend et al. highlighted the importance of remotely monitoring vital signs [9]. A monitoring architecture for real-time patients is proposed, which includes: body sensor networks (including EEG sensors), electronic patient records, and an SMS messaging service as a data transfer mechanism. Through a web portal, the data of the physiological state of the patient is displayed, as well as a service via SMS to provide alerts to medical personnel in case of emergencies. Although the proposed system allows the collection of summary information on vital signs through SMS, it does not allow the management of information associated to epilepsy.

Thangavelu et al. proposed a series of signal processing algorithms for the detection of epileptic seizures which are implemented through the analysis of EEG signals in a mobile environment. These algorithms were tested in a simulated Body Area Network (BAN) using the Emotiv EEG device. The main disadvantage of the proposed system is that it does not integrate or implement an EHR system and it can't be used in real Tele-EEG services because Emotiv is not a medical device.

Shoeder et al. presented a pilot tele-neurology service implemented in a hospital in Colombia [10]. The study assessed patient's satisfaction with the neurological tele-consultation service and establishes the human and technical requirements for its implementation and evaluation. The pilot study was performed with 20 patients. The proposed service provided only a tele-consultation service, not involving the collection and analysis of clinical examinations such as the EEG, nor the integration with an EHR.

Borja et al. described the design, implementation and evaluation of the reliability of an EEG system for signal acquisition and visualization [11]. In this work, a system for the visualization of EEG signals was implemented, however the number of EEG channels is limited (4 in total) due to hardware restrictions. In addition the information collected is not managed by any EHR.

3 Methods

The development process was guided through the Scrum [12] framework. It included in-depth interviews with a neuropediatrician and EEG technician, and the observation of the health services provision in an EEG clinic. The Electronic Health Record (EHR) technology used for the construction of the system was Bahmni (https://www.bahmni.org), an open source distribution of the OpenMRS (Open Medical Record System) framework [13].

3.1 Identification of Software Requirements

The software requirements elicitation process began with in-depth interviews [14] conducted with a neuropediatrician through a protocol of questions. This protocol was defined to generate discussion and exchange of opinions. The objective of the interview was to understand the conventional procedure of collecting and managing both clinical and EEG data in the context of the diagnosis of epilepsy, as well as to know the needs of the neuropediatrician concerning the remote diagnosis of epilepsy. The interview was recorded in audio format and an informed consent was signed.

In order to get firsthand information about the procedure for collecting clinical data and EEG exams, an observation was performed at the neuropediatrician's medical office, in which regular EEG exams are normally taken to the patients.

Based on the activities described above and subsequent meetings with the neuropediatrician, the software requirements of the system were identified. Below is a summary of the EEG data collection process as it was formalized in this stage of the development.

1. Patient data collection (5 min): Patient clinical information is gathered by the clinics technical staff and the collected data is registered in the BWAnalysis[1] software, which is used both for the recording of clinical data and for the recording of the EEG signals. The registered data are full names, identification document, date of birth, gender, weight, height, medical doctor, medication, health provider, and previous clinical events.

2. Location of electrodes (20 min): 24 electrodes are located in total (22 in the scalp and 2 in the chest) and the impedance of each one is verified through the BWAnalysis software, to ensure that they have proper contact. The electrodes are located according to the 10/20 positioning standard using the BWII-EEG[2] device.

3. Taking the EEG exam (30 min): The signals are captured in three different assemblies, these are configured in the software beforehand. Each assembly (lasting ten minutes) determines which group of electrodes is activated for recording the

---

[1] Computer Software developed by Neurovirtual, which is distributed with the BWII-EEG device.
[2] FDA certified Medical device for the recording of EEG signals.

signals. During assembly one, patients are hyperventilated; during the assembly two, flash stimulation is provided, and during assembly three, opening, ocular closure, and auditory stimulation is provided. Following, the signals are stored and annotations are made when an event that alters the signal (artefact) occurs, for example body movements or coughing.

4. Test Reporting: An EEG test report is created by the neurologist and delivered to the patient after 15 business days. It includes some clinical recommendations, for example changing patient's medication, or ordering additional tests required for possible clinical interventions.

The identified software requirements were specified in fifteen user stories (US) to have more precise descriptions regarding functionality, effort estimation, and responsibility.

According to the software requirements, the Tele-EEG system should allow the management of patients and clinical data, the registration of EEG exams, the reporting of EEG test results, and the management of appointments. It should operate in a telemedicine environment, in which one or more technicians take EEG exams on patients in the same or different geographical location. Subsequently, one or more neurologists should be able to review the registered data and exams in the system, and report results independent of his/her geographical location. On the other hand, the platform should facilitate the scheduling of appointments for EEG exams.

Three actors interact in the system: The EEG technician, who records the clinical data and EEG exams, and also schedules appointments; the neurologist, who reviews the EEG exams and reports the results; and the system administrator, who is responsible for managing users, as well as the general maintenance of system configurations.

The system is especially useful when it is employed for taking EEG exams in geographically disperse or low-income rural areas, where there is no presence of neurologists.

3.2 Technology Used

OpenMRS [13] is a Java-based and open source electronic medical record system. It provides a data model, which is included in the platform's API. The API works like a "black box" hiding the complexities of the data model and ensuring that the applications and modules that use the API work with a similar set of business rules. At the heart of OpenMRS there is a dictionary of concepts, on which all the management of clinical information is based. OpenMRS is built to support modules, which can be used by software developers to modify the behavior of the system. This technology was chosen because it is the most used open source EHR in the world. It has a strong developers and support community, and several technical functionalities.

Bahmni (http://www.Bahmni.org) is an open source framework built as a JavaScript application on top of the OpenMRS (http://www.openmrs.org) data model and application program interface. Bahmni objective is to satisfy the needs of hospitals in low-resource environments by taking advantage of many other open source technologies. Bahmni uses OpenERP (https://www.odoo.com/) for billing and inventory management, and OpenELIS (http://www.openelis.org/) for laboratory management [4].

Taking into account the above, Bahmni was selected as the base technology for the construction of the Tele-EEG system because it is integrated with OpenMRS, it is of general purpose, configurable, and adaptable to any workflow of a hospital. It not only offers the possibility of implementing hospital information systems (HIS) through personalized configurations with JSON files (Bahmni configuration files), but it is also possible to modify the source code of the framework to adapt aspects not supported by the configuration files.

In order to meet the identified software requirements, only the OpenMRS component which is integrated into the Bahmni JavaScript application was deployed. The OpenERP and OpenELIS components were not used because the identified requirements didn't include billing or laboratory management needs.

3.3 Development Process

The development of the Tele-EEG system called NeuroEHR was carried out under the Scrum framework through the four following events: Sprint Planning, in which the software requirements to be implemented on each sprint were selected; Sprints, in which the system was implemented using three iterations; Sprint Review, which reviewed the functionality of the system in each iteration, and Sprint Retrospective, which allowed to evaluate the development process and introduce improvements to it.

In the first sprint, the user interfaces of the entire system were designed and the user management module was implemented; in the second sprint, the modules for patient management and exam management were implemented. Finally, in the third sprint the results reporting and appointment management modules were implemented. A neuro-pediatrician was present during the entire implementation process to clarify the software requirements when it was necessary and to validate the usability of the user interfaces.

4 NeuroEHR

NeuroEHR is a web telemedicine platform built on the Bahmni framework that allows the scheduling of appointments, the registration of clinical data, and EEG exams by technical personnel in any geographical area. It also allows the remote reading of EEG tests, and reporting of results related to the diagnosis of epilepsy. In this way, NeuroEHR is useful in the diagnosis process of epilepsy in rural or low-income areas, solving the problem of medical coverage for these places where the presence of neurologists is not feasible. The following section describes the architecture and software features of the aforementioned Tele-EEG system.

4.1   System Architecture

The system architecture is based on the Bahmni architecture [4] which is a client-server one (see Fig. 1).

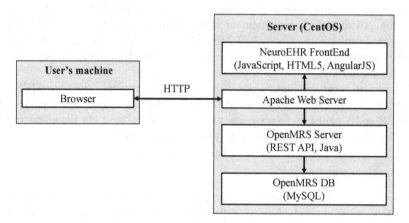

Fig. 1. NeuroEHR architecture.

The *User's machine* component represents the personal computers of the technicians and neurologists, who access NeuroEHR through a *Browser* with Internet connection.

The *Server* is responsible for providing the necessary services for the operation of the Tele-EEG system. *NeuroEHR FrontEnd* is the web application with which users interact to make use of the functional characteristics of the system. *Apache Web Server* provides the necessary HTTP services so that users can access the system through the web. *OpenMRS Server* allows the storage and management of all clinical information. *OpenMRS DB* represents the database where all the information collected by the system is stored.

4.2   Source Code

Four repositories of Bahmni located at GitHub (https://github.com/bahmni) related to the management of clinical information with OpenMRS were taken as a basis and a fork operation was performed on each of them, obtaining four new projects. These were adapted to meet the requirements of NeuroEHR. Below is a short description of the resulting repositories and their location on GitHub.

NeuroEHR: This project contains the FrontEnd of the system. It is an application based on AngularJS, which is used by the technicians and neurologists to record clinical data of patients, take and review EEG studies, and manage appointments for patients in a Tele-EEG environment, as mentioned earlier. This repository is available on https://github.com/neuromotic/hce-neuromotic-openmrs-module-bahmniapps.

OpenMRS Modules: It contains the modules that provide NeuroEHR with the necessary OpenMRS services for the management of clinical information. This project is written in Java and available at: https://github.com/neuromotic/hce-neuromotic-bahmni-core.

Back-End: This project written in Java provides several utilities necessary for the operation of the web platform. Available at: https://github.com/neuromotic/hce-neuromotic-bahmni-java-utils.

System configuration: Set of JSON files that allow the configuration of some aspects of the system modules at runtime, without the need to re-compile services. Available at: https://github.com/neuromotic/hce-neuromotic-default-config.

4.3   Main Features of NeuroEHR

To use the Tele-EEG System, each user must log in using the account provided by the system administrator. The main functions of the system are described below.

Recording EEG Studies. Before starting with EEG recording, the technician records the patient's personal data (see Fig. 2). Subsequently she/he performs the procedure of recording EEG signals using a medical device. At the end of the study, the technician records the clinical data of the patient, and a single EEG file is generated (see Fig. 3). From this moment the data and the exam will be available for a neurologist to review them and to report the results.

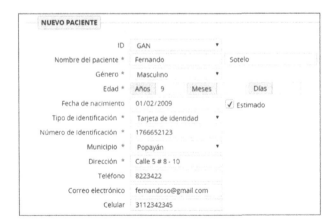

Fig. 2. Patient registration in NeuroEHR (fictitious data).

Examen EEG
Peso (Kg)
28
Altura (Cm)
125
Medicamentos actuales
Ácido valproico
Divalproato de sodio
Valproato de magnesio
Carbamazepina
Oxcarbazepina
Fenitoina
Fenobarbital
Levetiracetam
Topiramato
Lamotrigina
Primidona
Etosuximida (3,4)
EPS
Asmet salud
Cafesalud
Caprecom
Coomeva
Emssanar
Nueva EPS
Saludvida
Sanitas
Histórico
Presenta movimientos involuntarios y pérdida de conciencia.
Tipo de EEG
Vigilia
Sueño
Grabación EEG
Subir archivo EEG
Visualizar examen EEG
Descargar examen EEG

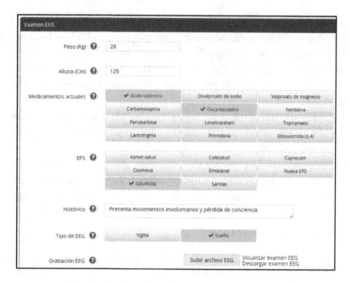

Fig. 3. Registration of EEG and clinical data.

Review of EEG Studies. The neurologist selects the exam that he/she wants to review, analyzes the patient's clinical data, and views or download the EEG test (see Fig. 4). The option visualize allows opening the EEG exam in the desktop application that has been previously configured into the system. At the time of reading the EEG signals, the neurologist can record annotations in the system, for example, normal body movements or abnormal signals related to epilepsy (see Fig. 5).

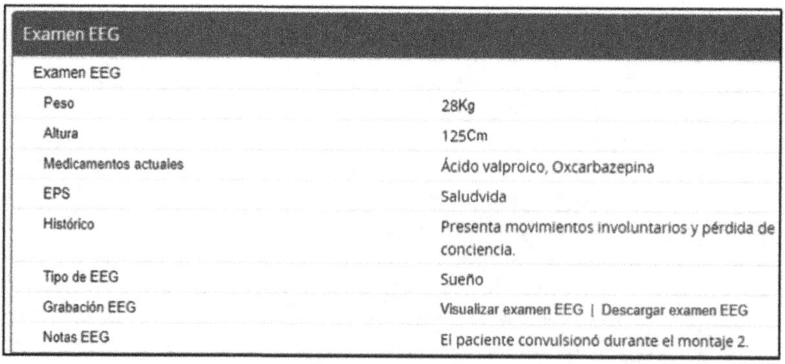

Examen EEG
Examen EEG
Peso
28Kg
Altura
125Cm
Medicamentos actuales
Ácido valproico, Oxcarbazepina
EPS
Saludvida
Histórico
Presenta movimientos involuntarios y pérdida de conciencia.
Tipo de EEG
Sueño
Grabación EEG
Visualizar examen EEG | Descargar examen EEG
Notas EEG
El paciente convulsionó durante el montaje 2.

Fig. 4. Visualization of clinical and EEG data.

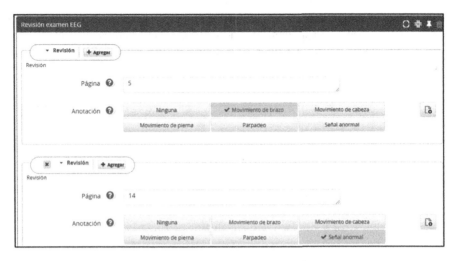

Fig. 5. Record of EEG test annotations.

EEG Test Report. Once the neurologist has finished reading the EEG exam and recording the examinations that he considers pertinent, he/she can record the report of the study. This is generated in PDF and contains the neurologist's concept of the presence or absence of epileptic seizures in the patient (see Fig. 6).

Fig. 6. EEG test report.

Management of Appointments. This functionality facilitates the scheduling of EEG exams. Before scheduling appointments, the schedules and practices available for this purpose are defined. When scheduling an appointment the patient, location, date, and time are selected (see Fig. 7).

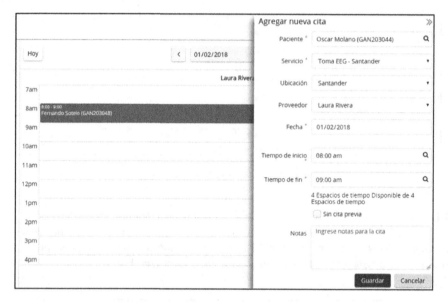

Fig. 7. EEG exam scheduling (fictitious data).

5 Discussion and Conclusions

The paper presents the development process of NeuroEHR, an open source EHR system for the management of patient information, encounter scheduling, remote registration and subsequent analysis of EEG studies. Through qualitative in-depth interviews and observations, particularly the participation of a neuropediatrician in all the phases of the development, the resulting implemented system was adapted to real needs in relation to the remote diagnosis of epilepsy. This Tele-EEG system has the potential to benefit hospitals or communities in low or middle income countries, contributing to the solution of the problem given by the limited availability of specialized professionals.

As it was demonstrated in the previous state of the art analysis section, there is a lack of Tele-EEG systems supported on open technologies and able to be integrated into Electronic Health Record (EHR) information systems. The above is very relevant in LMIC countries, especially because high cost and low availability of neurology services for the diagnosis and management of epilepsy. The base technology used for the development of the NeuroEHR system (Bahmni) provided the required functionality, also the scalability to integrate the OpenMRS component into a customizable web application by means of configuration files and modification to the source code. This allowed an easy adaptation of the system requirements to the open source platform, therefore decreasing the implementation effort required.

The system is currently being used in the context of the NeuroMoTIC project [15], in which a pediatric EEG data set is being created and annotated, and one Machine Learning Classifier is being trained to support the neurologist in the diagnosis of epilepsy in children [16]. So far, 100 pediatric EEGs have been collected using the NeuroEHR system and 4 of these were diagnosed with the presence of epilepsy. A training dataset has been created with 13 segments of EEG with epileptiform events and 7 segments of normal signals. After the algorithms had been trained, and the classification and relevance algorithms had been proposed, an intelligent component will be created and integrated to the system as a new OpenMRS component. The Intelligent component would help the neurologist in identifying patterns of suspicious signs of epilepsy (epileptiform events such as peaks and low waves), which will allow him to increase the efficiency in the process of reading EEG tests. Furthermore, as it is part of the NeuroMoTIC project, the implementation of a pilot Tele-EEG intervention in rural areas at the Department of Cauca, Colombia, aiming at demonstrate the NeuroEHR system´s feasibility to increase the opportunity of epilepsy cases confirmation is foreseen. As future work, the usability and performance of the system will also be evaluated.

Acknowledgements. The work is funded by a grant from the Colombian Agency for Science, Technology, and Innovation Colciencias – under Call 715- 2015- "Convocatoria para Proyectos de Investigación y Desarrollo en Ingenierias", project: "NeuroMoTIC: Sistema móvil para el Apoyo Diagnóstico de la Epilepsia", Contract number FP44842-154-2016.

References

1. Mental health: strengthening our response. http://www.who.int/mediacentre/factsheets/fs220/en. Accessed 13 Apr 2018
2. Diez Datos sobre la salud mental. http://www.who.int/features/factfiles/mental_health/mental_health_facts/es/index9.html. Accessed 13 Apr 2018
3. Ministerio de Salud y Protección Social: Guía de Práctica Clínica (GPC) para la prevención, diagnóstico, tratamiento y rehabilitación de los Pacientes con Epilepsia en el Contexto Colombiano, Bogotá, Colombia (2013)
4. Velez, A., Eslava-Cobos, J.: Epilepsy in Colombia: epidemiologic profile and classification of epileptic seizures and syndromes. Epilepsia **47**, 193–201 (2006)
5. Amaya, J., et al.: Estudio de disponibilidad y distribución de la oferta de médicos especialistas, en servicios de alta y mediana complejidad en Colombia. Doc. técnico GPES/1682C-13. Dispon. en (2013). https://www.minsalud.gov.co/salud/Documents/Observatorio%20Talento%20Humano%20en%20Salud/DisponibilidadDistribuci%C3%B3nMdEspecialistasCendex.pdf
6. Campos, C., et al.: Setting up a telemedicine service for remote real-time video-EEG consultation in La Rioja (Spain). Int. J. Med. Inform. **81**, 404–414 (2012)
7. Celi, L.A., Sarmenta, L., Rotberg, J., Marcelo, A., Clifford, G.: Mobile care (moca) for remote diagnosis and screening. J. Health Inform. Dev. Ctries. **3**, 17 (2009)

8. Insuasty, D.F., Ceron, R.E., López, D.M.: A mobile system for the collection of clinical data and EEG signals by using the sana platform. Stud. Health Technol. Inform. **200**, 116–123 (2014)
9. Townsend, B., Abawajy, J., Kim, T.-H.: SMS-based medical diagnostic telemetry data transmission protocol for medical sensors. Sensors **11**, 4231–4243 (2011)
10. Shoeder, N.M., Gaona Barbosa, I.A., Rodriguez Velásquez, N., Vergara, J.P.: Teleneurología para el seguimiento de pacientes epilépticos prueba piloto en el Hospital de San José. Bogotá DC, Colombia. Reper. Med. Cir. **21**, 285–290 (2012)
11. Borja, G., Ortega, T., Romero, A.: Diseño e implementación de un equipo para la adquisición y visualización en pc de señales electroencefalográficas. PROSPECTIVA **8**, 21–28 (2010)
12. Schwaber, K., Beedle, M.: Agile Software Development with Scrum. Prentice Hall, Upper Saddle River (2002)
13. Wolfe, B.A., et al.: The OpenMRS system: collaborating toward an open source EMR for developing countries. In: AMIA Annual Symposium Proceedings, pp. 1146–1146 (2006)
14. Sjøberg, D.I.: Guide to Advanced Empirical Software Engineering. Springer, Alemania (2008). https://doi.org/10.1007/978-1-84800-044-5
15. Proyecto NeuroMoTIC, https://neuromotic.unicauca.edu.co/. Accessed 13 Apr 2018
16. Mera-Gaona, M., Vargas-Canas, R., Lopez, D.M.: Towards a selection mechanism of relevant features for automatic epileptic seizures detection. Stud. Health Technol. Inform. **228**, 722–726 (2016)

Approach of an Active Defense Protocol to Deal with RAT Malware

A Colombian Case Study Against njRAT Campaigns

Fernando Quintero$^{(\boxtimes)}$ ⓘ, Eduardo Chavarro$^{(\boxtimes)}$ ⓘ,
Giovanni Cruz$^{(\boxtimes)}$ ⓘ, and Carlos Fernández$^{(\boxtimes)}$ ⓘ

CSIETE - Corporación para la Investigación en Seguridad de la Información en
Tecnologías Emergentes, Medellín, Colombia
{fernando.quintero,eduardo.chavarro,giovanni.cruz,
carlos.fernandez}@csiete.org
https://www.csiete.org

Abstract. Organizations have become infrastructure and information dependent, and any problem that affects those assets can compromise the organization's operations. Incident handling and malware research requires new
strategies focusing on cyber defense in a way that allows researchers, incident
responders and authorities to react preventively to mitigate high damaging
attacks. The results of this research are a guideline of an active defense protocol
to contain Remote Access Trojan (RAT) malware attacks, identifying proac-
tively weaknesses on generic, open source or leaked code used for Trojan
infection campaigns, and thus developing an effective response protocol to
contain and stop the threat with a limited resource investment. This protocol
does not replace traditional national protocols required by local authorities to
report cyber security incidents; however, some mechanisms to deactivate
Command and Control (C2) servers, can reduce effectiveness of operations
based on malware related threats faced in Colombian and other countries around
the globe.

Keywords: Malware · Remote Access Trojan · njRAT · Computer crime
Active security model · Offensive countermeasure · Network security
Command and control server · Incident response

1 Introduction

1.1 Cybercrime

Information is one of the main assets for organizations and its protection is an implicit
objective for the organization's management [1]. Although information security standards are implemented to protect information, companies are targeted by attackers,
which also include citizens and ICT consumers as targets.

The attackers are not passive but developing techniques and tools that make life
easier. They use tools that go through perimeter controls to stay within organizations

© Springer Nature Switzerland AG 2018
J. C. Figueroa-García et al. (Eds.): WEA 2018, CCIS 915, pp. 431–445, 2018.
https://doi.org/10.1007/978-3-030-00350-0_36

and from there controlling their operations to obtain data at rest or in transit that can be transacted in the black market.

According to the report about the Impact of Digital Security Incidents published by the Colombian Ministry of ICT (MINTIC), in 2016 more than 50% of the Colombian companies interviewed registered between 1 and 5 digital incidents, and approximately 30% of the companies reported between 6 and 100 incidents. The report highlights that 5% of the companies registered over 1.000 incidents, with a global number of more than 100 thousand incidents in 2016 [2]. Other reports show an average of up to 540.000 incidents in Colombia with a loss of more than 6 billion dollars [3].

The Russian company of cybersecurity services, Kaspersky Lab, presented an overview about cybercrime in Latin America for 2017, pointing out that it found 677 million cyber threats in a time lapse of 8 months (January to August) that could be interpreted as an average of 117 attacks per hour and 33 per second [4].

Risks and threats to information security in companies are evident. Only in Colombia, in 2015, the Department of Cybercrime of the National Police received 7118 complaints from cyber victims, which represents a 40% increase compared to 2014. Economic losses derived from these acts represent the 0,14% of the gross domestic product, according to the Worldwide Bank (2014); this means, about US$500 million approximately [5].

1.2   Malware

Malware [6] is any piece of software designed for the specific purpose of performing malicious activities within the devices that they compromise. Malware can have the ability to spread automatically or manually, where this last one represents a higher risk, since a threat that arrives specifically to the organization is considered a targeted attack.

Among the preferred tools of the attackers are the RAT (Remote Access Trojan), considered a malware with great potential to control devices remotely and through a centralized station known as Command and Control (C2). The scope of the application for RAT-type tools is continuously increasing, impacting organizations, employees and users. However, the tools that are used to infect users to access information that gives revenue to attackers, are getting diverse and its functionalities are growing.

Malware focuses mainly on user manipulation techniques by means of email, spoofing or theft of government and private companies' mailboxes, as indicated on 2016–2017 Police's Cybernetic Center from Colombia [7]. In the first quarter of 2018, campaigns directed to Colombian users using a remote access Trojan identified as njRAT was identified. This is an open source RAT configurable and with enough functions to compromise information [8].

1.3   Rats Campaigns

RATs are used in campaigns with life cycles that begin with the infection of users that then become bots and remain operative as long as the sample of malware used is not detected by antivirus controls. The process of a campaign begins when the attacker sends a massive email, which impersonates a government mail request or an update, then the victim user is asked to download a file and open it and when he does so the malware generates mechanisms to remain inside of the infected device, be it a tablet, cell phone, laptop or desktop, installed in different places, creating shortcuts, impersonating installed programs in order not to be easily detected. It also has the ability to hide in active processes and erase traces of its executions at the memory level.

The installed RAT converts the infected device into a BOT, which works as a program that is controlled remotely by C2, that is managed by the attacker. The campaign begins and the attacker starts earning money using several mechanisms, for example, the theft of credentials, cryptocurrency wallets and credit cards, spamming from the devices, performing DDoS attacks for which they charge a sum to the client who buys the service.

The survival mechanism of the campaign consists in updating the bots, making them undetectable and making connections from one IP address to the next where the command and control are hosted. The success of a campaign depends on how long the mechanism of infection lasts, the number of users who have been infected and therefore the retribution (profit) obtained from the process.

2   Current Defense Strategy

2.1   Standard Procedure for Containment and Mitigation

In the Colombian industry, companies have a standard mechanism to report cybercrime [9]. The report to Internet Service providers and/or local authorities of domains names and IP addresses used by attackers in the campaigns. Foreign third-party companies protect the identity of those who register their services and this is problematic because it prevents identifying the attackers properly.

Deactivation or seizing of IP addresses supporting C2 servers is a procedure that must be requested only to authorities in Colombia, and it will depend on the diligence of the authorities and service providers to proceed. This process can take a long time, 6 months or more unfortunately because of its urgent nature. Also, a report generated to dynamic DNS providers contact services are not always a solution to switch off malicious C2 domains.

The majority of cases are not resolved, allowing the attackers to act in impunity and cause significant losses for the victims. This is why a new way of dealing with this type of computer attacks is proposed.

3   Proposed Protocol for Active Defense Against RAT

3.1   Active Incident Response

Methodologies for an active response to cyber security incidents is not a new subject and it has been addressed by governments all around the world. This concept not only focuses on counter-attack, but on developing strategies that demotivate and identify the malicious actors, their tactics, capabilities and tools [10].

According to a study from George Washington University [11], sets of activities for an active defense framework allow counteracting different stages in the attack phases, affecting the possibilities of the attackers in the preparation, intrusion and security breakdown. Figure 1 shows active defense jobs and their impact on the stages of the attack.

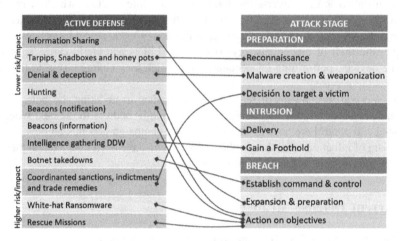

Fig. 1. Impact of active defense in cyber-attacks [11].

By taking down C2 servers communications from and to infected clients (bots) will deactivate, and it forces the attacker to have to obtain new resources and change their strategy, increasing the recovery time and making the attack strategy less resilient and more expensive.

This proposal defines activities that can be deployed against malware campaigns to identify C2 servers and malware installed in a victim, which could give ideas to deactivate these kinds of servers in order to minimize the damage caused. It reduces the time to take down a malware campaign, compared to local authority's procedures and decreases the response time of international requests based on collaborative protocols or a legit complaint against service providers.

3.2 Steps to Make an Active Defense Against RAT

The protocol developed interprets the way in which a defender could develop an analysis of the attacks in order to identify weaknesses within the attackers' environment, to perform an effective active defense as a response strategy to this type of cyber incidents.

Identify the Malware Sample

Cybercriminals in a single campaign usually implement standard procedures to select a RAT, an open source or leaked RAT code, free dynamic dns, hosting in compromised servers, domain names for C2 server and the whole elements to infect and affect citizens [12]. These common elements allow the identification of patterns that help identify the type of malware used and potential attackers. The tools that are used by cybercriminals are reused using the same variant (type) of RAT in most of their campaigns, improving their evasion using obfuscation and encryption techniques.

The use of free analysis sandboxes[1], can provide[2] an overview of the type of sample you are dealing with. Basic analysis tools such as *file, gdb, strings*, allow the identification of the architecture and possible text strings in the binary.

Permanent Monitoring

The permanent monitoring is part of the traffic analysis exercise, where the behavior of the sample in relation to the outside world will be observed, that is, if the malware connects to a C2 or downloads additional binaries from some Internet site.

It is important to keep track of connection patterns and requests to different network protocols. In general, the protocols dns, http, ftp can be an observed with tools like those in the suite sysinternals[3] and traffic analyzers like Wireshark[4].

Search for Vulnerabilities

The search of vulnerabilities is carried out both in the bot sample and in C2, since in most cases weaknesses are found in the protocol that connects these components. It is also possible to find weaknesses directly in the bot or in C2, which provides extra possibilities of exploitation and access to information about the attacker's environment. The most common vulnerabilities are:

- Weakness in the communication protocol
- Authentication and authorization failures
- Buffer Overflows in different components

Create Proofs of Concept and Exploits

Once the vulnerabilities have been identified, the process of exploiting them is automated, with the aim of having programs or quick scripts that help to give an immediate response. It is necessary to use a flexible programming language such as python or ruby and do the necessary tests to guarantee that the elaborated proofs will work in a real attacker's environment.

Develop the Active Defense Plan

In this step, in the cases in which the attacker is faced, a plan must be carefully selected to use a tool to counter and demotivate the attacker's environment and the attack, causing frustration to disable your cybercriminal operation. Among the actions contemplated are:

- Geolocation (GPS/WiFi) of the attacker
- Dismantling the new addition of bots to C2

---

[1] https://www.hybrid-analysis.com/.

[2] https://app.any.run/.

[3] https://live.sysinternals.com/.

[4] https://www.wireshark.org/.

- Achieve a denial of service against C2
- Achieve a massive disinfection of bots in devices
- Achieve remote access to the C2 or to the attacker's station.

Document the Case

Documenting the process generates a knowledge base of effective responses to these types of threats, and it will also maintain a continuous update on the techniques used to defeat attackers. In the documentation, it is also important to add response times and impact mitigation at the organizational level.

Finally, it is a good practice to document and share vulnerabilities, proof of concepts and exploits created for a given threat, so that they can be studied and improved by the academic community and the industry.

4   Case Study: njRAT in Colombia

In this section, the protocol was implemented against njRAT (v0.7d) malware on the campaigns against Colombia to detain them and test the active defense protocol during an incident.

4.1   Infection Campaign Against Colombia - Q1-2018

During the first quarter of 2018, it was determined that several attacker groups were using the same version of njRAT to control infected users. This RAT was deployed to infect users within different companies in order to take control of the compromised machines, steal passwords and execute DDoS attacks. There were at least three major campaigns targeting online banking services in the country. Around 10 malware samples were collected during campaign.

The samples were identified as MSIL/Bladabindi by AV engines, that are an open source malware, originally written in Microsoft .NET language, created in 2012 and cataloged as one of the 300 most known RATs in Latin America [13]. This RAT includes functions to control botnets, download, upload and file execution, remote command execution, windows registry read and write, screen capture, keylogging, webcam capture.

4.2   Global Malware Activity

According to reports from Kaspersky Lab, in the last quarter of 2017, MSIL/Bladabindi was reported in LATAM with Brazil as the most compromised country by this kind of malware. Colombia was identified as the 32nd country in the world with a low number of reports. In the first quarter of 2018, Colombia raised to 8th place in the world, and was the second country in reports for MSIL/Bladabindi in LATAM (Tables 1 and 2).

Table 1. Bladabindi Q4-2017.

Position	Country	Users
1	Brazil	90
2	Russian	85
3	Algeria	35
4	Thailand	34
5	Germany	25
6	India	25
7	France	19
8	Saudi Arabia	18
9	Egypt	15
32	**Colombia**	2

Table 2. Bladabindi Q1-2018.

Position	Country	Users
1	Brazil	145
2	Algeria	43
3	India	35
4	Russian	28
5	Germany	24
6	Egypt	23
7	Thailand	19
8	**Colombia**	17
9	Saudi Arabia	14
10	Spain	14

4.3 Active Defense Protocol Implemented

In the first quarter of 2018 in Colombia, during the wave of njRAT campaigns and after the difficulty of stopping the campaign using traditional channels, a request was received to work in conjunction with the technical staff of some companies, with the objective of detaining the computer threat. It was decided to put into practice the developed active defense protocol.

Identify the Malware Sample

During the stage of recognition of the threat, different samples of the njRAT malware were collected and analyzed, together with identification of connections made to C2 servers used in the campaigns, that confirm C2 IP addresses in Colombia and the use of services in the United States. Identification is done using antivirus signatures and looking for patterns of behavior already documented on the Internet. Some indicators of compromise are shown in Table 3.

Table 3. C2 servers in Colombia and USA using njRAT for 2018-Q1.

MD5 sample Bladabindi	C2 server	CO	USA
37d2b5281b6118155bb27fec0cc8966d	181.61.169.237	X	
25ce4a3901029a1a2dab41c0050fca13 01b791955f1634d8980e9f6b90f2d4c0 2f943d10cde37ea3c331dc61520d293d	23.105.131.187, 174.127.99.215		X
05673fa013236130c3c1e68c18f4bb44	186.112.199.203	X	
37ba434dd2e887fd122b0139abf3a855	186.119.57.208	X	
26c129f51a10816b261f73d5e3b2557e f90a54bb0f5db31eb1b8b2ac409b96d1	191.109.37.128, 190.67.132.99, 186.112.195.41	X X	
6ae912d6fd007f49ab01a23d91245305 c04f2bab82ef5491750fb55b452f4e78	191.109.59.131, 186.112.203.198, 159.65.76.143	X	X

Permanent Monitoring

A systematic monitoring of malware campaigns in Colombia on the first quarter of 2018 was done, validating samples related to njRAT attacks and tracing C2 servers used by these campaigns, this continuous monitoring permitted to identify patterns used by cybercriminals and the selected version of RAT. This was possible implementing a laboratory scenario used to analyze communications between C2 server and infected clients. The way to perform this process is by running the RAT malware sample in a sandbox and monitoring the outgoing network traffic, to identify which is the C2 where it connects. As also analyzing the network traffic, which allows to identify if the communication mechanism used is encrypted or uses a specific pattern.

Indicators of Compromise

For each sample obtained and analyzed, indicators of compromise (IoC) were generated, supporting its classification and confirming their relationship with njRAT.

- IP addresses related to C2 servers.
- Installation paths for malware on operating systems.
- Persistence mechanisms (register, boot files)
- IP addresses for possible attackers.
- Dynamic domains names used for different campaigns.

Malware and C2 Requests/Responses Identification

With the study of different samples, it was possible to identify that this RAT uses a vulnerable communication protocol between infected clients and C2. Each packet builds a frame for the message using the following pattern:

<Message length (byte)> <Command> <Field Separator> <Command Parameters>

According to requested commands, some parameters are encoded using base64 as shown in Fig. 2.

```
155.11|'|'|aG9zdDFfRDA1NTA5OUM=|'|'|IE11WIN7|'|'|IEUser|'|'|
155                                   message length
11                                    Command
|'|'|                                 Separator
aG9zdDFfRDA1NTA5OUM=                  Base64 enconded parameter
IEUser                                Clear Parameter
```

Fig. 2. Exchange frame between client and C2 server infected with njRAT.

All communications begin from client side (infected machine/bot), with a request to C2 server with data about the operating system, session username, hostname, and other fields. This message is immediately answered by the server using a specific format, with the CAP command to take a screenshot of the client as can be seen in Fig. 3.

Fig. 3. Communication establishment between bot and C2 server.

Table 4. Some of the most important commands used.

C2 Commands	Description	Client Commands	Description
CAP|'|'|	Screen capture	PLG	Feed active processes list
EX|'|'|proc|'|'|	Processes request	post|'|'|	Send a file to C2
EX|'|'|tcp|'|'|	TCP connections request	get|'|'|	File request from C2
EX|'|'|srv|'|'|	Services request	un|'|'|~	Uninstall malware
EX|'|'|rs|'|'|	Remote Shell		
rn|'|'|exe|'|'|	File execution		
Ex|'|'|fm|'|'|dw|'|'|	File download		
Ex|'|'|fm|'|'|up|'|'|	File Upload		
ret|'|'|	Passwords list		
Kl	Key Logger		
un|'|'|~	Uninstall malware		

The PLG command, sent from the client side, does not require additional parameters and C2 servers will answer to them. If there is a response then there is a C2. This command was used to create a script for detecting specific field separators used by a njRAT version.

Search for Vulnerabilities and Proofs of Concept

In this step, a sample of the presumed exact version used by the attackers is obtained, and a vulnerability analysis process is carried out in order to counter the threat displayed in the victims from a technical level. With a static and dynamic analysis approach, with a vulnerability analysis process, a defender could identify weaknesses in the version njRAT 0.7d used by the attackers. The weaknesses that were found are not public until this moment and it's a contribution to the community that works in incident response and active defense. Proof of concept can be found in the github of the csiete[5] organization.

---

[5] https://github.com/csieteco/njRatActiveDefense.

Identify the Existence of a C2 njRAT

Using the PLG command it is possible to receive a positive response when a C2 is hosted in the scanned IP. In Colombia, it is very common for attackers to use their own workstations to manage C2 instead of dedicated servers or VPS. The following python script achieves the detection of C2 and give as response the field separator used in the protocol.

```
njRATdetector.py:
    ...
    client.send(str(len('PLG'))+'\x00'+'PLG')
      print 'Waiting for the answer'
    ...
    delimiter = response.split('PLG')[1].split('\x00')[0]
        print "NjRAT answer found!!!: " + delimiter
    ...
```

This script works against njRAT because C2 server does not confirm the existence of a preliminary connection between the client and the server, who sends the response immediately with the communication pattern. View Fig. 4.

Fig. 4. Communication pattern for PLG command on nJRAT.

C2 Denial of Service

The first communication from client to server is produced using "ll" command. This request feeds the administration form on the C2 side to identify infected clients and select commands to perform over them. Sending two or more "ll" requests using the same socket, with the same structure of the connection message, will generate a *System. ArgumentException* exception in the C2 server application causing its immediate shutdown.

The njRATDoS.py script takes 5 to 10 s to takedown a C2 server and it's possible to execute it for a prolonged period so attackers won't be able to reload its admin console.

Through the execution of denial of service techniques (DoS) based on RAT issues, it is possible to halt any activity executed from C2 server regardless of the domain name, IP address, location or server protection. This procedure does not require to be carried out by authorities nor does it require the intervention of the hosting or dynamic domain-name-server providers.

```
njRATDoS.py:
    ...
    def attack():
      print "\nATTACK: Cause DoS"
    for i in range(2):
        client.send(str(len(hello))+'\x00'+hello)
        client.close()
        print "KO"
    ...
```

Sending two or more requests will produce a communication reset from server side as shown in Fig. 5.

Fig. 5. DoS procedure against njRAT C2 server.

C2 Arbitrary File Upload

One of the features of njRAT is the ability to send and receive files from users. Although this command is initiated from the server side, an infected machine uses post command to create a new socket and send files without C2 server request, this is identified as an arbitrary file upload. Once C2 server receives a post request from the victim, it will prepare a socket for file transfer and will save the file using its njRAT download path. Through this active defense vector, it is possible to achieve the following events that affect the attacker's resources.

- Send enough traffic so that the transfer limit is reached in attacker's server or the storage disk is fulfilled, thus generating a degradation in the attacker's infrastructure.
- Search for the execution of a file loaded into C2 server, which may be possible at the moment only if the attacker executes it interactively (human interaction).

It is possible to increase execution probability by using transliteration techniques based on the name of the file that will be created on the C2 server, confusing attackers for them to execute the file. For this case, a right-to-left technique [14] was implemented in a script to modify the appearance of the file trying to spoof its file extension.

By using the proposed procedures for uploading files to the C2 server, it is possible to access privileged information, enabling the identification of infected users and attackers behind the threat, allowing the construction of alerts to inform the pertinent stakeholders for the apprehension of attackers or for the protection of the systems and users compromised. This is the python code to upload arbitrary files to the C2.

```
njRATupload.py:

...

def post(client):
    f=open(file,"rb")
    s=f.read(size)
    post_msg = []
    post_msg.append("post")
    post_msg.append(b64filename) # b64(file)
    post_msg.append(str(size)) # File size
    post_msg.append(localip+':'+str(localport))
    post = delimiter.join(post_msg)
    client.send(str(len(post))+'\x00'+post)
    response = ""
    print "Post send, waiting for ok"

...
```

This script can be executed because C2 servers do not verify the existence of a request for file transfer and will prepare the socket for file transfer once the client sends a post request with the corresponding parameters. The client sends connection parameters to the server and starts a session for file transfer as show in Fig. 6.

Fig. 6. Messages exchange for arbitrary file upload to C2 server.

Massive Bot Uninstaller

By seizing C2 server dynamic domain name or IP Address, an uninstall command can be sent so compromised clients will remove malware from auto run paths and malware file will be deleted from systems. This can be done send the command "un<field separator>~" as registered on Table 4, "Client Commands".

It is possible to create a script to open a listening port and act as a C2 server, wait for njRAT bot requests, and once received this request, send an uninstall command to clean infected machines automatically. This can be done by using a *Sinkhole DNS* server or using the arbitrary file upload vulnerability to C2 servers as described in the last paragraph, the payload will kill njRAT server process, create a server for listening and will send uninstall command to all requesting clients.

```
njRATuninstaller.py:

    ...

    s.bind((host, port))
    s.listen(500)                 # 500 clients
    while True:
        clientSocket, addr = s.accept()
        print("got a connection from %s" % str(addr))
        currentTime = time.ctime(time.time()) + "\r\n"
      mssg = '''un|'|'|~'''
        clientSocket.send(str(len(mssg))+'\x00'+mssg)
        time.sleep(1)
        print(" - Infected client on %s uninstalled" % str(addr))
        clientSocket.close()

    ...
```

Each infected client, that connects to this server will receive the order to uninstall the njRAT malware.

Develop the Active Defense Plan
The main objective of the affected organizations was to stop in the shortest possible time the attack that was causing hundreds of infections inside their facilities. The date in which the incident response team was contacted was the third active day of the incident. The strategy used in this Colombian case was planned like this:

1. Build a payload that allowed using geolocation using WiFi networks. Using the found vulnerability it is possible to upload a PDF (with the payload) file to the C2 that is expected to be opened by the attackers.
2. Intermittent service C2 is caused by using the proof of concept of the first vulnerability, causing the attackers to lose their C2 management, forcing them to open the application continuously after crashing.
3. Before the movement and change of IP or domain names by the attackers, the identification script is executed, making a sweep of the ISP range address that the attackers have been using, finding the C2 again.
4. A false server was built, making use of the provided script, where the requests of the infected users were redirected, achieving a massive disinfection in a matter of minutes.

The information collected was documented and sent to the relevant entities and stakeholders to take action in the case. With this plan, it was possible to identify with a precision of ten meters, the physical place where the attackers were found, giving as a result a residential address in Bogotá, Colombia.

With the collected evidence, it was possible to alert the authorities of the model and serial of the computer equipment of the attackers, as well as the complete identification of the hardware including MAC addresses of the different network cards, wireless and wired. The incident was stopped in just four hours, giving an effective response to the incident presented.

Document the Case
Documentation is an important process, as well as knowledge obtained for the organization itself, as well as to have immediate reaction mechanisms validated, which can be in the hands of the blue teams (CSIRTS, PSIRTS, CERTS) of the organizations. In this case, the approach of the active defense protocol is shared through this literature, which is expected to be useful for the scientific community and industry interested in the active defense field.

5   Considerations and Future Work

This procedure is an approach to the implementation of a cyber security strategy based on an active defense for a specimen of a specific malware called njRAT, which was used intensively in different malware campaigns in Colombia in Q1-2018.

There are many matters to explore in the active defense field and it is necessary, for example, to find more weaknesses (such as remote exploits) that will make them cease their activities, thus achieving a prompt disarticulation.

It is proposed, as future work, to create a way to standardize and automate the protocol and also the documentation of elements of the active defense. There would be documentation that could be consigned in a repository and thus support the work of the incident response teams CSIRT, CERT that fight against cybercrime.

Finally, within the framework to generate active defense actions against cybercrime threats, it is necessary to review the legal implications of carrying out this type of actions, depending on each country and their current legislation, especially if they are actions that are carried out in parallel to open judicial cases or in legal departments within a company.

6   Conclusions

The currently used procedures for reporting malicious dynamic domains, IP addresses, and services hosting the C2 servers do not generate adequate results in an effective response to attending to an incident and can allow attackers to increase their ability to create damage over time. Through the experience gained by implementing the suggested protocol and the different attack vectors analyzed, it is concluded that the active defense protocol is effective in containment activities and that it speeds up the deactivation of the C2 servers.

During the case study, the response to incidents using active defense strategies initially required an investigation, analysis and preparation; however, once the response team is prepared with the appropriate procedures and tools, response times will improve.

The topics related to the legal or moral aspects of the investigation are at the discretion of each one of the readers of this document. The purpose of this is to propose a strategy that, while not openly disseminated in the field of active defense, does represent an approach to the work done in the practical field when it comes to mitigating the impact that such a threat can cause.

References

1. Monsalve-Pulido, J.A., Aponte-Novoa, F.A., Chaves-Tamayo, D.F.: Estudio y gestión de vulnerabilidades informáticas para una empresa privada en el departamento de Boyacá (Colombia). Fac. Ing. **23**(37), 65–72 (2014)
2. Organización de Estados Americanos: MINTIC y BID, Impacto de los Incidentes de seguridad digital en Colombia (2017). https://publications.iadb.org/bitstream/handle/11319/8552/Impacto_de_los_incidentes_de_seguridad_digital.pdf
3. Correa, C.A.P., Díaz, H.P.: Las amenazas informáticas: peligro latente para las organizaciones actuales. Rev. GTI **6**(16), 85–97 (2007)
4. Kaspersky: 33 ataques por segundo: Kaspersky Lab registra un aumento de 59% en ataques de malware en América Latina, 12 Septiembre 2017. https://latam.kaspersky.com/blog/33-ataques-por-segundo-kaspersky-lab-registra-un-aumento-de-59-en-ataques-de-malware-en-america-latina/11265/
5. Vidal Londoño, J.H.: Una nueva experiencia en seguridad hacking ético, Bachelor's thesis, Universidad Militar Nueva Granada (2017)
6. Bettany, A., Halsey, M.: What is malware? In: Bettany, A., Halsey, M. (eds.) Windows Virus and Malware Troubleshooting, pp. 1–8. Apress, Berkeley, CA (2017). https://doi.org/10.1007/978-1-4842-2607-0_1
7. Amenazas del cibercrimen en Colombia 2016–2017. Centro cibernético Policial. Policía Nacional de Colombia. https://caivirtual.policia.gov.co/sites/default/files/informe_amenazas_de_cibercrimen_en_colombia_2016_-_2017.pdf
8. NjRAT Source Code. https://github.com/AliBawazeEer/RAT-NjRat-0.7d-modded-source-code. Accessed 16 July 2018
9. Mattica, Colombia. https://mattica.com/colombia-los-seis-pasos-a-seguir-cuando-es-victima-de-un-delito-informatico/. Accessed 16 July 2018
10. John, S.: Offensive Countermeasures – The Art of Active Defense. 2nd edn (2017)
11. Center for Cyber and Homeland Security (CCHS) George Washington University: Into the Gray Zone, The Private Sector and Active Defense Against Cyber Threats, October 2016. https://cchs.gwu.edu/sites/g/files/zaxdzs2371/f/downloads/CCHS-ActiveDefenseReport FINAL.pdf
12. Díaz, F.: Hispasec Una al día, Continuos ataques a usuarios colombianos por XtremeRAT. https://unaaldia.hispasec.com/2017/05/continuos-ataques-usuarios-colombianos.html
13. Valeros, V.: The 300 most well known RATs of the last 30 years, March 2018. https://www.veronicavaleros.com/blog/2018/3/12/a-study-of-rats-third-timeline-iteration
14. Suignard, M.: Unicode Technical report #36, Unicode Security Considerations, 19 September 2014. http://unicode.org/reports/tr36/#Bidirectional_Text_Spoofing

Towards a Computational Tool to Facilitate the Scheduling of Elective Surgeries in a Healthcare Institution

Carolina Saavedra-Moreno[1]([⊠]) [iD], Fabián Castaño[2] [iD],
Luis Corredor[1], and Andrés García-León[1]

[1] Facultad de Ingeniería, Universidad de Ibagué, Ibagué, Colombia
{carolina.saavedra,andres.garcia}@unibague.edu.co,
2320131064@estudiantesunibague.edu.co
[2] School of Management, Universidad de los Andes, Bogotá, Colombia
fa.castano47@uniandes.edu.co

Abstract. This paper describes the process followed for designing a computational tool to improve the scheduling of surgeries in a regional healthcare institution where the availability of surgeons and medical staff is limited and heavily constrained. The goal is to analyze the characteristics of the system so as to design the structure of the master surgical schedule and select and appropriate set of rules aiming at reducing the waiting time for elective and ambulatory procedures and increasing the use of the rooms. In first place, the characteristics of the demand are studied by collecting and analyzing the information recorded during a two-year time lapse. Then, this information is used as an input to imitate the characteristics of the process through a discrete event system simulation model which can be used to analyze the performance of the system when different strategies are adopted. In particular, easy-to-use rules of thumb, adapted to the simplicity of the studied system are analyzed. For example, offline and online scheduling strategies and combination of these with operatory blocks (defined as a time dedicated exclusively to a given specialty) are studied. Then, upon the basis of the results obtained, a user-friendly computer interface is designed such that the process, that was predominantly carried out by hand, can be automated while improving systems performance and reducing the effort devoted by the personnel in charge.

Keywords: Operating room scheduling · Rules-of-thumb
Discrete event systems simulations

1 Introduction

Some studies suggest that, in Colombia, operating rooms report up to 40% of the total income perceived by healthcare institutions equipped to provide such services [1]. In addition, it is known to be the area that contributes the most to the costs drivers in hospitals. Several reasons can be argued as the origin of such findings, however an inefficient use of resources seems to be the law in healthcare institutions, especially in low income countries where investments out of the core business (*e.g.* technological

© Springer Nature Switzerland AG 2018
J. C. Figueroa-García et al. (Eds.): WEA 2018, CCIS 915, pp. 446–458, 2018.
https://doi.org/10.1007/978-3-030-00350-0_37

platforms and IT) are often scarce. As a consequence, it is not rare to find that complex tasks as nurse rostering, appointments scheduling and operating theatre planning are carried out by hand, without the support of specialized tools leading to optimize the use of such valuable resources [2].

Operating room scheduling is one of those challenging tasks that very often face schedulers within healthcare institutions without having the appropriate tools. It is common to find that no automated tools are available for such a purpose and the way it is carried out follows what can be seen as somehow inefficient methods [1]. As a consequence, the process becomes heavily time consuming, alongside leading to presumably suboptimal schedules that do not necessarily balance the needs of the different areas so as to satisfy demand and contribute to provide a timely attention to patients.

Because of its nature, operating room planning and scheduling problems have attracted a lot of attention within the Operations Research community. The problem is not only complex from the computational point of view, but in addition it poses some specific challenges specifically related to the characteristics of healthcare organizations. It seems that no two hospitals have the same set of constraints; moreover, the characteristics of the services offered, the legal restrictions, the availability of specialized personnel and technologies, pose extra-challenges when designing schedules that optimize the use of resources [3].

Surgeries scheduling in Colombian health care institutions, as in many countries, is subject to a large number of conditions and restrictions that limit efficiency and often implies that patients cannot receive attention when this is needed. One of the main problems identified rely on the fact that specialized personnel is scarce, a problem that is remarkably notorious in medium and small size cities with up to 500 thousand inhabitants. According to Amaya [1], in Colombia about 55% of hospitals do not account with the personnel necessary to provide the services offered in a timely manner. Therefore, most of the few remaining physicians located in the regions must be shared among different health care providers, working under hiring schemes in which the doctors have the greatest bargaining power and are in a position to impose conditions regarding the schedules and times that they will work for a given institution. Consequently, the adoption of advanced scheduling procedures frequently does not suit hospitals conditions, what often leads to the adoption of simple schemes, which in practice can be easily modified to adapt the system to rapidly changing conditions.

It is possible to find that in public and private health institutions there are still strong weaknesses regarding the adoption of technological platforms used for activities such as resources planning [2]. Computer developments tailored to the institutions and even some general purpose ERP have been adopted by institutions that have the economic muscle, and accounts with the human and technological resources for their implementation. However, it has also become evident that there is a clear advantage in the developments *made-at-home* as a response to hospitals own conditions. This is due partly to the fact that each institution can operate under very different schemes which, consequently, limits the applicability of general purpose developments. From this perspective, it is important to propose computational alternatives that facilitate the task of designing schedules in health institutions with these characteristics, and also allow to improve quality indicators such as the opportunity of care and the use of the rooms.

This research aims at optimizing the scheduling of surgeries in the operating room theatres in a regional healthcare institution. The goal is to analyze the system characteristics so as to generate a tailored computational tool that can be used for the personnel in charge to improve decision making processes and the access to health care services for the outpatients coming to the institution. Basic aspects as demand, suitable scheduling rules and schemes used to provide services are evaluated to be later embedded within a computational tool with the purpose of facilitating the process previously carried out by hand.

2   Operating Room Planning and Scheduling

Surgery cases scheduling consists in the determination of the date and time for performing the surgical cases, in such a way that the availability of the personnel, equipment and technology required for performing such procedures is synchronized in an adequate manner [4]. This problem has been long time attracting researchers, leading to a wide availability of methods frequently suited to particular situations, a response to the fact that hospital constraints may vary significantly between institutions and healthcare systems [5].

Several levels of decision may be involved in the particular task of appropriately plan and organize the way surgeries are to be performed in hospitals operating theaters [6]. In particular, strategic, tactical and operational levels are visible and determine the nature of the decisions to be taken and the difficulty of generating a plan that satisfies parties expectations [3]. At the strategic level, a typical objective is to define the offer of hospital procedures according to the available or forthcoming resources, taking into account aspects as the estimated demand for such services and restrictions usually related to financial resources. The tactical level typically involves the development of master surgery plans, in which the assignment of operating theatres time is decided and priorities are assigned for procedures to be executed in each room. Finally, at the operative level, the sequences are established, and surgeries are assigned for their attention during the corresponding time frames [6]. The boundaries between these major categories, however, may vary considerably between different contexts.

The literature on operating room planning and scheduling exhibits a wide range of solution methodologies that are retrieved from the domains of operations management and operations research. Exact approaches based on linear and/or integer programming are probably the most widespread approaches proposed from a theoretical perspective for planning operating theatre surgeries [7–12]. Nevertheless, the difficulty faced for solving such problems often leads to the adoption of heuristic methods that conduct to approximate solutions in a prudential time [13, 14].

Approaches adopting alternative perspectives have been also studied [4, 14]. In particular it is common to find that authors explore strategies that imitate the way the scheduling procedure is carried out within the hospitals and propose improvements applied directly to the process, rather than defining completely new approaches that can be sometimes difficult to adopt in practice. One of such approaches consists in reserving an amount of operating room time (namely blocks) for procedures of either specific surgeons or medical specialties [5, 9, 15]. Several criteria can be used to assign such blocked time, a decision often taken in the tactical level that can lead to an inefficient use of rooms time while, in contrast, making the scheduling process easier to execute.

A different approach consists in evaluating the performance of the systems under different scenarios seeking to identify the one that is most suitable to the actual conditions and constraints faced for the hospitals [9]. Simulating the system and/or study the mathematical properties of scheduling rules under some given conditions is common. In this way, it is expected to contribute to improve the efficiency of both, the scheduling process and the use of resources. Molina et al. [15] study an applied problem where the programming of surgeries in a hospital is required. With this purpose, the authors adopt the use of heuristics to assign patients to waiting lists with the intention of assigning an intervention date and an operating room. A large number of alternative heuristics and test instances guide authors towards a robust conclusion about the most appropriate mechanisms to address the problem.

Several strategies can be used for scheduling operating room theatres that can differ enormously in their application and that may require more or less sophisticated technologies for their adoption. The so-called online methodologies, are carried out in real time, in which the dates, rooms and starting of surgery start are assigned immediately when the request arrive. Waiting lists (offline) are adopted often in ambulatory and elective settings, where the patient can wait for confirmation of the appointment and moment when the surgery will take place. Under this approach, a surgery is scheduled by the institution once it has accumulated enough requests produce a program that can use resources more appropriately.

As previously stated, technological platforms are barely used for accompanying the scheduling processes in hospitals. In particular in low income countries very often this task is completely carried out by hand only supported by a piece of paper, a notebook or a bulletin board where the sequence of the surgeries is presented once an appointment has been confirmed. The process implies synchronizing patients requests with the availability of the human and technical resources required for performing these procedures [1].

3 System Description and Proposed Models

This article describes the procedure followed to construct a computational tool for facilitating the scheduling process within a regional institution in Colombia. The process involves first the exploration of suitable approaches or procedures to schedule the surgeries requests. In this way, several important aspects are analyzed: (i) the demand patterns (ii) stochastic nature of procedures durations, (iii) and external constraints mostly related with the availability of specialists that obligates to renegotiate the time frames offered by them to the institutions. The goal, as defined by personnel in charge, is to reduce patients waiting time and increase rooms' utilization. This research mainly deals with planning and scheduling procedures that apply to an outpatient setting. This means that the research is focused on elective patients for whom the surgery can be planned in advance.

The study is carried out for a private hospital, which provides high complexity health services, and is located in a medium size city of Colombia. The institution considered has a limited number of specialists working under a full-time contract. Consequently, besides to the limited availability of specialists in the region, the institution usually must adapt to the available schedules provided by these (external) personnel and not necessarily to the requirements of the institution.

When the hospital personnel was first approached, there was not a clearly defined procedure that can be easily imitated to reproduce the surgeries scheduling process executed in the studied institution. There were no technological tools available for scheduling surgeries in the operating theatres and the process was mainly based on chief nurse intuition who, based on the knowledge of procedures and medical staff, decided on the right timings for performing a given procedure. However, it was not clear the criteria used to allocate appointments to the patients.

While scheduling the surgeries, the date and time for performing the surgical procedure is defined. This is a manual process which is carried out in an online fashion. The process main inputs are the requests specifications and the availability of both the surgeons suitable to perform the procedures and the rooms. The final decision depends mostly on reaching an agreement between the surgeon and the chief nurse in charge of programming the operating rooms. The process considers the availability of the room, the anesthesiologist and the team of physicians on duty who should support the surgical procedures. It is the surgeon who provides an estimation of the surgery duration and so the room time that should be reserved for a given procedure. A typical objective, as described by the personnel in charge, was to increase the utilization of the operating theatres, avoiding overtime in the operating rooms and reducing the lead times (waiting time for a patient requesting a procedure). A simple representation of the process is depicted in Fig. 1.

3.1 Analyzing Demand Patterns and System Characteristics

The firsts step consisted in analyzing the characteristics of the demand in detail. As previously indicated, technological platforms were almost inexistent for most of the processes carried out within the institution, so the records were collected from paper-based archives where these were deposited in the books corresponding to previous years. Two years of information were analyzed; the data collected includes information about all the procedures including name, specialty, the start and end time of the procedures (including anesthesia and operation), the doctor who performed the procedure and the date of the appointments. With this information, the behavior of the demand was analyzed for the different surgical services offered by the institution and the proportion of time that should be dedicated to serve each of these specialties.

Although there are many different procedures carried out within the institution, these were only grouped by specialty for the analysis. No distinction was made between medical doctors who performed the surgical procedures. The duration of the procedures belonging to the same specialty was analyzed as if there were generic surgeries for which the duration ranges between the times required for the different procedures.

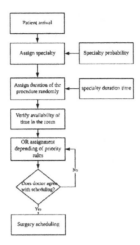

Fig. 1. A conceptual model for the scheduling process in the studied hospital

3.2   Proposed Improvements to the Scheduling Process

According to the characteristics observed in the demand patterns and the analysis of the surgical cases durations, several strategies are proposed to be evaluated as the actual method to be implemented in practice by the hospital. In particular, there were considered options aligned with what can be seen as possible for the hospital staff. In this sense, priority rules-of-thumb were the basic option to study; it was also planned to investigate about the effect of reserving an amount of operating room time (blocks) dedicated exclusively for cases of specific surgeons or highly demanded medical specialties. Both, for the free and the blocked time the theoretical priority rules that were appropriate to the context of the institution studied were [10, 12, 13]:

- First fit: The surgery is scheduled in the first room that has available time
- Best fit: The surgery is scheduled in the room that has enough time to accommodate it but has the least time available from among the possible options.

The combination of parameters was selected according to what is considered practicable from the perspective of institution personnel and that lead to improvements in the indicators related to the scheduling process, in particular opportunity of care average and percentage operation room utilization average. The average opportunity of care measures the time elapsed between the moment when a procedure is requested and the actual date when it is scheduled to take place. Percentage room utilization measures the proportion of the operating room time scheduled for performing procedures. Some combinations were just discarded as those were not logical, *e.g.* either First Fit or Best Fit are only useful when a list of requests is available (offline). Finally, only one of the combinations that were equivalent was considered, *e.g.* Non-sorted (FIFO) First Fit online or offline. The Table 1 presents the final set of scheduling scenarios. Scenarios evaluated include current scheduling process (scenario 1), current scheduling using operating blocks (scenario 2) and a combination of First Fit and Best Fit approaches together with the adoption of different priority rules and operating blocks. The latter were considered in the scenarios considering that about 70% of surgeries carried out belong to only two specialties. As previously stated, online and offline (waiting lists) scenarios were also considered. When the usage of waiting lists was considered, the surgeries to be programmed were sorted according to the estimated duration (decreasing or increasing).

Table 1. Proposed scheduling scenarios

Scenario	Priority rule	Online vs. Offline	Sort	Operating blocks
1	First Fit	Online	FIFO	No
2	First Fit	Online	FIFO	Yes
3	First Fit	Offline	Decreasing	Yes
4	First Fit	Offline	Increasing	Yes
5	Best Fit	Online	FIFO	Yes
6	Best Fit	Offline	Decreasing	Yes
7	Best Fit	Offline	Increasing	Yes

3.3 A Discrete Event System Simulation Model to Evaluate Surgery Scheduling Rules

In order to evaluate the performance of the systems when faced to the different scenarios proposed in Sect. 3.2, a discrete event systems simulation model was proposed. The model imitates the process as it is currently carried out by the chief nurse, but it includes those specific elements associated to the different rules proposed to improve the process.

In the simulation model, the process begins with the arrival of a request for a surgery. The amount of surgeries generated for each specialty is proportional to the demand observed during the time lapse during which demand was analyzed, *i.e.* according to the historical demand for the different services offered. Then, a duration of the procedure is assigned randomly; in this way, it is possible to avoid considering specific details of the procedures to be performed. This process imitates the time estimated for performing a procedure as it is currently provided by doctors and the chief nurse. Once this information is known, the availability of time in the room is verified, and the respective assignment is made depending on the priority rule evaluated. In this phase a probability of rejection by the surgeon is incorporated into the model, to simulate the actual procedure, where medical doctor's available time depends on external factor not controlled by the hospital. Finally, the model considers the time required for preparing the room for a new procedure and considers that there are surgeries for which there is a significant risk of contamination, increasing the time required as a consequence of the cleaning process once the surgical procedures has finished.

To analyze the results obtained by the model a steady state simulation model is considered and, as recommended by Banks et al. [16], 10% of the total time was selected as the warm-up time, after which statistics were collected. A first group of experiments showed that the total execution time required to run the model assuming time periods of up to ten years was sufficiently short to perform simulations with multiple replicates.

3.4 Results and Conclusions

The analysis of the information collected from the records during the period of time under study suggests that operating theatres receive mainly elective patients (ambulatory and hospitalized). Only 13% of the admissions corresponded to emergency patients. The most demanded specialty in the system is plastic surgery. During the time period analyzed, it was found that plastic and aesthetic surgeries required about 65% of the total time rooms were in use. Some other important specialties were orthopedics and general surgery consuming about 9% and 8%, respectively, of the operating theatres time (see Fig. 2).

As previously indicated, the duration of the surgeries was characterized after grouping procedures according to the specialties. Then, goodness-of-fit tests were carried out aiming at identifying the distribution that better suits the duration for each specialty. There were some specialties for which a good fitness was not obtained for any distribution; a possible reason for this lies on the fact that there were not enough procedures during the studied time period to find a good fit. In the latter case, either uniform or triangular distributions were adopted, using as an input the opinion provided by the experts within the hospital.

Performance indicators results over the proposed scenarios are displayed in Table 2. In first place, the Bonferroni approach was used to rank the alternatives that better perform in terms of the opportunity of care criterion, the one having a higher priority as indicated by hospital staff [16]. In particular, the results suggest that scenario 3 is the ones that better fit hospital goals. Not only the expected waiting times are shorter in comparison to the remaining scenarios, but also the distribution of the waiting time is more compact, suggesting smaller probabilities of long waiting times. The results showed that there is not a difference in opportunity of care across the scenarios (offline and online) that used First Fit rule without operating blocks. Similarly, the scenarios 3 and 4 present little difference in the indicator when waiting lists were sorted with increasing or decreasing surgeries duration. Considering the opportunity of care standard deviation, the results evidenced that scenarios of First Fit had a deviation smaller to 4 days approximately, unlike scenarios of best fit scheme that had an opportunity of care standard deviation over 6 days. In all the evaluated scenarios, the distributions of the waiting times show a significant bias to the right, meaning that there exists a non-neglectable probability of waiting for the surgery a time longer than the represented by the mean.

The results evidenced that using the Best Fit rule increases opportunity of care indicator. A plausible explanation may be given if it is considered that this rule tries to fill the operational blocks as much as possible. Nevertheless, a possible disadvantage is that it can leave empty blocks in the less distant days, while waiting for a procedure that improves the use of operating rooms on a given day; however, and it might be possible that this never happens. Then, as time progresses it is possible that some days finish with a low utilization. On the other hand, the First Fit scheme, tends to be programmed in the days closest to the current date, filling all available spaces in the present, therefore, blocks that can be used in the moment when it is needed. The implementation of blocks in the most demanded surgeries improves opportunity of care indicator significantly. Unlike the current situation, it is no longer necessary to negotiate with the doctor the date and time of surgery, but, on the contrary, these parameters are included in the operational blocks. Thus, it is possible to give flexibility to the programming of low frequency surgeries, knowing operating room availability spaces that are not assigned to specialties of high demand.

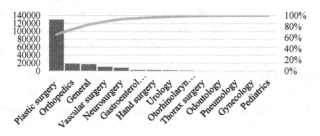

Fig. 2. Total operating room theatre time (minutes) required for the specialties

Table 2. Performance indicators of assessing scenarios

Scenario	Opportunity of care average	Opportunity of care standard deviation	% rooms utilization average
1	4.83	3.84	54.8
2	5.73	3.19	57.0
3	4.93	4	56.6
4	4.94	4.06	54.5
5	6.65	6.65	60.1
6	6.7	6.79	58.0
7	7.01	7.4	61.1

4   A Computational Tool for Operating Room Theatre Scheduling

The final phase of the research included the construction of the computational tool in NET-BEANS 7.3.1 framework employing Java Language. The guidelines of Decree 0256 of 2016 issued by the Ministry of health of Colombia concerning to what should be reported and tracked from operating room theaters, including quality and performance criteria, were also considered. The computational tool was developed in three steps. In the first step, the functional requirements were established considering the guidelines provided by the Ministry of health. In the second step, a data base was consolidated to record the information of the patients and their illness. Simultaneously this data base considered all surgeons with their time frames and the capacity of the surgery rooms; it also considered the blocked time that should be used for a particular specialty. The third step took in account the functional requirements to apply the selected rules-of-thumb and design a graphic machine-human interface. Finally, the performance of the computational tool was validated by considering the information provided by the hospital staff.

a) Window to record the information of the patient

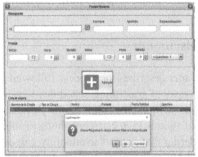

b) Window to record the information of operating blocks and waiting lists

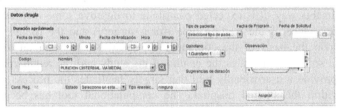

c) A window of Surgery menu

Fig. 3. Window panels in the proposed tool

The computational tool possesses a menu with four modules: patients, physicians, surgeries and indicators. The menu Patients allows to introduce the information about the patient (see Fig. 3a) which is recorded in the data base. A similar function has the menu Physicians related to the surgeons. The menu Surgery is used for the assignment (see Fig. 3c). In this module the operating blocks for specialties are created (see Fig. 3b).

Figure 4 presents a conceptual model of the scheduling process. The process starts when the user loads the information of the patient and the surgeon to schedule the surgery. The computational tool shows minimum, maximum and average time duration of surgery based on historical data, user enter approximate duration manually. If surgery is scheduled in a block it is included within a waiting list. When the waiting list is complete, typically when at the end of the labor day, surgeries are schedule by following the selected priority rule (First Fit sorted by Longest Processing times). The computational tool validates the availability of the surgery room. When surgery is not included in an operating block it programs the surgery in the first space available. It is important to highlight that the computational tool does not schedule a surgery if a surgery room is busy, and the user has the option to schedule manually, cancel a procedure or postpone a surgery, when it is necessary. If it is required to re-program a surgery, this is done by relocating the surgery at the first position of the waiting list. Finally, the Menu Indicators was created to generate reports for the different criteria established, the schedule of surgeries, surgeons and patients. Information can be provided back to users in the form of pdf-files.

5   Discussion

This paper describes the process followed to construct a computational tool to facilitate the process of generating schedules in a healthcare institution with serious limitations in terms of human resources. In particular, the research explored the use of simple rules-of-thumb that can contribute to alleviate the difficulties faced when planning, considering that doctors availability can be quite limited, and the systems performance might be deteriorated as a consequence of this fact.

The contribution of the research was twofold. First, the system characteristics are studied through discrete event systems simulations and the process is analyzed so as to have a reliable support for selecting the appropriate scheme that better suits the hospital conditions. In this way, it is expected contribute to improve some metrics related to systems performance as the waiting time (for a surgery) and the rooms utilization. Secondly, upon the basis of the computational study a computational tool is constructed. The software integrates the results of the study and the requirements of the hospital to provide a user-friendly tool that largely facilitates the process of creating schedules within the studied hospital. The computational tool has been designed according considering also the guidelines of the Ministry of health and some

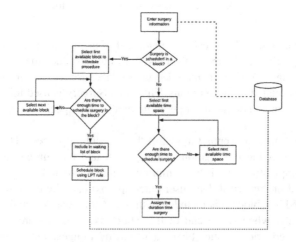

Fig. 4. A conceptual model of the computational tool.

constrained conditions. The operation of the computational tool does not require personnel highly trained in informatics. In particular, it is designed to be used by nurses, seeking to reduce the time these devote to perform some of the administrative tasks they have in charge.

As a future work, it is proposed to evaluate the impact of the designed software in the hospital. In particular, it will be interesting to check whether it satisfies the actual needs of the institution, and if it appropriately deals with the diverse set of problems typically faced by the chief nurse in charge of the process. In addition, it is proposed to evaluate if the systems performance metrics have improved as a consequence of the adopted scheduling rules and explore strategies leading to integrate easily changes observed in the demand patterns and the hospital conditions.

Acknowledgement. We thank the Universidad de Ibagué for funding this study under the project entitled "Formulation and validation of heuristics for optimizing the customer service in flexible configurations in the Tolima region" identified with the Code 16-465-INT and the Colombian Administrative Department of Science, Technology and Innovation (COLCIENCIAS) for supporting the participation of Fabián Castaño through the Grant 784-2017.

References

1. Amaya, J.L.: Estudio de disponibilidad y distribución de la oferta de médicos especialistas, en servicios de alta y mediana complejidad en Colombia, Bogotá (2013)
2. Velasco, N., Amaya, C.: Logística hospitalaria: lecciones y retos para Colombia. In: La salud en Colombia: logros, retos y recomendaciones, Uniandes, Bogotá, Colombia, p. 576 (2012)
3. Choi, S., Wilhelm, W.E.: On capacity allocation for operating rooms. Comput. Oper. Res. **44**, 174–184 (2014)
4. Dexter, F., Traub, R.D.: How to schedule elective surgical cases into specific operating rooms to maximize the efficiency of use of operating room time. Anesth. Analg. **94**, 933–942 (2002)
5. Herring, W.L., Herrmann, J.W.: A stochastic dynamic program for the single-day surgery scheduling problem. IIIE Trans. Healthc. Syst. Eng. **1**, 213–225 (2011)
6. Cardoen, B., Demeulemeester, E., Beliën, J.: Operating room planning and scheduling: a literature review. Eur. J. Oper. Res. **201**(3), 921–932 (2010)
7. Rachuba, S., Werners, B.: A robust approach for scheduling in hospitals using multiple objectives. J. Oper. Res. Soc. **65**(4), 546–556 (2014)
8. Pradenas, L., Matamala, E.: Una formulación matemática y de solución para programar cirugías con restricciones de recursos humanos en el hospital público. Ingeniare. Rev. Chil. Ing. **20**(2), 230–241 (2012)
9. Fei, H., Meskens, N., Chu, C.: A planning and scheduling problem for an operating theatre using an open scheduling strategy. Comput. Ind. Eng. **58**(2), 221–230 (2010)
10. Zhang, B., Murali, P., Dessouky, M.M., Belson, D.: A mixed integer programming approach for allocating operating room capacity. J. Oper. Res. Soc. **60**(5), 663–673 (2009)
11. Pham, D.N., Klinkert, A.: Surgical case scheduling as a generalized job shop scheduling problem. Eur. J. Oper. Res. **185**(3), 1011–1025 (2008)
12. Kuo, P.C., Schroeder, R.A., Mahaffey, S., Bollinger, R.R.: Optimization of operating room allocation using linear programming techniques. J. Am. Coll. Surg. **197**(6), 889–895 (2003)

13. Guido, R., Conforti, D.: A hybrid genetic approach for solving an integrated multi-objective operating room planning and scheduling problem. Comput. Oper. Res. **87**, 270–282 (2017)
14. Molina, J.M., Framiñán, J.M., Pérez, P., León, J.M.: Modelos para la resolución de la programación de quirófanos. In: 3rd International Conference on Industrial Engineering and Industrial Management, pp. 1356–1365 (2009)
15. Zenteno, A.C., Carnes, T., Levi, R., Daily, B.J., Price, D., Moss, S.C., Dunn, P.F.: Pooled open blocks shorten wait times for nonelective surgical cases. Ann. Surg. **262**(1), 60–67 (2015)
16. Banks, J., Carson, J.S., Nelson, B.L., Nicol, D.M.: Discrete-Event System Simulation, 5th edn. Pearson, London (2010)

Design and Implementation of a Modular Optical System of Perimeter Activity Detection for Military Posts of the Colombian National Army - Phanton Fox

Fabian Garay$^{(\boxtimes)}$ ⓘ, Sebastián Puerto, Jose Jiménez,
and Jorge Rodríguez

Escuela de Infantería – Ejército Nacional de Colombia, Bogotá, Colombia
fsgarayr@correo.udistrital.edu.co,
ul802147@unimilitar.edu.co, {cienciatecnologia.esinf,
jorgerodriguezmonroy}@cedoc.edu.co

Abstract. The Colombian National Army conducts military operations against armed groups aimed at defending sovereignty, independence and territorial integrity. One of the armed groups strategies involved the creation of groups called "pisa-softs", whose mission was to infiltrate the patrols and kill the sentinels. Various responses were developed to stop this type of attacks; One of them makes use of technological tools with programmable electronic devices and the use of sensors. A review of perimeter activity detection devices to detect intruders with systems applicable to hostile environments to define the most practical technology for building an effective device usable in the military posts. Subsequently, the functional modules of the device were defined, including a PIC microcontroller, a module with four infrared sensors, a receiving module and a tablet under Android for enhanced Tablet can be used for its construction. The result is a tool capable of generating a tactical advantage to military posts with a data reception at 60 ± 5 m and high sensitivity of 80% to 90% for intrusion detection.

Keywords: Optical detection · Military posts · Perimeter activity
Sensors

1 Introduction

Within the context of the armed conflict in Colombia there are different GAOs (organized armed groups), which for a period of approximately 52 years have tried to seek the political power of the state through weapons [1], one of the strategies to weaken the military forces It is the use of "pisa-softs". As described in the April 2015 article in the newspaper the "Espectador", the "pisa suave" camouflages itself on the trail, then crawls and attacks the sentries, its objective, to behead it [2].

In a post-conflict context, there is no talk of a stable and lasting peace since there are other armed actors that interrupt total security for the country, which is why today there

© Springer Nature Switzerland AG 2018
J. C. Figueroa-García et al. (Eds.): WEA 2018, CCIS 915, pp. 459–467, 2018.
https://doi.org/10.1007/978-3-030-00350-0_38

is talk and threat in national security. To that end, threats have been identified such as organized armed groups that obstructs the peace of the Colombian environment [3].

The early alarms are a deterrent measure that allows the units to be alerted to the intruder's proximity, in this case to the calls to softness, which are used within the technique of enslavement. About the units in adverse operations, either in movement of the enemy, either offensive or reconnaissance.

Previously, similar devices have been implemented in the case of an optical fiber intrusion detection system for railway safety, which is designed to protect a perimeter area from some type of access that is not authorized as the system that has come. in this document, but what characterizes and makes the system better is the low cost of infrared sensors with respect to FBGs connected by fiber optic cables. In addition, the cables are arranged to travel around the perimeter, differentiating communication by radio frequency, which generates more expenses and signs during the installation of the system [4].

Looking to improve these problems, the Phanton Fox was designed, consisting of an integrated system of motion detection sensors, a long-range communication, rechargeable devices with extended time, and easy access and management to the user's control platform.

2   Devices Developed for the Detection of Perimeter Activity

This section describes others technological developments that have been implemented to perimeter activity detection, which have been applied considering the specific characteristics of the conditions places of application and the technology applied. These applications represent potential comparisons points for the development of the device of the national army; also, the differences of said previous developments with respect to the device proposed in this document are set forth.

2.1   Perimeter Surveillance System for Marine Farms and Similar

This invention relates to a system comprising one or more detection nodes, formed by a radar, an image-processing system and GPS identification means, and comprising a detection system for friendly boats, whose data is sent via internet connections to a database associated with a server, with a web application which can be accessed remotely via a terminal, be it a mobile telephone, computer, tablet or similar, a server associated with an alarm center [5]. This system requires an internet connection, which makes the military context inapplicable.

2.2   Safety Canvas for the Perimeter Protection of Lots and Premises in General Against the Income of Intruders with Criminal Intensions

In this allows activating alarm devices when detecting the cutting or breaking of the canvas by intruders in order to commit thefts, this canvas is installed covering the perimeter surrounding the land of the properties to be protected and have a wire that extends following a zigzag development along and across the canvas, thus defining a passive sensor circuit that is connected to electrical or electronic alarm devices, which are activated automatically when the wire is cut or disconnected [6]. This application requires a physical connection, that do not permissive in a military post.

2.3   Perimeter Vibration Detection System and Method

This system uses first and second vibration sensor assemblies. The first vibration sensor assembly is installed at a first depth below a ground surface. The second vibration sensor assembly is installed relative to the first vibration sensor assembly at a horizontal distance away from the first vibration sensor assembly and/or at a second depth below the ground surface, where the second depth is different than the first depth [7]. In this system, is necessary are connected to a computer system for calculate a location of a vibration source, and this not is possible for the military application.

2.4   Improved Intrusion Detection System and Method

This invention operates in a restricted mode, for restricting access to areas. The system assigned permissions by an administrator which allows access or disallows access to specific regions of a building. The system further has intrusion detection sensors such as motion detectors and window or door contacts for ascertaining to presence of an individual [8]. This system cannot be applied for the detection of soft feet, since the identity of an individual is determined from entering an access code upon entry to the premises or an RFID device carried by the individual, and its use is directed to the protection of buildings.

3   Methodology: Device Design

For the design of the Fox Phantom it was necessary to make a preliminary study of the sensors, microcontrollers and materials necessary for the elaboration of it, to obtain a device that meets the main objective, which is easy to transport, with good autonomy, that can support all the climates to which it can be exposed. Next, the design stages for the device will be explained.

3.1   Stage 1: System Structuring

Based on the requirements established for the project, a block diagram was reached as shown in Fig. 1, which was the starting point for development. With this block diagram, it can visualize the structure of the perimeter activity detection system, which is composed by the sensing and reception modules.

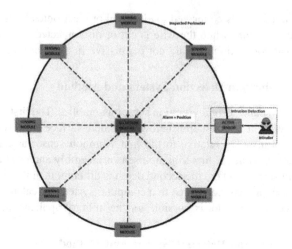

Fig. 1. Solution block diagram.

3.2   Stage 2: Sensing Module

The sensor module will carry a microcontroller (PIC18F26K22), four infrared sensors (EKMC1603112), an accelerometer (LSM330DLC), a GPS (L86), a Synapse module (RT100) and a 5000 mA lithium-ion battery.

These elements described above will be connected as shown in the block diagram of Fig. 2, to detect the intruder and send the necessary information to the receiving module to alert.

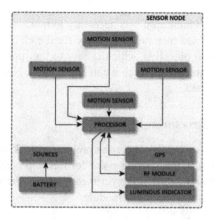

Fig. 2. Block diagram sensing module.

Figures 2 and 3 show the architecture of the perimeter activity detection system, where the internal structure of the two modules is evidenced by means of a block diagram.

3.3   Stage 3: Reception Module

The reception module will have a Synapse module (RT100), a Bluetooth module (SPBT2532C2.AT2) and a 5000 mA lithium-ion battery.

In this stage a unique system is implemented for the reception of the information from the Sensor Modules which establishes a connection via Bluetooth with the Android application as shown in Fig. 3.

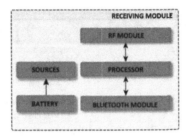

Fig. 3. Block diagram reception module.

3.4   Stage 4: Trimble ASCII Interface Protocol (TAIP)

The protocol based on ASCII characters of the Table 1, is used due to its easy handling and the quality of being able to program a desired speed for us, which in our specific case helps us to reduce the loss of data, when each information could represent the death of a soldier. The information submission format is:

$$> ABB\{C\}[; ID = DDDD][; *FFFF] <$$

Table 1. ASCII characters for the information submission format.

ID	Meaning
>	Start a new message
A	Message qualifier
BB	Two characters for the message identifier
{C}	Data chain
[DDD]	ID of the device that sent the message
*FFFF	CRC-16 in hexadecimal (Optional 2-character checksum)
<	End of message

3.5   Stage 5: Android Visualization and Control System

The interface will make it easier for the user to interact with the different functions of the device and to execute its functions in a simpler and more functional way. It was designed in a friendly and easy to use way. In Fig. 4 it shows the GUI of application.

The Android application can be installed on any mobile device (Tablet or Cellular) with Android operating system. In the interface, the user will have access to the display of coordinates, battery status of each module, connection status between sensor module and receiving module, verification of the status of each of the sensors, alarm notifications, control of the led and vibrator indicators.

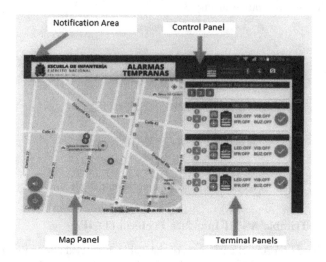

Fig. 4. Graphic interface of the application with its 4 main elements.

In this part all the information of the alerts that were activated is stored, leaving a record that facilitated the supervision of the activity in the period that is active.

4 Test Protocol

The main objective of the test protocol for the Phanton Fox was to analyze the device in any environmental condition that may arise, to find possible errors that the device has in their application for the military posts.

A main part of the preparation of the protocol was the identification of the most important device variables, such as climatic conditions, the autonomy, the maximum distance of the reception and sensing modules, and finally, was established a relationship between climate and sensitivity to achieve the standardization of the percentage of sensitivity, and thus achieve greater precision when using the device. To understand the above. See Table 2.

With the variables already defined, the scenarios and events necessary to obtain the correct information must be specified. With respect to the climate, extreme climates must be taken into account in which in Colombia, due to their diversity, patrols can be confronted, so previous two different places are chosen to carry out the protocol the first place is the desert of the Tatacoa obtaining a dry environment and with temperatures up to 43 °C, and the second place is chosen a Sumapaz region where its environment is humid with temperatures up to 5 °C, but to obtain different conditions, the hours required to do the tests must be taken into account, choosing the following events:

- The event on the day from 10:00 a.m. to 2:00 p.m., since in this period there is a high level of light, and a higher temperature for the case of the Infantry Battalion No. 27.
- The event on the day from 6:00 a.m. to 10:00 a.m., because there is a high light level at these hours and a low temperature for the case of the Infantry Battalion No. 1.
- The event on the night from 8:00 pm to 11:00 pm, because at this time the sun was already hidden, and the lighting conditions are limited.

Table 2. Variables for the test protocol.

Name	Description
Weather	The climatic conditions in which the Phanton Fox device does not work correctly must be validated
Sensitivity	Sensitivity is the variation of time with which the infrared sensor emits a beam of light and receives it, if the intruder causes the light beam to return, in the Android application it is possible to standardize by placing the minimum time the sensor supports, assigning it 0% and the maximum time 100%. It must be concluded what is the percentage of sensitivity necessary for each environmental condition
Electric charge of the devices	The aim is to find the exact autonomy in continuous operation of the Phanton Fox device
Distance	It is sought to find the maximum distance between the Central Module and the Sensor Module in different environments

5   Results and Discussion

5.1   Performance of the Device Under Climatic Conditions Variables

On sunny days with high temperatures the device worked stably with a high sensitivity percentage of 80% to 90%. For rainy days with low temperatures the device works in a more unstable way with a low sensitivity percentage of 10% to 30%.

On days with strong winds and low temperatures it is expected that the device worked in an unstable manner with a low sensitivity percentage of 30% to 40%. On cloudy days with low temperatures the device worked stably under percentages of high sensitivity of 90% to 100%.

5.2   Device Degree of Protection

In laboratory tests, the protection level of the device was corroborated with respect to its resistance to water and dust for the sensing and reception modules, resulting in an IP55 degree of protection under the international standard IEC 60529 Degrees of Protection.

5.3   Charging and Discharging the Device's Battery

The charging time of the modules averages 6 h per module from 0% to 100%. The discharge time of the modules is on average 72 continuous hours from a 100% load to 0%.

5.4   Operating Distance

The range of reach of the sensing and reception module is unstable from 60 m to 70 m where if the distance is less than 60 m the connection is good, if the distance is between 60 m and 70 m the connection is unstable and if the distance is greater the connection is totally lost. Also, the accelerometers of the sensor modules are activated at an average acceleration of $12 \, \text{m/s}^2$.

6   Conclusions

Regarding the operation of the Modular Optical System of Perimeter Activity Detection, on sunny days, the sensors work correctly by the available light, so the intruders' detection was not inconvenient to reach 100% of the detections in the field test. However, when the rains were present, the detection index results were reduced because the amount of water that interferes with the sensors, so the sensitivity of motion detection had to be increased to compensate, obtaining a detection percentage of 92%.

For other weather conditions such as days with strong winds or cloudy, the sensors efficiency was reduced, accuracy and scope in the intruders' detection can be solved in the same way, by increasing sensitivity levels to avoid false detection alarms. The device is suitable for use in hostile environments such as those common for military posts, for which it has IP55 protection that is available in operation in these environments, however, for future applications is necessary apply additional protection to allow it to submerge the modules.

The device has a discharge time of approximately 72 h, which is not enough for a military post, so it must be maximized so that it can be applied in areas where there is no electricity and because the provisions are received every 15 days. Finally, the maximum distance to which each sensor module can be positioned before the receiver stops detecting them, is 60 m, this could be maximized so that it detects intruders at the maximum range of some firearms that is of 150 m and thus reduce the effectiveness of surprise enemy attacks.

References

1. Ríos Sierra, J., Cairo Carou, H.: Breve historia del conflicto armado en Colombia. Los Libros de la Catarata, Madrid (2017)
2. El Espectador: Así actúan los "pisa suave" en las Farc, encargados de degollar a soldados. https://www.elespectador.com/noticias/judicial/asi-actuan-los-pisa-suave-farc-encargados-de-degollar-s-articulo-555506
3. Defensoría Delegada para la Prevención de Riesgos de Violaciones a los Derechos Humanos, SAT: Grupos Armados Ilegales y nuevos escenarios de riesgo en el posacuerdo, Bogotá D.C. (2017)
4. Catalano, A., et al.: An optical fiber intrusion detection system for railway security. Sens. Actuators A Phys. **253**, 91–100 (2017). https://doi.org/10.1016/J.sNA.2016.11.026
5. Hernandez Belda, H.O., Collazos Carrera, A., Leret Verdú, A.C.: Sistema de Vigilancia Perimetral de Cultivos Marinos y Similares (2017). https://patentscope.wipo.int/search/es/detail.jsf?docId=WO2017060543
6. Calanna, C.A., Acs, R.E.: Lona de Seguridad para la Protección Perimetral de Lotes y Predios en General Contra el Ingreso de Intrusos con Intensiones Delictivas (2016). https://patentscope.wipo.int/search/es/detail.jsf?docId=AR10511144&redirectedID=true
7. Turnbull, R.C., Brown, T.D., Horvath, S.P., Turnbull, N.R.: Perimeter vibration detection system and method (2017). https://patentscope.wipo.int/search/es/detail.jsf?docId=WO2017048347&redirectedID=true
8. Greenberg, Z., Rettig, D.A.: Improved intrusion detection system and method (2017). https://patentscope.wipo.int/search/es/detail.jsf?docId=GB191880247&recNum=1&office=&queryString=ALL%3A%282540880%29&prevFilter=&sortOption=Fecha+de+publicación%2C+orden+descendente&maxRec=12

A Programming Model for Decentralised Data Networks

Joaquín F. Sánchez(✉)®, Jorge A. Quiñones, and Juan M. Corredor

National University of Colombia, Bogotá, Colombia
{jofsanchezci,jaquinonesg}@unal.edu.co

Abstract. In this article, we present the description of a programming language model based on Interaction Nets. With this base model, an explanation of its pertinence is made to model a programming language that helps the construction of decentralised systems (For the article, ad hoc networks are considered). Four interactions are presented, where the flexibility of the language is shown using native libraries and functions. The paradigm that is proposed is a multi-paradigm that combines the use of functions, software agents, and the use of libraries.

Keywords: Ad hoc networks · Self- assembly · Networks
Net interactions

1 Introduction

The programming languages are tools developed along the computation history to interpret the reality of a situation toward a computing device and, in this way, to give solutions to problems and conditions that require the execution of quick and reliable operations [1,6,9,18]. Furthermore, with the passing of years, the networking computer systems have evolved. First, there were centralized systems, which have a robust and defined architecture. In the '90s, fixed telephony lost ground against mobile telephony, and the data transmission component over these networks was added [12,17]. In the 2000s, the evolution of the fixed network systems passed toward wireless and mobiles networks, where apps have been transforming the way of not only doing computation, but also of connecting devices and people [11]. Following this trend, where the computing devices are mobiles with significant processing features and memory, the current processing clouds are going to evolve to become mobile clouds with stochastic, dynamic, and distributed elements. [7,10].

In this way, a new paradigm in computing systems is coming, and the challenges to overcoming the system design and conception must generate new ideas and viewpoints to approach to the solution of the problems they face. The purpose of language will be to address the design challenges of a decentralized system of devices belonging to mobile clouds, and it is necessary to think about a tool through which the physical and logical setting of the system components are possible.

© Springer Nature Switzerland AG 2018
J. C. Figueroa-García et al. (Eds.): WEA 2018, CCIS 915, pp. 468–479, 2018.
https://doi.org/10.1007/978-3-030-00350-0_39

The proposed tool is a programming language that incorporates the fundamentals of the operation of a decentralized system and, in consequence, contains native functions that allow the adaptation of the components to provide required services to users. If attention is focused on wireless networks, specifically on an ad-hoc network, some challenges to guarantee the adequate network functioning need to be solved. In nodes management, aspects of transmission power control, frequency spectrum, the right use of the battery, the memory resource, and the processing capability should be managed, and this requires a suitable programming language that considers the dynamics of the operations of these factors [10,13]. When studying the dynamics of decentralized systems whose interactions define the behavior of the system [16,19], the adaptation as a consequence of self-organization concept might be the way to design a programming language. The idea is to face the challenges of the startup of the required functions to make the system works correctly, and its functioning might depend on the services offered to the system users [8].

The contribution of this article is the presentation of a programming language prototype used in the construction of ad hoc networks, using the Interaction Nets as a form of inspiration for the design.

In Sect. 2, the interaction nets model is introduced, which is the basis of Sect. 3, which describes four interactions related to an ad hoc network. In Sect. 4 an interaction is the realisation with a prototype programming language is presented. Finally, in Sect. 5, the conclusions are given.

2   Base Model: Interaction Nets

The convenience of this computational model to represent local interactions in decentralised data networks is a function of the participating nodes of these networks. A node can have a number n of communication interfaces depending on the application for which it is intended, and each communication it makes with another node or other nodes is an action that generates a result [5,14]. For instance, a transmission of a packet burst, from node A to node B. The configuration is an IP address and a port number. Node A generates interaction with node B when the transaction has done. The net's interaction model is based on the idea of computing as an interaction. Yves Lafont in 1990 proposed this model. [4,15].

The description of the system is as follows:

– A set Σ of symbols used to build networks.
– An set R of rules called interaction rules.

Network: A network N on Σ is a graph where the symbols of Σ give the labels of the nodes. A node is called an agent, and a link between two agents is called a connector. So networks are graphs that connect agents through connectors.

Active Pairs: The active pairs are equal to a pair of agents (α, β) that belong to a set of symbols. An interaction rule is composed of an active pair on the left side and a network on the right side. The rules must meet two conditions:

- Both left and right side must have the same interfaces.
- In a rule set R, there is a maximum of one rule for each pair of agents.

The interaction nets model is similar to other formal models for the definition of programming languages, such as the lambda calculus for functional languages or the *pi* calculation for parallel processes. In this article, we show how we obtain the components of a programming paradigm oriented to decentralised networks by using process algebra tools. However, other aspects of decentralised networks must be considered in order to complete the paradigm.

The model can use several notations:

- $A \bowtie B \to N$: Active pair A and B produce an interaction in a network N
- $foo(A, B)$: A function foo that acts on A and B and creates an interaction.
- Graphic notation

The following describes four essential aspects to take into account for this type of network:

- Self-configuration: in this context, configuration refers to the way the network is set up, and not only the configuration of an individual device. Nodes and applications can configure and reconfigure themselves automatically under any, predictable or unpredictable, condition with minimal or no human intervention. Self-configuration expects to reduce the effects of networks dynamics to users [2,3,16]. *The language achieves this by building functions to monitor the state of the network nodes. The functions handle agents for these actions.*
- Self-deployment: preparation, installation, authentication and verification of every new network node. It includes all procedures to bring a new node or applications into operation. Besides, self-deployment try to find strategies to improve both coverage and resource management in networking tasks [2,3,16]. *The language has native functions that manipulate routing actions and management information.*
- Self-optimization: utilisation of measurements and performance indicators to optimise the local parameters according to global objectives. It is a process in which the configuration of the network is adapted autonomously and continues the network environment regarding topology, resources, and users [2,3,16]. *The language is a tool to build agents that measure the state of the network.*
- Self-healing: Execution of routines that keep the network in the steady state and prevent possible problems from arising. These methods can modify configuration and operational parameters of the overall system to compensate failures [2,3,16]. *The language creates verification scripts of the components of the network to perform healing processes.*

3 Programming Model: Language Interactions

Based on the definition of Interaction Net and considering the nature of decentralised networks, the decision was taken to model interactions between agents in order to solve different challenges arising from the construction of the programming language. Since we want the scheme to generate local interactions, the designed interactions are:

- An agent sending a message to another agent, and being confirmed.
- An agent sending a ping message to another agent or a system element.
- Taking into account the communication specification between the FIPA agents, the proxy interaction is: a transmitter wants the receiver to make a selection of other agents to send a message or a service.
- Propagate: A transmitter wants the receiver to select other agents to send a message or service.

Below are the models:

3.1 An Agent Sending a Message to Another Agent, and Being Confirmed

This action defines two agents: A and B. Other agents are also used to complement the interaction. Figure 1 depicts this interplay.

- Agent A: send the message.
- Agent B: receive the message and send the confirmation.
- Mess is an agent with the action of the message.
- Ack is an agent with the confirmation action.

The set $\Sigma = \{A, B, mess, ack\}$
The rules of interaction are:

1. $A \bowtie B \rightarrow mess$: sent a message
2. $A \bowtie B \rightarrow ack$: an affirmative confirmation is received
3. $A \bowtie B \rightarrow \sim (ack)$: received a negative confirmation
4. $A \bowtie 0 \rightarrow \sim$: sent a message without a receiver.

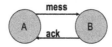

Fig. 1. The interaction between agent A and agent B. A message is sent, and a confirmation is received

3.2 An Agent Sending a Ping Message to Another Agent or a System Element

This action occurs between two agents: a transmitting agent which sends a ping to a receiving agent or a system device. Figure 2 represents interactions between them.

- Agent A: send the ping
- Agent B: receive the ping and send the confirmation
- Ping: is an agent with the action of ping
- Ack is an agent with the confirmation action.
- X: is another element of the system.

The set $\Sigma = \{A, B, ping, ack, X\}$
  The rules of interaction are:

1. $A \bowtie B \rightarrow ping$: sent a ping
2. $A \bowtie B \rightarrow ack$: an affirmative confirmation is received
3. $A \bowtie B \rightarrow\sim (ack)$: received a negative confirmation
4. $A \bowtie X \rightarrow ping$: sent a ping another element of the system
5. $A \bowtie X \rightarrow ack$: an affirmative confirmation is received
6. $A \bowtie X \rightarrow\sim (ack)$: received a negative confirmation
7. $A \bowtie 0 \rightarrow\sim$: sent a ping without a receiver.

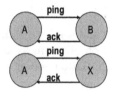

Fig. 2. The interaction between agent A and agent B. A ping is sent, and a confirmation is received. It shows the possibility that A sends a ping to another device in the system, X is used to identify the other device.

3.3 Propagate

This interaction consists of Agent A sending a message to Agent B that aims to send the information to other agents in the system. The message is from an agent with the action of the message to n agents and represents the n agents of the system. Figure 3 shows that interaction.

- Agent A: send the message.
- Agent B: receive the message and send the confirmation.
- Mess is an agent with the action of the message.
- $Mess_n$ is an agent with the action of the message to n agents
- $\otimes$ represents the n agents of the system
- Ack is an agent with the confirmation action.

The set $\Sigma = \{A, B, mess, mess_n, \otimes, ack\}$
  The rules of interaction are:

1. $A \bowtie B \to mess$: sent a message
2. $A \bowtie B \to ack$: an affirmative confirmation is received
3. $A \bowtie B \to \sim (ack)$: received a negative confirmation
4. $A \bowtie 0 \to \sim$: sent a message without a receiver
5. $A \bowtie B \to mess_n \bowtie \otimes$: agent A sends a message to agent B and sends it back to the n agents of the system
6. $mess_n \bowtie \otimes \to ack$: there is a positive confirmation of the receipt of the message from the n agents of the system
7. $mess_n \bowtie \otimes \to \sim (ack)$: there is a negative confirmation of the receipt of the message from the n agents of the system
8. $mess_n \bowtie 0 \to \sim$: there are no agents in the system to send the message
9. $mess_n \bowtie B \to mess_n \bowtie \otimes$: is the action of agent B of resends the message to the n agents of the system.

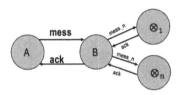

Fig. 3. The base interaction is to send a message from A to B, but B has the option of propagating this message to the other agents of the system. Each agent of the system uses the interaction. The rules are similar for each interaction, and the purpose is to send the message that B received from A

3.4   Proxy Interaction

This interaction consists of Agent A sending a message to Agent B whose purpose is to send the information to other agents of the system who are authorised to receive the information. Figure 4 indicates that interaction.

- Agent A: send the message.
- Agent B: receive the message and send the confirmation.
- Mess is an agent with the action of the message.
- $Mess_n$ is an agent with the action of the message to n agents.
- $Mess_k$ is an agent with the action of the message to k authorized agents
- $\otimes$ represents the n agents of the system.
- Ack is an agent with the confirmation action.

The set $\Sigma = \{A, B, mess, mess_n, mess_k \otimes, ack\}$
  The rules of interaction are:

1. $A \bowtie B \to mess$: sent a message
2. $A \bowtie B \to ack$: an affirmative confirmation is received

3. $A \bowtie B \to\sim (ack)$: received a negative confirmation
4. $A \bowtie 0 \to\sim$: sent a message without a receiver
5. $A \bowtie B \to mess_n \bowtie \otimes$: agent A sends a message to agent B and sends it back to the k agents of the system
6. $mess_k \bowtie \otimes \to ack$: there is a positive confirmation of the receipt of the message from the n agents of the system
7. $mess_k \bowtie \otimes \to\sim (ack)$: there is a negative confirmation of the receipt of the message from the k authorized agents of the system
8. $mess_k \bowtie 0 \to\sim$: there are no agents in the system to send the message
9. $mess_k \bowtie B \to mess_k \bowtie \otimes$: is the action of agent B of resends the message to the k authorized agents of the system.

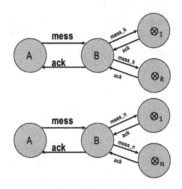

Fig. 4. This interaction is similar to the propagation interaction but is modified depending on the target agents. Only the agents k $(k \in n)$ receive the message of A. Which is classified by B

4   Real Work

The preliminary tests allow the establishment of an ad hoc network on embedded devices (Raspberry Pi). The network turns on, and the environment is switched on for communication between agents. Next, the following tests are carried out:

- Establish the ad hoc network
- A pinging agent
- An agent that sends information from sensors to a web service
- Share the Internet from one node to the other nodes of the network

4.1   Establish the Ad Hoc Network

This function enables the option to establish the network quickly with the desired parameters for its operation and little physical manipulation of the nodes.
The code that is used to make the power on the network, the environment, and the communication between agents are the following:

```
importar network.adhoc #import library
do_adhoc() # function call system
importar agent.environment #import library
a=Environment() # initialize environment
a=Environment(12345) # socket set up
```

The description of the interaction is:

1. $do\_adhoc(A, B) \rightarrow Net_{adhoc}$
2. $Environment(A, B) \rightarrow Enviroment(Socket)$

This interaction is simple since it handles four agents and it is represented in Fig. 5. Agent A and agent B are the devices that help to turn on the network. The do_adhoc agent or function is responsible for enabling the requirements to be turned on by the ad hoc network. The environment agent creates the environment in the network and receives, as a parameter, the socket number for the communication between the agents.

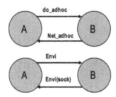

Fig. 5. The interaction is divided in two, one happens when the ad hoc network is turned on, and the other is when the environment (*Envi*) is turned on for communication between agents. In the environment (*Envi*), it receives a socket (*sock*) parameter to receive the information

4.2   A Pinging Agent

This function works as a tool to know if other agents or other devices are on in the network. The code used to create this tool is:

```
importar mas.__init__ #import library SMA

funcion ping(dir) #creation ping function
    x = PingAgent(dir)
    x.start()
end

log("test ping")
a = ping(192.168.2.1) #Execution of the function
```

This interaction is the execution of the model described in Sect. 3.2. The creation of a PingAgent is accepted as an IP address parameter. The internal function of this agent is to create the ping message and send it to the address as the parameter. The description of the interaction is:

1. $ping(A, X) \rightarrow ack$
2. $ping(A, X) \rightarrow \sim (ack)$

4.3 An Agent that Sends Information from Sensors to a Web Service

This application is more elaborate than the previous ones. The data given by the sensors are humidity, temperature, and GPS position. The most convenient scheme is Agent A, which receives the data from the sensors, then sends it to Agent B, which is responsible for making the connection to the Web service. We must remember that the applications run on a network with raspberry pi; this facilitates the manipulation of the information of the sensors.

We have created native functions of the programming language, which serve as support for some procedures. The native function of this application is the reading of the sensors. It has been called the "Measurement Agent". The code for this interaction is:

```
importar mas.__init__

funcion dataSensor(identifier, description, times)
    x = ExecuteScript() # The agent that turns on the rutine
    x.start()
end

log("test Data Sensor")
a = dataSensor(1, MeasurementAgent, 10)
```

The *dataSensor* function receives an identifier as parameters, and an agent turns on the sensors sometimes to execute the transmission of data to the Web service. The description of the interaction is:

1. $dataSensor(A, B) \rightarrow dataSensor(B, SW)$
2. $dataSensor(B, SW) \rightarrow ack| \sim (ack)$
3. $dataSensor(A, B) \rightarrow dataSensor(B, SW)$
4. $ExecuteScript(A, MA) \rightarrow MA(device)$
5. $ExecuteScript(A, MA) \rightarrow ack| \sim (ack)$
6. $MA(device) \rightarrow data$

4.4 Share the Internet from One Node to the Other Nodes of the Network

This interaction is the most powerful application in the ad hoc network. Several additional services can be offered on the internet channel to convert the network into a more flexible system to meet possible user requirements. The interaction described in Sect. 3.3 is well suited to this application.

The code for this interaction is

```
importar mas.__init__

funcion internet(identifier, description, times)
    x = ExecuteScript()
    x.start()
end

log("test Internet")
a = internet(1, CycleCallBash, 1000000)
```

For this application, we have used the ExecuteScript agent. In this case, however, the CycleCallBash agent executes the native function that modifies the configuration of the node to create a bridge interface and share the internet service.

The description of the interaction is:

- $internet(A, B) \rightarrow CycleCallBash(A)|ack| \sim (ack)$
- $internet(B, \otimes_n) \rightarrow internet(A, B)|ack| \sim (ack)$
- $CycleCallBash(A, device) \rightarrow ExecuteScript(A, device)$
- $ExecuteScript(A, device) \rightarrow data$

5   Conclusions

In this article, we have presented a programming language model with the intention of adapting it to the nature of decentralised networks. The nets interaction model is used as a basis for the programming paradigm. The advantage of the nets interaction computing model lies in the fact that interaction is seen as a form of computing. The new paradigm model views the characteristics of decentralised networks as a structural part of its conception. Thus, in the construction of the language, which is a DSL made in ANTLR, it has been thought to use functions as fundamental structures of language. On the other hand, the use of libraries and native functions that give the programming language the necessary flexibility in the construction of decentralised networks is also considered.

The description is made of the fundamental interactions of the programming language, and its application on the DSL in use is shown. The system of modules gives suitable results. We can build native functions of a sophisticated degree that are synthesised from the proposed programming language. The intention is the construction of a tool to streamline the process of building ad hoc networks, which are networks of a decentralised nature whose modules were built for the language.

On the other hand, the described models are simple and easy to implement. Thinking about the functioning of decentralised networks (for this work, ad hoc networks), the model considers interactions between two nodes (local interactions), and the agent schema can be seen with a control system for each node.

Thus, the definition of the agent on a node must also be part of the programming paradigm.

In conclusion, the paradigm proposed in this article is a multi-paradigm that considers the use of the following elements: net interaction, functions, agents, and a library management structure. It is expected that in future tests on ad hoc networks, language as a tool will serves to manipulate elements at the node level, such as handling the data traffic load or bandwidth allocation for particular flows.

References

1. Aho, A.V.: Compilers: Principles, Techniques and Tools (for Anna University), 2nd edn. Pearson Education India (2003)
2. Dressler, F.: Self-Organization in Sensor and Actor Networks. Wiley, Hoboken (2008)
3. Dressler, F.: Self-organization in ad hoc networks: overview and classification. Univ. Erlangen, Dept. Comput. Sci. **7**, 1–12 (2006)
4. Fernández, M.: Models of Computation: An Introduction to Computability Theory. Springer, London (2009). https://doi.org/10.1007/978-1-84882-434-8
5. Fernández, M., Mackie, I.: A calculus for interaction nets. In: Nadathur, G. (ed.) PPDP 1999. LNCS, vol. 1702, pp. 170–187. Springer, Heidelberg (1999). https://doi.org/10.1007/10704567_10
6. Fister, I., Mernik, M., Hrnčič, D.: Implementation of the domain-specific language easytime using a LISA compiler generator. In: 2011 Federated Conference on Computer Science and Information Systems (FedCSIS), pp. 801–808. IEEE (2011)
7. Fitzek, F.H., Katz, M.D.: Mobile Clouds: Exploiting Distributed Resources in Wireless, Mobile and Social Networks. Wiley, Hoboken (2013)
8. Gershenson, C.: Design and control of self-organizing systems. CopIt ArXives (2007)
9. Grune, D., Van Reeuwijk, K., Bal, H.E., Jacobs, C.J., Langendoen, K.: Modern Compiler Design. Springer, New York (2012). https://doi.org/10.1007/978-1-4614-4699-6
10. Loo, J.H., Mauri, J.L., Ortiz, J.: Mobile Ad Hoc Networks: Current Status and Future Trends. CRC Press, Boca Raton (2011)
11. Nitti, M., Girau, R., Atzori, L.: Trustworthiness management in the social internet of things. IEEE Trans. Knowl. Data Eng. **26**(5), 1253–1266 (2014)
12. Ortiz, A.M., Hussein, D., Park, S., Han, S.N., Crespi, N.: The cluster between internet of things and social networks: review and research challenges. IEEE Internet Things J. **1**(3), 206–215 (2014)
13. Palos, S., Kiviniemi, A., Kuusisto, J.: Future perspectives on product data management in building information modeling. Constr. Innov. **14**(1), 52–68 (2014)
14. Perrinel, M.: On context semantics and interaction nets. In: Proceedings of the Joint Meeting of the Twenty-Third EACSL Annual Conference on Computer Science Logic (CSL) and the Twenty-Ninth Annual ACM/IEEE Symposium on Logic in Computer Science (LICS), p. 73. ACM (2014)
15. Pinto, J.S.: Sequential and concurrent abstract machines for interaction nets. In: Tiuryn, J. (ed.) FoSSaCS 2000. LNCS, vol. 1784, pp. 267–282. Springer, Heidelberg (2000). https://doi.org/10.1007/3-540-46432-8_18

16. Prehofer, C., Bettstetter, C.: Self-organization in communication networks: principles and design paradigms. IEEE Commun. Mag. **43**(7), 78–85 (2005)
17. Pureswaran, V., Brody, P.: Device democracy: saving the future of the internet of things. IBM Corporation (2015)
18. Sheng, W., et al.: A compiler infrastructure for embedded heterogeneous mpsocs. Parallel Comput. **40**(2), 51–68 (2014)
19. Zhang, Z., Long, K., Wang, J.: Self-organization paradigms and optimization approaches for cognitive radio technologies: a survey. IEEE Wirel. Commun. **20**(2), 36–42 (2013)

Fighting Adversarial Attacks on Online Abusive Language Moderation

Nestor Rodriguez and Sergio Rojas-Galeano[✉]

School of Engineering, Universidad Distrital Francisco José de Caldas,
Bogotá, Colombia
srojas@udistrital.edu.co

Abstract. Lack of moderation in online conversations may result in personal aggression, harassment or cyberbullying. Such kind of hostility is usually expressed by using profanity or abusive language. On the basis of this assumption, recently Google has developed a machine-learning model to detect hostility within a comment. The model is able to assess to what extent abusive language is poisoning a conversation, obtaining a "toxicity" score for the comment. Unfortunately, it has been suggested that such a toxicity model can be deceived by adversarial attacks that manipulate the text sequence of the abusive language. In this paper we aim to fight this anomaly; firstly we characterise two types of adversarial attacks, one using obfuscation and the other using polarity transformations. Then, we propose a two–stage approach to disarm such attacks by coupling a text deobfuscation method and the toxicity scoring model. The approach was validated on a dataset of approximately 24000 distorted comments showing that it is feasible to restore the toxicity score of the adversarial variants. We anticipate that combining machine learning and text pattern recognition methods operating on different layers of linguistic features, will help to foster aggression–safe online conversations despite the adversary challenges inherent to the versatile nature of written language.

Keywords: Abusive language moderation · Adversarial attacks
Text pattern recognition

1 Introduction

User-generated-comments are arguably one of most appealing features of social networks and other platforms for online conversation, allowing users to engage in debate and exchange of opinions on common topics of interest, openly and freely. This kind of digital freedom of speech enables user to express not only their reasons but also their emotions and some people may misuse it to turn their discussion into personal aggression or abuse intended to ridicule, distort or confuse other's opinion, avoiding factual–based debate in favour of opinion manipulation by means of fake news, libel and personal or social group hostility, an scenario now commonly–referred as post–truth politics [1].

© Springer Nature Switzerland AG 2018
J. C. Figueroa-García et al. (Eds.): WEA 2018, CCIS 915, pp. 480–493, 2018.
https://doi.org/10.1007/978-3-030-00350-0_40

Emotion–guided arguments may lead easily to radicalism in political, religious, ethnic, sport or minorities views, which in turn may result in comments coloured with personal aggression, harassment or cyberbullying [2–4]. This kind of hostility is becoming a cause of concern in online communities and hence, the question arises about the need to detect and block such behaviour with automatic moderation tools. In this direction, Google Counter-Abuse Technology Team has launched *Perspective*, a tool to identify the degree of abusive language contained in a written comment, by using crowd–sourcing and machine learning models trained on large samples of respectful and aggressive conversations [5]. One assumption is that usually abuse is expressed in terms of harshness or swearing, and thus the model recognises, among many other features, to what extent rude language is poisoning a comment, thus obtaining its "toxicity" score.

The toxicity model performed remarkably well on diverse hot topics such as US Presidential election, Brexit and climate change; however it has been suggested recently that its detection mechanism can be heavily defeated using adversarial strategies that corrupt the input text sequence with typographic or polarity manipulation [6]. On some comments available for demonstration in the *Perspective* website [5], it was shown in that study for example, that the insulting statement "They are liberal idiots who are uneducated" (toxicity score: 90%), becomes a mild comment when written as "They are liberal idiots who are uneducated" (toxicity score: 15%). Similarly, the rude sentence "It's stupid and wrong" (toxicity: 89%), remains rude even if negated: "It's not stupid and wrong" (toxicity: 83%). The number of variations that can be obtained with these adversarial strategies is combinatorial, and therefore training a machine learning model would be impractical even with large amounts of available examples.

In this paper a counter–attack strategy is devised; it consists of firstly pre–processing the input with a recently proposed text deobfuscation method [7] so as to transform it back into its original representation, and subsequently feeding this corrected text to the toxic scoring model. Our results indicate that this approach is able to effectively restore the intended toxic score of the corrupted text given by *Perspective*, suggesting that combining pattern recognition methods and machine learning models is a feasible approach to disarm such kind of adversarial attacks.

2   Materials and Methods

2.1   Google's Toxicity Model

The Google *Perspective* (GP) model aims to asses to what extent a comment may be poisoning a conversation towards an aggressive or abusive outburst: it screens the text of a comment to compute a toxicity score on a scale from 0 ("safe") to 1 ("very toxic"). The model was built based on a large–scale sample of real polite and aggressive comments, using crowd–sourced annotations to train machine learning classifiers (logistic regression and neural networks, with bag–of–words features, see [5] for details). Here, toxicity is understood as the use of rude, disrespectful or distressing language referring to personal, political, ethnic, religious or any other social condition (sex preferences, sport club supporter, etc.) that may affect negatively the views or feelings of other persons.

2.2 Adversarial Attacks

Within the machine learning community, an adversarial framework refers to inputs deliberately designed to manipulate the expected behaviour of a prediction model [8,9]. The adversary usually picks data from distributions different to those assumed when training the model, thus defeating its prediction capabilities. The attacks usually consist of corrupted features or distorted inputs. In our problem of interest, two adversarial attacks on the GP toxic model have been recently highlighted [6], which we formally characterise as follows.

Obfuscation Attack. In this attack the adversary obfuscates portions of the text sequence that is commonly associated to aggressive content, such as insults or swear words. The obfuscation takes advantage of the robustness of the human mind to recognise corrupted variants of text. Such edits can be: misspellings or symbol substitution, letter repetition, fake punctuation (inserting dots, commas or blanks within letters in the words). As a result, the text becomes disguised from its original character codification whilst still conveying its meaning. These kind of obfuscations has been identified as homoglyph substitution and bogus segmentation anomalies [7].

Polarity Attack. In this attack the adversary uses grammatical negation of an offensive comment which the model still recognises as toxic. This is achieved by simply negating toxic terms effectively swapping the polarity of the comment to its opposite meaning or emotional intent. For example, if the toxic term is an adjective, the polarity change occurs when inserting in the text the particle "*not*" before the word. The modified comment still contains the aggressive term, misleading the model to compute high toxic scores despite its apparent neutrality. We remark that the adversarial intensity of the strategy can be worsen by combining the two attacks within the same comment, i.e. negating obfuscated versions of toxicity terms.

2.3 Dataset Preparation

The GP website [10] provides a sample of comments gathered from online surveys on three delicate topics: US Election (45 comments), Brexit (61) and Climate change (49). The comments' text along with scores obtained with the GP toxicity model are available. So we collected those with toxicity scores higher than 60%, obtaining a subset of 24 comments that we labeled as {usel01,..., usel10, brex01,..., brex07, clic01,..., clic07} (for a complete list, see Appendix).

We subsequently prepared datasets conveying the two types of adversarial anomalies, namely obfuscation attack and polarity attack. For the first attack, 1000 variations of each comment were randomly generated by isolating toxic terms in order to obfuscate them with a number of edits including homoglyph substitution, bogus segmentation and letter repetition (using the same protocol as [7]). The isolation of toxic terms was made as explained in the next subsection.

The number of edits applied to each term was controlled with a corruption rate $p \in \{50\%, 99\%\}$. Thus, for each character in the isolated term a uniformly-distributed random number $r \sim \mathcal{U}(0,1)$ was sampled; if $r < p$ the character was kept unchanged, otherwise one of these edits was applied (with their respective probabilities): an homoglyph substitution (60%), a bogus segmentation (30%) or a fake letter repetition (10%). In this way, we obtained two datasets, `obfuscation-50` and `obfuscation-99` consisting of 24,000 obfuscated toxic comments each (see examples in Table 1). With respect to the homoglyph edits utilised in the obfuscation attack, we defined substitution lists encompassing a subset of the ASCII encoding set, as depicted in Fig. 1.

Now, the second dataset (`polarity`) was obtained by inserting negation predicates within each comment. Thus, the size of this dataset is 24 negated comments. Although possible, we refrained from generating obfuscated variants of these comments as the aim of this attack was to investigate the effect of the polarity change achieved by the negated predicates alone. Table 1 also shows examples for this attack.

2.4   Toxic Term Isolation

We identified a list of toxic terms contained in the original comments as follows: for each comment in the original dataset, we scanned every single word with the toxicity model; those scoring higher than 50% were added to the list. Regarding

Table 1. An excerpt of adversarial examples from the datasets.

Topic	Attack	ID	Text sequence
US Election	None (original)	usel01	If they voted for Hilary they are idiots
	obfuscation-50	usel01-098	If they voted for Hilary they are !d10ts
	obfuscation-99	usel01-295	If they voted for Hilary they are i;;d-I0t_5
	polarity	usel01'	If they voted for Hilary they are NOT idiots
Brexit	None (original)	brex03	They are stupid and ignorant with no class
	obfuscation-50	brex03-381	They are st.VPId and ignorNt with no class
	obfuscation-99	brex03-120	They are s7uuupi-d, and 1g,Nooooora,n t with no class
	polarity	brex03'	They are NOT stupid and NOT ignorant with no class
Climate change	None (original)	clic01	They have their heads up their ass
	obfuscation-50	clic01-688	They have their heads up their AS5
	obfuscation-99	clic01-512	They have their heads up their a**$s
	polarity	clic01'	They have their heads NOT up their ass

Table 2. The lists of toxic terms and their negated predicates.

Toxic term	Negated predicate	Toxic term	Negated predicate
idiots	not idiots	awful	not awful
stupid	not stupid	in hell	not in hell
the worst	not the worst	morons	not morons
screw you	don't screw you	terrible	not terrible
suck	don't suck	a shame	not a shame
stupidity	no stupidity	racist	not racist
sexist	not sexist	supremacists	not supremacists
assholes	not assholes	ignorant	not ignorant
a moron	not a moron	nationalists	not nationalists
rubbish	not rubbish	up their ass	not up their ass
uneducated	not uneducated	an idiot	not an idiot
an abortion	not an abortion		

the negated predicates, such list was built by preceding each word within the toxic term list, with the particle *not* if it was an adjective or noun, or *do not* if it was a verb. The resulting lists are shown in Table 2.

2.5 Disarming the Adversarial Attacks

The method we propose to address the adversarial attacks is illustrated in Fig. 2; it basically consist of filtering the corrupted comment prior to feeding the toxicity model, by means of the deobfuscation approach introduced in [7]. Such normalisation filter requires a list of target vocables written in plain English, that are to be searched within the input text. The approach then uses an approximate string matching algorithm to find occurrences of the vocables, either verbatim

Fig. 1. Homoglyph substitution lists. For each letter of the English alphabet in the inner orange ring, the corresponding list of substituting symbols are shown in the outer blue ring. The blank character "␣" indexes the lists of bogus segmentators.

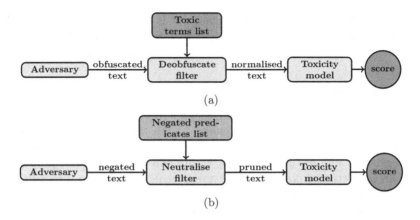

Fig. 2. Disarming the adversarial attacks. The adversary comment is preprocessed in order to provide a suitable input to the toxicity model. (a) Obfuscation attack: the preprocessor is a deobfuscation filter fed with a list of toxic terms; if any obfuscated variant is found, the filter replaces them with their plain English version. (b) Polarity attack: the preprocessor is a neutralisation filter fed with a list of negation predicates; if any of these are found in this case the filter removes them from the input text.

copies or variants resulting from the homoglyph substitution, bogus segmentation or symbol repetition. Matching occurrences are corrected and the resulting sequence is accordingly fed to the GP toxicity model.

We defined two correction schemes, namely a *deobfuscation* filter or a *neutralisation* filter, depending on the kind of attack, obfuscation or polarity, respectively. In the former, the vocabulary consists of a list of toxic terms that when obfuscated are not recognised by the model, thus lowering the toxicity of the comment whilst still conveying its aggressive tone; therefore here the filter corrects the input by replacing obfuscated occurrences with their corresponding plain English versions. In contrast, the neutralisation filter uses as vocabulary a list of negated predicates of such toxic terms; here the input is corrected by removing (i.e. pruning) plain or even obfuscated occurrences of these predicates, effectively switching the polarity of the comment towards a neutral attitude by expurgating references to (negated) toxic content. These two vocabularies correspond to those of Table 2.

3   Results

3.1   Experimental Setup

We used to APIs to apply the toxicity model and the deobfuscation filter, available from the Perspective Web Service [10] and the TextPatrol Web Service [11], respectively. Besides, we developed an experimental command-line tool to process the dataset of comments by invoking the APIs in order to produce an output text file including, for each comment, toxicity scores and execution times of the GP model alone and the combined TP+GP method. The command-line tool was written using the Go programming language, it is open source and is available at the repository https://gitlab.com/textpatrol/gp-tp-experiment, from where the datasets used in our experiments can also been downloaded.

3.2 Obfuscation Attack

Let us examine first the results of toxicity scores reported in Fig. 3. The figure comprises three plots corresponding to the three topics: usel*, brex* and clic*. Each plot in turn combines the scores obtained in both datasets, obfuscation-50 and obfuscation-99, within two reflected panels (upper and lower half, respectively; notice that the y-axis scale ranges from 0 to 1 in both directions). Three sets of values are depicted in these plots: toxicity of the original comments (red squares) and average toxicities of the 1000 variants of each comment, as obtained by the GP model (green bars) and by the TP+GP method (amber bars).

On the one hand, the red squares in the figure (GP scores on original comments) show that toxicity scores for every comment is nearly 1.0, except for usel09 and usel10, scoring lower toxicities closer to 0.9. The latter two comments contain toxic terms related to superlatives or adjective derivations (*racist, supremacist, sexist, stupidity*) whereas the remainder comments (usel01-usel08 and brex* and clic*) incorporate either insults or swearing (*idiot, stupid, asshole, moron, screw you*), which highlights the assumption of the model that toxicity is stressed by the use of profanity terms.

On the other hand, the green bars in the figure (average GP scores on obfuscated comments) exhibit a common pattern associated with the vulnerability of the model to the obfuscation attack: toxicities decrease to levels closer to or lower than 0.5 (18 out of 24 cases in obfuscation-50 and 22 out of 24 in obfuscation-99). If a moderator were to apply a reasonable cut–off of less than 0.7 toxicity to consider a comment as safe, then all but one of the toxic obfuscated categories would have been accepted by the model as non–toxic. This pattern strongly substantiate the preliminary results reported in [6], regarding the weakness of the model to this kind of attack.

Additionally, the amber bars in the figure (average TP+GP scores on obfuscated comments) show that our approach is able to restore toxicity scores to their original levels. There it can be seen that on obfuscation-50 the differences between the TP+GP and the original scores differ in less than 0.03 in all but three cases: brex01 (0.11), brex07 (0.11) and clic07 (0.15). Similarly, on the more deceitful obfuscation-99 dataset, where essentially the entire sequence of toxic terms occurrences are corrupted, the reduction in the scores is again less than 0.03 in all but four cases: usel09 (0.05), brex01 (0.21), brex07 (0.22) and clic07 (0.26). In this case, a moderator with the aforementioned 0.7 toxicity cut–off would correctly reject all the cases as toxic. Besides, the evidence indicate that also in all cases of obfuscation, the average drop of toxicity incurred by the GP model is significantly larger than that the average drop obtained by the TP+GP method ($p < 0.001$).

In order to further corroborate the effectiveness of the proposed method in disarming the obfuscation attack, Fig. 4 illustrates radial frequency histograms

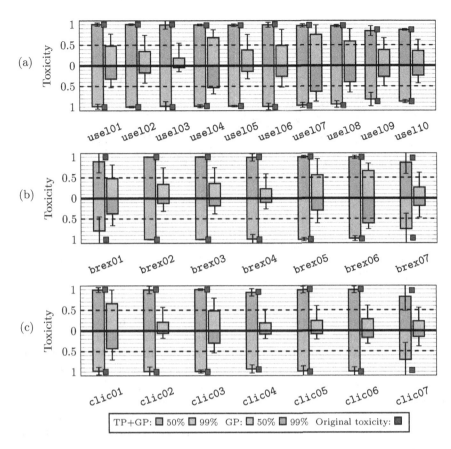

Fig. 3. Toxicity scores for the obfuscation attack. In each plot the upper half panel shows average toxicities obtained for comments obfuscated with a 50% corruption rate (`obfuscation-50` dataset) whereas the reflected lower half panel reports toxicities with a 99% corruption rate (`obfuscation-99` dataset). Bars indicate the average was taken over 1000 variants in their respective comment category (whiskers being standard deviations) whilst squares indicate the toxicity values of a single observation, i.e. those of the original comments. (a) US Election. (b) Brexit. (c) Climate change. (Color figure online)

of the proportion of obfuscated instances correctly scored with at least the original toxicity, from the total 1000 variants (red area) of each comment ID. It can be seen how on the `obfuscation-50` dataset the TP+GP method (amber area) is able to correctly score a large proportion of comments in all topics. This pattern is replicated in the `obfuscation-99` dataset, although proportions slightly decline due to the higher corruption level, which, as it was said before, yields more acid attacks because almost the entire toxic sequences are altered.

It is worth noting in Fig. 4, that the GP model alone is able to recognise correctly some proportion of the variants in the `obfuscation-50` dataset (left

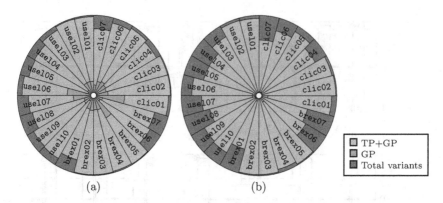

(a)   (b)

Fig. 4. Effectiveness in disarming the obfuscation attack. These radial histograms show the proportion of obfuscated comments correctly scored with at least the same toxicity of the original comment, out of 1000 variants (red area), as obtained by GP model (green) and TP+GP method (amber). (a) `obfuscation-50`. (b) `obfuscation-99`. (Colour figure online)

panel, green sectors), particularly obfuscations of `usel06`, `brex05` and `clic01`. On closer examination we found that the toxicity of the two former comments (`usel06` and `brex05`) comes from the insult *"moron"* (see Table 3) and that for this particular sequence of letters the list of homoglyph substitutions are simply their upper–and lowercase versions (see Fig. 1); thus, a possible explanation of why the GP model is able to detect some variants is because given a low corruption rate (50%) some of them would be simply the same word with intermixed case (e.g. *"mORoN"*, *"MoROn"*, etc.), and it is very likely that the GP API makes a lower case conversion before feeding the comment to the model. The case of the recognised `clic01` variants may be explained because its toxicity is originated from the term *"ass"* (in its offensive meaning, see Table 3); notice that homoglyphs for these characters include non-letter symbols (see Fig. 1), but due to the shortness of the offensive term (just 3 letters) along with the low corruption rate (50%) it is very likely that a number of variants are identical to the original or a mixed-case version as before.

On the other hand, in the more acid `obfuscation-99` attacks (right panel of Fig. 4) harder obfuscated variants will be found more frequently, hence the dilution of the green sectors. Moreover, we observe that the longer the toxic sequence and the more toxic terms are included in the original comment, the stronger the deception effect of the obfuscation attack. Take for example `usel10` which contains 3 toxic terms, one of which is 12-letters long; in this case, the proportion of recognised variants by the GP model alone is tiny. Combine that with more frequent bogus segmentations due to higher corruption rates, resulting in the toxic recognition ability of the GP model to further weaken, as it is noticeable in the radial histogram of the `obfuscation-99` dataset. The TP+GP approach in contrast, is able to still recognise a large proportion of variants despite the intensity of the attack.

Let us focus now on processing time. Figure 5 shows average runtimes of the 1000 repetitions for GP model and TP+GP method in each category. Here the first observation is that the effectiveness of the proposed method in disarming the obfuscation attack, comes at the expense of an increase in runtime. This is due of course to the additional preprocessing step that executes the deobfuscation filter. The trend in the plot shows that the TP+GP nearly doubles the time taken by GP model alone. The second observation is that the average runtimes for each set of comments are quite similar in both obfuscation-50 and obfuscation-99, a reasonable behaviour considering that since the obfuscation may add extra characters (bogus segmentators or fake letter repetitions) only to the toxic terms, the overall comment length may vary but not drastically, and the time cost of the deobfuscation method depends only on the length of the screened text [7].

The last observation is related to the variability of the results, indicated by the whiskers in the plots. At first glance these deviations may seem large; nonetheless recall that the experimental pipeline was built using two web-service APIs, one for GP and another one for TP, respectively. In such setting the execution of the experiments need to take into account network latencies and server availability (in some cases the GP web service replied with a 400 Bad Request or 502 Bad Gateway error codes; these executions were excluded from the reported average runtimes: 651 in obfuscation-50 and 506 in obfuscation-99 out of their corresponding 24,000 variants).

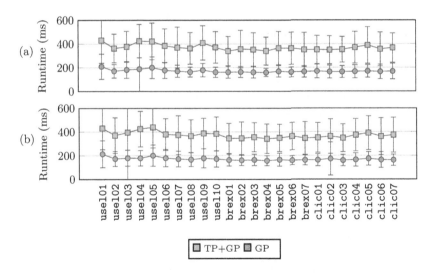

Fig. 5. Average runtimes for the obfuscation attack experiment, GP model (green) vs. TP+GP method (amber). (a) obfuscation-50. (b) obfuscation-99. (Color figure online)

3.3 Polarity Attack

The results of the polarity attack experiment are summarised in Fig. 6; recall that the `polarity` dataset contains a single negated variation per comment, hence the figure reports single executions ({`usel01'`,...,`clic07'`}). These scores indicate the negated versions were assessed by the GP model with high toxicities (although lower than their respective original comments). The TP+GP method on the contrary, obtains toxicities levels mostly below 0.5, except for some comments that incidentally contain toxic content not initially identified as such at the beginning of our study, but incorporated into newer versions of the GP model (e.g. terms like "*dishonest*" in `usel04` or "*short-sighted*" in `clic06`, not included in the vocabulary lists of Fig. 2).

The rationale of this behaviour is that the toxicity model is trained on the assumption that the comments would be coherently written, in a grammatical sense. Thus it simply checks weather toxicity features and patterns are identified within the comment and not if it is correctly constructed. To illustrate this point, let us analyse the effect of the neutralise filter on comment `usel01'`: *If they voted for Hilary they are NOT idiots.* Using GP, this comment scores a 86% toxicity score (very close to the score of the original aggressive comment), which when removing the negated offensive term (*If they voted for Hilary they are*) plunges to a 25% toxicity level; in other words, GP would identify the trimmed sentence as safe, despite its dubious grammar soundness.

The TP+GP approach takes advantage of the aforementioned assumption, by simply removing subsequences matching the list of negated predicates. One may argue however, that the trimmed comment is not comparable with the negated one, as the former may become a grammatically malformed sentence (due to the removed predicates). The reason we proceeded that way is we wanted to preserve as far as possible the authentic source content, allowing the filter to remove but not to alter or add new content *ad libitum*. An alternative approach would have been precisely to replace, instead of to remove, the matching negated predicates with non–negated synonyms (e.g. *not awful → wonderful, not idiot → clever*);

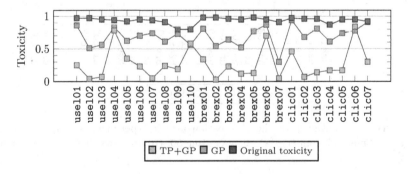

Fig. 6. Toxicity scores for the polarity attack, as obtained by GP model (green) vs. TP+GP method (amber) in the 24 negated comments of the `polarity` dataset. Toxicities of the original comments are also shown (red). (Color figure online)

as a result, correctly constructed toxic–trigger–free comments would have been obtained. Hence, their scores would also have dropped down to the safety region (in this example *If they voted for Hilary they are clever*, obtained a 24% toxicity, almost equalling the trimmed sentence). We note in passing that runtimes of this experiment resembled those of the obfuscation attack in the sense that TP+GP nearly doubled GP processing time (data not shown).

4   Discussion and Conclusion

We have shown how adversarial manipulation of the text sequence in user comments is able to deceive robust machine learning models of aggressiveness assessment. These attacks take advantage of the reconstruction capacity of the human brain when reading corrupted text, an of course, of the grammatical and semantical complexities of language as a communicating device. The large combinatorial number of variants that can be derived with these stratagems makes unfeasible to train a model to recognise them. Thus we propose to alleviate the attacks by preprocessing the comment at the character level, so as to restore its natural representation and/or polarity before feeding the aggressiveness model.

Nonetheless, we reckon that as long as adversaries will keep hardening their attacks, ensuring hostility–free, respectful and opinionated online discussion environments would require more sophisticated pipelines of text analysis operating on different linguistic levels, ranging from sequence to linguistic to semantic to sentiment analysis; lower level processing would provide useful features to higher level analysis, which of course, may prove more difficult to handle. To illustrate this point, take for example figures of speech such as sarcasm, irony or satire that may use toxic content as a legitimate rhetorical device. What is more, it has been recognised that aggression is strongly related to arising causes of concern such as cyberbullying, harassment, racism, post-truth opinion forming, and mind state manipulation towards violence [3,12,13]; hence, robust toxicity detection will have significant implications for casual, legal or political issues in online communities and we believe is rightly worthy of further research efforts.

Disclaimer: Original comments and modified variants shown in Tables 1 and 3 and in other sections of this paper, were gathered or derived from their original source [10] for research purposes; they do not represent the views of the authors.

Appendix. Original Comments

Table 3 shows the original aggressive comments extracted from the GP Website [10] with their toxicity scores obtained at the beginning of this study (notice that since GP is continuously refining its model by learning from new examples, these scores may have varied over time). The terms triggering toxicity are indicated in bold type and were found as explained in Sect. 2.4.

Table 3. Original aggressive comments extracted from [10].

ID	Comment text sequence	Toxicity	Length
usel01	If they voted for Hilary they are **idiots**	0.90	40
usel02	It was **awful**. People are **stupid**	0.90	32
usel03	I respect it but they are **stupid**	0.89	32
usel04	Liberals are **idiots**. Why in the **hell** would u vote for a person like Hillary Clinton. She believes in stealing, she's dishonest and believes it's okay for an **abortion** to be done at 9 months. She's **awful**	0.87	202
usel05	Donald trump is the **worst** person to be president. This election really showed how **stupid** the U.S. is	0.85	101
usel06	Anyone who voted for Trump is a **moron**	0.81	38
usel07	**Screw** you trump supporters	0.79	26
usel08	It was a **terrible**. Both sides **suck**, but Trump REALLY is scary	0.72	61
usel09	It is a **shame** that Donald Trump was elected. You can never underestimate the **stupidity** of middle America	0.67	105
usel10	Good job voting for a **racist**, **sexist** guy who's putting white **supremacists** in the white house. Have fun	0.67	103
brex01	Anti democratic **assholes**	0.95	24
brex02	**Ignorant** and **stupid**	0.93	19
brex03	They are **stupid** and **ignorant** with no class	0.91	42
brex04	It's **stupid** and wrong	0.89	21
brex05	you **morons**	0.92	10
brex06	**idiots**. backward thinking people. **nationalists**. not accepting facts. susceptible to lies	0.80	89
brex07	It's **rubbish**	0.69	12
clic01	They have their heads up their **ass**	0.93	35
clic02	How can you be so **stupid**?	0.91	25
clic03	They are liberal **idiots** who are **uneducated**	0.90	43
clic04	They're **stupid**, it's getting warmer, we should enjoy it while it lasts	0.86	71
clic05	Climate change is happening and it's not changing in our favor. If you think differently you're an **idiot**	0.84	105
clic06	I think those people are **stupid** and short-sighted	0.84	49
clic07	They're allowed to do that. But if they act like **assholes** about, I will block them	0.78	83

References

1. Dale, R.: NLP in a post-truth world. Nat. Lang. Eng. **23**(2), 319–324 (2017)
2. Hosseinmardi, H.: Survey of computational methods in cyberbullying research. In: Proceedings of the First International Workshop on Computational Methods for CyberSafety. ACM, New York (2016)
3. Burnap, P., Williams, M.L.: Us and them: identifying cyber hate on Twitter across multiple protected characteristics. EPJ Data Sci. **5**(1), 11 (2016)
4. Nobata, C., Tetreault, J., Thomas, A., Mehdad, Y., Chang, Y.: Abusive language detection in online user content. In: Proceedings of the 25th International Conference on World Wide Web (2016)
5. Wulczyn, E., Thain, N., Dixon, L.: Ex machina: personal attacks seen at scale. arXiv preprint arXiv:1610.08914, February 2017
6. Hosseini, H., Kannan, S., Zhang, B., Poovendran, R.: Deceiving google's perspective API built for detecting toxic comments. arXiv preprint arXiv:1702.08138, February 2017
7. Rojas-Galeano, S.: On obstructing obscenity obfuscation. ACM Trans. Web **11**(2), 12:1–12:24 (2017). https://doi.org/10.1145/3032963
8. Laskov, P., Lippmann, R.: Machine learning in adversarial environments. Mach. Learn. **81**(2), 115–119 (2010)
9. Samanta, S., Mehta, S.: Towards crafting text adversarial samples. arXiv preprint arXiv:1707.02812 (2017)
10. PerspectiveAPI: Jigsaw (2017). https://www.perspectiveapi.com. Accessed 26 May 2018
11. TextPatrolAPI: TPLabs (2017). https://api.textpatrol.tk. Accessed 26 May 2018
12. Stone, T.E., McMillan, M., Hazelton, M.: Back to swear one: a review of English language literature on swearing and cursing in western health settings. Aggress. Violent Behav. **25**, 65–74 (2015)
13. Hosseinmardi, H., Mattson, S.A., Ibn Rafiq, R., Han, R., Lv, Q., Mishra, S.: Analyzing labeled cyberbullying incidents on the instagram social network. In: Liu, T.Y., Scollon, C., Zhu, W. (eds.) Social Informatics. LNCS, vol. 9471, pp. 49–66. Springer, Cham (2015). https://doi.org/10.1007/978-3-319-27433-1_4

Power and Energy Applications

Simulation of a 14 Node IEEE System with Distributed Generation Using Quasi-dynamic Analysis

Luis Felipe Gaitan[1,2(✉)], Juan David Gómez[1,2(✉)],
and Edwin Rivas Trujillo[1,2(✉)]

[1] Ingeniería Especializada S.A., Medellín, Colombia
{luis.f.g, juan.d.g, erivas}@ieee.org
[2] Universidad Distrital Francisco José de Caldas, Bogotá, Colombia

Abstract. In this article, an electrical system with a study case is presented within the Colombian industrial electric sector in order to identify the changes in the electrical variables of a electrical network with distributed generation (DG). To achieve this, each present load in the 14-node IEEE system was modelled as daily demand curve of the Colombian industrial electric sector. In first place, the power dispatch of the 14-node IEEE system with DG was optimized through the particle swarm method. Afterwards, Quasi-Dynamic simulations were implemented throughout a 24-h period in the different nodes of the system with the purpose of estimate the transformers and line losses as well as the variations in the power and voltage profiles in the system nodes. DG systems supply effectively the demanded power however the voltage and power profiles resulting from Quasi-Dynamic simulations do not show significant changes in the behavior of the electrical network.

Keywords: Distributed generation · Particle swarm optimization
Quasi-dynamic simulation

1 Introduction

The definition of the term Distributed Generation (DG) depends on each country's legislation [1, 2]. As an example [3] defines DG as the production of electric energy close to the consumption centers connected to a Local Distribution System (LDS). This new electricity generation scenario leads to economic and technical changes in the system. From a technical standpoint, power-flow and economic dispatch optimization studies are carried out before and after the inclusion of distributed generation to assess the changes caused by the inclusion of these new generation systems. The power-flow was developed based on Quasi-Dynamic simulations during a 24-h period in the different nodes of the electric power system. These types of simulations allow identifying and analyzing the parameters that vary in the electric network over time, as well as estimating the transformers and line losses.

The basic idea of "Quasi-Dynamic" methods is to consider different time scales in nature throughout the whole process simulating shorter timescale processes between

© Springer Nature Switzerland AG 2018
J. C. Figueroa-García et al. (Eds.): WEA 2018, CCIS 915, pp. 497–508, 2018.
https://doi.org/10.1007/978-3-030-00350-0_41

longer transitions. Different authors point out that these methods not only improve the fidelity of the simulation in the general process, in comparison with the quasi-static methods, but also decrease the processing time of the dynamic simulations since it is not necessary to solve the whole differential equations that the models have [4–7].

2 Simulation of the 14-Node IEEE System with Distributed Generation

The 14-node IEEE system is a representation of Mid-Western USA electrical system of 1962. This power system's data were entered in the IEEE Common Data Format in August 1993 and hence, the reported simulation data in [8] was replicated. The 14-test node IEEE system has 11 loads, 5 generators, 17 transmission lines and 3 power transformers [9].

2.1   Modification of the Transformers

The 14-node IEEE system is conceived originally without losses in its windings. In the simulation scenarios in the case studies, the loss value was adjusted according to Colombian Technical Norm (NTC) 819 of Electro techniques, Self-cooling Three-phase Transformers and Submerged in Liquid, Current without load, Losses and Short-circuit voltage [10]. This norm only considers transformers up to 10 MVA, so the losses present in the 100 MVA transformers' copper windings were adjusted to 76 kW based on the Eq. 1 of the aforementioned norm.

$$Losses\ without\ load = 8,3104 * P_{nominal}^{0,792} \tag{1}$$

$$Losses\ without\ load = 8,3104 * 100000\ KVA^{0,792} \tag{2}$$

$$Losses\ without\ load = 76317,11\ KVA \tag{3}$$

2.2   Modification in the Loads

For each load present in the 14-node IEEE system, a daily demand curve was modeled and the Colombian industrial electric sector's demand curve [11] was included since it represents the potential users that would have the economic power to acquire and generate electricity independently thereby profiting from eventual discounts and assistance offered from the Colombian government.

2.2.1   Modeling the Distributed Generation Systems

The DG systems included in the 14-node IEEE system generate electrical energy from non-conventional renewable energy sources such as photovoltaic or eolical generation systems. These DG nodes are modeled with the Static Generator tool from DIgSI-LENT® Powerfactory software which models DG technologies that are connected to the network through an inversor [12, 13].

The power value of this generator is 0.9 inductive. To determine the values of the generators' active power and apparent power, the active power of the spot-type load from the original power system is taken as the reference value. The power is calculated according to Eq. 4.

$$P = S \cdot Power\ Factor \tag{4}$$

The DG systems begin their power dispatch at 14:00:00 h in the day and end dispatch at 18:00:00, attending to the second peak in the typical demand curve of industrial load.

To simulate the DG nodes, two new electrical barrages were added to the nodes with spot-type charges through a "Breaker/Switch". Figure 1 shows how the load and the new generators are connected in the 14-node IEEE system. The power values in the new generators included are related in Table 1.

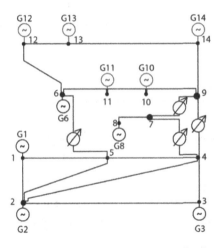

Fig. 1. Schematic of the modified 14-node IEEE system with distributed generation used in the study case. Source: Elaborated by the author.

2.2.2   Modeling the Transformers for the Alternative Generators

A transformer is modeled whose function is to adjust the voltage level present at the exit of the alternative generator (Node "Farm") and the level of voltage present in the original power system (Node "Generator"). Another feature included in the new transformers is that the losses will be about 3% and their star connection in Neutral Cero (YN-YN-0). The other values are maintained in the default values generated by DIgSILENT® Powerfactory.

Table 1. Capacity of the generators added to 14-node IEEE system

Generator	Active power [MW]
Generator 10	9.00
Generator 11	3.50
Generator 12	6.10
Generator 13	13.5
Generator 14	14.9

2.3   Simulation Scenarios

To identify the impact of DG in power systems, two simulation scenarios were established:

2.3.1   Conventional Scenario

In this operation scenario, only the *"Breaker/Switch"* that connect the *"Load"* nodes are activated. These nodes are associated with spot-type loads present in the original power system.

Table 2. Types of nodes in the 14-node IEEE system in the conventional and distributed generation scenarios.

Node	Conventional scenario	DG scenario
1	Generation	Generation
2	Generation – Load	Generation – Load
3	Generation – Load	Generation – Load
4	Load – Substation	Load – Substation
5	Load – Substation	Load – Substation
6	Generation – Substation – Load	Generation – Substation - Load
7	Substation	Substation
8	Generation	Generation
9	Load – Substation	Load – Substation
10	Load	Generation – Load
11	Load	Generation – Load
12	Load	Generation – Load
13	Load	Generation – Load
14	Load	Generation – Load

2.3.2   Distributed Generation Scenario

In this operation scenario, only the *"Breaker/Switch"* that connect the *"Load"* and *"Generator"* nodes are activated. In [14], it is defined that, when adding a generation source to the distribution network, the maximum injection of power for new sources must be guaranteed during analysis (Table 2).

Table 3. Type of nodes in the 14-node IEEE system in the conventional and distributed generation scenarios.

Conventional scenario			DG scenario		
Gen	P (MW)	$/MWh	Gen	P (MW)	$/MWh
G1	143.684	560.251	G1	130.963	511.616
G2	70.026	314.410	G2	44.455	210.018
G3	50.000	247.600	G3	39.431	201.761
			G10	9.000	22.662
			G11	3.500	8.775
			G12	6.100	15.324
			G13	13.500	34.115
			G14	14.900	37.694

Hence, throughout the simulations, the Distributed Generation sources delivered 100% of their installed capacity. In Fig. 4, the schematic of the modified 14-node IEEE system can be seen with the DG included in the study. The power values of these systems are indicated in Table 3.

3   Economic Dispatch Optimization

Before the Quasi-Dynamical simulation, the economic dispatch optimization is performed in two simulation scenarios with the premise that DG delivers the total of its available generation, in the highest peak of the energetic demand curve to minimize generation costs. In the optimization process, the particle swarm optimization (PSO) [15, 16] method is used with MATLAB software's Particle Swarm Optimization Toolbox [17]. Since this toolbox is referred to in various research projects [18–22]. In [23], the equations to solve the optimization problem are defined:

1. Total cost function of the combustible:

$$f(P_G) = \sum_{i=1}^{N_g} f_i(P_{Gi}) \qquad (4)$$

2. Active power with the quadratic cost function:

$$f_i(P_{Gi}) = a_i P_{Gi}^2 + b_i P_{Gi} + c_i \qquad (5)$$

Where:

$f(P_G)$ is the total production cost in $/hr.
$f_i(P_{Gi})$ is the combustible cost function for unit i in $/hr.
$a_i\, b_i\, c_i$ are the combustible cost coefficients of unit i.
P_{Gi} is the real power delivered by unit i in MW.

Coefficients a, b and c were adjusted so that the generators were dispatching at 100% of their capacity. The optimization results are summarized in Table 3.

4 "Quasi-Dynamic" Simulation

The "Quasi-Dynamic" models have been used in different researches. For instance, they are used in the earthquake studies to overcome the inconvenient of quasi-static simulation methods [4, 5]. In the field of Electrical Engineering, "Quasi-Dynamic" methods are proposed for the simulation of cascade power switches [6] and the simulation of photovoltaic systems with the purpose of estimating its components [24]. The basic idea of "Quasi-Dynamic" methods is to consider different time scales in the nature during the entire simulation process by defining shorter time scale processes between longer neighboring transitions. In [13, 25, 26] it is indicated that this method enhances the fidelity of the simulation in the overall process, in comparison to quasi-static methods and the processing time is diminished that dynamic simulations have, since it does not require to solve all the differential equations.

DigSILENT® Powerfactory includes a tool dedicated to the calculation of the power flow that varies in time, called "Quasi-Dynamic" simulation. The "Quasi-Dynamic" simulation uses the parameters that vary in the system over time [13]. To assess the behavior of the 14-node IEEE system with distributed generation sources, the voltage, active and reactive power profiles are plotted over a 24-h period once the optimization process of the economic dispatch has been performed. Additionally, the losses in the transformers and lines are presented for the conventional and DG scenarios.

To visualize the simulation results, the 14-node IEEE system was divided into two zones, each one with 7 nodes: zone 1 contains nodes 1 to 7; zone 2 contains nodes 8 to 14. In Sects. 4.1 to 4.3, the most significant voltage and power variations are listed in the scenarios described in Sect. 2.4.

4.1   Variation in the Voltage Profile

The voltage variations are illustrated in Fig. 2. In Zone 2, there is a significant increase in the voltage level of nodes 9 to 14 during the DG scenario. In this scenario, there is a voltage drop during the first peak of the demand curve since the loads demand a considerable amount of power that, up to that point, is only being supplied by the conventional generation systems. The DG input into the system does not represent significant changes in the system's voltage profiles.

4.2   Variation in the Active Power Profile

Variations in the active power profiles are illustrated in Fig. 3. The modification implemented on the system does not imply significant changes in the levels of active power. In this zone, there is a significant increase in the voltage level of nodes 9 to 14 during the DG scenario.

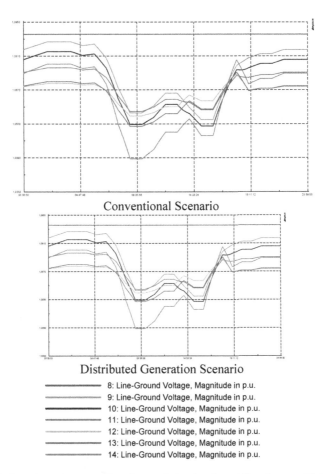

Conventional Scenario

Distributed Generation Scenario

——————— 8: Line-Ground Voltage, Magnitude in p.u.
——————— 9: Line-Ground Voltage, Magnitude in p.u.
——————— 10: Line-Ground Voltage, Magnitude in p.u.
——————— 11: Line-Ground Voltage, Magnitude in p.u.
——————— 12: Line-Ground Voltage, Magnitude in p.u.
——————— 13: Line-Ground Voltage, Magnitude in p.u.
——————— 14: Line-Ground Voltage, Magnitude in p.u.

Fig. 2. Variations in voltage profile of zone 2 (nodes 8 to 14). Source: Elaborated by the authors

4.3 Variation in the Reactive Power Profile

Variations in the reactive power profiles are illustrated in Fig. 4. Optimization does not imply significant changes in the levels of reactive power. As the power levels demanded by the loads increase, in the conventional scenario during the first peak of the day, there is a reduction in the reactive power levels in nodes 1, 2, 3 and 4 which adopt their initial values after both peak demands of the day. During the day's peak values, there is a considerable increase in the reactive power levels especially in those nodes. In the DG scenario, the reactive power levels that were seen in the conventional scenario are also presented but they do not surpass the levels reached at the start of the day. The peak representing the reduction in the demanded power level is also present while the GD is still active.

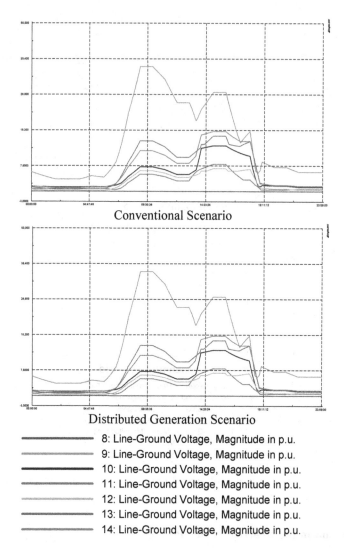

Conventional Scenario

Distributed Generation Scenario

──────── 8: Line-Ground Voltage, Magnitude in p.u.
──────── 9: Line-Ground Voltage, Magnitude in p.u.
──────── 10: Line-Ground Voltage, Magnitude in p.u.
──────── 11: Line-Ground Voltage, Magnitude in p.u.
──────── 12: Line-Ground Voltage, Magnitude in p.u.
──────── 13: Line-Ground Voltage, Magnitude in p.u.
──────── 14: Line-Ground Voltage, Magnitude in p.u.

Fig. 3. Variations in active power profile of zone 2 (nodes 8 to 14). Source: Elaborated by the authors

5   Results Analysis

5.1   Variations in the Transformers' Losses

In Table 4, the percent difference between the losses that occur in the conventional and distributed generation scenarios is shown with a variation up to 76.5%.

In this simulation scenario, there is a reduction in the system transformers' losses up to 76.53%.

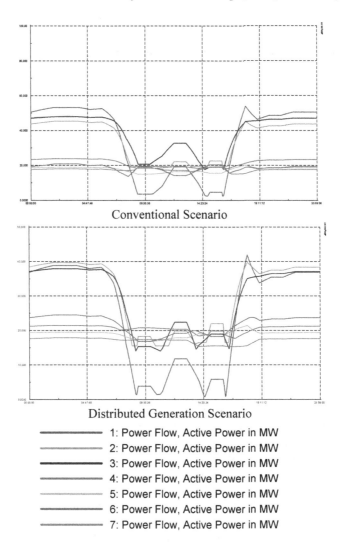

Conventional Scenario

Distributed Generation Scenario

1: Power Flow, Active Power in MW
2: Power Flow, Active Power in MW
3: Power Flow, Active Power in MW
4: Power Flow, Active Power in MW
5: Power Flow, Active Power in MW
6: Power Flow, Active Power in MW
7: Power Flow, Active Power in MW

Fig. 4. Variations in active power profile of zone 2 (nodes 8 to 14). Source: Elaborated by the authors

Table 4. Percent difference losses' in transformers between conventional and distributed generation scenarios.

Lines	Losses [kW]
Transformer 4–7	−63.04%
Transformer 5–9	−72.61%
Transformer 7–8	−20.88%
Transformer 7–9	−75.92%
Transformer 4–9	−76.53%

5.2 Transmission Lines Losses Variations

In Table 5, the percent difference between losses in both scenarios are listed.

Table 5. Percent variation in line losses

Lines	Losses [kW]
Line 1–2	−4.42%
Line 1–5	−35.57%
Line 10–11	44.13%
Line 12–13	−63.29%
Line 13–14	−65.04%
Line 2–3	−4.61%
Line 2–4	−44.72%
Line 2–5	−54.82%
Line 3–4	446.49%
Line 4–5	1.15%
Line 6–11	−48.79%
Line 6–12	−89.58%
Line 6–13	−85.03%
Line 9–10	−8.43%
Line 9–14	−78.55%

In this case, there is an excessive increase in the losses for lines 3–4. Due to the location of the new generators, the line increased the current flow from 30 to 58 Amperes which directly affects the losses in those lines.

The Distributed Generation simulation scenario has a reduction in the line losses up to 89.58%. The lines with a significant losses increase are lines 10–11, 3–4, 9–10, with 44.13%, 446.49% and 22.56% respectively.

The increase in lines 9–10 and 10–11 is caused by bidirectional power flows due to the location of generation units in nodes 10 and 11. There is an excessive increase in losses for line 3–4 due to the location of the new generators. The line increased the current flow from 30 to 58 Amperes which has a direct impact in the losses presents in those lines. Line 3–4 is a clear evidence that, if the location of new DG units is not adequate, losses can rise significantly affecting the operation the line.

6 Conclusions

The DG systems supply effectively the demanded power. The voltage and power profiles resulting from the "Quasi-Dynamic" simulation do not show considerable changes in the behavior of the electrical network. In the Distributed Generation scenario, the introduction of the DG to the system leads to an average reduction of 49.95% losses for most lines and an average reduction of 61.8% losses for the system transformers. Accordingly, the changes in the current flows of this system are the cause of this since they are present in the nodes of the new generation technologies. Hence, there is an increase in the currents present in the lines which leads to an increase in losses.

A previous study of the optimal location of DG in the systems, with the purpose of determining the location and size of multiple sources of DG and minimizing the total power losses of the system, would multiply the advantages of including DG restricting the number of lines that suffered more losses.

References

1. Godoy, G.A.C.: Impacto De La Generación Distribuida En La Operación De La Distribución. Universidad De Chile, Facultad De Ciencias Físicas Y Matemáticas, Departamento De Ingeniería Eléctrica, Santiago de Chile (2013)
2. Sarabia, F.: Impact of distributed generation on distribution system. Department of Energy Technology, Faculty of Engineering, Science and Medicine, Aalborg University, Aalborg (2011)
3. Congreso de Colombia: Ley 1715 de 2014: Por medio de la cual se regula la integración de las energías renovables no convencionales al Sistema Energético Nacional (2014)
4. Rice, J.: Spatiotemporal complexity of slip on a fault. J. Geophys. Res.-Solid Earth **98**, 9885–9907 (1993)
5. Zoller, G., Holschneider, M., Ben-Zion, Y.: Quasi-static and quasidynamic modeling of earthquake failure at intermediate scales. Pure Appl. Geophys. **161**, 2103–2118 (2004)
6. Yao, R., Huang, S., Liu, F., Zhang, X., Zhang, X.: A multi-timescale quasi-dynamic model for simulation of cascading outages. IEEE Trans. Power Syst. **31**(4), 3189–3201 (2016)
7. Habib, A.H., Disfani, V.R., Kleissl, J., de Callafon, R.A.: Quasi-dynamic load and battery sizing and scheduling for stand-alone solar system using mixed-integer linear programming. In: de IEEE Conference on Control Applications (CCA), Buenos Aires, Argentina (2016)
8. Electric Power System Analysis & Nature-Inspired Optimization Algorithms, Power Flow, August 2016. http://www.al-roomi.org/power-flow
9. Rojas, E.M.S.: Detección de áreas débiles respecto a la estabilidad de tensión en tiempo real utilizando lógica difusa. Universidad de Cuenca, Cuenca, Ecuador (2013)
10. Instituto Colombiano de Normas Técnicas y Certificación, ICONTEC, NTC 819, Norma Tecnica Colombiana 819, Electrotecnia. Transformadores Trifásicos Autorefrigerados Y Sumergidos En Liquido. Corriente Sin Carga, Pérdidas Y Tension De Cortocircuito, ICONTEC (1995)
11. Castaño, S.: Redes de distribución de energía. Universidad Nacional de Colombia, Manizales (2009)
12. Pedraza, A., Reyes, D., Gómez, C., Santamaría, F.: Impacto de la Generación Distribuida sobre el Esquema de Protecciones en una Red de Distribució, Universidad Distrital Francisco Jose de Caldas (2015)
13. GmbH DIgSILENT: DIgSILENT PowerFactory Version 15 User Manual (2014)
14. Hernández, F.P.: Localización de fallas en alimentadores primarios de distribución de energía eléctrica considerando incertidumbres en la carga y con presencia de Generación Distribuida. Universidad Tecnológica De Pereira, Pereira (2013)
15. Schutte, J.F.: Particle Swarms in sizing and global optimization, University of Pretoria (2001)
16. Eberhart, R., Kennedy, J.: Particle swarm optimization. In: de Proceedings of IEEE International Conference on Neural Networks, vol. 4, pp. 1942–1948 (1995)

17. Birge, B.: Mathworks (2006). https://www.mathworks.com/matlabcentral/fileexchange/7506-particle-swarm-optimization-toolbox
18. Rambharose, T.: Mathworks, Noviembre 2010. https://www.mathworks.com/matlabcentral/fileexchange/29565-neural-network-add-in-for-psort
19. Danaraj, R.: Mathwoks, Marzo 2014. https://www.mathworks.com/matlabcentral/fileexchange/46002-optimal-power-flow-by-vector-pso
20. Danaraj, R.: Mathworks, Agosto 2008. https://www.mathworks.com/matlabcentral/fileexchange/20984-pso-solution-to-economic-dispatch
21. Danaraj, R.: Mathworks, Marzo 2009. https://www.mathworks.com/matlabcentral/fileexchange/23491-improved-pso-program-to-solve-economic-dispatch
22. Mathworks: Mathworks, Diciembre 2009. https://www.mathworks.com/matlabcentral/fileexchange/25986-constrained-particle-swarm-optimization
23. Frank, S., Rebennack, S.: A Primer on Optimal Power Flow: Theory, Formulation, and Practical Examples, Golden (2012)
24. Habib, H., Disfani, V.R., Kleissl, J., de Callafon, R.A.: Quasi-dynamic load and battery sizing and scheduling for stand-alone solar system using mixed-integer linear programming. In: de IEEE Conference on Control Applications (CCA), Buenos Aires, Argentina (2016)
25. Nuñez, J.: Comparacion Tecnica Entre Los Programas De Simulacion De Sistemas De Potencia DigSILENT PowerFactory y PSSS/E (2015)

Computational Tool for Simulation and Automatic Testing of a Single-Phase Cascaded Multilevel Inverter

Oswaldo Lopez-Santos[(⊠)] ⓘ, Julián R. Corredor,
and Diego F. Salazar

Universidad de Ibagué, 730001 Ibagué, Colombia
oswaldo.lopez@unibague.edu.co

Abstract. This work describes in detail a computational tool designed to study performance indicators of a four-stage transformer-based single-phase cascaded multilevel inverter. The proposed system integrates simulation, on-line measurement, control and signal processing providing automating testing functionality to optimize the performance of the inverter with base on indicators such as Total Harmonic Distortion (THD), partial and global efficiency and power balance between the stages. The computational component of the tool was developed in LabVIEW providing not only didactic interactivity with the user through the Human-Machine Interface (HMI) but also a reliable interconnection with the power converter and the instruments of the experimental setup. The hardware component was developed integrating the power converter prototype, an acquisition card and electronic circuits providing measurement, conditioning, digital control and gate driving functions. Experimental results obtained from automatic tests are presented showing potentiality of the tool to support research activities related with this type of power converters.

Keywords: Cascaded multilevel inverter · Automatic testing · LabVIEW
Computational tool

1 Introduction

Electronic power conversion is one of the most relevant areas of technological development in the world. This is mainly due to the need of power converters to build more electric transportation systems [1], high voltage direct current (HVDC) transmission systems [2], grid connected power generators using renewable energies [3], storage of energy in batteries and freewheeling systems [4], and many other applications [5]. Today, majority of these devices operate commuting power semiconductors at high frequencies using a control method well known as Pulse Width Modulation (PWM) which allows a simple and reliable implementation of many control techniques. However, in order to convert direct current (DC) to alternative current (AC), multilevel topologies using other switching strategies have attracted attention of researchers and engineers. Although practically all of the known multilevel inverter topologies are more complex that the bridge based PWM inverter topologies, the absence of output

© Springer Nature Switzerland AG 2018
J. C. Figueroa-García et al. (Eds.): WEA 2018, CCIS 915, pp. 509–522, 2018.
https://doi.org/10.1007/978-3-030-00350-0_42

filters and the use of lower frequencies to commutate semiconductors are advantages that have made them a promising alternative. As a result, these topologies are preferred today in high power applications in which the cost of the control is considerably lower in comparison with the cost of the elements in the power circuit [6, 7]. Although transformer based cascaded multilevel inverter topologies have higher cost, weight and size compared with other topologies, the use of isolation transformers may even be mandatory because of reliability and robustness requirements. Then, the study of this kind of topologies is focused on increasing its performance and facilitates its manufacturability. Key aspects guiding research in this field are the use of a lower number of components, unification of stress of the semiconductor elements, increasing of the controllability to extend its use to power conditioning and integration of renewable energies to the grid [8, 9].

Computed aided test platforms for inverters can be used not only to facilitate experimental work in research but also to apply automatic test protocols in manufacturing, reducing the process time in both cases. Industry applications are related with engineering characterization and design validation, high volume production, incoming inspection, failure analysis and others. Additionally, the use of software allows analyze the behavior and performance of the power converters using online data storage and analysis, short and long term monitoring, report generation, among other specialized functions [10, 11]. Depending of the complexity of each power converter, an automatic test platform must be more or less specialized. However, Human-Machine-Interface (HMI), data acquisition (DAQ), visualization and data storage are minimal characteristics for all of them. The use of LabVIEW in development of this kind of applications is mainly justified by the simultaneous need of visualization, control and data acquisition functions which can be easily implemented because of its graphical programming language [12–15].

This paper presents a computational tool developed as a part of a real-time test platform applied in the study of a single-phase transformer-based four-stage multilevel inverter. This tool contributes in the improvement of characteristics of the inverter such as power quality, efficiency and power equalization between stages. In this particular case, the studied topology of the multilevel inverter can operate with multiple possible switching patterns (SP) obtaining the levels that make up the output voltage signal. Also, the use of these different SP implies different distribution of the total power among the stages and also different values of efficiencies (global and per stage). For this, the tool allows automatically changing the SP of the four inverter stages measuring currents and voltages at the input and output of each stage as well as the input and output of the inverter. Although off-line algorithms can be used to obtain the optimal SP, the platform help to model voltage drops, power losses and then, to improve the models used in optimization algorithms.

The rest of the paper is organized as follows: a Sect. 2 gives fundamentals, characteristics and principle of operation of the studied multilevel inverter. After that, Sect. 3 is devoted to describe the hardware configuration of the test platform as a whole while Sect. 4 details the software component including simulation algorithms, functions of the HMI and mathematical expressions used for computations of the performance indicators. Experimental results are presented in Sect. 5 and finally, conclusions and future work are presented in Sect. 6.

2 Transformer Based Cascaded Multilevel Inverter

2.1 Description of the Studied Inverter

Cascaded topologies are the simplest way to implement multilevel inverters because they consider the independent use of conventional H-bridges operating as power stages with a series connection at the output side. Transformer based versions of cascaded multilevel inverters allow to obtain galvanic isolation between power stages and then the input of different power stages can be the same. Asymmetric version of these inverters has as main property the use of DC sources with different amplitudes in order to increase the number of levels on the output signal [16, 17]. In case of the studied converter, output transformers of each stage provides in addition to the galvanic isolation, required gains to obtain asymmetrical operation having only one DC source. As it is depicted in Fig. 1, the studied converter is composed of four stages, each of one composed of one H-bridge which output is connected to the primary side of a power transformer. Input side of the H-bridges is common and is connected to the DC source. The secondary sides of the transformers are connected in series in such a way that the output voltage of the inverter is obtained as the sum of the output voltages of the stages.

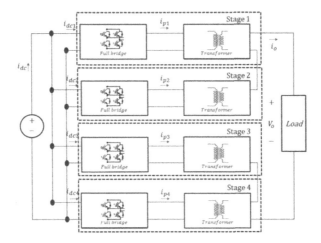

Fig. 1. Schematic diagram of the studied multilevel inverter with galvanic isolation.

2.2 Properties of the Converter Operation

By using four cascaded stages, the output voltage of the inverter is computed as

$$v_o(\omega t) = v_1(\omega t) + v_2(\omega t) + v_3(\omega t) + v_4(\omega t) = \sum_{k=1}^{4} v_k(\omega t). \tag{1}$$

Where $v_k(t)$ is the output voltage of each stage which is defined by:

$$v_k(\omega t) = V_{dc}T_{Rk}S_{Fk}, \tag{2}$$

where V_{dc} is the magnitude of the DC input voltage, T_{Rk} is the voltage transformation ratio of each k stage, and S_{Fk} is a parameter taking values -1, 0 or 1 depending of the SP generated by the control. Then, outputs of the inverter stages are three-level voltage signals which when summed generate a sinusoidal output voltage with M positive integer levels. For a desired output voltage $v_{oref}(\omega t) = V_{max}\sin \omega t$, relation between the signal of M positive levels and the amplitude of the output waveform is $K_m = V_{max}/M$. Figure 2 shows a quarter-period of the stepped sine signal obtained at the output of the inverter together with sinusoidal envelopes defining the phase angles θ_m to jump from a level to the following one. To exemplify, a value of $M = 5$ was considered. Because of the symmetry of the sinusoidal signal, the second half of the positive semi-cycle is obtained by inversely reproducing the first half semi-cycle, and the negative semi-cycle is obtained by multiplying by -1 the voltage levels used in the positive semi-cycle.

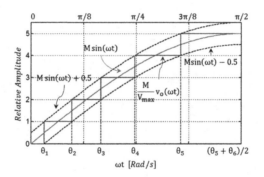

Fig. 2. Stepped sine signal design.

The stepped sine signal observed in Fig. 2 represents the output voltage of the inverter when a number of five positive levels is selected (This value is used only for explanation purposes). The intersection with the ωt axis, named as θ_m determines the end of the m interval and the starting point of the following interval, so that it can be expressed in radians for m = 1, 2, 3... M as follows:

$$\theta_m = \sin^{-1}\left(\frac{2m-1}{2M}\right) \tag{3}$$

Then, each level is defined for the interval $[\theta_m, \theta_{m+1}]$.

3   Description of the Hardware Component

Figure 3 depicts the proposed test platform and its interconnection with the multilevel inverter. As it can be observed, inverter is fed by a programmable DC source XLN6024 whose voltage and limited current are defined using two signals generated by analogue output channels of the acquisition card (NI-USB-6008). The power inverter has been implemented using four MOSFET IRFZ44, and a transformer for each stage. Transformer turn ratios are 1:1.4, 1:1.82, 1:2.08, and 1:2.34, which specify the following input to output RMS voltage relations: 28.0 to 39.2 V, 28.0 to 50.9 V, 28.0 to 58.2 V and 28.0 to 65.5 V. These relations and voltage were defined using (1) and (2) in order to obtain a signal of 31-levels (M = 15) with an amplitude of $120\sqrt{2}$ V when the inverter is fed by a nominal voltage of 36 VDC.

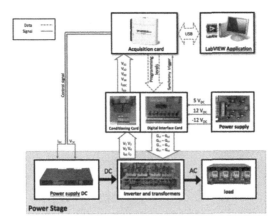

Fig. 3. Block diagram representing the hardware component of the proposed automatic test platform.

The output of the inverter is connected to a programmable load SLM-AC-300VA which is manually configured for each applied test. A printed circuit board (PCB) was designed to allocate a microcontroller unit PIC16F877 generating the gate signals for the four converter stages and also to receive configuration provided by the software application through a four line parallel communication protocol which loads the SP of the inverter as a table at the start of the test. Operating on-line, microcontroller generates a synchronization signal (square signal at the same frequency of the output signal) which defines the clock to start data acquisition and visualization. The same PCB allocates eight drivers IRS2004 providing the gate signals of MOSFET introducing the requiring dead times. Measurements are obtained by using four dedicated PCB, each of one integrating isolated closed-loop hall-effect transducers measuring voltages (LV-20P) and currents (CAS-6P), two of each type. Input and output voltages and currents of the inverter are measured as well as input voltage and input current at the input of the transformer of each inverter stage (12 measurements in total). Control and measurement circuits are fed by PTN04050A and PTN04050C non-isolated DC-DC converters providing +5, +12 and −12 V.

4 Description of the Software Component

4.1 Software Functions

To describe the software component of the test platform, it was sectioned in functions as it is depicted in the Unified Modeling Language (UML) diagram in Fig. 4. Two main parts are highlighted: theory 1, theory 2 and didactic (Interactive simulation section) and SCADA (Supervisory control and data acquisition section).

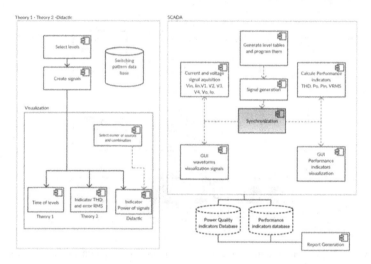

Fig. 4. UML diagram representing components of the LabVIEW applications

The following are brief description of the software components which are directly related with the corresponding human machine interface (HMI) in Fig. 5:

Theory 1: This section allows simulating the building of the stepped sine signal by configuring a desired number of levels. A slide control is provided in order to give a visual tracking of the segments of the signal (time duration of each level). The main objective is to facilitate the understanding of the signal generation process. In order to give a comprehensive visualization with real-time experience, SP are previously stored in a database which is accessed by demand (Top-left frame in Fig. 5).

Theory 2: This section provides the user with a complete overview of the waveforms of the inverter. The output signal of each stage is synchronously visualized with the output of the inverter as the sum of these signals. Then, user can activate or deactivate the presence of each stage regarding fault scenarios. Additionally, this section evaluates the THD and the RMS of the output signal as a function of the number of inverter stages (1–6) and the number of levels (1–17).

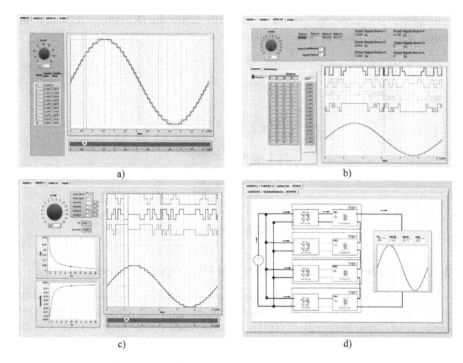

Fig. 5. HMI of the software: (a) simulation of multilevel output signal considering different number of output levels, (b) simulation of the four inverter stage signals for different number of inverter stages and output voltage levels; (c) simulation of the four inverter stage signals for different number of output levels and computing the THD and RMS values of the output signal, (d) visualization of measured output voltage signal and real power measurements.

Didactic: This section allows the user to build, both the output signal of the inverter and change the number of levels, number of converter stages and the used SP. Also, the HMI of this section allows to known the redundancy obtained to reproduce each signal level. Visualization in this section includes waveforms and computation of power distribution between stages.

SCADA: This section of the software allows the user to visualize the waveforms acquired by the system computing THD and power balance as main indicators. HMI provided by this component also gives the values of the real power in all connection points of the inverter.

4.2   Additional User Functions

As it is depicted in Fig. 6, the software component of the test platform has been developed considering two types of users (Local tester user and Remote supervisor user). Local user has access to all of the provided functions while remote supervisor can only access to the HMI. In addition to the functions mentioned above, the user can configure the web access to the system, manually define the DC voltage applied to the inverter and save manually or automatically a set of measurements.

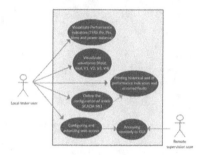

Fig. 6. Case of use diagram of the MLI test platform.

4.3 Computation of Power, Efficiency and Power Quality Indicators

Considering that signal analysis and visualization is required at steady state and no transient behaviors are studied, the system acquires signals at a rate of 9.6 kS/s (160 samples at an output frequency of 60 Hz) capturing each signal every two cycles at the output frequency. Current and voltage waveforms of the DC side of the inverter are measured as $i_{dc}(k)$ and $v_{dc}(k)$. Acquired samples are stored in vectors $\mathbb{I}_{dc}$, and $\mathbb{V}_{dc}$ respectively, which are multiplied element-by-element to obtain the vector $\mathbb{P}_{dc}$. Then, average power at the input side is computed as follows:

$$P_{dc} = \frac{1}{160} \sum_{k=1}^{160} \mathbb{P}_{dc} \tag{4}$$

Voltage and current waveforms at the input of the isolation transformers are acquired as $v_{ix}(k)$ and $i_{ix}(k)$ for $k = [1, 2, \ldots, 160]$ and $x = [1, 2, 3, 4]$ storing 160 samples for each signal in the vectors $\mathbb{V}_{i1}$, $\mathbb{V}_{i2}$, $\mathbb{V}_{i3}$, $\mathbb{V}_{i4}$, $\mathbb{I}_{i1}$, $\mathbb{I}_{i2}$, $\mathbb{I}_{i3}$ and $\mathbb{I}_{o4}$ respectively. These values are multiplied element-by-element to obtain vectors $\mathbb{P}_{ix}$. Then, average power at the input sides of the inverter stages is computed as follows:

$$P_{ix} = \frac{1}{160} \sum_{k=1}^{160} \mathbb{P}_{ix} \tag{5}$$

Finally, voltage and current waveforms at the AC side are acquired as $v_o(k)$, $v_{ox}(k)$ and $i_o(k)$ for $k = [1, 2, \ldots, 160]$ and $x = [1, 2, 3, 4]$ storing signals in the vectors $\mathbb{V}_o$, $\mathbb{V}_{o1}$, $\mathbb{V}_{o2}$, $\mathbb{V}_{o3}$ and $\mathbb{V}_{o4}$ and $\mathbb{I}_o$ respectively. RMS values are determined as:

$$V_{ORMS} = \sqrt{\frac{1}{160} \sum_{k=1}^{160} (\mathbb{V}_o \cdot \mathbb{V}_o)}$$

$$I_{O_{RMS}} = \sqrt{\frac{1}{160} \sum_{k=1}^{160} (\mathbb{I}_o \cdot \mathbb{I}_o)}$$

By defining the vectors $\mathbb{SS}$ and $\mathbb{CS}$ as a sine and a cosine waveforms sampled for 160 elements, RMS values of the fundamental components of current and voltages are obtained from the Fourier series expansion by using the following expressions:

$$V_{O_{RMS}} = \frac{1}{160} \sqrt{\frac{1}{2} \left[\left(\sum_{k=1}^{160} V_o \mathbb{SS} \right)^2 + \left(\sum_{k=1}^{160} V_o \mathbb{CS} \right)^2 \right]}$$

$$I_{O_{RMS}} = \frac{1}{160} \sqrt{\frac{1}{2} \left[\left(\sum_{k=1}^{160} \mathbb{I}_o \mathbb{SS} \right)^2 + \left(\sum_{k=1}^{160} \mathbb{I}_o \mathbb{CS} \right)^2 \right]}$$

From this, apparent power is easily computed as:

$$S = V_{O_{RMS}} I_{O_{RMS}} \tag{6}$$

Power computation at the AC side was developed using principles of electrical power in presence of harmonic content [18, 19]. Harmonic RMS components are:

$$V_{O_h} = \sqrt{V_{O_{RMS}}^2 - V_{O_1}^2}$$

$$I_{O_h} = \sqrt{I_{O_{RMS}}^2 - I_{O_1}^2}$$

From which, real power can be computed as:

$$P_o = \frac{1}{160} \sum_{k=1}^{160} V_o I_o \tag{7}$$

THD-R of the output current and voltage are:

$$THD_v = \frac{V_{O_h}}{V_{O_{RMS}}} \tag{8}$$

$$THD_i = \frac{I_{O_h}}{I_{O_{RMS}}} \tag{9}$$

Then, the Power Factor (PF) is obtained as:

$$PF = \frac{P_o}{S} \tag{10}$$

Power equalization quadratic error is evaluated as:

$$Error_x = \left(\frac{P_{ix}}{\sum_{k=1}^{4} P_{ik}} - 0.25 \right)^2 \tag{11}$$

Efficiencies are computed as:

$$\eta_{dc-ac} = \frac{P_{i1} + P_{i2} + P_{i3} + P_{i4}}{P_{dc}} \tag{12}$$

$$\eta_{transf} = \frac{P_o}{P_{i1} + P_{i2} + P_{i3} + P_{i4}} \tag{13}$$

$$\eta_o = \frac{P_o}{P_{dc}} \tag{14}$$

Accuracy of computations defined by expressions (4)–(14) is affected by discretization (sampling) and quantization errors. This is mainly due to the fact that some of the analyzed signals have unipolar and bipolar transitions which do not have coincidence with sampling events and then they are delayed one sample or less in the obtained discrete time signal. In order to evaluate that error and solve the concert about its effect in the performance of the test, some simulations were performed using MATLAB considering the sampling rate defined above (9.6 kS/s), quantization to 10 bits and measurement gain defined to acquire each signal covering the 80% of the total acquisition range (−10 to 10 V) when converter operates at nominal conditions. Figure 7 shows the waveforms of voltages of the inverter comparing their continuous time and discrete time versions. Deviation is assessed by using the Mean Average Error (MAE) (in absolute value) which takes values between 2 and 22 V. Firstly, as it can be observed in the output voltage (sum of the stage voltages), the effect of the error is compensated because of the symmetry of the signal (a pulse error has its symmetrical reflection with opposite sign).

5   Experimental Validation

To validate the support provided by the developed test platform, experimental results were obtained from application of designed automatic tests. Figure 8 shows photography of the complete experimental setup showing visualization in the HMI of the SCADA module of the software. Some automatic tests were performed in order to obtain results validating the good performance of the system and also verifying that expected errors do not affect considerably the computed performance indicators.

5.1   Simulated and Experimental Results

Several tests have been realized in order to assess accuracy of measurements and computation of the platform for different operational conditions of the inverter.

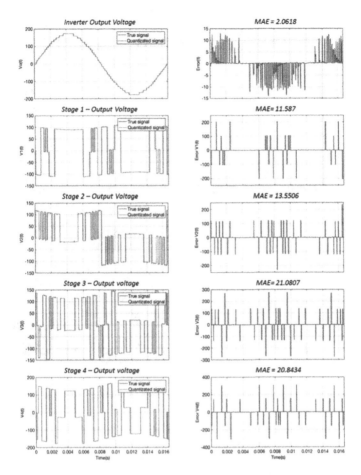

Fig. 7. At the left side, output signals of the inverter and the individual inverter stages with and without sampling; and, at the right side Mean Absolute Error (MAE) comparing both signals.

Experiments were selected from a database including results for different SP, power levels and power factor (inductive and capacitive). In all experiments, THD and real power measurements were realized using a Power Analyzer Fluke 43B. An automatic test can be described by means of the following step by step procedure:

- Configure the load connected at the output of the inverter to have linear or nonlinear behavior at a desired power (External and defined by the user).
- Transfer a SP to the control board of the prototype (by demand of the user).
- Define a DC input voltage and a DC current limitation to be configured in the programmable source (on-line defined by the user).
- Capture measurements of THD and real power at different conditions.

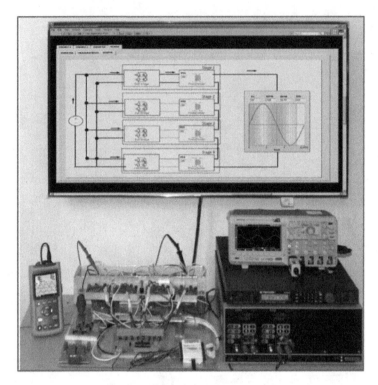

Fig. 8. Photography including converter prototype and test platform in operation.

Measurements obtained with SCADA system have been compared to theoretical results, simulated results and measured results from instruments at it is listed in Table 1. It is possible to observe that the SP computationally synthesized has coherence with simulation and theoretical prediction since differences in assessed indicators are expected because the theoretical model is ideal, simulation uses only resistive parameters in MOSFET and the real converter has other unknown parasitic elements.

Table 1. Comparison between theoretical, simulated and experimental results.

Experiment #: load selected SP	THD				Power equalization error			
	Theor.	Sim.	Meas.	Comp.	Theor.	Sim.	Meas.	Comp.
Exp. 1: 250 W optimal SP	2.63%	2.90%	1.90%	1.86%	4.20%	4.53%	5.30%	9.60%
Exp. 2: 131 W optimal SP	2.63%	2.90%	3.00%	2.92%	4.20%	5.20%	10.4%	11.8%
Exp. 3: 100 VA FP: 0.95 optimal SP	2.63%	2.93%	0.90%	0.96%	4.20%	4.84%	9.80%	9.30%
Exp. 4: 250 W No optimal SP	2.63%	2.93%	3.20%	3.10%	28.51%	93.14%	132.0%	158.0%

6 Conclusions and Future Work

Development of an automatic test platform used to support research related with a particular architecture of DC-AC power electronic converter was presented. Proposed system allows applying all the possible switching patterns to an asymmetrical multi-level inverter by means of a simple selection of the user, which considerably facilitates test and measurement process. Errors introduced in measurement and visualization module of the software application due to discretization and quantization were analyzed confirming that the selected sampling method works adequately despite of it operates asynchronously with respect to the switching edges. Experimental and simulation results were presented and compared confirming applicability of the tool.

With the use of this tool, it will be possible to identify experimentally the parasitic elements of the circuit from voltage drops and power losses, allowing complementing the ideal model and in consequence a more accurate contribution of the experiments in the study of optimization algorithms.

Acknowledgements. This work was supported by project 16-454-SEM *Universidad de Ibagué* and *Gobernación del Tolima* under *Convenio de cooperación 1026- 2013* - Scientific Culture. The presented results were obtained with the assistance of students from the Research Hotbed on Control and Power Electronics (SICEP), Research Group D + TEC, Universidad de Ibagué, Ibagué-Colombia.

References

1. Zheng, Y., Dong, Z.Y., Xu, Y., Meng, K., Zhao, J.H., Qiu, J.: Electric vehicle battery charging/swap stations in distribution systems: comparison study and optimal planning. IEEE Trans. Power Syst. **29**(1), 221–229 (2014)
2. Jung, J.J., Cui, S., Lee, J.H., Sul, S.K.: A new topology of multilevel VSC converter for a hybrid HVDC transmission system. IEEE Trans. Power Electron. **32**(6), 4199–4209 (2017)
3. Chung, I.Y., Liu, W., Cartes, D.A., Collins, E.G., Moon, S.I.: Control methods of inverter-interfaced distributed generators in a microgrid system. IEEE Trans. Ind. Appl. **46**(3), 1078–1088 (2010)
4. Jiang, W., et al.: Flexible power distribution control in an asymmetrical-cascaded-multilevel-converter-based hybrid energy storage system. IEEE Trans. Ind. Electron. **65**(8), 6150–6159 (2018)
5. Khoucha, F., Lagoun, S.M., Marouani, K., Kheloui, A., Benbouzid, M.E.H.: Hybrid cascaded h-bridge multilevel-inverter induction-motor-drive direct torque control for automotive applications. IEEE Trans. Ind. Electron. **57**(3), 892–899 (2010)
6. Boussada, Z., Elbeji, O., Benhamed, M.: Different topologies and control techniques of multilevel inverter: a literature survey. In: Proceedings International Conference on Green Energy Conversion Systems (GECS), Hammamet, pp. 1–5 (2017)
7. Seth, N., Goel, V., Kulkami, R.D.: Three phase innovative multilevel inverter topologies for research and industrial applications: a review. In: Proceedings of International Conference on Nascent Technologies in Engineering (ICNTE), Navi Mumbai, pp. 1–6 (2017)
8. Farakhor, A., Reza Ahrabi, R., Ardi, H., Najafi Ravadanegh, S.: Symmetric and asymmetric transformer based cascaded multilevel inverter with minimum number of components. IET Power Electron. **8**(6), 1052–1060 (2015)

9. Shankar, J.G., Edward, J.B., Neeraja, E.: Performance evaluation of a nine level cascaded multilevel inverter with single DC source for photovoltaic system. In: Proceedings of Innovations in Power and Advanced Computing Technologies (i-PACT), Vellore, pp. 1–8 (2017)
10. Chroma System Solutions: Power conversion: C8000 Power Conversion Automated Test Platform. https://www.chromausa.com/automated-test-systems/power-conversion. Accessed 11 Apr 2018
11. OPAL-RT Technologies: OP1200 OPAL-RT Lab-Scale MMC Test Bench: Modular Multilevel Converter (MMC) Test Bench. https://www.opal-rt.com/wp-content/themes/enfold-opal/pdf/L00161_0014.pdf. Accessed 11 Apr 2018
12. Lopez-Santos, O., Arango-Buitrago, J.S., González-Morales, D.F.: On-line visualization and long-term monitoring of a single-phase photovoltaic generator using SCADA. In: Figueroa-García, J.C., López-Santana, E.R., Ferro-Escobar, R. (eds.) WEA 2016. CCIS, vol. 657, pp. 295–307. Springer, Cham (2016). https://doi.org/10.1007/978-3-319-50880-1_26
13. Lidozzi, A., Di Benedetto, M., Sabatini, V., Solero, L., Crescimbini, F.: Towards LabVIEW and system on module for power electronics and drives control applications. In: Proceedings of the 42nd Annual Conference on IEEE Industrial Electronics Society, Florence, pp. 4995–5000 (2016)
14. Xuejun, X., Ping, X., Sheng, Y., Ping, L.: Real-time digital simulation of control system with LabVIEW simulation interface toolkit. In: Proceedings of the 26th Chinese Control Conference, Hunan, pp. 318–322 (2017)
15. Hapeez, M.S., Baharom, R., Zainuddin, I.N.A., Hamzah, N.R., Hamzah, M.K.: Automated measurements of power electronics research test rig for investigation of single-phase matrix converter operating as a controlled rectifier. In: Proceedings of the IEEE Symposium on Industrial Electronics & Applications, Kuala Lumpur, pp. 938–941 (2009)
16. Yang, K., Lan, X., Zhang, Q., Tang X.: Unified selective harmonic elimination for cascaded h-bridge asymmetric multilevel inverter. IEEE J. Emerg. Sel. Top. Power Electron. (2018, in press)
17. Saeedian, M., Adabi, J., Hosseini, S.M.: Cascaded multilevel inverter based on symmetric–asymmetric DC sources with reduced number of components. IET Power Electron. 10(12), 1468–1478 (2017)
18. Shaffer, R.A.: Fundamentals of Power Electronics with MATLAB. Charles River Media, Boston (2007)
19. Akagi, H., Watanabe, E.H., Aredes, M.: Instantaneous Power Theory and Applications to Power Conditioning, pp. 1–379. IEEE Press. Wiley (2007)

Analysis of Exact Electrode Positioning Systems for Multichannel-EEG

Mónica Rodríguez-Calvache(✉) ⓘ, Andrés Calle, Sara Valderrama,
Isabel Arango López, and José David López ⓘ

SISTEMIC, Engineering Faculty, Universidad de Antioquia UDEA,
Calle 70 No. 52-21, Medellín, Colombia
monicav.rodriguezc@gmail.com

Abstract. Electroencephalography (EEG) consists on the recording of brain electrical activity along the scalp surface. The potentials generated in the brain are acquired using electrodes covering the head. This method is efficient, but in most cases the operator should deal with bad locations and slipping, which generate motion artifacts and localization errors in posterior brain imaging and connectivity analyzes. The aim of this work is to elaborate a reference framework addressed to the currently available electrode positioning methods for EEG in terms of efficiency, viability, and placement error. With this purpose, different procedures for electrode localization were considered in this study: manual methods, EEG-caps, Magnetic Resonance Imaging EEG electrode localization, digitization, 3D laser scanner, and photogrammetry. We found that the method with higher accuracy is digitization; but it requires a controlled environment and the system itself is expensive. In terms of implementation time, the 3D hand-held laser scanner and photogrammetry provided the better results and can be used in uncontrolled clinical environments.

Keywords: 3D hand-held laser scanner · Digitizer
EEG electrode positioning · EEG-cap · Photogrammetry · MRI

1 Introduction

EEG is the most widely used technique for studying the dynamics of the human brain. It has been established as a relevant tool in psychology and neurology, mainly because it can register several brain conditions in a non-invasive and safe way, with an excellent temporal resolution and at a low price [1]. Currently, several brain analysis techniques require estimating the location of the sources of neural activity at cortical level (commonly known as brain imaging): connectivity analysis, brain state classification, brain computer interface, among others. EEG brain imaging requires a model of the electrical propagation through the head related to the exact coordinates of the electrodes. The precision in the localization of the electrodes is one of the parameters that most influence the

© Springer Nature Switzerland AG 2018
J. C. Figueroa-García et al. (Eds.): WEA 2018, CCIS 915, pp. 523–534, 2018.
https://doi.org/10.1007/978-3-030-00350-0_43

correct behavior of the brain imaging algorithms due to the high non-linearity of the electromagnetic field propagation [2]. Thus, inaccuracies in the coordinates of electrodes may severely affect the quality of the EEG analysis. This problem grows when reconstructing neural activity from deep brain areas [3]. Additionally, the time needed to place the electrodes is an important factor because the fatigue and compliance of the subjects affect both research and medical studies, especially when children and clinical population are considered. Then, a technique for fast placement of sensors with low localization error is desired.

According to the international positioning 10–20 system (or its variations for high density configurations: 10–10, 10–5), the electrodes must be placed in a standardized system able to recover information in terms of brain regions [4]. This system aims for a common interpretation of results obtained from EEG data, as well as providing information of the neuro-anatomical correlation that allows comparisons among intra- and inter-subject studies [5]. Moreover, current neuroimaging software (SPM12 [6], FieldTrip [7], EEGLAB [8], etc.) include this configuration by default.

An standardized positioning system does not guarantee a correct placement of electrodes. Then, different methods have been proposed to guarantee their correct positioning or to provide an accurate location regardless their ideal location. In this paper, six of these methods are analyzed: manual methods, EEG-caps, Magnetic Resonance Imaging (MRI) localization methods, digitization, 3D hand-held laser scanner, and photogrammetry. We compare these methods with a summary of different research works in terms of the reported error and the time consumed by each method for placing the electrodes.

Manual methods do not require specialized equipment, the operator uses tools such as a compass, calipers [9], or digital calipers [10]. Manual methods show good results in terms of positioning accuracy and are less expensive than other methods that require specialized equipment. However, most manual methods require placing the electrodes in a regular standard pattern such as the 10–10 system [10], which may be restrictive. Additionally, if these methods could be too time consuming for high-resolution EEG studies, and they are also highly dependent on the operator's skills. The EEG-cap is the most common solution for the time-consuming process of manually placing the electrodes. However, Atcherson et al. [11] concluded that using this method without any other electrode positioning tool is not recommended for source localization analysis, because it is not accurate among subjects.

The MRI localization methods use the scanned images for determining the EEG electrodes location. These methods are accurate and reproducible, but they require a special type of electrodes not sensitive to magnetic fields [12] and the fixation is performed with an structural image that additionally consumes time (around 20 min). These two requirements make this approach impractical as it is expensive in time and funding.

The digitization is the most commonly used technique and it has been reported to be sufficiently accurate. It consists on interpolating the sensor location with a pointer and beacons. However, both electromagnetic and ultrasound digitization alternatives require a controlled environment because these systems are sensitive to environmental conditions such as temperature, humidity, or electric fields; and in addition, their hardware and software are expensive [13,14]. Similarly, the 3D laser scanner could be used for localizing EEG sensors with an equivalent accuracy and a better repeatability than the electromagnetic digitizer, with the advantage of being able to be used in uncontrolled clinical environments [15]. However, it is more expensive than digitization.

Finally, Photogrammetry is a method that allows determining the EEG electrode positions, shapes, and sizes. Studies on this approach are commonly divided in four categories: multiple cameras in a geodesic array that capture images of multiple views [16], a single rotating camera [17], a single camera with mirrors [18], and novel methods that use a Microsoft Kinect [19]. These methods have demonstrated to be a good option in time consumption, and some of them could be feasible for clinical environments. But their price or availability (Microsoft Kinect has been discontinued, for example) may be challenging for a wider used.

This short overview shows how each of the analyzed techniques comes with advantages and disadvantages. A trade of among flexibility, price, time, and accuracy (in terms of placement error) would also depend on the needs of each user. In this work, we aim to analyze each of these techniques and provide a comprehensive analysis useful for users to select the best tool depending on their own needs. This paper is composed by three sections: It begins with a description of these EEG electrode positioning techniques. Then, the following section contains the discussion about these methods, including their advantages and disadvantages. Finally, the conclusions derived from this analysis are presented in the final section.

2   EEG Electrode Positioning Methods

2.1   Manual Methods

In [9], the authors proposed a direct measurement technique that used different simple tools such as calipers for measuring the distances between each electrode and three reference landmarks (Nasion, left and right pre-auricular points), which did not lie on a single plane. With these measurements, they calculated the Cartesian coordinates of each electrode placed on the head. The authors developed a low expensive method. In addition, with this method they were able to find the best fitting sphere for the electrode position, useful when a multi-sphere volume conductor is used in the EEG brain imaging method. This method became the standard for co-registration between structural MRI and EEG. Nearly all current co-registrations are performed with the same three reference landmarks.

The authors of [9] performed their simulations using a spherical head model with a radius of 100 mm, with the center located on the coordinates (10 mm, 0 mm, 40 mm) for x, y, and z, respectively. Such coordinates correspond to the average values used in practice. They calculated the reference distances, and corrupted them adding Gaussian noise with zero mean and different standard deviation values. The authors concluded that for standard deviations of 2.5 mm and 4 mm, the dipole position errors were approximately 4 mm and 10 mm, respectively.

Another research [10] showed an efficient technique to calculate the 3D coordinates from any array. The authors systematically laid out according to the regular pattern 10–10 standard position electrode system with a set of only 14 direct measurements. Using the 10–10 standard position system [20], the head shape can be approximated by five planes defined by electrode positions, in this way: (1) F7-Fz-F8; (2) T7-F7-FPz-F8-T8; (3) T7-Cz-T8; (4) T7-P7-Oz-P8-T8, and (5) P7-Pz-P8. To determine the dimensions of the coronal planes (F7-Fz-F8, T7-Cz-T8, P7-Pz-P8) and horizontal planes (T7-F7- FPz-F8-T8, T7-P7-Oz-P8-T8), 8 of 14 inter-electrode distances had to be measured. To determine the spatial relationship between these planes 6 of 14 inter-electrode measurements were used. To fit the arcs of the five planes along the head's surface, the authors generated ellipses whose curvatures were determined by the coordinates of the points they intersected. The intersections of these ellipses form angles that are determined from the direct measurements produced one basic 10-10 standard grid representation of the head. The positions were calculated by appropriately subdividing the ellipsoidal curves and extrapolating [10].

The efficiency benefit of this last method increases as the number of electrodes increases. This because the same 14 measurements are necessary independently of the number of electrodes. This method takes less than six minutes to determine the placement of 128 electrodes whereas the magnetic field digitization method takes more than 15 min. Additionally, it is at least 5 times less expensive than the magnetic field digitizer when a good quality 12-inch digital caliper is used [10]. However, of course, this method determines the position of the sensors a priori, being sensitive to operator errors.

2.2   EEG-Caps

Manual EEG electrode montages require considerable time for multi-channel configurations and they are sensitive to placement errors as the sensor locations are determined a priori. Hence, some manufactures have generated caps that involve electrodes placed in a pre-defined montage [5]. The EEG-Caps are available in different layouts. The most common range from 16 to 256 channels. They also have different sizes (commonly small, medium and large) to accommodate different head sizes. These caps are designed to provide fast, consistent and cost-effective electrode applications. Some concerns on this system come from its adaptability to actually fit different head shapes and sizes, and on the variance in the selected scalp locations for the electrodes [21].

The study performed in [11] describes the variability of the positions of 15 electrodes in a custom made Neuromedical cap with 72 mounted electrodes. The electrodes were digitized in three separate sessions for 10 participants. They obtained a three-dimensional variability of up to 12.7 mm. The authors found two negative consequences of EEG-caps: (1) the shifting caused by the weight of the bundled electrode wires, and (2) the skewing of the posterior electrode positions when they are rubbed against a pillow or a chair headrest. They also noted that the reported variability of electrode locations in EEG caps may have implications for brain imaging methods. Then, the use of EEG caps may be harmful for most cortical source localization methods [11].

2.3 MRI-Based Electrode Localization Methods

In [22], the authors presented a method to visualize the EEG electrodes in a magnetic resonance image (MRI). The electrodes used in the study were acrylic capsules with 15 or 20 mm in height and 12 mm in diameter, and were placed in a standard 10–20 positioning system with an additional Fpz location. The MR images showed the location and shape of the electrodes. The EEG electrodes locations were manually segmented on the two-dimensional axial image. This method allowed direct measurements of the electrodes positions and the distances from any MRI visible anatomical structure placed in the scalp.

Another research [12] shows an automatic method for localizing and labeling the EEG electrode using MRI. The authors initially validated the method with a phantom head and then with volunteers and patients in a clinical environment. This method was compared with electromagnetic digitization. The results suggest that the proposed method provides better reproducibility, but both methods have equal accuracy (without statistical differences). In addition, automation makes this a highly reproducible and easy to handle method in a routinely clinical environment. However, to perform the localization process it is necessary to use a magnetic resonator together with a special electrode set, which makes this an expensive task; and a time consuming one if the study does not require the structural MRI.

2.4 Digitization

Electromagnetic: The 3D coordinates of the EEG electrodes and the position of the nasion and pre-auricular points are obtained using this 3D device, which takes the measurements with three receivers placed on the head of the subject. The receivers are positioned and oriented by a transmitter that produces an electromagnetic field. The location of the receivers allows free motion of the head during the digitization process. The digitization of the sensor locations is made by pointing a pen shaped device called "Stylus" on the targeted point, and validating it by pressing a button. The system is composed of the transmitter, the receivers and the stylus, all connected to a central processing unit [10].

One of the advantages of the digitizer, called the Fastrack system (Polhemus Inc., Colchester, VT, USA), is the short time to determine the electrode positions. Specifically, the mean time to digitize 64 electrodes is lower than 10 min. According to the manual, the theoretical accuracy of Fastrack is 0.75 mm in a sphere of 1.5 m of diameter centered on the transmitter. In practice, some authors indicate that the mean error is about 6.8 mm [23]. The results in other studies showed that the precision ranging from 0.1 mm to 8 mm depends of the measurement conditions [14], being more than 4 mm prohibitive for brain imaging purposes [24].

Two main difficulties to use the system in clinical applications are that it is highly sensitive to environmental conditions [14], and that the presence of metallic objects disturbs the measurements [25]. Additionally, comparing it with manual methods, the software used to calculate the positions is private and expensive, which increases the cost of the overal technique [10].

Ultrasound: In the ELPOS system, the 3D Cartesian coordinates and the distances between the generator and receiver can be estimated by measuring the time that a sonic impulse takes from a sound generator, with which the user touches the electrode (Stylus), to a receiver (microphone). When an ultrasound digitization device is used, the system records the relative position of each electrode. The system has some advantages, such as the possibility of sensing the head shape of the subject in 3D coordinates for correlating with data from imaging methods, and that the subject can freely move the head during the digitization [13].

Same as in the electromagnetic digitizer, when the user touches each electrode (even slightly) it changes the real position and therefore the digitized values. But the main flaws of both methods are that they are expected to be used in controlled environmental conditions [10], and the cost of the software.

2.5   3D Hand-Held Laser Scanner

The use of a hand-held 3D laser scanner is described in [15]. This method is commonly used for inspection, digitization of models, interactive visualization, and human body scanning, as well for EEG electrode localization. The proposed system is handy, useful and establishes spatial reference with a resolution of 0.05 mm. This system does not need any positioning device to integrate 3D measurements in a global coordinate system if the subject is moving [26].

The study presented in [15] showed that the 3D laser scanner could be used for EEG sensors localization with an equivalent accuracy (from metrological and clinical perspectives) and a better repeatability than the electromagnetic digitizer. In [27], the authors evaluated the effectiveness of the 3D hand-held laser scanner when the scanner acquired the EEG sensor positions and the scalp mesh was obtained from the MRI scan. The mean time for the digitization of 64 electrodes and 3 landmarks was 53 s, and the mean residual error of the sensors co-registration was 2.11 mm. They compared the expended time results of the presented method with an electromagnetic digitizer, an ultrasound digitizer, and a photogrammetry system that obtained 8, 10, and 4 min 30 s to digitize 67, 61, and 22 sensors respectively. These results suggest that the laser scanner is an accurate and fast technique, although its cost is higher than the digitizer.

2.6   Photogrammetry

A photogrammetric method called Geodesic Photogrammetry for Localizing Sensor Positions (GPS) is described in [16]. The system uses a software to mark the coordinates of sensors in the images using a mouse or a graphic pointing device. The user saves the images and the software processes the data in an off-line and eventually automated way. Finally, the digitizing results provide the locations of each electrode. In [16], the simultaneous acquisition of images was performed using cameras in a geodesic array. A sensor localization system was designed by the authors with the purpose of achieving a rapid acquisition of electrode positions with minimal time and cooperation required from the patient. The proposed GPS system was compared with electromagnetic digitization method. Both methods gave accurate results but the mean error of the electromagnetic digitizer was 0.25 mm lower than the GPS.

The authors of [16] show that the mean localization error for the electromagnetic digitizer method was 1.02 mm, which is smaller than the mean localization error obtained when comparing between manual and digitization methods. For that case, the average error reported was 3.6 mm for digitization [10]. The authors attributed the difference to the methodology used to acquire the data, and to the environmental conditions during the experiments [16].

Other authors have improved this model by using a single camera. A rotating single digital camera was used in [17] to capture the EEG electrodes locations. In this experiment, a plastic head model and stickers were used to represent the electrodes on the head. After registration, a shape- and color-based pattern recognition algorithm was used. Another single camera photogrammetry system was developed in [23]. As the system presented in [17], the experiment was developed with a shape- and color-based pattern recognition algorithm implemented over a plastic head model and stickers. The authors used the combination of two planar mirrors and the digital camera to take a faster (3 min) acquisition of images with multiple angles. The algorithm was developed in MATLAB [28], it basically consisted in reading the image, converting the colors (red, yellow, green, blue, and purple) to black, and other colors to white. Subsequently, the pixels that did not belong to electrodes were removed and the objects corresponding to the electrodes were selected. Finally, the radios of the electrodes were computed and their nomenclature was identified. The electrode recognition and localization was automatically performed in a computer software.

This method has a maximum reported error of 1.19 mm [18], which is acceptable for brain imaging purposes. The authors suggested that the method has the potential to be accepted in practical clinical diagnosis because the system is easy to use, non-expensive, and the subjects do not require to stay for long time during the registration. However, using multiple cameras or a single rotating one can generate inconsistency on images, because the patient could move the head while the cameras take images [18].

Another photogrammetry system for fast localization of EEG electrodes is presented in [19]. This method used four 3D labels and a Microsoft Kinect. The Kinect provides 3D information of the scene with a two-camera system. The method was developed to achieve accurate calibration results by recovering depth information using a Depth Map In-painting Algorithm. The authors reported an average error of 1.07 mm.

Finally, in [29] the authors developed an alternative photogrammetry method, using a digital single-lens reflex (SLR) camera combined with an open-source software called janus3D, which implements different computer vision techniques. The authors reported an error of 0.8 mm. Additionally, this system allows acquiring the fiducial markers for both EEG and MEG devices.

3 Comparative Analysis of Methods

Table 1 provides a comparative analysis of the EEG electrode positioning approaches presented here, with information reported by the authors on their research. The table shows reported information about error distances and time consumption (time-number of electrodes). Note how the electromagnetic digitizer has been used as gold standard by several authors, but each of these works has reported a different mean error [10,12,16].

Despite the variety of sensor placement and location available, manual methods are still used for low density EEG systems (less than 32 electrodes). Although not having variations in 20 years, they provide good accuracy. However, to get faster results, faster manual methods require that the electrodes to be placed in a regular pattern (10–10 standard position) over the head [10]. While the system proposed by [9] required usually 1 h for measuring the coordinates of each electrode position, the method described in [10] required an average of 5.66 min, that is less than the magnetic digitization (7.95 min). In terms of localization accuracy, the technique proposed by the authors is more accurate (3 mm) than the magnetic digitizer (5 mm), too. But training the operators to make the manual positioning should be accounted as extra financial expenses and time.

The manual placement of electrodes has been replaced with EEG-caps on most high density systems [5]. The position of the electrodes in these caps is fixed, so they avoid expending time determining the sensor locations. Moreover, caps seem to be simpler and faster to implement than more advanced methods. Another advantage is that the caps are useful in less controlled environments and thus can be easily deployed [21]. However, they are not too precise (Their mean error is 12.7 mm) [11], mainly because the shape and size of different heads vary from the standard cap sizes, and developing subject specific caps is impractical.

The first electronic device (and the most popular nowadays) device for sensor location is the Digitizer, either electromagnetic or ultrasound based. The former is not recommended for use in clinical environments due to the interference with metallic object and some sensitive devices, while the latter is sensitive to environmental factors such as temperature and humidity [10]. These methods are commonly used as gold standard, but mostly because of their market availability. Although they promise to be precise, they are time consuming as they require to digitize each electrode individually [16], and their price is high compared to other approaches, mostly because of the commercial software that they need to process the data.

Table 1. Summary of reported mean error and time consumption to determine the exact EEG electrode positioning of different systems reported in the literature.

Year	Authors	Methodology	Error	Time consumption-number of electrodes
1991	De Munk et al. [9]	Manual method	4 mm* 10 mm*	60 min −128
1998	Le et al. [10]	Electromagnetic Digitizer	3.6 mm	15 min −128
		New Manual Method [10]	3 mm	6 min −128
		Old Manual Method [9]	4 mm* 10 mm*	60 min −128
2005	Russell et al. [16]	Electromagnetic Digitizer	1.02 mm	25–35 min −128
		Photogrammetry-GPS	1.27 mm	15–20 min −128
		Ultrasound Digitizer		25–35 min −128
2007	Atcherson et al. [11]	EEG caps	12.7 mm	
2008	Koessler et al. [12]	ALLES	2.91 mm ± 2.29 mm (SD)	
		Electromagnetic Digitizer	2.18 mm ± 1.6 mm (SD)	
2010	Engels et al. [14]	Electromagnetic Digitizer	0.1 −8 mm	
2010	Koessler et al. [15]	Electromagnetic Digitizer	0.759 mm **	
		3D Handheld Laser Scanner	0.892 mm **	
2011	Koessler et al. [27]	3D Handheld Laser Scanner	2.11 mm	0.88 min −67
		Electromagnetic Digitizer		8 min −67
		Ultrasound Digitizer		10 min −61
		Photogrammetry		4.5 min −22
2011	Qian and Sheng [18]	Photogrammetry-Single camera	1.19 mm	8 min −67
2014	Dalal et al. [23]	Electromagnetic Digitizer	6.8 mm	
2014	Zhang et al. [19]	Photogrammetry-Kinect	1.07 mm	
2017	Clausner et al. [29]	Photogrametry-SLR camera	0.8 mm	
		Electromagnetic Digitizer	6.1 mm	

* Found errors for corrupted positions when adding Gaussian noise with zero mean and SD values of 2.5 mm and 10 mm, respectively.
** RMSE: Root Mean Squared Error. SD: Standard Deviation.

There are other approaches with some success but still not as popular as the Digitizer. The next one would be the MRI based localization, which requires a special type of electrode. Comparing the MRI localization method with respect to the electromagnetic digitizer, it provides better reproducibility and equal accuracy without statistical differences [12]. The main advantage of this approach is the possibility of using the same sensors on functional studies, acquiring simultaneous fMRI-EEG data; and actually, brain imaging highly benefits from structural MRI head models [30]. However, the price of these special EEG sensors make it prohibitive for most EEG users.

Other approaches are based on optical sensors. The results of the 3D hand-held laser scanner show that it had an equivalent accuracy compared to the electromagnetic digitizer, but with better repeatability [15]. Additionally, the 3D hand-held laser scanner showed better results (0.795 mm vs. 0.892 mm) in terms of the Root Mean Squared Error (RMSE) compared to the electromagnetic digitizer [15]. Additionally, the registered data provided by the scanner could be directly introduced in source localization studies. Because of its easy use and fast digitization time, this method can be employed in a standard medical environment (no special room or illumination required) without risk of false labeling due to human errors [15]. The main drawbacks of this method are its price and market availability.

Other optical systems are based on cameras (photogrammetry systems), and contrary to the previous methods, works on this respect present ways of manufacturing home-made devices. The GPS is easy to use and it does not require any device touching the subject. While the electromagnetic and ultrasound methods require 25–35 min to digitize the electrodes and another 15 min to re-digitize if an electrode looks poorly placed, the GPS system takes 15–20 min to mark the sensor positions of 128 electrodes. In terms of mean error, the electromagnetic digitizer had better results than GPS with 1.02 mm vs. 1.27 mm respectively [16], which is not significant for most purposes. Finally, the single camera method reported in [18] has a maximum error of 1.19 mm and the reported in [29] has a maximum error of 0.8 mm. The single camera system is a better option in terms of time consumption than GPS. The elapsed time of the single camera methods to whole localization procedure is about 3 min, and the camera calibration takes about 1 min [18].

4   Conclusion

In this work, we present and analyze six commonly used approaches for providing a correct EEG sensor placement. This process must be practical, accurate, fast, and reproducible. Although traditional EEG event related potential analysis is robust to sensor location errors, current brain imaging techniques are more sensitive to them.

In terms of time consumption, our analysis suggests that the 3D hand-held laser scanner is the fastest alternative, followed by photogrammetry. In terms of mean localization error, the photogrammetry, the electromagnetic digitizer, and the 3D hand-held laser scanner showed similar results. Finally, in terms of price the photogrammetry is usually cheaper than the other approaches (excluding manual methods). Indeed, if the system is hand-made, it may be cheaper than most commercial EEG-caps. In conclusion, the photogrammetry is the best cost-effective method for EEG electrode placement, because it requires few time to determine the electrode locations, it presents minimum localization errors, it can be used in non-controlled environments (such as hospitals), it is not expensive, and it does not require any device touching the subject.

Acknowledgement. This work was partially supported by Colciencias Grant 111577757638.

References

1. Müller-Putz, G.R., Riedl, R., Wriessnegger, S.C.: Electroencephalography (EEG) as a research tool in the information systems discipline: foundations, measurement, and applications. Commun. Assoc. Inf. Syst. **37**(1), 46 (2015)

2. Baillet, S., Mosher, J., Leahy, R.: Electromagnetic brain mapping. IEEE Signal Process. Mag. **18**(6), 14–30 (2001)
3. Beltrachini, L., von Ellenrieder, N., Muravchik, C.H.: General bounds for electrode mislocation on the EEG inverse problem. Comput. Methods Programs Biomed. **103**(1), 1–9 (2011)
4. Jurcak, V., Tsuzuki, D., Dan, I.: 10/20, 10/10, and 10/5 systems revisited: their validity as relative head-surface-based positioning systems. Neuroimage **34**(4), 1600–1611 (2007)
5. Towle, V.L., et al.: The spatial location of EEG electrodes: locating the best-fitting sphere relative to cortical anatomy. Electroencephalogr. Clin. Neurophysiol. **86**(1), 1–6 (1993)
6. Wellcome Centre for Human Neuroimaging: SPM12-Statistical Parametric Mapping (2016). http://www.fil.ion.ucl.ac.uk/spm/software/spm12
7. Oostenveld, R., Fries, P., Maris, E., Schoffelen, J.M.: Fieldtrip: open source software for advanced analysis of MEG, EEG, and invasive electrophysiological data. Comput. Intell. Neurosci. **2011**, 1 (2011)
8. Delorme, A., Makeig, S.: EEGLAB: an open source toolbox for analysis of single-trial EEG dynamics including independent component analysis. J. Neurosci. Methods **134**(1), 9–21 (2004)
9. De Munck, J., Vijn, P., Spekreijse, H.: A practical method for determining electrode positions on the head. Clin. Neurophysiol. **78**(1), 85–87 (1991)
10. Le, J., Lu, M., Pellouchoud, E., Gevins, A.: A rapid method for determining standard 10/10 electrode positions for high resolution EEG studies. Electroencephalogr. Clin. Neurophysiol. **106**(6), 554–558 (1998)
11. Atcherson, S.R., Gould, H.J., Pousson, M.A., Prout, T.M.: Variability of electrode positions using electrode caps. Brain Topogr. **20**(2), 105–111 (2007)
12. Koessler, L., et al.: Automatic localization and labeling of EEG sensors (ALLES) in MRI volume. NeuroImage **41**(3), 914–923 (2008)
13. Echallier, J., Perrin, F., Pernier, J.: Computer-assisted placement of electrodes on the human head. Electroencephalogr. Clin. Neurophysiol. **82**(2), 160–163 (1992)
14. Engels, L., De Tiege, X., de Beeck, M.O., Warzée, N.: Factors influencing the spatial precision of electromagnetic tracking systems used for MEG/EEG source imaging. Neurophysiol. Clin./Clin. Neurophysiol. **40**(1), 19–25 (2010)
15. Koessler, L., Cecchin, T., Ternisien, E., Maillard, L.: 3D handheld laser scanner based approach for automatic identification and localization of EEG sensors. In: Engineering in Medicine and Biology Society (EMBC), 2010 Annual International Conference of the IEEE, pp. 3707–3710. IEEE (2010)
16. Russell, G.S., Eriksen, K.J., Poolman, P., Luu, P., Tucker, D.M.: Geodesic photogrammetry for localizing sensor positions in dense-array EEG. Clin. Neurophysiol. **116**(5), 1130–1140 (2005)
17. Baysal, U., Şengül, G.: Single camera photogrammetry system for EEG electrode identification and localization. Ann. Biomed. Eng. **38**(4), 1539–1547 (2010)
18. Qian, S., Sheng, Y.: A single camera photogrammetry system for multi-angle fast localization of EEG electrodes. Ann. Biomed. Eng. **39**(11), 2844 (2011)
19. Zhang, J., Chen, J., Chen, S., Xiao, G., Li, X.: Multimodal spatial calibration for accurately registering EEG sensor positions. Comput. Math. Methods Med. **2014**, 1–7 (2014)
20. Sharbrough, F., Chatrian, G., Lsser, R., Luders, H., Nuwer, M., Picton, T.: Guidelines for standard electrode position nomenclature bloomfield: American EEG society. Technical report (1990)

21. Hairston, W.D., et al.: Usability of four commercially-oriented EEG systems. J. Neural Eng. **11**(4), 046018 (2014)

22. Yoo, S.S., et al.: 3D localization of surface 10–20 EEG electrodes on high resolution anatomical MR images. Electroencephalogr. Clin. Neurophysiol. **102**(4), 335–339 (1997)

23. Dalal, S.S., Rampp, S., Willomitzer, F., Ettl, S.: Consequences of EEG electrode position error on ultimate beamformer source reconstruction performance. Front. Neurosci. **8**, 42 (2014)

24. López, J., Penny, W.D., Espinosa, J., Barnes, G.R.: A general bayesian treatment for MEG source reconstruction incorporating lead field uncertainty. NeuroImage **60**(2), 1194–1204 (2012)

25. Hummel, J., et al.: Evaluation of a new electromagnetic tracking system using a standardized assessment protocol. Phys. Med. Biol. **51**(10), N205 (2006)

26. Éric, S.P., Gagné, P.l., Caron, A.T., Beaupré, N., Tubic, D., Hébert, P.: Hand-held self-referenced apparatus for three-dimensional scanning. US Patent 8,082,120 (2011)

27. Koessler, L., Cecchin, T., Caspary, O., Benhadid, A., Vespignani, H., Maillard, L.: EEG-MRI co-registration and sensor labeling using a 3D laser scanner. Ann. Biomed. Eng. **39**(3), 983–995 (2011)

28. The MathWorks: MATLAB users guide (1998)

29. Clausner, T., Dalal, S.S., Crespo-García, M.: Photogrammetry-based head digitization for rapid and accurate localization of EEG electrodes and MEG fiducial markers using a single digital SLR camera. Front. Neurosci. **11**, 264 (2017)

30. Hallez, H., et al.: Review on solving the forward problem in EEG source analysis. J. Neuro Eng. Rehabil. **4**, 46 (2007). https://doi.org/10.1186/1743-0003-4-46

The Impact of Residential Demand Response in the Active Power Balance of an Isolated Microgrid: A Case of Study

Dahiana López-García[1][✉], Adriana Arango-Manrique[2],
and Sandra X. Carvajal-Quintero[1]

[1] Faculty of Engineering and Architecture, Department of Electrical,
Electronic and Computer Engineering, Research Group Environmental Energy
and Education Policy – E3P, Universidad Nacional de Colombia,
Manizales, Colombia
dahlopezgar@unal.edu.co

[2] Department of Electrical and Electronic Engineering, Grupo de Investigación
en Sistemas Eléctricos de Potencia - GISEL, Universidad del Norte,
Barranquilla, Colombia
adrianaarango@uninorte.edu.co

Abstract. Integration of variable generation sources such as the renewable energy resources and the operation by isolated microgrids involves technical issues related to the reliability and the quality of the electricity supply. Indeed, the small inertia of the isolated microgrids with the integration of variable generation is a challenge faced in the operation of these electricity supply systems. One way to tackle these problems is through demand response programs. In this perspective, this paper first presents a bibliographical review of the importance of the provision of frequency control services by the demand-side and some international experiences related, and later it is present a case of study, in which we assess the effects of high penetration levels of variable generation, specifically solar PV generation, in the power balance of the microgrid, and we evaluate some proposed demand response mechanisms, focused on the active participation of residential users, that respond to variations of the system's frequency, showing that residential demand response has the potential to reduce the frequency variations that occur during the day, while increasing the use of renewable generation sources immersed in the microgrid.

Keywords: Demand response · Isolated microgrids · Power balance
Frequency control

1 Introductory Remarks

Integration of distributed generation whose primary source is predominantly renewable energies, which are characterized by their variability and intermittency, makes it necessary to have new mechanisms that allow maintaining in real time the frequency of the system in an acceptable range [1–3].

Conventionally, frequency regulation has been provided only by generation units, but this paradigm is changing due to the inclusion of storage technologies and the flexibility of demand to respond to events or variations in a system indicator [2, 4].

© Springer Nature Switzerland AG 2018
J. C. Figueroa-García et al. (Eds.): WEA 2018, CCIS 915, pp. 535–547, 2018.
https://doi.org/10.1007/978-3-030-00350-0_44

In this sense, demand response can be understood as changes in the electricity comsumption in comparison with a baseline, due to variations in the electricity price over time, or due to incentives designed to flatten the demand curve [5–7]. The possibility of changing the consumption patterns allows to schedule displacements and load reductions that would help to maintain the balance demand-supply in isolated microgrids. At the same time, demand flexibility makes it feasible to respond to events that compromise the continuity of the supply [5].

In this paper we evaluate some of the effects of demand response, focused on residential users, in the active power balance of isolated microgrids, for this purpose, in Sect. 2 a bibliographic review of the importance of the provision of frequency control by demand side is made, showing some related international experiences. Then, in Sect. 3, the study case and the proposed demand response mechanisms are presented. Later, Sect. 4 shows the results extracted from the case of study and their respective analysis, and finally, Sect. 5 presents the concluding remarks.

2 Demand Response and Frequency Control

Penetration of renewable energy is growing rapidly in the world, and its integration brings with it challenges related to the reliability and high volatility of the electricity supply, challenges that are easily visible in the operation of isolated microgrids [8, 9].

Achieve a flexible operation of an isolated microgrid with the integration of variable generation sources requires a coordinated operation of all the resources immersed in the electrical system (generation, demand, storage). This coordination would allow having a reliable, sustainable and secure electricity supply, that may massify the inclusion of energy resources with a reduced carbon footprint [10].

Microgrid operation is like the operation of an electrical power system that depends largely on the constant balance between generation and demand, achieved by the up/down ramping of synchronous generators [11]. However, in the operation of isolated microgrids, there is not the large-size generation to maintain inertia, and with the introduction of variable generation, the paradigm of controlling generation to match demand is no longer sustainable [11].

For this reason, it is necessary to have new mechanisms to maintain supply-demand balance, and therefore the frequency of the system in real time [1–3]. In this regard, demand response is a key element in the operation of isolated microgrids, because of its potential for maintaining the efficiency in the electricity supply, the active power balance and the reliability of the system [12–14].

Demand response is characterized by its flexibility and its ability to make changes in consumption profiles [5, 9, 15, 16]. Thus, flexibility of demand response, in many cases, allows to have faster load reductions than the up/down ramping of the synchronous generation plants (thermal or hydraulic) [17–19], so demand response has the potential to mitigate the variability and intermittency of renewable generation [2, 20], keeping the frequency of the system within operational ranges.

On the other hand, the electrification of rural or isolated areas is one of the predominant problems of electrification worldwide [21]. Most countries have focused on increasing the coverage of access to electricity supply without paying special attention to whether the implemented solutions are sustainable in the short and medium term [22]. On this subject, the operation by isolated microgrids offers the possibility of coordinating distributed energy resources, to maintain a continuous electricity supply. Consequently, it is required to have the flexibility that the demand, the storage systems and the generation units immersed in the isolated microgrid can provide in terms of active power, with the aim of maintaining the frequency within the operational ranges [5, 23–25].

Internationally, there have been isolated microgrids in the research field, in which the energy management model, the behavior of the variable source, among others characteristics, are analyzed [26].

Kythnos microgrid, located in Greece, is an isolated microgrid that supplies the electricity of 12 houses. The control of this microgrid is based on frequency monitoring for battery management. In addition, a load disconnection control is performed when the battery charge level is very low [26].

Hartley Bay located in Canada is a remote coastal village which operates an isolated microgrid that supplies electricity to a native community of 170 members. It relies on a set of three diesel generators, two of 420 kW and one of 210 kW to provide electricity to 20 commercial buildings and 62 residential units. Given the low efficiency of the 210-kW generator, a demand response program has been deployed to use the generator as little as possible, thus optimizing the diesel dispatch. The demand response system has been included in the commercial buildings and is composed by 20 variable thermostats and twelve load controllers, and it has been able to reduce the peak demand by 15% [27].

In the west coast of Scotland, Isle of Eigg has a high renewable content power microgrid. The project has been successful at integrating multiple renewable energy sources into a community system. The system is composed of 110 kW of hydro power, 24 kW from wind turbines and 32 kW of solar PV. The introduction of renewable energy sources is supported by load side management with energy monitors installed in all properties and droop control of the system, based on battery charge level and frequency [27].

Fort Collins microgrid in Colorado represents about 10–15% of Fort Collins' entire distribution system. Technologies in the project include solar PV, combined heat and power, microturbines, fuel cells, electric vehicles, thermal storage, load shedding, and demand-side management. Demand response occurs through heating, cooling, and ventilation rescheduling using existing controls and building automation systems.

Huatacondo microgrid located in Chile supply electricity to 30 families approx. This microgrid combines a 150 kW diesel generator, together with 22 kW tracking solar PV system, a 3 kW wind turbine, a 170 kWh battery, and an energy management system [27]. To compensate the fluctuations of variable energy sources, there is a demand management program that responds to deviation signals from a grid indicator. In addition, a social SCADA was implemented to characterize the energy needs of users [28].

Table 1 shows a summary of the main characteristics of the microgrids previously described. The programmed demand response category refers to those mechanisms designed to encourage displacements or reductions of load using hourly rates, such as Time-Of-Use rates, social incentives or other mechanisms that seek the voluntary participation of the community to reduce the risk of disconnections. The automatic demand response category refers to automatic limitations or disconnections of non-critical loads at times in which the continuity of supply is compromised.

Table 1. International experiences of isolated microgrid operation with demand response mechanisms. Source: Compilated by author based on [26–28].

Microgrid	Generation and electrical storage systems						Demand response	
	PV	Diesel	Hydro	Wind	ESS	CHP	Programmed	Automatic
Kythnos	x	x			x			x
Hartley Bay		x					x	x
Isle of Eigg	x		x	x				x
Fort Collins	x				x	x	x	x
Huatacondo	x	x		x	x		x	

International experiences with active demand participation are focused on the communities' contribution to the use of resources and productivity [29]. But, there are no mechanisms for taking advantage of demand flexibility to avoid disconnections when events of supply-demand unbalance occur.

To provide ancillary services, like frequency control with demand flexibility, regulation is incipient in the operation by isolated microgrids, so the implementation of specialized controls to provide this ancillary service is still being developed and studied.

3   Case of Study

The study case analyzed corresponds to an isolated microgrid with four hydro generation units of 1,0 kVA and four PV generation units of 350 kWp. The analyzed system is shown in Fig. 1.

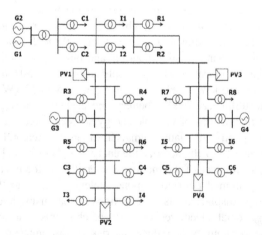

Fig. 1. One-line diagram of the analyzed microgrid. Source: Compiled by author.

The location of PV generation units was determined following the methodology proposed in [34], which aims to reduce congestion and losses, while keeping the voltage profile between allowable ranges, by including distributed generation in the system.

Additionally, the primary frequency control of the four hydroelectric units is performed by means of the IEEEG3 modeled governor, which is a general purpose linearized turbine governor model [30].

A typical load curve of Colombian Andean region, of aggregation of residential, commercial and industrial consumption, was used as the load shape of the system (Fig. 2).

The generation curve of the solar photovoltaic systems corresponds to a daily generation curve taken from the database of Universidad Nacional de Colombia -Sede Manizales and it is shown in Fig. 3. This generation scenario was selected due to the high variability of the power generation and because its tendency is not fully predictable.

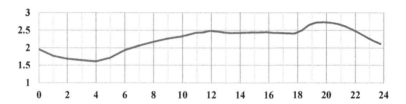

Fig. 2. Demand curve in MW of the microgrid in a 24-hours period. Source: Compiled by author based on [31].

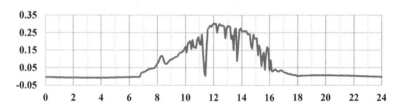

Fig. 3. Solar photovoltaic generation curve used for the scenarios with solar PV generation in a 24-hour period. Source: Compiled by author based on the PV database of Universidad Nacional de Colombia – Sede Manizales.

The inclusion of the solar PV generation curve induce fluctuations in the frequency of the system, which is translated into an extension of the range in which the frequency varies during the day. These frequency fluctuations depend not only on the variability of power production due to climatic conditions, but also depend on the percentage of the system installed capacity corresponding to solar PV generation. Therefore, to narrow the frequency of the system to a more limited range, and thus reducing the risk of power outages, two scenarios for the implementation of demand response programs are proposed, focusing on the residential loads of the system:

- **Load shifting/load shaping (Scenario 1):**
  This scenario seeks to flatten the residential demand curve, by shifting demand from peak hours (6:00 p.m. to 10:00 p.m) to off-peak hours in which the generation from solar PV resources is available. In this scenario, the total energy of the residential demand curve remains constant for the simulated day of operation.
- **Automatic load limitation (Scenario 2):**
  In this scenario, it is intended, automatically, to limit a percentage of the residential load of the system when low-frequency thresholds are exceeded. This load limitation is considered as a limitation in the current, by means of measurement concentrators located in the transformers that supply electricity to these loads. For this operation scenario, the two mechanisms shown in Table 2 are proposed. Each mechanism automatically limits the specific power percentage when a certain frequency threshold is exceeded.

Table 2. Demand response mechanism for the second scenario. Source: Compiled by author.

Case	Threshold [Hz]	Demand response mechanism		
		Variation type	[%]	User type
Case 1	59.85	Load decrease	10%	Residential
Case 2	59.90	Load decrease	5%	Residential
	59.85	Load decrease	5%	Residential

It is important to note that the load displacements can be carried out with the reprogramming of non-vital domestic activities, such as the washing cycle, the recharging of electronic devices, etc. [3]. While, the load limitation may refer to the increase of temperature of the refrigerators and air conditioners, or to the disconnection of circuits previously selected by the user [3]. However, the selection of residential loads that would allow this kind of demand response action is beyond the scope of this paper.

For the dynamic simulation of the microgrid, in a time horizon of 24 h, the RMS/EMT simulation toolbox of the specialized DIgSILENT Power Factory software was used. This simulation is often used to analyse grid stability when there are changes in generation and load and mid-term and long-term transients under both balanced and unbalanced conditions [32].

4 Results

4.1 Frequency Response to Different Levels of Solar PV Integration

Figure 4 shows the frequency of the system at different levels of integration of solar generation. The integration level is calculated as the percentage of the installed capacity of the system that corresponds to solar PV generation units.

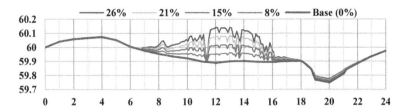

Fig. 4. Frequency response to different integration levels of generation from solar PV. Source: Compiled by author

It is important to highlight that sudden changes in frequency can decrease the reliability of the system, increasing the probability of occurrence and the severity of power outages. In addition, it is possible to show that with a massive installation of solar PV generation, the frequency of the system is not only compromised in the demand peak hours, which is inherent to all electrical grids but also could be compromised in the peak of solar PV generation.

The results presented in Sects. 4.2 and 4.3 correspond to scenarios with an integration of 26% of solar PV generation.

4.2   Scenario 1: Load Shifting/Load Shaping

Figure 5 shows the original demand curve (blue line) and the proposed demand curve (red line) for the residential charges of the microgrid. This proposed curve reduces the peak residential demand, which happens between 18:00 and 22:00, by 10% and shifts the energy reduced to the period between 10:00 and 14:00. This proposed curve is an application of the load shaping mechanism, which is a type of demand response that encourages electrical consumption when the generation from solar PV units is abundant and discourage it when it is not [33].

For this microgrid, changes proposed in residential demand curve are translated into very little changes in the total demand curve (see Fig. 6). The 10% reduction in the peak of residential demand is reflected in only a 1.5% decrease in the total demand peak.

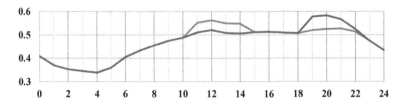

Fig. 5. Original (blue line) and proposed (red line) demand curve in MW of the aggregated residential loads in a 24-hours period. Source: Compiled by author (Color figure online)

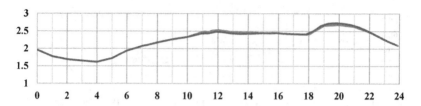

Fig. 6. Original (blue line) and obtained (red line) demand curve in MW of the microgrid in a 24-hours period. Source: Compiled by author (Color figure online)

However, even if the changes in the total demand curve were not highly significant; when making the proposed changes in the residential demand curve, the frequency of the system, shown in Fig. 7, is positively affected by a narrowing in the range in which it varies during the day.

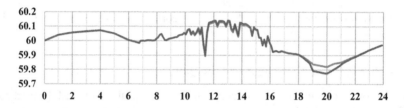

Fig. 7. Original (blue line) and obtained (red line) frequency in Hz of the microgrid in a 24-hours period. Source: Compiled by author (Color figure online)

4.3   Scenario 2: Automatic Load Limitation

Figure 8 shows the changes in the residential demand curve that occur with the implementation of the demand response mechanism proposed in case 1 (red line) and in case 2 (yellow line).

Case 1 performs an automatic load limitation of 10% of the current load when the frequency of the system reaches the under-frequency threshold of 59.85 Hz. This load limitation remains active as long as the frequency remains below the said threshold, and it consists in a limitation of 10% of the consumption baseline. For this case of study, only a load cut is performed, on residential loads, due to the performance of the demand response mechanism proposed in case 1, this load reduction takes place at 18:44 and remains active until 21:00.

On the other hand, Case 2 performs an automatic load limitation of 5% of the current load when the frequency of the system reaches the under-frequency threshold of 59.9 Hz and an automatic load limitation of 5% of the current load when the frequency of the system reaches the threshold of 59.85 Hz. These load limitations remain active as long as the frequency remains below its respective threshold. For this study case, two load reductions are made in the residential loads due to the performance of the demand response mechanism proposed in case 2, The first load limitation, corresponding to the threshold of 59.9 Hz, takes place at 18:06 and remains active until 22:15; the second load limitation, corresponding to the threshold of 59.85 Hz takes place at 18:47 and remains active until 21:10.

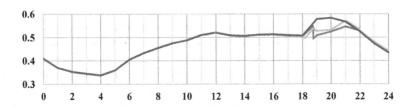

Fig. 8. Original (blue line) residential demand curve and resultant demand curve to mechanisms proposed in Case 1(red line) and Case 2 (yellow line) in MW of the aggregated residential loads in a 24-hours period. Source: Compiled by author (Color figure online)

Figure 9 shows system frequency, both for the base scenario (blue line), and for the scenarios in which the demand response mechanisms proposed in case 1 (red line) and in case 2 (yellow line) are implemented.

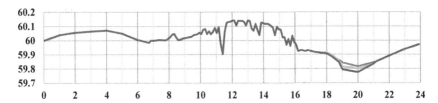

Fig. 9. Original (blue line) frequency and resultant frequency behavior to DR mechanism proposed in case 1 (red line) and case 2 (yellow line) in Hz in a 24-hours period. Source: Compiled by author (Color figure online)

The best frequency response occurs with the implementation of the demand response mechanism proposed in case 1. In addition, with the implementation of this case is only necessary to carry out a 10% load reduction for 2.27 h, while with the mechanism proposed in case 2, it is necessary to make two reductions of 5%, one with a duration of 4.15 h, and the other with a duration of 2.39 h. However, it is necessary to highlight that it is possible that the load reduction triggered by case 1 implies a greater impact on domestic activities and possibly a decrease on the users' comfort; but it would be necessary to carry out additional studies to identify which mechanisms are better accepted by consumers.

Also, it would be convenient to add an extra level in both demand response mechanisms, in which residential demand responds to frequency excursions below the 59.8 Hz threshold, however, with the level of solar integration analyzed, and with the implementation of the demand response mechanisms proposed above, the frequency

does not exceed this value and therefore it is not possible to evaluate the appropriate
level of load limitation.

4.4 Results Summary

Table 3 shows some of the most relevant results of each proposed scenario. Here, the
proposed demand response mechanism is briefly described, and it is presented the
minimum and maximum value of the range in which the frequency varies during the
day, in both the base case and the case in which the proposed mechanism is implemented. In addition, the total daily energy reduction (as a percentage of the base
aggregate demand curve) for each scenario is presented. It is necessary to emphasize
that, the lower the energy of the daily demand curve compared to the original curve, the
greater the impact on the user's domestic activities.

Table 3. Summary of the most relevant results of each scenario. Source: Compiled by author.

Scenario & case		Proposed mechanism	Total energy reduction [%]	Frequency variation range [Hz]	
				Before	After
Scenario 1	Case 1	Shift of demand of 10% from peak hours to off-peak hours in which the generation from solar PV resources is available	0.037	59.78 60.14	59.82 60.13
Scenario 2	Case 1	Automatic load limitation of 10% when the frequency exceeds the sub-frequency threshold of 59.85 Hz	0.440	59.78 60.14	59.82 60.14
	Case 2	Automatic load limitation of 5% when the frequency exceeds the sub-frequency threshold of 59.80 Hz, and additional limitation of 5% when the frequency exceeds the sub-frequency threshold of 59.85 Hz	0.466	59.78 60.14	59.80 60.14

5 Concluding Remarks

The obtained results show that the high flexibility of the demand and its capability to
adjust the demand curve allows the demand, from a technical point of view, to provide
frequency control services to the microgrid, keeping the frequency variations within a
more limited range. This is translated into an accurate active power balance, which
reduces the probability of occurrence and severity of power outages.

Based on the obtained results from the evaluation of the first scenario of the study
case, it is possible to affirm that the load shifting, by means of encouraging electrical
consumption when the generation of solar PV units is abundant and by discouraging
consumption when it is not, has the potential to improve the reliability of the system
and narrow the range in which the frequency varies daily, which could guarantee

greater continuity in the electricity supply and a greater use of the renewable energy resources immersed in the microgrid.

The study case shows the potential of the active participation of residential users to improve the continuity and quality of electricity supply. The active participation of this type of users would also allow increasing the use of the renewable generation sources of the region, thus reducing the environmental impact of the production and commercialization of electricity in isolated areas.

The results of the two proposed scenarios: the automatic mechanisms of load limitation or disconnection, which require the acquisition of specialized measurement and control equipment, and the load shifting, which can be achieved by diverse means such as of the incentive payment and socialization of the community, allow to highlight that both have the potential to reduce the frequency variations that occur during the day, while increasing the use of renewable generation sources immersed in the microgrid.

Based on international experiences and considering the results obtained from the evaluation of the case of study, it can be affirmed that the active participation of the demand could increase the reliability and continuity of the supply in an isolated microgrid. But the mechanisms of participation implemented must be adapted to the technical, economic and social conditions in which the electrical system is developed.

The operation by isolated microgrids with the integration of renewable energy resources is a possible solution for electrification of isolated areas. However, it is necessary to include demand for this type of solutions, in order to maintain a continuous service with acceptable standards of quality and sustainability, and with the aim to enhance the use of the primary resources of the regions, with the massification of distributed generation from renewable sources.

Acknowledgements. The research for this paper was supported by Universidad Nacional de Colombia through the research department of Manizales – DIMA as part of the project "Evaluación del impacto de la remuneración de la generación distribuida y la demanda por la prestación de servicios de soporte técnico en el sistema de distribución eléctrico colombiano", code 39039, developed by Environmental Energy and Education Policy – E3P research group.

References

1. Anderson, C.L., Cardell, J.B.: A decision framework for optimal pairing of wind and demand response resources. IEEE Syst. J. **8**, 1104–1111 (2014)
2. Federal Energy Regulatory Commission. Assessment of Demand Response & Advanced Metering, pp. 1689–1699, December 2015
3. Cappers, P., Mills, A., Goldman, C., Wiser, R., Eto, J.H.: Mass market demand response and variable generation integration issues: a scoping study (2012)
4. Behrangrad, M.: A review of demand side management business models in the electricity market. Renew. Sustain. Energy Rev. **47**, 270–283 (2015)
5. Federal Energy Regulatory Commission. Benefits of Demand Response in Electricity Markets and Recommendations for Achieving Them (2006)
6. Lebel, G., et al.: Distributed and coordinated demand response for frequency-controlled reserve supply. In: PowerTech 2015, pp. 2–6. IEEE, Eindhoven (2015)

7. Palensky, P., Dietrich, D.: Demand side management: demand response, intelligent energy systems, and smart loads. IEEE Trans. Ind. Inform. **7**, 381–388 (2011)
8. Meyn, S., Barooah, P., Busic, A., Chen, Y., Ehren, J.: Ancillary service to the grid using intelligent deferrable loads. IEEE Trans. Autom. Control **60**, 2847–2862 (2014)
9. Eid, C., Codani, P., Perez, Y., Reneses, J., Hakvoort, R.: Managing electric flexibility from distributed energy resources: a review of incentives for market design. Renew. Sustain. Energy Rev. **64**, 237–247 (2016)
10. Brown, R.E., Freeman, L.A.A.: Analyzing the reliability impact of distributed generation. In: Proceedings of IEEE Power Engineering Society Transmission and Distribution Conference, vol. 2, pp. 1013–1018 (2001)
11. Barooah, P., Bušić, A., Meyn, S.: Spectral decomposition of demand-side flexibility for reliable ancillary services in a smart grid. In: Proceedings of Annual Hawaii International Conference on System Sciences, March 2015, pp. 2700–2709 (2015)
12. Parvania, M., Fotuhi-Firuzabad, M., Shahidehpour, M.: Optimal demand response aggregation in wholesale electricity markets. IEEE Trans. Smart Grid **4**, 1957–1965 (2013)
13. Shao, S., Pipattanasomporn, M., Rahman, S.: Demand response as a load shaping tool in an intelligent grid with electric vehicles. IEEE Trans. Smart Grid **2**, 624–631 (2011)
14. Shafie-Khah, M., Fitiwi, D.Z., Catalao, J.P.S., Heydarian-Forushani, E., Golshan, M.E.H.: Simultaneous participation of demand response aggregators in ancillary services and demand response exchange markets. In: Proceedings of IEEE Power Energy Society Transmission Distribution Conference, July 2016, pp. 1–5 (2016)
15. Observatorio Industrial del Sector de la Electrónica Tecnologías de la información y Telecomunicaciones. Smart Grids y la Evolución de la Red Eléctrica. Fedit 1–82 (2011)
16. Neves, D., Brito, M.C., Silva, C.A.: Impact of solar and wind forecast uncertainties on demand response of isolated microgrids. Renew. Energy **87**, 1003–1015 (2016)
17. Schisler, K., Sick, T., Brief, K.: The role of demand response in ancillary service markets. In: IEEE Transmission and Distribution Conference and Exposition, pp. 1–3 (2008). https://doi.org/10.1109/tdc.2008.4517087
18. Ma, O., et al.: Demand response for ancillary services. IEEE Trans. Smart Grid **4**, 1988–1995 (2013)
19. Wang, Q., et al.: Review of real-time electricity markets for integrating distributed energy resources and demand response. Appl. Energy **138**, 695–706 (2015)
20. Brooks, A., Lu, E., Reicher, D., Spirakis, C., Weihl, B.: Demand dispatch. IEEE Power Energy Mag. **8**, 20–29 (2010)
21. International Energy Agency - IEA.: Energy for All: Financing access for the poor (Special early excerpt of the World Energy Outlook 2011). World Energy Outlook 2011, vol. 52 (2011)
22. Bhattacharyya, S.C.: Energy access programmes and sustainable development: a critical review and analysis. Energy. Sustain. Dev. **16**, 260–271 (2012)
23. North American Electric Reliability Corporation - NERC. Accommodating High Levels of Variable Generation (2008)
24. Shariatzadeh, F., Mandal, P., Srivastava, A.K.: Demand response for sustainable energy systems: a review, application and implementation strategy. Renew. Sustain. Energy Rev. **45**, 343–350 (2015)
25. Narimani, M.R., Nauert, P.J., Joo, J.-Y., Crow, M.L.: Reliability assesment of power system at the presence of demand side management. In: 2016 IEEE Power and Energy Conference at Illinois (PECI), pp. 1–5. IEEE (2016). https://doi.org/10.1109/peci.2016.7459222
26. Hatziargyriou, N.: Microgrids: Architectures and Control (2014). https://doi.org/10.1002/9781118720677

27. Berkeley Lab. Microgrids at Berkeley Lab. https://building-microgrid.lbl.gov/huatacondo. Accessed 30 Jan 2018

28. Núñez, O., Ortiz, D., Palma-Behnke, R.: Microrredes en la red eléctrica del futuro – caso Huatacondo. Cienc. y Tecnol. **29**, 1–16 (2013)

29. Euei Pdf. Mini-grid Policy Toolkit. Rep vol. 69 (2014). http://www.euei-pdf.org/en. https://doi.org/10.1017/cbo9781107415324.004

30. Argonne - National Laboratory. Review of Existing Hydroelectric Turbine-Governor Simulation Models (2005)

31. XM Expertos en Mercados. Propuesta Pronóstico de Demanda CND (2017). http://www.xm.com.co/Pages/PropuestaPronosticodeDemandaCND.aspx. Accessed 19 July 2017

32. DIgSILENT GmbH. DIgSILENT PowerFactory 15 - User Manual (2013)

33. Perez, R., et al.: Achieving very high PV penetration – the need for an effective electricity remuneration framework and a central role for grid operators. Energy Policy **96**, 27–35 (2016)

34. Afkousi-Paqaleh, M., Abbaspour-Tehrani Fard, A., Rashidinejad, M.: Distributed generation placement for congestion management considering economic and financial issues **92**, 193–201 (2010)

Event-Triggered Digital Implementation of MPPT for Integration of PV Generators in DC Buses of Microgrids

Oswaldo Lopez-Santos[1]([⊠]) [iD], María Merchán-Riveros[1] [iD], and Germain Garcia[2]

[1] Universidad de Ibagué, 730001 Ibagué, Colombia
oswaldo.lopez@unibague.edu.co
[2] LAAS-CNRS, Univ. Toulouse, Toulouse, France

Abstract. This paper presents an event-triggered approach to optimally implement a Maximum Power Point Tracking (MPPT) algorithm into a Digital Signal Processor (DSP). The proposed method allows improving the amount and distribution of time required for executing control tasks. The used nested loop control architecture has an outer loop of MPPT generating the conductance reference used by an inner loop which regulates the input conductance of a DC-DC converter. This last loop enforces a sliding-mode loss-free-resistor behavior for the power converter by means of a simple hysteresis comparator. Computations required by the MPPT algorithm are synchronously executed by the two possible commutation events produced by the inner loop during a switching period. Then, the acquisition of signals must be activated only at an instant before each one of the switching events, releasing the most of the time to implement other tasks. This last characteristic and the use of a nested loop control architecture facilitate the integration of the other essential control functions for photovoltaic (PV) generators in microgrids. Simulation and experimental results confirm the high potetialities of this implementation approach.

Keywords: Photovoltaic generator · Microgrids · Event triggered control
MPPT · Digital signal processor

1 Introduction

Solar photovoltaic (PV) is the renewable energy source (RES) preferred for distributed generation (DG) because, it allows modular, scalable and flexible implementation in both small and medium scale power systems. PV generators are integrated with other RES, energy storage systems (ESS) and local loads, configuring complex but flexible systems named microgrids [1–3]. These structures support one of the two possible natures of the electrical energy: direct current (DC) or alternative current (AC). Although AC-coupled microgrids allow direct integration into the grid, DC and hybrid (DC and AC) microgrids have been highly studied and developed recently because they also facilitate autonomous operation with high reliability and efficiency. Interconnection of the different elements that compose microgrids are made in DC distribution

© Springer Nature Switzerland AG 2018
J. C. Figueroa-García et al. (Eds.): WEA 2018, CCIS 915, pp. 548–560, 2018.
https://doi.org/10.1007/978-3-030-00350-0_45

buses which has standard regulated voltage levels classified as either low voltage DC (LVDC) or extra LVDC (ELVDC) [4, 5].

Power conversion stage of a PV generator is commonly composed by the solar array and a DC-DC converter. The topology of the power converter depends of the amount of power, input and output voltage levels (PV array and DC distribution bus), and other particular requirements needed by the application [6]. On the other hand, control stage needs to use a Maximum Power Point Tracking (MPPT) algorithm to keep optimized the power extracted from the solar panels [7, 8]. Although the most efficient operation mode implies the use of the MPPT, other possible environmental and energy profile scenarios can require the use of two additional modes: limited power mode (LP-mode) or voltage regulation mode (VR-mode). In limited power mode, PV generator delivers an amount of power defined by a superior control level. On the contrary, operating in the voltage regulation mode, the PV generator regulates the voltage of the DC distribution bus controlling the amount of power that it can provide [9–11]. The function of a MPPT algorithm in the control of a PV generator is to enforce the impedance at the input port of the DC-DC power converter to be equal to the impedance of the panel array in order to obtain maximum power transfer at the maximum power point. Most of the known MPPT algorithms use a single loop architecture in which the duty cycle of a constant frequency pulse width modulator (PWM) is generated by the control to be directly applied. Nevertheless, although these methods are simple, they are also less flexible and less attractive in the context of microgrids. Nested loop architectures use an inner loop (primary level) regulating the input current of the converter to a value given by the outer loop (secondary level) with the aim to operate in one of the three modes mentioned above (MPPT, LP and VR modes) [12]. Indistinctly of the employed method, the DC-DC converter is controlled at the input port leaving only free the current of the output port since it is connected to a regulated voltage DC bus [13]. Implementation of the MPPT method for a PV generator can be performed by using only analogue electronics, giving same advantages for cost, reliability and even efficiency [14, 15]. However, digital implementation could be necessary because, MPPT function must be combined with other control functions and because measurements required by the inner computations can be also used for high-level supervision and management algorithms [16–19].

Many of the digital devices available in the market include specialized modules of PWM, simultaneous multiple channel analogue to digital conversion (ADC) and other hardware modules, facilitating control of motor drives and other established industrial applications [20, 21]. However, only a few of them incorporate hardware comparator modules facilitating implementation of hysteresis based controllers [22]. In that context, in most cases, the performance is severely affected by an inappropriate sampling rate. In order to overcome this limitation and simultaneously minimize the computational cost related with digital implementation of control strategies, the called event-triggered (ET) control also called event-based control can be applied [23, 24]. This technique is especially suitable for applications where processing resources are limited because it is possible to avoid unnecessary execution of some computations or routines saving processing time which can be employed by other functions. In a digital control system using ET control, computations to obtain output values are only triggered by the occurrence of an event. In addition, the use of ET control can improve considerably the performance of digitally implemented hysteresis based controllers because the error introduced by the sample and hold tasks is minimized.

In this paper, the control employed to obtain MPPT is based on the application of the Sliding Mode Loss-Free-Resistor concept (SM-LFR), which consists in enforcing a resistive behaviour at the input port of the converter while the output port operates as a power source [25, 26]. The main difference of this nonlinear control with respect to the ones based on PWM is the operation of the converter at variable switching frequency which adds complexity to the discrete time approach [27–30]. Despite this important specificity, digital implementations of current controllers using similar approaches have been proposed so far in the literature [31]. This work is focused on an innovative digital implementation of an ET-MPPT synchronized with the variable switching frequency of a converter controlled via sliding mode. The rest of the paper is organized as follows: Sect. 2 presents description of the PV generation system and the proposed control implementation. Theoretical fundamentals and design considerations of the control system are analysed in Sect. 3. Validation of the proposal, one using simulated results is proposed in Sect. 4 and the other using experimental results in Sect. 5. Finally, conclusions are presented in Sect. 6.

2 General Description of the System Control Scheme

A block diagram of a PV generator using the proposed event-triggered digital control approach is depicted in Fig. 1. It is possible to differentiate a DC-DC converter connected at the input port to a PV array and at the output port to a DC voltage source representing a LVDC bus of a microgrid. The algorithm is represented into the frame named as digital device which corresponds to the control stage. As it can be noted into this frame, implementation of the proposed control implies the use of two Analogue-to-Digital Conversion (ADC) channels, one for the inductor current of the converter i_L (DC-DC converter must have a series inductor in the input port) and another for the voltage of the PV array v_p. Only one digital output is required for the control signal u which is used to trigger sampling functions. The inner loop of the control has been represented in a frame named as LFR (Loss-Free-Resistor) in which the system is waiting for two events which we will call on-event and off-event:

$$on - event \rightarrow i_L > i_{ref} + \Delta \rightarrow u = 0$$
$$off - event \rightarrow i_L < i_{ref} - \Delta \rightarrow u = 1 \text{ '}$$

being 2Δ the width of a hysteresis band imposed around the current reference value i_{ref}. In steady state, the average value of the inductor current is equal to the output current of the PV module i_p while the ripple component is absorbed by a coupling capacitor.

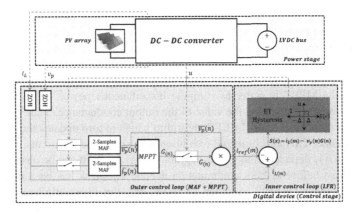

Fig. 1. General scheme of the PV generator using the proposed control implementation.

With this simple implementation, the input current of the DC-DC converter is regulated. The switching frequency of the converter results defined by the rising edge events of u, independently of the way in which the algorithm is implemented. Because of Δ is constant, the switching frequency (also the sampling frequency) depends on the operation point of the converter which in turn is function of the environmental conditions of the PV array. As it can be noted, there are differentiated two sampling frequencies in the block diagram (samples of each one noted with (n) and (m)). Samples denoted with (n) are obtained once each switching period of the converter and samples denoted with (m) are obtained at the maximum sampling rate of the digital device. Figure 2 shows the expected triangular shape of the inductor current waveform related with events of the control signal u when a jump of the current reference i_{ref} is produced from i_{ref1} to i_{ref2}.

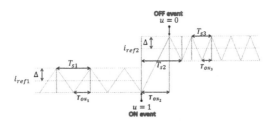

Fig. 2. Detail of the input inductor current waveform for a change in the reference value.

The current reference of the inner control loop is provided by the SM-LRF control and is computed as $i_{ref} = G \cdot v_p$, where G is the desired conductance. In this case, that value is given by the MPPT algorithm which in turn requires average measurements of the voltage and current of the PV array. As it is shown in Fig. 1, current and voltage signals are averaged using two-sample moving average filters (MAF) [32, 33], having that these two values for the current correspond to the two limits of the hysteresis band.

Triangular shape of the current waveform ensures that the way to compute the average is accurate. In the case of the voltage, averaging only allows reducing the effect of the high frequency ripple due to commutations which is not really significant.

Understood as a sequence of tasks, immediately after the control signal u turns on, SMA algorithm is executed updating the values of the averaged current and voltage required by the MPPT in order to compute instantaneous power. After that, MPPT algorithm is executed updating the value of the output conductance. That value is used right away in order to execute the LFR algorithm which in turn updates the value of the current reference. This synchronized execution of tasks based on events affecting the control signal u is depicted in the time diagram of Fig. 3a. As it can be observed, a task is executed just before of both commutation events. This task has been denominated "waiting for event (WFE)" in order to show that the event triggered control is implemented performing ADC and comparison only during these intervals. WFE intervals are required because of the variation of the switching frequency, or in other words because of the no uniformity in the occurrence of the events. The length of the WFE intervals is computed to absorb the uncertain difference between switching frequencies for the entire operational range of the converter. Figure 3b show the way in which the on and off intervals are optimally used to execute multiple tasks (tasks 1–4).

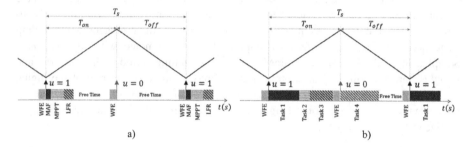

Fig. 3. Detail of the event-triggered execution of computational tasks.

The time required by the four tasks is considerably lower that the switching period and then an important time interval is free of task and can be used to implement control algorithms to increase the capabilities of the photovoltaic generator. In the case of microgrids, MPPT task of the outer loop can be replaced by a power regulation loop using the same set of variables or also can be replaced by a voltage regulation loop to control the DC bus voltage, in such a case, measurement of the output voltage will be required. Summarizing, outer loop is executed once per period and in consequence operates in discrete time at a variable switching rate.

3   Theoretical Fundamentals and Design Considerations

To apply the proposed control, the DC-DC converter must have a series inductor connected at the input port. Additionally, as it can be noted in Fig. 4, a coupling capacitor C is required for reducing the effect of ripple current in the lifetime of the

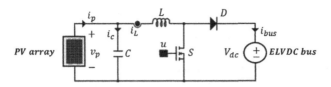

Fig. 4. Power stage of the PV generator integrated into a DC bus of a microgrid.

panels. These two constrains allow the use of the boost, Cûk, SEPIC and other quadratic converters. In this study, a boost converter is considered for the simplicity of the analysis. A DC source type load is connected at the output port of the converter representing an ELVDC bus of a microgrid. Operating in continuous conduction mode, the boost converter can be described by the differential equation system (1)–(2).

$$\frac{di_L}{dt} = \frac{1}{L}v_p - \frac{1}{L}V_{dc}(1-u) \tag{1}$$

$$\frac{dv_p}{dt} = \frac{1}{C}i_p - \frac{1}{C}i_L, \tag{2}$$

where i_p is the output current of the solar panel, V_{dc} is a constant value. If a sliding mode is induced by means of the surface $S(x) = i_L - i_{ref} = i_L - gv_p$, then, by applying the equivalent control approach, the equilibrium can be expressed as:

$$\overline{i_p} = \overline{v_p}G \tag{3}$$

$$u_{eq} = 1 - \frac{\overline{v_p}}{V_{dc}}, \tag{4}$$

where G is the average value of the variable g which is given by the outer loop of the control. u_{eq} represents the average value of the control signal u which is constrained between 0 and 1. Then, u_{eq} can be seen as the duty cycle of the converter. Like theoretical concept of sliding motion implies an infinite switching frequency, a hysteresis band of $\pm\Delta$ is used in order to implement the following switching law:

$$u = \begin{cases} 0 \ if \ S(x) > \Delta \\ 1 \ if \ S(x) < \Delta \end{cases} \tag{5}$$

As a consequence, switching period is defined as $T_s = t_{on} + t_{off}$. By considering constant slopes in the current of both intervals t_{on} $(u=1)$ and t_{off} $(u=0)$, time intervals can be derived as it is shown in Table 1.

Table 1. Mathematical procedure used to compute switching frequency

On interval $(u=1)$	Off interval $(u=0)$
$L\frac{di_L}{dt} = L\frac{\Delta}{t_{on}} = \overline{v_p}$	$L\frac{di_L}{dt} = L\frac{\Delta}{t_{off}} = \overline{v_p} - V_{dc}$
$t_{on} = \frac{L\Delta}{\overline{v_p}}$	$t_{off} = \frac{L\Delta}{V_{dc} - \overline{v_p}}$

$$T_s = \frac{L\Delta}{\overline{v_p}} + \frac{L\Delta}{V_{dc} - \overline{v_p}} = \frac{L\Delta V_{dc}}{\overline{v_p}(V_{dc} - \overline{v_p})} \tag{6}$$

Then, switching frequency is computed as:

$$f_s = \frac{\overline{v_p}(V_{dc} - \overline{v_p})}{L\Delta V_{dc}} \tag{7}$$

As it can be noted in (7), switching frequency depends on v_p and then on the environmental conditions. However, the expected variation of v_p is constrained by the value of conductance g which in turn is given by the MPPT algorithm. As it is illustrated in Fig. 5 where I–V characteristic of a PV module is represented for four irradiance values into the set $S = [S_{min}, S_{max}]$, conductance values are constrained into the set $g = [g_{min}, g_{max}]$ and in consequence, output voltage of the panel keeps into the set $v_p = [v_{plmin}, v_{pmax}]$. Therefore, as it can be also noted, voltage is always close to the open circuit voltage V_{OC}. This induces possible variations into a range of approximately a 25% of V_{OC} and then values above 60% of V_{OC}. Although these values have been deduced approximately, the behavior in the real case is very close.

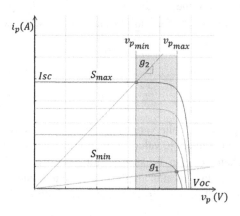

Fig. 5. PV module characteristic regarding operation limits of the converter in voltage and conductance.

Switching frequency is then constrained into the set $f_s = [f_{s_{min}}, f_{s_{max}}]$ and in consequence, the sampling period will be constrained into the set $T_s = [T_{s_{min}}, T_{s_{max}}]$. On the other hand, considering (4), duty cycle will be constrained into the set $D = u_{eq} = [D_{min}, D_{max}]$. Then, uncertainty with respect to the length of the time intervals t_{on} and t_{off} can be absorbed by including a variable interval t_{aux} into t_{off} and t_{on} in such a way that $T_s = T_{s_{min}} + t_{aux}$. In the implementation of the algorithm this time corresponds to the execution time of the routine WFE.

4 Implementation of the Control into the DSP

Implementation of the proposed control was accomplished using a DSP TMS320F28335 involving MPPT proposed in [34]. ADC module of the DSP is configured to 12 bits [35] using two acquisition channels. A single channel of General-Purpose Input-Output (GPIO) module [36] is used to carry out the signal u to the MOSFET driver. The same output is used as flag for the external interrupt service routine (EISR) generating the trigger to execute MAF, LFR and MPPT routines. The Enhanced Capture module (ECAP) [37] is used to measure the sampling frequency in order to update its value for the MPPT algorithm and compute difference equations of integrators. Implementation for DSP architecture is depicted in Fig. 6.

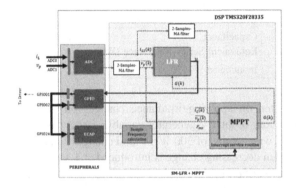

Fig. 6. Diagram describing the architecture of the proposed control into the DSP.

As a complement to the time diagram presented in Fig. 3 of Sect. 2 and the above description of the DSP implementation, the flowchart of the complete control is depicted in Fig. 7. As it can be expected, programming of the controller can be easily accomplished following this flowchart.

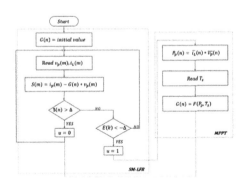

Fig. 7. Even triggered MPPT algorithm flowchart.

5   Simulated Results

To validate the proposed control several simulations were performed in PSIM software using model configured as the solar panel BLD80-36P and the MPPT introduced in [34]. Parameters of the converter and PV module are listed in Table 2.

Table 2. Simulation parameters used in PSIM

Element	Parameter	Symbol	Value	Units
Solar panel module (BLD80-36P)	Maximum power	P_{mp}	80	W
	Open-circuit voltage	V_{oc}	21.6	V
	Short-circuit current	I_{sc}	5.17	A
	Voltage at maximum power	V_{mp}	4.58	A
	Current at maximum power	I_{mp}	17.5	V
Capacitor	Capacitance	C	18	μF
	Equivalent Series Resistance (ESR)	R_c	1.9	mΩ
Inductor	Inductance	L	120	μH

The test consisted on applying irradiance changes on the solar module model regarding the behaviour of the PV generator variables. As it can be observed in Fig. 8, the irradiance starts with a value of 300 W/m^2 and changes suddenly to 800 W/m^2 at 2 s. After that, a sudden decreasing change is introduced at 4 s arriving to a final value of 600 W/m^2. As it is verified in the zoom of the power waveform for the three steady states of the test, system reaches the maximum power point. It is worth to mention that simulations involves errors of quantization and also discretization using the variable frequency of the sample and hold, which indicates that proposed implementation can be successfully carry out in a real DSP. Also, application of disturbances allows to known the response of the control in cases in which the commutation is not uniformly defined by the hysteresis band. As it is expected, there are no undesirable behaviors during transient response because minimum on and off periods are constrained digitally and then spurious commutations are not possible.

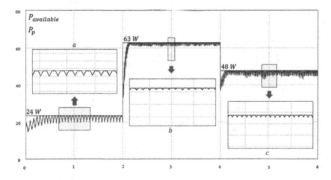

Fig. 8. Simulated results showing instantaneous power compared with maximum available power.

6 Experimental Results

In order to validate the proposed implementation with real constraints of the digital device and the power converter, a 100 W prototype of PV generator was tested in laboratory. The single-switch quadratic boost converter employed is composed by two Super Junction MOSFET APT94N60L2C3, two Silicon Carbide Schottky Diode C3D06060A, one inductor 1140-121K-RC (120 µH) and two input coupling capacitors C4ATHBW4900A3LJ (2 × 9 µF). Driver circuit for MOSFET was implemented using simple transistor based totem-pole circuits. Inductor current is measured by using an isolated closed-loop hall-effect transducer CAS-15-NP while voltage is measured using a simple voltage divider. Experimental setup for experimental test is composed by a solar panel BLD80-36P, a programmable load ITECH IT8512B+ configured as voltage source, an oscilloscope using a current probe.

In Fig. 9, inductor current is shown together with gate signal of the MOSFET and two digital signals generated from the DSP in order to observe execution of WFE routines corresponding to the on and off trigger events (2 × 5 µs) and also time interval required to execute MAF, LFR and MPPT algorithms (8 µs) when the converter operate at a switching frequency of 12.5 kHz.

Figure 10 shows measurements of current and voltage at the output of the solar panel. As it can be noted, power waveform shows the typical doubling frequency behaviour with respect to the voltage and current waveforms which verify operation at the maximum power point. Algorithm shows its typical efficiency around 99.8%.

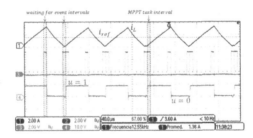

Fig. 9. Experimental results: showing execution times for algorithm routines.

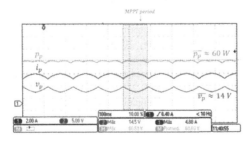

Fig. 10. Experimental results for PV module operating at a maximum power point of 60 W.

7 Conclusions

A novel implementation of the control of a PV generator into a DSP has been proposed in this paper. The event-triggered approach is developed using a nested loop architecture which allows improving computational cost and facilitate implementation of other outer controllers empowering its use in microgrid applications. As it was demonstrated using simulation and experimental results, the proposed implementation does not affect MPPT performance. The proposed architecture can be indistinctly employed to control power converters in the field of renewable energies especially in those in which boost converter based topologies are preferred. Although the idea was not emphasized throughout the paper, this implementation favors simple development of controllers designed on the basis of the sliding modes allowing taking advantage of its robustness and rapid response and also promoting its massive use in the future.

Acknowledgements. This research is being developed with the support of the *Departamento Nacional de Ciencia, Tecnología e Innovación COLCIENCIAS* under contract *CT 018-2016*. The results were obtained with assistance of students of the Research Hotbed on Power Electronic Conversion (SICEP), Grupo D+TEC, Universidad de Ibagué.

References

1. Jiayi, H., Chuanwen, J., Rong, X.: A review on distributed energy resources and MicroGrid. Renew. Sustain. Energy Rev. **12**(9), 2472–2483 (2008)
2. Lidula, N.W.A., Rajapakse, A.D.: Microgrids research: a review of experimental microgrids and test systems. Renew. Sustain. Energy Rev. **15**(1), 186–202 (2011)
3. Ustun, T.S., Ozansoy, C., Zayegh, A.: Recent developments in microgrids and example cases around the world—a review. Renew. Sustain. Energy Rev. **15**(8), 4030–4041 (2011)
4. IEEE 946-2004 (Revision of IEEE 946-1992): Recommended Practice for the Design of DC Auxiliary Power Systems for Generating Systems. Accessed 15 May 2018
5. IET Standards: Code of Practice for Low and Extra Low Voltage Direct Current Power Distribution in Buildings (2015)
6. Alsharif, R., Odavic, M.: Photovoltaic generators interfacing a DC micro-grid: design considerations for a double-stage boost power converter system. In: Proceedings of 18th European Conference on Power Electronics and Applications (EPE), Karlsruhe, pp. 1–10 (2016)
7. Bendib, B., Belmili, H., Krim, F.: A survey of the most used MPPT methods: Conventional and advanced algorithms applied for photovoltaic systems. Renew. Sustain. Energy Rev. **45**, 637–648 (2015)
8. Onat, N.: Recent developments in maximum power point tracking technologies for photovoltaic systems. Int. J. Photoenergy **2010**, 1–11 (2010). Article ID 245316
9. Abdelsalam, K., Massoud, A.M., Ahmed, S., Enjeti, P.N.: High-performance adaptive perturb and observe MPPT technique for photovoltaic-based microgrids. IEEE Trans. Power Electron. **26**(4), 1010–1021 (2011)
10. Seyedmahmoudian, A., Oo, M.T., Arangarajan, V., Shafiullah, G.M., Stojcevski, A.: Low cost MPPT controller for a photovoltaic-based microgrid. In: Power Engineering Conference (AUPEC), Perth, pp. 1–6 (2014)

11. Yuan, W., Yang, J., Sun, Y., Han, H., Hou, X., Su, M.: A novel operation mode for PV-storage independent microgrids with MPPT based droop control. In: Proceedings of IEEE 3rd International Future Energy Electronics Conference (IFEEC), Kaohsiung, pp. 936–941 (2017)

12. Lopez-Santos, O., García, G., Martinez-Salamero, L.: Derivation of a global model of a two-stage photovoltaic microinverter using sliding-mode control. In: Proceedings of IEEE 13th Brazilian Power Electronics Conference (COBEP), Fortaleza, pp. 1–6 (2015)

13. Lopez-Santos, O.: Contribution to the DC-AC conversion in photovoltaic systems: module oriented converters, pp. 1–248. Ph.D. dissertation, Institut National de Sciences Apliquées (INSA) de Toulouse (2015)

14. Maity, S., Sahu, P.K.: Modeling and analysis of a fast and robust module-integrated analog photovoltaic MPP tracker. IEEE Trans. Power Electron. **31**(1), 280–291 (2016)

15. Leyva, R., Alonso, C., Queinnec, I., Cid-Pastor, A., Lagrange, D., Martinez-Salamero, L.: MPPT of photovoltaic systems using extremum - seeking control. IEEE Trans. Aerosp. Electron. Syst. **42**(1), 249–258 (2006)

16. Reza Tousi, S.M., Moradi, M.H., Basir, N.S., Nemati, M.: A function-based maximum power point tracking method for photovoltaic systems. IEEE Trans. Power Electron. **31**(3), 2120–2128 (2016)

17. Levron, Y., Shmilovitz, D.: Maximum power point tracking employing sliding mode control. IEEE Trans. Circuits Syst. I Regul. Pap. **60**(3), 724–732 (2013)

18. Cabal C., et al.: Adaptive digital MPPT control for photovoltaic applications. In: Proceedings of ISIE IEEE International Symposium on Industrial Electronics, Vigo, pp. 2414–2419 (2007)

19. Jiang, Y., Qahouq, J.A.A., Haskew, T.A.: Adaptive step size with adaptive-perturbation-frequency digital MPPT controller for a single-sensor photovoltaic solar system. IEEE Trans. Power Electron. **28**(7), 3195–3205 (2013)

20. Microchip Technology. dsPIC30F4011/12 Data Sheet: High Performance Digital Signal Controllers, pp. 1–228 (2005)

21. Techakittiroj, K., Aphiratsakun, N., Threevithayanon, W., Nyun, S.: TMS320F241 DSP boards for power-electronics applications. AU J. Technol. **6**(4), 168–172 (2003)

22. Bosque, J.M., Valderrama-Blavi, H., Flores-Bahamonde, F., Vidal-Idiarte, E., Martínez-Salamero, L.: Using low-cost microcontrollers to implement variable hysteresis-width comparators for switching power converters. IET Power Electron. **11**(5), 787–795 (2017)

23. Donkers, M.C.F., Heemels, W.: Output-based event-triggered control with guaranteed $\mathscr{L}_\infty$-gain and improved event-triggering. In: Proceedings of 49th IEEE Conference on Decision and Control (CDC), Atlanta, pp. 3246–325 (2010)

24. Rathore, N., Fulwani, D.: Event triggered control scheme for power converters. In: Proceedings of 42nd Annual Conference on IEEE Industrial Electronics Society (IECON), Florence, pp. 1342–1347 (2016)

25. Cid-Pastor, A., Martinez-Salamero, L., El Aroudi, A., Giral, R., Calvente, J., Leyva, R.: Synthesis of loss-free-resistors based on sliding-mode control and its applications in power processing. Control Eng. Pract. **21**(5), 689–699 (2013)

26. Haroun, R., El Aroudi, A., Cid-Pastor, A., Martinez-Salamero, L.: Sliding mode control of output-parallel-connected two-stage boost converters for PV systems. In: IEEE 11th International Multi-Conference on Systems Signals & Devices (SSD), Barcelona, pp. 1–6 (2014)

27. Marcos-Pastor, A., Vidal-Idiarte, E., Cid-Pastor, A., Martinez-Salamero, L.: Digital loss-free resistor for power factor correction applications. In: Proceedings of 39th Annual Conference of the IEEE Industrial Electronics Society (IECON), Vienna, pp. 3468–3473 (2013)

28. Marple, S.L., Marple, S.L.: Digital Spectral Analysis: with Applications, vol. 5. Prentice-Hall, Englewood Cliffs (1987)
29. Golestan, S., Ramezani, M., Guerrero, J.M., Freijedo, F.D., Monfared, M.: Moving average filter-based phase-locked loops: performance analysis and design guidelines. IEEE Trans. Power Electron. **29**(6), 2750–2763 (2014)
30. Lopez Santos, O., et al.: Analysis, design and implementation of a static conductance-based MPPT method. IEEE Trans. Power Electron (2018, in Press). https://doi.org/10.1109/tpel.2018.2835814
31. Texas Instruments: TMS320x2833x, Analog-to-Digital Converter (ADC) Module (2007)
32. Texas Instruments: TMS320x2833x, 2823x system control and interrupts (2007)
33. Texas Instruments: TMS320x2833x, 2801x, 2804x Enhanced Capture (eCAP) Module (2007)
34. Hua, C., Lin, J., Shen, C.: Implementation of a DSP-controlled photovoltaic system with peak power tracking. IEEE Trans. Ind. Electron. **45**(1), 99–107 (1998)
35. Youssef, A., Telbany, M.E., Zekry, A.: Reconfigurable generic FPGA implementation of fuzzy logic controller for MPPT of PV systems. Renew. Sustain. Energy Rev. **82**, 1313–1319 (2018)
36. Patel, S., Shireen, W.: Fast converging digital MPPT control for photovoltaic (PV) applications. In: Proceedings of IEEE Power and Energy Society General Meeting, Detroit, pp. 1–6 (2011)
37. Safari, A., Mekhilef, S.: Simulation and hardware implementation of incremental conductance MPPT with direct control method using cuk converter. IEEE Trans. Ind. Electron. **58**(4), 1154–1161 (2011)

Integration of Distributed Generation in Demand Response Programs: Study Case

Luis A. Arias[1], Edwin Rivas[2], Francisco Santamaria[2], and Andres D. Quevedo[2(✉)]

[1] Faculty of Engineering, Universidad Autónoma de Colombia,
Bogotá, Colombia
lincarias@yahoo.com
[2] Faculty of Engineering, Universidad Distrital Francisco José de Caldas,
Bogotá, Colombia
{erivas, fsantamariap}@udistrital.edu.co,
adquevedor@correo.udistrital.edu.co

Abstract. In this paper a strategy for integration of Distributed Generation (DG) in Demand Response (DR) program is proposed. This strategy allows users of DR increase both the number of participation or the manageable power in disconnecting power program along the day. This paper explores the improvements of voltage profile in an IEEE node test feeder when a DR program is deployed and additionally a DG supply is including, but in a different approach since this power DG supply do not will be injected directly to distribution network but else this one going to be an additional power of DR program in the users that have DG available.

Keywords: Demand response program · Distributed Generation
Distribution network · Energy market · Energy utilities · Integrating strategy

1 Introduction

DR programs reflect changes in end-user electricity consumption, user consumption patterns in response to changing electricity prices over time or to encourage less use of electricity at times of high electricity prices or also to ensure security of supply when the reliability of the system is threatened [1].

The International Energy Agency notes that the demand energy management by users is the key factor to reduce the global consumption, and even states that on rational and efficient consumption scenarios the global energy demand toward 2035 could be reduced by half of the projected [2]. The possibility of managing consumption from the demand side has been pointed out as the desired management "instrument" for energy systems, especially in distribution networks due to different factors, such as the liberalization of the electricity supply market [3].

This liberalization allows any consumer, in addition to controlling their consumption, to acquire energy among different existing companies or to benefit from a "fee-based" supply scheme. Through which the consumers acquire energy from suppliers, paying integral tariff composed by a fixed fee depending of power contracted

© Springer Nature Switzerland AG 2018
J. C. Figueroa-García et al. (Eds.): WEA 2018, CCIS 915, pp. 561–572, 2018.
https://doi.org/10.1007/978-3-030-00350-0_46

and a variable fee depending of consume, these tariff are published in official state bulletins and whose prices are updated periodically [4]. As an example, in the California market, there are different demand response programs designed to allow end-users to contribute with load energy reduction individually or through a demand response provider [5].

This paper explores the improvements of voltage profile in an IEEE test feeder when a DR program is deployed and DG supply is included. The power supplied by DG is not injected directly into the distribution network, but represents an additional power of the DR program for users with DG available.

The paper is organized as follows: Sect. 2 describes the main characteristics of demand response programs; Sect. 3 shows the line segment data, power parameters for loads in the IEEE test feeder and the users that participate in the demand response program; Sect. 4 describes the operation details of the DR program and the strategy to include the renewable DG supply; Sect. 5 exposes the results and discussion. Finally, Sect. 6 gives the main conclusions about the potential of proposed DG supply integration strategy and the technical improvements obtained.

2 Demand Response Programs Based on Incentives

The DR programs based on incentives have as main objective to reduce peak demand, offering to users pays or penalties according to the program in which they participate [6, 7]. Among the main programs of this kind are:

- Demand offer: In this program energy is sold at the stock price and participates in the economic dispatch.
- Direct load control: There is an aggregator agent that perform the cuts remotely when it is considered appropriate, aiming improve reliability of the system in high demand hours [8].
- Emergency: When an emergency event is announced and its duration time or load cut is defined, the load cut is performed voluntarily and there is not penalty.
- Curtailable load: Similar to emergency case but disconnections is not voluntary and penalties for non-fulfilment may be imposed [9].
- Demand as a resource of capacity: The suppliers perform load reductions in the face of contingencies, non-fulfilment may result in penalties.
- Frequency control: It is used when demand and supply mismatch is presented, the reserve is spinning reserve if it can act quickly and non-spinning reserve if it takes more than ten minutes [10].
- Regulation services: Demand increase or decrease in response to real time signals send by the system operator.

3 Test Network: IEEE 34 Node Test Feeder

In this paper the IEEE 34 node test feeder was selected as electrical test network. Figure 1 shows the radial topology of the distribution network. The demand for the loads is defined by the standard model de IEEE 34 nodes. The minimum load of users that has less than 5 kW was modified and fixed at 5 kW. The three users on which the management of DR and DG resources is implemented are highlighted in light gray.

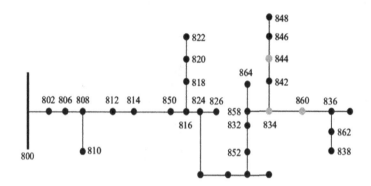

Fig. 1. IEEE 34 node test feeder for testing DR program and DG inclusion

Line segment data are shown in Table 1.

Table 1. Line segment data for IEEE-34 Network

Section	Length (km)	Section	Length (km)	Section	Length (km)
800–802	0.786	824–826	0.092	844–846	0.111
802–806	0.527	824–828	0.026	846–848	0.016
806–808	0.982	828–830	0.623	850–816	0.009
808–810	0.178	830–854	0.016	852–832	0.003
808–812	1.143	832–858	0.149	854–852	1.123
812–814	0.906	832–888	0.003	854–856	0.711
814–850	0.003	834–842	0.009	858–834	0.178
816–818	0.052	834–860	0.062	858–864	0.049
816–824	0.311	836–840	0.026	860–836	0.082
818–820	1.468	836–862	0.009	862–838	0.148
820–822	0.419	842–844	0.041	888–890	0.322

The parameters for the loads in the IEEE network are shown in Table 2. The ten users that participate in the demand response program during a day are underlined and bold. The criteria to select those users was the active power.

Table 2. Power parameters for loads in the IEEE-34 network

Load	Power		Load	Power	
	Active (kW)	Reactive (kVAr)		Active (kW)	Reactive (kVAr)
816	5	2.5	824	24.5	12
842	5	2.5	806	27.5	14.5
864	5	2.5	802	27.5	14.5
856	5	2.5	846	34	17
854	5	2.5	**840**	**47**	**31**
828	5.5	2.5	**830**	**48.5**	**21.5**
832	7.5	3.5	**836**	**61**	**31.5**
810	8	4	**822**	**67.5**	**35**
808	8	4	**848**	**71.5**	**53.5**
862	14	7	**820**	**84.5**	**43.5**
838	14	7	**834**	**89**	**45**
818	17	8.5	**860**	**174**	**106**
826	20	10	**844**	**432**	**329**
858	24.5	12.5	**890**	**450**	**225**

In Table 3 is shown the manageable power of each user participating in the DR program. According to national and international standards and regulations, the level of manageable power defined for users correspond to 5–7% of its installed capacity according DR Europe program 2015 in international context [11, 12]. Three of the users selected for DR program have DG, two with a renewable resource (photovoltaic system) and one with a microturbine.

Table 3. Parameters of the users participating in the DR program

USER	Installed capacity (kW)	Manageable power (kW)	DG type	DG power (kVA)
840	47	3.2	–	
830	48.5	3.395	–	
836	61	4.27	–	
822	67.5	4.725	–	
848	71.5	5.005	–	
820	84.5	5.915	–	
834	89	6.23	Photovoltaic	10
860	174	12.18	Photovoltaic	15
844	432	30.24	–	
890	450	31.5	Microturbine	125

For each user, a direct load control has been designed based on a programmable logic controller (PLC), which can be controlled directly by the aggregator or by the user, depending on what is established in the contract.

To illustrate how is the actuation dynamics to interrupt or carry out load shedding of users a base test scenario has been proposed, where 10 users committed to participate in the DR program, according to contract established previously with aggregator. Each user has been characterized taking into account the following parameters: installed capacity, manageable power, presence of DG and its power and finally the hours of participation of each user along the day in the DR program according the interruptility contract. In Table 4 are shown the hours of participation of the DR program for each user in the base test scenario.

Table 4. Hours of user participation in the DR program, according to their interruptibility contract

Hour user	1	2	3	4	5	6	7	8	9	10	11	12
840	1	1	1	1	0	0	0	0	0	0	1	0
830	1	0	0	0	0	1	1	0	0	1	0	0
836	0	1	0	1	1	0	0	0	0	0	0	0
822	0	0	1	0	0	1	0	0	0	0	0	1
848	1	0	0	0	0	0	1	0	0	0	1	0
820	0	0	0	0	1	0	0	0	0	0	0	0
834	0	0	1	0	0	1	1	1	1	1	1	0
860	0	0	0	0	0	0	0	0	1	1	0	1
844	0	0	0	0	0	0	0	1	0	0	1	0
890	1	0	1	0	0	0	0	1	0	0	0	1
Hour user	13	14	15	16	17	18	19	20	21	22	23	24
840	0	0	0	0	0	0	0	0	0	0	1	0
830	1	0	0	0	1	0	0	0	0	0	0	0
836	0	1	0	1	0	0	0	0	1	0	0	0
822	0	0	1	0	0	0	0	0	0	0	1	1
848	1	0	0	0	0	0	1	0	1	0	1	1
820	0	0	0	1	1	1	0	0	0	0	0	1
834	0	1	0	0	0	1	0	0	0	1	1	0
860	0	0	0	0	1	0	1	1	0	1	1	0
844	1	0	1	0	0	0	0	0	1	1	0	1
890	0	1	0	0	0	0	0	1	0	0	0	0

Note: 1- Disconnectable power available,
0-Disconnectable power unavailable

Users can choose different hours in a demand response service. Participation during a day does not exceed 8 h because users do not usually participate in rates higher than 30% throughout the day if their comfort is affected [13].

As a base case it is assumed that the load control is executed by the aggregator. In this paper the result of the DR program are evaluated for the peak hour (Hour 22). The devices available to do the load management for each user for the hour 22 are shown in Table 5.

Table 5. Devices used by the available users at 22 h to manage their load.

User	Manageable power (kW)	Manageable loads	Quantity	Power per unit (kW)	Total power (kW)
834	6.23	Elevator	1	9.5	9.5
		Lighting system	40	0.064	2.56
		Entry phone	10	0.024	0.24
860	12.18	Elevator	1	9.5	9.5
		Air conditioning	2	3.91	7.82
844	30.24	Electric stair motor	2	2.5	10
		Cargo elevator	2	14.7	29.14
		Lighting system	60	0.030	1.8

4 Operation of the DR Program Including DG

4.1 Base Test Scenario

As described earlier, the DR program works all day; however, this paper the detailed operation of the DR program is presented for the 22:00 h. In addition, it was established that the disconnectable power required by the network operator at this time is 40 kW.

According to the information provided in Table 4, users 834, 860 and 844 are available to meet the requirement of the network operator, as follows: User 834 decreases consumption by 6 kW, the user 860 decreases its consumption by 10 kW and the user 844 decreases its consumption by 24 kW.

4.2 Direct Load Control Strategy

According to the requirements, the aggregator will disconnect loads until reaching 40 kW, although, if required, the aggregator can disconnect the 48.65 kW corresponding to total manageable power by the three users in this time. The operation of the direct load control strategy from the aggregator to user 834 is presented below, in response to the request to reduce consumption. The user 834 participates with a disconnection of 6 kW during the hour 22, which means reducing his energy consumption by 6 kWh.

In order to achieve the reduction of energy consumption, the stepped disconnection of a group of 40 luminaires and the reduction of the consumption of an elevator are proposed. With respect to the stepped disconnection of the 40 luminaires, these were divided into 5 groups of 8 luminaires to perform a better control. Table 6 shows how staging was done to disconnect the luminaires in 10-min steps. The energy not consumed by the luminaires during the hour is evaluated with Eq. 1.

$$P_{cons} = \frac{\sum_{i}^{n}(P_{inti}) \cdot (t_{inti})}{60} \tag{1}$$

Where:

P_{inti}:   Power consumed in the interval (in W)
t_{inti}:   Interval time (in minutes)
P_{cons}:   1280 W

Considering that luminaires consumption is 2560 W along the hour is the same as during each interval time the luminaries consumes 427 W, means that with luminaires management control is possible decrease the power from 2560 W to 1280 W, that is to say a saved energy consumption of 1280 Wh. The power saving by the luminaires is shown in Fig. 2, the sum of power consumed during the hour 22 corresponding to the 1280 W which must manage the aggregator.

Table 6. Steps to disconnect different luminaire groups from the user 834

GROUP OF LUMINAIRES	TIME STEPS (MINUTES)					
	0-10	10-20	20-30	30-40	40-50	50-60
G1						
G2						
G3						
G4						
G5						

☐ ACTIVE LUMINAIRE   ■ INACTIVE LUMINAIRE

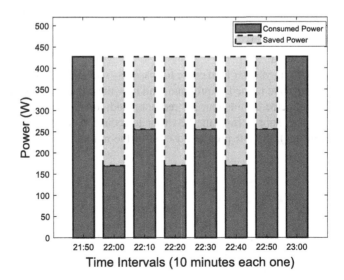

Fig. 2. Power consumption due to luminaires of user 834 during the hour 22.

To complete a saving of 6 kWh it is necessary to ensure an additional reduction of 4.71 kWh. To achieve this goal, the 9.5 kW elevator will be controlled by the use of a variable frequency drive (VFD). The mechanism operates from Eq. 2.

$$P = \frac{(T) \cdot (n)}{9.54} \tag{2}$$

Where:

P: Power of the electromechanical elevator system (in kW)
T: Torque of the electromechanical elevator system (in Nm)
n: Revolutions per minute of the electric motor, RPM

The RPM of the elevator motors are proportional to the frequency of the network, according to Eq. 3

$$n = \frac{(f)(60)}{p} \tag{3}$$

Where:

f: Electrical network frequency (in Hz)
p: Number of magnetic poles of motor

According to the datasheet of the elevator, for an ascent speed of 2.8 m/s and a nominal RPM of electromechanical system of 600 RPM at 60 Hz, the power consumption is 9.5 kW. This power should be reduced to 4.24 kW to achieve the objective of the DR program. To achieve this reduction, it was established that the best option is to vary the frequency from 60 to 30 Hz, maintaining the same torque and obtaining a nominal ascent speed of 1.4 m/s, which is within the admissible limits for commercial elevators.

In summary, by managing the energy consumption in the group of luminaires and in the electromechanical elevator device, a reduction of 6 kW is achieved at the request of the DR program for the hour 22. For the users 860 and 844, similar management strategies were proposed.

In Fig. 3 is shown the power load curve for base test scenario (black line) of each of the nodes who participate in the DR program, and how the curve is modified according to DR program contracted for the hour 22 (red line), additionally the case when the DR program uses the DG supply from the 834 user to reduce even more the aggregated load curve (green line), the DR program use all of the nominal power of the DG.

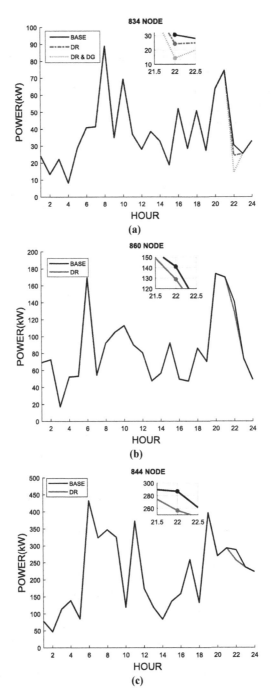

Fig. 3. Base, DR and DG loads curves for users that participate in the DR program at 22 h, (a) 834 Node, (b) 860 Node and (c) 844 Node (Color figure online)

5 Analysis of Results

In order to carry out the power flows for the three scenarios (base, DR and DR & DG), the IEEE network was implemented in the DigSilent® software. In Fig. 4 is shown the voltage levels in all the nodes of the system for the first two scenarios at hour 22. It is observed that the voltage drop is greater as the nodes are farther away from the substation. 14 nodes have tensions below the minimum level allowed by the Colombian regulation (0.9 p.u).

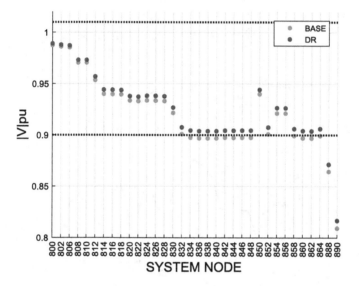

Fig. 4. Voltage levels of the system in the base and DR scenarios at 22 h

When the DR program acts, the power decreases by 40 kW (6 kW of user 834, 10 kW of user 860 and 24 kW of user 844), which is equivalent to reducing 3.24% of the total power of the system. An improvement in the voltage level of all nodes is observed, of the 14 nodes that had a voltage level below the allowed, only the nodes 888 and 890 are maintained in this state.

The following scenario proposes the inclusion of DG, for which the DG available in user 834 will be included. As part of the DR program, in this case the user can increase his manageable power up to the agreed value plus the DG supply, that is, user 834 goes from disconnecting 6 kW to disconnecting 16 kW at 22 h.

In Fig. 5 is shown that the inclusion of DG does not significantly modify the voltage levels of the system and only a small change is observed in the nodes close to the 834. This is due to the fact that the disconnected power only represents 4.05% of the total demand at hour 22.

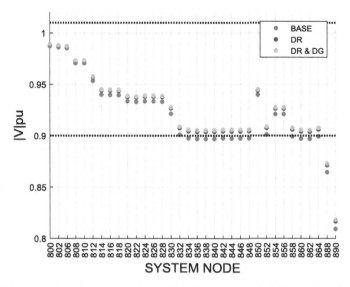

Fig. 5. Voltage level of the system when both DR program and DG are taking into account

6   Conclusions

With participation of users in DR programs, the voltage level of the users and their neighbors is improved depending on the load reduction. For the study case, the branch circuits beginning from user 832 improve with the use of DR program and a slight improvement is observed when the DG is used to decrease the power demand of the circuit.

The strategy of increasing the participation of users with DG sources in DR programs allows to improve the voltage levels; it also excludes the need for synchronization required when there is a direct connection between the DG and the distribution network.

Inclusion of DG as complement of DR programs results as effective way to reduce energy orders to generation power plants and avoids inconveniences related to direct connecting DG elements to electrical networks.

References

1. Shen, B., Ghatikar, G., Lei, Z., Li, J., Wikler, G., Martin, P.: The role of regulatory reforms, market changes, and technology development to make demand response a viable resource in meeting energy challenges. Appl. Energy **130**, 814–823 (2014). https://doi.org/10.1016/j. apenergy.2013.12.069
2. International Renewable Energy Agency: Renewable power generation costs in 2014 (2015)
3. CAISO, Goodin, J.: Demand Response & Proxy Demand Resources. Mechanical Engineering, pp. 1–3 (2011). 9

4. International Energy Agency IEA: Energy Technology Perspectives 2014 Energy Technology Perspectives 2014 (2014). https://doi.org/10.1787/energy_tech-2010-en
5. Behrangrad, M.: A review of demand side management business models in the electricity market. Renew. Sustain. Energy Rev. **47**, 270–283 (2015)
6. Fotouhi Ghazvini, M.A., Faria, P., Ramos, S., Morais, H., Vale, Z.: Incentive-based demand response programs designed by asset-light retail electricity providers for the day-ahead market. Energy **82**, 786–799 (2015). https://doi.org/10.1016/j.energy.2015.01.090
7. Wijaya, T.K., Vasirani, M., Villumsen, J.C., Aberer, K., Generation, A.L.: An economic analysis of pervasive, incentive-based demand response, pp. 331–337 (2015)
8. Lu, S., et al.: Control strategies for distributed energy resources to maximize the use of wind power in rural microgrids. In: IEEE Power Energy Society General Meeting, pp. 1–8 (2011). https://doi.org/10.1109/pes.2011.6039787
9. Koliou, E., Eid, C., Chaves-ávila, J.P., Hakvoort, R.A.: Demand response in liberalized electricity markets: analysis of aggregated load participation in the German balancing mechanism. Energy **71**, 245–254 (2014). https://doi.org/10.1016/j.energy.2014.04.067
10. Bayat, M., Sheshyekani, K., Hamzeh, M., Rezazadeh, A.: Coordination of distributed energy resources and demand response for voltage and frequency support of MV microgrids. IEEE Trans. Power Syst. **31**, 1506–1516 (2016). https://doi.org/10.1109/TPWRS.2015.2434938
11. Singh, S.N., Ostergaard, J.: Use of demand response in electricity markets: an overview and key issues. In: 2010 7th International Conference on the European Energy Mark (EEM), pp. 1–6 (2010). https://doi.org/10.1109/eem.2010.5558728
12. Comisión de Regulación de Energía y Gas (2016). Creg025-2016.pdf
13. Rahman, M.M., Arefi, A., Shafiullah, G.M., Hettiwatte, S.: A new approach to voltage management in unbalanced low voltage networks using demand response and OLTC considering consumer preference. Int. J. Electr. Power Energy Syst. **99**, 11–27 (2018). https://doi.org/10.1016/j.ijepes.2017.12.034

Adaptive Sampling Frequency Synchronized Reference Generator for Grid Connected Power Converters

Oswaldo Lopez-Santos[1]([⊠]) [iD], Sebastián Tilaguy-Lezama[1], and Germain Garcia[2]

[1] Universidad de Ibagué, 730001 Ibagué, Colombia
oswaldo.lopez@unibague.edu.co
[2] LAAS-CNRS, Univ. Toulouse, Toulouse, France

Abstract. This paper introduces a simplified method for digital generation of high-quality references required for control of single-phase grid-connected (GC) power converters, which can generate synchronized sinusoidal waveforms at the same frequency of the input signal or its harmonics. Therefore, its application can be useful for active power filtering, high power factor rectification, and grid integration of renewable energy sources. A hybrid analog-digital implementation is proposed integrating an Adaptive Sampling Frequency Moving Average Filter (ASF-MAF) and a discrete-time Proportional-Integral (PI) controller into a Digital Signal Processor (DSP) operating with a sampling frequency defined by an external hardware-based Voltage Controlled Oscillator (VCO). The main advantages attributed to the method are immunity to harmonic content, accuracy in computations despite of frequency changes, flexibility to produce phase displacements and reduced computational cost. Performance of the proposal was verified by means of simulation and experimental results.

Keywords: Sinusoidal reference generation · Adaptive sampling frequency Grid connected converter · Grid synchronization · Power converters

1 Introduction

From the phase controlled rectifiers until the more recent applications in power quality conditioning, grid connected (GC) converters require frequency and phase measurements as references to operate adequately. However, the way in which these measurements are obtained or used can be different from one application to another. For example, line-commutated controller rectifiers require knowing the zero crossing of the grid voltage in order to have a reference to generate the firing angles of thyristors [1]. In other cases, for example in high power factor (HPF) rectifiers [2], active power filters (APF) [3] or grid-connected photovoltaic (PV) generators [4], frequency and phase of the grid voltage are required to generate reference waveforms to control the shape of the current extracted or injected into the grid.

The first and simplest open-loop technique to get synchronized references from grid voltages is zero crossing detection (ZCD). This technique considers zero crossing as an

© Springer Nature Switzerland AG 2018
J. C. Figueroa-García et al. (Eds.): WEA 2018, CCIS 915, pp. 573–587, 2018.
https://doi.org/10.1007/978-3-030-00350-0_47

event giving an absolute reference to generate control signals. The main disadvantage of ZCD is sensitivity to noise and harmonic content because the zero crossing can take place a lot of times in a period deteriorating considerably the reliability of the system [5]. After many years in application and some improvements, this solution continue being acceptable [6]. Because of the proliferation of industrial electronics in the last decades, nonlinear behavior in currents of distribution systems accentuated, affecting the quality of voltage, and consequently calling for a rethinking of synchronization systems. As the most used closed-loop technique, the phase looked loop (PLL) is today established thanks to efforts of researchers comparing existing methods and improving them to increase the robustness to deal with frequency, phase, amplitude, harmonic content, noise and DC offset disturbances [7, 8].

The basic but not obligatory architecture of the PLL includes a phase detector (PD), a loop filter (LF) and a voltage controlled oscillator (VCO). The PD is a signal comparator which gives information about the phase error considering a value of zero as reference. Although the PD can be implemented using an improved ZCD avoiding asymmetries or deformities, its use is not recommended. This leads to the use of PD based in mathematical computations such as multiplication (product-type PD), quadrature shifting (quadrature signal generation based PD, QSG [9]) or trigonometric function transformation [10] among others. Product-type PD is preferred because of its simplicity but it has as drawback the need of a LF of high order or high rejection capability in order to eliminate ripple component at double frequency. One of the techniques employed to obtain improved phase comparison can be also useful for orthogonal signal generation (OSG) which consist on having references with phase shift of exactly 90° [11]. The simplest way to obtain that result is to implement a time delay equivalent to the needed phase shift. However, as expected, accuracy of this method is very sensitive to frequency changes. The use of derivatives allows obtaining phase displacement with some immunity to frequency variation but system becomes sensitive to noise. By using adaptive frequency in the implementation of a digital PLL, the phase displacement can be associated to an exact number of samples which is easily accomplished using a memory stack and offers a very good performance in comparison with the other mentioned approaches. Additionally, it is worth to mention that this property can be very useful in the case of three phase or multiphase systems in which also accurate phase displacements are required (power rectifiers and inverters).

The simplest LF that can be used in PLL is a first order low pass filter in series with a proportional integral (PI) controller enforcing zero phase error. To improve the performance and robustness of the closed-loop, more complex LF techniques have been proposed, and among them, it is important to highlight the use of discrete Kalman filter (DKF) [12], complex coefficient digital [13], digital Butterworth and adaptive notch filters (ANF) [14]. Naturally, implementation of all of these techniques increases considerably the computational cost of the PLL system. Other interesting technique which has been widely applied as low pass filter in digital versions of PLL is the moving average filter (MAF) [15, 16]. A MAF computes the average of a constant number of previous samples acquired during a time window whose width is approximately one period of the input signal. When a constant sampling frequency is used, the period of the grid cannot be divided into an integer number of sampling periods which implies a loss of accuracy. Although some estimation methods can help to overcome this drawback keeping constant the sampling frequency, adaptive sampling frequency MAF (ASF-MAF) is a more effective solution [17]. ASF can be obtained by approximating the number of samples per cycle to the nearest value or, on the contrary by adapting the sampling frequency. Both alternatives make considerably complex the implementation of the synchronization system.

Most of the PLL configurations mentioned so far are implemented digitally using microcontrollers or digital signal processors (DSP). However, the more widely applied digital PLLs (DPLLs) in power electronics are based on the use of common integrated PLL integrated circuits (IC) such as CD4046 and 74LS297 [18, 19]. These ICs incorporate PC and VOC modules and provide connections for external compensation loops or external frequency dividers. As drawback, this type of PLL cannot give a notion of the amplitude of the input signal and hence its use in many applications is limited. Internal modules of these PLL ICs can be used separately and then they can be incorporated in other control loops as it is performed in this work.

A first version of our hybrid analog-digital implementation of reference generation uses an IC-based PLL generating the clock to reproduce a discretized sine waveform previously stored in the memory of a microcontroller [20]. This implementation has been successfully tested in the control of the output stage of a solar microinverter [21–23], and later with the integration of active filtering function in the same device [24]. Although, it is simple and effective, the main drawback of this work is that the phase detector was based on ZCD. This paper presents a new proposal in which the references generator is completely implemented into a DSP using an external analog VCO module (CD4046 IC) in order to produce the sampling rate for digital control algorithms. Main advantages of the proposal are simplicity, immunity to harmonic content and frequency disturbances, possibility to generate accurately shifted orthogonal signals, reduced processing time and low memory expense. Additionally, internal functions developed for PLL can be also used for other control algorithms facilitating computations obtained from per cycle signal analysis (mean values, RMS values, total harmonic distortion (THD), power factor (PF) and others).

The rest of the paper is organized as follows: Sect. 2 presents a general description of the proposed synchronized reference generator. After that, in Sect. 3, the control loop developed to ensure phase and frequency synchronization is analysed and subsequently digital implementation is discussed in Sect. 4. Simulation results regarding rejection of phase and frequency disturbances are presented in Sect. 5. Experimental results testing the system with both ideal and distorted grid voltage conditions are presented in Sect. 6. Finally, conclusions are presented in Sect. 7.

2 General Description of the System

A general block diagram representing a grid connected converter controlled using a digital control incorporating the proposed synchronized reference generator is depicted in Fig. 1. The reference generator is embedded into the DSP together with a digital PLL and the control algorithms. The PD of the PLL receives measurement of the grid voltage $v_g(t)$ and compares it with the internally generated orthogonal reference $r_q(t)$. The output of the PD is averaged by the MAF obtaining a representation of the phase shift which is in turn processed by a digital PI (DPI) controller in order to enforce synchronization in frequency and phase. Output of the DPI controller is taken out of the DSP through the hardware digital PWM module (DPWM). High frequency component of PWM signal is eliminated using a low pass filter (LPF), allowing using the mean value as input of an external VCO to generate the base sampling frequency for all task into the DSP. In addition to the above mentioned orthogonal signal $r_q(t)$, reference generator produces the waveforms $r_x(t)$ which in turn are used as references for the control of the GC converter. Like the control of the converter is embedded in the DSP, analog to digital conversion of voltage and current measurements $v_x(t)$ and $i_x(t)$ is also incorporated in order to generate the control signals $u_x(t)$.

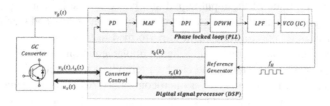

Fig. 1. Block diagram of the proposed reference generator integrated into the control of a power converter.

3 Mathematical Analysis and Modeling

To model dynamic behaviour of the system, simplified transfer functions of PD, MAF, PI, PWM, LPF and VCO components are obtained. Thereby, a loop transfer function of the PLL can be obtained facilitating design of compensator.

3.1 Linear Model of the PD

As conventionally, the grid voltage with harmonic content can be defined as:

$$v_g(t) = V_{g1}\sin \omega_o t + V_{g3}\sin(3\omega_o t + \phi_3)\ldots + V_{gn}\sin(n\omega_o t + \phi_n), \tag{1}$$

where $\omega_o = 2\pi f_o$ is the fundamental frequency of the grid voltage. The orthogonal reference generated by the system is defined as:

$$r_q(t) = \cos(\omega t + \phi), \tag{2}$$

where $\omega = 2\pi f$ with $f \neq f_o$ and $\phi \neq 0$. A product-type PD is used to compare the input signal $v_g(t)$ with the orthogonal signal $r_q(t)$. Having that the signal $r_q(t)$ has only a frequency component which is close to the fundamental frequency of the $v_g(t)$, it is easily to demonstrate that the product of $r_q(t)$ with the harmonic content of $v_g(t)$ give components beyond double of the grid frequency. Then, it is obtained that:

$$pd(t, \phi) = r_q(t)v_g(t) \approx \frac{V_{g1}}{2} \left[\underbrace{\sin((\omega_o - \omega)t - \phi)}_{LF} + \underbrace{\sin((\omega_o + \omega)t + \phi)}_{HF} \right] \quad (3)$$

As it can be noted, HF term has only a frequency component almost at the double of the grid frequency. Then, this term is not considered in the model of the PD. By defining $\Delta f = f_o - f$, it can be obtained that:

$$pd(t, \phi) \approx \frac{V_{g1}}{2} \sin 2\pi \Delta ft \cos \phi - \frac{V_{g1}}{2} \cos 2\pi \Delta ft \sin \phi \quad (4)$$

For values of ϕ and Δf close to zero, $pd(t, \phi)$ can be approximated as:

$$pd(t, \phi) \approx V_{g1} \pi \Delta ft - \frac{V_{g1}}{2} \phi \quad (5)$$

By applying the Laplace transform, it is obtained that:

$$PD(s) = \underbrace{V_{g1} \pi}_{K_{pd}} \frac{1}{s} \Delta F(s) + \underbrace{0.5 V_{g1}}_{K_\phi} \Phi(s) \quad (6)$$

By constraining possible phase variations of the closed loop system lower than $\pi/4$, then, gain of the transfer function $PD(s)$ will vary in the interval between $2.22V_g$ and $3.14V_g$ approximately. Then, to obtain a linear model a gain in the middle of this interval can be selected considering the rest of the range as an uncertainty.

3.2 Linear Model of the MAF

Definition of moving average filter can be mathematically represented by:

$$maf(t, \phi) = \frac{1}{T_w} \int_{t-T_w}^{t} pd(t, \phi)dt, \quad (7)$$

being T_w the filtering window period. This value is time variant because it is working with an ASF-MAF. When the system is completely synchronized, the time window corresponds to the grid voltage period. Transfer function is given by:

$$MAF(s) = \frac{1 - e^{-T_w s}}{T_w s} PD(s) \quad (8)$$

However, because the presence of the delay in the transfer function makes difficult the mathematical analysis, the first order Pade's approximation is applied, obtaining:

$$MAF(s) = \frac{2}{T_w s + 2} PD(s) \tag{9}$$

3.3   Linear Model of the PI Controller

The simplest PI control structure is used to ensure that phase error will be zero. K_p and K_i are the proportional and integral constants respectively.

$$PI(s) = \left(\frac{K_p s + K_i}{s}\right) MAF(s) \tag{10}$$

3.4   Linear Model of the PWM Module

The output signal of the controller is get out of the DSP using the DPWM module, a second order Laplace transform is considered:

$$PWM(s) = \underbrace{\left[\frac{1 - 0.5T_{pwm}s}{\left(1 + 0.5T_{pwm}s\right)^2}\right]}_{K_{pwm}} MAF(s), \tag{11}$$

where T_{pwm} is the frequency of the triangular carrier signal [24].

3.5   Linear Model of the LPF

The first order low pass filter of expression (12) is used to eliminate the high frequency component of the PWM providing the input of the external VCO. We have:

$$LPF(s) = \left(\frac{T_f}{T_f s + 1}\right) PWM(s), \tag{12}$$

where T_f defines the time constant of the filter.

3.6   Linear Model of the VCO

Although the external VCO generates a high frequency square signal into a range constrained by minimum and maximum frequencies and hence its behavior is proportional but nonlinear, its dynamic behavior is obtained by linearization as:

$$VCO(s) = \frac{K_{vco}}{N} LPF(s), \tag{13}$$

where N is the number of samples per cycle of the grid voltage signal [20].

3.7   Closed-Loop of the Overall System

The loop transfer function (14) is obtained by series connection of the single transfer functions of the PD, MAF, PI, PWM, LPF and VCO elements of the system. The resulting close-loop of the synchronization system is depicted in Fig. 2.

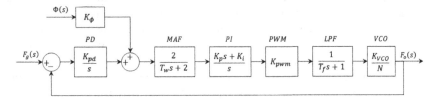

Fig. 2. Block diagram of the continuous time model of the PLL.

$$
L(s) = \left(\frac{K_{pd}V_g}{s}\right)\left(\frac{2}{T_w s + 2}\right)\left(\frac{K_p s + K_i}{s}\right)\left(\frac{T_f}{T_f s + 1}\right)\left(\frac{1 - 0.5T_{pwm}s}{(1 + 0.5T_{pwm}s)^2}\right)\left(\frac{K_{vco}}{N}\right)
$$

$$(14)$$

K_p and K_i parameters has an influence on the closed loop stability, robustness and dynamic performance of the system. Synthesis of these parameters can be accomplished using robust control techniques but this result is not part of this paper.

4   Discrete-Time Implementation

The implementation of the most of PLL is today performed into a DSP. In Fig. 3, it is depicted a detailed block diagram of the hybrid analog-digital implementation here proposed. Functions represented into the shaded box are the algorithms programmed into the DSP whereas other functions represent external electronic circuits. The first digital stage into the DSP is a digital bidirectional (up-down) counter (DBC), which increments or decrements the integer value every time an interruption is produced by a rise edge in the signal given by the external VCO (f_H).

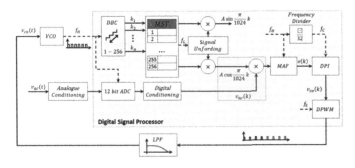

Fig. 3. Detailed discrete time implementation of the proposed reference generator.

A table composed of 256 registers of eight bits in which a quarter of sinusoidal waveform is stored off-line into the memory (MST). As it will be demonstrated bellow this resolution is sufficient to obtain a correct behavior of the system preserving computational resources. The values in the table are obtained by different pointers (counters) whose rate and direction depends of the required reference. A pointer producing the quadrature reference for the PLL is needed for many applications. Because the generated signals are built using only a quarter of the samples required in a period, reconstruction needs an unfolding function which is responsible for differentiating positive and negative half-cycles. Simultaneously, measurement of the grid voltage is obtained by the hardware module of analog to digital conversion (ADC). After a simple digital conditioning, the sampled grid voltage $v_{ac}(k)$ is multiplied by the quadrature reference $A cos \frac{\pi}{1024} k$ configuring the product-type PD. The MAF takes the output of the PD obtaining the 1024 samples summation. To guarantee the window size, in every execution of MAF, the new sample is added and the oldest is subtracted. Finally, the average is calculated taking the summation and dividing by the total number of samples. Later, this result is used by a digital PI controller, which is sampled 32 times slower to the sampling frequency given by the external VCO ($f_c = f_s/32$). This synchronized undersampling in the PI control allows obtaining adequate constants K_p and K_i less susceptible to rounding by quantization. Finally, the control action is getting out the DSP through a PWM module with a frequency f_{pwm}. The duty cycle of the output signal brings the information required by the external VCO.

4.1 Algorithm for DSP Programming

The real implementation of the abovementioned digital functions is performed using algorithms programmed into the DSP. Although some tasks are really executed sequentially, many of the functions used in this application are performed by hardware modules embedded in the DSP which involve few programs and memory resources [25–27]. Figure 4 presents the general flowchart of proposed reference generation system highlighting the importance of the external interruption in the execution of algorithm, and likewise, the way in which analog-to-digital conversion and updating of the generated signals are executed at the same time. Also, after executing MAF and DPI algorithms, the PWM task is started (hardware task) and the system enters in a waiting period in which control functions can be performed.

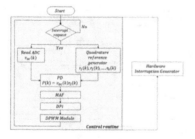

Fig. 4. Main flowchart of the synchronized reference generator

In Fig. 5, two of the main subroutines of the proposed implementation depicted in Fig. 4 are extended. The first one is the waveforms generator (Fig. 5a), which reads data stored in the memory using different pointers to build sinusoidal signals. In Fig. 5b, it is shown the MAF process execution in which the sum of the elements of an N + 1 size vector is stored while the new sample is added and the oldest is subtracted.

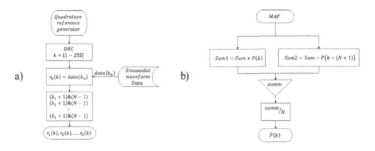

Fig. 5. Subroutines of system building blocks

5 Simulated Results

To validate the proposed control several simulations was performed using the solar module model of PSIM software which has the parameters listed in Table 1.

Table 1. System parameters used in simulations

Parameter	Symbol	Value	Units
Nominal grid voltage	$V_{g\,max}$	$120\sqrt{2}$	V
Nominal frequency	f_o	60	Hz
PI proportional gain	K_p	1.6628	–
PI integral gain	K_i	4.545	–
Controller average time sampling	T_{sc}	0.523	ms
Digital frequency divider	N	1024	–
PWM time constant	T_{pwm}	3.4133	μs

Results presented in Fig. 6 correspond to the comparison of transient response of the discrete system and its linear model during input frequency changes. Firstly, at 0 s, system starts from 55 Hz to find its operation point at 63 Hz. One second after, frequency of the input signal is changed to 57 Hz and the output frequency moves quickly to the new operation point (in less than two cycles) showing a slower displacement in phase (at least 20 cycles). After that, at 2 s, frequency of the input signal suddenly changes to 60 Hz. As it can be analysed, dynamic response in both cases is similar. Figure 7 depicts dynamic response of the system when phase disturbances are applied. At the beginning of simulation, the phase of the input signal and the output signal are equal but not the frequency. Then, it can be observed the same transient behaviour as in Fig. 6. After that, a positive phase shift of 22.5° is applied on 1 s and later, other negative phase shift of 11.25° is applied at 2 s. As it can be noted in the transient response, both disturbances are rejected in approximately 100 ms.

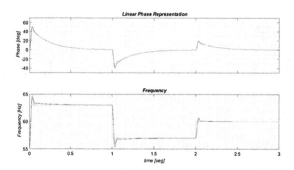

Fig. 6. Transient responses of PLL signals when frequency disturbances are applied in the grid voltage.

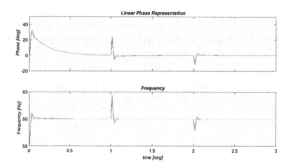

Fig. 7. Transient responses of inner system signals when phase disturbances are applied in the grid voltage.

6 Experimental Results

6.1 Experimental Setup

To assess dynamic response of the proposed system, a software application was developed in LabVIEW in order to generate two waveforms with different phase, harmonic content and amplitude. Application allows download discrete signals into a microcontroller (dsPIC30F4011) which in turn reproduce signals using PWM channels [24]. The application and the microcontroller communicate through an acquisition card NI USB-6008. By complaining interface and microcontroller capabilities, programmable AC source Keysight AC6802A is controlled producing sudden changes in frequency, sudden phase displacements and distorted conditions.

Reference generation system is implemented into a digital signal processor TMS320F28335. Additional electronics correspond to the external VCO (CD4046) and the needed LPF implemented using conventional LM324 operational amplifiers. To obtain oscilloscope captures of the digital references the PWM module of the DSP was used. However, it is important to mention that conventionally these references would not come out of the DSP. Figure 8a shows the experimental set-up together with the prototype of the proposed system. Measurements in experiments are obtained using an oscilloscope Tektronix MSO2014B with one isolated 20:1 attenuated voltage probe measuring the output voltage of the programmable source. Figure 8b shows the experimental set-up together with the prototype of the proposed system.

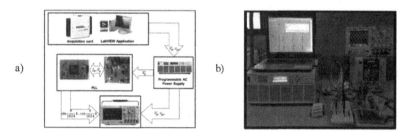

Fig. 8. (a) Block diagram of the experimental test bench; and (b) experimental setup in laboratory.

6.2 Experimental Results for Frequency Disturbances

Transient response of the system facing of frequency disturbances was tested by applying increasing and decreasing sudden changes using the programmable source emulating the grid voltage. Firstly, system was settled to operate at 60 Hz and after that an increasing change of 5 Hz suddenly is applied. The new operation point at 65 Hz was achieved after a settling time of around 50 ms. A maximum frequency deviation of 1.2 Hz was observed as overshoot. Approximately 500 ms later, a new sudden change was applied returning the system to its initial operational frequency of 60 Hz. As it can be observed in Fig. 9, dynamic behavior in both cases is very similar.

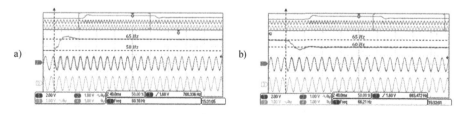

Fig. 9. Response to frequency changes: (a) from 60 to 65 Hz; and (b) from 65 to 60 Hz.

6.3 Experimental Results for Phase Disturbances

Transient response of the systems submitted to of phase disturbances was tested by generating a signal jumping between two signals at the same frequency but with a phase of 45° between them. Jumps between signals are applied just at a zero crossing. In both cases, system recuperates synchronization after five cycles of the fundamental frequency showing a maximum deviation of 5 Hz (Fig. 10).

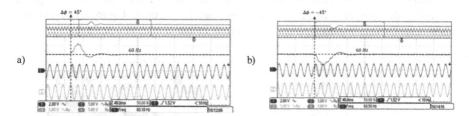

Fig. 10. Response to phase changes: (a) abrupt change of 45°; and (b) abrupt change of −45°.

6.4 Experimental Results Under Distorted Grid Voltage Conditions

Having demonstrated the good dynamic performance of the system in face of disturbances of frequency and phase, the parameter that remains to evaluate is the capability of the system to synchronize itself and produce references when the grid voltage is distorted. Then, as it is listed in Table 2, three tests were applied to evaluate this immunity response. The test 1 corresponds to ideal conditions in which there is no harmonic content. Tests 2 and 3 correspond to highly distorted grid voltages.

Table 2. Grid voltage waveform definition for the test

Test 1: Undistorted grid voltage (THD = 0%)
$v_g(t) = 170 \sin 120\pi t \, \text{V}$
Test 2: Distorted grid voltage (THD = 87.9%)
$v_g(t) = 170 \sin 120\pi t + 136 \sin(360\pi t + 45°) + 51 \sin 600\pi t + 34 \sin(840\pi t - 170°) \text{V}$
Test 3: Distorted grid voltage (THD = 112%)
$v_g(t) = 170 \sin 120\pi t + 136 \sin(360\pi t + 80°) + 102 \sin(600\pi t + 170°) + 85 \sin(840\pi t + 70°) \text{V}$

Figure 11a shows two signals generated by the system when test 1 is applied. Phase displacement is signaled with dotted lines to show accuracy of the expected phase shift. In Fig. 11b, the two signals generated by the system when test 2 is applied, one with the same phase and frequency of the grid voltage and the other corresponding to the second harmonic of the grid also synchronized at null phase. In this case, distorted signal is shown simultaneously with its fundamental component. Figure 11c show the same signals but corresponding to test 3.

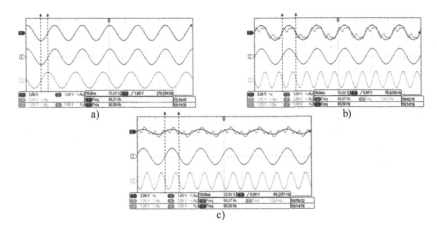

Fig. 11. Immunity to distorted grid voltage: (a) test 1, (b) tests 2, and (c) test 3.

7   Conclusion

A hybrid digital-analog implementation of an adaptive sampling frequency synchronized reference generator was presented in the paper. The main difference between the proposed method and the known methods is the use of an external VCO into the PLL to generate the sampling frequency for all the tasks into the DSP. This characteristic reduces computational cost aiding to increase the reliability. As it was presented, although the system integrates two filters in the loop (digital MAF and analog LPF), dynamic response of the closed loop is comparable with other more complex methods. Generation of the signal is very simple and then multiple signals can be obtained simultaneously without the use of complex computations. Several tests demonstrated effectiveness, robustness and accuracy of the proposed system.

Acknowledgements. This work was supported by *Universidad de Ibagué* under project #14-315-INT, *Gobernación del Tolima* under Convenio de cooperación 1026- 2013, project #16-406-INT, and *Departamento Nacional de Ciencia, Tecnología e Innovación COLCIENCIAS* under contract CT 018-2016.

References

1. Cirstea, M.N., Giamusi, M., McCormick, M.: A modern ASIC controller for a 6-pulse rectifier. In: Proceedings of 10th Annual IEEE International ASIC Conference and Exhibit, Portland, pp. 335–338 (1997)
2. Huber, L., Irving, B.T., Jovanovic, M.M.: Review and stability analysis of PLL-based interleaving control of DCM/CCM boundary boost PFC converters. IEEE Trans. Power Electron. **24**(8), 1992–1999 (2009)
3. Busada, C.A., Chiacchiarini, H.G., Balda, J.C.: Synthesis of sinusoidal waveform references synchronized with periodic signals. IEEE Trans. Power Electron. **23**(2), 581–590 (2008)

4. Hadjidemetriou, L., Yang, Y., Kyriakides, E., Blaabjerg, F.: A synchronization scheme for single-phase grid-tied inverters under harmonic distortion and grid disturbances. IEEE Trans. Power Electron. **32**(4), 2784–2793 (2017)
5. Hsieh, G.-C., Hung, J.C.: Phase-locked loop techniques: a survey. IEEE Trans. Ind. Electron. **43**(6), 609–615 (1996)
6. Zheng, L., Geng, H., Yang, G.: Fast and robust phase estimation algorithm for heavily distorted grid conditions. IEEE Trans. Ind. Electron. **63**(11), 6845–6855 (2016)
7. Lu, C., Zhou, Z., Jiang, A., Luo, M., Shen, P., Han, Y.: Comparative performance evaluation of phase-locked loop (PLL) algorithms for single-phase grid-connected converters. In: Proceedings of IEEE 8th International Power Electronics and Motion Control Conference, Hefei, pp. 902–907 (2016)
8. Ferreira, R. J., Araújo, R.E., Peças-Lopes, J.A.: A comparative analysis and implementation of various PLL techniques applied to single-phase grids. In: Proceedings of the 2011 3rd international Youth Conference Energetics (IYCE), Leiria, pp. 1–8 (2011)
9. Golestan, S., Guerrero, J.M., Vasquez, J.C.: Single-phase PLLs: a review of recent advances. IEEE Trans. Ind. Electron. **32**(12), 9013–9030 (2017)
10. Zhang, Q., Sun, X.D., Zhong, Y.R., Matsui, M., Ren, B.Y.: Analysis and design of a digital phase-locked loop for single-phase grid-connected power conversion systems. IEEE Trans. Ind. Electron. **58**(8), 3581–3592 (2011)
11. Han, Y., Luo, M., Zhao, X., Guerrero, J.M., Xu, L.: Comparative performance evaluation of orthogonal-signal-generators-based single-phase PLL algorithms—a survey. IEEE Trans. Power Electron. **31**(5), 3932–3944 (2016)
12. Moreno, V.M., Liserre, M., Pigazo, A., Dell'Aquila, A.: A comparative analysis of real-time algorithms for power signal decomposition in multiple synchronous reference frames. IEEE Trans. Power Electron. **22**(4), 1280–1289 (2007)
13. Silva, S.M., Lopes, B.M., Filho, B.J.C., Campana, R.P., Bosventura, W.C.: Performance evaluation of PLL algorithms for single-phase grid-connected systems. In: Proceedings of IEEE Industry Applications Conference, vol. 4, pp. 2259–2263 (2014)
14. Golestan, S., Ramezani, J.M., Gerrero, J.M., Freijedo, F.D., Monfared, M.: Moving average filter based phase-look loops: performance analysis and design guidelines. IEEE Trans. Power Electron. **29**(6), 2750–2763 (2014)
15. Wang, J., Liang, J., Gao, F., Zhang, L., Wang, Z.: A method to improve the dynamic performance of moving average filter based PLL. IEEE Trans. Power Electron. **30**(10), 5978–5990 (2015)
16. Golestan, S., Guerrero, J.M., Vasquez, J.C.: Nonadaptive window-based PLL for single-phase applications. IEEE Trans. Power Electron. **33**(1), 24–31 (2018)
17. Wang, L., Jiang, Q., Hong, L., Zhang, C., Wei, Y.: A novel phase-locked loop based on frequency detector and initial phase angle detector. IEEE Trans. Power Electron. **28**(10), 4538–4549 (2013)
18. Fairchild Semiconductor: CD4046: Micropower Phase-Locked Loop, pp. 1–14 (2002)
19. Texas Instruments: Digital Phase-Locked Loop Using SN54/74LS297, pp. 1–19 (1997)
20. Lopez-Santos, O., Garcia, G., Avila-Martinez, J.C., Gonzalez-Morales, D. F., Toro-Zuluaga, C.: A simple digital sinusoidal reference generator for grid-synchronized power electronics applications. In: Proceedings of IEEE Workshop on Power Electronics and Power Quality Applications (PEPQA), Bogota, pp. 1–6 (2015)
21. Lopez-Santos, O., Garcia, G., Martinez-Salamero, L., Avila-Martinez, J.C., Seguier, L.: Non-linear control of the output stage of a solar microinverter. Int. J. Control **90**(1), 90–109 (2017)

22. Lopez-Santos, O., Tilaguy-Lezama, S., Rico-Ramirez, S.P., Cortes-Torres, L.: Operation of a photovoltaic microinverter as active power filter using the single phase P-Q theory and sliding mode control. Ingeniería **22**(2), 254–268 (2017)
23. Lopez-Santos, O., Cortes-Torres, L., Tilaguy-Lezama, S.: Discrete time nested-loop controller for the output stage of a photovoltaic microinverter. In: Figueroa-García, J.C., López-Santana, E.R., Ferro-Escobar, R. (eds.) WEA 2016. CCIS, vol. 657, pp. 320–331. Springer, Cham (2016). https://doi.org/10.1007/978-3-319-50880-1_28
24. Ye, T., Dai, N., Lam, C.S., Wong, M.C., Guerrero, J.M.: Analysis, design, and implementation of a quasi-proportional-resonant controller for a multifunctional capacitive-coupling grid-connected inverter. IEEE Trans. Ind. Appl. **52**(5), 4269–4280 (2016)
25. Texas Instruments: TMS320x2833x, 2823x enhanced pulse width modulator (ePWM) module (2009)
26. Texas Instruments: TMS320x2833x, 2823x reference guide: system control and interrupts (2010)
27. Texas Instruments: TMS320x2833x, analog-to-digital converter (ADC) module (2007)

Software Assisted Energy Efficient and Flexible WDM-PON Access Networks

Luis Albarracín[1](✉) [iD], Imene Sekkiou[2] [iD], Beatriz Ortega[2] [iD],
Francisco Chicharro[2] [iD], José Mora[2] [iD], and Gustavo Puerto[1] [iD]

[1] Universidad Distrital Francisco José de Caldas, Bogotá, Colombia
lfalbarracins@correo.udistrital.edu.co,
gapuerto@udistrital.edu.co
[2] Universidad Politécnica de Valencia, Valencia, Spain
imsek@doctor.upv.es, bortega@dcom.upv.es,
frachilo@upvnet.upv.es, jmalmer@upv.es

Abstract. This paper presents the architecture of a green and flexible WDM-PON access network. We propose the segmentation of a broadband source into smaller frequency windows by means of a wave shaper filter. A central controller commands the configuration of physical network parameters such as the optical bandwidth delivered by the filter and the modulation format of the service to be transported in the network. Different optical bandwidths were defined for the experimental demonstration and two modulation formats were evaluated in our approach. Results found an effective bandwidth of 3 GHz for optical bandwidths below 1 nm. Broader optical pass bands reduce the bandwidth but improve the signal quality measured in the receiver due to a relative higher average optical power available in the photo detector.

Keywords: Optical slicing · SDN · WDM-PON

1 Introduction

Globalization, competitiveness and the technological demands of a modern world, pose key challenges to the telecommunications industries worldwide, and that is when they promise us a new generation, which implies low energy consumption and infrastructure costs. According to the Cisco Visual Networking Index (VNI) Report on Global Mobile Data Traffic 2016–2021, by 2021 in the world there will be around 5.500 million mobile phones. The exponential increase in mobile users, smartphones, broadband Internet connections, the Internet of Things paradigm and the increased consumption of mobile video will multiply fixed and mobile data traffic by seven over the next four years [1]. In the same way, the statistics portal *Statista* indicates that the global mobile data traffic point to a continuous growth of the transport information featuring monthly numbers above 30 million terabytes from 2020 [2]. In this scenario the use of optical fibers for the transmission of radio signals is postulated as a promising solution for the improvement of capacity in access networks. The current state of art shows the high possibilities of development and viability of the convergence processes between wireless networks and fiber optic networks. This type of convergent

© Springer Nature Switzerland AG 2018
J. C. Figueroa-García et al. (Eds.): WEA 2018, CCIS 915, pp. 588–595, 2018.
https://doi.org/10.1007/978-3-030-00350-0_48

processes, in addition, has the great advantage of being able to use the current infrastructure used in wireless networks, reducing costs and deployment times. The convergence processes respond to previously mentioned access needs as well as alternatives in the provision of services such as triple play, trends in cloud computing [3], Distributed Antenna Systems (DAS) [4], and in general to an environment with increasingly users that demands quality of telecommunications services, which essentially use fiber optics as transmission line and radio systems to enable wireless access and mobility.

In accordance with the above, data traffic will need technological solutions that support the transport of huge volumes of information in the segment of the access network. Thus, optical fibers, Wavelength Division Multiplexing (WDM) and the recent paradigm known as Software Defined Networking in which the control plane is separated form the data plane in order to centralize the network control and management [5, 6] appear in order to take advantage of the enormous capacity of the optical spectrum and to counteract the limitations existing in traditional access systems.

In the context of access networks, passive optical networks (PON) are based on a scheme called passive photonic loop [7], where the Central Office (CO) contains a transmitter that emits a wavelength channel to be distributed among the different clients of the PON. This architecture generates low Operational Expenditure (OpEx) and Capital Expenditure (CapEx) due to the passive nature of the distribution device in the Optical Distribution Network (ODN). However, the fact of transporting a single wavelength limits the capacity of the current PON networks. Current proposals to increase the bandwidth in access networks are based on the use of binary nonreturn-to-zero and duobinary-based transmission [8], optical amplification in the ODN [9] and avalanche photodiodes (APD) in order to improve the power balance in the network [10]. In this context, a foreseeable evolution of the current optical access networks would consist on solutions based on WDM. These systems have multiple transmitting lasers that operate at different wavelengths, for that reason the complexity of a network architecture and the costs are higher compared to a traditional PON.

This paper proposes a WDM-PON network in which a software-controlled wave-shaper filter enables the partitioning of a broadband light source to provide different wavelengths in an efficient and lower cost. The approach allows the transport of fixed and mobile services in an WDM environment by optimizing the network resources according to the capacity and services demanded while offering flexibility in the resource allocation and energy savings according to the traffic granularity that is required to transport in the access segment. The paper is organized as follows, Sect. 2 presents the architecture description that include the network concept and implementation details. Section 3 describes the results obtained in the conducted experimental measurements and Sect. 4 summarises the paper.

2   Architecture Description

Figure 1 shows the software-assisted approach for a WDM PON network in which the broadband spectrum of an optical source (BBS) is segmented in a WaveShaper filter (WVS). The pass band of this filter can be adjusted in both central frequency and bandwidth. Then, according to the data transport requirements, different wavelength slices may feed an Electro-Optical Modulator (EOM) via the optical switch. In this context, the SDN controller commands the right instructions to control the WVS in order to set a given bandwidth on a certain central wavelength. The combination of the WVS and the optical switch provide flexibility to the system as the resources are allocated depending on the current demand. The granularity is given by assigning different modulation formats to an Orthogonal Frequency Division Multiplexing (OFDM) transported signal. Thus, low profile traffic might be transported onto a QPSK format whereas high bandwidth traffic would be assigned a multi-level modulation format such as 16-QAM or 32-QAM. This operation is performed in the Arbitrary Waveform Generator (AWG). As the approach uses only one optical source for the generation of multiple wavelengths, the system provides energy savings features, unlike the standard WDM systems in which for each wavelength a laser source is needed. Thus, the potential towards providing truly cost-effective and green features in the access segment is feasible.

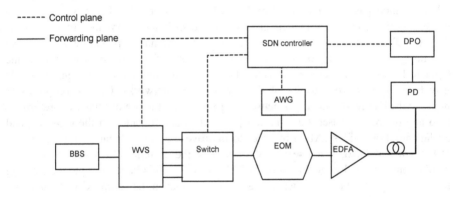

Fig. 1. Proposed network model.

2.1 Implementation Details

The experimental setup is depicted in Fig. 2, where a BBS launches a broadband signal from 450 nm and 2400 nm to the WVS that is centered at 1550 nm. From this broadband signal, optical bandwidths of 1 nm, 3 nm, 6 nm and 8 nm were set in the WVS and used as optical sources to the 20 GHz-EOM. The WVS is a fully programmable, flat-top optical filter with bandwidth programmable in 1 GHz increments from 10 GHz up to the whole C band and center frequency programmable in 1 GHz increments also over the whole band. The system response is evaluated in terms of the bandwidth modulation that provides the fact of using broadband optical sources. Therefore, a vector Network Analyzer (VNA) feeds the system with frequencies from 10 MHz up to 30 GHz. The optical modulated signal is amplified previously to be transmitted through the optical fiber link. Inset (a) in Fig. 2 shows the optical power at the output of the WVS, after the EOM and also after the amplification in the Erbium Doped Fiber Amplifier (EDFA) for different optical bandwidths set by the WVS. After fiber transmission, the signal is detected in the Photo Diode (PD) and analyzed in the VNA. Inset (b) in Fig. 2 shows the signal detected when a 3 nm bandwidth signal has been transmitted through 2 km of optical fiber. The layout of the implementation for the experimental demonstration is shown in Fig. 2.

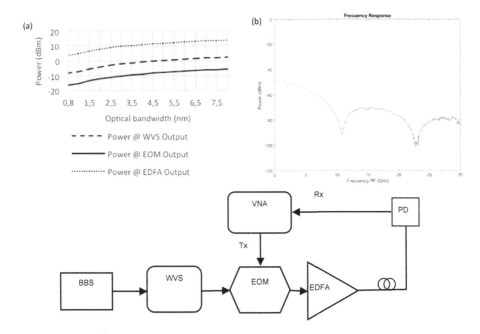

Fig. 2. Layout for the experimental demonstration of the proposed system. Inset (a): optical power measurement as a function of the WVS optical bandwidth. (b) Transfer function for a 3 nm bandwidth signal after propagation over a 2 km fiber link.

3 Results and Discussions

Figure 3 shows the measured RF modulation bandwidth as a function of the optical bandwidth given by the WVS and different fiber transmission lengths. Results show that long fiber spams penalizes the usable bandwidth due to the significant impact of the fiber dispersion that affects the broadband wavelength channels [11]. In this context, an optical bandwidth of 1 nm supports a modulation frequency of up to 3 GHz for fiber spams of 1 km (dotted-dash trace). As the fiber length and the optical bandwidth increase, the effective range of modulation frequencies decrease as can be seen in the continuous trace of Fig. 3 that corresponds to a 3 nm optical bandwidth and 2 km of fiber transmission. This bandwidth is measured for a 3 dB threshold in different transfer functions as can be seen in inset (a) for an optical bandwidth of 1 nm at 1 km and inset (b) for an optical bandwidth of 6 nm at 2 km.

The resulting band pass was evaluated by transmitting two different services using OFDM transport over 1 km optical link. One service was modulated onto a QPSK

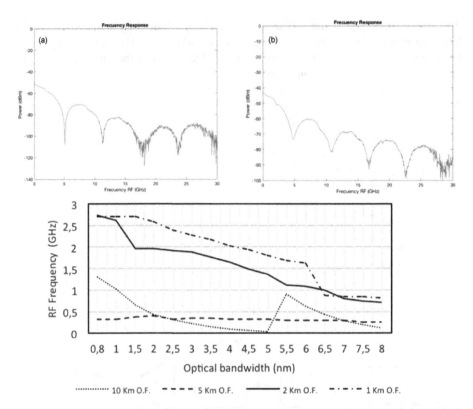

Fig. 3. Experimental results: effective bandwidth modulation as a function of the optical bandwidth for different link lengths. (a) 1 nm optical bandwidth and 1 km of fiber. (b) 6 nm optical bandwidth and 2 km of fiber.

modulation format and a second service onto a 16-QAM modulation as can be seen in Fig. 4, which shows the obtained constellations for both services. These constellations correspond to the transmission of both radiofrequency services at 1 GHz, 2 GHz and 3 GHz respectively modulating an 8 nm optical bandwidths. Despite of obtaining an even performance for both modulation formats transmitted at different frequencies, it can be observed that the fiber transmission causes higher penalties on the 16-QAM service. This is due to the fact that higher modulation formats transport more bits per symbol and therefore it needs more energy per bit in order to assure a proper signal to noise ratio at the receiver. The Error Vector Magnitude (EVM) was evaluated for both services, results in Fig. 5 shows the performance for the QPSK service, note that the EVM remains steady at an average value of 30%. Note that as the optical bandwidth is broader, the obtained results are improved.

Finally, the EVM per subcarrier and EVM per symbol were measured for the QPSK service transported onto a subcarrier of 1 GHz. Figure 6(a) shows the results for a 3 nm optical bandwidth, Fig. 6(b) depicts the results for an optical bandwidth of 6 nm and Fig. 6(c) shows the performance when the optical bandwidth was of 8 nm. These results show that the EVM improves, as the optical bandwidth is broader due to the

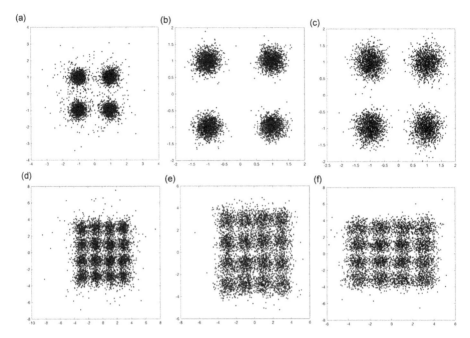

Fig. 4. Experimental results: measured constellations for two different services. (a) QPSK at 1 GHz. (b) QPSK at 2 GHz. (c) QPSK at 3 GHz. (d) 16-QAM at 1 GHz. (e) 16-QAM at 2 GHz and (f) 16-QAM at 3 GHz.

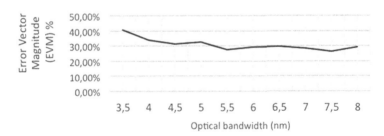

Fig. 5. Experimental results: EVM performance for the QPSK service transmitted at different optical bandwidths.

relative higher optical power within the available optical bandwidth, as seen in Fig. 2 (a). Note that for a 3 nm bandwidth the EVM is around 45% whereas 6 nm and 8 nm reduce the EVM up to 29%. However, despite of the improvement of the signal-to-noise ratio of broad optical bandwidths, still the dispersion prevents the system to reach lower EVM values. In order to mitigate the dispersion effect, the system can employ the solution proposed in [12], in which a Mach-Zehnder based interferometric structure is placed before the modulation in order to reduce the optical bandwidth.

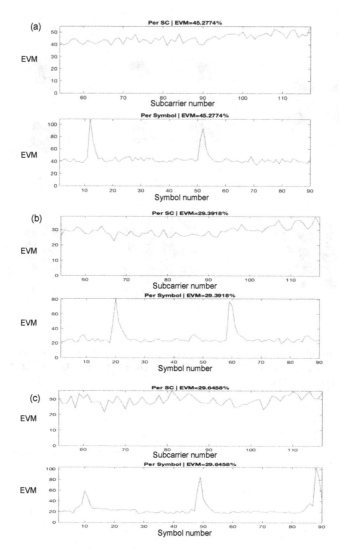

Fig. 6. Experimental results: EVM per subcarrier and EVM per symbol for the QPSK service at 1 GHz transmitted at different optical bandwidths. (a) 3 nm. (b) 6 nm. (c) 8 nm.

4 Conclusions

This paper presented an approach towards the definition of reconfigurable optical networks based on the Software Defined Networking paradigm. In our proposal, a controller commands the optical bandwidth configuration of a wave shaper filter in order to set different pass bands obtained from a broadband optical source. According to the conducted measurements, better power responses are obtained at frequencies below 1 GHz. Nevertheless, it depends on the optical bandwidth set by the wave shaper. The narrower the bandwidth in the wave shaper filter, the better the response in the receiver as expected from dispersion penalty. However, narrow optical bandwidths leads to a lower average power at the receiver, thus a trade-off between optical power and dispersion for a given optical bandwidth was found in order to meet a target signal quality. According to the constellation figures measured at the receiver, the 16-QAM modulation is only recommended when the central frequency is 1 GHz or below for a correct equalization of the received signal. The measured EVM did not show significant difference regarding the subcarrier frequency for a QPSK service. In order to improve the EVM performance, further approaches must be employed to compensate the dispersion impact.

References

1. https://www.cisco.com/c/en/us/solutions/collateral/service-provider/visual-networking-index-vni/complete-white-paper-c11-481360.pdf
2. Statista GmbH: Datos móviles: previsión del tráfico global 2017-2021 | Estadística. Statista GmbH (2016). [En línea]. https://es.statista.com/estadisticas/600634/prevision-del-trafico-total-de-datos-moviles-a-nivel-mundial-2016. Accessed 30 Jan 2018
3. Maier, M., Rimal, B.P.: Invited paper: the audacity of fiber-wireless (FiWi) networks: revisited for clouds and cloudlets. China Commun. **12**(8), 33–45 (2015)
4. Chanclou, P., et al.: How does passive optical network tackle radio access network evolution? IEEE/OSA J. Opt. Commun. Netw. **9**(11), 1030–1040 (2017)
5. Talli, G., et al.: Technologies and architectures to enable SDN in converged 5G/optical access networks. In: 2017 International Conference on Optical Network Design and Modeling (ONDM), Budapest, pp. 1–6 (2017)
6. Pakpahan, A.F., Hwang, I.S., Nikoukar, A.: OLT energy savings via software-defined dynamic resource provisioning in TWDM-PONs. IEEE/OSA J. Opt. Commun. Netw. **9**(11), 1019–1029 (2017)
7. Alimi, I.A., Teixeira, A.L., Monteiro, P.P.: Toward an efficient C-RAN optical fronthaul for the future networks: a tutorial on technologies, requirements, challenges, and solutions. In: IEEE Communications Surveys & Tutorials, vol. 20, no. 1, pp. 708–769. Firstquarter (2018)
8. van Veen, D.T., Houtsma, V.E.: Proposals for cost-effectively upgrading passive optical networks to a 25G line rate. J. Lightwave Technol. **35**(6), 1180–1187 (2014)
9. Yin, S., van Veen, D., Houtsma, V., Vetter, P.: Investigation of symmetrical optical amplified 40 Gbps PAM-4/Duobinary TDM-PON using 10G optics and DSP. In: Proceedings of Optical Fiber Communication Conference and Exhibition (2016)
10. Houtsma, V., van Veen, D., Gnauck, A., Iannone, P.: APD-based duobinary direct detection receivers for 40 Gbps TDM-PON. In: Optical Fiber Communications Conference and Exhibition (OFC), Los Angeles, CA (2015)
11. Grassi, F., Mora, J., Ortega, B., Capmany, J.: Experimental evaluation of the transmission in a low cost SCM/WDM radio over fibre system employing optical broadband sources and interferometric structures. In: 2009 11th International Conference on Transparent Optical Networks, Azores, pp. 1–4 (2009)
12. Grassi, F., Mora, J., Ortega, B., Capmany, J.: Subcarrier multiplexing tolerant dispersion transmission system employing optical broadband sources. Opt. Express **17**, 4740–4751 (2009)

Real-Time Frequency-Decoupling Control for a Hybrid Energy Storage System in an Active Parallel Topology Connected to a Residential Microgrid with Intermittent Generation

Alexander Narvaez[1,2(✉)] ⓘ, Camilo Cortes[1] ⓘ, and Cesar Trujillo[2] ⓘ

[1] Universidad Nacional de Colombia, Bogotá, Colombia
caacortesgu@unal.edu.co
[2] Universidad Distrital Francisco José de Caldas, Bogotá, Colombia
{anarvaez, cltrujillo}@udistrital.edu.co

Abstract. This paper presents a study by simulation of the performance of a Hybrid Energy Storage System (HESS) integrated to a residential microgrid. The storage system is composed of li-ion battery units and supercapacitors connected in a parallel active topology. An optimization-based real-time frequency-decoupling control strategy is used for the power split and for the assignation of the high-frequency and low-frequency energy components to the storage mediums. The simulation system emulates a photovoltaic generation source with typical intermittence of the injected power, the typical loads of a residential electric grid, and a HESS.

Keywords: Energy storage system · Hybrid energy storage system
Lithium-ion battery · Supercapacitor · DC/DC bidirectional converter

1 Introduction

A small-scale electric sub-system, capable of operating in both grid-connected or island-mode with respect to the electric system, and containing renewable generation sources, Energy Storage Systems (ESSs) and interconnected home loads is known as a residential microgrid [1]. The proliferation of renewable and clean power sources, such as wind turbines or solar panels, makes necessary the use of ESS to solve the problems related to the intermittent nature of their power generation [2]. Battery Energy Storage Systems (BESS) have been commonly used for this kind of applications.

However, it has been demonstrated that storing intermittent energy from renewable sources results inefficient and could reduce the battery lifetime [3]. In order to solve this problem, combinations of different storage technologies have been studied. An ESS that uses two or more energy storage mediums is known as a Hybrid Energy Storage System (HESS). The idea of using HESSs is attractive because of the potential use of the operational benefits of each storage technology [4]. The total power flow is intended to be divided into an average component assigned to a "high energy" storage

© Springer Nature Switzerland AG 2018
J. C. Figueroa-García et al. (Eds.): WEA 2018, CCIS 915, pp. 596–605, 2018.
https://doi.org/10.1007/978-3-030-00350-0_49

device, and a dynamic component (rapid power fluctuations) assigned to a "high power" storage device. Nevertheless, the implementation of a HESS depends on technical and economic factors, which compromise their feasibility in some cases.

One of the most used HESS configurations is the combination of batteries (high energy) and supercapacitors (high power), which has been studied since the late 90s [5]. Most applications of HESS have taken place in electric vehicles [6], although some of them have also been implemented in wind turbines [4, 7], as well as in photovoltaic systems [3], and UPS [8]. Some advantages of the combination of batteries with supercapacitors are the extension of battery lifetime [9], the capability of a fast energy storage [10], a better performance of the storage system for intermittent sources of energy [3, 7] and a smaller environmental impact [11].

The main objective of the present study is to implement an optimization-based real-time frequency-decoupling control strategy for a HESS in an active parallel topology connected to a residential microgrid, with the inclusion of an emulated solar generator and a realistic behavior in its generated power. The paper is organized as follows: a short explanation of the topologies for the interconnection of batteries and supercapacitors in a HESS is exposed in Sect. 2. Section 3 shows a detailed description of the system under study, the system transfer functions and the controllers for the implemented control strategy. Section 4 presents the simulation results. Finally, some conclusions are presented in Sect. 5.

2   Topologies for the Interconnection of Batteries and Supercapacitors

There are three families of topologies for the interconnection of the storage technologies in a HESS: passive, semi-active, and fully active topologies. In a passive topology, the storage technologies are directly interconnected, while in an active connection the storage elements are connected via DC-DC converters, whose operational modes could be designed to function unidirectionally or bidirectionally, depending on the nature or the requirements of the HESS [12]. In a semi-active topology, only one of the storage devices is connected through a DC-DC converter, or a single converter is used to connect the load to the pre-connected storage devices.

Several studies have compared the different topologies for the interconnection of batteries and supercapacitors. For instance, a potential application in residential microgrids was presented in [13]. In this study, two semi-active topologies were used with the aim of prolonging the lifetime of batteries, using the supercapacitor for reducing the dynamic component of the current from a pulsed current load to the batteries. The main conclusion of this study was that the chosen topologies could be tuned for the reduction of the dynamic part of the power flows from and to the battery. However, the use of an intermittent generation source with power flow oscillations in a wide frequency range demands an interface capable of properly distributing the average and dynamic part of the source current into the battery and into the supercapacitor, respectively. Based on the previous analysis, an active topology and a more structured control strategy are needed in order to design a HESS for a real application in a residential microgrid.

Parallel Active Hybrid Topology: The parallel active Hybrid topology is commonly used to take advantage of the operational characteristics of every storage device connected in a HESS. The additional DC-DC converter associated to the "high power" storage device helps to operate the supercapacitor in a broader voltage range, and hereby the storage capacity is best used [14]. For example, for a voltage variation range between 50% and 100% of SC rated voltage, the stored energy will vary from 25% to 100% of its rated energy. The related topology is shown in Fig. 1.

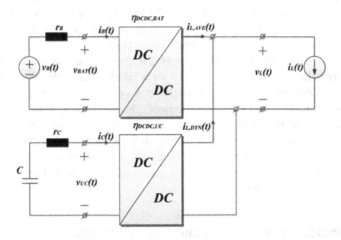

Fig. 1. Parallel active hybrid topology [15].

In addition to the higher costs, the main drawback of the parallel active topology is its complexity in terms of the control strategies, not only for a suitable energy management, but also for the power flow decomposition. Among the several options of the control strategies for the energy management in a HESS [14], an optimization-based real-time frequency-decoupling control strategy has been selected for the present study. With respect to the characteristics of a residential microgrid, a real-time control strategy allows the controllers to operate with an independent control decision, without central controllers and communications. It provides better reliability and scalability of the entire system [16].

An example of this method has been recently presented in [17, 18]. Authors propose an Extended Droop Control strategy to autonomously separate the dynamic part of the power flows during sudden load changes. The dynamic component is assigned to the supercapacitor and then the high-frequency fluctuations due to sudden load changes, emulated by a step function current source, are compensated. In addition, other control objectives such as the system stability and a suitable voltage regulation are achieved. A Low Pass Filter (LPF) and a High Pass Filter (HPF) are included in a third control loop of each DC converter. As a result, these virtual filters manage to soften the rapid current change forced by the step function. However, intermittences of a PV source with a defined range of time variation demand a different sizing of SC and a different virtual filters design.

The injected power of a PV generator is proportional to the solar irradiance and temperature. Figure 2 shows some measures of irradiance in a cloudy day in the Tropical Zone.

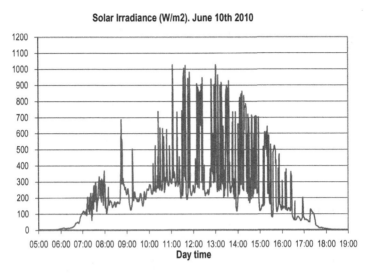

Fig. 2. In situ measurements in a cloudy day in the tropical zone. Faculty of sciences laboratory. Universidad Nacional de Colombia

3 HESS in a Residential Microgrid with Intermittent Generation. System Description

The main goal of a HESS in a microgrid with intermittent generation is to separate the average and the dynamic parts of the injected power and assign them to the storage technologies, both of them with complementary characteristics in terms of energy and power densities. Consequently, the objective of the present work is to implement an optimization-based real-time frequency-decoupling control strategy for a HESS in an active parallel topology connected to a residential microgrid, with the inclusion of an emulated solar generator and a realistic behavior in its generated power.

Large variations in the injected power of a PV generator, with irradiance similar to the one showed in Fig. 2, have been measured in a time range of 3 to 5 s. Based on these measurements, the square-shaped current source shown in Fig. 3 is chosen for the emulation of a PV source.

An active parallel topology of a HESS, such as the one described in the previous section, is integrated in a typical residential microgrid architecture, as shown in Fig. 4.

The HESS is intended to be placed in a DC residential microgrid with a rated capacity of 5 kW. Physical models of li-ion batteries and supercapacitors are included in the software PSIM 11.0.1. The li-ion battery bank has a capacity of 6.2 kWh. The SC module has a rated voltage of 240 V and a Capacitance of 7.8 F. This capacitance was calculated based on the duration of the intermittences of the injected current and their

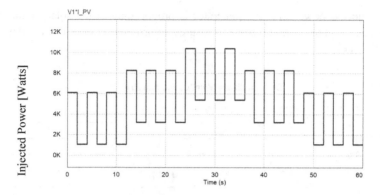

Fig. 3. Injected power emulation of a PV generator.

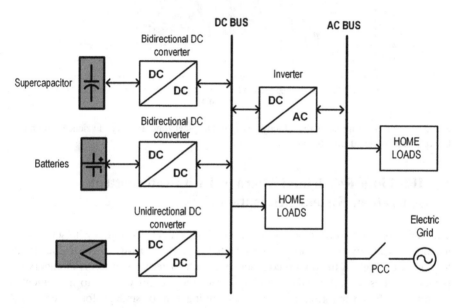

Fig. 4. Architecture of the residential microgrid under study

associated energy. Higher values of this suitable capacitance will not cause wide voltage variations in the terminals of the SC, which would not justify the use of an active topology. However, large variations in SC voltage imply an effective conversion ratio of the SC converter in order to guarantee a good stability and a good voltage regulation.

For the integration of each storage technology, a non-isolated bidirectional half-bridge DC/DC converter has been chosen (Fig. 5). This PWM bipolar switching converter topology works as a boost converter when the storage systems are in discharging mode and as a buck converter when they are in charging mode. The chosen control strategy for the converter is an ACC double-loop control [19]. This control algorithm is suitable for a regulated current source, and it is commonly used in methods of charging and discharging batteries. Table 1 shows a summary of the elements used in the converters.

Table 1. DC/DC battery and SC converter parameters

Variable name	Variable	Battery converter	SC converter
Rated power	Pn	5 kW	7 kW
Rated voltage	Vout	360 V	360 V
Rated input voltage	Vbat	144 V	120–240 V
Nominal current	In	13.9 A	19.44 A
Δ IL_max	ΔIL_max	1.4 A	1.94 A
Switching freq	fs	4 kHz	12 kHz
Filter inductance	L	6 mH	3 mH
Filter capacitor	C	470 µF	180 µF

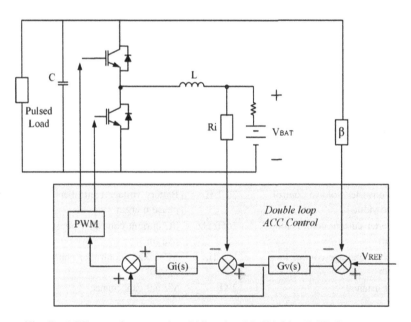

Fig. 5. ACC control strategy in a bidirectional half-bridge DC/DC converter

The switching frequency in the SC converter is higher than the used in the battery converter. This higher frequency allows us to adjust the bandwidth of the controllers in the control loops, especially in the voltage control loop, and provide the SC converter with a faster dynamics. At the same time the rated power of the SC converter should be also higher because of the power assignment to this storage medium.

For the design of the controllers and the calculations of the elements of the converter, the computational tool SISOTOOL of MATLAB has been used. Because of stability criteria, the current controllers are between 5 to 10 times faster than voltage controllers. Additionally, for all the controllers, the phase margin is higher than 50 degrees. The main transfer functions of the system under study, developed in [20], as well as some other parameters of the implemented control strategy are shown in Table 2.

Table 2. Transfer functions of interest for control of the DC converter.

Function	Transfer function		
Duty cycle to inductor current	$Gid(s) = \dfrac{\hat{i}_L(s)}{\hat{d}(s)}\Big|_{\hat{v}_i=\hat{i}_o=0} = \dfrac{V_{DC}+(1-D)Z_{DC}I_{Lbat}}{sL+(1+D)^2Z_{DC}}$		
PWM modulator gain	$F_M = 1$		
Current loop gain	$T_i(s) = Gid(s)\,R_i\,G_i(s)\,F_M$		
Control voltage to inductor current	$ILC(s) = \dfrac{\hat{i}_L(s)}{\hat{v}_c(s)}\Big|_{\hat{v}_i=\hat{i}_o=0} = (1+G_i(s))\dfrac{F_M\,Gid(s)}{1+T_i(s)}$		
Inductor current to output voltage	$G_{vi}(s) = \dfrac{\hat{v}_{DC}(s)}{\hat{i}_L(s)}\Big|_{\hat{v}_i=\hat{i}_o=0} = \dfrac{V_{DC}Z_{DC}(1-D)-Z_{DC}sL\,I_{Lbat}}{V_{DC}+(1-D)Z_{DC}\,I_{Lbat}}$		
Control voltage to output voltage	$V_{oc}(s) = \dfrac{\hat{v}_{DC}(s)}{\hat{v}_c(s)}\Big|_{\hat{v}_i=\hat{i}_o=0} = ILC(s)G_{vi}(s)$		
Voltage loop gain	$T_V(s) = \beta\,V_{oc}(s)\,G_v(s)$		
Current controller	$G_i(s) = \dfrac{w_i\left(1+\frac{s}{w_{z1}}\right)}{s\left(1+\frac{s}{w_{p1}}\right)}$		
Voltage controller	$G_v(s) = \frac{w_i}{s}$		
Voltage sensor gains	$\beta = 1$	Current sensor gains	$Ri = 1$
Battery converter current control loop bandwidth	625 Hz	Battery current controller phase margin	65.8°
Battery converter voltage control loop bandwidth	34.3 Hz	Battery voltage controller phase margin	77.9°
SC converter current control loop bandwidth	1660 Hz	SC current controller phase margin	70.1°
SC converter voltage control loop bandwidth	155 Hz	SC voltage controller phase margin	60.1°
Virtual resistance	2 Ω	Virtual capacitance	5 F

4   Simulation Results

This section presents the simulation results using the software PSIM 11.0.1. These simulations were tested on the system described in Sect. 3. The complete schematic circuit is shown in Fig. 6. The load and the PV current source emulator are connected to the DC bus and are represented in the element marked as LOAD. The output voltage is nearly constant over the 360 V due to the double loop control strategy implemented in each converter. An extra filter capacitor has been added to the terminals of the battery in order to reduce the ripple of the inductor current and the high frequency oscillations due to the sudden changes of load. The values of the virtual resistance and capacitance, shown in Table 2, are selected with a time constant closely related to the duration of the intermittences in the power generation.

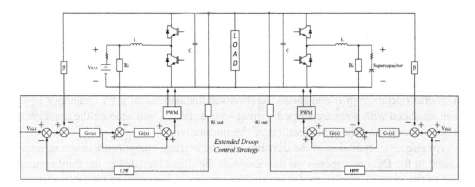

Fig. 6. System schematic with the implemented control strategy

Figure 7 shows the simulation plots of the implemented system. Figure 7a) shows the injected current (green) as a sum of the PV emulator current shown in Fig. 3, and the load current (purple) with an important step in 30 s. The injected current is divided into the converters in parallel as expected. The dynamic component is assigned to the SC and the average component to the battery. These plots are shown in Fig. 7b). Drastic variations in the total current do not immediately change the battery current; therefore, the electrical stress in the battery is considerably reduced.

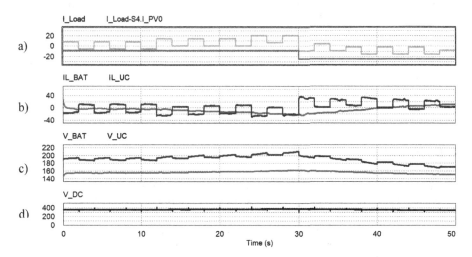

Fig. 7. Simulation plots of a HESS in an active topology. (a) Injected current in the DC bus. (b) Battery and SC current plots. (c) Voltage in terminals of the battery and the SC. (d) Voltage in the DC Bus (Color figure online)

As mentioned in Sect. 2, one of the most important advantages of a parallel active topology is that using a converter for the SC makes possible to best manage its stored energy. Thus, it is necessary to vary the voltage in the terminals of the SC. Figure 7c) shows the voltage in terminals of the battery and the supercapacitor. This plot shows a SC voltage variation between 70% and 90% of the rated voltage of SC.

5   Conclusions

An optimization-based real-time frequency-decoupling control strategy has been implemented for the control of a HESS in a parallel active topology for a residential microgrid operating in island mode. Real power fluctuations of a PV generator have been emulated with a square shaped current source, taking into account the associated injected energy and the time duration of the intermittences.

An effective separation of the dynamic and the average components of the injected current in the DC bus depends on the design of the filters included in the third control loop of the implemented control strategy. However, it is important to take into account that the dynamics of the SC converter should be higher than the dynamics used for the battery. Larger bandwidths for voltage and current controllers of SC normally imply the convenience of using a higher switching frequency for the SC converter.

A parallel active topology allows to manage better the stored energy in the SC due to the possibility of varying the voltage in the terminals of SC with a DC converter as interface to the DC bus.

A suitable value of SC will depend on two main factors: first, the energy associated to the intermittences of the injected current, and second, the ratio conversion of the used DC converter.

Future work contemplates to integrate a second level control strategy and a practical implementation of the designed HESS in a realistic residential microgrid.

Acknowledgment.   First author thanks Universidad Distrital Francisco José de Caldas for the financial support in his doctoral studies through the study commission contract N° 000101-2016.

The third author thanks the National Fund for the financing of science, technology and innovation "Francisco José de Caldas Fund" of the Administrative Department of Science, Technology and Innovation - COLCIENCIAS, for the financial support to the present work (Contract: FP44842 - 031 2016).

References

1. DOE, Summary Report: 2012 DOE Microgrid Workshop (2012)
2. Trujillo, C., et al.: Microrredes eléctricas, 1st ed. Universidad Distrital Francisco José de Caldas, Bogotá (2015)
3. Kan, S.Y., Verwaal, M., Broekhuizen, H.: The use of battery-capacitor combinations in photovoltaic powered products. J. Power Sources **162**(2), 971–974 (2006)
4. Chowdhury, M.: Grid integration impacts and energy storage systems for wind energy applications—a review. In: IEEE Power and Energy Society General Meeting, pp. 1–8 (2011)

5. Dougal, R.A., Liu, S., White, R.E.: Power and life extension of battery-ultracapacitor hybrids. IEEE Trans. Compon. Packag. Technol. **25**(1), 120–131 (2002)

6. Khaligh, A.: Battery, ultracapacitor, fuel cell, and hybrid energy storage systems for electric, hybrid electric, fuel cell, and plug-in hybrid electric vehicles: state of the Art. IEEE Trans. Veh. Technol. **59**(6), 2806–2814 (2010)

7. Mendis, N., Muttaqi, K.M., Perera, S.: Management of battery-supercapacitor hybrid energy storage and synchronous condenser for isolated operation of PMSG based variable-speed wind turbine generating systems. IEEE Trans. Smart Grid **5**(2), 944–953 (2014)

8. Lahyani, A., Venet, P., Guermazi, A., Troudi, A.: Battery/supercapacitors combination in uninterruptible power supply (UPS). IEEE Trans. Power Electron. **28**(4), 1509–1522 (2013)

9. Bolborici, V., Dawson, F., Lian, K.: Hybrid energy storage systems. IEEE Ind. Appl. Mag. **20**(4), 31–40 (2014)

10. Ortúzar, M., Moreno, J., Dixon, J.: Ultracapacitor-based auxiliary energy system for an electric vehicle: implementation and evaluation. IEEE Trans. Ind. Electron. **54**(4), 2147–2156 (2007)

11. Sanfélix, J., Messagie, M., Omar, N., Van Mierlo, J., Hennige, V.: Environmental performance of advanced hybrid energy storage systems for electric vehicle applications. Appl. Energy **137**, 925–930 (2014)

12. Etxeberria, A., Vechiu, I., Camblong, H.: Hybrid energy storage systems for renewable energy sources integration in microgrids : a review. In: Power Electronics Conference International, pp. 532–537 (2010)

13. Narvaez, A., Cortes, C., Trujillo, C.L.: Comparative analysis of topologies for the interconnection of batteries and supercapacitors in a hybrid energy storage system. In: IEEE 8th International Symposium on Power Electronics for Distributed Generation (2017)

14. Bocklisch, T.: Hybrid energy storage systems for renewable energy applications. Energy Procedia **73**, 103–111 (2015)

15. Kuperman, A., Aharon, I.: Battery-ultracapacitor hybrids for pulsed current loads: a review. Renew. Sustain. Energy Rev. **15**(2), 981–992 (2011)

16. Guerrero, J.M., Chandorkar, M., Lee, T., Loh, P.C.: Advanced control architectures for intelligent microgrids; Part I: decentralized and hierarchical control. IEEE Trans. Ind. Electron. **60**(4), 1254–1262 (2013)

17. Xu, Q., Hu, X., Wang, P., Xiao, J., Tu, P., Wen, C.: A decentralized dynamic power sharing strategy for hybrid energy storage system in autonomous DC microgrid. Ind. Electron. IEEE Trans. **64**(7), 5930–5941 (2017)

18. Xu, Q., Xiao, J., Hu, X., Wang, P., Lee, M.Y.: Decentralized power management strategy for hybrid energy storage system with autonomous bus voltage restoration and state of charge recovery. IEEE Trans. Ind. Electron. **64**, 7098–7108 (2017)

19. Singh, R.K., Chauhan, N.S., Mishra, S.: A novel average current-mode controller based optimal battery charger for automotive applications. In: 2012 International Conference on Devices, Circuits and Systems, ICDCS 2012, pp. 135–139 (2012)

20. De La Fuente, D.V., Rodriguez, C.L.T., Garcera, G., Figueres, E., Gonzalez, R.O.: Photovoltaic power system with battery backup with grid-connection and islanded operation capabilities. IEEE Trans. Ind. Electron. **60**(4), 1571–1581 (2013)

Analysis of Control Sensitivity Functions for Power System Frequency Regulation

Julian Patiño[1,2(✉)] [iD], José David López[3] [iD], and Jairo Espinosa[4] [iD]

[1] Departamento de Ingeniería Eléctrica, Facultad de Ingeniería y Arquitectura, Universidad Nacional de Colombia, Manizales, Colombia
japatin0@unal.edu.co
[2] I. U. Pascual Bravo, Calle 73 No. 73A - 226, Medellín, Colombia
[3] Engineering Faculty, Universidad de Antioquia UDEA, Calle 70 No. 52-21, Medellín, Colombia
josedavid@udea.edu.co
[4] Departmento de Ingeniería Eléctrica y Automática, Facultad de Minas, Universidad Nacional de Colombia, Medellín, Colombia
jespinov@unal.edu.co

Abstract. This work studies the behavior of the Control Sensitivity Functions derivated from the frequency regulation structure in power systems. Here, we explore the performance of the sensitivity functions in the presence of changes in the parameters of frequency regulation and power system components. A one-area power system is employed as the simulation benchmark. Results of frequency-domain analysis with Bode plots highlight the more significant parameters for Load Frequency Control and the different changes in sensitivity functions.

Keywords: Control sensitivity functions · Power systems
Frequency regulation

1 Introduction

The electricity sector is undergoing significant changes worldwide. Factors such as the proliferation of isolated systems with the possibility of connecting to the network and equipped with storage systems (microgrids) [17], the progressive incorporation of electric vehicles, the installation of equipment based on power electronics to control and manage networks (FACTS), and the application of automation and advanced information technologies configure what is usually called the smart grid [2]. These factors, together with the unavoidable integration of unconventional energy sources, pose new challenges for the operation and control of electric power systems, mainly because these factors introduce power and load unbalances that affect the stability on the power system frequency.

Frequency constitutes a significant operational parameter for power systems, establishing a direct relationship with the speed of rotation of conventional synchronous generators. Some electrical phenomena such as power outages, fluctuation in demanded power, variations in renewable energy sources or transmission

© Springer Nature Switzerland AG 2018
J. C. Figueroa-García et al. (Eds.): WEA 2018, CCIS 915, pp. 606–617, 2018.
https://doi.org/10.1007/978-3-030-00350-0_50

line losses [5] modify the generation and load equilibrium, producing frequency changes in the standard operating values. These phenomena raise the need for control strategies maintaining the system frequency inside the corresponding operational frame. Frequency control scheme for power systems is composed by the damping actions of speed variations of synchronous units by machine inertia, and by primary (Load Frequency Control, LFC) and secondary (Automatic Generation Control, AGC) control structures returning frequency to standard operating ranges in the presence of disturbance events [1].

Frequency control has been a significant topic of research for electrical power systems [3,13,15,16,18]. This work explores the analysis of the so-called Control Sensitivity Functions [20] of the frequency regulation system as a tool for obtaining information useful for controller design. The use of Control Sensitivity Functions for power system analysis has been shown in [22], for the control of an electrically powered steering system through a robust H_∞ controller designed with mixed sensitivity technique. Also, model uncertainties have been studied with complementary sensitivity functions in the development of robust stabilizers for power systems [12]. Robust control is the main topic of application of sensitivity functions in power systems, with reported works in control schemes for doubly fed induction wind generators [11], and solar power generation systems [4]. Also, the use of sensitivity analysis in the assessment of power system stability using small-signal techniques is described in [21].

The specific application of sensitivity functions in frequency control derives from the design of robust controllers using H_∞ methodologies [3]. Related applications with Bode plots for the dynamic study of power system frequency regulation with integration of renewable energy sources (mainly wind farms) are reported in [6,9,10,15]. Also, sensitivity-like expressions and transfer functions were developed in [7,8] for the parametric analysis of the frequency control scheme in power systems. This paper extends the work first reported on [14], where the Control Sensitivity Functions for a single area power system were derived and studied. Here, we explore the behavior of the sensitivity functions in the presence of changes in the parameters of frequency regulation and power system components. Results of frequency-domain analysis with Bode plots highlight the more significant parameters for Load Frequency Control and the different changes in sensitivity functions.

This paper is structured as follows. We begin with a short explanation of the Control Sensitivity Functions extracted from the control systems theory. Next, we describe the frequency regulation for power systems and define the Sensitivity Functions from this structure. Using Bode plots, we analyze the effects of parameter variations in the derived Sensitivity Functions for frequency control in computer simulations for a single area power system with conventional machines. We finish discussing the results and presenting final remarks.

2   Sensitivity Functions in Control Systems

Linear time-invariant (LTI) systems are a class of dynamic systems that can be represented by linear, constant-coefficient, differential equations. Transfer

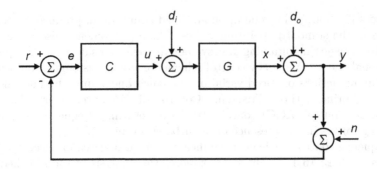

Fig. 1. Generalized structure of a control system with a basic feedback loop [20]

functions and block diagrams represent these LTI systems [20]. Consider a control system with a basic feedback loop and without measurement filter, as shown in the block diagram of Fig. 1. Two blocks are representing the system: the controller C and the plant G. Four external signals influence the feedback loop: the reference value r, the disturbance d_i at the plant input, the output disturbance d_o, and the measurement noise n. Error signal e is the signal feeding the controller block C for the generation of control action u. Finally, signal y denominates the process output. From Fig. 1, the following expressions denoting the signal relationships can be obtained using block algebra:

$$U = \frac{C}{1+GC}R - \frac{GC}{1+GC}D_i - \frac{C}{1+GC}D_o - \frac{C}{1+GC}N$$
$$Y = \frac{GC}{1+GC}R + \frac{G}{1+GC}D_i + \frac{1}{1+GC}D_o - \frac{GC}{1+GC}N \tag{1}$$

In both Fig. 1 and Eq. (1) Laplace variable s has been omitted for simplicity. In Eq. (1) some transfer functions are the same; these are denominated as the *Control Sensitivity Functions* determining system dynamic performance. The four sensitivity functions are given by the following transfer functions [20]:

- Sensitivity S(s), offering an estimation of the disturbance rejection capabilities of the system.

$$S(s) = \frac{1}{1+G(s)C(s)} \tag{2}$$

- Complementary Sensitivity $T(s)$:

$$T(s) = \frac{G(s)C(s)}{1+G(s)C(s)} \tag{3}$$

- Disturbance Sensitivity $S_i(s)$:

$$S_i(s) = \frac{G(s)}{1+G(s)C(s)} \tag{4}$$

– Control Sensitivity $S_o(s)$:

$$S_o(s) = \frac{C(s)}{1 + G(s)C(s)} \tag{5}$$

These Control Sensitivity Functions concentrate characteristical information related to the dynamic behavior of the system, such as disturbance impacts, the performance of the control action and reference signal tracking [20]. Both static (low frequencies) and dynamic (high frequencies) studies can benefit from these descriptions of the system. Moreover, Control Sensitivity Functions are intrinsically related among them through the expressions shown below:

$$S(s) + T(s) = 1 \tag{6}$$

$$S_i(s) = G(s)S(s) = \frac{T(s)}{C(s)} \tag{7}$$

$$S_o(s) = C(s)S(s) = \frac{T(s)}{G(s)} \tag{8}$$

The relationships described by Eqs. (6) to (8) imply that the tuning of a determined controller $C(s)$ is not shaping the Control Sensitivity Functions. Conversely, those restrictions highlight the requirement of trade-off compromises between the different control goals. Designer criteria are of paramount importance for the selection of the proper control scheme concerning the performance objectives.

3   Control Sensitivity Functions for Frequency Regulation in Power Systems

3.1   Description of Frequency Control System

In electrical systems under normal operating conditions, the generators are rotating in synchronism, and together they generate the total demanded energy [1]. Since electrical energy can not be stored in large quantities, if the power consumed by the load increases but the mechanical power provided by the turbines remains constant, the increase in demand can only be compensated for the stored kinetic energy [1]. This effect supposes a decrease in the rotation speed of the generators and a frequency falls on the system, directly related to said speed. As the demand is continuously changing, a control system is required to automatically adjust the power generated in each generation unit while keeping the frequency within certain operational limits [19]. Frequency control scheme for power systems is formed by the damping effects of speed variations of synchronous machines by the inertia, and by primary (Load Frequency Control, LFC) and secondary (Automatic Generation Control, AGC) control structures returning frequency to standard operating ranges in the presence of disturbance events [1]. A simple representation of the Frequency control for a single area

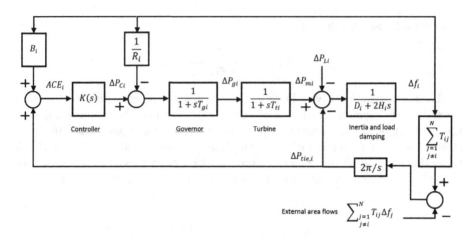

Fig. 2. Block diagram for frequency control structure in power system including only one machine for a regulation area i (based on [3])

power system is shown in Fig. 2. The complete derivation of the system can be found in [3].

In Fig. 2, $\Delta P_m(s)$ is the variation $[p.u]$ in the mechanical power of generating units, $\Delta P_l(s)$ represents the load changes $[p.u]$, $\Delta f(s)$ denotes the per-unit frequency deviation, the adjusted inertia characteristic for the area is H $[s]$, and D is known as the load damping constant [3]. R is the speed drop of the machines, $K(s)$ is the secondary control block (usually, and for this work, $K(s) = -k_I/s$) and $B_i = D_i + 1/R_i$ is an adjusted gain denominated as the frequency bias of the area. Finally, T_{ti} and T_{gi} denote the corresponding time constants of the respective turbine and governor first-ordel models.

3.2   Derivation of Control Sensitivity Functions for Frequency Regulation Structure

The Frequency regulation structure in Fig. 2 can be expressed as the classic feedback control system of Fig. 1 after the application of certain block operations. Assuming the simplification $r = d_i = n = 0$, the system of Fig. 3 is reached [14]. The output signal y for this resulting control structure is Δf_i, the change in electrical frequency for a given area i without transferred power to other areas (isolated).

From Fig. 3, we can see how the plant G groups the blocks corresponding to total inertia of the area i and the turbine-governor system. Also, the controller C is combining the effects of both primary and secondary actions in power system frequency control. Moreover, we have to note how the output disturbance d_o shows the load deviations filtered through the load damping and the total inertia of the system. This filtering effect can be seen in Eqs. (9) and (10):

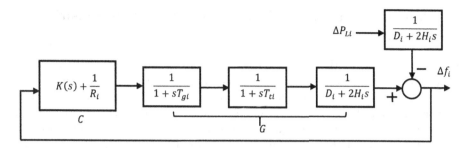

Fig. 3. A single area power system frequency regulation scheme seen as a generalized feedback control system [14]

$$C = K(s) + \frac{1}{R_i} = \frac{-k_i B_i}{s} + \frac{1}{R_i} \tag{9}$$

$$d_o = -\Delta P_L \left(\frac{1}{D_i + 2H_i s} \right) \tag{10}$$

The relationship between the process frequency $\Delta f(s)$ and the load disturbance signal $\Delta P_L(s)$ is defined by transfer function $G_f(s)$ in Eq. (11):

$$G_f(s) = \frac{-\frac{1}{2H_i s + D_i}}{1 + \left(K(s) + \frac{1}{R_i} \right) \frac{1}{T_g s + 1} \frac{1}{T_t s + 1} \frac{1}{2H_i s + D_i}} \tag{11}$$

The control sensitivity functions according to the frequency regulation structure of Fig. 3 are [14]:

$$S(s) = \frac{1}{1 + \left(K(s) + \frac{1}{R_i} \right) \left(\frac{1}{T_g s + 1} \frac{1}{T_t s + 1} \frac{1}{2H_i s + D_i} \right)} \tag{12}$$

$$T(s) = \frac{\left(K(s) + \frac{1}{R_i} \right) \left(\frac{1}{T_g s + 1} \frac{1}{T_t s + 1} \frac{1}{2H_i s + D_i} \right)}{1 + \left(K(s) + \frac{1}{R_i} \right) \left(\frac{1}{T_g s + 1} \frac{1}{T_t s + 1} \frac{1}{2H_i s + D_i} \right)} \tag{13}$$

$$S_i(s) = \frac{\frac{1}{T_g s + 1} \frac{1}{T_t s + 1} \frac{1}{2H_i s + D_i}}{1 + \left(K(s) + \frac{1}{R_i} \right) \left(\frac{1}{T_g s + 1} \frac{1}{T_t s + 1} \frac{1}{2H_i s + D_i} \right)} \tag{14}$$

$$S_o(s) = \frac{K(s) + \frac{1}{R_i}}{1 + \left(K(s) + \frac{1}{R_i} \right) \left(\frac{1}{T_g s + 1} \frac{1}{T_t s + 1} \frac{1}{2H_i s + D_i} \right)} \tag{15}$$

4 Effects of Parameter Variations in Control Sensitivity Functions of LFC

We are interested in the behavior of the sensitivity functions in the presence of changes in frequency regulation parameters and power system components. After the parameter variations, sensitivity functions are studied with magnitude Bode plots in absolute units (*abs*). As the simulation benchmark, a power system frequency regulation from a single area one-machine system like the one in Fig. 3 is selected. System parameters for the base case are taken from [19]: $T_g = 0.2$ *sec*, $T_t = 0.5$ *sec*, $H = 5$ *sec*, $R = 0.05$ *p.u* and $B_i k_i = 7$. System includes an integral secondary controller for the AGC. Then, these values are changed and the control sensitivity functions are obtained for the updated parameters.

4.1 Variations in Inertia H

The effects of the change of inertia H in the control sensitivity functions of the frequency regulation system are depicted in Fig. 4. As the inertia is decreased gradually, the control sensitivity functions present more prominent peaks of magnitude. These effects signal a performance degradation in the frequency regulation structure and highlight the importance of the inertia for frequency control purposes.

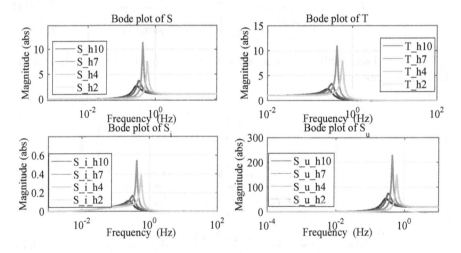

Fig. 4. Effects of the variation of inertia H in the control sensitivity functions of frequency regulation system

4.2 Variations in Load Damping D

The effects of the change of load damping D in the control sensitivity functions of the frequency regulation system are depicted in Fig. 5. Load damping is a parameter representing the impact of the frequency-dependent loads in the frequency regulation structure. The simulations show the minimal effect of D in the sensitivity functions. This behavior is due to the lack of frequency-dependent loads in the power systems, and show the limited value of load-damping for frequency regulation at these penetration levels.

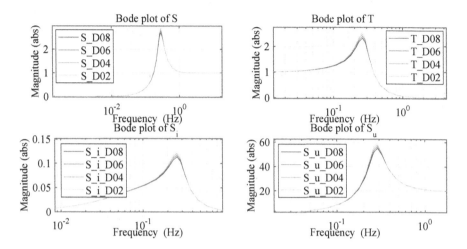

Fig. 5. Effects of the variation of load damping D in the control sensitivity functions of frequency regulation system

4.3   Variations in Turbine Time-Constant T

The effects of the change of turbine time-constant T in the control sensitivity functions of the frequency regulation system are depicted in Fig. 6. The results show how the control sensitivity functions suffer from performance degradation with the increase of time-constant T. This behavior causes an increased delay in the response of the system controllers caused by the slower action of the machines.

4.4   Variations in Speed Droop R

The effects of the change of speed droop R in the control sensitivity functions of the frequency regulation system are depicted in Fig. 7. The parameter R represents the response capability of the machines, the operational margin for changing rotational speed and contribute to primary regulation. In this way, as expected, the performance of the control system improves as the speed drop increases.

4.5   Variations in Controller Integral Gain k_i

The effects of the change of controller integral gain k_i in the control sensitivity functions of the frequency regulation system are depicted in Fig. 8. As the controller integral gain k_i increases, the only sensitivity function with significant

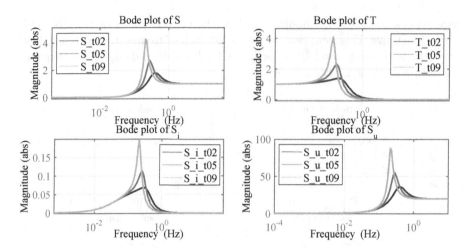

Fig. 6. Effects of the variation of the turbine time-constant T in the control sensitivity functions of frequency regulation system

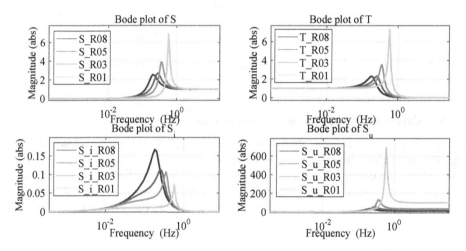

Fig. 7. Effects of the variation of the speed droop R in the control sensitivity functions of frequency regulation system

change is S_i. This behavior makes sense because the disturbance rejection is improved with the adequate tuning of the secondary controllers for frequency regulation.

5   Conclusions

This work analyzed the impacts of parametric variations in the Control Sensitivity Functions of frequency regulation in power systems. The inertia H caused the

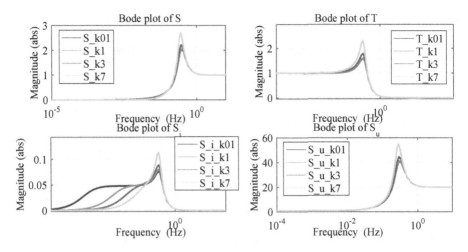

Fig. 8. Effects of the variation of the controller integral gain k_i in the control sensitivity functions of frequency regulation system

most significant effect on the performance of frequency control loops. Reduction of this parameter significantly diminishes the system's opposition to frequency variations, even reaching an amplifying effect of power disturbances at maximum value. This fact suggests that in the case of inertia variations for the system, both the integral action and the proportional gain of the controller given by the machine speed *droop* need to be adjusted.

On the other hand, the negligible impact of load damping D suggests the lack of influence of this parameter in frequency regulation. Also, the increase in the time constant of the turbine represented a significant delay in the response of the control system.

The variations in speed droop and integral gain showed that, even when the control parameters were adjusted for the diminishing inertia, disturbance rejection performance decreased as evidenced by control sensitivities. There has to be particular attention to the essential design considerations for the tuning of control parameters, as these determine the disturbance rejection capabilities and the ability for minimizing the steady-state error in frequency deviations.

Acknowledgement. Colciencias supported contributions of J. Patiño through the program "Convocatoria 528 – Convocatoria Nacional para Estudios de Doctorados en Colombia 2011".

References

1. Anderson, P.M., Fouad, A.A.: Power System Control and Stability. IEEE Press Power Engineering Series. Wiley-IEEE Press, Hoboken (2002)
2. Barrero-Gonzlez, F., Milans-Montero, M., Gonzlez-Romera, E., Roncero-Clemente, C., Gonzlez-Castrillo, P.: El Control de Potencia y Frecuencia en los Sistemas Elctricos Multirea. Revisin y Nuevos Retos. Revista Iberoamericana de Automtica e Informtica Industrial RIAI **12**(4), 357–364 (2015). https://doi.org/10.1016/j.riai.2015.07.001
3. Bevrani, H.: Robust Power System Frequency Control. Power Electronics and Power Systems, 2nd edn. Springer, New York (2014). https://doi.org/10.1007/978-0-387-84878-5
4. Chen, J., Yang, F., Han, Q.L.: Model-free predictive $_{infty}$ control for grid-connected solar power generation systems. IEEE Trans. Control Syst. Technol. **22**(5), 2039–2047 (2014). https://doi.org/10.1109/TCST.2013.2292879
5. Duque, E., Patino, J., Velz, L.: Implementation of the ACM0002 methodology in small hydropower plants in Colombia under the clean development mechanism. Int. J. Renew. Energy Res. **6**(1), 21–33 (2016)
6. Horta, R., Espinosa, J., Patino, J.: Frequency and voltage control of a power system with information about grid topology. In: 2015 IEEE 2nd Colombian Conference on Automatic Control (CCAC), pp. 1–6. IEEE (2015)
7. Huang, H., Li, F.: Sensitivity analysis of load-damping characteristic in power system frequency regulation. IEEE Trans. Power Syst. **28**(2), 1324–1335 (2013). https://doi.org/10.1109/TPWRS.2012.2209901
8. Huang, H., Li, F.: Sensitivity analysis of load-damping, generator inertia and governor speed characteristics in hydraulic power system frequency regulation. In: Power Engineering Conference (AUPEC), 2014 Australasian Universities. pp. 1–6, September 2014. https://doi.org/10.1109/AUPEC.2014.6966474
9. Li, W., Joos, G., Abbey, C.: Wind power impact on system frequency deviation and an ESS based Power filtering algorithm solution. In: Power Systems Conference and Exposition, 2006, PSCE 2006, pp. 2077–2084. IEEE PES, October 2006. https://doi.org/10.1109/PSCE.2006.296265
10. Luo, C., Far, H., Banakar, H., Keung, P.K., Ooi, B.T.: Estimation of wind penetration as limited by frequency deviation. IEEE Trans. Energy Convers. **22**(3), 783–791 (2007). https://doi.org/10.1109/TEC.2006.881082
11. Ma, X., Yang, H., Zeng, G., Yin, Q., Yuan, L.: Robust controller design of doubly fed induction wind generator based on IMC theory. Yi Qi Yi Biao Xue Bao/Chin. J. Sci. Instrum. **37**(11), 2528–2535 (2016)
12. Mosskull, H.: Performance and robustness evaluation of dc-link stabilization. Control Eng. Pract. **44**, 104–116 (2015). https://doi.org/10.1016/j.conengprac.2015.06.011
13. Pandey, S.K., Mohanty, S.R., Kishor, N.: A literature survey on load–frequency control for conventional and distribution generation power systems. Renew. Sustain. Energy Rev. **25**, 318–334 (2013). https://doi.org/10.1016/j.rser.2013.04.029
14. Patino, J., Espinosa, J.: Control sensitivity functions of frequency regulation for a one-area power system. In: 2017 IEEE 3rd Colombian Conference on Automatic Control (CCAC), pp. 1–6, October 2017. https://doi.org/10.1109/CCAC.2017.8276460
15. Patino, J., Valencia, F., Espinosa, J.: Sensitivity analysis for frequency regulation in a two-area power system. Int. J. Renew. Energy Res. **7**(2), 700–706 (2017)

16. Ruiz, S., Patino, J., Espinosa, J.: PI and LQR controllers for frequency regulation including wind generation. Int. J. Electr. Comput. Eng. (IJECE) **8**(6) (2018). http://www.iaescore.com/journals/index.php/IJECE/article/view/11840

17. Ruiz, S., Patino, J., Marquez, A., Espinosa, J.: Optimal design for an electrical hybrid microgrid in Colombia under fuel price variation. Int. J. Renew. Energy Res. **7**(24), 1535–1545 (2017). http://ijrer.com/index.php/ijrer/article/view/6128/pdf

18. Ruiz, S., Patino, J., Espinosa, J.: Load frequency control of a multi-area power system incorporating variable-speed wind turbines. In: Conference Proceedings of XVII Latin American Conference in Automatic Control, Medelln, Colombia, pp. 447–452 (2016)

19. Saadat, H.: Power System Analysis. PSA Publishing, United States (2010)

20. Skogestad, S.: Multivariable Feedback Control: Analysis and Design. Wiley, Hoboken (2005)

21. Vesti, S., Oliver, J.A., Prieto, R., Cobos, J.A., Suntio, T.: Simplified small-signal stability analysis for optimized power system architecture. In: 2013 Twenty-Eighth Annual IEEE Applied Power Electronics Conference and Exposition (APEC), pp. 1702–1708, March 2013. https://doi.org/10.1109/APEC.2013.6520526

22. Wang, H., Xu, Z., Li, Z., Shang, Z., Zhang, H.: Analysis of electric power steering control based on S/T method. In: Fifth World Congress on Intelligent Control and Automation (IEEE Cat. No.04EX788), vol. 1, pp. 582–585, June 2004. https://doi.org/10.1109/WCICA.2004.1340642

Author Index

Printed in the United States
By Bookmasters